LAW AND WAR

LAW AND WAR

An American Story

PETER MAGUIRE

COLUMBIA UNIVERSITY PRESS • NEW YORK

Columbia University Press
Publishers Since 1893
New York   Chichester, West Sussex

Copyright © 2001 Columbia University Press
Library of Congress Cataloging-in-Publication Data
Maguire, Peter H.
　　Law and war: an American story / Peter Maguire.
　　　p.　cm.
　　Includes bibliographical references and index.
　　ISBN 0–231–12050–8 (cloth) — ISBN 0–231–12051–6 (paper)
　　1. War crimes.　2. War (International law).　3. Nuremberg War Crime Trials, Nuremberg, Germany, 1946–1949.　4. United States—Foreign relations—20th century.　I. Title.
K5301 .M34 2000
341.6'9—dc21　　　　　　　　　　　　　　　　　　　　00–031442

Columbia University Press books are printed on permanent and durable acid-free paper.
Printed in the United States of America
c 10 9 8 7 6 5 4 3 2 1
p 10 9 8 7 6 5 4 3 2

This book is dedicated to the memories of
Telford Taylor (1908–1999),
Marty Hoey (1951–1982),
Robert Ross (1955–1999),
and the very much alive
James Patrick Shenton.

Contents

Acknowledgments

I began this book as a junior at Bard College in 1986 at the prompting of German history professor John Fout, who encouraged me to find out more about my great-grandfather's tenure as a judge at the Nuremberg trials. Others at Bard College who were supportive in the early years of this project include: Robert Koblitz, Peter Skiff, Mark Lytle, Karen Greenberg, William Preston, Leon Botstein, Sanjeb Baruah, and the late Mary McCarthy.

I continued my research on the Nuremberg trials as a graduate student in history at Columbia University, where I was very fortunate to be assigned James Patrick Shenton as my advisor. Jim guided me through the political minefields of contemporary academia with the wisdom and *sangfroid* that he gained on the battlefields of Europe during World War II. Whether it was from a hospital bed or on the road guiding historical tours, Jim made time for me, and I will always be grateful.

Another individual who played a key role in this project was the late Nuremberg prosecutor Telford Taylor. For more than a decade, Telford made himself available for interviews and casual conversations. He allowed me to attend his laws of war class at Columbia Law School. Most of all, I was inspired by Telford Taylor's intellectual courage. Whether he was attacking Joseph McCarthy at West Point or telling North Vietnamese leaders that they too were committing war crimes during a wartime visit to Hanoi, Telford Taylor called them as he saw them, irrespective of the political consequences. While we didn't agree on some things, in the end he supported and encouraged this study long after others had given up on it. Telford died in May 1998, but his life's work and memory live on. I only wish that he could have lived to see the publication of this book, as he was working on a similar one when he died. Jonathan Bush, Telford Taylor's biographer, was also extremely helpful, and I owe him a great debt for his helpful and constructive criticism.

Anders Stephanson was my most important intellectual advisor in graduate school and beyond. In an age of academic microspecialization, I was extremely fortunate to study under someone whose intellectual repertoire is both broad and deep. Anders helped me to make sense of the vast literature on war and statecraft and in the process to see how American policy broke from European tradition. He never lost faith in my work, and for this I will always be grateful. Others I would like to thank for various forms of support and inspiration at Columbia include: Ron Grele, John Danaher, Mary Marshall, Ed O'Donnell, Walter Friedman, Dan Hulsebosch, Gordon Spencer, Ken Jackson, and James Chace.

I would like to thank Lydia Wills of the Artists Agency for her early support of my work and her efforts on my behalf. I had an opportunity to examine West German disdain for the Nuremberg trials and the importance of the Cold War on American war crimes policy more closely after graduate school. In 1995 I was hired by documentary film producer Robert Ross to work on a German documentary about Nuremberg's IMT produced by Bengt von zur Mühlen of Chronos Films and Michael Kloft of Speigel TV in 1995. I spent a large part of the summer of 1995 in Berlin working with German war crimes scholar Jörg Friedrich. This study was greatly enriched by the time that I spent in Berlin with Friedrich and Kloft in the summers of 1995 and 1996. Without the help of Robert Ross, Michael Kloft, Jörg Friedrich, and Otto Kranzbühler, my book would be significantly less thorough and I would have passed over a number of unpleasant realities about Nuremberg and West Germany. I would also like to thank Martin Splichal and Johanna Sophia for helping me translate a number of German secondary sources.

The American Nuremberg trial participants generously gave of their time. Former IMT and subsequent proceedings prosecutor, author of one of the most comprehensive studies of the international trial (*Inside the Nuremberg Trial*), Drexel Sprecher, was very helpful over many years. William Caming helped me to get a better sense of my great-grandfather and his role in the Ministries case. Walter Rockler candidly described the impact of the Cold War on the trial. Ben Ferencz helped me learn more about John McCloy's Peck Panel and forced me to reconsider some of my early and more simplistic views on John McCloy. The late Robert Kempner was also helpful in the earlier stages of this project. A number of my great-grandfather's former legal associates helped me to get to know Robert Maguire, the man. Thanks to Alfred Hampsten, Randolph Kester, and James Brand Jr. Judge Maguire's children were also extremely helpful in locating his letters from Germany. Betty Frankus, Connie and Joseph Wilson, and Robert Maguire Jr. all greatly added to my understanding of my great-grandfather and his experience in Nuremberg. My uncle Gil Maguire also read numerous drafts and offered very constructive criticism.

The students in my seminar on the law and theory of war at Columbia University also helped me to distill my ideas on law and war. A special thanks goes to William Gouveia, Dan McDorman, Greg Lembrich, David Van Geyzel, and Brit West. In the fall of 1995, I gave a paper at the Carnegie Council on Ethics and International Affairs, and benefited from the comments of Barton Bernstein and Akira Iriye. I was fortunate to be placed on a panel with Lt. Col. Conrad Crane of West Point, who taught me a great deal about bombing the professional military's view of the laws of war. Conrad introduced me to Lt. Col. Gary Solis, who read an earlier draft of this book and greatly increased my knowledge of and appreciation for the professional military's views of law, war, duty, and honor. My work has been greatly enriched by my interaction with America's professional soldiers.

In 1998, Susan Gillespie and Leon Botstein invited me to host a conference at Bard College entitled "Accounting for Atrocities Fifty Years After Nuremberg." I would like to thank Bard and all the conference participants. A special thanks goes to Jörg Friedrich, Jonathan Bush, Richard Goldstone, Conrad Crane, and Chinua Achebe for their particularly inspired papers.

I want to express my gratitude to the many scholars, lawyers, and journalists who read and commented on parts or all of this study over the last decade: Ron Steel, Brian DiSalvatore, William Finnegan, Ron Olson, Werner Koenig, Thomas Schwartz, Marc Trachtenberg, John Willand, and Michael Coles. A special thanks goes to Bob Primeaux, an enrolled member of the Standing Rock Sioux tribe and a traditional Elder of the Hunkpapa Treaty Council. Our discussions in the summer of 1999 greatly added to my knowledge of America's Indian Wars.

Others who helped more than they will ever know: Mike Cundith, George Greenough, Anthony Edgeworth, Ian Warner, and Mike Perry.

I owe a special debt to Mark, Dotty, and Fritz Johnson of Portland, Oregon, who provided me with a bit of peace and quiet and a place to write on the Oregon coast in 1992 and 1993. Seaside Point and Chris Cowan—generosity I will always be grateful for. Frank Opperman and Mary Kennedy were also extremely helpful in the final stages of the book. I would also like to thank Kate Wittenberg and James Burger of Columbia University Press for their help. To my editors, Rebecca McLennan and Leslie Kriesel, thank you for your patience and perseverance.

My parents, Joan Tewkesbury and Robert Maguire, both generously supported me and this project. Finally, to my wife, Annabelle Lee, whose unconditional love, faith, and support made the completion of this book possible.

LAW AND WAR

INTRODUCTION

When I was twelve, the Oregon Bar Association held a special memorial session in the chambers of the U.S. District Court of Oregon to honor my recently deceased great-grandfather, Robert Maguire. I had never been to a funeral or a trial, and the stark wood-paneled chambers and the somber demeanor of the old men in their black robes filled me with equal parts fascination and fear. After gaveling the court into session, the judge announced "the presence in the courtroom of the following members of Mr. Maguire's family." I grew increasingly nervous as he ran down the list: "Mrs. Robert F. Maguire; Robert F. Maguire Jr."—I winced, waiting for my name—"Peter Maguire, a great-grandson; Robert F. Maguire III, grandson . . ." Just as my breath began to return, the door of the judge's chambers opened slowly and a young woman entered pushing a wheelchair, in which sat a very haunting old man.[1]

For a brief moment my young mind began to reel. Was this the corpse of my great-grandfather? My father, recognizing the ten-thousand-yard stare, reassured me that the man in the wheelchair was former Supreme Court Justice William O. Douglas, not my great-grandfather. He added that the two men had agreed on very little, but that today was a day past differences were set aside. The only time I had ever met Robert Maguire was at my grandfather's house in Ventura, California. I was very young, but I remember his stately demeanor contrasting starkly with the southern Californian environs. One by one the children were taken to his knee and introduced with a solemn handshake. Though the judge was very old, his mind was razor sharp and he was very stylish in a three-piece, gray pinstripe suit.

At first glance, Robert Maguire appeared to be a typical conservative Republican. However, he was the son of two very atypical Americans. His mother, Kate or Kitty, was the daughter of L. H. Harlan, one of Ohio's leading intellectuals. She was described in her obituary as "a pioneer social worker in the United States." Robert's high school thesis, "John Mitchell and the Miners," reflected his upbringing: "The United States will see the greatest conflict of the world. Where capital is strongest there will be the fight, conservatism against progress. . . . Future generations will call upon John Mitchell as the man who gave the death blow to . . . industrial slavery. . . ." (Robert Maguire, "John Mitchell and the Miners" [circa 1903], Betty Maguire Frankus Papers, Portland, Oregon).

During high school Robert Maguire taught himself shorthand. In 1905 he received a civil service clerkship in Washington, D.C.; during the day he worked as a court reporter and at night he attended Georgetown University Law School. After receiving his L.L.B. in 1909, Maguire took a job with the U.S. Land Service and was sent to Oregon to work as a border marker. The slight twenty-one-year-old was issued a horse, a gun, and a badge and thrown headlong into the rough-and-tumble disputes of eastern Oregon. In 1910, Robert Maguire married Ruth Kimbell of Massachusetts and moved to Portland, Oregon, where he had just been named Assistant U.S. Attorney. For several years, Maguire honed his skills as a trial lawyer, and in 1915, he entered private practice with Edwin Littlefield. The majority of the firm's work involved representing large insurance companies.

Robert Maguire led two legal lives. Although he had become what today would be described a "corporate lawyer," he remained a public-spirited jurist. In 1917, he was appointed Standing Master in Chancery of the Federal Court of Oregon, a position he would hold for the next thirty-three years. Oregon Supreme Court Justice Randolph Kester stated, "It was the first appointment of its kind ever made in Oregon. . . . The object of appointing such a judicial official is to expedite the work of the federal courts" (interview by author, tape recording, Portland, Oregon, 19 March 1987). Throughout the 1920s, Robert Maguire worked on behalf of the infant Oregon Bar Association and was named the Oregon Bar Association's first president in 1929. His professional rise continued throughout the 1930s, and Maguire seemed destined for a seat on the Oregon Supreme Court. Clients such as Union Pacific allowed him to earn a large salary, while his post as Master in Chancery and bar association prominence gave his voice more resonance than a corporate lawyer could normally expect. When the clouds of war gathered over Europe in the late thirties, Maguire echoed the sentiments of his favorite statesman, Winston Churchill, arguing that Hitler's incursions needed to be met with force. When the war ended, he supported the idea of a European recovery program, but had no idea that he would actively participate in it.

As the memorial continued, Robert Maguire was described by his colleagues as "one of the finest if not the finest trial lawyer in the Pacific Northwest," a man of "rocklike integrity." What piqued my curiosity was a one-sentence biographical detail: "In 1948 he served as a Judge of the U.S. Military Tribunal for the War Crimes Trials in Nuremberg, Germany."[2] That was the first time I had heard of the Nuremberg trials.

After the ceremony, we were led through the crowd and into the judge's chambers. From there, we were taken to an even deeper recess, and steered to the foot of a wheelchair and introduced to former U.S. Supreme Court Justice William O. Douglas. He took my hand and did not release it immediately. When he looked into my eyes, I was reminded of that first encounter with Robert Maguire.

I proudly regaled my fifth-grade classmates with my great-grandfather's historical significance. But my pronouncements were met with the same dull response someone receives for bragging that their forefathers sailed aboard the *Mayflower*. A few years later, when my ninth-grade history class staged a trial of Napoleon Bonaparte, I jumped at the opportunity to play the French leader. It was with a great sense of purpose that I cynically argued that sovereign leaders are immune from prosecution.

My first serious attempt to obtain more information about the Nuremberg trials was in junior high school. Although there were books on the subject, Robert Maguire could not be found in the group photos or the indexes. When I pressed my father and grandfather for details, they could only respond that "he was a judge at Nuremberg" and point to a faded black-and-white photograph on the wall of three black-robed men sitting in front of a large American flag.

Over the years my curiosity about the trials grew. It was not until college that I reluctantly told a political science professor about the family's claims. He informed me that after the international tribunal, there had been a subsequent series of American trials at Nuremberg. When I asked German history professor John Fout if he knew anything about the American trials, he took me to the library, where we found fifteen formidable-looking green books. We took them down and began to search.

Each volume had a picture of a three-man tribunal and their biographical information. As I scanned the tomes, my heart began to sink—we had checked nine of twelve cases and still no Robert Maguire. Then suddenly my professor said, "Yes, he does sort of look like you," and handed me one of the volumes. I looked down and there was Robert F. Maguire staring at me once again. It was the same picture that hung in my grandfather's hallway. His case was number 11, the *United States Government v. Ernst von Weizsaecker*, also known as the Ministries case.

My subsequent research efforts yielded an undergraduate thesis and raised many more questions than I could possibly answer. The most puzzling discovery was a 1953 U.S. High Commission Report on Germany. Buried deep in the report was a chart of charges, pleas, and sentences. The chart seemed suspiciously overcomplicated. However, there was one column that was straightforward. It was headed: "In custody as of February 30, 1952." When I looked at the Ministries case, I noticed that, despite a number of lengthy sentences, none of the defendants remained in prison after 1952. Even stranger was the number of death sentences that had been reduced to prison terms.

William Manchester's *Arms of Krupp* gave me a first, rather sensational account of the war criminal amnesty of the early 1950s. In an attempt to solve this and other mysteries, I contacted former Nuremberg chief counsel Telford Taylor. Our first meeting was in his Morningside Heights office in 1987; he was seventy-nine, I was twenty-two. When I produced the chart, Taylor put on his glasses and carefully studied it. He agreed that the sentences had been reduced way beyond the controversial McCloy decisions. However, he could offer no explanation why.[3]

Law and War is an attempt to transcend the simple oppositions of real-ism and idealism, positivism and natural law, liberalism and conservatism, might and right. During the 1990s, "war crimes" very much returned to center stage. If Nuremberg provides the legal and symbolic framework, its lessons remain unclear. In part, this is because what that name repre-sents is really a series of contradictory trials that lead to no single, simple conclusion.

It is my contention that over the course of the twentieth century, the United States attempted to broaden the laws of war to include acts that had previously been considered beyond the realm of objective judgment. During the early twentieth century, American leaders argued that law would replace blind vengeance as a means of conflict resolution. The apogee of this movement came at Nuremberg in 1946. In order to pro-vide a better context for America's radical post–World War II war crimes policy, it is necessary to see how the U.S. conception of international law differed from its European predecessor.

Generally speaking, after the Thirty Years War (1618–48), the era of the modern nation-state began.[4] European leaders viewed international politics as a never-ending and ever-changing struggle in which sovereign-ty and the national interest were the highest political ideals.[5] Americans tended to view war more like a contest in which total victory was the ulti-mate objective. The notion that enemies and their policies could be crim-inalized was not uniquely American; however, American lawyer-states-men gave this idea its greatest impetus. After I examined the larger history of conflict resolution, it became obvious that the *U.S.-Dakota War Trials*, the trial of Captain Henry Wirz, the Dachau trials, and the Yamashita case were examples of traditional postwar political justice and that the Nuremberg trials were the anomaly. Under the traditional rules, the victor has no historical obligation to extend a wide latitude of civil rights to the vanquished. After reading Hans Delbrück, Michael Howard, Charles Royster, David Kaiser, John Keegan, and the more extreme views of J.F.C. Fuller, on the history of war and conflict resolution, I began to see the American Civil War and the two World Wars as excep-tional events that had raised the stakes of international conflict. After reading German military political and legal theorists like Carl von Clausewitz, Heinrich von Treitschke, and Friedrich Meinecke on interna-tional politics, and Carl Schmitt on the concept of "neutrality," I began to realize how radical and threatening America's punitive occupation policies, outlined in Joint Chiefs of Staff Directive 1067, must have appeared to post–World War II Germans.[6] Impressions, as my former professor Robert Jervis pointed out, are often more important than empirical facts, because they can be shaped to conform to the observers' preconceptions and expectations.

However, it was the foreign policy of my own country that made me question the sincerity of America's commitment to the new principles of international conduct that we had so aggressively advocated during the first half of the twentieth century. Although the second half of this book will focus very sharply on the Nuremberg trials, first I will take a step backward in order to examine America's unique historical relationships with law and war. The episodic histories in the first three chapters help to establish a much larger historical, legal, and political context from which the Nuremberg trials stand out as the legal, political, and historical revolution that they were intended to be. This three-dimensional, multidisciplinary approach is absolutely necessary if one is to enter the storm where war, law, and politics swirl and oscillate in a constant state of flux. As Otto Kirchheimer argued so eloquently, political justice is not illegitimate by its very nature; however, he warned that this is a high-risk arena where the line between "blasphemy and promise" is a very fine one.

America's political ideology posed unique problems for U.S. foreign policy. It became increasingly difficult to justify an expansive, essentially imperialistic foreign policy within the framework of an egalitarian political ideology. As America grew into a regional and later a global power, this simple hypocrisy evolved into a more profound duality. More than the obvious gap between words and deeds, from the beginning, there was a tension between America's much-vaunted ethical and legal principles and its practical policy interests as an emerging world power. In his book *American Slavery, American Freedom*, Edmund Morgan argues that the simultaneous rise of personal liberty and slavery on the North American continent was the great paradox of the first two centuries of American history.

What also became clear, long before the United States even gained independence, was that the "others," in this case the slave population and North America's native inhabitants, would pay the greatest price for American freedom. Whether it was the Algonquin and the Pequot in the northeast, the Sioux in the Dakotas, or the Chumash in California, U.S. expansion cost American Indians their civilization. Initially colonial leaders deemed both slaves and Indians "barbarians" and "savages" and refused to grant them their natural rights. They would however, grant them financial credit; as much as the West was won with blood and iron, it was won with whiskey, dependence, and debt. However, from the point of view of early American leaders, these dualities were neither problematic nor paradoxical until well into the twentieth century. So what emerges quite naturally, even organically, are two sets of rules for war. When U.S. soldiers faced British and other European armies, they fought according to the customary European rules, with few exceptions. However, when American settlers and soldiers squared off against foes they deemed "savage" or "barbarian," they fought with the same lack of restraint as their adversaries. The "barbarian" distinction allowed early U.S. leaders to offer messianic justifications for everything from the forcible seizure of the American West to the brutal suppression of those unwilling to give in to the ever-increasing demands of a land-hungry American population. Although they did not hesitate to use force, early American leaders were careful to legalize their seizures in the form of treaty law. After reading Dee Brown's sad and moving account of the fall of traditional North American Indian civilization, *Bury My Heart at Wounded Knee*, I was shocked not so much by the flagrant use of force as by the U.S. government's inability to honor either its treaties or its word. Carol Chomsky's excellent article on the Minnesota Indian War of 1862 and the trials and executions that followed was extremely helpful. Sven Lindquist's provocative study of the role of colonial warfare in European history, *Exterminate All the Brutes*, was also extremely helpful.

In 1862, for a brief moment, the United States simultaneously fought Sioux Indians in Minnesota and Confederate armies in the South. Although the Confederacy would not be crushed until 1865, comparing the U.S. government's treatment of the two groups of vanquished foes is very telling and again points to the fact that America fought according to different sets of rules depending on its adversaries. However, this was consistent with the military practices of the European powers, who fought formal restrained wars against one another and operated with a freer hand in their colonial wars. After 1860, the Indian Wars entered a more brutal, final stage in which American Indians were settled onto reservations. Those who refused were deemed hostile and hunted down by specially trained cavalry units like the one led by Colonel Chivington at Sand Creek in 1864. This policy successfully cleared the American frontier for settlement and reached a sad and inevitable apogee at Wounded Knee in 1890.

All of this was justified with a home-grown American doctrine of innate superiority that matured into the messianic political ideology of Manifest Destiny by the late nineteenth century. However, by 1898, American foreign policy was crossing into a new and uncharted territory. It was one thing to justify domestic atrocities on the ground of innate inferiority, but similar justifications would not work on the global stage. After the United States soundly defeated Spain in Cuba, the new imperial power faced one in a series of moments of truth—an either/or situation: either the United States would free Spain's former colonies in the Caribbean and the Philippines, or it would reimpose colonialism in its own name. When American leaders attempted to justify their absorption of the former Spanish colonies with the doctrine of Manifest Destiny, the argument was unconvincing both at home and abroad. American statesmen would require new and more sophisticated justifications in the coming years, and where ideology had failed them, law would serve them.

The American duality was embodied in Secretary of War Elihu Root, whose appointment in 1899 marked an important moment in the history of U.S. foreign policy. As Secretary of War he was an outspoken advocate of the new codes of international law like the Hague Agreements of 1899 and even an international court, but he had no qualms about using Manifest Destiny to justify a brutal colonial war in the Philippines. Richard Drinnon's *Facing West* was extremely helpful in outlining the similarities between America's conduct in the Indian Wars and the Philippine War. American President Theodore Roosevelt dismissed the Philippine calls for independence by claiming that granting it would be like granting independence to an "Apache chief."

However, much of the American public was unconvinced by their leaders' official explanations. In order to contain the public dissent and the outcry over American conduct in this brutal war, the Secretary of War ordered a number of war crimes trials for American officers like Major Littleton Waller and General Jacob Smith in Manila in 1902, after the war had been largely won. Although the court went through all the proper motions, the charges were hazy and in the end, the sentences were extremely light. Secretary of War Root used law as a strategic device in order to quell a public relations problem that threatened to undermine American foreign policy. Elihu Root also employed what would become the favorite "device" of the strategic legalists—he used post-trial, nonjudicial means to further reduce already lenient sentences. In other words, once the public had been served its "justice," the sentences were quietly reduced behind the scenes. Root learned how to use the law to further his client's interests irrespective of facts and laws on Wall Street. In the case of the Philippines, everyone from his biographer and noted international lawyer Phillip Jessup to biographer Godfrey Hodgson to journalist Jacob Heilbrunn pointed to Root's use of his considerable legal skills to deny charges that were basically true. In fact, one of the major arguments of this book is that the American lawyers who came to shape and dominate twentieth-century U.S. foreign policy employed and interpreted international law in an extremely cynical manner. By "strategic legalism" I mean the use of laws or legal arguments to further larger policy objectives, irrespective of facts or laws, as Root pointed out: "It is not the function of law to enforce the rules of morality."

Throughout the early twentieth century, a long line of Wall Street–trained American lawyer-statesmen took the lead in pushing for radical new codes of international conduct that threatened by implication to undermine many of the traditional European rules of statecraft. The Europeans resisted these efforts, and no country more vehemently than Germany. Their representatives at the 1899 and 1907 Hague conferences made it clear that they wanted no part of the new international laws and courts. Above all, the Germans viewed war, not law, as the value-free means of dispute resolution. They rejected the "neutrality" of international law and any international court. To the leaders of the Second Reich, in the arena of international affairs there were only friends and enemies, and the only sacred international political principle was sovereignty. As a result of these views, American lawyer-statesmen like Elihu Root deemed Germany "the great disturber of world peace."

World War I was a very different kind of war, in both scale and aims. With the American entry in 1917, it was fully transformed into a crusade against German tyranny, or as Elihu Root described it, "A battle between Odin and Christ." The emergence of democracy and total war in the late nineteenth century began to erode Europe's customary rules of warfare. The popular support required for total war also included a vilification of the enemy, and by the twentieth century, amnesties for wartime atrocities were being replaced by more punitive approaches. With the defeat of Germany came a window of opportunity for U.S. leaders to transform international relations along the lines advocated by American lawyer-statesmen like Elihu Root. Germany was not only labeled with war guilt but also fined with reparations. Most dramatic of all, by indicting the former Kaiser Wilhelm and attempting to put him on trial, the world powers crossed a threshold, challenging the sanctity of sovereignty.

The American duality was alive and well at the Paris Peace Conference and even in the fine print of the Treaty of Versailles. This time American President Woodrow Wilson and his Secretary of State Robert Lansing personified it. While President Wilson was attempting to overturn many of the traditional European rules of statecraft, Robert Lansing and colleague James Brown Scott stood unequivocally against the trial of the Kaiser, the punishment of the "Young Turks" for their genocide of over one million Armenians, and more generally, the expansion of international law. Like Elihu Root, both men were extremely successful Wall Street lawyers who argued that the prosecution of individuals for war crimes would imperil America's postwar strategic interests. In this case, Lansing was concerned that a breakdown of the old German social and political order could lead to a Bolshevik takeover. Another facet of the American duality was buried in a single, very significant amendment to the Treaty of Versailles. Although the League of Nations proposed outlawing colonialism and extending natural rights on a global basis, the United States was allowed to preserve its right to hemispheric intervention under the terms of the Monroe Doctrine.

The Leipzig trials, held in the German *Reichsgericht* in 1921, provide yet another example of a new form of twentieth-century political justice— strategic legalism. Unlike the General Jacob Smith case, where the U.S. government acted voluntarily, in the Leipzig trials the Germans were forced to prosecute their soldiers under the terms of the Versailles Treaty. But as in the Jacob Smith case, the Germans were no strangers to strategic legalism. They coupled stern and solemn judgments with very light sentences that also were subject to post-trial, nonjudicial modification. German authorities simply allowed convicts to "escape" after their trials.

The interwar period saw a flurry of American-inspired international legal efforts, the most radical of which was the Kellogg-Briand Pact of 1928. Elihu Root was near the end of his life by now and he had passed the torch to his apprentice, Henry Stimson. Not only had Stimson begun his career in Elihu Root's Wall Street law firm, he was a forceful advocate of the revolutionary new treaties. After the Japanese seized Manchuria in 1931, Henry Stimson declared, in what would come to be known as the Stimson Doctrine, that the United States reserved the right of "nonrecognition" for governments that did not come to power through what it considered to be "legitimate means."

The rise of National Socialism in Germany came at a time when European leaders were both war weary and unprepared to confront an aggressive regime willing to couple bad-faith diplomacy with military force. The Rhineland, Austria, and Czechoslovakia were taken over with minimum force, maximum bluff, and all the diplomatic trappings. Moreover, Hitler forced occupied nations like Czechoslovakia to accept the Munich Agreement or face destruction. In between more naked acts of aggression, as we shall see, Hitler's diplomats employed their own form of strategic legalism by providing careful, legal justifications for each takeover.

So by the late 1930s, Hitler had, for all intents and purposes, rendered the Treaty of Versailles null and void. Certainly one of the overlooked tragedies of World War II is the fate of Poland. Not only were Polish civilians of all religions killed, but Allied leaders failed to keep their word both during and after the war. The Poles suffered the horror of both Nazi and Soviet occupations. Once Hitler had obtained the goals he outlined in *Mein Kampf*, Poland became the site of Nazi Germany's unique contribution to the twentieth century—the death camp. However, unlike the residents of Indian reservations of the American West or the U.S. *reconcentrado* camps in the Philippines, the inmates of these camps were "less than slaves." If they could not be worked to death, they were killed with cold precision.

It would become very clear after the war that the Nazis fought according to different sets of rules, depending on their theater of operations. As Sven Lindqvist observes, "In the war against the western powers, the Germans observed the laws of war. Only 3.5 percent of English and American prisoners of war died in captivity, though 57 percent of Soviet prisoners of war died." In the East, the Third Reich waged a war of annihilation. The records left behind by the *Einsatzgruppen* and other sadistic execution squads like the *Dirlewanger* Regiment provide ample evidence that the Nazis spared few during Operation Barbarossa. However, on the Western Front, with a few famous exceptions, American

POWs were treated far better by the Germans than by the Japanese. Roughly 27 percent of the American POWs in Japanese captivity died, while only 3–5 percent died in German and Italian captivity. Japanese contempt for the weak, defeated, and defenseless led to carnivals of atrocity that lasted for weeks in Asian cities like Nanking and Manila, where tens of thousands of women were raped and hundreds of thousands of civilians slaughtered. Books by Iris Chang, Sheldon Harris, Yuki Tanaka, John Dower, and Hal Gold helped me to better understand the contempt that the Japanese military forces displayed toward the weak and the vanquished.

However, it was the Third Reich's systematic aggression and the killing of millions of European Jews that motivated American lawyer-statesmen like Murray Bernays and Henry Stimson to find a way to try German leaders. Because the Nazis had so carefully bureaucratized and legalized not just their invasions but even their killings, this posed new and insurmountable challenges for the traditional laws of war. Germany's Jews were German nationals; the atrocities committed against them, no matter how horrific, were outside the jurisdiction of the laws of war. Punishment for the defendants was absolutely dependent on legal innovation, or as many would later argue, *ex post facto* law. Once the defeat of the Third Reich was imminent, the advocates of a punitive peace were led by Henry Morgenthau. The U.S. State Department objected to this plan, favoring German rehabilitation (for similar reasons to those employed by Robert Lansing after World War I) to prevent the expansion of the Soviet sphere of influence. It was left to American lawyer-statesmen, led by Henry Stimson, to argue that German leaders should be tried under the interwar nonaggression treaties like the Kellogg-Briand Pact. The protrial faction was a fragile coalition of second- and third-generation lawyer-statesmen like Henry Stimson and John McCloy and liberal New Dealers like Telford Taylor and Robert Jackson.

Once the protrial faction emerged victorious from the internecine domestic battle in Washington in 1945, it had to convert very skeptical European allies to the idea that the trials would do more than render justice; they would also serve to "reeducate" the German people. While the American lawyer-statesmen were able to get the Allies to agree to charge German leaders under the radical new rules of statecraft that the United States had been pushing since at least 1907, ironically, they were unable to convert their scattered domestic critics on the right and the left. By 1945, the U.S. State Department was already resurrecting Nazi intelligence infrastructure and operations in order to get a jump on the Soviet Union's efforts along similar lines.

However, this posed unique problems for U.S. foreign policy because military defeat was not the sole objective of the American war effort. U.S. leaders committed themselves to radical and wide-ranging social reform policy called "denazification." Although this was unlike anything Europeans had ever seen, it was all too familiar to Americans south of the Mason-Dixon Line, who had undergone a similarly resented postwar reconstruction after the Civil War. The German postwar reconstruction was founded upon the assumption that if only the Allies could somberly present evidence of Hitler's war guilt, Germans would recognize and acknowledge the criminality of their leadership. It turned out to be significantly more complicated than this.

While the Nuremberg trial is often referred to in the singular, there were actually three major trials, all different in scope and meaning. As American political scientist Quincy Wright pointed out in the 1950s, the Nuremberg trials provided a fresh setting for positivists and natural advocates to settle old scores. The leading American historian of the International Military Tribunal, Bradley F. Smith, concludes that although the trials were in many ways hypocritical, in the end their collective judgments were conservative and on the whole quite sound. Although British historians John and Ann Tusa take a harder view of Robert Jackson and the Americans, they too have a favorable view of the trials. German historians Werner Maser and Jörg Friedrich point out important flaws in the trials and most important, how the Soviet inclusion tainted the proceedings in the eyes of many Germans.

Nuremberg's International Military Tribunal (IMT), the first trial, continues to be the most popular model for contemporary international criminal courts and the central object of inquiry for almost all books on the subject. Between November 20, 1945 and September 30, 1946, a four-nation international court indicted twenty-two of Nazi Germany's highest ranking survivors under a radical indictment that included charges of aggression or crimes against peace, crimes against humanity, and conspiracy. The tribunal sentenced twelve men to death, seven to prison terms, and acquitted three. Initially the international court was planning to try more cases against German military and civilian leaders. Because of U.S.-Soviet tensions, however, President Truman was advised by the IMT's

Chief Prosecutor, Robert Jackson, not to participate in another international trial. Instead, the President asked OSS Colonel and IMT prosecutor Telford Taylor to create and staff American courts in Nuremberg to try the remaining high-level war criminals. Armed with an indictment modeled on the IMT's, American lawyers and judges tried one hundred eighty-five men in twelve cases at Nuremberg's Palace of Justice between 1947 and 1949. What initially interested me in these trials was the conspicuous absence of secondary sources about them. These were the more interesting trials because the courts were forced to address the same vexing questions as the IMT had, in far less certain cases, long after the passions of war had cooled. As the Cold War intensified, a new American duality emerged as political concerns began to eclipse moral and legal ones.

In trying to obtain even the most basic information about the American Nuremberg trials, I found a glaring historiographic omission—the absence of a single English-language study. With the exception of *Telford Taylor's Final Report to the Secretary of the Army on the Nuernberg War Crimes Trials*, books like Joseph Borkin's *The Crime and Punishment of I. G. Farben*; Josiah Dubois's *The Devil's Chemists*; William Manchester's *The Arms of Krupp*; more recently, Ian Buruma's *The Wages of Guilt*; and Richard von Weizsäcker's *From Weimar to the Wall* examine specific cases, but none offers a comprehensive analysis of the subsequent proceedings and war criminals' changes of fate during the mid-1950s. In German there is more literature, Jörg Friedrich's *Das Gesetz Des Krieges* being by far the most comprehensive account of any single American Nuremberg trial.

The American Nuremberg trials resembled the IMT in a number of ways. In addition to punishing the guilty, the American courts intended to create an irrefutable record of Hitler's Third Reich. Defendants were not simply charged with violations of the customary rules of war, they were subject to the same unprecedented standards of international conduct as the defendants at the IMT. Military leaders, politicians, lawyers, doctors, businessmen, and bankers faced charges of aggression, conspiracy, and crimes against humanity. Each case produced a voluminous historical record composed of documentary evidence and testimony. The transcripts of the final American Nuremberg trial alone ran to 28,000 pages. The defendants included industrialist Alfried Krupp, diplomat Ernst von Weizsäcker, *Einsatzkommando* Otto Ohlendorf, Field Marshal Wilhelm von List, Judge Rudolf Oeschey, and many other high-ranking Third Reich officials. Originally Telford Taylor had hoped to try as many as three hundred individuals. However, by 1949 it was clear that these punitive policies did not fit with the new American plan for West Germany.

Initially, I was interested in the final American trial at Nuremberg because my great-grandfather had been a judge. I quickly learned that *United States v. Ernst von Weizsaecker* was an extremely complicated case that brought charges against twenty-one high-ranking Nazis from all sectors of the Third Reich. The Ministries case could best be described as a Cold War IMT. Its roster of defendants included Ernst von Weizsäcker, SS General Walter Schellenberg, banker Emil Puhl, industrialist Wilhelm Keppler, Chief of the Reich Chancellery Hans Lammers, Reich Minister of Public Enlightenment Otto Dietrich, SS General Gottlob Berger, and fourteen others.

The American Nuremberg trials and especially the Ministries case would serve as yet another "moment of truth" that would test America's commitment to the trials themselves and their international legal legacy. The prosecution charged former State Secretary Ernst von Weizsäcker with the radical and recent crime of aggression (crimes against peace) for his role in the Nazi takeover of Czechoslovakia. His five-man defense team included his son Richard, who would later serve as the President of the Federal Republic of Germany and one of the most eloquent spokesmen of his generation. This was the only American court to convict under the controversial aggression charge. However, the decision was not unanimous: Judge Leon Powers blasted the majority decision in his dissenting opinion.

Few historians have attempted to consider the Nuremberg trials within the context of America's larger post–World War II war crimes policy. The first thing that becomes apparent is that the Nuremberg trials compare very favorably to the trial programs run by the various branches of the American military. The most glaring victor's justices came in the Yamashita case and the Malmedy trials. These proceedings occured immediately after the war when passions had not yet cooled; the cry for vengeance outweighed considerations of due process. This was postwar military justice, after all.

Aside from a single French trial in 1947 (Hermann Roechling), the only other court to employ a Nuremburg-like indictment was the International Military Tribunal Far East ("Tokyo Trial"). The eleven-man international tribunal arraigned twenty-eight of Japan's military and civilian leaders on May 3, 1946. Although Emperor Hirohito was not among the defendants, they did include Hideki Tojo and a number of other military and political officials. After two and a half strife-filled years, the court sentenced seven men to death and seventeen to life in prison on November 4, 1948. Three of the eleven judges filed dissenting opinions. Justice Radhabinod Pal of India issued a scathing dissenting opinion that found all of the accused not guilty on every count of the indictment. Fueled by anti-imperialism, Pal wrote, "It would be sufficient for my present purpose to say that if any indiscriminate destruction of civilian life and property is illegitimate in warfare, then . . . this decision to use the atom bomb is the only near approach to the directives of . . . the Nazi leaders." In an effort to place the Nuremberg trials within the context of post–World War II war crimes adjudication, I have included summary analyses of the IMT, IMTFE (Tokyo Trial), and a few of the more significant military cases. The published secondary works of Bradley F. Smith, John and Ann Tusa, Robert Conot, Eugene Davidson, Drexel Sprecher, James Willis, Thomas Schwartz, Telford Taylor, Frank Lael, John Dower, James Weingartner, Frank Buscher, Phillip Piccigallo, James Bosch, Howard Levie, Michael Marrus, and John Pritchard were particularly helpful.

I then go on to examine the paroles of convicted war criminals in West Germany and Japan during the 1950s carried out by the U.S. Army (low level) and the State Department (high level). What interests me here is the clash between the geopolitical need for "reconciliation" with new and important allies and the traditional U.S. commitment to principles of law and human rights. Many West Germans, their leaders included, found the Nuremberg manner of punishment and parole confusing, unprecedented, and ultimately legally illegitimate. In the end, the United States and the Federal Republic found a face-saving way of resolving the war crimes question to West Germany's advantage. The ensuing story of how some of the worst war criminals of World War II were quietly paroled is worth telling. It is widely known that Rudolf Hess and the other IMT defendants were shown little mercy under quadripartite control in Berlin's Spandau Prison. How did the war criminals in the western prisons (Werl, Wittlich, and Landsberg) fare?

After I read Frank Buscher's groundbreaking study, *The American War Crimes Program in Germany*, and spent some time at the National Archives reading the State Department legal advisor's war crimes files, my eyes were opened to a far more complex picture that consisted of many levels of activity. In 1951, less than two years after the last Nuremberg sentence was handed down, U.S. High Commissioner John McCloy ordered the first large-scale sentence reductions; he has provided a convenient scapegoat for historians ever since. Although McCloy's justifications for the sentence reductions were weak and often disingenuous, his actions were nowhere near as dramatic as the releases that came after 1953.

With the exception of Buscher's study, most of the accounts of war crimes clemency focus too heavily on John McCloy and his motives. What Buscher so powerfully demonstrates is that by 1953, American leaders viewed the war criminals as a political question they wanted to resolve as quickly and quietly as possible. For German views on the subject I relied on Jörg Friedrich, Norbert Frei, Anna and Richard Merrit, Thomas Schwartz, Jeffrey Herf, and Verene Botzenhart-Viehe.

My real education on the German side of these questions began in the summer of 1995, when I was hired as a historical advisor for a Chronos Films documentary entitled *Nuremberg: A Courtroom Drama* with German historian Jörg Friedrich under the direction of Spiegel Television's Michael Kloft. Not only did we watch all the American and Soviet footage of the trials, but Kloft interviewed everyone from Telford Taylor to Markus Wolf to Louise Jodl. I was able to interview Nuremberg's most successful defense attorney, Otto Kranzbühler, in the summer of 1996. After representing Admiral Doenitz, Alfried Krupp, and many other prominent defendants at Nuremberg, Kranzbühler advised Chancellor Adenauer on the war crimes question throughout the 1950s. He proudly described how he engineered both the early releases of Germany's most notorious war criminals and the official West German nonrecognition of the legal validity of the original sentences. Friedrich and I carefully examined the treaties restoring German sovereignty in the early 1950s and found the final and official German expression of illegitimacy in paragraphs 6.11 and 7 of the Paris Treaty on the Termination of the Status of Occupation of 1952. Buried in the paragraph regarding war criminals, just as Kranzbühler had told us, is a confusing caveat. In it the West German government, in a roundabout way, refused to accept the legal validity of not only the Nuremberg trials but all of the Allied war crimes trials.

I returned to the National Archives in College Park, Maryland in 1997 and, thanks to the help of archivist Martin McCaan, found the secret correspondence between the State Department legal advisors and the American members of the various war crimes parole boards. This new material demonstrates how American leaders caved in to official West

German pressure to release war criminals and as a result cast a shadow of doubt over the legal legitimacy of those trials in Germany. Many argue that however misguided the war crimes clemencies were, they did not detract from "the lessons of Nuremberg." I reject this view. In 1958, a parole board composed of Germans and Americans released the final four war criminals. Three of the four men had been members of the *Einsatzgruppen*, sentenced to death by an American tribunal at Nuremberg in 1948.

American clemency board member Spencer Phenix wrote State Department Assistant Legal Advisor John Raymond a telling memo on the eve of the decision: "I can answer all your questions and between us we can reach substantial agreement on what can and should be done to get this bothersome problem quietly out of the way where it will no longer complicate international relations." Because the question of war crimes clemency was usually linked to German rearmament, it created the impression that the United States was trading war criminals for German rearmament.

Did America fail to punish convicted German war criminals due to a lack of resolve? Or were there more serious internal problems with the Nuremberg approach to war crimes adjudication? It is my contention that a number of international political factors combined to force American and Allied authorities to abandon their controversial war crimes policy. In the United States, many scholars continue to point to the Allied war crimes trials, especially Nuremberg's IMT, as the centerpiece of a successful reeducation effort. The American flight from the radical and punitive policies of the occupation period coincided with the release and social reinstitution of prominent war criminals like Alfried Krupp and Ernst von Weizsäcker. This sent a powerful message to the West German body politic. The question was further confused when President Eisenhower asked West Germany to rearm under the EDC Treaty in the early 1950s. The abrupt and often contradictory shifts in American foreign policy reopened the question of Nuremberg's legitimacy in West Germany. Finally, we are left with two Nuremberg myths: the American myth of the redemptive trial and the German myth of the victor's justice.

Chapter One

THE END OF LIMITED WAR

Today, there is a tendency to romanticize both the chivalric era and
the early years of the European state system as more humane times,
when soldiers were governed by codes of honor and civilians were not
targeted for wanton destruction.[1] However, what is often overlooked is
that the gentlemanly rules of war outlined by both Christian scholars and
the Heralds applied only to warriors of the same race and class. When
invasive "others" like Norsemen and Muslims descended on early European states, the only law of war was survival. The roots of this duality can
be traced to Christianity and its paradoxical and incongruous relationship with armed violence.[2] In order to protect and spread their pacific
faith, early Christian leaders were forced to condone and justify violence.
As military historian Michael Howard points out, neither the laws of
nations nor "warriors' honor" applied "when Norsemen were raging
through the land like devouring flames."[3] In wars against pagans, no
holds were barred, no prisoners were taken; and this was in keeping with
the *guerre mortale* doctrine.

Although America had no Norsemen or Magyars, it did have an

indigenous population of at least five million scattered across the continent.[4] The Seneca, Sioux (or Lakota, as they call themselves and are now
commonly known), Iroquois, Cheyenne, Arapaho, Apache, Chippewa,
Nez Perce, and numerous others had lived free, according to their own
rules, for thousands of years. However, even in America there was freedom only for some, and this was consistent with Jefferson's original vision.
According to nineteenth-century American historian Frederick Jackson
Turner, the first period of U.S. history was spent clearing and pacifying
the western frontier—no small feat, and one that required equal parts
determination and brutality.[5]

What were the moral implications of forcibly uprooting America's
native inhabitants for the "Citty upon a Hill," the republic founded upon
the principles of "liberty and justice for all"? As Walter McDougall notes
in *Promised Land, Crusader State*, "The evidence that the colonists believed
that America was a holy land (that is 'set apart') is so abundant as to be
trite. Governor John Winthrop: 'to Consider that wee shall be as a Citty
upon a Hill, the eies of all people are uppon us.' "[6] A previous generation
of European leaders had been content to invoke the divine right of God
or king to justify war and territorial acquisition, but American leaders
outwardly scorned the European model of power politics. However, from
the beginning, the United States was founded and built upon a contradiction. As Edmund Morgan observes in *American Slavery, American Freedom*,
the simultaneous development of both slavery and freedom on the American continent is the "central paradox" of sixteenth- to nineteenth-century American history.[7] As with the slaves, if American leaders denied the
Indians their humanity, they could deny them their natural rights. Before
there were "war criminals," there were "barbarians," "heathens," and
"savages" who did not qualify as equals in the arena of "civilized warfare."

From the beginning, America's founding fathers considered the American Indians barbarians. The second President of the United States, John
Adams, described Indian warfare in a 1775 letter: "The Indians are
known to conduct their Wars so entirely without Faith and Humanity,
that it will bring eternal infamy. . . . To let loose these blood Hounds to
scalp Men and to butcher Women and Children is horrid."[8] "Humanity,"
or in this case, a lack thereof, provided the justification that allowed European and U.S. armies to occupy territory and exploit it unhindered by the
restraints of the traditional European rules of statecraft. The early Amer-

ican settlers granted their continent's native inhabitants no natural rights;
Puritan leader Reverend Cotton Mather put it very bluntly: "To think of
raising these hideous creatures into our holy religion! . . . All was diaboli-
cal among them."[9]

The American frontier and especially the northern plains were
inhabited by fierce and seasoned Indian warriors whom military historian John Keegan counts "among the most remarkable of all the world's
warrior peoples." By the end of the eighteenth century they possessed
horses and guns and "combined their use into terrifyingly effective military practice. . . . It is difficult to think of any other pre-literate ethnic
group which has made so rapid and complete a transition from primitive to sophisticated warriordom in so short a space of time."[10] Stephen
Longstreet makes a similar point in *Indian Wars of the Great Plains*. "The
Indian, long before napalm, made total war. It was his ritual right, his
sense of tribal sportsmanship to take horses and women—in key with
his vision of the world, his guiding spirits."[11]

Many of the American tribes lived in "hard primitive" societies in
which war played an important role. "War had, of course, also been central to the way of life of many of the Indian tribes since time immemori-
al. Indian warfare, however, generally took forms quite different from
those known to Europeans," writes John Keegan, describing the significance of war in Sioux Indian culture. He points to the role of hostage
taking: "A dominant motive in their style of their warfare, however, was
the taking of captives, to be adopted into the tribe as a replacement for a
casualty if thought worthy, to be tortured to death if not; it was bravery
under torture that usually determined the captive's fitness for adoption."
Keegan goes so far as to say that of all the opponents it faced in the eighteenth and nineteenth centuries, the U.S. Army had the most difficult job
in the American plains: "the enemies of the British and French . . . cunning, tough, and brave though they were—did not approach the Plains
Indians in qualities of harsh individual warriordom."[12]

American settlers faced fearsome foes who shared none of their ethical
assumptions about life and death, much less war. Because the customary
laws of war forbade guerrilla warfare, the taking of hostages, and the
massacre of civilians, the early colonists and the U.S. government never
recognized the legitimacy of the American Indian resistance. Historian
William Fowell remarks on the differing perceptions of war: to the American mind, the so-called Indian raids "amounted simply to massacre, an

atrocious and utterly unjustifiable butchery of unoffending citizens." However, says Dr. Fowell, the Sioux were fighting for national survival according to their own time-honored customs: "The Indian, however, saw himself engaged in war, the most honorable of all pursuits, against men who, as he believed, had robbed him of his country and his freedom."[13]

Colonial leaders had no qualms about slaughtering those tribes that resisted the colonists' "civilizing" influence. As early as 1675, colonists nearly wiped out the Algonquin Indians for attacking and destroying colonial settlements in what would come to be known as King Philip's War.[14] In the end, King Philip, the Algonquin Indian leader, was captured and killed. His head was exhibited in Plymouth for the next twenty years, and his wife and children were sold as slaves in the West Indies.[15] Reprisal would become the key word in America's emerging Indian policy. Tribes that refused American demands were subjected to harsh punitive measures.

America's first President, George Washington, ordered Major General John Sullivan to "chastize" hostile Iroquois in a May 31, 1779 letter. President Washington wanted the Indian villages "not merely overrun but destroyed. But you will not by any means, listen to any overture of peace before the total ruin of their settlements is effected." Washington wanted to establish a precedent of terror and believed that American national security demanded it: "Our future security will be in their inability to injure us . . . and in the terror with which the severity of the chastizement they receive will inspire them."[16] Major General Sullivan shared his commander-in-chief's view that "the Indians shall see that there is malice enough in our hearts to destroy everything that contributes to their support."[17]

In 1792, George Hammond, the first British ambassador to the United States, asked Thomas Jefferson what he "understood as the right of the United States in Indian soil?" Jefferson responded, "We consider it as established by the usage of different nations into a kind of jus gentium (Law of Nations) for America," arguing that while the United States would treat the invasion of Indian territory by "any other white nation" as an act of war, America assumed "no right of soil against the native possessors." Hammond was utterly unconvinced by Jefferson's earnest claims and told him that the British believed the United States planned "to exterminate the Indians and take their lands." Jefferson replied defensively, "On the contrary, our system was to protect them, even against our own citizens: that we wish to get lines established with all of them, and have no views even of purchasing any more land of them for a long time."[18] However, the U.S. government's actions would tell another story.

When Thomas Jefferson became President in 1801, the duality of American frontier policy became clear for all to see. Contradicting the position he had presented to the British diplomat in 1792, the United States began to undergo a massive territorial expansion during his presidency. The precedent for America's nineteenth-century Indian policy can be found in an 1803 letter from President Jefferson to Indiana Territory Governor William Henry Harrison. It outlined a uniquely American form of conquest—credit and debt: "To promote this disposition to exchange lands, which they have to spare and we want, we shall push our trading uses, and be glad to see the good and influential individuals among them run in debt, because we observe that when these debts get beyond what individuals can pay, they become willing to lop them off by a cessation of lands."[19] The American plans for conquest were passive-aggressive and indirect by design. The President noted the importance of appearances and encouraged Governor Harrison to soothe the Indians "by liberalities and sincere assurances of friendship." Jefferson's objective was to "finally consolidate our whole country to one nation only." However, he realized that time was running out: "The crisis is pressing; whatever can now be obtained must be obtained quickly."[20] By 1812, less than two decades after Jefferson's pledge to the British ambassador, the United States had acquired 109,884,000 acres of former Indian territory, and its slave population had grown to more than 1.2 million.[21] As Alexis de Toqueville observed in the 1830s, "The Americans are already able to make their flag respected; in a few years, they will make it feared."[22]

To early American leaders, owning land was a question of establishing "dominion" over it; because most of America's native tribes were hunters, their relationship with the land did not qualify as ownership. In a September 23, 1818 letter to Judge William Tudor, John Adams described the American expansion in these terms: "Shall we say that a few handfulls of scattering tribes of savages have a right of dominion and property over a quarter of this globe capable of nourishing hundreds of millions of happy human beings? Why had not the Europeans a right to come and hunt and fish with them?"[23] However, was sustenance all that the American settlers sought? What were the implications of this massive territorial expansion for the American Indians?

Senator Benjamin Leigh of Virginia was more candid than most when he described the significance of America's westward spread in 1824:

> It is peculiar to the character of this Anglo-Saxon race of men to which we belong, that it has never been contented to live in the same country with any other distinct race, upon terms of equality; it has invariably, when placed in that situation, proceeded to exterminate or enslave the other race in some form or other, or, failing that, to abandon the country.[24]

James Madison seemed to recognize the American paradox in an 1826 letter: "Next to the case of the black race within our bosom, that of the red on our borders is the problem most baffling to the policy of our country."[25] Even as late as 1831, the legal status of the American Indians was unclear. Supreme Court Chief Justice Marshall called the various tribes "domestic dependent nations" in *Cherokee Nation v. Georgia* (1831):

> The Indians are acknowledged to have unquestionable and heretofore an unquestioned right to the lands they occupy until that right shall be extinguished by a voluntary cessation to the Government. It may well be doubted whether those tribes which reside within the acknowledged boundaries of the United States can with strict accuracy be denominated domestic dependent nations. They occupy territory to which we assert a title, independent of their will, which must take effect in point of possession when their right of possession ceases; meanwhile they are in a state of pupilage. The relations with the United States resemble that of a ward to his guardian. They look to our Government for protection; rely upon its kindness and its power; appeal to it for relief to their wants, and address the President as their great father.[26]

American Indian historian Vine Deloria Jr. best describes the Indians' ambiguous international legal status: "Marshall, building on this foundation of domestic dependency, interposed a limited sovereignty enjoyed by the Indian nations to prevent the state of Georgia from extending its power over the Cherokee Nation's lands." However, Indians' legal rights meant little if the federal government was unwilling to uphold the court's decisions. "Andrew Jackson's refusal to enforce Marshall's decision gave mute testimony that, if the tribes had legal rights affirmed by the highest court in the land, their political status made it easy to void such rights."[27]

After a successful war against Mexico, the United States took possession of Texas and California. With the discovery of gold in California in 1848, wagon trains filled with hopeful settlers streamed west onto "the permanent Indian frontier." What the U.S. government did not take by treaty, the settlers simply occupied. The American Indians would soon learn that under the white man's law, possession by squatting could be translated into ownership. Not surprisingly, many native tribes were unwilling to give up their land without a fight. By the time Minnesota became a state in 1860, the various bands of Sioux had sold more than 24,000,000 acres of their territory to the U.S. government.[28] Two treaties signed by Sioux leaders in 1837 and 1851 relieved them of 90 percent of their property in exchange for annuity payments from the American government. The 1851 treaty promised a lump-sum payment that the Sioux had still not received by 1862.[29]

The situation in Minnesota was exacerbated during the 1850s by more than 150,000 settlers who moved into the state and, in many cases, pushed onto land reserved for the Sioux as "permanent Indian frontier."[30] Often the government's annuity payments went straight to frontier traders for supplies already purchased on credit. When the Sioux chiefs demanded to be paid directly, the traders refused to extend them further credit. In the summer of 1862, the situation reached a point of crisis.

Due to crop failure and the drastically reduced hunting grounds, many Santee Sioux were going hungry and turned to their chief Little Crow for help. This leader was in a very precarious position because he had a foot in each world. Although he was the son and grandson of Santee chiefs, Little Crow decided that resisting the white expansion would be futile. After a tour of American cities, he returned to Minnesota, joined the Episcopal church, built a house, and even started to farm. Little Crow not only signed the two treaties surrendering Sioux territory but had even been to Washington to meet "the Great Father," President Buchanan.[31]

Although Little Crow had become a "model Indian" in the eyes of the white men, as the summer of 1862 dragged on and no payments arrived, even he began to lose faith in the American government. In July, he led several thousand Santee to Upper Agency to collect their government annuity payments and to purchase food and other supplies.

However, when the payments did not arrive, a rumor began to circulate that the U.S. government had spent all their gold in the Civil War.[32] Little Crow approached the U.S. Indian Agent, Thomas Galbraith, and asked why his people could not be issued food instead of gold if the storehouses were full and they were starving. Galbraith refused the Santee chief's request and called in one hundred U.S. soldiers to guard the storehouses. On August 4, more than five hundred Santee surrounded the soldiers in Upper Agency.[33] Overwhelmingly outnumbered, the U.S. soldiers watched as the Indians took flour and other basic supplies. Little Crow was still not satisfied and demanded on August 13 that Galbraith distribute more supplies in the neighboring settlement, Lower Agency.[34]

Two days later, on August 15, Little Crow and several hundred of his followers arrived in Lower Agency. However, this time the Indian Agent refused to distribute goods.[35] Little Crow tried to reason with Agent Galbraith: "We have waited a long time. The money is ours, but we cannot get it. We have no food, but here are these stores, filled with food. We ask that you, the agent, make some arrangement by which we can get food from the stores. . . . Or else we may take our own way to keep ourselves from starving. When men are hungry, they help themselves." The Indian Agent said nothing; however, storekeeper Andrew Myrick responded derisively, "So far as I am concerned, if they are hungry let them eat grass or their own dung."[36] This public insult, coupled with Little Crow's failure to obtain food, cost the Santee leader the trust of his own people.

On August 17, 1862, four Sioux braves attacked and killed a group of settlers near Acton, Minnesota.[37] Late that night, Little Crow was awakened and informed of the massacre. He warned of harsh reprisals for the killings. "No Santee's life would be safe, not after these killings. . . . It was the white man's way to punish all Indians for the crimes of one or a few." The braves called for a preemptive strike before the settlers' reinforcements could arrive: "The Santees might as well strike first instead of waiting for the soldiers to come and kill them. It would be better to fight the white men now while they are fighting among themselves far to the south."[38]

Little Crow did not want to go to war and mocked the braves: "You are full of the white man's devil water. You are like dogs in the Hot Moon when they run mad and snap at their own shadows." He warned his militant followers that the whites were "like the locusts when they fly so thick that the whole sky is a snowstorm. . . . Kill one—two—ten, and ten times ten will come to kill you. Count your fingers all day long and white men with guns in their hands will come faster than you can count."[39] When the warriors began to question their leader's bravery, Little Crow quieted them with a grim prophecy: "Braves, you are like little children—you are fools. You will die like rabbits when the hungry wolves hunt them in the Hard Moon of January."[40]

The war council continued through the night; although chiefs Little Crow and Big Eagle called for peace, they were shouted down by a firm majority set on vengeance. Finally, Little Crow reluctantly agreed to wage war and drive the settlers out of Sioux territory once and for all. However, the seventy-year-old chief realized that the war would soon escalate and issued another stern warning: "Blood has been shed, the payments will be stopped and the whites will exact a terrible revenge because women have been killed, but I will lead you."[41] That night Little Crow sent word to neighboring tribes that there would be an early morning surprise attack on Lower Agency.[42] The Santee would settle the score with the traders first.

The next morning at 6:00, Little Crow and other Santee gathered near the stores that would not extend them credit and waited for their signal. At 6:30, a young warrior named Wasu-ota ran toward Andrew Myrick's, shouting, "Now, I will kill the dog who would not give me credit."[43] Myrick ran into his store and up the stairs to the second floor. When the Indians set fire to the building, he jumped from a window. The shopkeeper's body was later found shot and scalped. Big Eagle entered Lower Agency after the massacre and saw him "lying on the ground dead, with his mouth stuffed full of grass, and the Indians were saying tauntingly: 'Myrick is eating grass himself.' "[44]

Very quickly, Minnesota settlers were forced to realize that the Sioux did not recognize the most basic distinction between soldier and civilian. In fact, torture and terror had deep precedents in native American military history. Settler Justina Kreiger was captured by the Sioux and recalled her ordeal in a book written at the time: "One of these inhuman savages seized . . . my niece, yet alive, held her up by the foot . . . while holding her there by one hand . . . he hastily cut the flesh around one of the legs . . . and then, by twisting and wrenching, broke the ligaments and bone, until the limb was entirely severed from the body, the child was screaming frantically, 'O God! O God!' "[45] Mary Schwandt was fourteen when the Sioux killed her family and took her prisoner: "When I screamed . . . one of the fiends struck me on the mouth with his hand, causing the blood to flow very freely. They then took me out by force, to an unoccupied tepee . . . and perpetrated the most horrible and nameless outrages upon my person. These outrages were repeated, at different times during my captivity."[46]

When settlers from the nearby Beaver Creek settlement loaded their wagons and fled, they had barely traveled a mile before they were surrounded by painted Santee warriors. After they surrendered their wagons and livestock, the Indians opened fire on them. Two settlers tried to surrender under a white flag; according to a witness, "Wedge and Henderson held up a white cloth, but it was not regarded, and Wedge was shot dead, and Henderson lost the fingers off one hand. The Indians then came up and pulling the bed with Mrs. Henderson on it to the ground, set fire to it. One of the infant children was beaten to death over the wagon wheel, and thrown in the fire, the other was cut to pieces and thrown in piecemeal."[47]

If the American Indians employed these methods against one another, why should the American settlers be exempt? Historian William Fowell observes, "He [Sioux] was making war on the white people in the same fashion in which he would have gone against the Chippewa or the Foxes."[48] As the Lower Agency massacre was in progress, the Santee leader rode into town and became angry because his men were too busy looting and not intent enough on killing. According to Minnesota historian Marion Satterlee, Little Crow entered the settlement and ordered his men to shoot the remaining survivors.[49] While generally critical of the Sioux, Satterlee, writing in 1921, described their decision to wage war thus: "With true Indian sagacity they made certain that no trouble was expected, and that there was no probability of their plans miscarrying. It is but just to state, that very many of these Indians were unwilling attendants. But the orders of the Soldiers Lodge were imperative and absolute, disobedience meant dishonor, heavy penalty even instant death, if enforced."[50]

Forty-seven settlers managed to escape the slaughter at Lower Agency thanks to the heroic efforts of a ferryman named Herbert Millier.[51] The survivors traveled thirteen miles downstream toward the federal garrison at Fort Ridgely, where Company B of the Fifth Minnesota Voluntary Infantry Regiment was stationed. Captain John Marsh and forty-six mounted U.S. soldiers intercepted the fleeing settlers and rode for Acton. The relief party was ambushed long before it reached its destination. Captain Marsh tried to escape by crossing a river, but he was struck by cramps and drowned.[52] Sergeant John Bishop managed to straggle back to Fort Ridgely with twenty-four survivors. The Santee made a key strategic error at this point by not pressing their advantage and capturing the American fort. Little Crow was in favor of attacking and argued that as warriors, they had to engage and defeat the soldiers. However, the young braves wanted to attack the undefended town of New Ulm, loot the storehouses, and capture more civilians. Once again, Little Crow was overruled.[53]

The Sioux rampage in Minnesota came as an especially unwelcome distraction to President Abraham Lincoln. The President was trying to rally the Union Army after poor initial outings against the Confederacy when Minnesota exploded into open warfare. A short front-page story in the August 22 edition of *The New York Times* announced, TROUBLE WITH THE INDIANS IN MINNESOTA. ATTACK ON THE WHITES—MEN, WOMEN, AND CHILDREN MASSACRED, ETC.[54] The story described the massacres at Acton and Lower Agency and said that four companies under the command of former Minnesota Governor Colonel Henry H. Sibley were on the way to relieve the embattled settlers.

Henry "Long Trader" Sibley and the Santee had a long history that went back to the governor's days as a trader on the Minnesota frontier. According to historian Dee Brown, "Of the $475,000 promised the Santee in their first treaty, Long Trader Sibley claimed $145,000 for his American Fur Company as money due for overpayments to the Santees." At the time, Santee leaders argued that Sibley's company had underpaid them. However, when they complained to their Indian Agent, Alexander Ramsey, he sided with Sibley.[55] In 1862, Ramsey was the Governor of Minnesota, and "Long Trader" Sibley was in charge of the Sixth Minnesota Regiment.

On August 23, nearly 600 painted Santee warriors descended on the settlement of New Ulm. During the next 30 hours, 34 settlers died; 60 were wounded in the valiant defense of their town.[56] Although the Sioux succeeded in burning 190 buildings, they were unable to capture or destroy the settlement. On August 24, New Ulm was evacuated as 2,000 settlers set out in a convoy of 153 wagons for Manakato, nearly 30 miles away.[57] The August 24, 1862 *New York Times* described the conflict: THE

INDIAN MASSACRES—Terrible Scenes of Death and Misery in Minnesota—Five Hundred Whites Supposed to Be Murdered—The Sioux Bands United Against the Whites.[58]

The Minnesota Indian War would be headed by Army Major General John Pope, who had suffered an embarrassing defeat at the second Battle of Bull Run on August 6. On August 30 he received orders from President Lincoln to go to the northwest territories to put down the uprising.[59] General Pope was outraged by the Santee attacks on civilians, particularly the raping and killing of women and children. He informed Colonel Sibley that the Sioux needed to be "badly punished" and ordered him to carry out reprisals before any surrender was accepted or any settlement was made: "The horrible massacres of women and children and the outrageous abuse of female prisoners, still alive, call for punishment beyond human power to inflict. There will be no peace in this region by virtue of treaties and Indian faith." General Pope was very explicit about his intentions. "It is my purpose to utterly exterminate the Sioux if I have the power to do so and even if it requires a campaign lasting the whole of next year. Destroy everything belonging to them and force them out to the plains, unless, as I suggest, you can capture them." He considered the Indians outside the circle of humanity: "They are to be treated as maniacs or wild beasts, and by no means as people with whom treaties of compromises can be made."[60] Colonel Sibley seems to have been emboldened by General Pope's aggressive orders: "I am glad to perceive that you have so just an appreciation of the magnitude of the war in which we are engaged with the Sioux or Dakota, the most warlike and powerful of the tribes on this continent."[61]

Once advance troops from the Sixth Minnesota Regiment began to arrive, the Santee retreated up the Minnesota Valley with more than 100 prisoners and set up a camp 40 miles north of Upper Agency.[62] With 1,450 men and two cannons, Colonel Sibley set out for Little Crow's camp on September 19. The wagon train was ambushed near the Yellow Medicine River, and although Little Crow succeeded in drawing the soldiers into his trap, he was unable to overrun Colonel Sibley's forces. When the U.S. troops opened fire with their cannon, six Santee were killed instantly by a direct hit and 15 were wounded.[63] Overwhelmed by the American soldiers' firepower, the Indians began to retreat into the woods. Colonel Sibley was horrified when he arrived at the battlefield and found his soldiers scalping dead Santee warriors and issued an immediate order: "The bodies of the dead, even of a savage enemy, shall not be subjected to indignities by civilized and Christian men."[64]

Not only did Colonel Sibley win a victory on the battlefield, he began surrender negotiations with Sioux leaders. On September 7, 1862, Little Crow left this message for him:

> For what reason we have commenced this war I will tell you. It is on account of Major Galbraith. We made a treaty with the government, and beg for what we do get, and can't get that till our children are dying with hunger. It is the traders who commenced it. Mr. A. J. Myrick told the Indians that they could eat grass or dirt. Then Mr. Forbes told the Lower Sioux that they were not men.

Colonel Sibley offered this response: "LITTLE CROW—You have murdered many of our people without a sufficient cause. Return me the prisoners under a flag of truce, and I will talk with you then like a man."[65]

Although many Santee would surrender in the coming months, Little Crow would not be among them. He wanted to continue the war and fled deep into the wilderness of northern Minnesota. His son-in-law, Rda-in-yan-ka, delivered his message: "I am for continuing the war, and am opposed to the delivery of the prisoners. I have no confidence that the whites will stand by any agreement they make if we give them up."[66] Little Crow pointed to the Santee's sad history of relations with the U.S. government and the American settlers. "Ever since we treated with them, their agents and traders have robbed and cheated us. Some of our people have been shot, some hung; others placed upon floating ice and drowned." Little Crow claimed that the war had been avoidable, but due to the unpopularity of the treaties he had negotiated and signed, he had lost much of his standing among his own people. "The older ones would have prevented it if they could, but since the treaties they have lost all their influence."[67] By early September, Little Crow realized that events had gained too much momentum and was resigned to his fate. "We may regret what has happened, but the matter has gone too far to be remedied. We have got to die. Let us, then, kill as many of the whites as possible, and let the prisoners die with us."[68]

By the end of September 1862, hundreds of Santee had surrendered to Colonel Sibley, who in turn promised that he only sought to punish those who had committed atrocities against civilians.[69] Once 1,200 Sioux were in government custody, Sibley established a five-man Court of Inquiry to "try summarily the Mulatto, and Indians, or mixed bloods, now prisoners . . . and pass judgment upon them, if found guilty of murders or other outrages upon Whites, during the present State of hostilities of the Indians." The colonel planned to execute the guilty immediately to create a spectacle of vengeance that would serve as a deterrent against future attacks: "An example is . . . imperatively necessary and I trust you will approve the act, should it happen that some real criminals have been seized and promptly disposed of."[70] The Sioux were not charged with violations of the customary laws of war because the U.S. government did not consider them lawful combatants. To grant them the status of legitimate belligerents would have been to recognize their sovereignty and their inherent right to wage war.

The chairman of the Court of Inquiry was a missionary named Stephen Riggs who had worked with the Sioux since 1837.[71] These "trials" were so summary that it is difficult to even describe them as such. The court offered a plea bargain to a mulatto named Godfrey who was married to a Sioux woman and had fought with the Indians, earning the sobriquet, "he who kills many." Godfrey would testify in fifty-five cases, and even though he was known to have killed many settlers at Upper Agency, his sentence was commuted in exchange for his testimony.[72] On the first day, the Military Commission sentenced ten to death and acquitted six. The Court of Inquiry would try as many as forty-two Santee in a single day![73]

General Pope approved of the speedy trials, but warned that he would sanction no treaties with the Indians. He now had sufficient troops at his disposal to "exterminate them all, if they furnish the least occasion for it."[74] Because some of the Sioux had not yet given themselves up, Colonel Sibley postponed the executions so as not to discourage their surrender.[75] General Pope wrote General Henry Halleck to find out if he needed further authorization before proceeding with the executions. On October 10, Minnesota Governor Ramsey wrote to President Lincoln requesting "nothing less than the removal of the whole body of Indians to remote districts, far beyond our borders."[76] On October 17, Colonel Sibley received a dispatch from Lincoln that stated in no uncertain terms that no executions would take place until the President personally had reviewed the death sentences.

After the Santee surrendered, Lincoln faced problems commonly found when war, law, and politics converge. His most immediate concern was the need for an immediate postwar show of vengeance against the Indians in order to prevent vigilante retribution on a much larger scale. By early November, public opinion was divided over the fate of the Santee. The mood in Minnesota was best summarized by an article in the *St. Paul Press:* "The business has been dispatched with celerity, as many as forty cases having been tried per day in some instances. . . . Besides, no individual injustice is probably done, as ninety-nine hundredths of these devils are guilty, and witnesses in their favor would be as useless as teats on a boar."[77] However, in the cities of the northeast, far from the threat of Indian invasion, *The New York Times* editorial page urged the government to show "mercy" to the Sioux. Now that the war was over, the paper opined that "the whole thing seems to have been but a burst of rage on the part of the redskins, incited by the atrocious injustice to which they had been subjected." The indiscriminate killings were "the work of a few bad men among them."[78] The *Times* urged the U.S. government to move the Sioux out of Minnesota, away from irate settlers seeking revenge. In the end, the Court of Inquiry tried 394 Santee, and found 303 guilty and sentenced them to death.

It appeared that nothing short of a mass execution would satisfy the citizens of Minnesota. DEATH TO BARBARIANS IS THE SENTIMENT OF OUR PEOPLE read the *Minnesota Messenger* on November 11. Minnesota Senator Morton Wilkinson wrote President Lincoln and warned him that "the Outraged people of Minnesota will dispose of these wretches without law. These two people cannot live together. We do not want to see mob law inaugurated in Minnesota."[79] A few weeks later, when a wagon train of Indian prisoners passed, a group of settlers attacked them with pitchforks, scalding water, and rocks. An army bayonet charge finally dispersed the crowd, but not before a Santee baby was torn from the arms of his mother and killed by the mob.[80] Late on the night of December 4, several hundred settlers gathered to attack the prison camp, but were quickly surrounded and disarmed by soldiers.[81]

President Lincoln was in a very difficult position. He was clearly torn between the need to maintain the most minimal standards of justice and the demands of contemporary politics. Would he be able to satisfy all of his constituencies? If the Indians were not punished, what message would that send the settlers? If the U.S. government were to execute all 303 San-

tee, what message would that send the rest of America's Indian population? The U.S. Commissioner of Indian Affairs, William Dole, visited
Minnesota and characterized the sentences as "more of the character of
revenge than of punishment."[82] The interrogator, Reverend Riggs, urged
the President to draw a distinction between those braves who were
involved in combat and those who murdered and tortured civilians.[83]

On December 6, President Lincoln announced his final decision.
"Anxious to not act with so much clemency as to encourage another outbreak on the one hand, nor with so much severity as to be real cruelty on
the other, I caused a careful examination of the records of the trials to be
made." He ordered the execution of only those Santee "proved guilty of
violating females" and those "who were proven to have participated in
massacres as distinguished from participation in battles."[84] This reduced
the number of death sentences from 303 to 38.[85]

On December 22, Reverend Riggs translated President Lincoln's decision to the prisoners: "Their Great Father at Washington . . . has come to
the conclusion that they have each been guilty of wantonly and wickedly
murdering his white children. And for this reason he has directed that
they each be hanged by the neck until they are dead, on next Friday."
Riggs went on to urge the Indians "to seek their salvation in God," and he
"put Protestant and Catholic priests at their disposal."[86] According to the
St. Paul Daily Press, the captive Santee did not react to the news of their
impending executions with surprise: "Several Indians smoked their pipes
composedly during the reading, and we observed one in particular who,
when the time of the execution was designated, quietly knocked the ashes
from his pipe and filled it afresh with his favorite Kinnekinnick."[87] When
one reporter spoke with the Indians, he found them a rather stoic bunch.
"When the condemned are talked to on that subject they say, 'Kill me, kill
me. I would kill you if I had you.' " The reporter recognized that to the
Sioux brave, war was a calling, a *raison d'etre*: "He would prefer death by
the slow, lingering torture, such as none but an Indian can devise and execute, to a death on the gallows."[88] On the day before the executions the
condemned sang, danced, and met with male relatives.[89]

A crowd of settlers began to gather as a small army of carpenters
worked around the clock constructing a giant, 4-sided scaffold, custom
designed to hang all 38 men at once. This was a late example of the old
style of corporal punishment. Under the traditional model, as French
philosopher Michel Foucault points out so graphically in *Discipline and*

Punishment, "public torture and execution must be spectacular, it must be seen by all as its triumph."[90] On December 25, 1862, the sale of all intoxicants was banned for 48 hours and martial law was imposed. Early on the morning of December 26, the condemned Santee began their haunting death chants as 1,400 soldiers kept the crowd of 3,000 spectators at bay.[91] At 10:00 a.m., the convicts were unshackled, hooded, and led up the stairs of the hanging platform. Some continued to sing death hymns and held hands with their neighbors. The army drummer signaled the moment of execution with three beats and William Duley, a man whose family had been killed in the massacre, cut the rope. At that moment a cheer came from the soldiers and settlers who had come to witness this spectacle of punishment.[92] More than nine years later, it was admitted that two of the men hanged were not on President Lincoln's list. However, this mattered little: by 1863 the State of Minnesota was offering a $25 bounty for the scalp of any Sioux. Although Little Crow escaped the hangman's noose, he was shot and mortally wounded on July 3, 1863 by two settlers out hunting deer.[93] His killers were given a $500 bounty for the Santee chief's remains. His skull and scalp were preserved and put on display in St. Paul.[94]

This early attempt to apply law to war (even though the U.S. government did not consider the ongoing battles with the Indians a war) produced a primitive form of political justice. Guilty convictions were based on rumor and hearsay. Individuals were singled out for punishment in order to quench the domestic population's thirst for vengeance. The alternative would have been mob violence. Although he presided over the largest mass execution in American history, Abraham Lincoln probably averted a larger bloodbath. This was by far the simplest form of political justice because there was no presumption of fairness or impartiality. A few especially odious and well-deserving felons were singled out for public prosecution and punishment, after which the rest were given formal or informal amnesties for wartime atrocities. The outcome was largely known before the trial began, so the "legal" proceedings became part of the spectacle—hence the term "show trial." German legal theorist Otto Kirchheimer describes primitive forms of political justice like the *U.S.-Dakota War Trials* case as "a spectacle with prearranged results." However, Kirchheimer makes a subtle and often overlooked point, warning that any trial "presupposes an element of irreducible risk for those involved" and "even in the administration of injustice there are gradations." Above all, Kirchheimer warns that "justice in political matters is more tenuous than in any other field of jurisprudence, because it can so easily become a mere farce."[95]

The questions in the *U.S.-Dakota* trials were less about guilt and innocence than about the manner of punishment and the spectacle of public execution. At the same time as the Indian wars, the U.S. Army was engaged in another war against a different foe, fought according to a different, significantly more formal set of rules. During the time of the 1862 Indian War in Minnesota, Union General Henry Halleck read excerpts from a lecture on the laws of war in *The New York Times*. The author was Francis Lieber, a professor of history, political science, and law at Columbia College. It was ironic that the United States, at the beginning of one of the world's first modern wars, was turning to an old Prussian soldier for advice. A veteran of the Battle of Waterloo, the Battle of Namur, and the Greek War of Independence, Lieber was well schooled in the traditional rules of war.[96] How would its laws apply to a new form of war that was fast erasing the distinction between soldier and civilian? General Halleck wrote Professor Lieber in December 1862, requesting a definition of guerrilla war; Lieber replied with two essays, one on guerrilla warfare and another that would form the basis for the Lieber Code. As Geoffrey Best observes, "What could be got away with in wars against 'Red Indians' and Mexicans would not wash in a contest with Southern gentlemen."[97]

The War Department's board had decided to revise and update the rules of land warfare and appointed Lieber to prepare a draft. The Lieber Code, known as General Order No. 100, was approved by President Lincoln on April 24, 1863. Lieber's 159 articles covered very traditional and practical subjects like guerrilla warfare, captured enemy property, and the treatment of prisoners.[98] The code was significant because it marked the first time in Western history that the government of a sovereign nation established formal guidelines for the conduct of its army in the field. However, the rules were really a codification of long-standing Western military customs.[99]

Most significantly, the Lieber Code drew a sharp line between civilian and soldier. Article 22 states: "Nevertheless, as civilization has advanced during the last centuries, so has likewise steadily advanced, especially in war on land, the distinction between the private individual belonging to a hostile country and the hostile country itself."[100] However, like all warrior's codes, the Lieber Code contained significant loopholes. Francis

Lieber's experience as a soldier probably informed his decision to define "military necessity" very broadly. For example, a commander was not obliged to give quarter to enemy soldiers if the lives of his men were in danger. Article 27 left a key gray area that granted broad and vague powers under the doctrine of retaliation: "The law of war can no more wholly dispense with retaliation than can the law of nations, of which it is a branch. Yet civilized nations acknowledge retaliation as the sternest feature of war."[101] Article 24 distinguished between "barbaric" and "civilized" military practices: "The almost universal rule in remote times was, and continues to be with barbarous armies, that the private individual of the hostile country is destined to suffer every privation of liberty and protection and every disruption of family ties. Protection was, and still is with uncivilized people, the exception."[102]

Because the federal government refused to recognize the sovereignty of the Confederacy, it did not consider the Rebel Army lawful combatants. However, given the Confederates' early battlefield successes, the Union had no choice but to grant them *de facto* recognition by largely observing the laws of war on the battlefield. Even though the United States considered the Confederates rebels, they were not "others" who stood outside the circle and so not considered barbaric. This distinction was reserved for racial and cultural others who flouted the military customs of the West. The Confederates were both white and American.

Although the Lieber Code was a clear outline of European norms, it already appeared to be outdated in comparison to contemporary military practices. Ironically, this effort to limit the ravages of war came at a time when armed conflict was growing increasingly destructive and unlimited. The Civil War was nothing less than a preview of the bloody "total" wars of the coming century. None of the prudent restraint of the old European warlords was shown by American generals at Shiloh, Antietam, Gettysburg, and dozens of other bloody battles that left more than 600,000 Americans dead.[103] Writing in 1867, John DeForest captured America's fratricidal spirit in his novel, *Miss Ravenel's Conversion from Secession to Loyalty*: "The excitement of Germany at the opening of the Thirty Years' War, of England previous to the Cromwellian struggle, was torpid and partial in comparison with this outburst of a modern, reading, and swiftly informed free democracy." DeForest conveyed the notion that this conflict was unique and that "from the St. Lawrence to the Gulf there was a spiritual preparedness for slaughter which was to end in such a murderous contest as should make ensanguined Europe rise from its thousand battlefields to stare and wonder."[104]

Above all, what the Civil War demonstrated was that the military was no longer the praetorian guard of the political elite. Instead, it was an instrument of democracy, and democratic political leaders could not be content to win a limited military victory and strike an advantageous diplomatic solution. Instead, President Lincoln sought an unconditional surrender and an overthrow of the preexisting political and social structure in the South.[105] Military historian J.F.C. Fuller blames democracy and conscription for a return to tribal warfare: "Primitive tribes are armed hordes, in which every man is a warrior, and because the entire tribe engages in war, warfare is total."[106] The losers were not simply defeated on the battlefield; their entire social structure was overturned.

The two generals who finally secured victory for the Union did not only defeat the Rebel Army. They also waged war against southern society, civilians included. Cities were destroyed and infrastructure demolished. As George Nichols, Sherman's aide-de-camp, noted, "the only possible way to end this unhappy and dreadful conflict . . . is to make it terrible beyond endurance."[107] General Sherman, on the eve of his invasion of South Carolina, mentioned the Union Army's desire not only to win but also to settle the score. "The whole army is burning," he wrote, "with an insatiable desire to wreak vengeance upon South Carolina. I almost tremble at her fate, but feel that she deserves all that seems in store for her."[108] In Sherman's mind, the rebels deserved to suffer for starting the war.

As Charleston went up in flames, Sherman remarked: "They have brought it on themselves." When Confederate General John Bell Hood warned his adversary of the implications of his actions, Sherman informed him that "war is cruelty and you cannot refine it. Those who brought war into our country deserve all the curses and maledictions a people can pour out."[109] Until then, though, "we are not only fighting hostile armies, but a hostile people, and must make old and young, rich and poor, feel the hard hand of war."[110] General Sherman was among the first of his generation to realize that modern war could not be waged without the support of the domestic population. They needed to be beaten and demoralized before their army would collapse. His "war is hell" dictum was a harbinger of things to come. J.F.C. Fuller attaches great importance to Sherman's march on Atlanta: "Nothing like this march had been seen in the West since the maraudings of Tilly and Wallenstein in the Thirty Years War. . . . Terror was the basic factor in Sherman's policy, he openly says so."[111]

However, William T. Sherman did not believe in punitive peace treaties. He wrote: "When peace does come, you may call on me for anything. Then I will share with you the last cracker."[112] The defeat of the Confederacy was followed by a costly and hugely ambitious social engineering plan known as Reconstruction. Again, northern troops did more than defeat the Confederate Army on the battlefield; they toppled the government and social institutions that lay at the root of the entire southern belief system as well.[113] Punishment for wartime atrocities was swift and sure and, like the *U.S.-Dakota War Trials*, provides an excellent example of primitive political justice.

When the war ended and photographs of skeletal-looking Union POWs appeared in northern newspapers, there was a resounding cry for vengeance. On August 23, 1865, a Union Military Commission charged the commandant of Andersonville Prison in Georgia under a thirteen-count indictment.[114] Henry Wirz was a Swiss immigrant who had married a woman from Kentucky and fought for the Louisiana volunteers. He was severely wounded in the Battle of Seven Pines and lost the use of his right arm. After the battle he was promoted to captain for "bravery on the field of battle." In 1862, Wirz commanded a prison camp in Richmond. Later that year he served as a diplomatic emissary for Jefferson Davis in Berlin and Paris. Wirz returned to the Confederacy in 1864 and was ordered to serve as commandant of Andersonville Prison.[115]

Andersonville was designed to hold a maximum of 10,000 men, but by August 1864, captives from Sherman's army and the Eastern Theater pushed the prison's population to 33,000. An average inmate's daily rations were down to a few tablespoons of salt, beans, and a half pint of unsifted cornmeal.[116] The only source of water was a brackish stream fouled by human excrement and corpses. A southern woman who surveyed the camp from an observation tower was horrified: "My heart aches for these poor wretches. Yankees though they are, I am afraid God will suffer some terrible retribution to fall upon us for letting such things happen. If the Yankees should ever come . . . and go to Anderson and see the graves there, God have mercy on the land."[117] By the summer of 1864, Union soldiers in Confederate camps were dying by the thousands of gangrene, scurvy, dysentery, and starvation. When intelligence reports filtered back to the North about the conditions in the Confederate prison camps,

Secretary of War Stanton condemned the Confederacy in the strongest terms: "The enormity of the crime committed by the rebels cannot but fill with horror the civilized world. . . . There appears to have been a deliberate system of savage and barbarous treatment."[118]

The majority of the counts in *The Trial of Captain Henry Wirz* charged the camp commandant with personally murdering or abusing inmates. The most far-reaching count of the indictment accused Wirz of having been part of a conspiracy led by Confederate President Jefferson Davis that sought

> to impair and injure the health and to destroy the lives, by subjecting to great torture, and suffering, by confining in unhealthy and unwholesome quarters, by exposing to the inclemency of winter and to the dews and burning sun of summer, by compelling the use of impure water, and by furnishing insufficient and unwholesome food, of a large number of federal prisoners . . . to the end, that the armies of the United States might be weakened and impaired.[119]

Due to the lack of evidence, the conspiracy charge was not easily proven. Although the government presented 160 witnesses, none of the alleged victims were named. This made it impossible for witnesses to substantiate their claims.[120]

Like the *U.S.-Dakota* trials, *The Trial of Captain Henry Wirz* provided a dramatic spectacle of vengeance. Unlike the Indian braves who taunted death, Henry Wirz proved a pathetic sight in the courtroom. Due to gangrenous wounds, he was unable to sit in a chair and viewed the proceedings lying on a couch.[121] The witnesses painted a Hieronymus Bosch-like portrait of a squalid, overcrowded, and lawless camp. Dr. John C. Bates, a surgeon at Andersonville, described "20,000 or 25,000 prisoners crowded together; some had made holes and burrows in the earth; . . . found them suffering with scurvy, dropsy, diahorea, gangrene, pneumonia and other diseases." The strain of gangrene at the camp was so potent that "if a person should perchance stump a toe or scratch the hand, the next report to me was gangrene."[122] Bates "saw men lying partially naked, dirty and lousy in the sand; others were crowded together in small tents. . . . Clothing we had none; the living were supplied with the clothing of those who had died. Of vermin and lice there was a prolific crop." The prisoners lived in a Hobbesian state of nature and did little to help one another: "There was much stealing among them. All lived for himself."[123] Another surgeon at Andersonville described the prisoners as "the most horrible specimens of humanity I ever saw."[124]

Prison guard Nazareth Allen and Captain John Heath testified to Wirz's use of stocks, the deadline, and whippings. Wirz took special delight in unleashing his vicious pack of hounds on escaped prisoners. According to Captain Heath, "one of them got away and the hounds were put upon his scent; the man was discovered up a tree, and a pistol was fired at him; Wirz commanded him to come down; the man asked that the dogs might not be permitted to bite him; however, he was attacked when he descended, biting at his legs; Wirz did not call the hounds off."[125] Union prisoner Abner Kellog described a prisoner in August of 1864 standing at the Andersonville gate with a "sore on him as large as the crown of my hat, filled with maggots, fly-blown; the sergeant asked Capt. Wirz to have the man carried to the hospital; No, said Wirz; let him stay there and die. The man was afterward carried as a corpse."[126]

On October 18, Henry Wirz attacked the government's murder charges: "In no instances were the name, date, regiment, or circumstances stated in the specifications, and in the whole mass of testimony."[127] His second defense strategy would be employed by Germans nearly a century later: Wirz argued that he was only following orders. "I now bear the odium, and men who were prisoners there seem disposed to wreak their vengeance upon me for what they have suffered, who was only the medium, or I may better say, the tool in the hands of my superiors."[128] Wirz pleaded not guilty to all charges on the ground that he had merely "followed the orders" of General John Winder: "I think I may also claim as a self-evident proposition that if I, a subaltern officer, merely obeyed the legal orders of my superiors in the discharge of my official duties, I cannot be held responsible for the motives that dictated such orders."[129] The prosecution countered that "superior orders" was no excuse and in no way mitigated Henry Wirz's guilt: "General Winder could no more command the prisoners to violate the laws of war than could the prisoners do so without orders. The conclusion is plain, that where such orders exist both are guilty."[130]

On October 24, the court ruled that Captain Henry Wirz was guilty of "conspiring . . . against the United States, against the laws of war, to impair and injure the health, and to destroy large numbers of Federal prisoners" and sentenced him to death. There are unconfirmed reports

that Wirz was offered a plea bargain—if he had agreed to name Confederate President Jefferson Davis in the conspiracy to kill Union soldiers, his
life would be spared. The death sentence was confirmed by President
Andrew Johnson on November 3, 1865.[131] Once again an especially odious war criminal was singled out for summary "justice" and the victors
were able to vent their wartime passions in a powerful public display.

The *U.S.-Dakota War Trials* (1862) and the trial of Captain Henry Wirz
(1865) provide excellent examples of traditional, limited, and punitive
political settlements. Both cases were tried by victor regimes with monop-
olies on political and military power. The expression *vae victis* or "woe to
the conquered" best describes this type of primitive and punitive settlement. Traditionally there had never been a presumption of fairness or
impartiality, only a very public spectacle of vengeance followed by an
amnesty for wartime acts. American leaders would attempt to give legitimacy to this type of proceeding by adding legal trappings to something
that had traditionally only been about revenge. On November 11, 1865,
the spectacle was completed as Henry Wirz walked to gallows constructed just outside Washington's Old Capital Prison. Union soldiers lined the
walls and chanted, "Wirz, remember Andersonville!"[132] Henry Wirz was
portrayed in southern accounts as a hero and a martyr. But as James
McPherson points out in *The Battle Cry of Freedom*, "These defenders of
the South doth protest too much. . . . As for the comparison of Andersonville with Johnson's Island, the mortality of southern prisoners at the
latter was 2 percent—and at Andersonville, 29 percent."[133]

Probably more important than the trial of Captain Henry Wirz was
the fact that the Lieber Code was fast providing the foundation for a body
of treaty law codifying the customary rules of war.[134] Francis Lieber's prediction that General Order No. 100 "will be adopted as a basis for similar
works for the English, French, and Germans" soon came true.[135]
Although it was heartening that Prussia adopted the Lieber Code in 1870
to govern its forces in the Franco-Prussian War, the American Civil War
had shown a new, horrible face of conflict—industrial total war. Sherman
had blurred the all-important line between soldier and civilian to win the
war for the Union. It was ironic that the new international humanitarian
laws came at a time when America's Indian wars were entering their most
brutal phase.

In November 1864, about six hundred Cheyenne and Arapaho Indians
established a winter camp at an elbow-shaped bend at Sand Creek. The

Indians had enjoyed good relations with the American army commander, Wyn Koop, at the nearby fort, and he had granted them permission to camp at the Creek.[136] In late November, Koop was replaced by Major Anthony, who immediately ordered the Indians to surrender all of their weapons. Anthony told the Cheyenne and Arapaho chiefs that they would be safe at Sand Creek as long as they flew the American flag.[137] He also informed the Indian leaders that their rations would be cut in half and gave them permission to leave the area to hunt buffalo. Many of the braves departed for the hunting grounds and some of the Arapaho headed south, as they did not trust "the red-eyed soldier."[138] On November 27, reinforcements arrived from the Third Colorado Regiment under the command of a Methodist minister named Colonel J. M. Chivington. The six-hundred-man cavalry force had been formed specifically to fight Indians.[139]

Colonel Chivington had barely gotten off his horse before he informed Major Anthony that the time for "wading in the gore" had come.[140] Although Chivington wanted to attack the Indian camp at Sand Creek, there was dissent to the brash newcomer's bloodlust. Captain Silas Soule, Captain Joseph Cramer, and Lieutenant James Conner reminded their commanders of their promises to the Indians. The dissenting officers argued that an attack on the Sand Creek camp "would be murder in every sense of the word."[141] Colonel Chivington cursed the officers— "Damn any man who sympathizes with Indians"—stating, "I have come to kill Indians, and believe it is right and honorable to use any means under God's heavens to kill Indians."[142]

On November 28, at 8:00 P.M., seven hundred mounted American soldiers moved out in four columns under Colonel Chivington's command. He was reported to have ordered them "to kill and scalp all, big and little; nits make lice."[143] In addition to their rifles, the Colorado Regiment had four mountain howitzers.[144] Colonel Chivington grew impatient with his Indian guide and rousted a rancher named Robert Bent from bed to lead the Third Colorado Regiment to the Indian camp. Bent was married to a Cheyenne woman, and his three sons were camped with their Indian relatives at Sand Creek.[145] Of the six hundred or so Indians at the camp, two thirds were women and children. Most of the warriors were away hunting buffalo according to Major Anthony's instructions.[146]

The Cheyenne and Arapaho felt and heard the hoofbeats before they saw the mounted soldiers approaching at a full gallop. The Indians all began to run to an American flag and a white flag that were flying prominently on a lodgepole in front of Chief Black Kettle's encampment. The rancher noted the presence of the flags, "in so conspicuous a position that they must have been seen."[147] Bent's son watched the mounted American soldiers descend upon the camp. "I looked towards the chief's lodge, holding the pole, with the flag fluttering. . . . I heard him call to his people not to be afraid, that the soldiers would not hurt them; then troops opened fire from two sides of the camp."[148]

This was a full-scale massacre in which no quarter was given and no prisoners were taken. When twenty or thirty women were found hiding in a hole, they sent out a young girl with a white flag on a stick; "she had not proceeded ten steps when she was shot and killed. All the squaws in that hole were afterwards killed."[149] Not content with simply killing the Indians, many soldiers dismounted and set about mutilating the bodies in what would become one of the darkest episodes in the annals of American military history. The bodies were not just scalped in a number of instances; female genitals were cut off and worn as hatbands or stretched over saddlebows.[150] One soldier bragged that he planned to make a tobacco pouch out of the penis and testicles of the leader White Antelope. Another recalled, "I saw one squaw cut open with an unborn child, as I thought, lying by her side. Captain Soule after told me that such was a fact. . . . I heard one man say that he had cut out a woman's private parts and had them for exhibit on a stick."[151]

Colonel Chivington would later claim that his forces had killed 400 to 500 Indian warriors at Sand Creek. In truth the Third Colorado Regiment killed only 28 men; the other 105 dead were women and children.[152] No matter, the former Methodist minister returned to Denver a hero, and the 100 Indian scalps collected by Chivington's forces were put on display in a Denver theater. British historian Hugh Brogan makes a telling observation about nineteenth-century U.S.-Indian relations: "The records of the American past re-echo with denunciations of the fiendishness of the savages, just as the Negroes were accused of insatiable lust, bloodlust and criminal propensities of all kinds . . . but the Christians themselves raped, scalped, looted, murdered, burned, and tortured, the very deeds by which they justified their contempt and loathing for the Indian."[153] After the Sand Creek Massacre, the Cheyenne, Arapaho, and Sioux tribes called for a war of revenge on the white men. This would speed the destruction of traditional American Indian life because attacks on frontier outposts were followed by increasingly brutal reprisals by the U.S. Army. One of

Geronimo's U.S. army captors remarked candidly, "His crimes were retail, ours wholesale."[154]

The Sioux got some revenge in 1866, when they lured an entire regiment of American soldiers into a canyon and killed and scalped all eighty members of the Twenty-Seventh Infantry (Captain William Fetterman's).[155] When the news reached Washington, General William T. Sherman outlined the final phase of America's Indian policy in a letter to his trusted comrade in arms, General Ulysses S. Grant. Sherman wanted to take his total war strategy one step further on the American plains: "We must act with vindictive earnestness against the Sioux, even to their extermination, men, women, and children. Nothing else will reach the root of this case."[156] After General Custer's defeat at Little Big Horn in 1876, General Sherman received presidential authority to assume control of the Sioux reservations and treat the inhabitants as prisoners of war.[157]

The U.S. government maintained that the Sioux had violated the treaty of 1868, which had granted them reservations in the Black Hills of South Dakota and on the Powder River. A new Indian Commission led by Newton Edwards, Bishop Henry Whipple, and Reverend Samuel Hinman traveled to the reservation to meet with Indian leaders. The Commission wanted them to sign over their rights to the Black Hills in exchange for a piece of arid land on the Missouri River. Chief Red Dog reminded the Americans that "it is only six years since we came to live on this stream where we are living now and nothing that has been promised us has been done."[158] One of the chiefs pointed out that he had been moved by the Great Father in Washington five times, and each time he had been promised that he would never be moved again: "I think that you had better put the Indians on wheels and you can run them about whenever you wish."[159] According to the terms of the 1868 treaty, any changes in Sioux reservation boundaries required the signatures of three quarters of the tribe's males. This vote would be impossible to obtain because more than half of the warriors were off the reservation with the more militant leaders, Sitting Bull and Crazy Horse.[160]

The Commission gave the chiefs a week to discuss their proposal and called all Indians off the reservation "hostile." Now, "only friendly Indians were covered by the treaty."[161] When the Sioux refused to sign over the Black Hills and their hunting grounds on the Powder River, the American delegation threatened to cut all their government rations. Faced with the starvation of their women and children, chiefs Red Cloud and Spotted Tail signed the new additions to the 1868 treaty.[162]

Historian Hermann Hagedorn, author of *Roosevelt in the Badlands*, wrote in 1921, "In the conflict between white and red, the Indians were not always the ones who were most at fault." Hagedorn described the Indian wars of the 1880s as "a peculiarly atrocious warfare. Many white men shot whatever Indians they came upon like coyotes, on sight; others captured them, when they could, and, stripping them of their clothes, whipped them till they bled."[163] Future American President Theodore Roosevelt had an even less forgiving view of the American Indians he encountered during his travels in the west. In 1886, he wrote: "I suppose I should be ashamed to say that I take the Western view of the Indian. I don't go so far as to think that the only good Indians are dead Indians, but I believe nine out of ten are, and I shouldn't like to inquire too closely in the case of the tenth." Roosevelt drew what in his mind was a telling parallel. "Turn three hundred low families of New York into New Jersey, support them for fifty years in vicious idleness, and you will have some idea of what the Indians are. Reckless, revengeful; fiendishly cruel, they rob and murder . . . the defenseless, lone settlers on the plains."[164]

The Indian wars reached their sad and inevitable apogee at Wounded Knee on December 29, 1890 when Colonel James Forsythe, leading the late George Armstrong Custer's Seventh Cavalry Regiment, opened fire with rifles and four Hotchkiss guns firing a shell a second on the four hundred Sioux camped at Wounded Knee Creek.[165] When the smoke had cleared and a three-day blizzard passed, at least three hundred Sioux were dead from wounds and exposure. Black Elk best summarized the significance of the Wounded Knee Massacre for his people: "I can see that something else died there in the bloody mud, and was buried in the blizzard. A people's dream died there. It was a beautiful dream."[166] Twenty-six Congressional Medals of Honor were awarded to members of the reconstituted Seventh Cavalry for their actions at Wounded Knee.[167]

Chapter Two

THE CHANGING RULES OF WAR AND PEACE

In fittingly paradoxical fashion, the United States, the country that brought the world total war and drove the American Indians to the brink of extinction, was simultaneously advocating stringent new codes of conduct for the rest of the world. Though the major legal efforts of the late nineteenth and early twentieth centuries differed in tone, they grew logically from the American code.[1] By the late nineteenth century, the efforts to limit war with law grew more intellectually adventurous. In 1898, Russia's Czar Nicholas II called for a conference on the limitation of armaments.[2] Representatives of twenty-six states met at the Hague in 1898. The United States delegation included Andrew White, Seth Low, Stanford Newell, Admiral Alfred Thayer Mahan, and Fredrick William Hols. Like the Lieber Code, most of the Hague Conventions that resulted from the conference were practical measures designed to mitigate excessive suffering in war. Rules were laid down relating to the treatment of prisoners, casualties, and spies. Technical issues such as flags of truce, capitulation, armistice, and neutrality were also dealt with.[3] Three of the conference's declarations addressed technological developments that fell outside the previously accepted rules of war. Bombing from balloons was prohibited for a period of five years and the use of poison gas was banned.

American statesmen wanted to go further: they were not content to codify customary military laws and wanted to reform statecraft itself.[4] The American delegation hoped to create a permanent international court where signatories to the Hague Conventions "would resort for a settlement of . . . differences which could not be adjusted by diplomatic negotiations, and were not of a character compelling or justifying war."[5] The Americans argued that arbitration would eventually replace war as the most common means of conflict resolution. This view was based on the assumption that delinquent or aggressive states could be treated under international law the same way as criminals were handled under domestic law.[6] However, this was a difficult proposition. Was there a "community" of nations, and how could they punish grave human rights violations without a monopoly on state power? The Americans would have to dislodge the keystone of the European state system—sovereignty—to implement their radical new plan. If they could not revoke sovereign immunity, their plan stood no chance.

German leaders were incensed by the implications of the American plan, and they were not about to cede at the bargaining table what they had won on the battlefield. The leadership of the Second Reich believed that treaties to limit arms and provide for "neutral" arbitration of disputes negated their most important strategic advantage: the ability to mobilize and strike more quickly and effectively than any other nation. The Germans also rejected the concept of neutrality, arguing that in international politics there were only friends and enemies. Outnumbered and surrounded by hostile neighbors, Prussia was among the first nations to recognize the need for developing a practical relationship with war rather than attempting to eliminate it altogether. Late to enter the game of colonialism, Germany would oppose America's attempt to rewrite the rules of international affairs.

At one point during the Hague Conference, a German representative voiced opposition to a permanent court of arbitration on the ground that such an idea was too radical for his government to accept. The German delegation refused to sign the relevant convention until they had hamstrung the proposed court with limitations. The most significant omission in the final draft was of the phrase "obligatory arbitration." Although the spirit of the convention remained unchanged, it was no longer binding.[7]

Colonel von Schwarzhoff, the military member of the German delegation at the Hague, rejected mandatory disarmament and instead advocated preparedness and self-reliance: "As for compulsory military service,
which is intimately associated with these questions, the German does not
regard it as a heavy burden but a sacred patriotic duty, to the performance of which he owes his existence, his prosperity, his future."[8] Historian John Keegan wrote, "The truth of Europe's situation at the turn of
the century lay rather with the German than the American."[9]

The 1898 Hague Conference saw the beginning of an American
attempt to broaden the laws of war to include acts that had previously
been considered beyond the realm of objective judgment. Francis Lieber
was a soldier; he accepted war as a constant in human affairs and had
hoped only that his code would help to mitigate its ill effects. What
occurred at the Hague was the tentative first attempt to go beyond laws
regulating war to laws governing the conduct of international relations.
At the vanguard of this movement were American lawyer-statesmen like
Elihu Root and Joseph Choate who had come of age far from the Byzan-
tine power struggles and diplomatic double-crossing that characterized
international relations under the European public law. Choate, the American representative at the Hague, claimed war was "an anachronism, like
dueling or slavery, something that international society had simply out-
grown."[10] However, again there was a paradox or duality inherent in the
American position.

By 1893, Fredrick Jackson Turner had deemed the American frontier
closed; to Turner this marked the end of "the first period of American
history."[11] Historian John Fiske, one of America's earliest evolutionists,
coined the term "Manifest Destiny" in an 1880 speech. He believed that
the American Anglo-Saxon was "one of the dominant races of the
world" and that "The day is at hand when four-fifths of the human race
will trace its pedigree to English forefathers, as four-fifths of the white
people in the United States trace their pedigree to-day." Fiske freely
admitted the American duality in foreign policy, or as he put it, "the
seeming paradoxes," and conceded that "the possibility of peace can be
guaranteed only through war."[12] A messianic justification for the American expansion was offered by Reverend Josiah Strong in his hugely popular 1885 book, *Our Country*. Strong, the head of the Christian Home Mission, described America as "Time's noblest offspring"[13] and predicted a
"final competition of the races."[14] Many Manifest Destiny advocates were

drawing explicitly or implicitly on the recent work of Charles Darwin to justify American expansion. In *The Descent of Man* (1871), Darwin had predicted that "at some future period, not very distant as measured by centuries, the civilised races will almost certainly exterminate, and replace, the savage races throughout the world." According to nineteenth-century German nationalist scholar Heinrich von Treitschke, the laws of war only applied to wars between European nations: "International law becomes phrases if its standards are also applied to barbaric people. To punish a Negro tribe, villages must be burned, and without setting examples of that kind, nothing can be achieved. If the German reich in such cases applied international law, it would not be humanity or justice but shameful weakness."[15]

To secular advocates of Manifest Destiny like John Fiske, it was self-evident that non-Anglo-Saxons like the American Indians must either accept America's civilizing influence or face extinction: "So far as relations of civilization with barbarism are concerned to-day, the only serious question is by what process of modification the barbarous races are to maintain their foothold upon the earth at all. While once such people threatened the very continuance of civilization, they now exist only on sufferance." In his book, *The Beginnings of New England*, Fiske argued that American colonists had been fully justified in slaughtering the Indians because they were "barbarians." He believed that in wars against "savages," Western armies could fight with significantly less restraint; women and children were fair game. Fiske believed that "the annihilation of the Pequots can be condemned only by those who read history so incorrectly as to suppose that savages, whose business is to torture and slay, can always be dealt with according to methods in use between civilized peoples. . . . If the founders of Connecticut, in confronting a danger which threatens their very existence, struck with savage fierceness, we cannot blame them." Finally, Fiske justified any military action taken against savages and barbarians on the ground of racial superiority: "The world is so made that it is only in that way that the higher races have been able to preserve themselves and carry on their progressive work."[16] In 1885, John Fiske's Manifest Destiny speech was published by *Harper's* magazine, and soon the historian was in Washington lecturing President Rutherford B. Hayes, Secretary of State William Everts, General William T. Sherman, John Hay, and others. Fiske reported to his wife, "I have got all the brains of Washington to hear me, and they are delighted."[17]

By 1898, Admiral Alfred Thayer Mahan's plan for the U.S. expansion, outlined in his influential 1890 book, *The Influence of Sea Power upon History*, was unfolding nicely as the United States was rapidly acquiring overseas territories in both the Pacific (Hawaii and Samoa) and the Caribbean. After crushing the Spanish in Cuba, American leaders had to decide what to do with Spain's other colonial war prize, the Philippine Islands. San Juan Hill veteran Theodore Roosevelt remarked to Senator Henry Cabot Lodge in a June 24, 1898 letter, "Mahan and I talked the Philippines . . . for two hours;" all agreed that the United States "could not escape our destiny there."[18] The most vexing questions revolved around the Spanish possession of the islands. Twenty-nine-year-old revolutionary leader Emilio Aguinaldo believed that if, with U.S. assistance, he ousted the Spanish from the archipelago, it would become an independent republic. However, once the Spanish were defeated, President McKinley refused to grant independence to the Philippines.[19] Aguinaldo and a group of prominent Filipinos refused to accept the American assumption of power and declared the Philippines an independent republic on June 18, 1898. The rebel leader implored his people: "Filipino citizens! We are not a savage people; let us follow the example of the Europeans and American nations. . . . Let us march under the flag of Revolution whose watchwords are Liberty, Equality, and Fraternity!"[20]

President McKinley's decision to send a 59,000-man expeditionary force to crush Aguinaldo and the movement for Philippine independence raised a number of difficult questions for the young republic. The obvious disparity between words and deeds—the champion of liberty and self-determination fighting to thwart independence and reimpose colonialism—forced American leaders to justify the duality. In the language of Manifest Destiny, America was not engaged in colonialism; instead, the United States was rescuing the natives from their own barbarism. At the time, one American wrote, "What America wants is not territorial expansion, but expansion of civilization. We want, not to acquire the Philippines for ourselves, but to give the Phillipines free schools, a free church, open courts, no caste, equal rights to all."[21] European critics were less bothered by the substance of American policy than the style. Britain's *Saturday Review* commented: "There have been more wicked wars than this . . . but never a more shabby war. . . . Of all that curious mixture of sentiments, noble and ignoble, out of which the war with the Filipinos sprang, only the element of hypocrisy seems to have retained its original vigor." At roughly the same time, General Horatio Herbert Kitchener and his troops mowed down approximately 11,000 Sudanese soldiers in the Battle of Omdurman in 1898. The British lost less than 100 soldiers. It was clear that the new laws of war did not apply universally. Whether it was the U.S. Army fighting the Sioux on the American plains or the European armies fighting in Africa, western armies fought with few restraints in nineteenth-century colonial wars. In a speech at Albert Hall, Lord Salsbury stated: "One can roughly divide the nations of the world into the living and the dying . . . the living nations will fraudulently encroach on the territory of the dying."[22]

When McKinley appointed international law advocate and New York corporate lawyer Elihu Root Secretary of War in 1899, it marked the beginning of a new legalist era in American foreign policy. Political scientist Judith Shklar has defined "legalism" as "the ethical attitude that holds moral conduct to be a matter of rule following, and moral relationships to consist of duties and rights determined by rules." Root best articulated the American lawyer-statemens' view of the relationship between law and public policy in an 1899 letter: "It is not a function of law to enforce the rules of morality."[23]

The choice of a Wall Street lawyer to conduct a colonial war says a great deal about the convergence of law and war in twentieth-century American foreign policy. As America's global aspirations grew, so did the need for justifications more sophisticated than Manifest Destiny. American leaders would learn to wield law as a political tool like any other. Those who used it most effectively had learned their trade on Wall Street, where what could be justified legally did not have to be justified morally.[24] America's lawyer-statesmen would try to apply these same tactics to foreign policy and their "strategic legalism" would grow into their dominant "nonideological" ideology.[25] As the United States became a global power, a two-sided relationship with international law developed, and what began as the simple hypocrisy of the age grew into a more profound and lasting duality. There was a tension between the ethical and legal principles that American leaders espoused and the actual conduct of American foreign policy. At moments of crisis and contradiction, American leaders attempted to rephrase complex moral questions into apolitical disputes that required only the application of law to a set of facts. Was it that simple? As Shklar points out, "Here legalism is projected into the greater political environment of multiple and competing ideologies."[26] American leaders were no longer content to use law for primitive forms of political justice; they were growing more ambitious, and now had the power to back their words with force.

When asked what a lawyer knew about managing a foreign war, the Philippine Civil Governor, William Howard Taft, commented, "I don't want a man who knows about war and the army. I want a lawyer to handle the problems of the new islands."[27] Roosevelt pointed out that Elihu Root was an unlikely choice for Secretary of War, the work was "really out of his line," but wrote, "Root is taking hold of his work in just the right way. He went into it "only because he felt the task was so serious, so difficult and of such vital importance to the nation."[28] In his first public speech as Secretary of War on October 7, 1899, Root flatly rejected the calls for Filipino independence. He put forward the argument that there were no Philippine people, only tribes of barbarians scattered throughout the archipelago. As with America's Indians, if he could deny them their civility, he could deny them their natural rights and take over their territory. In his first press conference, the new Secretary of War asked, "Well, whom are we fighting? Are we fighting the Philippine nation? No!" He declared, "There is none. There are . . . more than sixty tribes . . . all but one ready to accept American sovereignty."[29] Root phrased the American acquisition as a legal question, one of contracts and titles, not people and sovereignty: "Gentlemen, the title of the America to the island of Luzon is better than the title we had to Louisiana."[30] He declared that the Jeffersonian principle that a government derives its just powers from the consent of the governed did not apply to the Filipinos because they were simply unfit for self-government: "Nothing can be more misleading than a principle misapplied. . . . Government does not depend on consent. The immutable laws of justice and humanity require that people shall have government, that the weak shall be protected, that cruelty and lust shall be restrained, whether there be consent or not."[31]

Secretary of War Root tried to cast the new American soldier less as a warrior than as an ambassador of democracy and Christianity—a social worker with a Springfield rifle: "I claim for him the higher honor that while he is as stern a foe as ever a man saw on the battlefield, he brings the schoolbook, the plow, and the Bible. While he leads the forlorn hope of war, he is the advance guard of liberty and justice, of law and order, and peace and happiness."[32] The task of restraining the "cruelty and lust" of the Philippine insurgents fell to the U.S. military.

The leaders of America's expeditionary force had a more sober assessment of their foes. Many in the Philippine campaign had fought in America's nineteenth-century wars, like General Henry Lawton, the veteran of twenty-six Civil War battles who received the Congressional Medal of Honor and was best known for capturing Geronimo in 1886. General Lawton was in awe of his adversaries in the Philippines: "They are the bravest men I have ever seen. . . . These men are indomitable. . . . At Bacoor Bridge they waited until Americans had brought their cannon to within twenty-five yards of their trenches."[33] He paid his adversaries the ultimate compliment and in the process contradicted Secretary Root's glib assessment of the situation: "Such men have a right to be heard. All they want is a little justice. . . . What we want is to stop this accursed war." Henry Lawton was shot and killed by a sniper's bullet in San Mateo on December 18, 1899.[34]

Winning this undeclared war was not as easy as American political leaders had imagined. The insurgent forces, despite their inferior weaponry, proved to be fierce and terrifying adversaries. The Filipinos had a great deal of experience in fighting invading armies. When the Spanish tried to disarm them, they simply replaced their knives with rattan sticks and the martial art of escrima was born. Although they used firearms whenever they could, the guerrillas' favorite method of attack was with a bolo or machete-type knife in each hand. Charles Burke Elliott described the Philippines' Moro tribesmen in 1916 as "not open and fair in fight, and frequently resorts to what white men regard as improper methods of attack." The Moros' wavy-bladed Kris knives "are often prized for their service in having killed a great number of persons, and the selling price is established accordingly. Individuals have an uncomfortable habit of getting into a religious frenzy and running amok among the Christians. A Moro who goes juramentado and runs amok often finds many victims before he is killed."[35]

Some of Aguinaldo's orders (captured by the Americans) described a different style of war, far removed from the gentlemanly rules of engagement outlined by Francis Lieber: "The Chief of those who go on to attack the barracks should send in first four men with a good present for the American commander. They should not, prior to the attack, look at the Americans in a threatening manner. To the contrary . . . the attack should be a complete surprise with decision and courage."[36] Three men and a man dressed as a woman would enter the camp and attack only with their bolos: "The Sandatahan should not attempt to secure rifles from their dead enemies, but shall pursue slashing right and left until the Americans surrender."[37] Aguinaldo then ordered six men to nearby rooftops; when retreating American troops passed underneath, the insurgents were to drop furniture, boiling oil, molasses, and red-hot iron on them.[38] Because the Filipinos responded to the American invasion with the brutal strategy of guerrilla warfare, the distinction between soldier and civilian began to disappear. There were a number of instances where the insurgents used the Americans' self-restraint to their strategic advantage, for example, raising a white flag and then opening fire on the approaching Americans.[39]

Although there is no formal record of a policy of not taking prisoners, the U.S. government's own casualty list raises a troubling question: Was the army refusing to grant quarter to the Philippine guerrillas? In March of 1899, Brigadier General Lloyd Wheaton left Manila and traveled south down the bank of the Pasig River. One week later, General Wheaton and his men reached Laguna de Bay Lake. In that week, according to the U.S. Army, 2,500 Filipinos were killed or wounded and 36 Americans were killed.[40] One soldier described the offensive in a letter home: "In the path of the Washington regiment and Battery D of the Sixth Artillery there were 1,008 dead niggers and a great many wounded. We burned all their houses. I don't know how many men, women and children the Tennessee boys did kill." An infantryman from Tennessee recalled, "They would not take any prisoners."[41] Another army private recalled General Wheaton's reprisal for a Philippine atrocity: "Last night one of our boys was found shot and his stomach cut open. Immediately orders were received by General Wheaton to burn the town and kill every native in sight, which was done."[42] Private Barnes's letter to his brother provides strong evidence that the distinction between soldier and civilian had disappeared in the Philippines. "I am probably growing hard-hearted, for I am in my glory when I can sight my gun on some dark skin and pull the trigger. Should a call for volunteers be made for this place do not be so patriotic as to come here."[43]

During the bloodiest battles of the American Civil War, the ratio of dead to wounded soldiers was never any higher than 1:5. At Gettysburg, for example, 2,834 were killed and 13,709 wounded. Even in

Great Britain's brutal Boer War, the dead-to-wounded ratio was 1:4. In the Philippines the ratio of dead to wounded guerrillas was an astounding 5:1, five dead for every wounded man.[44] As early as 1899, soldiers like Captain Edwin Boltwood wrote that "On more than one battlefield they were treated like Indians. At Caloocan I saw natives shot down that could have been prisoners, and the whole country around Manila set ablaze with apparently no other object than to teach the natives submission by showing them that with the Americans war was hell."[45]

In December 1900, Secretary of War Elihu Root announced that the United States would adopt the "methods which have proved successful in our Indian camps in the West" to defeat the insurgents.[46] On December 20, General Arthur MacArthur placed Philippine civilians under martial law. The United States resettled much of the population into concentration camps throughout the island chain. This action was not unlike the methods employed by the Spanish in Cuba and the British in South Africa. Natives found outside of the resettlement camps were considered hostile and often fired upon. The soldiers relied on a favorite Spanish torture technique called "the water cure" to get information from prisoners. Three to five gallons of water mixed with salt were funneled down the throat and nose of the victim, coupled with a few blows to the stomach; this made even the hardest guerrillas talk.[47]

When reporters tried to file stories about the harsh nature of this war, they were censored. The journalists became so enraged by the U.S. government's attempts to silence them that in February 1900, eleven reporters sent a letter by regular mail (to avoid army censors) to Hong Kong. It read:

> The undersigned, being all staff correspondents of American newspapers stationed in Manila, unite in the following declaration: We believe that, owing to official despatches from Manila made public in Washington, the people of the United States have not received a correct impression of the situation in the Philippines, but that these despatches have presented an ultra-optimistic view that is not shared by the general officers in the field. . . . We believe the despatches err in the declaration that "the situation is well in hand," and in the assumption that the insurrection can be speedily ended without a greatly increased force.[48]

When Carl Shirz reported the atrocities in the American press, he described U.S. policy as based on "deceit, false pretense, brutal treachery to friends . . . without parallel in the history of the republics."[49] By 1900, prominent citizens were lining up against the American annexation of the Philippines. The anti-imperialist outcry was led by Andrew Carnegie, Samuel Gompers, William Jennings Bryan, Mark Twain, and others who wondered how the brutal suppression of an indigenous independence movement served American interests.

When President McKinley was assassinated in 1901, Vice President Theodore Roosevelt assumed the Presidency. A veteran of the Spanish-American War, Roosevelt had no moral qualms about annexing the Philippines. Like Senator Lodge and Senator Albert Beveridge, he was a confident exponent of Manifest Destiny. The new President believed that "our whole national history has been one of expansion." Barbarians either accepted the uplifting and civilizing influence of the United States or faced extinction: "The Barbarians recede or are conquered . . . that peace follows their retrogression or conquest, is due solely to the power of the mighty civilized races which have not lost the fighting instinct."[50] Senator Beveridge argued that "God has been preparing the English-speaking and Teutonic peoples for a thousand years for nothing but vain and idle self-admiration? No! He has made us the master organizers of the world where chaos reigns."[51]

President Roosevelt considered the war against Spain "a great anti-imperialist stride."[52] Like Secretary Root, Roosevelt compared the Filipinos to native Americans and in doing so placed them outside the category of legitimate combatant: "Of course the presence of our troops in the Philippines . . . has no more to do with military imperialism than their presence in the Dakotas, Minnesota and Wyoming during the many years which elapsed before the final outbreaks of the Sioux were definitely put down." To Roosevelt, granting independence to Aguinaldo "would be like granting self-government to an Apache reservation under some local chief."[53] On March 23, 1901, Emilio Aguinaldo was captured in an elaborate ruse and the war entered its most brutal phase. By 1901, the last insurgent strongholds were the island of Samar and southern Luzon. American generals like Lloyd Wheaton recommended that the United States emulate the colonial methods that the Europeans "found necessary . . . through centuries of experience in dealing with Asiatics." According to Wheaton, "Unexampled patience was exercised throughout the department in the treatment of these savages, habitually violating all the laws of war as known to civilized nations."[54]

September 26, 1901, was an exciting day for the seventy-four American soldiers stationed at the small garrison at Balangiga on the island of Samar. The American soldiers were about to receive their first mail in four months. The American commander, a "puritanical Irish Catholic" captain named Thomas Connell, was in the process of "cleaning and civilizing" the town. The Filipino mayor asked Connell if men could "work off back taxes" by laboring for the Americans. When Connell agreed, the mayor contacted rebel leader Vicente Lukban, who "transferred one hundred of his best bolomen" to masquerade as laborers. Captain Connell believed that by cleaning up the town, it would give it "a semblance of civilization."[55] The guerrillas worked peacefully for two weeks before they decided to strike.[56] The American mailboat arrived in the evening of September 26 with the news of President McKinley's assassination. Captain Connell ordered his men to make preparations for a memorial service in honor of the fallen President the next day.[57] The following morning, after a 6:30 A.M. reveille, the troops began to eat in an outdoor dining area a few hundred feet away from their rifles, which were stacked outside their barracks. When the church bell rang, a conch shell blew and hundreds of Filipinos descended on the camp swinging bolos and hatchets. Most of the officers were killed in their quarters; many in the dining area were still in their chairs when they were butchered alive. The cook armed himself with a cleaver and threw cans and pots of boiling water to stave off a blur of slashing bolomen. After Captain Connell was hacked to death in front of his men, Sergeant Breton took command of the American survivors and formed them into a British square formation, and killed approximately 250 Filipinos (in the end, 59 Americans were killed at Balangiga, 23 were wounded, and only six came away unscathed).

When the survivors from Company C arrived at the American garrison at Basey, the American commander, Captain Bookmiller, planned a reprisal mission. He led fifty-five men and the six uninjured survivors from Company C back to Balangiga aboard the gunboat *Pittsburgh*. When the Americans returned to the scene of the massacre, they found Captain Connell's corpse decapitated and a fire smouldering in his nearby head. Also missing was the finger on which he wore his West Point ring. The American troops happened to stumble upon a mass funeral for the Filipinos killed at Balangiga. The soldiers captured 20 men and ordered them to remove the Filipino dead from their freshly dug mass grave and to replace their bodies with those of the Americans. The soldiers built a giant fire to burn the Filipino dead. According to historian Stuart Creighton Miller, as the pyre's flames leaped in the background and the bodies burned, Captain Bookmiller read from the Bible: "They have sown the wind and they shall reap the whirlwind." Bookmiller then handed over the 20 prisoners to the survivors from Company C, and as they were being executed, Company G set the town ablaze. Captain Bookmiller reported back to Manila, "Buried dead, burned town, returned Basey."[58]

General "Hell Roaring" Jacob Smith was sent to Samar to put down Lukban's insurgents. Jacob Smith was another old Indian fighter who had participated in the Wounded Knee Massacre in 1890. Earlier in the war, then Colonel Smith told a group of reporters in the Philippines that fighting the Philippine rebels was "worse than fighting Indians." According to Miller, "he had already adopted the appropriate tactics that he had learnt fighting 'savages' in the American West, without waiting for orders to do so from General Otis." In the intervening years, Smith had made a name for himself as an aggressive leader. Traveling to Balangiga with General Smith was Marine Major Littleton Waller, in command of three hundred U.S. Marines.[59] When the relief party finally arrived at Balangiga, they saw a man hanging out of a window. His face was hard to make out because it was covered with swarming ants. Upon closer inspection, they could see that his eyes were gouged out, his face was cut from nose to throat, and the wound was filled with jam. When the Americans reached the scene of the slaughter at Balangiga, they were horrified by the sight that greeted them—hogs had dug up and partially eaten the American bodies that Captain Bookmiller and his men had carefully buried.[60] When a Major Combe entered the town, he found more atrocities: "a deep wound across the face of Lieutenant Bumpus had been filled with jam"; another man had "his abdomen cut open and codfish and flour had been put in the wound."[61]

According to Major Combe, the guerrillas had consistently and flagrantly violated the laws of war: "No prisoners of war were taken. Noncombatants were put to death. Poison was used. Flags of truce were not respected and persons traveling under their protection were killed."[62] After General Jacob Smith examined the carnage, he issued the following orders to Major Littleton Waller, "I want no prisoners. I wish you to kill and burn. The more you kill and burn, the better you will please me. The interior of Samar must be a howling wilderness." Even a seasoned veteran like Major Waller was shocked by Smith's order, and when he passed it on to Captain David Porter, he tempered it: "Porter, I've had instructions to kill everyone over ten years old. But we are not making war upon women and children, only on men capable of bearing arms. Keep that in mind no matter what other orders you receive."[63] Captain Porter was also present when Smith issued his order. He would later claim that the general's order was a reprisal for the Balangiga Massacre and that this was clearly allowed by Article 24 of the Lieber Code: "After describing the situation General Smith spoke of the 'need to adopt a policy that will create in the minds of the people a burning desire for the war to cease.' "[64] Smith was voicing what had been American policy for most of the war.

General Adna Chaffee described Jacob Smith as "an energetic officer" whose mission on Samar was "to disarm these people and to keep them disarmed, and any means to that end is advisable." General John Franklin Bell believed that "These people need a thrashing to teach them some good common sense."[65] On November 11, 1901, the *Manila Times* reported this account of General Smith's first ten days on Samar: "He already ordered all natives to present themselves in certain of the coastal towns saying that *those who were found outside would be shot and no questions asked.* The time limit had expired . . . and General Smith was as good as his word. The policy of reconcentration is said to be the most effective thing of the kind ever seen under any flag. All suspects including Spaniards and half-breeds were rounded up in big stockades and kept under guard."[66] Major Waller reported from Basey, "in accordance with my orders, destroyed all villages and houses, burning in all 165." General Smith recommended a decoration for Major Waller, who was "an officer of exceptional merit and carries out my wishes and instructions loyally and gallantly."[67]

News of General Smith's orders caused an uproar in the United States that threatened to derail Roosevelt's Philippine policy. On November 11, an American officer who served in the war wrote in a letter to the *Philadelphia Ledger*, "Our men have been relentless, have killed to exterminate men, women, and children, prisoners, and captives, active insurgents and suspected people, from lads of ten up, an idea prevailing that the Filipino was little better than a dog." On December 7, 1901, General John Franklin Bell announced that the time had come for reprisals. He argued that the Filipinos had violated twenty-six articles of the Lieber Code and that now the United States was justified under the Lieber Code to carry out reprisals to "severely punish, in the same or lesser degree, the commission of acts denounced in the aforementioned articles."[68] On January 13, 1902, Senator George "Frisbie" Hoar introduced a resolution calling for an examination of the American conduct of the war in the Philippines. After some foot dragging, Henry Cabot Lodge consented to the request and established a committee of seven senators to examine the charges. The committee would hear from Admiral George Dewey, Civil Governor of the Philippines William Howard Taft, General Ewell Otis, General Arthur MacArthur, a survivor from the Balangiga massacre, and a number of other Americans.

Much of the early testimony before the Senate committee was aimed at establishing the cruel and barbarous nature of the foe. Army Private Leroy Hallock described administering the water cure to a captured guerrilla. The impact of the private's testimony was lessened when Hallock claimed that after the guerrilla had been tortured, he confessed to roasting an American soldier alive before hacking him to death.[69] Irish-born Senator Tom Paterson of Colorado viewed the laws of war in racial terms: "When a war is conducted by a superior race against those whom they consider inferior in the scale of civilization, is it not the experience of the world that the superior race will almost involuntarily practice inhuman conduct?"[70] William Howard Taft concurred: "There is much greater danger in such a case than in dealing with whites. There is no doubt about that."[71]

However, it was the army's casualty lists that drew the most attention. General MacArthur had a difficult time explaining away the disparity in American and Philippine losses. Senator Patterson appeared dumbfounded by the army's own body count (800 killed and 30 wounded in one battle). MacArthur tried to argue that the numbers were inaccurate because the guerrillas, like the American Indians, recovered their wounded and weapons from the battlefield. Patterson pressed him about the statistics for the battles around Manila, "a total of killed and wounded of 3,204, against 112 Americans killed and wounded." General MacArthur replied tellingly, "If that is what the mathematics of the situation call for I presume it is true."[72] Senator Beveridge sensed trouble and interjected, "In battle the object is to kill and wound as many of the enemy as possible, and to put them out of action." "Yes," MacArthur replied. Senator Patterson attempted to steer him back to the original question: "Where you have a uniform disproportion in the killed and wounded of the two contending armies, anywhere from fifteen to one . . . does not that become pretty near slaughter instead of war?" "No, no," General MacArthur replied testily, "not when your adversary stands up and fights."[73]

In early January in the Philippines, Major Littleton Waller launched an ill-fated land campaign in which his troops got lost and ran out of supplies. When Waller and the remnants of his forces returned from the field, he charged eleven of his native Philippine porters with "treachery" and had them shot by a firing squad.[74] Major Waller informed his superiors that he had had "to expend eleven prisoners" just as the Philippine investigation was getting under way in Washington.[75]

Subsequently, Secretary of War Root cabled General Adna Chaffee and ordered a number of the participants to Manila:

> The President desires to know in the fullest and most circumstantial manner all the facts, nothing being concealed, and no man being for any reason favored or shielded. . . . The President intends to back up the army in the heartiest fashion in every lawful and legitimate method of doing its work, he also intends to see that the most rigorous care is exercised to detect and prevent any cruelty or brutality, and that men guilty thereof are punished. Great as the provocation has been in dealing with foes who habitually resort to treachery, murder, and torture against our men, nothing can justify or will be held to justify, the use of torture or inhuman conduct of any kind on the part of the American Army.[76]

Major Littleton Waller was brought before military court in Manila in March of 1902. According to Stuart Creighton Miller, Elihu Root was looking to use Waller as a scapegoat, "At least Root was eager to cast Waller in that role if the major would only cooperate and play the sacrificial victim." The anti-imperialist press in the United States had already condemned Waller as "the butcher of Samar" and compared him to Kitchener in the Boer War. Major Waller was tried by a court-martial led by Major General William Bisbee, Major Edgar Robertson, and three other cavalry officers. When the trial opened on March 7, 1902, Waller's defense attorney challenged the court's jurisdiction over him. Bisbee was sympathetic to Waller's argument and turned to Adna Chaffee, who ordered the court to reconvene and to try him for murder. Although

Waller admitted to the killings, he claimed that they were justified by both General Smith's orders and the laws of war. Waller told the court that he had personally witnessed similar executions of Arab cavalrymen in Alexandria in 1892 and Chinese Boxers in 1900. Waller planned to defend himself using General Orders No. 100, which authorized reprisals and described them as "the sternest feature of war." However, when General Jacob Smith appeared in court as a witness for the prosecution, he testified that Waller had acted on his own by executing the prisoners. A shocked Major Waller produced both General Smith's written orders and witnesses who convincingly refuted Smith.[77] Although he was found not guilty of murder and sentenced only to a loss of pay, he implicated Major General Jacob Smith, whose order to kill and burn was condemned in the strongest terms by the anti-imperialist press in the United States.

The headline of the April 8, 1902 *New York Journal* read, "KILL ALL: MAJOR WALLER ORDERED TO MASSACRE THE FILIPINOS. The media now focused their enmity on "Howling Jake," also known more simply as "The Monster." Now the United States would have to investigate General Jacob Smith to extinguish this controversy. Adna Chaffee suggested that General Smith simply say that he issued the orders under duress and that they were not meant to be taken literally. General Smith refused and argued that his action was totally justified under the Lieber Code. However, when President Roosevelt signed the indictment of Jacob Smith on April 21, 1902, he was not charged with murder or war crimes. Instead, he faced the far more benign charge of "conduct to the prejudice of good order and military discipline."[78] This was an entirely different type of political justice from that exercised in the Sioux and the Wirz cases; the Jacob Smith case would provide an early example of strategic legalism. Secretary Root would attempt to use the judicial machinery to quell a controversial political problem that threatened to undermine the larger objectives of American foreign policy. On a more basic level, the Roosevelt administration needed to close the gap between words and deeds in America's Philippine policy.

When the trial began, most of the witnesses were very friendly to General Smith and attempted to establish the savage nature of their foes and the "irregular" nature of the war. Lieutenant Baines testified: "All the natives that I have seen in the interior of Samar, outside of the towns, were what I consider savages; they were very low intelligence, treacherous, cruel; seemed to have no feeling, either for their families or for anybody else."[79] Lieutenant Hoover testified that the fighting ability of twelve-year-old guerrillas was sufficient to consider them both "legitimate and fearsome, maniacal adversaries."[80] Lieutenant Ayer testified: "When one gets to the interior among the tribes who live there, religious fanaticism, stolid indifference, and great personal bravery are conspicuously in evidence."[81]

Major Waller testified that under the laws of war he was not obliged to give quarter and pointed to the Lieber Code. "General Orders, No. 100, covers it. For instance, if in actual experience we find that certain bands give us no quarter, or surrender and then become treacherous immediately afterwards—and we had that experience several times—we had a perfect right under the laws of war to shoot anybody belonging to that band."[82] Waller said that he tempered General Smith's order: "Always when prisoners came in and gave themselves up they were saved, they were not killed—not slaughtered, at that time. But in the field, whenever they opposed us we fought until there was nothing else to fight."[83] Major Waller's testimony demonstrated how blurry the line between soldier and civilian was in guerrilla warfare.

Q: *What do you mean by insurrectos in the island of Samar?*
Waller: *I mean those people actually bearing arms against us or who were openly aiding or abetting the insurrection.*
Q: *Whether they had arms or not?*
Waller: *They all had arms. Even the women carried arms.*[84]

The court's ruling was consistent with Chaffee's view that General Smith "did not mean everything that his unexplained language implied." Upon hearing the court's decision, an unrepentant General Smith was reported to have turned to the press in the courtroom "to declare he meant every word and that burning and shooting 'the treacherous savages' was the only way to win the war." Although General Smith had been found guilty of the vague crime of "prejudicing officers," he was not sentenced and boarded a steamship bound for the United States on August 1, 1902. In a letter, President Roosevelt commented on the Smith case to a friend: "Inspector General Breckinridge happened to mention quite casually to me with no idea that he was saying anything in Smith's disfavor, that he met him [Smith] and asked him what he was doing, he responded, 'Shooting niggers.' Breckinridge thought this a joke. I did not." Back in Washington, Root concocted a scheme to have Smith declared "temporarily insane." Chaffee could not persuade the medical officers to back his plan. The proceedings of the general court-martial were submitted to President Theodore Roosevelt, who made the final ruling. The President qualified his decision:

> I am well aware of the danger and difficulty of the task our Army has had in the Philippine Islands and of the . . . intolerable provocations it has received from the cruelty, treachery, and total disregard of the rules and customs of civilized warfare on the part of its foes. I also heartily approve of the employment of the sternest measures necessary to put a stop to such atrocities, and to bring this war to a close.[85]

Roosevelt was careful to distinguish the American atrocities as exceptional events and praised the army's "wonderful kindness and forbearance in dealing with their foes." Smith's order was considered an "isolated incident," not a matter of policy. "Loose and violent talk by an officer of high rank is always likely to excite to wrongdoing . . . among his subordinates whose will are weak or whose passions are strong," Roosevelt wrote. General Smith's wrongdoing was mitigated by "a long career distinguished for gallantry and on the whole for good conduct. . . . I hereby direct that he be retired from the active list."[86]

Shortly after the trials, antiwar activists Moorefield Storey and Julian Cadman wrote a 119-page pamphlet analyzing Elihu Root's handling of the Philippines atrocities and concluded that the trials had been a farce. Storey wrote that Root "was silent in the face of certain knowledge and by his silence he made himself responsible for all that was done in his acquiescence. . . . Mr. Root, then is the real defendant in this case. The responsibility for what has disgraced the American name lies at his door."[87]

The War Department telegraphed a summary of the attack to the Secretary of War during a stop in Peoria, Illinois. Root argued that the guerrillas had violated the rules of "civilized warfare":

> The war on the part of the Filipinos has been conducted with the barbarous cruelty common among uncivilized races, and with the general disregard for the laws of civilized warfare. . . . Filipino troops have frequently fired upon our men from under the protection of flags of truce, tortured to death American prisoners who have fallen into their hands,

buried alive both Americans and friendly natives, and horribly mutilated the bodies of the American dead.

Root justified any American atrocities under the doctrine of reprisal:
"That such soldiers fighting against such an enemy, and with their own
eyes witnessing such deeds should occasionally regardless of their orders
retaliate by unjustifiable severities is not incredible."[88]

Elihu Root went on to defend the American military's "scrupulous
regard for the rules of civilized warfare, with careful and genuine consideration for the prisoner and non-combatant, with self-restraint, and
humanity, never surpassed, if ever equaled, in any conflict, worthy only of
praise, and reflecting credit upon the American people."[89] However,
when pressed, he offered a more complex defense for America's Philippine policy and, like John Fiske, pointed to the "history and the conditions of the warfare with cruel and treacherous savages who inhabited the
island" and offered two "precedents of the highest authority." These were
George Washington's 1779 order to General John Sullivan to carry out
reprisals against hostile Iroquois Indians and William T. Sherman's
reprisal order after the Fort Kearney Massacre in 1866. Historian
Richard Drinnon attaches great importance to Root's reference to these
precedents: "Now, in the process of ransacking the War Department
records for authorizations of terror, Root had unwittingly disclosed two
important and related truths. The first was that the national past contained authorizations of terror and could easily be made to share the guilt
of current killings, hurtings and burnings."[90]

Secretary of War Root wrote Senator Henry Cabot Lodge: "Every
report or charge of this description which has been brought to the attention of the War Department, has been made the subject of prompt investigation." He enclosed "the record of thirteen such inquiries in which the
results have been reported. You will perceive that in substantially every
case the report has proved to be either unfounded or grossly exaggerated."[91] In a personal letter to Lodge, Root tellingly described the trials in
Manila as "the token courts-martial of a total of ten officers." In the
Jacob Smith case, the strategic legalism came in the form of a vague
indictment, a sympathetic court, and a narrow reading of the laws of war
that in the end produced little more than a symbolic chastisement. This
action allowed the U.S. government to admonish a scapegoat and deem
the atrocities isolated incidents.

An important element of strategic legalism was and remains the public-private split. Once the public has been served its symbolic "justice," post-trial, nonjudicial legal "devices," like pardon, clemency, and parole, are used to mitigate the original, public sentence. The case of American Lieutenant Preston Brown provides a good example. He was tried in Manila, found guilty of killing a prisoner of war, and sentenced to five years of hard labor. However, after the trial, Secretary of War Root quietly reduced Brown's sentence to the loss of half his pay for nine months and a demotion in the army promotions list. Lieutenant Bissell Thomas was convicted of "assaulting prisoners and cruelty," what amounted to "acute torture"; he was fined $300 and given an official reprimand.[92] As historian Godfrey Hodgson points out, "It is hard to avoid the judgment that Root did know that things had gone badly wrong in the Philippines, and that he used his lawyer's skill with words to deny charges that were in substance true."[93]

By the time the United States prevailed in the Philippines, approximately 200,000 Filipinos and 5,000 Americans were dead.[94] The duality in America's relationship with international law was personified by Secretary of War Elihu Root. With no sense of hypocrisy or contradiction, Root defended America's brutal colonial acquisition on the narrowest positive legal grounds, while simultaneously advocating a radical expansion of international law. To men like Roosevelt and Root there was nothing odd about this duality or duplicity—they believed that equity only existed among equals. Again, there were clearly two sets of rules and American leaders were very candid about this until the twentieth century.

Many of the Americans who were beginning to turn their attention to international law were high-level international corporate lawyers from New York City. Senator Daniel Patrick Moynihan notes that even though the U.S. capital moved south, "The culture would remain in New York. One result was that much of the international affairs of the new nation continued in the hands of New York lawyers. This indeed gave a legalist cast to American foreign relations that was distinctive among nations."[95] In December 1904, Elihu Root addressed a group in New York and declared, "Today the United States is practically sovereign on this continent, and its fiat is law upon the subjects to which it confines its interposition."[96] Under the new strategic doctrine of Manifest Destiny, American leaders could create and enforce stern new rules for the rest of the world to follow while keeping a free hand in the Western Hemisphere.

In 1905, President Theodore Roosevelt negotiated an end to the Russo-Japanese War at the Lotos Club on Fifth Avenue in New York City. Encouraged by the success of this effort, Roosevelt called for a second conference at the Hague. The American delegation was led by Joseph Choate, General G. B. Davis, Admiral Charles Sperry, David Hill, General Horace Porter, and Dr. James B. Scott. The group was given special marching orders from (now) Secretary of State Root, who urged them to take the most "progressive" view and to "always keep in mind the promotion of this continuous process through which the progressive development of international justice and peace may be carried on."[97] Forty-four nations convened in the Hague in June of 1907. Because the first Hague Conference had more or less codified the practical rules of war, the second could address more radical issues like international arbitration.

When the American delegation pressed for an international court with compulsory jurisdiction, the Germans again refused to relinquish their national interests to such a court. Foreign Minister Bernard von Bülow ordered the German delegation to demand modifications to that convention—most significantly, the omission of all references to obligatory jurisdiction.[98] In the end, the second Hague Conference succeeded in further defining the rules of war and committing more nations to observing them, but again, America's more ambitious plans were foiled by German conservatism. It was obvious that the Germans were not comfortable with the American assumption that war could be judged legitimate or illegitimate. To them, it was an instrument of policy bound by its own set of rules. The *London Times* mockingly described the second conference as a gathering of wide-eyed utopians, insisting that "We do not believe that any progress . . . in the cause of peace, in the mitigation of the evils of war, can be accomplished by a repetition of the strange and humiliating performance which has just ended."[99]

Undaunted, Secretary of State Root said that the second Conference provided concrete evidence that the world "had entered upon a more orderly process." The objective of these conferences, he proclaimed, was to make "the practice of civilized nations conform to their peaceful professions."[100] Joseph Choate went one step further, describing the accomplishments of the conference in the grandest terms: "And so at last, after three centuries, will be realized the dream of Grotius, the founder of international law, that all civilized nations of the earth will submit to its dictates, whether in war or peace."[101] Choate's celebration of the "completion of a century of unbroken peace between ourselves and all of the other great nations of the earth" begs another question. What were the skirmishes with Indians, Mexicans, and Filipinos? Did they simply not count? The movement at the second Hague conference was really one for equity among established powers.

Because the German contingent was unwilling to consent to America's new conception of the international order, they were branded "troublemakers" by American leaders. In a 1909 letter to Andrew Carnegie, Root declared that "the obstacle to the establishment of arbitration agreements, to the prevention of war, to disarmament, to the limitation of armaments, to all attempts to lessen the suspicions and alarm of nations toward each other, is Germany, who stands, and has persistently stood since I have been familiar with foreign affairs, against that kind of progress." Elihu Root considered "Germany, under her present government, is the great disturber of peace in the world."[102]

In 1913, the United States prepared for a third Hague Conference, scheduled for 1914. Joseph Choate wished a "hearty Godspeed to the Conference and all its successors."[103] But the third conference never convened, as hopes for international peace were dashed by a bullet in Sarajevo. Although the American Civil War had provided a preview of twentieth-century military conflict, it had been only a dress rehearsal for the "war to end all wars." The colonial conflicts of the nineteenth century did not prepare European armies for the trench battles of the Western Front, where combat was no longer a matter of killing natives armed with rattan sticks and bolo knives.[104]

Modern democracy profoundly changed the nature and objectives of warfare in the nineteenth and especially the twentieth centuries. Major-General J.F.C. Fuller writes that

Speaking for their peoples, governments demanded extraordinary rewards for unprecedented national sacrifices. . . . Specifically, they sought either the total defeat and subjugation of the enemy, or a reorganization of the European and world community that would make war impossible—two goals which they proved unable to achieve.[105]

The outbreak of World War I in 1914 demonstrated how vulnerable international law was to the aggressive policies of a nation ready, willing, and able to employ military force. Once national survival was at stake, international law fell victim to military necessity or "*Kriegsraison.*" German Chancellor Bethman Hollweg candidly acknowledged this in an address to the Reichstag: "Gentlemen, we are now in a state of necessity, and necessity knows no law. Our troops have already entered Belgian territory. Gentlemen, that is a breach of international law. . . . A French attack on our flank on the lower Rhine would have been disastrous. Thus we were forced to ignore the rightful protests of the Government of Belgium."[106] Once it appeared to the Kaiser and the General Staff that war was inevitable, they launched their much-vaunted Schlieffen Plan, described by historian Andreas Hillgruber as a policy in which "military strategy . . . coerced foreign policy."[107] Germany planned to encircle France with a flanking movement and mount a rear attack in the west before engaging Russia in the east.[108] The problem with the plan was that it required a massive violation of Belgian neutrality (which had been guaranteed by a treaty in 1911 and reassured in 1913),[109] in which the English had taken a special interest. German leaders knew that their strategy would force a confrontation with England.[110]

The Schlieffen Plan failed to produce a quick victory. The Belgian army counterattacked on August 25 and forced their foes back to Louvain, Belgium. Over the next two days, the Germans killed more than two hundred civilians and burned parts of the old medieval city. They did not treat captured civilian combatants as prisoners of war but as "*franc-tireurs,*" people waging unlawful war against an occupying army and therefore not protected by the laws of war. The British press told horrendous tales of "Hunish atrocities" in Belgium. However, the "war crimes" were not as clear cut as the British and American press made them out to be.

The German government correctly argued that in order to be protected by the laws of war, armed opponents needed to be members of an identifiable and organized military force. Civilians could not offer armed resistance at one moment and later claim immunity on the ground that they were civilians.[111] The Bryce Report on German atrocities in Belgium gave currency to some of the most exaggerated stories of German atrocities. Five American newspaper correspondents attached to the German armies in Belgium cabled the Associated Press: "In the spirit of fairness we unite in declaring German atrocities groundless." However, the introduction to the German General Staff's *Manual of Land Warfare* (*Kriegsgebrauchim Landkriege*) contained several telling passages:

> A war energetically carried on cannot be entirely confined to acts against the enemy under arms and his means of defense, but it will tend also to cause the destruction of his materials and moral resources. No consideration can be given to the dictates of humanity, such as consideration for persons and property, unless they are in accordance with the nature and object of the war.[112]

When stories of "Hunish" illegal warfare filtered back to Great Britain, learned legal arguments fell on deaf ears. British Prime Minister Herbert Asquith described the German action as "a shameless holocaust . . . lit up by blind barbarian vengeance."[113] The failure of the Germans to secure a quick victory in Belgium gave England time to send troops to reinforce the French. The Russians also mobilized more quickly than anticipated and when they attacked Germany from the east, von Moltke recalled reinforcements meant for his end run through Belgium. Although the Russians were repelled, by the fall of 1914 the Germans were bogged down in France.

As the Western Front settled down to trench warfare, battalion after battalion manned the ladders and threw themselves "over the top," but infantry charges proved to be no match for the machine gun. During the first day at the Battle of the Somme, Great Britain lost 60,000 men.[114] In five months—July 1 to November 18, 1916—the British lost 419,654 and the French nearly 200,000.[115]

The term "war crimes" was first widely used during and after World War I. More often than not, war crimes accusations were propaganda designed to fuel the moral outrage necessary for modern war. Neither side was quick to prosecute war criminals because they feared reprisals.[116] A number of people in Britain and France began a movement that aimed to try the German Kaiser after World War I. The German government feared war crimes prosecutions for a different reason. The ever-practical General Staff believed that if common soldiers were encouraged to examine orders as international legal questions, military discipline would disintegrate.[117]

The Germans would soon find out that morality has a prudential role in any foreign policy. Even when their tactics were not clearly wrong, it mattered little.[118] Flagrant violations of the law of nations and insensitivity to the subsequent international outcry doomed the Reich in the now important court of public opinion. The very image of the stiffly formal Kaiser in his spiked helmet invited ridicule. Historian Andreas Hillgruber has observed:

> Public opinion in other European nations slowly came to sense a threat, less because of the goals of German foreign policy per se than the crude, overbearing style Germany projected on the international stage. Without this background, one cannot understand the truly radical hate for Germany and all things German that broke out in the Entente countries with the war of 1914.[119]

This lack of judgment was demonstrated in 1915 when German authorities captured Edith Cavell, the head of a nursing school in Brussels, and charged her with helping 600 British prisoners to escape. Under German military law, aiding and abetting the escape of the enemy was punishable by death.[120] Hours after Cavell confessed and was found guilty by a military court, she was shot by a firing squad.[121] As historian James Willis notes, Cavell's execution was a typical German miscalculation, "an example of a lack of sensitivity to world public opinion. . . . Even those sympathetic described the German action as one characterized by 'incredible stupidity.' "[122]

Technological advances posed vexing new questions for the laws of war. If the small German submarine fleet had observed existing regulations, the sailors would have signed their own death warrants. Maritime law required submarines to surface, warn the targeted ship of its imminent destruction, and allow the crew to lower the lifeboats before sinking the vessel. Although this sounded sporting enough, the early submarines were slow and frail, and the British were not passive victims of submarine aggression. The British Admiralty had issued standing orders for merchant vessels to ram German submarines.[123] Armed British merchantmen "used decoy ships to lure U-boats into traps, flew neutral flags, and rammed whenever possible any submarines that complied with international law by surfacing to warn British merchant vessels of imminent destruction."[124] Once the merchant vessels were armed they technically became warships. The situation was further complicated when the Associated Powers invoked the legal doctrines of retaliation and contraband without officially declaring a blockade.[125]

The most famous British war crime occurred in 1915 when a merchant ship, H.M.S *Barlong*, sunk German submarine *U-27* and shot the surviving crew members.[126] The German reprisal was swift and draconic. After a U-boat captured the British steamship *Brussels* on July 27, 1916, German POW authorities determined that British captain Charles Fryatt had attempted to ram a German U-boat a year earlier. Fryatt was tried by a German navy court-martial that declared him a franc-tireur who had committed a "crime against armed German sea forces." Captain Fryatt was tried, sentenced, and executed all on the same day.[127]

In June of 1916, the steamship *Llandovery Castle* was returning to England after having delivered wounded and sick Canadian soldiers to Halifax, Nova Scotia. The *Llandovery Castle* left Halifax for England with 258 crew members aboard. On the night of June 27, the ship was intercepted by German submarine *U-86*, captained by First Lieutenant Helmutt Patzig. The steamer was clearly marked with Red Cross flags and lights according to the Tenth Hague Convention of 1907. At 9:30 P.M., *U-86* fired a torpedo that hit the *Llandovery Castle* squarely, and the steamer sank in only ten minutes, 116 miles southwest of Fastnet, Ireland, in the middle of the deep, black Atlantic.[128]

Of the five lifeboats lowered by Second Officer Chapman, only three managed to escape from being pulled under by the sinking ship. The boat that contained Chapman was pulling survivors from the water when *U-86* surfaced and called for the lifeboats to pull alongside. When they didn't comply, a pistol shot was fired as a warning and the lifeboats pulled alongside the submarine. Captain Sylvester was taken aboard and accused of having eight American airmen on board the *Llandovery Castle*. Two Canadian medical corpsmen were also taken aboard the sub and questioned, but all three men denied that they were airmen and were released by First Lieutenant Patzig. *U-86* submerged, only to reappear and demand that two of the ship's officers come aboard for an interrogation. They were asked to explain why the ship had exploded so violently if it was not carrying munitions. Officers Chapman and Barton were released and the submarine disappeared for a second time. The third time, *U-86* surfaced like a great white shark and headed straight for Captain Sylvester's lifeboat. It veered slightly at the last moment and just managed to avoid the boat. The submarine then circled and made another close pass, and vanished into the depths. The survivors in the captain's lifeboat were rigging a small sail when they heard firing, and two shells sailed over their boat. Thirty-six hours later, one lifeboat was picked up by the British destroyer *Lysander*. Captain Sylvester and the 23 others in his boat were the only survivors of the *Llandovery Castle*.[129] The day after the sinking of the hospital ship, First Lieutenant Patzig of *U-86* held a meeting and made his crew swear to an oath of silence about the previous night's activities.

In January 1917, Germany accused the Associated Powers of using hospital ships to ferry troops and munitions; British officials claimed that the munitions were defensive.[130] The German government announced that due to what they considered to be a double standard by which its enemies could transport men and arms clandestinely while its submarines were required to surface before attacking, Germany would wage unrestricted submarine warfare; all ships would be sunk without warning. American President Woodrow Wilson claimed that the use of submarines violated the "law and principles of humanity" and that this would not be tolerated by the "civilized world."[131] It is interesting to note that Wilson did not invoke the laws of war but the laws of "humanity." As a result of the German resumption of unrestricted submarine warfare, the United States entered World War I on April 6, 1917. The war was no longer a value-free means of dispute resolution; it was now a contest between civilizations.

At the time, Secretary of State Elihu Root announced: "To be safe, democracy must kill its enemy when it can and where it can. The world cannot be half democratic and half autocratic. It must be all democratic or all Prussian. There can be no compromise. If it is all Prussian, there can be no real international peace."[132] Root advocated a muscular brand of American legalism that was prepared to use force to uphold the new treaties. He believed that if Germany's flagrantly illegal invasion of Belgium and conduct during the war were tolerated, the Hague rules and other advances in international law would be reduced to "mere scraps of paper." The survival of a democracy was dependent on its ability to deal with the problem "by destroying the type of government which has shown itself incapable of maintaining respect for law and justice and resisting the temptation of ambition."[133] By 1918, Root described World War I as nothing less than a battle between "Odin and Christ."[134]

There was much less clamor over massive atrocities committed outside of Europe. This pointed to a duality not only in American foreign policy but also in international law. Rather than expel or resettle Turkey's minority Armenian population, Turkish leaders chose simply to kill them. When Turkey's Ittihad allied with Germany, its "Young Turk" leaders enslaved the Armenians and forced them to build public works projects. By 1915, according to David Kaiser,

> the Young Turks decided . . . to solve the problem of the Armenian minority by exterminating the Armenians. . . . The government disarmed the Armenians of Anatolia in 1915 and announced its decision to deport them to Mesopotamia. But the deportation was only a pretext: the Turks shot Armenian men and marched the Armenian women and children into the mountains and the desert, where they starved to death. Between 1 and 1.5 million Armenians perished.[135]

The U.S. government was divided over its official response. Although the U.S. Ambassador to Turkey, Henry Morgenthau, spoke out against the massacres, the State Department took a different view. In 1915, the governments of France, Great Britain, and Russia declared the Turkish atrocities "crimes against humanity and civilization" and threatened to hold the ringleaders "personally responsible."[136] However, American leaders neither supported nor took actions against the perpetrators of the Armenian genocide. After the German government agreed to an armistice on November 11, 1918, the State Department emerged as the conservative voice on American war crimes policy.

When President Woodrow Wilson unveiled his revolutionary peace plan in 1918, war crimes were a minor detail. His outline for a new international political system was by far the most radical American attempt to dislodge the cornerstone of the old European state system—sovereignty. Wilson's "Fourteen Points" set out to model international relations after a modern constitutional democracy, complete with "consent of the governed, equality of rights, and freedom from aggression." Points 1 through 5 proposed the creation of an international system characterized by "open covenants, openly arrived at, freedom of navigation on the seas, equal trade opportunities and the removal of tariffs, general disarmament and an end to colonialism." Points 6 through 13 intended to spread "democracy" by advocating the self-determination of national minorities in Europe. Not to be upstaged by the call to end colonialism or disarmament, point 14 called for the construction of an international government, the League of Nations, to guarantee the "political independence and territorial integrity to great and small nations."[137] The League's covenant applied a variation of constitutional democracy to international conflict.

Rather than fight, nations would enter into arbitration and settle differences diplomatically with nonmilitary sanctions. In the event of war, the League was to coerce the parties into arbitration. The terms "just" and "unjust" were changed to the more up-to-date "lawful" and "unlawful." The procedure for a lawful war was laid out in the League's Charter: "The members of the League agree that if there should arise between them any dispute likely to lead to rupture, they will submit the matter either to arbitration or judicial settlement or to Inquiry by the Council, and they agree in no case to resort to war until three months after the award by the arbitration or the judicial decision, or the resort by the Council."[138] The traditional rules of the European state system were further challenged by the introduction of the concept of "war guilt."

When the Paris Peace Conference opened in January 1919, a "Commission on Responsibility of the Authors of War and the Enforcement of Penalties" was assigned to examine the war crimes question. A group of fifteen Allied international law experts was chaired by American Secretary of State Robert Lansing. Although the American President and his Secretary of State had very dissimilar views on international relations, in this instance they were in agreement because Wilson did not want his peace plan tainted by the demands of vengeance. As James Willis points out, "Lansing . . . opposed international punishment of war crimes, believing observance of the laws of war should be left to the military authorities of each state."[139] A few years prior, President Wilson's advisor Edward House wrote tellingly of the Secretary of State's international legal mindset, "He believes that almost any form of atrocity is permissible provided a nation's safety is involved."[140] The American representative used his legal skills—he was America's most successful international lawyer, after all—to frustrate the European efforts to try the Kaiser and in the process broaden the laws of war.

After two months of private meetings, the commission majority issued its "Reservations to the Majority Report" on March 29, 1919. This statement boldly rejected the doctrine of sovereign immunity and proclaimed the Kaiser accountable for: "(a.) Acts which provoked the world war and accompanied its inception. (b.) Violations of the laws of customs of war and the laws of humanity."[141] On April 4, 1919, American representatives Robert Lansing and James Brown Scott issued an extremely conservative dissenting opinion in the form of the American and Japanese "Reservations to the Majority Report." This critique of the proposed expansion of international criminal law would serve as one of the touchstones for war crimes trial critics in the coming century. Ironically, the Americans echoed arguments that had been made by German representatives at the 1899 and 1907 Hague Conferences. Their report argued that it was one thing to try Germans for violations of the laws of war, "a standard certain, to be found in books of authority and the practice of nations," but "the laws of humanity" were a different and entirely unprecedented matter: they "vary with the individual, which, if for no other reason, should exclude them for consideration in a court of justice, especially one charged with the administration of criminal law."[142]

The American "Reservations" endorsed the principle of sovereign immunity with no reservations or qualifications: "the Commission erred in seeking to subject Heads of State to trial and punishment by a tribunal to whose jurisdiction they were not subject when the alleged offenses were committed." According to the American reading, "war was and is by its very nature inhuman, but acts consistent with the laws and customs of war, although these acts are inhuman, are nevertheless not the object of punishment by a court of justice." Most important, Secretary of State Lansing concluded that "The essence of sovereignty was the absence of responsibility. When the people confided it to a monarch or other head of State, it was legally speaking to them only that he was responsible, although there might be a moral obligation to mankind. Legally, however, there was no super-sovereignty."[143]

On May 8, 1919, Lansing pointed out that although Wilson's radical peace plan "aroused public opinion of mankind and to respond to the idealism of the moralist they have surrounded the new alliance with a halo and called it 'The League of Nations,' " the League was a military alliance like any other, and its success or failure would depend on its ability to project force, not justice. "It is useless to close our eyes to the fact that the power to compel obedience by exercise of united strength of 'The Five' is the fundamental principle of the League." Although the

Secretary of State was referring to the American view of international law after World War I, his statement might just as easily apply to twentieth-century American foreign policy: "Justice is secondary. Might is primary."[144]

It was ironic that the Lansing-led American delegation rejected the trial plan with arguments that would have pleased the German Kaiser himself. Robert Lansing invoked the act-of-state doctrine to argue that as a sovereign, the Kaiser bore no legal responsibility. Moreover, Lansing considered the trial plan a blatant implementation of *ex post facto* law.[145] He objected to a trial, writing that "the practical standard of conduct is not moral or humane ideas but the necessity of the act in protecting the national existence or in bringing the war to successful conclusion."[146] The American reading of the laws of war was made with one eye to the East: "We have seen the hideous consequences of Bolshevik rule in Russia, and we know that the doctrine is spreading westward. . . . We must look to the future, even though we forget the immediate demands of justice. Reprisals and reparations are all very well, but will they preserve society from anarchy and give to the world an enduring peace?"[147] With logic and language that resemble that of the post-World War II period, Lansing warned that a punitive policy might also lead to a breakdown of authority that would "hinder the resistance to Bolshevism." He added that President Wilson "approved entirely of my attitude only he is more radically opposed than I am to this folly."[148]

The disparity in the public positions of President Wilson and his Secretary of State says a great deal about the duality of twentieth-century American foreign policy. While Wilson was attempting to rewrite the rules of statecraft, Lansing was unequivocally invoking the rules that the President sought to overturn. This conflict was captured in an amendment to the League of Nations Charter obtained by the United States to legitimize the Monroe Doctrine. While the European powers were restrained by new rules ending colonialism and supporting national self-determination, the United States retained a free hand in North America. Historian James Willis speculates that President Wilson acceded to British demands on the war crimes issue in order to obtain their support for the Monroe Doctrine amendment: "The close conjunction of decisions makes such a thesis not unreasonable. Wilson compromised on the Kaiser's trial on April 8, and on the evening of April 10, the British helped him override French opposition to the amendment."[149]

After much procrastination, the American delegation agreed to a retributive peace and signed the Treaty of Versailles' infamous "war guilt clause," which held Germany responsible for all of the war's damages.[150] Article 231 of the Treaty of Versailles provided a very specific legal basis for financial reparations: "The Allied and Associated Governments affirm and Germany accepts the responsibility of Germany and her Allies for causing all the loss and damage to which the Allied and Associated Governments and their nationals have been subjected as a consequence of a war imposed upon them by the aggression of Germany and her Allies."[151] Originally, President Wilson resisted the effort to brand Germany with war guilt, but French and British leaders forced him to compromise. Naming Germany an "aggressor" introduced the concept into international positive law. These two articles marked the formal end of the traditional European rules of statecraft and the beginning of a shift toward more discriminatory and subjective codes of international law.[152] According to legal theorists Paul Piccone and G. L. Ulmen, "The turn to a discriminatory concept of war and the criminalization of the enemy . . . Art. 227, which indicted the former German Kaiser, and Art. 231, containing the so-called 'war guilt' clause—certainly contributed to the concept of total war. But the most important factor in the transition from enemy to foe was the infusion of ideology into politics."[153] Under the old European state system, war was considered an instrument of policy whose ill-effects should be limited by the self-restraint of the soldiers on the battlefield. Did the American leaders really believe that war was a social wrong that should one day be outlawed?

Germans of all political persuasions were enraged by the war guilt clause and the effort to try the Kaiser. They urged their leaders to reject the *schmachparagraphen* or "shame paragraphs." Conflict over the treaty caused the downfall of one German cabinet and civil unrest. German President Fredrich Ebert signed the treaty only after determining military resistance was not an option.[154] Under Article 227 of the Treaty of Versailles, the Kaiser was threatened with a trial by an international court. He was charged not with specific war crimes but "a supreme offense against international morality and the sanctity of treaties."[155] Articles 228–230 called for trials for men accused of traditional war crimes. Unlike the conflict resolutions of old, the victors did not execute a handful of deserving felons and issue an amnesty for acts committed during wartime. Instead, they attempted to broaden the scope of international criminal law to hold individuals personally accountable for acts of nations.[156]

However, once again judicial resolution gave way to political considerations that prevented a trial for the Kaiser.[157] European leaders realized that due to domestic weakness, the German government might not be able to endure the humiliation of such a procedure. Even British Prime Minister Lloyd George faced the opposition of his king and began to think in terms of compromise. The Kaiser scoffed at the idea from the relative safety of Denmark: "A court which is impartial does not at present exist in Europe. Against a single person . . . such a proceeding cannot be initiated. It must be directed against all sovereigns and statesmen who partook in the war. . . . The procedure would mean a dishonoring of the principle of monarchy. . . . I do not have any guilt and do not recognize any court having jurisdiction over me."[158] On January 22, 1920, the Dutch government officially refused to extradite the Kaiser.[159]

On February 3, the victors called on the German government to live up to Article 228 of the Treaty of Versailles and hand over 854 men accused of war crimes. Among them were some of Germany's most venerated military leaders: Ludendorff, von Moltke, von Tirpitz, and von Hindenburg.[160] The German government refused and stated firmly, "the extradition of those blacklisted for a trial by an Entente court is a physical and moral impossibility."[161] However, the Germans did agree to try a limited number of men before the German Supreme Court (*Reichsgericht*) in Leipzig. The Associated Powers presented a revised list of 45 defendants.[162] The British had been careful to choose cases where the violations of the laws of war were flagrant; in most, the infractions had been documented by both sides. The British submitted three submarine cases and three prison camp cases. Immediately following World War I, First Lieutenant Helmutt Patzig of U-86 returned home to Danzig and vanished, leaving his subordinates to take the fall.[163] The political justice rendered by the Germans at the Leipzig Trials was similar to the strategic legalism the Americans practiced in the Jacob Smith case—a sympathetic show trial as an appeasement measure to provide symbolic justice and little more.

The Leipzig trials opened on May 23, 1921 in the Reichsgericht with Dr. Schmidt, the presiding judge, and his six colleagues, cloaked in crimson robes and berets, sitting around a horseshoe-shaped table.[164] Ludwig Dithmar and John Boldt, the submarine defendants, were the subordinate officers of the U-boat that sank the hospital ship *Llandovery Castle.* Both refused to testify on the ground that they had taken an oath of silence concerning the events of the night of June 27, 1916. Even the German court looked sternly upon the two officers' unwillingness to cooperate: "If the firing could be explained in any other way, it cannot be imagined that the agreement of the accused to maintain silence could prevent them from denying firing on the boats, without entering into other matters."[165] The testimony of other submarine crew members made it clear that First Lieutenant Patzig had attempted to cover up his action—not only did he alter the submarine's logs, he also changed the ship's course on the charts.[166]

Based on the testimony of Chapman and the other survivors, the court determined that "the lifeboats of the *Llandovery Castle* were fired on in order to sink them." The court ruled sternly in Patzig's case: "The firing on the boats was an offense against the law of nations. In war the killing of unarmed enemies is not allowed. . . . The killing of enemies in war is in full accordance with the will of the state that makes war . . . only in so far as such killing is in accordance with the conditions and limitations imposed by the Law of Nations."[167] The court determined that neither of the accused had actually fired on the lifeboats and thus the "principle guilt rests with Commander Patzig, under whose orders the accused acted." With some qualifications, the court accepted the defense of superior orders: "They should certainly have refused to obey the order. This would have required a specially high degree of resolution. . . . This justifies the recognition of mitigating circumstances in determining the punishment."[168] The defendants were sentenced to four years imprisonment each.

The decisions in the British cases against Karl Heynen and Emil Müller were equally schizophrenic. Karl Heynen was in charge of British POWs in a Westphalian coal mine. When the prisoners refused to work, he beat some of them. Emil Müller, a German prison camp commandant, was similarly charged with nine instances of personal cruelty. They were sentenced to ten and six months respectively. While the court sternly condemned the defendant's beatings of prisoners as "unworthy of a human being," nonetheless they concluded, "It must be emphasized that the accused has not acted dishonorably, that is to say, his honour both as a citizen and as an officer remains untarnished."[169]

The most uncomfortable moment of the Leipzig trials came when the court heard France's charges against Franz Stenger, a decorated German officer who had lost a leg to a French artillery shell.[170] The officer was accused of issuing a no quarter order and ordering his men to shoot prisoners in August 1914. Major Benno Cruscius, a German officer who had pointed the finger at Stenger, testified that he had received the order, carried it out, and passed it on. However, Stenger argued that his troops were fighting illegitimate combatants who did not observe the laws of war: "At mid-day, numerous reports had come in of the French method of fighting, feigning to be dead or wounded, or appearing offering to surrender and from the rear shooting with rifles and machine guns at troops that passed by."[171]

In his final statement before the court, Stenger declared: "I did nothing in the war except my duty and obligation to the leaders of the German fatherland, to my Kaiser, the Supreme War Lord, and in the interest of the lives of my fighting German soldiers."[172] The speech was met with wild applause and an acquittal.[173] His German accuser was not so fortunate—Major Crucius was sentenced to two years for "killing through negligence." The French prosecutors were heckled and spat upon by the unruly German spectators. After the defendants in three more of their cases were acquitted, the French withdrew from the trials. In the six British cases, five of the defendants were convicted; the French obtained only one conviction in their five cases.[174] In their one case, the Belgians charged Max Ramdohr, the head of the German secret police in Belgium, with torturing young boys. The court acquitted him and maintained that the stories were merely the products of overactive adolescent imaginations.[175] When Ramdohr was acquitted, the Belgians also withdrew from the trials.

Like the sentences in another trial conducted by a friendly regime, the Jacob Smith case (1902), the sentences in the *Llandovery Castle* case did not match the tone of the judgments. While the two defendants in the *Llandovery Castle* case were sentenced to four years, they were "accompanied to prison by a cheering crowd."[176] Also like the Jacob Smith case, the sentences would be modified with a crude form of strategic legalism—posttrial, nonjudicial sentence modification. Both Boldt and Dithmar "escaped" from prison with the help of their captors (in November 1921 and January 1922 respectively).[177] In 1922, the Associated Powers repudiated the compromise arrangement for the trials and reserved all formal rights under articles 228–230 of the Treaty of Versailles.[178] Their dissatisfaction with Germany's failure to meet the terms of the treaty moved

French leader Raymond Poincaré to occupy the Ruhr Valley with French and Belgian troops.

The traditional European rules of statecraft had been declining steadily since the late nineteenth century, and the Treaty of Versailles marked its end.[179] With the indictment of the former Kaiser and the war guilt clause came the return of a discriminatory conception of war. During the years following World War I, governments redoubled their efforts not merely to limit war but to outlaw it.[180] The effort to criminalize aggression was a secular reinterpretation of the just and unjust war doctrine. Both Grotius and Gentili recognized the necessity of punishing those who initiated unjust wars.[181] Professor Quincy Wright, one of America's leading international legal scholars at the time, considered the Peace of Paris revolutionary because of its juridical view of war. Man had passed through the "Grotian phase" in which war was considered a right, through the "Vattellian phase" in which war was a fact, and into a new phase in which war was a crime.[182]

The interwar period brought a flurry of legal efforts to restrict and even outlaw war.[183] During the 1920s there were several attempts to criminalize aggression. In 1927, the Assembly of the League of Nations declared "That all wars of aggression are, and shall always be illegal." A year later, the Sixth Pan-American Conference even declared war "an international crime against the human species."[184] However, by far the best-known piece of legislation was the Kellogg-Briand Pact or the Pact of Paris. Sixty-three nations signed the treaty on August 27, 1928. Article I stated: "The High Contracting Parties solemnly declare in the names of their respective peoples that they condemn recourse to war for the solution of international controversies, and renounce it as an instrument of national policy."[185] Yet the solemn pronouncement contained neither contractual obligations nor a criterion for aggression.[186] With no enforcement mechanism in place and an international unwillingness to back tough words with force, the Kellogg-Briand Pact was violated with impunity throughout the 1930s by Japan in China, the Soviet Union in Finland, Italy in Ethiopia and Spain, and Germany in Czechoslovakia. Some of the signatories were condemned, but none were punished.[187] America's lawyer-statesmen continued to push for a new set of international norms that aimed to one day outlaw war. The most important step on this path was the criminalization of an American definition of "aggression."

Henry Stimson, Elihu Root's heir apparent, had been well groomed for his assumption of power. Stimson was a second-generation American lawyer-statesman who began his career in Root's Wall Street law firm. Stimson's biographer, Godfrey Hodgson, traces his legal lineage: "Elihu Root was, with Joseph Choate, the acknowledged leader of the New York bar, a man whose life exemplified Stimson's instinct that . . . public service yields true glory. . . . Stimson grew up in admiration of men slightly older than himself—men like Theodore Roosevelt, Elihu Root, Albert Beveridge, and Brooks Adams." Stimson had served as President Taft's Secretary of War and as a colonel in World War I.[188] It is safe to assume that he shared the American lawyer-statesmens' desire to broaden the rules of statecraft. He considered the Treaty of Versailles' war guilt clause a turning point in the history of international relations and in 1932, as Secretary of State, he condemned the Japanese invasion of Manchuria as a violation of the Washington Conference Treaty of 1922 and the Kellogg-Briand Pact.[189] Like Elihu Root, Stimson believed that the new standards of international law needed to be upheld with force if necessary.

Henry Stimson unequivocally declared: "This country was one of the authors of one of the greatest changes in International Law that has ever taken place . . . the initiator of what has been called the 'Pact of Paris' or the Kellogg-Briand Pact."[190] On August 8, 1932, he denounced the Japanese as "lawbreakers." In Stimson's mind, the traditional rules of the European state system had been buried once and for all by the Treaty of Versailles: "Henceforth when two nations engage in armed conflict . . . we no longer draw a circle around them and treat them with the punctilio of the dueler's code. We denounce [the wrongdoers] as lawbreakers."[191] When the Secretary of State personally appealed to British Foreign Secretary John Simon to support the nonaggression treaty, according to *The Manchester Guardian*, Foreign Secretary Simon acted like "a lawyer picking holes in a contract in the interest of a shady client."[192] Appalled by Sir John's "weaseling" and the "mushy cowards" at the League of Nations, Stimson saw "no reason for abandoning the enlightened principles which are embodied in these treaties."[193]

Under Henry Stimson, a new passive-aggressive principle was added to the strategic legalists' arsenal. Now the United States reserved the right to invoke "nonrecognition" for nations that did not come to power through means it judged "legitimate."[194] Stimson attempted to force the Japanese to withdraw from Manchuria by issuing an ultimatum in 1932 that came to be known as the Stimson Doctrine. It was an American announcement of nonrecognition of "any situation, treaty or agreement which may be brought about by means contrary to the Pact of Paris." Godfrey Hodgson says American statesmen reserved the right to judge the parties in the conflict and to define "legitimate means."[195] Again, the new standards of international conduct were, to borrow a term from contemporary art, "site specific." To German legal theorist Carl Schmitt, the American redefinition of "recognition" was key to what he described as America's "economic imperialism." In Schmitt's estimation, such a doctrine was interventionist by its very nature: "It meant that the United States could effectively control every governmental and constitutional change in every country in the Western Hemisphere."[196] Paul Piccone and G. L. Ulmen wrote, "According to the Tobar Doctrine of 1907, only those governments should be recognized which are 'legal' in the sense of a 'democratic' constitution. In practice, what was meant concretely by 'legal' and 'democratic' was decided by the U.S., which defined, interpreted, and reinterpreted." According to Ulmen, for the United States in the twentieth century, "the source of its power, the secret of its historical actuality—aracanum—lies in international law."[197] Although American leaders supported advances in international law, the American foreign policy duality always loomed in the background and continued to cause conflicts of interest.

Although the Germans signed many of the radical treaties like the Kellogg-Briand Pact, their commitment to the new rules was questionable given the lack of respect the Schlieffen Plan had shown for the nonaggression treaty with Belgium. From the German point of view, after World War I, there was little left to lose.[198] If anything, Germany benefited greatly from the world's unwillingness to confront an aggressive nation. Adolf Hitler took advantage of the uncertain state of European politics and combined mendacious diplomacy with overwhelming force. What he could not browbeat out of world leaders, he took by storm. The Nazi effort was extremely sophisticated and used a number of modern political devices: propaganda, fifth columnists, legalism, military force, and the murder of civilians. In many ways, Nazi Germany was the "criminal nation" or "rogue state" by which all others would be judged. In 1940 and 1941, the *Wehrmacht's blitzkrieg* campaign conquered central and western Europe with a speed, precision, and "frightfulness" that would have pleased their Prussian forefathers. By the end of 1941, Germany controlled most of the European continent. Early in the Second World War,

Allied leaders accused the Germans and the Japanese of atrocities and treaty violations. Initially the charges looked similar to those leveled against the Kaiser during World War I—propaganda intended to rally domestic support. Because the Third Reich's future seemed so promising in the early 1940s, war crimes were not an issue; only victors prosecute war crimes cases. It was not until the Japanese attack on Pearl Harbor on December 7, 1941, that Americans were killed and the United States entered World War II.

In January 1942, representatives of nine Nazi-occupied nations met at the Court of St. James in London and announced their intention to punish Germans who committed crimes against civilians. The St. James Declaration was the first call for something other than traditional vengeance: "international solidarity is necessary to avoid the repression of these acts of violence simply by acts of vengeance on the part of the general public."[199] The declaration was also the first mention of trials. In addition to the occupied nations, the United States, Great Britain, and the U.S.S.R. also signed. On October 7, 1942, the Allies established the United Nations War Crimes Commission to collect war crimes evidence. The Commission was based in London and faced the logistical problem of investigating atrocities in occupied nations. Like the threats of World War I, these early pronouncements raised more questions than they answered.[200] In January 1943, at the Casablanca Conference, Roosevelt and Churchill called for the unconditional surrender of the Axis powers. The United States argued that the vanquished should be tried in legitimate courts of law under the antiaggression treaties that came after World War I.[201]

The first specific commitment to a war crimes trial came when the Foreign Secretaries of the United States, the Soviet Union, and Great Britain met in Moscow for a week in late October 1943. The resulting Moscow Declaration threatened "those German officers and men and members of the Nazi party who have been responsible for atrocities, massacres, and executions" with being "sent back to the countries in which their abominable deeds were done in order that they may be judged and punished according to the laws of these liberated countries." There was even a clause for the Axis leaders: "The above declaration is without prejudice to the case of the major war criminals whose offenses have no particular geographic localization and who will be punished by a joint decision of the governments of the Allies."[202]

As the ring tightened around Germany in the summer of 1944, American and British army officials drafted plans for the occupation. The American plan, "The Handbook of Military Government for Germany and the Interim Directive on Occupation Procedures," was not an outline of American occupational policy but merely a loose set of guidelines designed to get the army through the invasion and early occupation.[203] Earlier that year, U.S. Treasury Secretary Henry Morgenthau Jr. read Dean Acheson's "Report on Reparation, Restitution, and Property Rights—Germany," and came away convinced that the State Department was "soft and coddling" toward Germany.[204] This was the beginning of a long-running dispute within the U.S. government between those who favored a punitive peace and those who favored enlisting Germany as an ally against the Soviet Union. Up to this point, American leaders had followed the British, who favored the summary execution of German political and military leaders. They were less interested in elaborate forms of punishment than in postwar strategy. Very early on, the British and some within the U.S. State Department recognized that Germany would play a key strategic role in the postwar world.

The Treasury Secretary was the most forceful advocate of a vindictive peace: he wanted to severely punish Germany for its war crimes.[205] Morgenthau considered the German atrocities more significant than violations of the laws of war; in his mind, the Third Reich had broken more basic codes of human decency.[206] Morgenthau was a political veteran whose father had battled the State Department over the U.S. response to Turkish war crimes in 1915. Morgenthau understood the game and he had an ally in the Oval Office. President Roosevelt had either read or was briefed on the army proposals outlined in the handbook. In a memo to Secretary of War Stimson, Roosevelt described the proposals as "pretty bad" and sided with Morgenthau. FDR believed that the Germans had to understand the magnitude of their crimes: "Too many people here and in England hold to the view that the German people as a whole are not responsible for what has taken place—that only a few Nazi leaders are responsible. This unfortunately is not fact." The President endorsed the concept of collective guilt: "The German people as a whole must have it driven home to them that the whole nation has engaged in a lawless conspiracy against the decencies of modern civilization."[207]

On September 5, 1944, Henry Morgenthau delivered a memo to the President that contained his own ideas for postwar Germany. The Morgenthau Plan recommended that "the cauldron of wars," Germany's industrial regions of the Ruhr and Saar, be stripped of all mines and industry and be depopulated. The Saar was to go to France, while East Prussia and Silesia were to be surrendered to Poland and Russia, respectively. Morgenthau's larger objective was to transform Germany into a nation "primarily agricultural and pastoral in character."[208] Due process was not to be wasted on Germany's "arch criminals . . . whose obvious guilt has generally been recognized. . . . When identification has been made the person . . . shall be put to death forthwith by firing squad."[209] The military, however, had more traditional ideas about war crimes punishment. Eisenhower felt that a harsh peace was necessary.[210] In the summer of 1944, General Eisenhower suggested executing the entire German General Staff.[211] It is clear that Eisenhower was influenced by wartime passions, and these feelings grew as American forces liberated concentration camps and had a first-hand look at the effects of Nazi depravity.[212]

For a brief moment it seemed that a harsher version of the Treaty of Versailles would be imposed on Germany. The leadership of the U.S. Army, the agency in charge of the European invasion and occupation, was baffled by the Morgenthau Plan. The economic dismantling of Germany would create disorder and chaos, hampering both the invasion and the occupation. There was also something odd about a New York banker preparing orders "for what the American army considered the high point of the whole war—the actual invasion of Nazi Germany."[213] The initial success with which the Morgenthau Plan was greeted forced those who favored a trial to state their case more carefully. Many considered the plan a bureaucratic coup that invaded provinces controlled by the military and State Department. Because Morgenthau was Jewish, some in the War Department and especially the State Department considered his plan a "Judaic act of revenge" committed in the name of the United States.[214] But the debate concerned much more than the fate of German leaders; it was about the shape of the postwar peace. The opponents of the Morgenthau Plan were led in both mind and spirit by second-generation American lawyer-statesman Henry Stimson.[215]

Secretary of War Stimson thought the Morgenthau Plan flawed both morally and strategically, "a Childish folly! . . . a Beautiful Nazi program! This is to laugh!" With world leadership came responsibility—a certain *noblesse oblige*. The Treaty of Versailles seemed mild in comparison to Morgenthau's crude *vae victis*, yet the former had laid the foundations for dictatorship. In a memo to the President, Stimson wrote that "enforced poverty is even worse, for it destroys the spirit not only of the victim but debases the victor. It would be just such a crime as the Germans themselves hoped to perpetuate upon their victims—it would be a crime against civilization itself."[216] Historian Bradley F. Smith has pointed to the social conflict behind the Stimson-Morgenthau clash:

> The Secretary of War bore certain disdain for the marks of crude aggressiveness and new money that clung to Morgenthau. Stimson was a social anti-Semite, as were the vast majority of old family New York aristocrats in the 1940s. In a number of cases Stimson decried the fact that Morgenthau had taken the lead in advocating harsh peace terms. Specifically, he believed that this could rebound and provide ammunition for those who would attribute all stringent controls on Germany to a mere "Jewish" desire for revenge.[217]

When President Roosevelt left for the Quebec Conference on September 11, 1944, Treasury Secretary Morgenthau was the only high-ranking American representative to accompany him.[218] The main purpose of the conference among American and British leaders was to discuss the terms of American economic aid to Great Britain. When the subject of war criminals came up, the delegates agreed that summary execution was the best solution. On September 15, 1944, Churchill and Roosevelt initialed a draft of the Morgenthau Plan.

Although the British did not deny the existence of profound legal questions, they wanted to avoid the maelstrom where justice, politics, and public policy converged. The spokesman for the British position, Lord John Simon, offered a traditional plan that was more restrained than Morgenthau's. Unlike the Americans, the British candidly admitted that the treatment of the vanquished was and had always been a political question. The British labored under no fictions of due process and reeducation and did not consider an international trial a practical possibility. Lord Simon argued that these questions were inherently political and subjective; "apart from the formidable difficulties of constituting the Court, formulating the charge, and assembling the evidence, the question of their fate is a political and not a judicial question. It could not rest with judges, however eminent or learned, to decide finally a matter like this, which is of the widest and most vital public policy."[219] Although Morgenthau carried the day, this was only the first exchange in what Bradley F. Smith describes as "the Great German War on the Potomac."[220]

In meetings and memos, Secretary of War Stimson voiced disapproval of the "economic oppression" implicit in the Morgenthau Plan. He argued that vindictive peace treaties "do not prevent war" but "tend to breed war."[221] The Secretary of War favored a more Wilsonian approach and felt that punishment should not be the sole objective of the occupation. Allied treatment of the Nazi leaders should also serve an educational role. In a memo to Henry Morgenthau, Stimson described the benefits of a more judicious approach:

> It is primarily by the thorough apprehension, investigation, and trial of all the Nazi leaders and instruments of the Nazi system of state terrorism such as the Gestapo with punishment delivered as promptly, swiftly and severely as possible that we can demonstrate the abhorrence which the world has for such a system and bring home to the German people our determination to expiate it and all its fruits forever.[222]

President Roosevelt's views on the question of Nazi Germany's "arch-criminals" tended to reflect the ebb and flow of public opinion rather than a deep commitment to any one approach.

Six weeks prior to the 1944 presidential election, a draft of the Morgenthau Plan was leaked to the press. Many attacked it on the ground that it would embolden German resistance. Nazi Minister of Propaganda Joseph Goebbels declared himself the "number one war criminal" and urged his countrymen to fight to the death rather than face vindictive conquerors.[223] After the uproar, President Roosevelt distanced himself from the Morgenthau Plan. Although Stimson's most immediate threat was now gone, there was another fire to put out: Roosevelt had casually agreed with Churchill that Nazi leaders should be identified and executed.[224] When the Secretary of War learned of this vague promise, he set out to devise an alternative. It was out of this bureaucratic struggle that concrete plans for a trial emerged.

Henry Stimson had not lost faith in the rule of law. He felt that America held a unique position in human history. A transition to peace without vengeance would provide a stable foundation for the postwar world.[225] Stimson insisted the victors restrain their vindictive tendencies and try the vanquished because simple revenge would only give rise to a new version of the "stab in the back" myth. After World War I, German nationalists claimed their political leadership had stabbed the military leadership in the back by negotiating a peace. The Secretary of War's warning proved very prescient given the final outcome of American war crimes policy. He argued that summary justice would "create Nazi martyrs and an opportunity for revisionists and isolationists to claim once more that charges against the German enemy were fabrications."[226]

Stimson believed that a trial would force the German people to face an irrefutable record of Nazi atrocities and as a result they would undergo a national catharsis.[227] Like Civil War reconstruction, America's postwar occupation policies in Germany and Japan would try to meld social work with military occupation policy. "I am disposed to believe that, at least as to the chief Nazi officials, we should participate in an international tribunal constituted to try them."[228] However, the war was not over as long as the Wehrmacht could mount offensives in the West; the treatment of the losers was a premature question.

Although the Nazi crimes were known long before 1944, some recalled the tales of marauding Huns bayoneting babies during World War I and suspected that the stories of Nazi atrocities were similar exaggerations; others questioned reports from Jewish sources.[229] It was clear to Secretary of War Stimson that the Germans had committed singularly horrible acts and that they should be tried publicly. This would present the American lawyer-statesmen with their best opportunity of the twentieth century to translate their ideas into practice. American war crimes prosecutor Colonel Telford Taylor credited a coalition of American lawyer-statesmen and former New Dealers with "the assemblage of all these concepts in a single trial package." Taylor described the backgrounds of the "handful of American lawyers, all but Cutter . . . from New York City. Some of them (Stimson, McCloy) were what today we would call 'moderate' Republicans; several (Rosenman, Chanler, Herbert Weschler) were Democrats. Elitist and generally accustomed to personal prosperity, all had strong feeling of noblesse oblige."[230] These men had no qualms about pushing the army's Judge Advocate General aside, and most shared Stimson's belief that summary execution was only a topical solution. As Stimson later wrote, "we at last reach to the very core of international strife, and we set a penalty not merely for war crimes, but for the very act of war itself."[231]

Stimson's views were not shared by all his colleagues in Washington, but with patrons like President Roosevelt and salesmen like John McCloy, the American lawyer-statesmen were able to outmaneuver those they could not convert. The War Department intended to replace revenge with something altogether different. Stimson gave his reasoning in a letter to President Roosevelt:

> The method of dealing with these and other criminals requires careful thought and a well-defined procedure. Such a procedure must embody, in my judgment, at least the rudimentary aspects of the Bill of Rights. . . . The very punishment of these men in a manner consistent with the advance of civilization, will have all the greater effect upon posterity. Furthermore, it will afford the most effective way of making a record of the Nazi system of terrorism and of the effort of the Allies to terminate the system and avoid its recurrence.[232]

The task of planning the first war crimes trial was assigned to Assistant Secretary of War John McCloy, who passed it to Murray Bernays in the War Department's Special Projects Division. Bernays did not consider the laws of war broad enough to cover the scope of the Nazi crimes and stressed the need for legal innovation. He argued that "undoubtedly, the Nazis have been counting on the magnitude and ingenuity of their offenses, the number of offenses, the number of offenders, the law's complexity, and delay and war weariness as major defenses against effective prosecution. Trial on an individual basis, and by old modes and procedures would go far to realize the Nazi hopes in this respect."[233]

Bernays's greatest concern was that individuals could not be charged with the killing of German Jews, which was not by definition a war crime.[234] Civil wars and atrocities against the domestic population fell outside the laws of war. Not content to simply try individuals for recognized violations, Bernays proposed trying Nazi organizations for conspiring to commit aggressive war. He borrowed the thesis of Polish émigré and international legal expert Rafael Lemkin, who argued in *Axis Rule in Occupied Europe* that the SS, Gestapo, and other Nazi organizations were an international version of La Cosa Nostra, "a criminal organization of volunteer gangsters."[235] Legal theorist David Luban makes a similar observation: "The framers of Nuremberg were confronted with a new offense, the bureaucratic crime, and a novel political menace, the criminal state."[236] Under Bernays's broad-reaching proposal, the central crime from which all others sprang was a conspiracy to dominate the world.

Bernays wrote: "This conspiracy, based on the Nazi doctrine of racism and totalitarianism, involved murder, terrorism, and the destruction of peaceful populations in violation of the laws of war."[237] The concept of conspiracy would also close legal loopholes that might allow guilty men to escape punishment.[238]

There was nothing basic about the "Basic Objectives" of the Bernays Plan; they were in fact revolutionary. In a three-page memo, the second-string War Department lawyer challenged long-standing maxims of international relations. The first stated objective rejected the concept of sovereign immunity: "Alleged high interests of state are not acceptable as justification for national crimes of violence, terrorism and the destruction of peaceful populations."[239] Objectives two and three broadened the laws of war and issued a statement of collective German war guilt, "bringing home to the world the realities and menace of racism and totalitarianism; and . . . arousing the German people to a sense of their guilt, and to a realization of their responsibility for the crimes committed by their government."[240]

Murray Bernays shared Stimson's hope that a sober presentation of irrefutable evidence would serve an educational role. Again, social work would be wedded to jurisprudence. The War Department did not seek only to punish but also to reform and reeducate: "If these objectives are not achieved, Germany will simply have lost another war. The German people will not know the barbarians they have supported, nor will they have any understanding of the criminal character of their conduct and the world's judgment upon it."[241] Under the conspiracy plan, law was tailored to fit the unique crimes of the Germans. Although simple in theory, the plan was fraught with legal and political difficulties. Perhaps the greatest problem was that conspiracy was an unfamiliar concept in international and German constitutional law.[242] According to the Anglo-American definition, members and leaders of a group were responsible for the crimes of that group even if they did not actively participate in them. But even in American courts, where the concept was familiar, judges tended to narrow their interpretation. Murray Bernays advocated just the opposite.[243]

Criminal accessory, the Continental system's closest approximation to conspiracy, was far narrower than the American definition.[244] The conspiracy charge allowed the Allies to move up the chain of command, past triggermen who personally violated the rules of war. Theoretically, a conspiracy charge would open the way for a blanket conviction of hundreds of thousands of members of the SS and other Nazi organizations without trials. Although the severity of the penalty depended on the individual's crimes and the body of evidence against him, many were troubled by the notion that voluntary membership in one of the "criminal" organizations alone provided sufficient evidence for a guilty verdict. It looked to the naked eye as if a massive charge of collective guilt was being prepared in the name of the United States. Although the Allies warned Axis leaders of war crimes prosecutions, there was no mention of a criminal conspiracy.

On November 11, the Secretaries of State, War, and the Navy signed and delivered a memo to President Roosevelt that affirmed the conspiracy plan and suggested establishing a court by international treaty. In stark contrast to the British position, the American Secretaries favored a solution that separated the judicial from the political and were unwilling to agree that the two were inherently connected.[245] Henry Stimson viewed the trial as an educational device, arguing that

> Not only will the guilty of this generation be brought to justice according to due process of law, but in addition, the conduct of the Axis will have been solemnly condemned by an international adjudication of guilt that cannot fail to impress generations to come. The Germans will not again be able to claim, as they have been claiming with regards to the Versailles Treaty, that an admission of war guilt was exacted under duress.[246]

The Secretary of War attempted to combine the Bernays Plan with his own pet project.[247] During the war, several of the smaller, weaker Allied nations resurrected the idea of criminalizing "aggressive war." Now that it jibed with the Bernays additions, Stimson seized the opportunity to deem aggression the Nazi's "supreme crime."[248] Assistant Secretary McCloy concurred, declaring, "if all the main United Nations participated, it would give a serious precedent that might operate as an added deterrent to waging aggressive war in the future."[249]

The most significant criticism of the War Department plan came from President Roosevelt's trusted advisor, Assistant Attorney General Herbert Weschler. In two memos (December 29, 1944 and January 5, 1945), he recommended more conventional proceedings based on traditional war crimes charges. Weschler also criticized the revolutionary aspects of the Bernays Plan: "I doubt whether such a conspiracy is criminal under international law . . . the theory would involve that any overt act is criminal— in other words any soldier fighting to carry out the conspiracy becomes a criminal by reason of the conspiracy being made criminal. This would entail hopeless confusion."[250] Attorney General Francis Biddle also felt that the traditional war crimes case was sound; why risk turning the trials into a forum in which to debate vanguard issues of international law?[251] However, these points soon became moot; a military event and its political repercussions would force Franklin Roosevelt's position on war crimes policy and demonstrate the significant and incalculable role that domestic politics played in the development of American war crimes policy.

In the predawn hours of December 16, 1944, Germany's Sixth Panzer Army mounted a final offensive. The spearhead was led by Sepp Dietrich and Joachim Peiper. The forces were not only the battlefield component of the Waffen SS but Hitler's former SS bodyguards; these were Nazi Germany's black knights, who had proven themselves "red in tooth and claw" in the Soviet Union.[252] The German forces were attempting to traverse the Ardennes mountains and then advance to the Meuse River in order to split the Allied forces in the low countries and northern France. On December 18, after two days of slow going and sporadic combat, the commander of one of the battle group's tanks informed Peiper that a "mix-up" had occurred near Ligneauville; a tank gunner had "spontaneously" opened fire on a group of prisoners.[253] That same day a message was received by the U.S. First Army: "SS troops vicinity L8199 captured U.S. soldier, traffic M.P. with about two hundred other U.S. soldiers. American soldiers searched. When finished, Germans lined up Americans and shot them with machine pistols and machine guns. Wounded informant who escaped and more details to follow later."[254]

The U.S. Army recovered seventy-two frozen, bullet-riddled bodies. Compared to atrocities committed against Russians, Poles, and Jews, the shooting of seventy-two soldiers in the heat of battle does not seem as horrendous.[255] But these victims of the SS were American, and as historian James Weingartner notes, "the 'Malmedy Massacre' had entered the consciousness of the American people as an example of Axis barbarity alongside the bombing of Pearl Harbor and the Bataan 'death march.' . . . The symbolic significance was enhanced by the fact that not only were the criminals SS men but members of the First Panzer Division 'Leibstandarte SS Adolf Hitler,' the fuehrer's 'own.' "[256] The Malmedy Massacre convinced high-ranking American officials, including Attorney General Weschler that the Nazis were involved in a "conspiracy to achieve domination of other nations" with the help of criminal organizations like the Gestapo.[257] By January 1945, the tide had turned once and for all in favor of the War Department. President Roosevelt informed Secretary of State Cordell Hull that "The charges should include an indictment for waging aggressive warfare, in violation of the Kellogg-Briand Pact. Perhaps these and other charges might be joined in a conspiracy indictment."[258]

By 1945, a once civil discourse among various government agencies had turned into a no-holds-barred battle for control of war crimes policy. In January, the War Department was targeted for one final salvo from the conservatives of the Judge Advocate General and the State Department. After having his well-considered criticism unceremoniously brushed aside, Major General John Weir called on Harvard Law School Dean Edmund Morgan to assess the conspiracy and aggressive war charges. Morgan echoed Herbert Weschler in arguing that charging the Germans with conspiracy went far beyond the traditional laws of war and applied retroactive law in violation of the principle *nullum crimen sine lege* (no crime without prior law).[259] Morgan took a dim view of the plan:

> If the international crime of conspiracy to dominate by acts violative of the rules of war is created, could these acts by Germany against her own nationals be rationally considered as themselves punishable? A negative answer seems imperative. The conspiracy theory is too thin a veneer to hide the real purpose, namely, the creation of a hitherto unknown international offense by individuals, *ex post facto*.[260]

Weir and Morgan made strong cases for a more conservative approach, but they could not stem the surging political tide.

On January 22, 1945, the Secretaries of State and War and the Attorney General signed a memo proposing a war crimes plan that included the Bernays additions. On January 25, Secretary of War Stimson and President Roosevelt discussed the fate of the Axis leaders. Stimson held firm to his belief that the proceedings should do more than simply render justice: the trials would make an example of the Nazi leaders. Stimson wrote in his diary, "I told him [FDR] of my own view of the importance as a matter of record of having a state trial with records." President Roosevelt hedged throughout the discussions of war crimes policy. Stimson's inability to get a straight answer is apparent in his January 19 diary entry: "He [FDR] assented to what I said, but in the hurry of the situation I am not sure whether it registered."[261]

The Secretaries of State, War, and Treasury prepared another memo for the President to take to Yalta, in the hope that the Big Three would commit to joint proceedings against the Axis leaders. But the issue never made the agenda; the Third Reich was collapsing nearly as fast as the tripartite alliance and questions about the fate of the Axis leaders were eclipsed by larger issues—namely, the fate of Europe.[262] With the end of the war in sight, Stimson now had to sell the War Department plan to the Allies. The Americans had a strong bargaining position, and as long as reconstruction aid was forthcoming, France and England would surely indulge them.[263]

On April 4, 1945, Americans Samuel Rosenman, Ami Cutter, and the recently converted John Weir traveled to London to confer with the British about war crimes policy. Lord Simon, the British foreign secretary, attempted to force the Americans into accepting a more traditional arraignment plan with summary trials and executions for Hitler and his cohorts. The two delegations failed to agree, so the British submitted a plan to the War Cabinet and the United States submitted another to the President. On April 15, the War Cabinet issued a scathing response to Simon's proposal, claiming that it was not conservative enough and insisted on executions. Lord Chancellor Simon conveyed these sentiments to the Americans in an April 16 memo: "H.M.G. assume that it is beyond question that Hitler and a number of arch-criminals associated with him (including Mussolini) must, so far as they fall into Allied hands, suffer the penalty of death for their conduct leading up to the war and for the wickedness which they have either themselves perpetuated or have authorized in the conduct of the war."[264]

After President Roosevelt's death on April 12, Henry Stimson returned to the United States, where he met with President Harry Truman. Among other things (the atom bomb), they discussed war crimes policy. With none of the guile of his predecessor, the President told the Secretary of War that he approved of Stimson's plans for a trial.[265] Buoyed by this unequivocal support, Stimson moved forward at full speed. An American delegation (McCloy, Weschler, Cutter, and Weir) returned to London in late April. The British, led by Lord Simon, continued to push for a traditional plan.

Assistant Secretary of War John McCloy brushed the British resistance aside and called it "retrogressive." Instead, he urged them to seize the opportunity "to move forward" as part of a larger effort to bring "international law into action against the whole vicious broad Nazi enterprise."[266] McCloy felt that "Hitler and his gang had offended against the laws of humanity," and that the time had arrived to make an example of them.[267] According to British historians John and Ann Tusa, "McCloy's certainty and energy was hard to resist."[268] By the end of April, the Assistant Secretary had gained the support of French Premier Charles de Gaulle and Soviet Premier Josef Stalin. Faced with this *fait accompli*, the British gracefully conceded, announcing that "the United States has gone a long way to answer cabinet objections and [we have] signed on to the international trial."[269] What the American delegation lacked in precedent it compensated for in bargaining power. Although the protrial faction had outgunned their opponents, they had not gone very far in addressing their substantive criticisms.

President Harry Truman searched for someone to head the American delegation at the international trial. The President read a speech given by U.S. Supreme Court Justice Robert Jackson to the American Society of International Law on the day of Roosevelt's death. Jackson warned the United States of the implications of their words: "You must put no man on trial before anything that is called a court . . . under forms of judicial proceeding, if you are not willing to see him freed if not proved guilty. If you are determined to execute a man in any case, there is no occasion for a trial, the world yields no respect to courts that are merely organized to convict."[270] Truman appointed Justice Jackson to head the prosecution team. British war crimes prosecutor Sir David Maxwell Fyfe described Jackson as "a romantic of the law" who embraced "the traditions of natural justice, reason and human rights."[271] Although he was a New Yorker, Jackson came from a different background than the American lawyer-statesmen. In 1941, Jackson had addressed the Inter-American Bar Association in Havana on the subject of the laws of war. As U.S. Attorney General, he had argued that war could no longer be considered a right of states. Jackson explicitly rejected the traditional rules of the European state system and argued that they had been replaced by new concepts: "It does not appear necessary to treat all wars as legal and just simply because we have no courts to try the accused."[272]

Jackson looked toward an era governed by an American redefinition of international law.[273] Jackson not only rejected the doctrine of sovereign immunity and *raison d'etat*, he took the criminalization of aggression to its ultimate conclusion: "A system of international law which can impose no penalty on a law breaker and also forbids other states to aid the victim would be self-defeating and would not help . . . to realize man's hope for eternal peace."[274] Justice Jackson was a fitting leader for the Americans and would passionately advocate their revolutionary plan. Like Henry Stimson, he was intent on reforming international relations by criminalizing aggression.[275] He believed that a grand trial would set the tone for the postwar period and give greater meaning to the war. The vanquished would not be wantonly slaughtered. The fate of the Germans was contained in a telling euphemism that was part America and part Orwell: the Germans were to be "reeducated."[276]

Chapter Three

THE AMERICAN WAR CRIMES PROGRAM

The American plan for an international trial based on radical and untested international legal principles raised a number of difficult questions. Was accounting for atrocities in the aftermath of a total war a moral act or a political act? Did the rules apply to the victors as well as the vanquished? Would the inclusion of Stalinist judges cost the international tribunal its credibility?

In Japan, America's city-bombing campaign would not reach its atomic climax for many months. In the meantime, General Curtis LeMay had taken over XXI Bomber Command in 1944 and ushered in a new era of civilian death and destruction. British officer and military historian B. H. Liddell Hart was so appalled by city bombing that he described it as "the most uncivilized method of warfare the world has known since the Mongol devastations."[1] On a single night in March 1945, American planes dropped incendiary bombs that turned Tokyo into an inferno that burned out 16 square miles of the city and killed between 90,000 and 100,000 civilians. General LeMay had no qualms about waging war against civilian targets: "Nothing new about death, nothing new about death caused militarily. We scorched and boiled and baked to death more people in Tokyo on the night of 9–10 March than went up in vapor at Hiroshima and Nagasaki combined."[2] How would the new court rule on city bombing? Would Great Britain's Arthur "Bomber" Harris and American Curtis LeMay remain above the law?

Although the United States would wage total war against the Axis powers, the extermination of entire ethnic, racial, religious, and economic groups was never among America's wartime goals. However, similar claims could not be made for the Soviets. Stalinist participation in any trial left the Allies open to charges of employing a double standard, also known as *tu quoque*.[3] For this reason alone, it was shortsighted of the Secretary of War to adopt a tone and legal procedure that did not reflect the geopolitical realities of the post–World War II period. The belief that war crimes proceedings were not political was at best naive and at worst disingenuous, but certainly consistent with America's two-faced relationship with international law.

With the memory of Stalin's unique contribution to political justice, the 1936–1938 Moscow Show Trials, fresh in their minds, many of the foreign policy professionals in the State Department and the British Foreign Office shuddered at the thought of sharing a judges' bench with Stalinists. John Troutbeck of the British Foreign Office wrote a scathing memo about the proposed international trial: "Surely to have a Russian sitting in a case of this kind will be regarded as almost a high point of international hypocrisy." Troutbeck tried to wake his superiors from the moral amnesia that total war and an alliance with Stalin had required. He argued that Russia had waged a similar campaign of aggression "aimed at domination over other nations," which involved atrocities and persecutions that rivaled those of the Nazis. Even worse, the Soviet conquests had just begun: "Is not the Soviet Government employed today in that very same thing in Poland, the Baltic States, Turkey and Persia?. . . . There have been two criminal enterprises this century—by Germans and Russians."[4]

The fate of Poland was one of the many tragedies of World War II. During the glory days of the Molotov-Ribbentrop Pact, both Hitler and Stalin sank their talons into the geographically unfortunate nation. Eastern Poland was seen as the strong point of Stalin's *cordon sanitaire*, which extended from the Black Sea to Finland. Like the Jews, the Polish were subjected to "industrialized extermination, mass deportations, and police state terror."[5] While the *Wehrmacht* was cutting a swath through Central and Western Europe, Germany and the Soviet Union were bound together by the Molotov-Ribbentrop agreement. To make matters worse, the Soviets had shared in the spoils of the German conquest.[6] Only in 1941, after the Germans launched Operation Barbarossa, was Stalin forced to cast his lot with the Western Alliance.

The most politically damaging Soviet war crime was uncovered in the winter of 1943. A group of Russian laborers working for the Wehrmacht in the Katyn forest near Smolensk, Poland came across fresh human bones that had been dug up by wolves. The Germans exhumed 4,143 neatly stacked corpses buried in eight common graves; the largest was an L-shaped pit, 85 feet by 26 feet.[7] Small birch trees had been planted on top of the mass graves in an effort to render the site indistinguishable from the other scenic vistas overlooking the Dnieper River.

The Soviets had hoped to destroy the Polish intelligensia in an effort to "behead" the nation.[8] In April 1943, Nazi Propaganda Minister Josef Goebbels announced: "A report has reached us from Smolensk to the effect that the local inhabitants have mentioned to the German authorities the existence of a place where mass executions had been carried out by the Bolsheviks and where 10,000 Polish officers had been murdered by the BPU. . . . They were fully dressed, some were bound, and all had pistol shots to the back of the head."[9]

It was not so easy to dismiss this as yet another missive from Goebbel's Ministry of Propaganda; all evidence pointed to the Soviet Union. The bodies were found on territory the Soviets had previously occupied and the men had disappeared in 1940 while in Soviet custody. But the telltale piece of evidence was the manner of execution—one quick shot to the back of the head at close range. According to historian Allen Paul, this bore the fingerprints of the NKVD (Narodnyi kommissariat vnutrennikh del): "It was a vintage, Bolshevik technique developed in the early days of the revolution when Lenin's secret police, the Cheka, routinely shot so-called enemies."[10] The Soviets responded defensively to the accusations, but their denials were unconvincing, particularly to the Polish government in exile.[11] Although the massacre was troubling, Poland had other problems by 1945. The nation was in the process of being absorbed into the Soviet Union's sphere of influence. Would its British and American "friends" shirk the lofty principles of the Atlantic Charter and look the other way? (Between August 9 and August 13, 1941, Roosevelt and

Churchill met in Newfoundland to outline their war aims. The eight-point Atlantic Charter was a vague restatement of Wilsonian goals like collective security and national self-determination.)

The Allies faced a moral dilemma: should they act according to conscience and reveal the massacre as Stalin's own, or turn a blind eye in order to maintain strategic trim? The dilemma highlights the flexibility of morality in twentieth-century international politics. The odious task of informing the Polish leaders that they were about to be sold down the river in the name of strategy fell to Sir Owen O'Malley, British Ambassador to the Polish government in exile. In a confidential memo to the British War Cabinet, O'Malley wrote, "We have in fact perforce used the good name of England like the murderers used the little conifers to cover up a massacre. . . . May it not be that we now stand in danger of bemusing not only others but ourselves; of falling . . . under St. Paul's curse on those who can see cruelty and 'burn not'?" In the end, O'Malley justified the British move as a sort of moral triage: "If the facts of the Katyn massacre turn out to be as most of us incline to think, shall we vindicate the spirit of these brave unlucky men and justify the living to the dead."[12] The need to placate a key strategic ally forced Churchill and Roosevelt to aid Stalin in suppressing evidence and thwarting Polish efforts to expose the truth about the fate of their military elite.[13] This would not have posed such a problem had the Allies not transformed the war into a crusade against evil. If the new war crimes standards were applied across the board, none of the Allied nations would be exempt from prosecution.

However, by April 1945, all Allied atrocities were overshadowed by the grisly discoveries being made by American soldiers as they swept into formerly Nazi-held territory and liberated several Nazi concentration camps. On April 4 and 5, soldiers from Patton's Third Army accidentally discovered the Ohrdürf concentration camp. On the camp's outskirts, they found a large pit filled with charred, half-burned bodies. The Americans were also greeted by the inmates who had survived the ordeal. U.S. soldiers were both saddened and horrified by these living skeletons in striped uniforms. On April 11, American generals Dwight Eisenhower, George Patton, and Omar Bradley toured Ohrdürf. More than the lice-ridden dead, it was the systematic dehumanization that shocked the generals. General Eisenhower cabled Washington, "We are constantly finding German camps in which they have placed political prisoners where unspeakable conditions exist. From my own personal observation, I can state unequivocally that all written statements up to now do not paint the full horrors." General Eisenhower wanted American troops to visit the camp: "We are told that the American soldier does not know what he is fighting for. Now, at least, he will know what he is fighting against."[14] These were not even the worst Nazi concentration camps; the Nazi leaders had been careful to construct their archipelago of death camps in Poland.

As the liberation of the camps continued, captured German guards and officials were subjected to spontaneous reprisals. U.S. Army Rabbi Max Eichhorn was among the first to enter Buchenwald. He described his feelings at the time: "We cried not merely tears of sorrow. We cried tears of hate. Then we stood aside and watched while the inmates of the camp hunted down their former guards, many of whom were trying to hide in various parts of the camp." American veteran Fred Maercer watched a German soldier attempt to surrender to American forces. However, he was intercepted by an inmate with a large wooden club. The American soldiers watched as the inmate bludgeoned his former captor: "He just stood there and beat him to death. He had to—of course, we did not bother him."[15] American soldiers allowed the former inmates to kill as many as eighty German prisoners. As a result of the American treatment of their German POWs at Buchenwald, Heinrich Himmler issued this April 14, 1945 Order: "No prisoners shall be allowed to fall into the hands of the enemy alive. Prisoners have behaved barbarously to the civilian population at Buchenwald."[16]

After a prolonged attack on Munich, U.S. soldiers from the 45th Division of the 157th Infantry Regiment discovered the Dachau concentration camp on April 29. As the American soldiers approached the camp's gate, they were fired on by a last line of SS defenders. Near the train depot that abutted the camp, the soldiers were confronted by 40 open freight cars filled with stacked dead bodies in striped uniforms. Some of the soldiers retched from the sight and smell, while others openly wept. Bill Allison recalled his reaction: "We were just in a state of shock really, nobody had ever seen anything like that before. You know, I had been in the service and I had seen men die before. I've seen dead bodies, but not stacked up like cordwood."[17]

When the American soldiers stormed Dachau's interior, they were met by the inmates who had survived the horror. Again, American soldiers watched and even encouraged concentration camp victims to hunt down and kill their former captors. Many of the guards were shot in the legs before they were brutally beaten to death. American veteran Jack Hallett recalled, "Control was gone after the sights we saw, and the men were deliberately wounding guards that were available and then turning them over to the prisoners and allowing them to take their revenge." Hallett saw an American soldier give his bayonet to an inmate "and watched him behead the man. It was a pretty gory mess."[18] Several haunting photographs survive of the Dachau liberation; in one, two concentration camp inmates tower over a collapsed guard. The German is not yet dead, and by the looks on their faces, the inmates are savoring their revenge. In the background lies a mound of crumpled bodies—not dead camp victims but recently executed German soldiers. According to historian Robert Abzug, an American squad guarding 122 German prisoners spontaneously opened fire on their captives, killing them all.[19] Ironically, the Dachau concentration camp would soon serve as the site of the army's trial of the perpetrators of the Malmedy Massacre.

It is unlikely that American soldiers limited summary executions to Nazi concentration camp workers. Writer Paul Fussell served as an American infantry soldier in France before he was wounded by German artillery in 1945. This experience left him convinced that modern war was "the very quintessence of amoral activity with its mass murders of the innocents." The combat infantry veteran argues that war is "not an appropriate context for invoking moral criteria."[20] Fussell casually describes a massacre he participated in when he encountered a group of German soldiers trapped in a bomb crater: "Earlier there had occurred in F Company the event known as the Great Turkey Shoot. . . . In a deep crater in a forest, someone had come upon a squad or two of Germans, perhaps fifteen or twenty in all. Their visible wish to surrender—most were in tears of terror and despair—was ignored by the men lining the rim." All of the American soldiers simultaneously opened fire. "Laughing and howling, hoo-ha-ing and cowboy and good-old-boy yelling, our men exultantly shot into the crater until every man down there was dead."[21] Fussell considers his motives—"Perhaps some of our prisoners had recently been shot by the Germans. Perhaps some Germans hadn't surrendered fast enough and with suitable signs of contrition. (We were very hard on snotty Nazi adolescents.)"—and reflects on how World War II transformed him from California golden boy to cold killer: "Impossible for me, once so Pasadena special, not to feel as murderous and cool as the other young officers." Fussell suffered no remorse—quite the contrary: "The result was deep satisfaction, and the event was translated into an amusing narrative, told and retold over campfires all that winter."[22]

Meanwhile, far from the hostilities, in a conference room in London, Allied leaders were finalizing their plans for the trial of the German leaders. On May 28, 1945, an American delegation led by Robert Jackson and former OSS chief William Donovan left for London to hammer out the details of the international trial. Now the Americans had to convert the British, French, and Russians to their radical proposal.[23] The London Conference opened in early June 1945. Many of the beginning sessions were spent wrangling over fundamental differences in the Anglo-American and Continental legal systems.[24] The British and American legal systems were adversarial by nature: the prosecution filed a brief indictment in open court that contained no evidence and the judge knew only the general nature of the case. French delegate and Sorbonne professor of international law André Gros was shocked by the implications of the Anglo-American system.[25] The French objected to the presentation of evidence in open court "by the lawyers, who examine and cross-examine the witnesses and who may exploit and must confront the element of surprise." Under the Continental legal system, evidence was assembled by a court magistrate. If a sufficient basis for a trial was established, the dossier and the indictment were given to the court and the defendant. Judges, prosecutors, and defense attorneys worked together to arrive at the truth and reach a just decision.[26]

The Soviet insistence on a full presentation of evidence provided the first opportunity for American prosecutor Robert Jackson to make his distrust of the Russians publicly known. When Jackson informed his colleagues that this would not sit well with the American public, the French delegate retorted that their system ensured a fair trial and was "not designed to satisfy an ill-informed American public."[27] U.S.-Soviet differences came to an ugly head on July 1, when Soviet representative I. T. Nikitchenko issued a statement that overshadowed all procedural squabbles and seemed to justify the worst assumptions about the Soviet conception of justice. Nikitchenko announced that the defendants had already been convicted by political decree: "The fact that the Nazi leaders are criminals has already been established. The task of the Tribunal is only to determine the measure of guilt of each particular person and mete out the necessary punishment—the sentences."[28] As if this declaration of collective guilt were not enough, the Soviet representative spoke scornfully of the presumed "fairness" and "impartiality" of the Anglo-American system: "The case for the prosecution is undoubtedly known to the judge before the trial starts and there is therefore no necessity to create a sort of fiction that the judge is a disinterested person. If such a procedure is adopted that the judge is supposed to be impartial, it would only lead to unnecessary delays."[29] Nikitchenko's statements were a breaking point for Robert Jackson. He had harbored deep reservations about the Soviets from the start, but now he hoped that the Soviets would withdraw from the trial.[30]

On July 7, Robert Jackson and William Donovan traveled to Frankfurt to discuss the trial sites with General Lucius Clay and his political advisor, Robert Murphy. General Clay suggested Nuremberg as the site, for the practical reason that part of a courthouse and a jail were still standing. Although the city had been leveled by Allied bombs, the surrounding suburbs were intact and could house members of the court staff. There were also symbolic reasons for the choice: it was the site of the infamous Nuremberg Rallies and had lent its name to the laws that marked the beginning of the Nazi persecution of German Jews.[31]

Justice Jackson returned to London more antagonistic toward the Soviets than ever before. Although this was partially the result of his anti-Soviet feelings, the American negotiating position was strong. Of the twenty-two "major war criminals," the United States held ten, the British five; three more were in joint custody.[32] Unsurprisingly, the Americans were the least accommodating. The British were in no position to resist, as their government was in the midst of a transfer of power to the Labor Party.

When the delegations considered the crimes that would be charged, it quickly became obvious that the Americans would have to recapture old ground. French representative Professor André Gros objected to the aggression charge, contending that any such legislation would be *ex post facto* and offering American Secretary of State Robert Lansing's arguments from the Paris Peace Conference to support his claim. This, according to the Frenchman, undermined "any legal basis for imposing . . . criminal responsibility on individuals who launch aggressive wars."[33] Gros neatly summarized the disagreement by observing that "the Americans want to win the trial on the ground that the Nazi war was illegal, and the French people and other people of the occupied countries just want to show that the Nazis were bandits."[34]

Jackson dismissed the French and Russian reservations and the Lansing precedent: "I must say that sentiment in the United States and better world opinion have greatly changed since Mr. James Brown Scott and Secretary Lansing announced their views as to criminal responsibility for the first World War."[35] He claimed that punishing Germans was not the sole objective of the American proposal and seemed to imply that the same rules would apply to American soldiers: "If certain acts of violation of treaties are crimes, they are crimes, whether the United States does them or whether Germany does them, and we must be prepared to lay down the rule of criminal conduct against others which we would not be willing to have invoked against us."[36] The debate raged for five sessions of the conference (from July 19–25). Jackson believed that "there are some things worse for me than failing to reach an agreement and one of them is reaching an agreement that would stultify the position the United States has taken throughout."[37]

The British considered the Americans quarrelsome and felt that Jackson was trying to disrupt the conference. Patrick Dean of the Foreign Office described the American judge as "afraid of the Russians, particularly their method of trial."[38] British Treasury official R. S. Clyde shared Dean's view that "the kernel of the trouble has been his explicit distrust of the Soviets. . . . The Russians are not unaware of this; and I think have begun to question . . . whether he is seeking to codify international law for their discomforture."[39] On July 24, Robert Jackson cabled John McCloy and described the discussions in London in very bleak terms: "Our conference is in serious disagreement today over definition war crimes. All European powers would qualify criminality of aggressive war and not go along on view in my report to President."[40] Jackson met with Secretary of State James Byrnes, who told him that a four-power trial was preferable but that the final decision was Jackson's alone. At Potsdam, the Big Three discussed the war crimes negotiations in London. Stalin proposed naming the defendants, but President Truman refused to commit until he discussed the issue with Jackson. Though the two never spoke directly, a message was relayed via Roosevelt's close advisor, Judge Samuel Rosenman. On August 1, the Big Three met and agreed to try the major Nazi war criminals before an international tribunal. Article VII of the Potsdam

Agreement officially committed them to "bring those criminals to swift and sure justice."[41]

However, the conferees had not yet formulated the charges. When the American plan was tabled, the French and the Soviets launched into a now familiar series of critiques. They did not want the court to declare the innocence or guilt of the defendants. The Soviet representative, Nikitchenko, argued heatedly against "trying an organization to reach all of its members."[42] In the drafting session the charge was diluted to an accusation of "planning" or "organizing" specific crimes.

After a month of contentious meetings, representatives of the four powers signed the London Agreement. The actual "agreement" was little more than a restatement of the Moscow Declaration, announcing quadripartite support for "a trial of war criminals whose offenses have no particular geographic location, whether they be accused individually or in their capacity as members of organizations or groups or in both capacities."[43] The London Agreement Charter contained the charges, defined the rights of the accused, and outlined many of the procedural issues. Count 1 charged the defendants with "The Common Plan or Conspiracy." Count 2, however, charged them with the crime of aggression; the Soviet representative, Professor Tranin, had renamed it "Crimes Against Peace." Ironically, with this count, the delegates were reestablishing a traditional view of statecraft that upheld the sanctity and centrality of sovereignty. According to legal theorist David Luban, "by criminalizing aggression, the Charter erected a wall around state sovereignity and committed itself to an old European model of unbreachable nation states."[44] In Laban's view, the Nuremberg planners came to the brink of truly challenging the traditional rules of statecraft but in the end backed off.[45] They charged the German leaders with both aggression and "participation in the formulation or execution of a common plan or conspiracy to commit any of the foregoing crimes."[46] Count 3, "War Crimes," charged traditional violations of the laws of war, while under Count 4's "Crimes Against Humanity" category, the definition of war crimes was broadened so that the Germans could be charged with crimes against Jews and other civilians.[47]

The Americans believed that a "free and fair" trial would do more than simply render justice; it would also reeducate the German people after a decade of dictatorship. Traditionally, America's reform efforts had been aimed at non-European nations. While the Germans could accept total military defeat and occupation, "reeducation" at the knee of the Americans was another matter. For the first time since Napoleon, German soil was occupied by foreign armies. World War II had cost Germany millions of lives (not including German Jews and other persecuted minorities), and most of the nation's cities had been reduced to rubble by the Allied city-bombing campaign. For Germans in the eastern provinces, Stalin's retribution had only just begun.[48] However, by 1945, the German population was resigned to having their cities bombed, their POWs executed, and their territory plundered by a marauding Red Army. As German historian Jörg Friedrich points out, "None of this was justified by international law, nor by justice, nor by humanity. It was brute revenge. The Germans understood this perfectly. Reprisals had been their customary method of occupation."[49] However, what many Germans did not understand were the American social and political reform policies. According to Friedrich, "Nazi propaganda chief Josef Goebbels had announced that the Allied forces, if successful, would destroy the vanquished. So the public regarded the International Military Tribunal as the Allies' way of eliminating an enemy, just as trials had been used in the Third Reich."[50]

The ominous presence of Soviet purge trial prosecutor Andrei Vyshinsky in Nuremberg confirmed German suspicions that the international trial would be a primitive form of political justice, a theatrical prelude to the inevitable executions. This idea was not without merit, given Vyshinsky's opinions on the role of law. In his Stalin Prize–winning book, *Court Evidence in Soviet Law*, Vyshinsky argued against the presumption of innocence and advocated the admissibility of confessions induced by torture. Under the Stalinist model of political justice, defendants were tortured until they were willing to "confess" to their crimes in open court.[51] When the Soviet delegation showed a group of Americans, including Judge Francis Biddle, a film of a Soviet "war crimes trial" conducted in Kharkov in 1943, the Americans sat in stunned silence. The film showed starved and beaten German officers being hanged in front of a crowd of 40,000 cheering Russians. Biddle was appalled: "They are horrible, tortured, naked skeletons, the Kharkov defendants being hung in front of the crowds."[52]

Not only was the Soviet delegation personally overseen by Vyshinsky; there was also the Soviets' "Supervisory Committee for the Nuremberg Trials," which included the Soviet Union's chief prosecutor, K. P.

Gorschenin, and Minister of Justice, I. T. Golyakov. The American trial participants always believed that the Soviet delegation at Nuremberg had to clear all their decisions with Moscow. The record of a discussion between Andrei Vyshinsky and B. Z. Kobulov shows Moscow's concern over the inclusion of potentially embarrassing revelations. "Our people in Nuremberg at the moment are reporting to us on the attitude of the defendants under interrogation. Goering, Jodl, and other persons indicted are putting on a big show," said Kobulov. He was especially concerned about the "anti-Soviet diatribes" of defendant Raeder: "When Raeder was interrogated by the British he said that the Russians tried to convince him that he made his statements under pressure. His testimony was recorded on film." Vyshinsky offered a simple solution to counter these embarrassing attacks: "The chief prosecutor must interrupt the defendant where necessary and deny him the opportunity of making any anti-Soviet attacks."[53] By the time the trial was ready to begin, the Soviet delegation at Nuremberg had been provided with a "list of questions provided by Comrade Vyshinsky which are to be regarded as not permissible for discussion before the Tribunal." These topics included the Hitler-Stalin Pact and the fate of Poland.[54]

Although the IMT was now saddled with a revolutionary indictment, the Americans' views were by no means universally held.[55] Even before the outbreak of the Cold War, there was never a consensus on American war crimes policy, and the alliance between Republicans and Democrats would prove frail once the Cold War began in earnest. The American treatment of the vanquished was heavily influenced by both domestic and international politics. The laws outlined in the London Agreement Charter provided the legislative groundwork for a series of trials that would be unique in legal history. The highest-level war crimes courts (the International Military Tribunal at Nuremberg, the International Military Tribunal for the Far East, and the subsequent Nuremberg trials) were all loosely modeled after the London Agreement and Charter. Although the three indictments on which these trials were based (the London Agreement, the Tokyo Charter, and Control Council Law No. 10) differed in small ways, they all contained traditional war crimes charges in addition to the novel aggression, conspiracy, and crimes against humanity counts. Each court would have to rule independently on these parts of the indictment.[56]

The international trial at Nuremberg was the symbolic flagship of American and Allied war crimes policy. The Allied Control Council produced a list of defendants on September 30, 1945 that included some of the highest-ranking Nazi survivors: Hermann Goering, Walter Funk, Wilhelm Frick, Alfred Speer, Julius Streicher, Martin Bormann, Alfred Rosenberg, Joachim von Ribbentrop, Rudolf Hess, Constantin von Neurath, Franz von Papen, Hjalmar Schacht, Baldur von Schirach, Ernst von Kaltenbrunner, Wilhelm Keitel, Alfred Jodl, Eric Raeder, Karl Doenitz, Artur Seyss-Inquart, Fritz Sauckel, and Hans Fritsche. The defendants represented a good cross-section of both the military and the political leadership of the Third Reich.

In the days leading up to the trial, all of the German defense lawyers signed a petition challenging the legal validity of the International Military Tribunal. The November 19, 1945 petition argued that any state, "by virtue of its sovereignty, has the right to wage war at any time and for any purpose," while acknowledging the prosecution's challenge to the idea that "the decision to wage war is beyond good and evil." The defense lawyers accused the Allies of trying to reestablish the concepts of just and unjust war: "A distinction is being made between just and unjust wars and it is asked that the Community of States call to account the State which wages an unjust war and deny it, should it become victorious, the fruits of its outrage." They contended that the victorious powers were holding Germans to archaic standards of international conduct: "More than that, it is demanded that not only should the guilty State be condemned and its liability be established, but that furthermore those men who are responsible for unleashing the unjust war be tried and sentenced by an International Tribunal. In that respect one goes now-a-days further than even the strictest jurists since the early Middle Ages."[57] The petition went on to make more familiar *ex post facto* and *nulla poena sine lege* arguments and asked "That the Tribunal direct that an opinion be submitted by internationally recognized authorities on international law on the legal element of this Trial under the Charter of the Tribunal."[58] The IMT invoked Article 3, which disallowed any direct challenges to the tribunal's legal jurisdiction or a reopening of the debate over the legal validity of the proceedings. This single article precluded any further discussion of the trial's legal legitimacy. German attorneys would not forget this slight. It is also important to note that an influential segment of the German population rejected Nuremberg's legal validity from day one. Legal positivism was a German science, and it would provide the Americans with a worthy foe.

The courtroom in Nuremberg's Palace of Justice was filled to capacity on November 6, 1945, as the International Military Tribunal opened amid much fanfare. The twenty-one Nazi leaders sat in the stagelike defendants' dock. American novelist John Dos Passos described the scene: "The freshly redecorated courtroom with its sage-green curtains and crimson chairs seems warm and luxurious and radiant with silky white light. . . . Under them, crumpled and torn by defeat are the faces that glared for years from the front pages of the world."[59] The American prosecutors began by presenting Count 1 of the indictment. On November 21, Robert Jackson opened the prosecution's case for the United States. His first three sentences would not only be the most-quoted words spoken at the trials; for many, they would come to symbolize the Nuremberg trials:

> The privilege of opening the first trial in history for crimes against the peace of the world imposes a grave responsibility. The wrongs which we seek to condemn and punish have been so calculated, so malignant and so devastating, that civilization cannot tolerate their being ignored because it cannot survive their being repeated. That four great nations, flushed with victory and stung with injury, stay the hand of vengeance and voluntarily submit their captive enemies to the judgment of the law is one of the most significant tributes that Power ever has paid to Reason.[60]

The American prosecutor described "aggressive war" as "the greatest menace of our times."[61] The defendants and their lawyers were especially irritated when Jackson characterized them as "twenty-odd broken men."[62] He conceded that it was unfortunate that the victors were judging the vanquished; however, the American argued that "The world-wide scope of the aggressions carried out by these men has left but a few real neutrals."[63] Jackson believed that the victors' conduct in this trial would also be sternly judged: "We must never forget that the record on which we judge these defendants today is the record on which history will judge us tomorrow. To pass these defendants the poison chalice is to put it to our own lips as well."[64] While the prosecution admitted that the defendants were "the first war leaders of a defeated nation to be prosecuted in the name of law," he added, "they are also the first to be given a chance to plead for their lives in the name of law."[65] From the beginning it was clear

that the Americans planned to take the broadest view of the Nazi conspiracy. They would consider how each count of the indictment furthered
the larger Nazi agenda: "It is my purpose to open the case, particularly
under Count One of the Indictment, and to deal with the Common Plan
or Conspiracy to achieve ends possible only by resort to Crimes Against
Peace, War Crimes, and Crimes Against Humanity. My emphasis will not
be on individual barbarities and perversions which may have occurred
independently of any central plan."[66]

While the Americans basked in the warm glow of Jackson's rhetoric,
German defense attorneys like Otto Kranzbühler bristled: "He was a
good speaker without a doubt. Rhetorically good, but totally unrestrained
in exploiting emotions." The former German naval judge shared the view
held by many Germans in 1945 that the Nuremberg trial was just another
form of politics: "From the beginning I regarded it as a political matter, as
a continuation of war by other means, if you like. . . . At the time, I could
not imagine any rational reason for indicting these men. The Allies were
still our opponents with political objectives and one of those was this trial.
That was how I saw it then."[67]

In order to establish the broadest range of Nazi criminality, the American prosecutor introduced a diverse array of evidence. In addition to the
485 tons of German diplomatic documents discovered by the Allies in a
castle near Marburg, there was even more graphic evidence.[68] In a very
dramatic move, on November 29, 1945, the prosecution introduced Document 2430-PS, a one-hour documentary film about the Nazi concentration camps. The film showed the Allied liberation of Dachau, Buchenwald, and Bergen-Belsen. The defendants' dock remained lit as images of
emaciated bodies stacked in ditches flickered on the courtroom wall.
Some of the defendants, like Ribbentrop, Funk, and Frank, were visibly
shaken, while others, like Hjalmar Schacht and Hans Fritsche, turned
their backs to the screen.[69]

Great Britain's Attorney General, Sir Hartley Shawcross, opened the
British case on December 4, 1945. He offered the most adamant rejection
of the traditional rules of statecraft of all the Allied prosecutors. Shawcross maintained that sovereignty no longer provided blanket immunity
for national leaders: "The right of war was no longer the essence of sovereignty."[70] He argued that "practically the whole civilized world abolished war as a legally permissible means of enforcing the law or of changing it." He also attached great importance to prewar legislation like the

Kellogg-Briand Pact. "These repeated declarations, these repeated condemnations of wars of aggression testified to the fact that with the establishment of the League of Nations, with the legal developments which followed it, the place of war in international law had undergone a profound change. War was ceasing to be the unrestricted prerogative of sovereign states."[71] The British prosecutor anticipated many of the defense arguments and dismissed them out of hand. "Political loyalty, military obedience are excellent things, but they neither require nor do they justify the commission of patently wicked acts."[72]

The prosecution's key piece of evidence in their aggressive war case was the notes of Adjunct Colonel Friedrich Hossbach from a November 5, 1937 conference at the Reich Chancellery. According to the prosecution, it was there that Hitler introduced the concept of *Lebensraum* and offered various military scenarios that included the taking of Austria and Czechoslovakia. Many of the defendants criticized the prosecution for exaggerating the significance of this document. Hermann Goering stated with typical candor, "Nevertheless, some of these statements naturally do reflect the basic attitude of the Führer, but with the best intentions I cannot attach the same measure of significance to the document as is being attached to it here."[73]

The defendants had a much more pleasant day on December 11, when the prosecution introduced Document 3054-PS, a film entitled *The Nazi Plan*. This four-part film was mostly German footage, including scenes from Leni Riefenstahl's *Triumph of the Will*. Some of the defendants, Ribbentrop and Goering in particular, beamed. Goering joked that the film was so inspiring he was sure that Justice Jackson would now want to join the party.[74] The defendants' courtroom levity ended when the court readjourned in early January 1946 and *Einsatzgruppen* leader Otto Ohlendorf took the witness stand. Each of the four Einsatzgruppen (A–D) was attached to a German army and followed them into the Soviet Union with the specific intent of killing Jews and Communist Party officials.

The U.S. Army had discovered the Einsatzgruppens' daily "Morning Reports" at Gestapo headquarters in Berlin. The reports covered the period of June 23, 1941–April 24, 1942, during which, according to their own careful records, the Einsatzgruppen killed more than one million people. The "Morning Reports" provided some of the most damning evidence presented at Nuremberg. When asked how many people his men killed, Ohlendorf answered matter-of-factly, "In the year between

June 1941 and June 1942 the *Einsatzcommandos* reported 90,000 people liquidated." Ohlendorf confirmed that the figure included women and children.[75] His explanation of why he preferred his soldiers to shoot their victims reveals much about how guilt is diffused in a modern, bureaucratic state: "The aim was that the individual leaders and men should be able to carry out the executions in a military manner acting on orders. They should not have to make a decision on their own."[76] American prosecutor Telford Taylor remembers being amazed by Ohlendorf's casual ruthlessness: "He said it just that way, as if there was nothing remarkable about it. The whole audience was shocked."[77]

Telford Taylor cross-examined SS General Erich von dem Bach-Zelewski on January 7, 1946. The witness had been in charge of SS antipartisan units and killing squads like the Einsatzgruppen and reported directly to Heinrich Himmler. Bach-Zelewski was best known for overseeing the brutal repression of the Warsaw uprising in 1944. Earlier in the trial, American prosecutors had introduced a homemade, leather-bound book made by German Police Major General Stroop and entitled *The Warsaw Ghetto Is No More.* The book gleefully recounted the annihilation of more than 50,000 Polish Jews: "The resistance put up by the Jews and bandits could be broken only by the relentless and energetic use of our shock-troops by day and night." Stroop concluded his account with a summary of the killing done by Wehrmacht, Waffen SS, and Police: "Only through the continuous and untiring work of all involved did we succeed in catching a total of 56,065 Jews whose extermination can be proved. To this should be added the number of Jews who lost their lives in explosions or fires but whose numbers could not be ascertained."[78]

Taylor attempted to establish the fact that the Wehrmacht, irrespective of their leaders' vigorous denials, had played an integral role in brutal "antipartisan" campaigns in the Soviet Union. Taylor was also trying to prove that the execution squads' activities were coordinated by the German army's leadership. The American prosecutor asked Bach-Zelewski very simple, direct questions and carefully built his case fact by fact. "In the course of your duties did you confer with the commanders of army groups and armies on the Eastern Front?" The SS general's answer implicated the army leaders: "With the commanders of the army groups, not of the armies, and with the district commanders of the Wehrmacht." Taylor bore down on the witness: "Did the highest military authorities issue instructions that anti-partisan operations were to be conducted with severity?" "Yes," Bach-Zelewski replied. He claimed that because the German high command had not drafted detailed antipartisan orders, policy descended into "a wild state of anarchy in all anti-partisan operations." Taylor asked if the leaders of the German army were aware of this state of "anarchy." "The state of affairs was generally known. There was no necessity to make a special report about it, since every operation had immediately to be reported in all detail, and was known to every responsible leader," Bach-Zelewski replied. Taylor was fast emerging as one of the legal stars of the IMT; many took notice of his skill as a cross-examiner.[79]

Soviet prosecutor Yuri Pokrovsky next took up the questioning of Bach-Zelewski. He tried to prove that the havoc wrought by the Wehrmacht during the invasion of the Soviet Union was the result of a specific plan. However, the witness stuck to his story that the mayhem had happened for the opposite reason—the lack of a clear policy directive. According to the witness, it was nearly impossible to punish a soldier for atrocities committed in the Soviet Union: "orders emanating from the highest authorities definitely stated that if excesses were committed against the civilian population in the partisan areas, no disciplinary or judicial measures could be taken." The witness confirmed the fact that the Germans had waged an unrestricted war of annihilation in the Soviet Union. "I believe that these methods would definitely have resulted in the extermination of 30 million if they had been continued, and if developments of that time had not completely changed the situation."[80] Adolf Eichman's former assistant, Dieter Wisliceny, testified that European Jews were "all taken to Auschwitz and there to the Final Solution." The Soviet prosecutor asked, "Do you mean they were killed?" "Yes, with the exception of about twenty-five to thirty percent that were used for labor," the witness replied. Hermann Goering bristled in the defendants' dock, "What does the swine expect to gain by it? He'll hang anyway!"[81]

Although French prosecutor François de Menthon had been a member of his nation's resistance, many of his countrymen had collaborated with the Nazi-imposed Vichy government. De Menthon opened the war crimes case for the French on January 17, 1946. According to him, the Germans attempted to take the world back to the Middle Ages: "In the middle of the 20th century Germany goes back, of her own free will, beyond Christianity and civilization to the primitive barbarity of ancient

Germany." The French prosecutor contended that the Third Reich had "raised inhumanity to the level of principle."[82] De Menthon argued that "We are brought back . . . to the most primitive ideas of the savage tribe. All the values of civilization accumulated in the course of centuries are rejected, all traditional ideas of morality, justice, and law give way to the primacy of race, its instincts, its needs and interests."[83]

Soviet Major General Roman A. Rudenko was the last Allied prosecutor to give his opening address, on February 8, 1946. Rudenko anticipated the German defense claim that Operation Barbarossa was a "preventive" war: "In its attempts to conceal its imperialistic aims the Hitlerite clique hysterically shrieked, as usual, about a danger alleged to be forthcoming from the U.S.S.R. and proclaimed that the predatory war which it started against the Soviet Union with aggressive purposes was preventative war."[84] He mocked the Germans' defensive claims in classic Stalinist language—"Much as the fascist wolf might disguise himself in sheep's skin, he cannot hide his teeth!"[85]—and pointed to the many Nazi euphemisms for killing in a June 17, 1941 order signed by Heinrich Himmler's deputy Reinhard Heydrich: "the systematic extermination of Soviet people in fascist concentration camps in the territories of U.S.S.R and other countries occupied by the fascist aggressors was carried out under the form of 'filtration,' 'cleaning measures,' 'purges,' 'extraordinary measures,' 'special treatment,' 'liquidation,' 'execution,' and so on."[86]

Major General Rudenko offered this shocking (and probably exaggerated) inventory of the destruction wrought in the Soviet Union by marauding Nazi armies: "The German fascist invaders completely or partially destroyed or burned 1,710 cities and more than 70,000 villages and hamlets . . . or destroyed six million buildings."[87] According to the Soviet prosecutor, the German invasion left more than 25 million homeless and destroyed 40,000 hospitals and 65,000 of Russia's 122,000 kilometers of railroad tracks. In addition, Rudenko claimed that the German invaders killed seven million horses, 17 million head of cattle, 20 million pigs, and an astounding 110 million chickens. Rudenko put the cost of the German destruction at 679,000 million rubles.[88] He next catalogued the human cost of the Soviet invasion. The wanton slaughter of civilians by the Wehrmacht, the SS, and special killing squads like the Einsatzgruppen were clear violations of the traditional laws of war. The 1907 Hague Convention provided a clear precedent because it expressly forbade such blatant mistreatment of civilians and war prisoners. While the Germans had fought a cleaner war on the Western Front, on the Eastern Front they waged a war of annihilation that summoned memories of Count Wallenstein's ten-year rampage during the Thirty Years War.

Abram Suzkever, a Soviet Jew from Vilna, took the stand on February 27 and described what happened when the *Sonderkommandos* came to town. A subdivision of the Einsatzgruppen, these were killing squads, and even their victims knew this. The Dirlewanger Brigade was an especially notorious Sonderkommando group that was composed entirely of convicted game poachers and convicted felons. Their primary task was to hunt humans. Under questioning from the Soviet prosecutor, the survivor painted a chilling portrait: "The man-hunters of the *Sonderkommandos*, or as the Jews called them, the '*Khapun*,' . . . broke into the Jewish houses at any time of day or night, dragged away the men, instructing them to take a piece of soap and a towel, and herded them into certain buildings near the village of Ponari." When the men did not return, many of the city's 80,000 Jews went into hiding and the Germans hunted them down with packs of vicious dogs. The larger objectives of Nazi policy were not lost on their victims: "I have to say that the Germans declared that they were exterminating the Jewish race as though legally."[89] Suzkever's wife gave birth to their son in violation of a Nazi order that required all pregnant Jewish women to abort and all Jewish babies to be killed. Sympathetic doctors delivered the baby and hid him in one of the hospital rooms. When the witness approached the hospital, he saw that it was already surrounded by Sonderkommandos and that they were dragging sick and old people outside. Suzkever felt a cold rush of terror but had to wait until the soldiers left before he could go inside. When he found his wife, she was sobbing. "She saw one German holding the baby and smearing something under its nose. Afterwards he threw it on the bed and laughed. When my wife picked up the child, there was something black under his nose. When I arrived at the hospital, I saw that my baby was dead. He was still warm," he testified.[90] Of Vilna's original population of 80,000 Jews, the witness estimated that only about 600 survived. The Soviets introduced a film of their own that included footage of Nazi death camps in Poland and Warsaw Ghetto in Poland.[91]

German Field Marshal Wilhelm Keitel, next on the witness stand, attempted to shift the blame for Nazi atrocities to the SS. He was not unconvincing and appeared genuinely shocked and horrified by the concentration camp films. When prison psychiatrist Gustav Gilbert asked the

Field Marshal about them, he was unequivocal in his condemnation of the perpetrators: "It is terrible. When I see such things, I'm ashamed of being German!—It was those dirty SS swine!—If I had known I would have told my son, 'I'd rather shoot you than let you join the SS.' But I did not know.—I'll never be able to look people in the face again."[92] The Soviet prosecutor was unconvinced by Keitel's contrition and forced him to admit that Operation Barbarossa was a war of extermination. Under cross-examination on March 6 and 7, Rudenko reminded Keitel of the directive that he had signed in May 1941, a month after the beginning of the German invasion. It read, "one must bear in mind that in the countries affected human life has absolutely no value and that a deterrent effect can be achieved only through the application of extraordinarily harsh measures."[93] Rudenko asked Wilhelm Keitel if he recalled the order, and he replied affirmatively. The prosecutor focused his questioning on the phrase "human life has absolutely no value" and asked the Field Marshal to explain what this meant to him. Rudenko succeeded in getting the high-ranking German officer to admit that the German army fought in the east according to a different set of rules: "It does not contain these words; but I knew from years of experience that in the Southeastern territories and in certain parts of Soviet territory, human life was not respected in the same degree."[94]

When Hermann Goering finally took the stand on March 13, 1946, he basked in the spotlight. After months in captivity, he had slimmed down from 264 to 186 pounds, and more important, rid himself of a nasty Percodan-and-champagne habit.[95] It was clear from the moment that Goering was asked for his initial plea of guilty or not guilty that he would not play the game of Nuremberg. Unlike many of the other defendants, the former *Reichsmarshall* seemed proud of his role in Germany's National Socialist revival. Above all, Goering rejected the international legal presumptions of the Nuremberg trial and refused to abandon the traditional rules of the European state system.

Under the friendly questioning of defense attorney Otto Stahmer, Goering described why he considered the 1907 Hague Conventions to be outdated by the nature of modern warfare. He believed that due to the rapid expansion of technology, it was impossible to wage a modern war without violating any number of the Hague rules.[96] Legitimate targets, according to Goering, now included food supplies, infrastructure, and civilians. He compared World War II to the Boer War and the Russo-

Japanese War to show how the very nature of military conflict had changed. He stated that nothing had done more to undermine the laws of war than city bombing: "A war at that time between one army and another, in which the population was more or less not involved, cannot be compared with today's total war, in which everyone, even the child, is drawn into the experience of war through the introduction of air warfare."[97] Goering dismissed the accounts of Nazi atrocities: "Also whatever happened in the way of atrocities and similar acts, which should not be tolerated, are in the last analysis, if one thinks about it calmly, to be attributed primarily to the war of propaganda."[98]

Hermann Goering was especially incensed by the idea put forward by the prosecution that soldiers should examine orders as international legal questions: "How does one imagine a state can be led if, during a war, or before a war, which the political leaders had decided upon, whether wrongly or rightly, the individual general could vote whether he was going to fight or not, whether his Army corps was going to stay at home or not, or could say, 'I must first ask my division.' Perhaps one of them would go along, and the others stay at home!" In the end, he simply rejected the idea that law had any place in international politics: "In the struggle for life and death there is in the end no legality."[99]

Goering's testimony began to lose momentum on March 14, when he was questioned about Nazi policy toward the Jews. "After Germany's collapse in 1918 Jewry became very powerful in Germany in all spheres of life, especially political, general intellectual and cultural, and, most particularly, the economic spheres," Goering stated. Prominent German Jews "did not show necessary restraint and . . . stood out more and more in public life." He and the early National Socialists were especially incensed by modernist "degenerate art": "I likewise call attention to the distortion which was practiced in the field of art in this direction, to plays which dragged the fighting at the front through the mud and befouled the ideal of the brave soldier."[100] When Goering began to discuss the Nuremberg Laws, he tried to portray himself as a moderating influence on Hitler when it came to the treatment of Germany's Jews. "I suggested to him that, as a generous act, he should do away with the concept of persons of mixed blood and place such people on the same footing as German citizens." The defendant claimed that Hitler "took up the idea with great interest and was all for adopting my point of view," but before the plan could be implemented "came more troubled times as far as foreign policy was concerned."[101] Although Goering claimed that the Final Solution had not been planned in advance, he was significantly less gregarious when he was confronted with his July 31, 1941 communiqué to Reinhard Heydrich describing "a total solution to the Jewish question within the area of Jewish influence in Europe."[102]

After the friendly questioning from defense counsel, Otto Stahmer, Robert Jackson was eager to rein in the witness. He began his cross-examination on March 18, 1946. Jackson asked Goering about the Nazi abolition of Germany's parliamentary government. Goering's cynical candor seemed to disarm Justice Jackson. The American prosecutor asked, "After you came to power, you regarded it as necessary, in order to maintain power, to suppress all opposition parties?" The former Reichsmarshall responded affirmatively, "We found it necessary not to permit any more opposition, yes."[103] Jackson's frustration grew as quickly as Goering's confidence. When the American prosecutor asked the witness about Germany's secret plans to occupy the Rhineland, the defendant answered snidely, "I do not think I can recall reading beforehand the publication of the mobilization preparations of the United States."[104] Robert Jackson was beginning to lose his cool and appealed to the bench, "We can strike these things out. I do not want to spend time doing that, but this witness, it seems to me, is adopting, and has adopted, in the witness box and in the dock, an arrogant and contemptuous attitude towards the Tribunal which is giving him the trial which he never gave a living soul, nor dead ones either."[105]

With that exchange, Justice Lawrence adjourned the proceedings for the day. The next morning, Jackson again appealed to the bench to control the defendant: "The difficulty arises from this, Your Honor, that if the witness is permitted to volunteer statements in cross-examination there is no opportunity to make objection until they are placed on the record." Jackson argued that under Article 18 of the London Agreement Charter, the tribunal could "rule out irrelevant issues and statements of any kind whatsoever." Justice Lawrence asked Jackson, "What exactly is the motion you are making? Are you asking the Tribunal to strike the answer out of the record?" Jackson replied that the defendant's answers should be limited to the issues in question: "Well, no; in a Trial of this kind, where propaganda is one of the purposes of the defendant, striking out does no good after the answer is made, and Goering knows that as well as I." Lawrence gently overruled Jackson: "As to this particular observation of the defendant, the defendant ought not to have referred to the United States, but it is a matter which I think you might well ignore."[106]

The professional military were watching the case of Admiral Karl Doenitz very closely. Despite British objections, the Americans insisted on trying him. Although Doenitz was a devoted Nazi who had been handpicked by Hitler to serve as his successor, he made an unlikely war crimes trial defendant because the submarine war had been relatively clean. As in World War I, it was impossible for submarine commanders to warn armed merchant ships of their imminent destruction and then rescue the survivors. Even so, Germany had lost 650 submarines and 25,000 of its 40,000-man U-boat force.[107]

Former German naval judge Otto Kranzbühler had been personally selected by Admiral Doenitz to defend him. At the time, Kranzbühler "felt myself obligated, on the German side, to cooperate as much as possible."[108] Although Admiral Doenitz was an unrepentant Nazi who, like Julius Streicher, continued to admire Adolf Hitler, had he committed war crimes? Kranzbühler was able to point to the gap between the victors' professed standards and contemporary naval practices. The admiral would contend that the "merchant vessels" attacked by German submarines not only had been armed but also had been attacking German submarines. Therefore, the ships could no longer be considered neutral. This was very similar to the situation that arose during World War I.

Although *tu quoque* arguments were banned by Article 3 of the London Agreement Charter, Otto Kranzbühler found a way around this technicality. He submitted questionnaires to Admiral Chester Nimitz, the commander of America's Pacific fleet, and to the British Admiralty about Allied naval practices during World War II. Kranzbühler was trying to establish the fact that refusing to rescue survivors was not the same as ordering their killing. Both Nimitz and the British Admiralty admitted that they too waged unrestricted submarine warfare. Admiral Nimitz appeared to side with his former adversary:

> [Question]: *Was it customary for submarines to attack merchant men without warning?*
> [Nimitz]: *Yes, with the exception of hospital ships and other vessels under safe conduct voyages for humanitarian purposes. . . . On general principles, U.S. submarines did not rescue enemy survivors if undue additional hazard to the*

submarine resulted, or the submarine would be prevented from accomplishing its further mission. Therefore, it was unsafe to pick up many survivors.[109]

Admiral Doenitz also challenged the claim that he had ordered survivors killed and grew especially edgy when the prosecution raised the *Laconia* affair. In 1942, German U-boats sank the passenger ship *Laconia*. When the German commander realized his mistake, he radioed Admiral Doenitz, who immediately ordered the submarines to rescue the survivors and take them to the nearest port under a Red Cross flag. The German submarines surfaced, collected the survivors, and were towing the lifeboats to safety when two American B-24s passed overhead. The bombers circled and then began to strafe the flotilla. The planes sank one submarine and killed a number of survivors. After this event, Doenitz ordered his submarines not to pick up survivors. He became exasperated with the American prosecutors: "I saved, saved, and saved! I didn't see any help from you! . . . It was quite clear to me that the time had passed where I was able to be on the surface and do things like that. You had a very powerful air force against me."[110]

On April 15, 1946, Auschwitz commandant (1940–43) Rudolf Hoess took the witness stand. He had served as a concentration camp commander at Sachsenhausen before being transferred to Auschwitz in May of 1940. Located in Poland, Auschwitz held as many as 140,000 inmates while the witness was in charge. The camp's site was chosen because it was isolated and approachable by rail only. Although the town of Auschwitz was only three kilometers away, the 20,000 acres surrounding the camp had been leveled. The actual site was deep in the woods in a "prohibited area and even members of the SS who did not have a special pass could not enter it." When the trains arrived, the prisoners were first examined by doctors for their physical condition. According to the witness, "The internees capable of work at once marched to Auschwitz or to the camp at Birkenau and those incapable of work were at first taken to the provisional installations, then to the newly constructed crematoria."[111]

Defense attorney Dr. Kurt Kauffmann tried to push the majority of the blame onto Adolf Eichmann. Rudolf Hoess claimed that he had no exact idea how many inmates had been killed because only Eichmann was allowed to keep notes about the numbers exterminated. "Is it furthermore true that Eichmann stated to you that in Auschwitz a total sum of more than 2 million Jews had been destroyed?" asked Dr. Kauffmann.

"Yes," replied Hoess. In the summer of 1941, Hoess was summoned to a meeting in Berlin where he was to receive personal orders from SS Chief Heinrich Himmler. "He told me something to the effect—I do not remember the exact words—that the Führer had given the order for the Final Solution of the Jewish question. We, the SS, must carry out that order. If it is not carried out now then the Jews will later on destroy the German people."[112]

The low point in the IMT came when the Soviet prosecutor, acting on orders from Moscow, charged Nazi Germany with the murders of Polish officers at Katyn. General R. A. Rudenko announced, "One of the most important criminal acts for which the major war criminals are responsible was the mass execution of Polish prisoners of war shot in the Katyn forest near Smolensk by the German fascist invaders."[113] Even in 1946, most suspected that the Soviets had committed the massacre. All of the evidence pointed toward them: none of the documents found on the victims was dated later than May 6, 1940, during the time the U.S.S.R. controlled the area; moreover, the victims were dressed in winter clothes, and their hands were tied with cord manufactured in the Soviet Union.[114] According to German historian Jörg Friedrich, nothing did more to discredit the proceedings in the eyes of those they were trying to reeducate than the bogus Katyn charges. "The fact that the Soviet Union, an aggressive and genocidal state, was participating in a legal proceeding strengthened this belief. The masters of the gulag would convict the masters of Auschwitz for crimes against humanity."[115]

On April 1, much to the discomfort of the Soviet delegation, defense attorney Alfred Seidl questioned former Nazi Foreign Secretary Joachim von Ribbentrop about the Hitler-Stalin Pact. The Foreign Secretary went out of his way to implicate the Soviet Union: "In keeping with this understanding, the eastern territories were occupied by Soviet troops and the western territories by German troops after the victory. There is no doubt that Stalin can never accuse Germany of an aggression or of an aggressive war for her action in Poland. If it is considered an aggression, then both sides are guilty of it."[116] Von Ribbentrop outlined the Soviet demands—Finland, the Balkans, Bulgaria, and the naval outlets in the Dardanelles and the Baltic Sea. If this was not sufficiently embarrassing, on May 21, while questioning former German State Secretary Ernst von Weizsäcker, Seidl claimed to have a copy of the Hitler-Stalin Pact's secret protocol: "I have before me a text and Ambassador Gaus [Ribbentrop's senior legal advisor] harbors no doubt at all that the agreements in question are correctly set out in the text."[117]

Justice Lawrence interrupted the defense lawyer and reminded him that the document had been ruled out of evidence because of its unknown origin. However, Seidl had an affadavit from Dr. Friedrich Gaus stating that he had witnessed the document's signing in Moscow. Soviet prosecutor Rudenko exploded, "Your Honors! I would like to protest against these questions for two reasons. First of all, we are examining the matter of crimes of the major German war criminals. We are not investigating the foreign polices of other states." He claimed that the document was a forgery and had no evidentiary value. However, Justice Lawrence allowed Seidl to ask the witness, von Weizsäcker, "what his recollection is of the treaty without putting the document to him." The witness deftly summarized the salient details of the Pact's secret protocol from memory: "It is about a very incisive, a very far-reaching secret addendum to the nonaggression pact concluded at the time. The scope of this document was very extensive since it concerned the partition of spheres of influence and drew a demarcation line between areas which, under given conditions, belonged to the sphere of Soviet Russia and those which would fall in the German sphere of interest. . . . Finland, Estonia, Latvia, Eastern Poland and, as far as I can remember, certain areas of Romania were to be included in the sphere of the Soviet Union." Seidl asked if the secret addendum "contained an agreement on the future destiny of Poland?" "The secret agreement included a complete redirection of Poland's destiny," replied the former State Secretary. Although the court did not allow the introduction of the Hitler-Stalin Pact into evidence, on May 23, the *St. Louis Post-Dispatch* published the document.[118] On that day, General N. D. Zorya, the Soviet official in Nuremberg responsible for the slip-up that allowed Seidl to introduce the Molotov-Ribbentrop Agreement, was found dead from a single gunshot to the head. The Soviets regretfully informed Zorya's international colleagues that he had committed suicide at the Soviet residence in Nuremberg.[119]

The case of Minister of Armaments and War Production Albert Speer was growing increasingly complicated. Unlike Goering, who refused to play the game of Nuremberg, Speer admitted his guilt, cooperated with the prosecution, and labored to save his life both in and out of the courtroom. However, Speer had clearly violated the Geneva conventions by demanding and utilizing concentration camp inmates and POWs as slave laborers on various armament-related projects. He had visited the underground factories that produced the engines for the V-2 rockets and the jet engines for the Messerschmitt 262 airplanes.[120] Not only had Speer taken 30,000 concentration camp inmates from Heinrich Himmler, he had also instituted a program under which factory "slackers" were sent to the camps.[121] If this blatant misuse of slave labor were not enough, between October 18 and November 2, 1941, Speer had helped Adolf Eichmann with the forced evictions of 50,000 German Jews from Berlin under the Reich's "Slum Clearance" project. Speer would claim on the stand that "There was no comprehensive authority in my hands. . . . But I, as the man responsible for production, had no responsibility in these matters. However, when I heard complaints from factory heads or from my deputies, I did everything to remove the cause of the complaints."[122] Most incriminating was Albert Speer's presence at Himmler's famous Posen speech on October 6, 1943, on the "Final Solution." Himmler had even addressed the defendant directly as "party comrade Speer" during the speech.[123]

Although Speer pled weakly that he had considered assassinating Hitler in the final days of the war, his guilt was more certain than his innocence. However, on the stand he claimed to have had little knowledge of his personal friend Adolf Hitler's intentions and even said that he had never read *Mein Kampf*.[124] On June 21, 1946, under Soviet cross-examination, Speer testified, "I was in close contact with Hitler, and I heard his personal views; these views of his did not allow the conclusion that he had any plans of the sort which appeared in the documents here."[125] Compared to the "Statement of Remorse" read by Walter Funk on May 6, 1946, many thought Speer's testimony unconvincing. "I nearly died of shame," Goering quipped after Speer's attorney had shown his client's hand by asking Otto Ohlendorf under cross-examination if his old friend, Albert Speer, had ever mentioned his plans to assassinate Adolf Hitler. Goering vividly expressed his disgust: "To think that a German could be so rotten, just to prolong his wretched life—to put it crudely, to piss in front and crap behind a little longer." As far as Goering was concerned, they would all surely be executed; however, there was "such a thing as honour."[126]

Contrasting most sharply with Speer's upper-middle-class propriety was the dark presence of Julius Streicher. Journalist Rebecca West described Streicher during the trial as "the sort who gives trouble in parks."[127] An unlikely choice as a defendant in a major war crimes trial, Streicher had been the publisher of the racist and borderline porno-graphic Nazi periodical *Der Strumer*. However, he had not been involved in either policy making or military decision making, and the prosecu-tion would need to establish the fact that the periodicals he produced helped to create a climate conducive to carrying out the Final Solution. Of the defendants at Nuremberg, the former comic book publisher had scored the lowest on the I.Q. test given to all the prisoners.[128] Although Streicher expressed odious personal views, had he committed war crimes?

When the time came to rule, the IMT proved very conservative in applying the hotly debated conspiracy and aggression charges.[129] While the judges found eight (Goering, Hess, Ribbentrop, Keitel, Rosenberg, Jodl, Seyss-Inquart, Neurath, and Raeder) guilty of crimes against peace, they acquitted four of the charge (Fritzsche, Speer, Schacht, and Papen). The court offered no expansive definition of aggression, only vague refer-ences to "aggressive acts."[130] The cautious precedent of the IMT did not establish a definitive standard for aggression.[131] David Luban describes the IMT precedent as "resting on the shakiest of grounds."[132] When it came to the criminalization of the Nazi organizations, the IMT carefully distinguished between the SS and other organs of terror and the profes-sional soldiers. While the court criminalized the SS, SD, Gestapo, and Leadership Corps of the Nazi Party, they acquitted the General Staff, High Command, Reich Cabinet, and SA.[133]

Otto Kranzbühler remembered the day of the sentencing as "full of gloomy tension. We knew that we would reckon with a large number of death sentences."[134] On November 6, 1946, the IMT sentenced twelve men to death (Goering, Ribbentrop, Keitel, Kaltenbrunner, Rosenberg, Frank, Frick, Streicher, Sauckel, Jodl, Bormann, and Seyss-Inquart). The biggest surprises were the acquittals of Schacht, Papen, and Fritzsche. Speer's repentance and his guilty plea got him twenty years in prison, Doenitz received a ten-year sentence, and Rudolf Hess was sentenced to life in Spandau Prison. Because of this and other examples of what they considered leniency, the Soviet judges issued a dissenting opinion on the acquittals; the majority's decision not to criminalize the Reich Cabinet, the General Staff, and the High Command; and finally the Hess sen-tence.[135] Although the IMT sentenced Hermann Goering to hang, he had made other plans. Goering had befriended an American guard named "Tex" Wheelis and plied him with expensive gifts like a Bulova watch and a Mont Blanc pen. Because Wheelis had access to the prisoners' baggage room, he could find Goering's hidden cyanide capsules. Hours before his scheduled execution, the former Reichsmarshall was found dead in his cell from cyanide poisoning. He left a final letter: "This grand finale is typical of the abysmal depths plumbed by the court and prosecution. Pure theater, from start to finish! All rotten comedy!" Hermann Goering was unrepentant and self-aggrandizing until the end. "I would have let you shoot me without further ado! But it is not possible to hang the German Reichsmarshall. . . . I have therefore chosen the manner of death of the Great Hannibal."[136]

The other ten convicts were hanged by Master Sergeant John Woods of the U.S. Army on October 16, 1946. German historian Jörg Friedrich describes how some of the German public reacted to the Nuremberg verdicts:

> The Germans learned from posters on the street that their former leaders had been hanged at Nuremberg. In the last three months of the war, more than 700,000 German soldiers and civilians had lost their lives. Now people crowded around the pillars on which the posters hung, reading in silence that ministers, field marshals and police chiefs had also died. There were no signs of remorse. In Wuppertal, schoolgirls dressed in black on the morning of the execution; in Hamburg, people whispered that the British leaders responsible for the bombing of the city also deserved to hang.[137]

In terms of providing fallen foes with a legitimate forum, the IMT was unprecedented in modern history. The accused were informed of the charges filed against them and given access to the evidence, legal representation, and an opportunity to state their cases in open court. The court simply refused to rule in the case of the Katyn Massacre, and any mention of it was conspicuously absent from its judgment. The acquittals and even the Soviet dissents all bolstered the court's credibility. Above and beyond all else, Nuremberg provided an international legal inquiry that was unique in history. Due to the acrimony surrounding the London Agreement Charter, the court began and ended divided. An accidental result of this division were carefully considered judgments and dissenting opinions. One of the most significant challenges the judges faced was reconciling a number of differing interpretations of international law (Continental, Anglo, and American) and preventing the differences among them from undermining the trials.[138]

Was the Nuremberg judgment a primitive form of punitive political justice like the U.S.–Dakota War Trials and the Wirz case? Or was it a form of strategic legalism like the Jacob Smith case or the Leipzig trials? Or was Nuremberg's IMT a new form of twentieth-century political justice? It certainly contrasts sharply with the forms of political justice exercised by both the Soviets and the Nazis against their respective enemies. Compared to Stalin and Vyshinsky's 1930s Moscow purge trials or to Hitler's 1944 trial of the "Bomb plotters," Nuremberg stands up quite nicely.

Ironically, the quadripartite disagreements over war crimes policy prevented the kinds of strategic legalist nonjudicial sentence reductions that would become all too familiar in Germany and Japan during the 1950s. Moreover, the Soviets failed to turn Nuremberg into "a continuation of political warfare in judicial robes."[139] The IMT proved that successor trials were not farcical by their very nature. The Allies managed to punish the guilty and to create a strong documentary record of the German dictatorship.

However, in terms of reeducation, reform, and overall social engineering, the trials were less successful.[140] The lessons of Nuremberg were lost on war-weary Germans, many of whom had grown cynical and apathetic and considered the trial a form of ritual or political theater. Nonetheless, the assumption that trials could reeducate an entire nation proved both naive and erroneous.[141] Instead of embracing national guilt after surviving World War II, many Germans chose to become "blind in one eye": "German critics ignored—and continue to ignore—some distinctive characteristics of Nuremberg, such as due process of law. They glossed over the sober presentation of abundant evidence of German atrocities. Instead, they insisted that Nuremberg was legally flawed, with the reservation that the major Nazis got what they deserved," observes Friedrich.[142]

The IMT stands in stark contrast to the International Military Tribunal for the Far East (IMTFE) or the "Tokyo trial." On April 29, 1946, the IMTFE arraigned twenty-eight of Japan's military and civilian leaders under a 55-count indictment that included charges of crimes against peace and crimes against humanity. Although Emperor Hirohito was not among the defendants, they did include Hideki Tojo and a number of other high-ranking officials.[143]

Dutch judge B.V.A. Röling later described the Tokyo trial as "very much an American performance. . . . I didn't see it at the time, and I didn't see that there were more 'Hollywoodesque' things around than there should have been." The decision not to try the Emperor was made unilaterally by General MacArthur himself. The Soviets grew extremely suspicious about the American refusal to indict Hirohito. MacArthur argued that if the Emperor were tried like a common criminal, "the nation will disintegrate" and went on to claim that the United States would need a million additional troops to restore order. At lower levels, the Americans under the Supreme Commander Asia Pacific (SCAP) occupation government would attempt to purge the Japanese government of wartime functionaries as had been done in Germany.[144] Japan was undergoing a similar social reconstruction, and they hoped that the trial of the high-ranking Japanese would, like Nuremberg's IMT, serve as the centerpiece of the American reeducation effort. However, prosecuting Japanese leaders for war crimes would prove to be far more difficult.

The four-power Nuremberg court with a four-count indictment was simple in comparison to the IMTFE. That Tribunal was composed of eleven judges from Australia, Canada, China, France, the Philippines, the Netherlands, New Zealand, the Soviet Union, Great Britain, the United States, and India. Unlike the IMT, whose indictment (the London Agreement and Charter) was an international agreement, the IMTFE was established by a Proclamation issued by Allied Supreme Commander General Douglas MacArthur. The chief counsel for the Americans was a former criminal lawyer and New Dealer named Joe Keenan who overzealously pushed the Americans' broadened conception of international criminality. Keenan claimed that the trial "served as a cockpit for a death struggle between two completely irreconcilable and opposed types of legal thinking" (natural law and positivism).[145]

The presiding judge in the Tokyo trial was William Webb of Australia. Unlike Justice Lawrence, the presiding judge in the IMT, who was elected by his peers, Webb was appointed by General MacArthur. Years later, B.V.A. Röling, the justice from the Netherlands, described Webb as "completely unsure of his position"; this manifested itself in "dictatorial behavior toward his colleagues as well as toward the prosecutors and defense counsel."[146] Legal historian John Appleman writes, "After examining the proceedings of the International Military Tribunal at Nuremberg . . . the proceedings before the International Military Tribunal for the Far East seem strangely autocratic."[147]

The case for German aggression was more easily made than that for Japanese aggression; the mountains of captured German documents provided enough proof to make the crimes against peace charges arguable. The same charges were far less certain in the case of the Japanese because the prosecution lacked the same type of documentary evidence. And because Nuremberg's IMT had not defined standards of aggression, the IMTFE had to render independent judgment.[148] The indictment in the Tokyo trial was significantly more complicated than the IMT's London Agreement Charter. Crimes against peace were covered by Counts 1–36, murder by 37–52, war crimes and crimes against humanity by 53–55. This indictment was legally problematic in a number of respects.[149] Some of the defendants were charged with not having prevented war crimes—in other words, negative criminality. The fifty-fourth count of the indictment accused the defendants of having "deliberately and recklessly disregarded their legal duty to take adequate steps to secure the observance and prevent breaches" of the laws of war.[150] In other words, they were charged for what they didn't do. Others were accused of cannibalism: "On 10 December 1944 an order was issued from 18 Army Headquarters that troops were permitted to eat the flesh of Allied dead but must not eat their own dead."[151]

On May 6, U.S. Army defense lawyer Major General Bruce Blakney challenged the court's jurisdiction over the defendants because "war is not a crime."[152] Unlike the defense lawyers in the first Nuremberg trial, those in Tokyo were not forbidden from attacking the court's international legal legitimacy. During the first week of the trial, the defense filed more motions challenging the legal basis of the tribunal. They questioned the criminality of aggression under international law. Japanese defense counsel Kenzo Takayanagi rejected the validity of the charge on the grounds that the Kellogg-Briand Pact had a provision for self-defense and that the Japanese war effort had been an act of self-defense.[153] Takayanagi also cited Robert Lansing's now well-worn conservative rejection of aggression charges from the Paris Peace Conference.[154] Prime Minister Tojo accepted full responsibility for Japan's actions. In a 50,000-word statement, he argued that the attacks on Pearl Harbor, China, and

Indonesia, and other so-called acts of "aggression," were responses to an Allied policy that intended to slowly strangle the island nation with economic and military blockades. According to the defendant, the fact that the Japanese had fired the first shot was inconsequential when placed within the larger context of U.S.-Japanese relations of the 1930s and early 1940s.[155] Although the trial began in May 1946; due to the size of the court and the number of defendants, the prosecution case would take seven months to present and the entire trial would last more than two and half years. Only the Axis leaders faced the War Department's aggression, conspiracy, and crimes against humanity charges and as a result, Allied war crimes policy was uneven in a number of ways.

Because of the logistical requirements of two occupations, Allied policy possessed a strong ad hoc character; theater officials were often forced to interpret vague policies. Historian Kurt Tauber has offered this explanation for the confusion that resulted: "Without a clear unambiguous decision at the highest level in favor of one or the other course, there was uncertainty at the lower echelons, where policy is actually executed. The ambiguity was never entirely removed."[156] The end result was the emergence of a hydra-headed American war crimes policy. High-ranking Axis leaders were given elaborate trials and judged according to new standards of international law. Meanwhile, the overwhelming majority of war crimes cases were tried by the Allied military under military law in both Europe and in the Pacific. Of the 1,672 tried by the U.S. Army at the Dachau concentration camp, approximately two thirds of the defendants had been guards or personnel at the Buchenwald, Flossenburg, Mauthausen, Nordhausen, Hadamar, and Muhldorf concentration camps; another large group (1,000) was charged with lynching Allied pilots; and a small number were tried for the Malmedy Massacre.[157] In the Pacific theater, U.S. military courts tried 215 in Manila, 966 in Yokohama, and 116 in trials at the Kwajalein Atoll and Guam for traditional war crimes.[158]

There were two series of trials that would come back to haunt the Americans and help to discredit American war crimes policy. These trials were conducted by the U.S. army in both Asia and Europe. While the military courts were not up to the lofty standards of the international courts, they were examples of traditional, punitive political justice. But because the Americans had loudly and conspicuously committed themselves to higher standards for the IMT and the IMTFE, all of their trials would be judged by those standards.

The most famous victor's justice occurred in the Philippines in 1945, where General Douglas MacArthur evened the score with his former Japanese adversaries Tomoyuki Yamashita and Masaharu Homma. General Yamashita had earned fame and glory in 1943 when with only 30,000 men he overwhelmed 100,000 British troops at Malaya. Because Yamashita's popularity threatened to eclipse even Tojo's, the general was transferred to an inactive front.[159] But on October 20, 1944, Yamashita returned to Manila as Japanese Supreme Commander in the Philippines, in direct command of Japan's 14th Army. In January 1945, he declared Manila an open city because the flat, spread-out city with its highly flammable buildings would be difficult to defend.[160] General Yamashita retreated to Baguio, and beginning on February 3, 1945, 20,000 Japanese sailors and marines began to enter Manila and set about destroying the city and slaughtering its inhabitants. When the general heard about the atrocities nine days later, he radioed Admiral Iwabuchia (the commander of the navy) and ordered him to withdraw. However, the admiral was dead.[161] General Yamashita would later claim that he was unable to command the troops due to a breakdown in communications caused by the onslaught of the U.S. forces.

Two days before the trial began, defense attorney Frank Reel learned that the prosecution had added fifty-nine new charges to the indictment. Reel petitioned for more time to address the new charges, but this request was rejected.[162] A reception hall in the High Commissioner's residence in Manila was transformed into a courtroom, and the general was arraigned by a five-man military commission on October 8, 1945. General MacArthur charged that General Yamashita "unlawfully disregarded and failed to discharge his duty as commander to control the ops of the members of his command." MacArthur divided the crimes into three categories: starvation, executions, and massacres; torture, rape, murder, and mass executions; and burning and demolition without military necessity.[163]

Nuremberg this was not, and General MacArthur offered no apologies or excuses. The "American Caesar" did not feel compelled to observe any law but his own. The trial of his former adversaries was a throwback to traditional, punitive political justice. Not only did MacArthur select the judges and draft the trial procedure, all of the generals on the five-man legal commission were under his command, and none was a lawyer. Moreover, the tribunal was not "bound by technical rules of evidence."[164] One prosecution witness testified that the Japanese soldiers had bayoneted her, and lifted her shirt to display twenty-six bayonet-wound scars. Another testified that Japanese soldiers killed her young child in front of her. The witness began to shake her fist at the general and scream, "*Tandaan mo!* [Remember it!] Yamashita!"[165]

The prosecution did great damage not so much to their case but to the trial's reputation when they introduced a pseudodocumentary movie as the "evidence which will convict." The film showed an American soldier removing a piece of paper from the pocket of a dead Japanese soldier; the paper read (in English), "Orders from Tokyo." The narrator broke in: "We have discovered the secret orders to destroy Manila."[166] After the prosecution rested on November 20, the defense called Australian Norman Sparnom, the Allied chief translator in charge of captured Japanese documents. The defense attorney asked, "A film was shown before this committee in which a statement was made that the United States of America had captured an order from Tokyo for the destruction of Manila. Have you ever seen such an order among the captured documents?" "No, I have not," Sparnom replied.[167]

Yamashita's attorney, Frank Reel, did not challenge the evidence presented by the prosecution. Instead, he attempted to distance Yamashita from the atrocities committed in Manila, claiming that the general was thrown into a desperate situation in the Philippines. After Yamashita entered Manila, he immediately declared it indefensible and retreated to Baguio, 150 miles away. Throughout his trial, Yamashita maintained that he did not hear of the atrocities until more than a week after they had occurred.[168] Yamashita claimed,

> I absolutely did not order [any atrocities] nor did I receive the order to do this from any superior authority, nor did I ever permit such a thing . . . and will swear to heaven and earth concerning these points.[169] . . . The facts are that I was constantly under attack by large American forces, and I had been under pressure day and night. . . . I believe that under the foregoing conditions I did the best possible job I could have done. However, due to the above circumstances, my plans and my strength were not sufficient to the situation, and if these things happened, they were absolutely unavoidable. They were beyond anything I would have expected.[170]

On December 7, 1945, the fourth anniversary of the Japanese attack on Pearl Harbor, MacArthur's military commission announced its decision. General Reynolds described the atrocities as "not sporadic in nature but in many cases were methodically supervised by the Japanese officers and noncommissioned officers."[171] The second part of the opinion announced the most significant precedent to come out of the Yamashita case—"command responsibility"[172]—the idea that a commanding officer could be held accountable for the actions of his troops. Major General Russell Reynolds, Major General Clarence Sturdevant, Major General James Lester, Brigadier General William Walker, and Brigadier General Egbert Bullens sentenced Tomoyuki Yamashita to death by hanging. Yamashita maintained his innocence until the end: "I wish to state that I stand here today with the same clear conscience as on the first day of my arraignment, and I swear to my Creator and everything that is sacred to me that I am innocent of all charges made against me."[173]

America's highest court had been conspicuously silent on the question of war crimes until Frank Reel, Yamashita's attorney, appealed to the U.S. Supreme Court for a writ of *habeas corpus*.[174] In February 1946, the court upheld Yamashita's death sentence by a clear six-to-two margin. The majority based their ruling on the 1942 decision in *Ex parte Quirin*, which authorized congressional passage of the articles of war and sanctioned the use of military tribunals during wartime.[175] This ruling allowed the court's majority to avoid the substantive legal questions of the Yamashita case. Chief Justice Harlan Stone applied a narrow reading of the Constitution, concluding that it was not the court's responsibility to reexamine the case: "We do not here appraise the evidence on which petitioner was convicted. . . . These are questions within the peculiar competence of the military officers composing the commission and were for it to decide."[176]

Not all of Stone's Supreme Court brethren were willing to take such an easy way out: Justices Murphy and Rutledge issued strong dissenting opinions that did lasting damage to the reputation of the Yamashita case. Justice Murphy described the trial as "a practice reminiscent of that pursued in certain less respected nations in recent years" and went on to attack the logic of the army tribunal.[177] "We will judge the discharge of your duties," wrote Murphy,

by the disorganization which we ourselves created in large part. Our standards of judgment are whatever we wish to make them. Nothing in all history or in international law, at least as far as I am aware, justifies such a charge against a fallen commander of a defeated force. To use the very inefficiency and disorganization created by the victorious forces as the primary basis for condemning officers of defeated armies bears no resemblance to justice or to military reality.[178]

At the time, Robert Shaplen of *Newsweek* wrote, "In the opinion of probably every correspondent covering the trial the military commission came into the courtroom the first day with the decision already in its collective pocket."[179] Once General MacArthur received word that the U.S. Supreme Court had upheld the death sentence, he ordered Yamashita stripped of his uniform and decorations and hanged.

MacArthur's Manila tribunal arraigned Masaharu Homma on December 19, 1945; he too was charged with failure to control his troops. When American General Edward King surrendered to Homma's forces on Bataan on April 9, 1942, he was assured that his troops would be treated humanely. Between 80,000–100,000 American and mostly Philippine soldiers began the 80-mile walk to Bataan; 7,000 and 10,000 died or were killed by Japanese soldiers. Homma's trial lasted from January 3 to February 11, 1946. General Homma had few doubts about his postwar fate: "Win and you are the official army, lose and you are the rebels." He believed that "there is no such thing as justice in international relations in this universe." Unlike Yamashita, who was hanged, Homma was sentenced to death by firing squad. Again, the Supreme Court rejected Homma's lawyer's writ of *habeas corpus* by a six-to-two majority, with Rutledge and Murphy again issuing dissenting opinions.[180]

While it is important to note the legal irregularities in the Yamashita case, it is also important to keep in mind that legal guilt and moral guilt are two entirely different things. Japanese soldiers treated American POWs significantly worse than the Germans. Of the approximately 235,000 American and British POWs taken by Germany and Italy, approximately 4 percent died in captivity, whereas 27 percent of 132,000 British and American prisoners died in Japanese captivity.[181] Australian POWs suffered most as prisoners of the Japanese: of the 21,726 captured, 7412 or 34 percent died. While the Manila trials contained some glaring procedural flaws, Yamashita and Homma were the leaders of a losing army that wantonly and brutally slaughtered civilians throughout Asia. Japanese soldiers tended to view POWs with contempt for surrendering.

While the motives will never be known, it is clear beyond a reasonable doubt that in Nanking, Manila, Canton, and many other parts of Asia, civilians were killed almost for sport. In six weeks in Nanking, Japanese soldiers killed approximately 300,000 civilians and raped 20,000 women.[182] Two soldiers even engaged in a contest to see who would be first to behead 100 POWs, and the contest was closely monitored by a Japanese newspaper.

With the surrender of Japan came the discovery of the Japanese special warfare Units 731, 100, and 112. In a laboratory in Manchuria they conducted medical experiments on Chinese, Korean, and Russian POWs, similar to those the Nazis conducted at Dachau for the *Luftwaffe*. Prisoners were frozen alive, infected with syphilis, given transfusions of horse blood, subjected to vivisection with no anaesthesia, and given numerous x-rays to test the effects of radiation.[183] Although the Soviets captured the laboratories in Manchuria, most of the 3,600 doctors and technicians made their way back to Japan. The head of Unit 731, Lieutenant General Shiro Ishi, traded his research results to American authorities in exchange for immunity from prosecution for himself and his staff.[184] In his recent book, *Embracing Defeat*, John Dower contends that the U.S. government gave immunity to General Ishii and his men in infamous bacteriological warfare Unit 731, "Americans who controlled the prosecution chose to grant blanket secret immunity to . . . the officers and scientific researchers in Unit 731 in Manchuria. . . . The data gained from human experimentation once again became ammunition: this time in the bargaining room, rather than on the battlefield. The Japanese hoped to use their knowledge as a tool for gaining freedom from prosecution as war criminals."[185] Similar to Germany, war crimes prosecutions in Japan were extremely uneven.

If anything, the Yamashita case, like the *U.S.-Dakota War Trials* and the trial of Captain Henry Wirz, was an example of traditional, punitive political justice. The conquered had no choice but to submit to the judicial fiat of the victors. A soldier from an earlier era, MacArthur had few legal pretensions and considered professional military men bound by "warrior's honor." In the final opinion, MacArthur wrote that "The soldier, be he friend or foe, is charged with the protection of the weak and unarmed. It is the very essence and reason for his being. When he violates his sacred trust, he not only profanes the entire cult but threatens the very fabric of international society."[186] General Douglas

MacArthur's treatment of his former foe, although abhorrent when measured by the new standards of the U.S. War Department, was consistent with history.[187]

The Yamashita case raised questions about the laws of war in the twentieth century. Was the objective of modern total war to defeat the enemy's army on the battlefield, or to attack and demoralize their civilian population? If civilians had become legitimate targets, were the laws of war outdated by the expansion of military conflict? These questions were especially relevant in Germany. Many Germans considered the destruction of their nation's cities and infrastructure punishment enough. Even William T. Sherman had advocated a merciful peace after total war. However, for the perpetrators of the Malmedy Massacre, it appeared that there would be no mercy.

Due to the symbolic importance of the slaughter of surrendered American soldiers, the United States was under a great deal of pressure to identify and prosecute those who had committed the executions. American intelligence blamed the killings on the men of *Kampfegruppe* Peiper, and they were transferred to a century-old prison near Ludwigsberg called Schwabisch Hall for interrogations. The army investigation team soon became frustrated by the stonewalling of Joachim Peiper and his men. A suspiciously large number of them claimed the killings had been ordered by the now dead SS Commander Walter Pringel.[188] The interrogators, Lieutenant Colonel Burton Ellis and Lieutenant William Perl, were pressured by the army to begin the trial as soon as possible.[189] An Austrian lawyer who had been forced out of Vienna in 1938, Perl had been trained at the U.S. Military Intelligence Center in Fort Ritchie, Maryland. He returned to Europe as a U.S. Army interrogator. The interrogation of Paul Zwiggart, a twenty-two-year-old member of Kampfegruppe Peiper, was described by his attorney in an obviously biased but telling account years later.

After Zwiggart's six weeks of solitary confinement in Schwabisch Hall, a guard entered his cell and put a hood over his head.[190] He and the other prisoners were taken to the mock court through long corridors, down a flight of stairs; "suddenly heavy iron chains had been trailed near the prisoners which rattle must produce a corresponding psychological effect." According to the defense attorney, the men were forced to face the wall with their arms raised up. "During about twenty minutes, he received in that position kicks without any interruption. . . . That treatment continued further by thrashing until Zwiggart gave sufficiently in. Finally, First Lieutenant PEARL pulled with a sudden push the capuche from the head of the prisoner and insulted him, first of all, using diverse terms." The suspect was taken to a small room with "a writing-table in the middle of which a crucifix was placed and two burning candles on the left and the right." Zwiggart's attorney described the American "court" that "tried" him: "Behind the writing-table, an American officer . . . who was indicated as being the judge. On the left stood Mr. THON who was presented as attorney-general and on the right of the prisoner First Lieutenant PEARL had taken place whereby he indicated that he was personally his defender and that this event was an 'American summary court.' " Because Zwiggart refused to confess, he was "sentenced" to death. According to the prisoner, the day after the fictitious trial, an execution was solemnly staged by his American interrogators: "A cord was bound around the neck of the young Zwiggart—he still had the capuche over his head—and then he heard the voice of First Lieutenant PEARL who said that he had only one chance to save himself by pleading guilty for himselves and his comrades." Zwiggart finally signed a "statement" dictated by his interrogators.[191] One of the accused, Arvid Freimuth, hanged himself after Lieutenant Perl threatened to hand him over to the Belgians.[192]

By December, a torrent of confessions began to pour in to American interrogators. One German commander claimed that he had been ordered to take no prisoners.[193] A number of confessions indicated that this had been a standing order. Disobeying was not a simple proposition in the SS; one soldier recalled, "those who showed consideration to the enemy were shown no consideration by him [Pringel]. Pringel's method of showing displeasure with a subordinate had been to require him to go to battle exposed on the hull of a tank."[194]

The confession of Joachim Peiper provided the prosecution with a major break in their case. Like Yamashita, Peiper made no effort to challenge the facts of the case and candidly confessed his orders, which included "an order of the Sixth SS Panzer Army, with the contents that, considering the desperate situation of the German people, a wave of terror and fright should precede our troops."[195] Symbolically, Peiper was an important figure to both the Americans and the Germans. To the Americans he was an unrepentant Nazi, but to the Germans he was a decorated officer and war hero.

The confessions obtained at Schwabisch Hall provided enough evidence for the General Military Government Court to begin. On May 16, 1946, seventy-four Waffen SS veterans were charged with various violations of the laws of war. As in the Yamashita case, the defense team was at a huge disadvantage.[196] The army argued that the defendants were not prisoners of war but "civilian internees" accused of war crimes. According to this interpretation, the prisoners were not protected by the Geneva Convention of 1929; the tribunal had the power to create and employ any evidentiary standard it desired.[197]

When the first reports of forced confessions came in the spring of 1945, Theatre Judge Advocate Major Claude Mickelwait investigated the charges and established that some of the defendants had been punched or slapped by guards. However, there was no evidence of systematic torture, only "psychological duress."[198] Chief prosecutor Burton Ellis admitted that "all the legitimate tricks, ruses, and stratagems known to investigators were employed—stool pigeons, witnesses who were not *bona fide*."[199] The defense argued that since the confessions had been obtained before the defendants' status had been changed, they were inadmissible as evidence. The tribunal dismissed these motions.[200]

Although the eight-man General Military Government Court was the highest level of military justice, it labored under none of the presumptions of the Nuremberg trial. The prosecution was headed by Colonel Burton Ellis, while the defense would be handled by Wallace Everett Jr. The defense was at a major disadvantage: not only did Everett have no prior courtroom experience, he had to defend seventy-four men.[201] On May 16, 1946, the prisoners were led into a defendants' dock at the Dachau concentration camp. Die-hard Nazi soldiers like Sepp Dietrich, Joachim Peiper, Fritz Kramer, and Herman Preiss sat in the hastily constructed courtroom, their only decorations the large number-bearing placards draped ingloriously around their necks. The court was presided over by Brigadier General Josiah Dalbey. The indictment stated that the defendants, "at the vicinity of Malmedy, Honsfeld, Büllingen, Stavelot, Wanne and Lutrebois, all in Belgium, at sundry times between 16 December 1944 and 13 January 1945, willfully, deliberately and wrongfully permit, encourage, aid, abet and participate in the killing, shooting, ill-treatment, abuse and torture of members of the Armed Forces of the United States of America, then at war with the then Third Reich."[202]

Joachim Peiper attacked the prosecution for the way in which they obtained his confession.[203] He claimed that after five weeks of solitary confinement, he was told by interrogators that some of those killed by his troops were the sons of prominent American politicians and business-men. The cry for his head had grown so loud that not even the President of the United States could save him. However, if he cooperated with investigators, the army might spare his men. Peiper claimed that this was why he signed the confession of guilt prepared by Lieutenant Perl.[204] As for actual violations of the laws of war, he argued that those laws had been rendered obsolete by the realities of total war. Perl could elicit no remorse from the hardened combat veteran:

> Perl: *Well were your men so ill-trained in the rules of the Geneva Convention that they killed prisoners of war without orders?*
> Peiper: *In the answer on that question, it is the same as on the question before. During combat there are desperate situations, the answer to which is given out very fast to main reactions and which do not have anything to do with education and teaching.*[205]

Peiper fought in the courtroom with the same tenacity that had earned him the Iron Cross with the oak-leaf cluster. To Peiper, morality and restraint had no place in the final days of a total war; he pointed to the destruction wrought by British and American bombers on German cities: "Also, this order pointed out that the German soldiers should, in this offensive recall the innumerable German victims of the bombing terror. . . . At this meeting, I did not mention anything that prisoners of war should be shot . . . because those present were all experienced offi-cers to whom this was obvious."[206]

Joachim Peiper and Admiral Karl Doenitz became two of Germany's most important post–World War II martyrs. However, it was not only German nationalists who claimed that their military had been unjustifi-ably persecuted. A large portion of the world's professional military was beginning to close ranks on the subject of war crimes. Although Peiper was tried by the U.S. Army under military law, this mattered little, as such distinctions were lost on German nationalists who considered all of the Allied war crimes trials part of a "victor's justice."[207] The precedent most threatening to professional soldiers was the rejection of the superior orders defense; many believed that this would erode the military chain of command.

Like the Yamashita case, the Malmedy trial was initially a traditional example of punitive political justice. Although the format had to be updated to fit the twentieth century, the message remained the same. On July 16, after a five-week trial, Peiper, Dietrich, and forty-two of his men were sentenced to death; twenty-two others were sentenced to life in prison. Defense counsel John Everett followed the example of Yamashita's attorney, Frank Reel, and petitioned the U.S. Supreme Court for a writ of *habeas corpus*. Everett maintained that the confessions were obtained under physical and psychological duress.[298] Although the court rejected the argument, the fate of Kampfegruppe Peiper was by no means sealed. By the time the Malmedy trials and the international Nuremberg trial had concluded, it was late 1946, and the larger political landscape was changing rapidly. German war crimes were now overshadowed by the perceived threat of the Soviet Union, and American policy toward Germany began to reflect this change.

Chapter Four

A SHIFT IN PRIORITIES

Joint Chiefs of Staff Directive 1067 (approved by President Roosevelt on September 29, 1944) governed the initial phase of the occupation of Germany. Although the Morgenthau Plan had been rejected, JCS 1067 retained some of its punitive elements.[1] The policy aimed to demilitarize, denazify, and deindustrialize the vanquished nation, removing the threat by approaching it as a social problem. The German army had been crushed, so demilitarization was never an issue. This overwhelming task fell to U.S. Military Governor General Lucius Clay and the U.S. Military Government. Although the Americans were the most conspicuous advocates of reeducation, they were not alone. Prior to the defeat of the Third Reich, prominent European intellectuals like Thomas Mann had called for the reeducation of Germany. Even German historian Friedrich Meinecke called for some type of reform.[2] Although there was a consensus that Germany needed to be reformed, there was no agreement about how to achieve this. Americans like Justice Robert Jackson hoped that the trials would aid the American reeducation effort by establishing an empirical record of the Nazi crimes. The trials would prove to the German people that under an American-inspired system of justice, due process of law was extended to even the guiltiest.[3]

Although the Nuremberg trials were the highest-profile legal proceeding, by far the largest number of cases were tried by U.S. denazification courts. Given the immensity of their task, these courts did not live up to the Atlantic Charter's promise to arrest, detain, and remove Nazis from public office. On March 5, 1946, German states in the American zone of occupation enacted the De-Nazification Law, which established four levels of offenses by members of the recently criminalized Nazi organizations.[4] The implications of this vague commitment were both radical and enormous: a large percentage German population would have to be processed judicially.[5] Many Germans considered the American questionnaire, or *Fragebogen*, used to categorize them an intrusively detailed accounting of individual wartime activities. Like the war crimes trials, many saw the denazification program yet another manifestation of the Allied victors' justice. German historian Jörg Friedrich describes it as "a form of political purge" with "no basis in international law. The Hague rules of land warfare do not authorize an occupier to undertake any such interference in the enemy's domestic affairs."[6] More than 13.4 million Germans registered with denazification boards; 945,000 were tried by denazification courts, and 130,000 were found guilty under some category of law. Penalties were not very severe. Sentences ranged from ineligibility to hold public office to restricted employment, fines, and at worst, forced labor.[7]

The year 1946 was transitional in American foreign policy. Cold War historians agree that Secretary of State James Byrnes's Stuttgart speech on September 6 "renounced the more retributive elements of JCS 1067 and began to relax the external controls of the occupation in an effort to move Germany down the road to self-government."[8] From the beginning, the State Department had taken a dim view of the "vindictive" elements of JCS 1067 (war crimes trials, denazification). There was also the perception that high-placed Jews within the Roosevelt administration had tainted the American occupation with "blind vengeance." According to Peter Grose's recent book *Operation Rollback*: "By the summer of 1946, Washington's top military intelligence officers had abandoned the fervor of de-Nazification and were arranging for ex-Nazis with 'special' qualifications, such as expertise in rocket science and other high technology, to be excused from the indignities of prisoner-of-war status and join the service of the United States for the demands of the postwar era."[9]

Denazification underwent a significant shift in March 1946, when the U.S. military turned the program over to the German government. Many considered this an abandonment of the reeducation program, but General Clay argued that the best way for Germans to learn democracy was to live it.[10] Although denazification proceedings continued until 1949, they often appeared farcical under German administration. Former Assistant U.S. High Commissioner Benjamin Buttenweiser recalled that "some of the denazification trials were absolutely shocking mockeries . . . they were by no test a complete success. Many who were cleared I'm pretty sure were Nazis."[11] The results were predictable. Like Reconstruction after the American Civil War, the grand social engineering project known as reeducation was quickly and quietly winding down.

Industrial leaders Friedrich Flick and Alfried Krupp, diplomat Ernst von Weizsäcker, and bureaucrat Hans Lammers could not be handed over to the military because they had not violated the laws of war. Moreover, an important part of the American reeducation effort was to compile a record of Nazi atrocities that would withstand the test of time. This task remained unfinished.

By 1947, high-level war crimes policy was the greatest anomaly in American foreign relations. The Allied war crimes effort provided one of the first rallying points for Germany's post–World War II nationalists. Their relationship with the trials was beginning to resemble that of a previous generation of German nationalists with the Treaty of Versailles. The theme remained the same: the expansion of Bolshevism was "divine retribution" for the "unjust" treatment of Germany.[12]

Robert Jackson probably never doubted that the United States should conduct subsequent proceedings under the laws created for the IMT. On December 4, 1945, in a letter to President Truman, Jackson suggested that the United States begin to prepare for another series of high-level trials and that Colonel Telford Taylor be put in charge of the preparations.[13] In his report to President Truman, Jackson offered practical reasons why the United States should proceed alone: "A four-power, four-language, International trial, was inevitably the slowest and most costly method of procedure. The purposes of this extraordinary and difficult method of trial had been accomplished."[14] Jackson had distrusted the Soviets from the start, and now he had a reason to exclude them. He suggested that the

United States hold a series of trials modeled after the IMT, under the auspices of General Lucius Clay's U.S. Military Government.

Three military decrees brought the United States closer to these autonomous trials. Joint Chiefs of Staff directive 1023/10, issued in the summer of 1946, ordered the American Theatre Commander to identify, investigate, and apprehend all persons suspected of war crimes. Military Ordinance No. 7 established three-man tribunals to preside over the American trials and define the court's role. But the most important of the decrees was Control Council Law No. 10, which was, in effect, a mandate to take up where the IMT had left off. It was supposed to "give effect to the terms of the Moscow Declaration of 30 October 1943 and the London Agreement of 8 August 1945, and the Charter issued pursuant thereto in order to establish a uniform legal basis in Germany for the prosecution of war criminals."[15] Military Governor Lucius Clay was responsible for overseeing the American trials. A number of participants from the IMT joined the prosecution and defense staffs for the subsequent proceedings. Clay believed that the trials were an important part of the reconstruction and reeducation effort and argued that no new legal system could be established in Germany until all the vestiges of the previous one had been swept away.[16] Since the trials were under military law, all verdicts were subject to the Military Government's review and confirmation. Clay's commitment to the subsequent proceedings would soon be tested.[17]

The man directly in charge of the trials was Justice Jackson's deputy at the IMT, the recently promoted Brigadier General Telford Taylor. He had graduated from Harvard Law School in 1932, and for the next decade built a promising career, advancing through a number of legal positions within the New Deal. In 1939, he was appointed Special Assistant to Robert Jackson, then Attorney General. Taylor attracted the attention of Henry Stimson during "the Great German War on the Potomac" when he argued that a great trial had the potential to do more than simply render justice: "it would give meaning to the war."[18] Justice Jackson felt that the trial's high aspirations would not be compromised under Telford Taylor's leadership. Like those who had provided the impetus for the first trial, the prosecution staff possessed a disproportionate number of Harvard law school graduates, former New Dealers, and liberal Democrats.[19]

The most famous and, to some Germans, infamous prosecutor was neither a Harvard graduate nor a New Dealer. He was a German Jew named Robert Kempner. In the early 1930s, Kempner worked in the legal division of the Prussian police department. His opposition to National Socialism led to his expulsion from Germany. For Kempner, the trials were personal; he was settling old scores. "This trial started in 1930 in Berlin when I was Chief Legal Advisor of the Prussian Police. At the time I had my first fights with Hitler and his consorts. The people in Prussia tried to suppress the Nazi Party and to send Hitler, as a kind of enemy alien, back to Austria."[20]

After Robert Kempner was forced to emigrate to the United States from Germany in 1940, he began to collect war crimes evidence on behalf of the Justice Department. His first-hand knowledge of German law and government made him valuable to the IMT, where he served as both an interrogator and a prosecutor. When he interrogated Hermann Goering, the man who had stripped him of his German citizenship, Goering was startled to see his old adversary. Kempner recalled, "First he didn't want to answer me, he said, 'You are biased against me.' So I said to him, 'Reichsmarshall, I am not biased against you, I am very happy, you threw me out on February 3, 1933. If you hadn't done it I would have been smoke through a chimney.' "[21] However, many would become critical of Kempner's heavy-handed interrogation methods. In one well-documented incident, Kempner threatened to turn Nazi Foreign Minister Joachim von Ribbentrop's former legal advisor, Friedrich Gaus, over to the Soviet Union unless he was willing to cooperate.

> Kempner: *Well, things aren't as simple as that. The Russians are interested in you. Do you know that?*
> Gaus: *The Russians?*
> Kempner: *Yes, as a professional violator of treaties.*
> Gaus: *No, that is not correct in the least. My God.*
> Kempner: *Well, let's finish for today. I'll tell you something . . .*
> Gaus (interrupting): *Don't extradite me to the Russians.*[22]

In the summer of 1946, Telford Taylor prepared to try two to four hundred high-ranking suspected war criminals. Five additional courtrooms were added to Nuremberg's Palace of Justice. The defendants in this second series of trials were a diverse mix. Although the laws that ultimately composed the London Agreement Charter were written with the leaders of the Reich in mind, they were also designed to "cast a wider net" of criminality so that bankers, industrialists, and diplomats could be charged with war crimes. The problem facing the subsequent proceedings was that if a court rejected the prosecution's expanded definition of international criminality, the heart of a number of cases would be removed. In an effort to give the greatest amount of credibility to the decisions, Justice Jackson suggested that civilian judges should preside over the courts,[23] but was thwarted by the newly appointed Supreme Court Chief Justice Fred Vinson. Clay recalled, "Great difficulty was experienced in obtaining qualified jurists for the courts and our hope of substantial representation from the federal judiciary was dashed by Chief Justice Fred Vinson's decision that federal court judges could not be granted leave for the purpose. It took a considerable period of time to obtain qualified jurists from the state judiciary system to form six courts."[24]

Some of America's most prominent jurists were beginning to turn against the war crimes trials. More important than their specific opinions was the emergence of a general conservative position that flatly rejected the presumptions of the Nuremberg trials. Chief Justice Harlan Fiske Stone described the IMT as "a high-grade lynching party . . . a little too sanctimonious a fraud to meet my old-fashioned ideas." He was especially incensed by his colleague Robert Jackson's "pretense that he is running a court or proceeding according to common law."[25] Robert Taft had criticized the Nuremberg trials in 1946 on the ground that they "accepted the Russian idea of the purpose of trials." He believed that "By clothing policy in the forms of legal procedure, we may discredit the whole idea of justice in Europe for years to come."[26]

By 1947, the tone of the criticism had changed. Conservative congressmen like John J. Rankin launched a broader and more conspiratorial, anti-Semitic attack on the Nuremberg trials from the floor of the U.S. House of Representatives: "I desire to say that what is taking place in Nuremberg, Germany, is a disgrace to the United States. Every other country now has washed its hands and withdrawn from this saturnalia of persecution. But a racial minority, two in a half years after the war closed, are in Nuremberg not only hanging German soldiers but trying German businessmen in the name of the United States."[27] Many midwestern isolationists felt that prominent American Jews (like Henry Morgenthau) had a disproportionately large say in American policy toward Germany.

Although the Morgenthau Plan was their favorite example, Nuremberg was a close second.

On the diplomatic front, certain quarters within the State Department had opposed war crimes trials from the very beginning. Author of the Long Telegram and the famous "Mr. X" article published in *Foreign Affairs* magazine in 1947, George Kennan was a bitter critic of American war crimes policy. He later characterized the Germans under the American occupation as "sullen, bitter, unregenerate and pathologically attached to the old chimera of German unity."[28] To the architect of containment, the IMT was nothing more than a pretentious sham that created confusion and tarnished American foreign policy with hypocrisy: "The only implication this procedure could convey was . . . that such crimes were justifiable and forgivable when committed by the leaders of one government, under one set of circumstances, but unjustifiable and unforgivable, and to be punished by death when committed by another set of government leaders under another set of circumstances."[29] For the United States to turn a blind eye to the cruelties of the Russian Revolution, collectivization, purges of the 1930s, and wartime atrocities would "make a mockery of the only purposes the trials could conceivably serve, and to assume, by association, a share of the responsibility for these Stalinist crimes themselves."[30] Kennan favored traditional military justice:

> I personally considered that it would have been best if the Allied commanders had had standing instructions that if any of these men fell into the hands of Allied forces they should, once their identity had been established beyond doubt, be executed forthwith. But to hold these Nazi leaders for public trial was another matter. This procedure could not expiate or undo the crimes they had committed.[31]

George Kennan viewed the Nuremberg trials with "horror." He and others in the State Department objected to both the war crimes trials and the basic premise underlying the American reform and reeducation program outlined by JCS 1067. In a wartime memo to the European Advisory Commission in London, Kennan had written that "whether we like it or not, nine tenths of what is strong, able and respected in Germany has been poured into those very categories" slated for reform.[32]

Kennan did not consider the Nazi tactics unique; the Germans were Europeans, after all. He believed that Nazi atrocities in Eastern Europe and Russia were consistent with the "customs of warfare which have prevailed generally in Eastern Europe and Asia for centuries in the past, they are not the peculiar property of the Germans."[33] However, Kennan had certainly been wrong about the Nazis and their intentions in April 1941, when he was a State Department officer posted at the American embassy in Berlin. He downplayed accounts of Nazi atrocities: "It cannot be said that German policy is motivated by any sadistic desire to see other people suffer under German rule. . . . Germans are most anxious that their new subjects should be happy in their care."[34] George Kennan also exhibited a strange unwillingness to consider whether or not the Nazi atrocities were *sui generis*. In a telling passage from his postwar memoirs, he wrote: "If others wish, in the face of this situation, to pursue the illumination of those sinister recesses in which the brutalities of war find their record, they may do so; the degree of relative guilt which such inquiries may bring to light is something of which I, as an American, prefer to remain ignorant."[35] Kennan preferred "to remain ignorant" while colleagues like OSS Chief Allen Dulles and General Edwin Siebert continued to enlist former Nazis to aid America against the Soviets.

Reinhard Gehlen, a former Nazi intelligence officer, provided the United States with exaggerated estimates of Soviet power and motives in the years immediately following World War II. He had anticipated Hitler's defeat and a struggle between the United States and the Soviet Union. In early March 1945, Gehlen and his senior officers microfilmed all the *Fremde Heere Ost* (military intelligence section of the General Staff) holdings on the Soviet Union, placed the data in steel drums, and buried them in the Austrian Alps. Once this task was complete, the officers surrendered to American counterintelligence agents.[36]

According to the Potsdam Agreements, the United States was obligated to send individuals involved in "Eastern" activities back to the Soviet Union. However, Generals Edwin Sibert and Walter Bedell Smith considered these intelligence assets too valuable to hand over.[37] According to Harry Rositzke, former CIA head of espionage in the Soviet Union, "in 1946 [U.S.] intelligence files on the Soviet Union were virtually empty."[38] As a result of this lack of basic information, Gehlen played a disproportionately large role in shaping American perceptions of Soviet military capabilities and intentions.[39] According to historian Hugh Trevor Roper, Reinhard Gehlen "lived on the primacy of the Cold War and on the favor of those American and German governments which believed in the primacy of the Cold War."[40] Historian Mary Ellen Reese writes: "Looking back it is easy to say that after waking to the fact that their former ally was implacably hostile, the United States overreacted, that the Soviets were in no position to wage war. But the fact is that the Americans did not know the degree of Soviet preparedness, a lack which played into Reinhard Gehlen's hands."[41] By late 1946, a duality was emerging in America's occupation policy.

Most of the American Nuremberg tribunals were presided over by retired state supreme court judges. Prosecution counsel Drexel Sprecher recalled that "Some of them were very good. . . . On the other hand, there were some judges that weren't. The War Department didn't have any real means of checking them out. . . . It was difficult to recruit top level judges, the Nuremberg Trials were not front page stuff after the first trial."[42] By 1947, General Clay was under pressure from the Department of the Army to finish the trials, and he set July 1, 1948 as the target date for completion.[43]

On October 25, 1947, the first indictment was filed against Nazi doctors, and the American Nuremberg trials took up where the IMT had left off.[44] Case One, *United States v. Karl Brandt*, charged Nazi doctors with war crimes for conducting medical experiments on humans for the *Luftwaffe* at the Dachau concentration camp. Defendant Karl Brandt had been Hitler's personal doctor before he was made an SS Major General and named Reich Commissioner of Health and Sanitation, the highest medical position in the Third Reich. Other defendants included the *Wehrmacht's* Chief of Medical Services, Lieutenant General Siegfried Handloser; the head Luftwaffe medical expert, Oskar Schroeder; Chief SS Surgeon Karl Gebhardt; and tropical medicine expert Gerhard Rose.[45] The doctors conducted experiments in which conditions of high altitude were simulated in low-pressure chambers. Inmates were immersed in extremely cold water for hours at a time. The doctors also infected concentration camp inmates with malaria, typhus, and other diseases in order to test tropical medicine vaccines.[46] Many died as a result of the experiments. In addition, some of the defendants were involved with the secret euthanasia programs that eliminated what they described as "useless eaters." Most victims were old, deformed, insane, or ill.

Although the indictment included conspiracy and crimes against humanity charges, the Brandt case was fairly straightforward because the defendants' actions were clear violations of a number of the Hague and

Geneva Convention articles.[47] Because the defendants could not dispute the facts of the case, some offered a superior orders defense, while others claimed to have been powerless to prevent the crimes. Karl Brandt and Wolfram Sievers had the most difficulty justifying their actions. The two doctors had carefully inspected hundreds of live concentration camp inmates before selecting 112 Jews for the skeleton collection at the Reich University at Strasbourg. The live victims were measured and photographed, then killed and sent to Strasbourg for defleshing and preservation.[48]

The tribunal, headed by Judge W. B. Beals of Washington State, handed down its decisions on August 19 and 20, 1947. The court rejected the defense of superior orders and the defendants' claims that they had been powerless to prevent the crimes. The unanimous opinion declared: "The protagonists of the practice of human experimentation justify their views on the basis that such experiments yield results for the good of society. . . . All agree, however, that certain basic principles must be observed in order to satisfy moral, ethical and legal concepts."[49] Probably the most significant thing to come out of the Brandt case was a ten-point set of scientific standards that required medical research on human subjects both to be voluntary and to lead to "fruitful results for the good of society."[50] Today, this set of rules appears to have been one of the Nuremberg trials' most enduring legacies. The sentences only served to bolster the stern tone of the tribunal opinion: seven defendants were sentenced to death, five to life, and three to prison terms; seven were acquitted.[51]

Luftwaffe Field Marshal Erhard Milch was the only defendant in Case Two. He was charged with allocating slave labor and participating in the Luftwaffe's medical experiments at Dachau.[52] Milch was charged under three counts: slave labor, war crimes, and crimes against humanity. The defendant was head of Hitler's Central Planning Board, the agency established to govern wartime production. The former Field Marshal conceded that many of the orders he had followed were violations of international law. His defense was a combination of military necessity and superior orders: "It was my duty toward my people to maintain my allegiance. I had sworn an oath to keep allegiance to Hitler, too."[53] His counsel, Dr. Bergold, contended that any protest would have effectively sentenced Milch to death.[54] The superior orders defense would be heard many times in the coming months as various defendants argued that

under a dictatorship there was only one leader. When the tribunal handed down their decisions on April 17, 1947, Milch was found not guilty on
the charges relating to the medical experiments and guilty on the slave
labor charges. He was sentenced to life in a unanimous decision.[55]

The judgment in *U.S. v. Oswald Pohl et al.* (the Pohl case) came on
November 3, 1947. Eighteen leading members of the Economic and
Administrative Department of the SS were charged with crimes arising
from their duties as concentration camp administrators. Their section
was also responsible for the allocation of labor for concentration camps,
factories, and mines.[56] Although the indictment in the Pohl case contained crimes against humanity and conspiracy charges, as in the Brandt
case, the prosecution had a solid, traditional war crimes case. The majority of the concentration camp administrators could not contest the mountains of documentary evidence and offered variations of the superior
orders defense.[57] The tribunal ruled firmly and unequivocally: "It was a
national Reich-approved plan for deliberate and premeditated murder on
a large scale." The judges pointed to the Nazis' careful accounting of the
defendants' personal property: "After the extermination, the victim's personal effects, including the gold in his teeth, were shipped back to the concentration camp and a report of 'death from natural causes' was made
out."[58]

The court was not swayed by the defense arguments. Their opinion
read: "Under the spell of National Socialism, these defendants today are
only mildly conscious of any guilt in the kidnapping and enslavement of
millions of civilians. The concept that slavery is criminal per se does not
enter into their thinking."[59] Four were sentenced to death, three to life,
nine to various prison terms, and three were acquitted. The judgments in
the first three cases followed the cautious precedent of the IMT. The convictions were for violations of the laws of war, not the more novel legal
constructions of the War Department.[60] However, legally speaking, these
were relatively simple cases compared to the *U.S. v. Josef Altstoetter* (the Justice case), *U.S. v. Ernst von Weizsaecker et al.* (the Ministries case), *U.S. v.
Alfried Krupp et al.* (the Krupp case), *U.S. v. Friedrich Flick et al.* (the Flick
case), and *U.S v. Carl Krauch et al.* (the Farben case).

The tribunal in the Justice case, with Oregon's James Brand presiding,
handed down its judgments on December 3 and 4, 1947. Case Three
promised to be an important test case for the more radicial charges of the
indictment. Nazi judges, prosecutors, and ministerial officers were

accused of "crimes committed in the name of law." Because the highest-ranking Nazi legal officials were dead (Minister of Justice Otto Thierack, President of the *Reichsgericht* Erwin Bumke, and People's Court President Roland Freisler), three Under-Secretaries of the Reich's Justice Ministry were also indicted.[61] The defendants included Franz Schlegelberger, Curt Rothenberger, Herbert Klemm, Chief Public Prosecutor of the Reich Ernst Lautz, three Chief Justices from the "Special Courts," and judges from Hitler's infamous "People's Courts."[62]

The defendants were charged with conspiracy, war crimes, crimes against humanity, and membership in a criminal organization. The prosecution's opening statement charged them with "judicial murder and other atrocities, which they committed by destroying law and justice in Germany, and then utilizing the emptied forms of the legal process for persecution, enslavement, and extermination on a vast scale." Although they did not actually commit the crimes, the defendants were held accountable for them because they were committed pursuant to Nazi legal decrees. When the prosecution introduced the *Nacht und Nebel* (Night and Fog) decree, they argued, "The dagger of the assassin was concealed beneath the robe of the jurist.."[63]

Witness Herbert Lipps described defendant and former Nazi Judge Rudolf Oeschey's courtroom manner: "Defendants were insulted by Oeschey in the most abusive manner and death candidates were told by Oeschey right at the beginning of their session that they had forfeited their lives."[64] Defendant Curt Rothenberger described the relationship between politics and law in a wartime memo: "The independent judge is a sad remnant of a liberalistic epoch. Law must serve the political leadership." Defendant Schlegelberger's novel defense would be heard many times in the coming months. He claimed to have stayed in the Ministry of Justice in order to prevent the Justice Department from being absorbed by Himmler's SS.[65] Because the defendants could not deny the existence of the legislation they had written and enforced, they attacked the indictment on the ground that it applied retroactive law. This was a classic legal tactic that would serve the Germans well in the coming years—when the facts are against you, argue the laws; when the laws are against you, argue the facts; when both are against you, attack the other side.

When the tribunal handed down its decisions on December 4, 1947, it was clear that they would take the broadest reading of their mandate. The court unanimously rejected a traditional reading of international law and argued instead that "The force of circumstance, the grim fact of worldwide interdependence, and the moral pressure of public opinion have resulted in international recognition that certain crimes against humanity committed by Nazi authority against German nationals constitute violations not alone of statute but also of common international law."[66] The tribunal unanimously rejected the defense of necessity: "Schlegelberger presents an interesting defense, which is also claimed in some measure by most of the defendants. . . . He feared that if he were to resign, a worse man would take his place. . . . Upon analysis this plausible claim of the defense squares neither with the truth, logic, or the circumstances."[67] The tribunal also addressed the *ex post facto* arguments put forward by the defense:

> It would be sheer absurdity to suggest that the ex post facto rule, as known to constitutional states, could be applied to a treaty, a custom, or a common law decision of an international tribunal, or to the international acquiescence which follows the event. To have attempted to apply the ex post facto principle to judicial decisions of common international law would have been to strangle the law at birth.[68]

The decision in the Justice case would be one of the high points for those who favored a broadened conception of international criminality at Nuremberg. The tribunal sentenced Franz Schlegelberger, Oswald Rothaug, Herbert Klemm, and Rudolf Oeschey to life, six others to prison terms, and acquitted four.[69]

After presiding in the Justice case, Judge James Brand was asked to stay on for a second trial. He declined but recommended his colleague and friend from Oregon, Robert Maguire. The attorney was at an American Bar Association meeting in Cleveland when he received the invitation. Robert Maguire was "flattered and pleased" by the offer and assumed that it was "an opportunity which comes only once in a lifetime."[70] He returned to Portland and told his partners that he would need a six-month leave of absence. Although a conservative Republican, Maguire was sympathetic to the views of the War Department. His father, Frank Maguire, had been a theosophist who embraced evolution, socialism, and women's suffrage. His mother, Kate Maguire, had been a pioneer social worker in the United States. It was with great excitement and a sense of purpose that the attorney boarded a converted navy frigate and set sail for Europe.[71]

Robert Maguire saw himself as part of the vanguard of the American reform and reeducation effort. After two weeks at sea, he and his wife, Ruth, disembarked in Bremerhaven on November 21, 1947. As they drove to Nuremberg, Maguire was struck by the damage wrought by the Allied air war: "Bremerhaven, Bremen, Giessen, and Frankfurt were terribly knocked about by bombs. Bridges were in ruins . . . factories gutted by fire or crumpled by bombs, houses and building blocks a mess of ruins, railroad yards torn up, with twisted cars and locomotives rolled off the right of way. . . . A sad, sad sight."[72] When they arrived in Nuremberg, he was greeted by similar destruction; the city was "literally pulverized. I should say that more than 90 per cent of the buildings are piles of brick, stone, mortar, twisted pipes and wire."[73] Maguire's first order of business was a visit with James Brand; the two were reunited at Nuremberg's social hub, the Grand Hotel. They walked through the old city and talked about the trials. Brand was leaving in a matter of days and took this opportunity to pass the torch to his old friend.[74] However, Maguire would not be assigned to a case until December 19, 1947.

In late November 1947, Robert Maguire flew to Berlin, where he met with General Clay and was assigned to a tribunal. The other two judges on his court, Leon Powers and William Christianson, were retired state supreme court justices (from Iowa and Minnesota, respectively). After the judges had been convened as a tribunal, the Supervisory Committee of Presiding Judges assigned them Case Eleven, *The United States Government v. Ernst von Weizsaecker*, which would come to be known as the Ministries or *Wilhelmstrasse* case. The indictment was filed on November 1, 1947 against Ernst von Weizsäcker, Gustav Adolf Steengracht von Moyland, Wilhelm Keppler, Ernst Wilhelm Bohle, Ernst Woermann, Karl Ritter, Otto von Erdmannsdorff, Edmund Veesenmayer, Hans Heinrich Lammers, Wilhelm Stuckart, Richard Walther Darré, Otto Meissner, Otto Dietrich, Gottlob Berger, Walter Schellenberg, Schwerin von Krosigk, Emil Puhl, Karl Rasche, Paul Koerner, Paul Pleiger, and Hans Kehrl. Of all the American Nuremberg trials, the Ministries case most closely resembled the IMT. Robert Maguire described the various defendants:

The head men of the Foreign Office, the Gaulitier [sic] of the Auslandes [sic] Organization, said to be the framers of the fifth columns, two or three of the top party men, Generals in the S.S., the Finance Minister, the head of the Reich Chancellory, several of the Reich's Kommisars [sic] who had charge of Austria, Czechoslovakia, Poland, Holland, Belgium, Denmark, and Norway; the head of the Dresdner Bank and two of the leading industrialists.[75]

Among other things, the Ministries case explored the culpability of bureaucratic leaders in a totalitarian state. As Robert Jackson had remarked in his opening statement before the IMT, "whatever else we may say of those who were the authors of this war, they did achieve a stupendous work in organization."[76] In many instances these were the "CEOs" of the Third Reich—the efficient bureaucrats who translated Hitler's words into deeds. But had they committed war crimes?[77] The answer to that question depended on the court's reading of their legal mandate. The diplomats and fifth columnists were the best candidates for the aggression and conspiracy charges since the IMT. However, the prosecution faced a daunting task—convincing a conservative American court both that the aggression and conspiracy charges were valid and that the defendants had violated them. Case Eleven was the prosecution's last hope for a crimes against peace conviction.

Telford Taylor opened the prosecution's case on January 7, 1948. The Chief Counsel derisively referred to the defendants as "the gentlemen of the *Wilhelmstrasse*." He recognized that convictions for aggression in the Ministries case could bolster the IMT's aggression precedent. Taylor told the tribunal, "We have indicted in this case the chief civil executives of the Third Reich. . . . Without their administration and implementation, and without the directives and orders which they prepared, no Hitler, no Goering, could have planned and waged aggressive wars."[78] In this case more than any other, the prosecution aggressively pressed for multiple convictions under the aggression charge. However, up to this point the court had not convicted a single person for aggression. Of the thirty-five defendants charged in the Farben case, Krupp case, and the High Command case, none had been convicted.[79] The defense was fully aware of the prosecution's need for legal innovation. Defendant Ernst von Weizsäcker's son, Richard, stated that "The prosecution depended largely on principles established in the main Nuremberg Trial, which were not codified but were based largely on natural right."[80]

During Hitler's early campaign of lightning wars (1939–41), the Foreign Office provided lists of alleged violations of neutrality that served as pretexts for the various Nazi invasions.[81] Eight of the Ministries case defendants were career diplomats who had risen through the ranks of the German Foreign Office. The most important case would be that of former State Secretary Ernst von Weizsäcker. He entered the German Foreign Office in 1921 and served for seventeen years in Switzerland, Denmark, Norway, and Berlin. Although he would later claim to loathe the boorish Nazis, he was a German nationalist and shared many goals with them: the repudiation of the Treaty of Versailles, a return to the status of a great power, and rearmament.[82]

After accepting the post of State Secretary in 1938, von Weizsäcker lent his diplomatic expertise to help orchestrate the Third Reich's absorption of her neighbors. Although he would present evidence that he had helped the German resistance, many questions remained. Most difficult to explain would be two memos from Heinrich Himmler to von Weizsäcker that authorized the deportation of a total of 6,000 French Jews to Auschwitz. In 1943, the defendant was named Ambassador to the Vatican, where he remained until the end of the war. In addition to keeping the Pope silent on the Final Solution, von Weizsäcker played a key role in the deportation of Rome's Jews. He would present one of the most legally and morally complex defenses of the Nuremberg trials. The court would be forced to reexamine their definition of resistance given the unique circumstances of the Nazi dictatorship. The von Weizsäcker case would also highlight the differences between legal and moral guilt.[83]

Defendant Wilhelm Keppler was not a Foreign Office aristocrat but a Nazi true believer. In 1927, he joined the National Socialist Party as an economic advisor and never left. In 1936, he was named Plenipotentiary for Austria, where he organized Nazi fifth columnists and delivered Hitler's ultimatum to Austrian President Wilhelm Milkas.[84] On his role in the Anschluss, SS Chief Heinrich Himmler gushed, "I would like to express to you, Keppler, once more, in writing, how you have accomplished a very difficult task under very difficult conditions, so clearly and bravely for the Führer. I do not have to reassure you that it will be a joy for me to allow SS men to work under your leadership in the future for these tasks."[85] When Germany invaded Poland, Hitler demanded the return of Danzig and the emancipation of "oppressed" German minorities.[86] Keppler played an important behind-the-scenes role: he and defendant Veesenmayer incited border incidents so that Germany would have a pretext for invasion.

The other two State Secretaries, Steengracht von Moyland and Ernst Bohle, were responsible for similar acts of "Germanism beyond the borders of the Reich."[87] From his position at the *Auslandsorganization*, Bohle directed fifth column activities. The other four members of the Foreign Office were lower in rank. Under-Secretary of State Ernst Woermann acted as von Weizsäcker's man in the field. In Czechoslovakia he provided military and financial assistance to the Sudeten German Party; in Poland he helped fabricate border incidents.[88] Ambassador Karl Ritter and Ministerial Dirigent Otto von Erdmannsdorf organized the actions of pro-Nazi groups.

The second group of defendants were Reich ministers involved in domestic policies. The highest-ranking official was Chief of the Reich Chancellery Hans Lammers, who had been a National Socialist since 1922. Lammers was the author and signatory of "legal" decrees that aided the Nazi consolidation of power.[89] These included the Enabling Act and the Reich Defense Law, both of which allowed Hitler to dissolve Germany's constitutional government. Of all the defendants, Lammers was involved in the broadest range of activities—everything from the exploitation of occupied territories to directives on captured pilots.

State Secretary Otto Dietrich was Josef Goebbels's rival in the Ministry of Propaganda. In his post as Minister of Public Enlightenment, Dietrich orchestrated the misinformation campaigns that preceded each invasion. German newspapers were ordered to print headlines like CONCENTRATION OF CZECH TROOPS ON THE BORDERS OF SUDETEN-LAND.[90] He was also an arch anti-Semite; he wrote, "In everything it must be established that the Jews are to blame! The Jews wanted war! . . . Naturally, those reports that do not lend themselves to anti-Semitic propaganda must be adapted for use as anti-Semitic propaganda." Dietrich condemned the Allied city bombing campaign in the strongest terms: "The further material on hand regarding the cynical utterances of our enemies on the air war is to be emphasized with full force, thus underlining once again England's responsibility for the terror methods in the conduct of war. In doing so, the case of the American Murder Corporation is to be brought up once again as proof . . . the war criminal Churchill will one day receive his punishment for his historical guilt."[91] Reich Peasant Leader and Minister of Food and Agriculture Richard Darré was the author of the "blood and soil decree."[92] In a letter Darré bragged that he had "created the prerequisites which made it possible for the Führer to wage his war as far as food is concerned."[93] Other long-time National Socialists were State Secretary to the Reich Ministry of Interior Wilhelm Stuckart and Presidential Chancellor Otto Meissner.[94] The economic mobilization had been so successful in restructuring the German economy to withstand the pressures of war that Plenipotentiary of the War Economy Walter Funk was moved to comment, "It is known that the German war potential has been strengthened very considerably by the conquest of Poland. We owe it mainly to the Four-Year Plan, that we could enter the war economically so strong and well prepared."[95]

The third group of defendants were involved in Hermann Goering's "Four-Year Plan." Paul Koerner left his job as an industrial engineer in 1931 to work for Goering. This personal association helped him rise to a position of prominence within the Reich. He joined the SS in order to help Heinrich Himmler place SS men in other sectors of the government. In 1936, when the Office of the Four-Year Plan took control of the economy, Koerner was named State Secretary for the Four-Year Plan.[96] In 1936, *Reichsmarshall* Goering stated that in "all current business concerning the Four-Year Plan, I shall be represented by State Secretary Koerner."[97] During the 1940s, Koerner shifted his focus to exploiting the resources of occupied territories. He worked for the Economic Staff East and sat on the Central Planning Board with Albert Speer and Walter Funk. Defendants Paul Pleiger and Hans Kehrl served as industrial and economic experts under Koerner.

The fourth group of defendants consisted of bankers involved in a variety of Nazi enterprises. One defendant, Karl Rasche, held a top position at the Dresdner Bank, which liquidated seized assets for the Nazis and financed the construction of concentration camps with low- or no-interest loans.[98] Schwerin von Krosigk was in charge of fiscal mobilization for the Minister of Finance.[99] He imposed fines against German Jews that totaled one billion Reichsmarks; when individuals were unable to pay, their property was expropriated and sold. Krosigk was also named a successor in Hitler's will. The other banker, Emil Puhl, had been vice president of the Reichsbank. Puhl issued an eight-million-Reichsmark loan to aid the expansion of the SS; the loan was low interest and the terms included the right to defer payment as long as necessary. Puhl said: "We agree that the credit in question cannot be considered from the viewpoint of ordinary business."[100] The Reichsbank also received seventy-six shipments of dental gold from Auschwitz. By the end of the war its vaults held thirty-three tons of gold teeth, rings, and glasses worth more than 60 million Reichsmarks.[101]

The SS was represented by Gottlob Berger, Walter Schellenberg, and Edmund Veesenmayer. A former gymnastics instructor, Berger was an ardent anti-Semite and proponent of the Final Solution. He had been one of Heinrich Himmler's experts on racial selection for the SS. In a wartime article, he wrote, "We the National Socialists believe the Führer when he says that the annihilation of *Jewry* in Europe stands at the end of the fight instigated by the *Jewish* World Parasite against us as his strongest enemy."[102] Berger was one of Himmler's favored "twelve apostles." He would have the most difficulty distancing himself from his unofficial sponsorship of his old comrade, Oskar Dirlewanger. Berger interceded to have Dirlewanger released from prison in 1939 to serve under General Franco in the Spanish Civil War. When Dirlewanger returned to Germany, Berger reinstated him as an SS colonel. In 1940, Dirlewanger began to train a regiment of convicted game poachers and criminals to wage antipartisan warfare in Eastern Europe.

Even Heinrich Himmler was moved to comment on their brutality: "I told Dirlewanger to choose men from the concentration camps and habitual criminals. The tone in the regiment is, I may say, in many cases a medieval one with cudgels and such things. If anyone expresses doubts about winning the war he is likely to fall dead from the table."[103] In 1942, after an SS police judge advocate named Conrad Morgen noticed a staggeringly high number of convictions for looting and assault among members of the Dirlewanger regiment, he inquired further. Morgen heard stories of Oskar Dirlewanger entertaining his men by injecting Jewish women with strychnine in the officers' mess hall and watching their death struggles.[104] Morgen issued a warrant for Dirlewanger's arrest, but once again his guardian angel, Gottlob Berger, intervened. Berger wrote Himmler in June of 1942, "Better to shoot two Poles too many than two too few. A savage country cannot be governed in a decent manner." Adolf Hitler concurred with Berger's view: "As it is, a poacher kills a hare and goes to prison for three months. Personally, I would take the fellow and put him in one of the guerrilla companies of the SS." Dirlewanger was awarded the Knight's Cross and given a second battalion so that by 1943, he commanded a brigade of approximately 4,000 men.[105]

Walter Schellenberg was a Waffen SS and former Police Brigadier General who went on to become the head of the military intelligence service of the SS and the Chief of Prisoner of War Activities on the eastern front. Schellenberg was a close personal friend and advisor of Heinrich Himmler until the end of the war. A fervent proponent of the Final Solution, he oversaw the capture of thousands of French Jews who were sent to Auschwitz. Schellenberg was also one of the few Nazis to mention "The Final Solution" in writing.[106] He had played an active role in the enforcement of the Commissar Order, as German historian Gerald Reitlinger writes: "it was found that the liquidation of Russian spies was handled by one of those pleasant little one-room offices of the RSHA and that this office came under Schellenberg's own foreign Intelligence service, AMT IV."[107] Although Schellenberg had gone out of his way to save a number of Jews from certain death in the last days of the war, would this mitigate his guilt?

Ministries case defendant Edmund Veesenmayer would have a very difficult time defending his wartime activities. Although he began in the Foreign Office, as the war progressed, he became a specialist in the deportation of Jews in nations occupied by the Third Reich. In September 1941, he signed a report recommending the deportation of Serbian Jews and then moved on to conduct similar operations in both Slovakia and Hungary. Veesenmayer was appointed Germany's Plenipotentiary in Hungary; he reported to both Ribbentrop in the German Foreign Office and Hans Kaltenbrunner in the Reich Main Security Office.[108] His main job between April and June 1944 was organizing the successful deportation of 381,600 Hungarian Jews to Auschwitz and other concentration camps.[109]

Unlike other contemporary examples of political justice, the Nuremberg trials worked from an unprecedented evidentiary base. Prosecutor Robert Kempner explained, "We had the documents and I had educated young officers, since 1941, on how to find the documents. This was very important from a political point of view because after the First World War the Allies had no documents."[110] Judge Maguire was struck by the quality of the evidence: "Our case is becoming very interesting, we are seeing the pages of history roll out from the confidential records made before the events occurred, and made by the main actors themselves."[111] As in the vast majority of the American Nuremberg trials, documentary evidence alone built a daunting *prima facie* case. The defense would have to raise doubts about the meaning of diplomatic correspondence in a dictatorship.

After the first week of the proceedings, Judges Maguire and Powers drove to Berchtesgaden. At their hotel, they were greeted by Hitler's court jester, "Putzi" Hafenstangel. Just as he had courted Hitler, Hafenstangel regaled his high-ranking audience with ribald tales of greed and decadence beyond their imagination.[112] The next morning the two judges made their way up the mountain in an army jeep, sloshing through mud and snow to Hitler's "Eagle's Nest" at Obersalzburg. Their tour guide was one of Hitler's former bodyguards, a battle-hardened SS veteran. Maguire wrote, "He had been in the German Army since he was fifteen, had won the Iron Cross in France and was transferred to the Waffen S.S. and for the last year of the war was a member of Hitler's bodyguard. He was a handsome youngster over six feet tall, spoke excellent English, and we enjoyed him very much."[113]

When the two judges reached Hitler's compound, they were struck by its opulence. Robert Maguire was moved to comment on the internal contradictions of National Socialism. "For a gentleman who was avowedly working for the good of the common people . . . he and his fellow workers did themselves very well indeed. There was a luxurious home for Hitler, one for Mussolini, one for Martin Bormann, another for Goering, and others for other top dogs; tremendous barracks for the bodyguard, covering acres of ground."[114] The Americans were more impressed by security provisions than by the structure itself. "I am of the opinion," Maguire reflected, "that if my efforts to save my countrymen necessitated bodyguards, tunnels, machine guns and the like to protect me from their enthusiasm, I would just let them stew in their own fat and go to perdition by their own road, free from interference on my part."[115] But Maguire's most important encounter with the remnants of the Third Reich was yet to come.

Among the first witnesses presented by the prosecution was Milada Radlova, daughter of Czechoslovakian President Emil Hacha. When President Hacha was summoned to Berlin in 1939 to discuss the future of Czech territory (Bohemia and Moravia), Radlova traveled to Berlin with him. She described an ominous late-night meeting with Hitler and Goering in the Reich Chancellory. According to Radlova, the Nazi leaders threatened to destroy Prague if Hacha did not capitulate. *The New York Times* described her testimony in the Ministries case:

Adolf Hitler and Hermann Goering shouted and threatened M. Hacha until, exhausted, he capitulated. . . . On his return at 5 A.M. the Czech was a broken man, pale and exhausted, the witness said. He informed her that he capitulated after Hitler had ranted and shouted for hours and Goering had assured him as an alternative to a signing of the proffered papers he would leave immediately and order the destruction of Prague by the Luftwaffe to demonstrate its efficiency to the Western powers.[116]

Further evidence on the pattern of German conquest was provided by the officials forced out during the Anschluss. Besides giving valuable evidence, these witnesses humanized the events. Theodore Hornbostel was head of the political division of the Austrian Foreign Office at the time of the Nazi takeover. Hornbostel refused to collaborate and as a result spent five years in a concentration camp. Judge Maguire was impressed by his somber demeanor: "He was very restrained in his testimony and his narration of what must have been most dramatic and tragic days of early March 1938."[117]

Next, the tribunal flew to Vienna, in the Russian zone of occupation, to take the deposition of former Austrian President Wilhelm Milkas, who was too sick and frail to travel to Nuremberg. Maguire was impressed by "the dramatic and tragic story of the fall of Austria, the delivery of the ultimatum, the actions of Keppler who was Hitler and Goering's agent in the affair, the forced resignation of Schuschnigg . . . the forced appointment of Seyss-Inquart."[118] In Austria, the Nazis coupled diplomatic demands with threats of force and Hitler staged a bloodless coup. But again, was this "aggression"? There was neither significant resistance nor actual military conflict. Did war crimes require actual combat? The fate of the aggression charges hinged on basic questions like these. The defense would contend that subversive diplomats like Ernst von Weizsäcker prevented war on the ground and should be viewed as heroes. Although they could not forestall the political takeover of nations like Austria and Czechoslovakia, they at least prevented their physical destruction.[119]

Encounters with men like Hornbostel and Milkas influenced the tribunal. These men had not supported the Nazi program until the eleventh hour and then, as the ship was sinking, joined the resistance. They had opposed Hitler from the beginning until the end. Maguire wrote, "Milkas is evidentially [sic] a man of high courage, he never resigned, he refused to recognize the Nazis, and he spoke with well justified bitterness of Austria's abandonment by the other nations."[120] What Milkas and Hornbostel provided for Maguire were standards against which to measure subsequent claims of resistance. The prosecution did not complete their cases until March. All of the participants at Nuremberg were distracted by the tumultuous political events of early 1948.

February 1948 marked yet another intensification in the Cold War. Two important events occurred that had a major impact on America's postwar foreign policy. The first was the Soviet takeover of Czechoslovakia. Up until 1948, the small nation was not clearly in the grasp of the Soviet Union. In mid-February, Klement Gottwald, leader of the Czech Communist Party, eliminated all opposition political parties. He then strengthened his hold on the government by filling the cabinet with fellow communists.[121] Military resistance was discouraged by the Red Army divisions poised on the border with the U.S.S.R. President Edward Benes and Foreign Minister Jan Masaryk were forced to surrender when a delegation of Soviet officials arrived in Prague. Two weeks later, Masaryk was dead; official Czech sources claimed he had committed suicide. Most people in the West believed that he had been murdered.[122]

A second major event occurred in late February: the Soviet Military Governor issued an order preventing access to Berlin. General Clay objected on the ground that this was a violation of the American right to access that had been assured by Marshal Zhukov. The next day the Soviets prevented freight from leaving Berlin.[123]

Lucius Clay had worked more closely with the Soviets than any other American official. Even as late as 1947, General Clay and Secretary of State James Byrnes remained convinced that cooperation with the Russians was possible. But Washington was moving in a different direction and expected General Clay to follow.[124] As the State Department became more and more involved in the affairs of Germany, Clay grew less and less comfortable with the direction of American policy. He attempted to resign in July 1947, writing in a letter to General Eisenhower, "I feel that State Department wants a negative personality in Germany. As you know, I can carry out policy wholeheartedly or not at all and there is no question left in my mind but that my views relative to Germany do not coincide with present policies."[125] Eisenhower shamed his old friend into staying on. According to Jean Smith, editor of General Clay's papers, "Clay got the message; henceforth, he realized that U.S. policy in Germany would march to a different drummer."[126]

Former Nazi spy Reinhard Gehlen and his operatives were still providing the Americans with estimates of Soviet military capabilities and intentions.[127] Gehlen was playing the Cold War to his advantage by making the United States rely so heavily on his organization for intelligence on the Soviet Union. The CIA's former head Soviet military analyst, Victor Marchetti, explained, "The agency [CIA] loved Gehlen because he fed us what we wanted to hear. . . . We used his stuff constantly, and we fed it to everybody else: the Pentagon; the White House; the newspapers. They loved it too. But it was hyped up Russian bogeyman junk, and it did a lot of damage to this country."[128] One can safely say that Gehlen's estimates were exaggerations, although that was not immediately obvious in 1948.

After these events, the Truman administration decided to reinstate the draft. Without an imminent threat to American national security, it was difficult to gain public support. Director of Army Intelligence Stephen Chamberlin met with General Clay in Berlin. Clay recalled, "He told me that the Army was having trouble getting the draft reinstated, and they needed a strong message from me that they could use in congressional testimony. So I wrote out this cable. I sent it directly to Chamberlin and told him to use it as he saw fit."[129] On March 5, the Director of Intelligence received General Clay's top-secret cable:

> For many months, based on logical analysis, I have felt and held that war was unlikely for at least ten years. Within the last few weeks, I have felt a sudden change in Soviet attitudes which I cannot define but which now gives me a feeling that it may come with dramatic suddenness. I cannot support this change in my own thinking with any data or outward evidence in relationships other than to describe it as a feeling of a new tenseness in every Soviet individual with whom we have official relation. I am unable to submit any official report in the absence of supporting data but my feeling is real. You may advise the chief of staff [Bradley] of this for what it is worth if you feel it is advisable.[130]

Clay was shocked and dismayed when the secret message was torn from context and leaked to the media (a portion of the cable first appeared in the *Saturday Evening Post*). He later recalled: "I assumed they would use it in closed session. I certainly had no idea they would make it public. If I had, I would not have sent it." But it was too late—the cable had had its desired effect. There was panic and alarm among civilians and officials; needless to say, the money for rearmament was allocated.[131] Historian Michael Howard later observed that a leaked "secret cable" became a new means by which American government officials could influence public opinion. This "was not to be the last occasion on which the American military were to try to influence congressional opinion by an inflated estimate of Soviet intentions and capabilities, but it may well have been the first and most significant."[132]

In its annual assessment of U.S. foreign policy, the State Department's Policy Planning Staff, headed by George Kennan, argued that America's reform and reeducation efforts in Germany had been a failure. The 1948 "Review of Current Trends in American Foreign Policy" declared: "we must recognize the bankruptcy of our moral influence on the Germans, and we must make plans for the earliest possible termination of those actions and policies on our part which have been psychologically unfortunate." The report also singled out the Nuremberg trials as a particular source of irritation and urged an end to them: "we must terminate as rapidly as possible those forms of activity (denazification, re-education, and above all the Nuremberg Trials) which tend to set us up as mentors and judges over internal German problems."

On June 18, 1948, President Truman approved George Kennan and his Policy Planning Staff's NSC Directive 10/2. The duality in American foreign policy was growing quickly.

> Political warfare is the logical application of Clausewitz's doctrine in time of peace . . . employment of all the means at a nation's command, short of war, to achieve its national objectives. Such operations are both covert and overt. They range from such overt actions as political alliances, economic measures . . . and "white" propaganda, to such covert operations as clandestine support of "friendly" foreign elements, "black" psychological warfare and even encouragement of underground resistance in hostile states.[133]

The Nuremberg trials' broadened conception of international criminality was challenged on February 19, 1948, when the tribunal in *U.S. v. Wilhelm List et al.* (the Hostage case) handed down their extremely conservative opinion. The Hostage case (Seven) and High Command case (Twelve) charged German generals with violations of the traditional laws of war (Case Twelve included aggressive war and conspiracy charges). The Hostage case accused senior Wehrmacht officers, including Field Marshal Wilhelm List and Lieutenant General Walter Kuntze, both of whom had commanded the Wehrmacht's Twelfth Army in Yugoslavia and Greece. Also charged was the head of the Second Panzer Army in Yugoslavia during 1942–43, General Lothar Rendulic. The other defendants were high-ranking German officers involved in atrocities against civilians in Yugoslavia, Albania, Norway, and Greece.[134] The court would examine the legality of defendant Maximilian von Weichs's 1941 "Hostage Order," which declared that one hundred Serbs would be shot for every German soldier harmed by partisans.[135] Accordingly, entire villages were burned while all the inhabitants were rounded up and slaughtered. Were these reprisals "proportional" to the crimes they sought to punish?

The four-count indictment charged German military leaders with traditional violations of the customary laws of war—the murder and mistreatment of civilians and the destruction of their property. Prosecutor Telford Taylor made the point that this was the first time since the IMT that German officers had been "charged with capital crimes committed in a strictly military capacity."[136] General Taylor admitted that in certain instances, reprisals were justified by the laws of war: "We may concede for purposes of argument that the execution of hostages may under some circumstances be justified, harshly as those words may ring in our ears." However, on the question of proportionality, the Germans had, in Telford Taylor's eyes, gone too far: "the law must be spared the shame of condoning the torrent of senseless death which these men let loose in southeastern Europe."[137]

Harry Wennerstrum, formerly of the Iowa Supreme Court, presided; all of the judges on the tribunal were midwesterners. This geographic distinction proved important, as the majority of the conservative judges came from the Midwest and the two most outspoken conservatives came from Iowa. Just as Judge Brand's opinion in the Justice case provided a model for those sympathetic to a broader view of international criminality, the opinion in the Hostage case became a model for conservative jurists at Nuremberg. The tribunal prefaced their judgment by explicitly narrowing their legal mandate—"it is not our province to write international law as we would have it,—we must apply it as we find it."[138] With many qualifications, the court rejected the idea that partisan or guerrilla forces were protected by the laws of war, and unanimously agreed that these groups fall into the same legal category as spies: "Just as a spy may act lawfully for his country and at the same time be a war criminal to the enemy, so guerrillas may render great service to their country and, in event of success, become heroes even, still they remain war criminals in the eyes of the enemy and may be treated as such." Finally, the tribunal ruled: "a civilian who aids, abets or participates in the fighting is liable to punishment as a war criminal under the laws of war. Fighting is legitimate only for the combatant personnel of a country. It is only this group that is entitled to treatment as prisoners of war and incurs no liability beyond detention after capture or surrender."[139]

Much to the chagrin of those nations occupied by the Third Reich, the tribunal, like the Lieber Code, defined "reprisal" very broadly: "The idea that an innocent person may be killed for the criminal act of another is abhorrent to every natural law. We condemn the injustice of any such rule as a relic of ancient times."[140] With this and other significant qualifications, the court concluded: "The occupant may properly insist upon compliance with regulations necessary to the security of occupying forces and for the maintenance of law and order. In accomplishment of this objective, the occupant may, only as a last resort, take and execute hostages."[141] The opinion in the Hostage case branded partisans "*franctireurs*" and provided few options for legitimate resistance under military occupation. "We think the rule is established that a civilian who aids, abets, or participates in the fighting is liable to punishment as a war criminal under the laws of war."[142]

The tribunal sentenced Field Marshal Wilhelm List and his successor, Lieutenant General Walter Kuntze, to life in prison; two defendants were acquitted, while the others were given terms of twenty years or less.[143] The court attempted to address the question of leniency in their opinion: "mitigation of punishment does not in any sense of the word reduce the degree of the crime. It is more a matter of grace than defense. In other words, the punishment assessed is not a proper criterion to be considered in evaluating the findings of the court with reference to the degree of magnitude of the crime."[144] Although the decisions in the Hostage case were very conservative, it would be wrong to assume that they were the result of political pressure. Members of the

American military seemed to sympathize with the plight of their German brethren. The once vindictive General Dwight Eisenhower testified in an affidavit that the German practice was not unique. The French had a similar decree "directing the shooting of five German hostages for every French soldier shot by snipers." These hostages were also shot without a trial.[145]

The judgment in the Hostage case marked a shift at Nuremberg. More courts began to adopt a conservative reading of Control Council Law No. 10. Politically, it was the safe thing to do because it was in line with America's overall German policy. A conservative position grounded in a positive reading of the laws of war was fast becoming the domain of midwestern judges. By 1948, the tension between some of them and the prosecutors and courtroom staff was growing. The prosecution team consisted of many Harvard Law School graduates and liberal New Dealers. Many in the courtroom staff (translators, etc.) were European, and some were Jewish. Some of the judges were suspicious and considered these individuals "vindictive." Years later, General Lucius Clay discussed this issue in his oral history:

> The British and French didn't have the same feeling towards the Nazis that we did. Neither one had a huge Jewish population that had developed a hatred you could well understand, which was true in this country. I'm not critical of it at all because I can understand how it developed. . . . Well, they went too far in their demands for denazification.

Clay described the American reconstruction program as "on the whole too vindictive a directive to have long suited the American people, because we're not a vindictive people."[146]

During the Hostage case there were some contentious exchanges between the prosecution and the bench. Although the issues tended to be trivial, the tone belied something deeper.[147] These long-simmering differences came to an ugly head on February 23, 1948, when the headline of the conservative *Chicago Tribune* read: IOWAN, WAR CRIMES JUDGE, FEELS JUSTICE DENIED NAZIS. Harry Wennerstrum, the presiding judge in the Hostage case, condemned the trial over which he had just presided as a "victor's justice" and placed the blame on the prosecution staff. Wennerstrum charged that "The high ideals announced as the motives for creating these tribunals have not been evident . . . the prosecution has failed to maintain objectivity aloof from vindictiveness, aloof from personal ambitions for convictions."[148] He went on to claim that the defendants were prevented from having a full and fair hearing because documents were not placed at the disposal of defense attorneys. Wennerstrum concluded by saying that if he had been aware of the character of the trials, he "would have never come."[149]

Although "vindictive" probably referred to Robert Kempner, the implicit target of this attack was Telford Taylor. Typically, the forty-year-old Brigadier General was a model of professional decorum; this time, he had been pushed too far. Although there had been strife between the prosecution and the judges during the proceedings, the presiding judge never made his deep reservations known. Wennerstrum waited until the day of his departure before granting an interview to Hal Faust of the *Tribune*. A friend of Taylor's in the U.S. Military Government's Press Office gave him the text of the article before wiring it to the United States for publication.[150] Ironically, General Taylor's response appeared in *The New York Times* on the same day as Wennerstrum's attack in the *Chicago Tribune*.

Brigadier General Taylor countered with a series of well-placed jabs. "If you in fact held the opinions you are quoted as expressing, you were guilty of grave misconduct in continuing to act in the case at all. In giving vent to these baseless slanders you have now fouled your own nest and sought to discredit the very judgment which you and your two distinguished colleagues have just rendered." Taylor took special offense at the charge that the trials were a victor's justice because the final task of rendering judgment was in the tribunal's hands:

> Your statement that these trials are teaching the Germans only that they lost the war to tough conquerors would be laughable if its consequences were not so likely to be deplorable. Your own tribunal, thanks to the wisdom, patience and judicial detachment of your colleagues, accorded the defendants a trial which can be an outstanding and sadly needed lesson to the Germans in respect to the rights of an accused person, and an unshakable demonstration that the Nuremberg trials are for justice, not for vengeance. The one great obstacle to your trial having this effect is the wanton, reckless nonsense which you yourself are quoted as uttering.[151]

The Chief Counsel pointed out the weakness of Wennerstrum's *ad hominem* attack: "Instead of making any constructive moves while you were here, you have chosen to give out a baseless, malicious attack during the last hours of your eight-month stay and then leave town rather than confront those whom you have so outrageously slandered." Taylor ended on a more personal note: "I would have used stronger language if it did not appear that your behavior arises out of a warped, psychopathic mental attitude. It is indeed fortunate that your unreasoning bias is so clearly on behalf of the defendants since, in that sense, it tends to reinforce the verdict of your tribunal rather than undermine it."[152]

This heated exchange reminded many Americans of the trials dragging on in their name. In Congress, Republican Representatives John Taber, Harold Knutson, Francis Case, and William Langer all believed that America's punitive war crimes policies were getting in the way of German reconstruction. Representative Taber contended that when he visited Germany, he found that "700,000 of their most active business people . . . were refused an opportunity to work because they were alleged to be Nazis." The Congressman's anti-Semitism was thinly veiled: "the trouble is that they have too many of these people who are not American citizens mixed up in those trials, and they are very hostile to Germans." Congressman Knutson asked, "Is it not just possible that these aliens who are employed by the Government to prosecute these cases do not want to let go of a good thing?" Taber agreed and added, "There is no question about that. On top of that, they do not have the right kind of disposition to create good will and get rid of the attitude that some of these people have had."[153] It was in Germany where the public American dispute over war crimes policy was read with the most interest and was perceived as a further indication of American "doubt" about their own war crimes program. General Taylor's prediction that Wennerstrum's charges "will be used by all the worst elements in Germany against the best" proved correct. A growing number of Germans viewed the second generation of critics' political attacks on the Nuremberg and Dachau trials as a sign that the Americans were abandoning their reform policies.[154]

It is telling that Wennerstrum's charges first appeared in the *Chicago Tribune*, while Taylor's response appeared in *The New York Times*. Diplomatic historian Thomas Schwartz notes the significance of this geographic distinction:

The conservative *Chicago Tribune*, with the remarks of Judge Charles Wennerstrum . . . made itself the mouthpiece of the critics of the Nuremberg trials. Wennerstrum's remark that 'some of the Nuremberg prosecutors had become Americans only in the last few years' provided further flammable material. This not subtle reference to the role which Jewish immigrants played in the prosecution apparently found its confirmation when it was reported Kempner had tried to intimidate a witness in the Ministries Case.[155]

War crimes historian Frank Buscher writes: "Wennerstrum's remarks to the *Chicago Tribune* were welcomed by German opponents of the war crimes program. Wennerstrum's action, primarily aimed at an American audience, kindled further German, anti-Nuremberg sentiments. For those Germans opposed to the trials, the fact that Americans were publicly debating these trials seemed to indicate a decreasing U.S. commitment to the proceedings."[156]

Proponents of the American Nuremberg trials were fortunate to have a spokesman as able as Telford Taylor. In the coming years he would be called upon numerous times to set the record straight. But more important, neither he nor General Clay caved in to growing political pressure to cut the proceedings short. Despite February's tumultuous events, the Ministries case moved forward at full speed. The prosecution presented its case throughout January, February, and March, introducing 3,442 documentary exhibits and the testimony of 70 witnesses. Because of external pressure, the court did its best to speed the proceedings. At one point, Maguire presided in order to ease Judge Christianson's burden. The tribunal also held night and weekend sessions.[157] When Robert Maguire was not in court, he was at home reading documents.

Despite the geopolitical shifts, Judge Maguire remained unswayed: "The object of these cases is not to take revenge on a defeated enemy, but it is to make clear to the world that those who plan and start aggressive wars and invasions of other countries and who inflict untold sorrow and loss to their neighbors cannot do so without being held personally responsible for these wrongs."[158] In words that could have come from Robert Jackson himself, Maguire wrote: "The goal sought is to set out by judicial process standards of International law and justice which it is hoped will be listened to and form finally an enlightened world opinion which will tend to prevent others from doing these things which we all know to be wrong." The conservative Republican remained unconvinced by the anti-Soviet siren song. He wrote in late March 1948, "I don't think Russia wants war, nor do I believe that for a sizable number of years, she could wage war, but that short of going to war she will do everything she can to get everything she can."[159] This view was not shared by all of the tribunal's members.

The first sign of a divergence of opinion within the tribunal came when Dr. Kubuschok of the defense offered a motion to dismiss Count 4 of the indictment (Crimes Against German Nationals 1933–1939) on the ground that it fell outside the court's jurisdiction. This was a major challenge, a test to see how this individual tribunal intended to interpret Control Council Law No. 10. In the Justice case, the court broadened the laws of war to include these acts. Their opinion read:

> It no longer can be said that violations of the laws of war are the only offenses recognized by common international law. The force of circumstance, the grim fact of world-wide interdependence, and the moral pressure of public opinion have resulted in recognition that certain crimes against humanity committed by Nazi authority against German nationals constituted violations not alone of statute but also of common international law.[160]

However, according to a "positivist" reading of the laws of war, the Nazi persecution of German Jews was not a war crime because it did not occur during wartime and the acts were committed by Germans against their own nationals. They may have been violations of German constitutional law, but they were not violations of a conservative reading of the laws of war.

Though opposed by the other two members of the tribunal, Judge Maguire did not want to dismiss the charge. He wrote to James Brand, the presiding judge in the Justice case, about the disagreement. Brand wrote back and urged his friend not to abandon his position: "I am especially glad to hear that you did not go along with your colleagues in their narrow construction of crimes against humanity committed by a government against its own nationals."[161] As he had done in the opinion of the Justice case, Brand shrugged off the charges of retroactivity: "I believe that it is too late in history for anyone to claim that governmentally organized persecution on racial, religious, or political grounds may not become a matter of international concern justifying punishment."[162] Judge Maguire was ultimately outnumbered and overruled; on March 26, 1948, Count 4 was dismissed. This was only a preview of the legal battles to come.

By the time the prosecution finished presenting their case, it was obvious that Judge Powers viewed his role and that of the court differently from Judge Maguire. If James Brand was Robert Maguire's role model, Harry Wennerstrum was Leon Powers's role model. During the debate over Count 4, Powers maintained that the acts of persecution had taken place prior to the outbreak of war; thus, they were not war crimes. Former prosecution counsel Walter Rockler was a young attorney who had served with the marines in the Pacific. He recalled, "There was another judge on the court—Powers—of whom I have a totally different view. . . . He thought maybe you could convict a man for outright murder at the point of a pistol, but everybody else was innocent." The prosecution rested its case on March 29, 1948, as the defense prepared to counter the numerous documentary exhibits introduced.[163]

By the time the Ministries case reconvened, a verdict had been rendered in Nuremberg's most sensational trial, the *Einsatzgruppen* case. These units were among the most brutal to fall under the black rubric of the SS. The twenty-four defendants were accused of killing more than one million people.[164] The prosecution's entire case consisted of captured documents that were among the most incriminating documentary evidence presented in any of the trials. This report from Minsk, Russia was typical: "In the city of Minsk, about 10,000 Jews were liquidated on 28 and 29 July, 6,500 of whom were Russian Jews—mainly old people, women and children." Waldemar Klingelhoefer reported from the Soviet Union in 1944: "Nebe ordered me to go from Smolensk to Tatarsk and Mstislavl to get furs for the German troops and liquidate part of the Jews there. The Jews had already been arrested by order of the *Hauptsturmfuehrer* Egon Noack. The executions proper were carried out by Noack under my supervision."[165] The weight of the evidence was such that the prosecution called no witnesses. Prosecutor Ben Ferencz took only two days to present 253 captured documents.[166] The political tides might be turning, but there were certain Nazi acts that were considered crimes under any circumstances.

Defendant Otto Ohlendorf gained a great deal of notoriety after his appearance at the IMT. When asked how many Jews his troops killed in

Crimea and the Ukraine, Ohlendorf calmly admitted, "Ninety thousand." Ohlendorf claimed that the killings were committed out of military necessity: "I believe that it is very simple to explain if one starts from the fact that this order did not only try to achieve security but also a permanent security for the reason that the children were people who would grow up and surely, being the children of parents who had been killed, they would constitute a danger no smaller than the parents."[167] When defendant Walter Blume was asked whether he knew the killing of civilians was contrary to the laws of war, he replied, "I already stated that for me the directive was the Fuehrer Order. That was my war law." Blume added a Cold War–inspired dig: "I was also fully convinced and am so even now, that Jewry in Soviet Russia played an important part and still does play an important part, and it has the especial [sic] support of the Bolshevistic dictatorship."[168]

In his closing statement, Telford Taylor outlined the five common defense arguments (reprisals, superior orders, no personal participation, military necessity, and the obsolescence of the laws of war).[169] Judge Musmanno's voice was charged with emotion as he read the verdict: "Although the principal accusation is murder and, unhappily, man has been killing man ever since the days of Cain, the charge of purposeful homicide in this case reaches such fantastic proportions and surpasses such credible limits that believability must be bolstered with assurances a hundred times repeated."[170] The court deemed the atrocities "so beyond the experience of normal man and the range of man-made phenomena that only the most exhaustive trial . . . could verify and confirm them."[171] The tribunal handed down the sternest rulings of all the American Nuremberg trials: thirteen death sentences, two life terms, five prison sentences, and one acquittal. The judges seemed especially incensed by the fact that cultured Europeans, like the former economist Otto Ohlendorf, were capable of such horrifying acts and offered a cultural justification for the severity of the sentences: "The defendants are not untutored aborigines incapable of appreciation of the finer values of life and living. Each man at the bar has had the benefit of considerable schooling. Eight are lawyers, one a university professor. . . . One, as an opera singer, gave concerts throughout Germany before he began his tour of Russia with the *Einsatzkommandos*."[172]

The court also addressed the Cold War–inspired defense arguments that equated the Allied city bombing with the crimes of the Einsatzgruppen. "Then it was charged that the defendants must be exonerated from the charge of killing civilian populations since every Allied nation brought about the death of non-combatants through the instrumentality of bombing." According to the opinion, whatever suffering German civilians had been subjected to was unfortunate collateral damage: "Any person, who, without cause, strikes another may not later complain if the other in repelling the attack uses sufficient force to overcome the original adversary. That is a fundamental law between nations as well."[173] The tribunal pointed out an important fact that clearly distinguished U.S. atrocities from those of the Third Reich—when Germany and Japan surrendered, the killing from above stopped. "The one and only purpose of the bombing is to effect the surrender of the bombed nation. The people of the nation through their representatives may surrender and with surrender, the bombing ceases, the killing is ended." In the case of the Third Reich, in most instances, with surrender, the numbers of civilians killed increased. "With the Jews it was entirely different. Even if the nation surrendered they still were killed as individuals."[174] An important objective of the Nuremberg trials was to create an irrefutable record of Nazi atrocities, and the American trials seemed to be on their way to accomplishing this. However, few of the war crimes were as clear cut as those of the Einsatzgruppen.

The case of Ernst von Weizsäcker was anything but clear. When German legal theorist Carl Schmitt was being interrogated at Nuremberg, he was asked by Robert Kempner what he thought of the fact that von Weizsäcker's initials appeared on so many incriminating documents. Schmitt appeared genuinely surprised:

> Kempner: *How do you explain that a diplomat like von Weizsaecker, as a state secretary, signed hundreds of such things?*
> Schmitt: *I would like to give you a nice answer. The question has great significance, a distinguished man like von Weizsaecker. . . . Only I must protect myself.*[175]

Ernst von Weizsäcker's lawyers claimed that the former State Secretary was "a Christian, an honest diplomat, a true patriot." They did not contest the fact that his initials were on a number of incriminating documents and instead argued that "political conditions under the Hitler dictatorship diminish the value of documentary evidence."[176] Under this reading of the law, things meant the exact opposite of what they appeared to mean. The defense contended that "a diplomatic document cannot be understood without expert interpretation and full knowledge of the historical and political facts." The prosecution derided the strategy as the "Dr. Jekyll and Mr. Hyde" defense.[177] With the exception of Alfried Krupp, Ernst von Weizsäcker launched the most sophisticated defense effort of the Nuremberg trials. The German diplomat's five-man team was led by Helmutt Becker and American Warren Magee. They were aided by Albrecht von Kessel, formerly of the German Foreign Office; Sigismund von Braun; and the defendant's son, Richard von Weizsäcker, the future President of the Federal Republic of Germany. The defense would contend that von Weizsäcker accepted the job of State Secretary as a "nonenrolled member" of the active German resistance.[178]

In 1938, Ernst von Weizsäcker reached a personal and professional crossroads when he was offered the job of State Secretary, officially second only to Joachim von Ribbentrop in the foreign policy establishment. Attorney Helmutt Becker attempted to portray his client as a leading member of the "political resistance" who used his position in the Foreign Office to soften the blow of Hitler's policies. This was done through the power of appointment and by leaking information about Hitler's plans to diplomats from other nations. Through the power of appointment, von Weizsäcker was also able to provide a safe harbor for officials conspiring against the Nazis.[179] The diplomat's defense team rejected the prosecution's narrow definition of resistance:

> 1). A resister is someone with a political philosophy, which, whatever it may be, is clearly and honestly opposed to the philosophy and ideology of Nazism. 2). Resistance requires active intent to remove Nazism from power and influence by revolutionary action or active participation in, incitement to, or preparation for such action. This would usually, if not necessarily, include political planning or preparation of a policy which is to replace the removed one. 3). Active prevention and/or sabotage of such measures and propaganda which made Nazism what it is.[180]

The defense faced a dilemma: some of the strongest evidence supporting von Weizsäcker's claims of resistance was the testimony of the members of the British Foreign Office with whom he claimed to have negotiated in 1938–39. According to Richard von Weizsäcker, "But now the British foreign office ordered these men to keep silent. Most of them obeyed to our detriment."[181] One British diplomat who stepped forward to defend von Weizsäcker was Lord Halifax, the former British Foreign Secretary.

The former State Secretary claimed that he accepted a promotion to State Secretary in an attempt to gain a better position to work from within. According to German diplomatic historian Klemens von Klemperer, "Weizsäcker no doubt pursued what Hans Ruthfels called a *Sonderpolitik* designed to protect the integrity of the Foreign Service and especially to counteract the aggressive plans of the Foreign Minister, von Ribbentrop, and thus prevent the great war."[182] Von Weizsäcker stated that more than anything else, he had wanted to prevent the outbreak of war. His son would later ask, "What price must a man pay for deciding not to abandon his post—and thus collaborate—in order to exert some influence from his position so as to change policy into something more acceptable and bring about change, or at least to prevent worse?"[183] In the end, the defense would concede that Ernst von Weizsäcker failed in his effort to preserve the peace but argued that he should be judged by his intentions.

The former State Secretary had played a central role in the German takeover of Czechoslovakia in 1939,[184] demanding concessions from the Czechoslovakian government for that nation's German population. At the same time, he instructed the leader of the Sudeten German Party, Konrad Heinlen, to reject the government's overtures in order to provide the Nazis with a pretext for intervening. When President Emil Hacha was summoned to Berlin, he was ordered to sign an agreement incorporating Bohemia and Moravia into the Reich. If Hacha refused, Czechoslovakia faced invasion.[185]

The defense would have the most difficult time with the charges under the rubric of crimes against humanity. The evidence consisted of a March 9, 1942 letter from Heinrich Himmler informing the Foreign Office of his intention to deport a thousand French Jews to Auschwitz. Von Weizsäcker was asked, point-blank, whether he had any objections— he had none. Two days later, a second request, to send another five thousand French Jews, arrived. The German embassy in Paris replied again, "no objection," and the response was initialed by defendants von Weizsäcker and Ernst Woermann. Ernst von Weizsäcker commented on the plight of Europe's Jews during cross-examination: "Hitler's persecu-tion of the Jews was considered by me from its inception to be a violation of all the rules and laws of Christianity. . . . As far as I was concerned, it was always a higher aim and interest which was of decisive importance; that is to work within the office in favor of peace and to overthrow the Hitler regime, because without peace and without the overthrow of the Hitler regime, the Jews could not be saved anyway."[186]

When the Nazis occupied Rome in 1943, Ernst von Weizsäcker was named ambassador to the Vatican. His main duty was to preserve a Faustian pact between the Third Reich and the Pope: the Nazis would respect the Vatican's "extraterritoriality" if the Pope remained silent about the Final Solution.[187] This pact was tested in the fall of 1943 when the SS began to round up Rome's Jews for deportation to Auschwitz. Ernst von Weizsäcker wrote Berlin in late October 1943 to report on the deportation:

> The Pope, although under pressure from all sides, has not permitted himself to be pushed into a demonstrative censure of the deportation of the Jews of Rome. Although he must know that such an attitude will be used against him by our adversaries . . . he has nonetheless done everything possible even in this delicate matter in order not to strain relations with the German government and the German authorities in Rome. As there apparently will be no further German action taken on the Jewish question here, it may be said that this mat-ter, so unpleasant as it regards German-Vatican relations, has been liq-uidated.[188]

Did Ernst von Weizsäcker cross an ethical point of no return? How far could the defense of necessity stretch?

The majority of the defendants charged with crimes against peace were members of the Foreign Office. Weizsäcker and Woermann were stationed in the main office, while Keppler, Veesenmayer, Ritter, and Erd-mannsdorf served as their field operatives. The latter group did the advance work for nearly all of the German invasions. What made the aggression charges relevant in Case Eleven was that the Nazis had gone to great pains to provide pretexts justifying each invasion. As Telford Tay-lor remarked in his opening statement, "These German diplomats of aggression, however, wore the mantle of diplomacy to cloak nefarious policies which were solely directed towards the realization of the criminal aims of the Third Reich. Their conduct violated every cardinal principle of diplomacy."[189]

Austrian Nazi leader Seyss-Inquart was furnished with a telegram asking the Germans to "send troops to put down disorder."[190] The takeover of Czechoslovakia was done in the name of the violated civil rights of Sudeten Germans. The invasion of Poland was justified by similar claims of aiding oppressed Germans and reclaiming long-lost territory. Once again, staged border incidents made it appear as if the Nazis were coming to the aid of beleaguered German ethnic minorities in foreign countries. Belgium, Holland, Luxembourg, and France were all accused of violations of neutrality.[191] The invasion of Russia was described as a preventative war. It was not as if the Germans had announced their intention to dominate Europe and employed only brute military force to achieve that end. The Nazis coupled bad-faith diplomacy with military force; the result was a brutally effective foreign policy.

By far Ernst von Weizsäcker's strongest support came in the form of testimony and depositions from credible character witnesses who claimed that the State Secretary had been in touch with Admiral Wilhelm Canaris and other resistance leaders. Hans Gisevius submitted an affidavit claiming the State Secretary spoke with General Beck, Lord Mayor Goerdeler, Admiral Canaris, General Oster, and Ambassador Ulrich von Hassell about the "overthrow of the regime."[192] Other dignitaries who testified on Ernst von Weizsäcker's behalf included Neils Bohr, Karl Barth, and General Canaris's widow. One witness who had a great impact on the tribunal was Bishop Eivind Bergrav, a leader of the Norwegian resistance. Bergrav had been captured and imprisoned by the SS; despite a terminal illness, he came to Nuremberg to testify in strong support of the former State Secretary:

> I know that Weizsaecker fought to preserve peace. I know that he remained in office, as I said, in an effort to prevent Nazi excesses and to bring about a just peace. I did this because of my strong feeling of the duty of helping the Tribunal to create full justice toward this man, and because it is my conviction that he is a man who has always been as much opposed to the Nazi regime as I myself have been.[193]

The trial was again interrupted by the Cold War on June 24, 1948, when the Soviets cut all access to Berlin. For several weeks it seemed that the United States and the U.S.S.R. might go to war. On July 19, General Clay sent a top-secret cable to Theodore Draper. The Military Governor no longer needed to be convinced of a Soviet threat. He reflected that "the world is now facing the most vital issue that has developed since Hitler placed his political aggression under way. In fact the Soviet government has a greater strength under its immediate control than Hitler had to carry out his purpose. Under the circumstances which exist today, only we can exert world leadership. Only we have the strength to halt this aggressive policy here and now."[194]

The blockade affected the trial in two ways. First, there was continued pressure from the War Department to bring the proceedings to a close. But by 1948, the Cold War had entered the courtroom. Visiting American politicians applied direct pressure on trial officials. Prosecutor William Caming recalled that

> Visiting Congressmen clearly conveyed the sentiment to the politically sensitive Military Government of the U.S. Zone under General Lucius Clay. That sentiment was also bluntly asserted to the prosecution staff and to the judges in private conversations and in the form of regret that the real enemy, Russia, was growing stronger and the trials were further weakening efforts to restore Germany to the necessary economic viability that would permit her to serve as a bulwark against communism.

Caming also mentioned a change in "the prosecutory climate": "The defendants and their counsel harped on the themes that the USA had made a grave mistake in intervening before Germany destroyed Russia; Bolshevism and its enmity to the West were the real threats."[195] After the Berlin blockade, the final resting place of many defense arguments was a combination of *tu quoque* and "we told you so." However, by 1948 these arguments had more resonance than similar objections leveled at the IMT in 1946. The Cold War rhetoric, coming from "responsible American statesmen," confirmed the darkest suspicions of German nationalists and die-hard Nazis. The Germans were masterfully playing the politics of the Cold War to their short-term advantage, displaying what Jörg Friedrich calls "retroactive opportunism."[196]

Defendant Hans Lammers's lawyer was none other than Alfred Seidl, who had gained notoriety during the IMT for releasing the secret portions of the Hitler-Stalin Pact. He described Lammers as the "notary public" of the Reich; even though the defendant's signature appeared on the Enabling Act and other important pieces of Nazi legislation, this meant little. It was an inversion of the *respondeat superior* defense. Seidl maintained that Lammers was not an "active" participant in the enforcement of these decrees, only the author.[197] Seidl made the most of the opportunities provided by the escalating Cold War, offering a revisionist interpretation of Operation Barbarossa:

> All these documents permit the conclusion, at least, that the Chief of the Reich Chancellory could be personally convinced in the year 1941 that the measures being taken by the Russians . . . would make necessary and would justify precautionary measures by the Germans. The development of international relations after the conclusion of World War II . . . has proved, in a way that could have hardly been expected or seemed possible, how justified Dr. Lammers was in his assumption.[198]

The Chief of Prisoner-of-War Activities, Gottlob Berger, had a difficult time covering up his wartime actions. Under cross-examination, Berger claimed that he had not heard of the Final Solution until after his capture. When the prosecution placed him at Posen in 1943 (during Himmler's speech on the Final Solution), his counsel offered the excuse that "he does not think the word 'extermination' was used with regard to Jews."[199] His attorney asked rhetorically: "Was it really only a craze for the 'master race' which claimed the blood of millions of people? Are there not still forces at work, the same as there were ten years ago—ideology which, in conjunction with military power of a dimension not even recognized today, are stretching out their claws to pull down everything in the turmoil of wild chaos?"[200] Berger's lawyer invoked the Cold War as a factor mitigating German guilt: "The struggle against Bolshevism was the leading motive of Berger's SS policy and it is on these grounds that the American prosecutor-in-chief is today indicting him on the charge of crimes against humanity. Perhaps the prosecution is unaware of the weakness of its position, but it may not be aware of the entire foundation on which it bases this charge, and events may take place tomorrow that force the prosecutor's own land to tread the same path in the near future."[201]

Those who had not violated the traditional laws of war had a much easier time defending themselves. Although former Propaganda Minister Otto Dietrich had led a "Campaign against world Jewry" on the radio, his attorney attributed this action to "wartime passions."[202] Von Krosigk, Puhl, and Rasche—the bankers who had helped finance the German rearmament and war effort—used a similar strategy. They admitted that they had aided the rearmament but questioned whether this was a crime. Even though Karl Rasche had been the chairman of the board of the Dresdner Bank and a member of Himmler's "Circle of Friends" who had actively participated in the economic plunder of Czech banks, his defense attorneys completely rejected the idea of a criminal conspiracy and assumed that the court would do the same. The fates of these three seemed more secure than those of any other defendants.[203] The IMT acquitted banker Hjalmar Schacht in the American trials, and the white-collar criminals received light sentences (in the Flick and Farben cases, and to a lesser extent in the Krupp case).[204]

Of all the American Nuremberg trials, the Flick (Five), Farben (Six), and Krupp (Ten) cases were the most dependent on a broadened conception of international criminality. The directors of the industrial companies were charged with playing a vital role in the German rearmament effort. The most conventional charge was mistreating slave labor, which the Hague Conventions expressly prohibited.[205] The entire board of directors (*Vorstand*) and its chairman, Hermann Schmitz, were indicted in the Farben case. In addition to the novel crimes against peace charge, the twenty-three industrialists were charged with plunder and spoliation, slavery and mass murder, conspiracy, and membership in a criminal organization.

Defendant Carl Krauch had been a confidant of and important advisor to Hermann Goering.[206] The I. G. Farben Company constructed and operated a "Buna," or synthetic rubber plant, on the premises of Auschwitz. The defendants sat on the board of directors and played integral roles in Germany's rearmament and the Four-Year Plan. The prosecution maintained that the "Four-Year Plan was a 75 percent Farben project."[207] Other defendants included the chairman of the board, Hermann Schmitz, and other board members, Georg von Schnitzler and Fitz Ter Meer.[208] The prosecution attempted to prove that most of the defendants had visited the I. G. Farben factory at Auschwitz and knew that inmates were being systematically killed and horribly mistreated. Defendants Ambros, Buetefisch, and Duerrfeld were all involved in the planning and execution of the Farben Auschwitz project. Defendant Ter Meer regularly discussed the allocation of slave labor with Auschwitz commandant Rudolf Hoess. Ernst Struss, the secretary of the I. G. Farben board, testified that he had heard from Farben's chief engineer at the Auschwitz plant "that before the burning, they were gassed."[209] A British POW who had survived Auschwitz provided especially dramatic testimony: "The population of Auschwitz was fully aware that people were being gassed and burned. On one occasion they complained about the stench of burning bodies." The witness found it laughable that the defendants were now claiming that they knew and saw nothing. "Of course, all of the Farben people knew what was going on. Nobody could live in Auschwitz and work in the plant, or even come down to the plant without knowing what was common knowledge to everybody."[210] This testimony undercut the defense claims of defendants like Otto Ambros, who visited the Auschwitz plant eighteen times yet maintained that he had no idea what was going on at the death camp. Further damning evidence was the testimony of the head of Farben's internal security, who claimed that in the final days of the war, he burned more than fifteen tons of incriminating documents.[211]

Counsel for the accused also offered the defense of necessity. Both Field Marshal Erhard Milch and industrialist Friedrich Flick testified that in Hitler's Third Reich, one had to utilize slave labor to meet production quotas or face the death sentence of "undermining fighting spirit."[212] This argument was most successful when the defense sought to portray their clients as white-collar executives: "Replace I. G. by I.C.I. for England, or DuPont for America, or Montecatini for Italy and at once the similarity will become clear to you."[213] The attorney for defendant Carl Krauch believed that the Cold War proved "How right Hitler was in this outline of his policy." Again, the defense offered a Cold War–inspired *tu quoque* argument, that the correctness of Hitler's policies was "confirmed by the political situation which has developed in recent months in Europe."[214]

The trial ended on May 12, 1948, and the tribunal was left to weigh 16,000 pages of transcripts, the testimony of 189 witnesses, and 2800 affidavits. It became clear that the decision would be split when Judge

Hebert asked for extra time to file a dissenting opinion.[215] When the judgment was handed down on July 29, 1948, the tribunal split along geographic lines, and once again the conservative push came from midwestern jurists. Judge Curtis Shake, former member of the Indiana Supreme Court, and Judge James Morris, former member of the North Dakota Supreme Court, were unconvinced by the evidence and acquitted all the defendants on the crimes against peace and conspiracy to commit crimes against peace charges. The tribunal majority imposed extremely light sentences[216] and rejected the aggression and conspiracy counts (1 and 4): "The prosecution, however, is confronted with the difficulty of establishing knowledge on the part of the defendants, not only of the rearmament of Germany but also that the purpose of rearmament was to wage aggressive war. In this sphere, the evidence degenerates from proof to mere conjecture."[217] The majority also accepted the defense of necessity: "There can be little doubt that the defiant refusal of a Farben executive to carry out the Reich production schedule or to use slave labor to achieve that end would have been treated as treasonous sabotage and would have resulted in prompt and drastic retaliation."[218]

The dean of the Louisiana State University Law School, Paul Hebert, concurred with most of the court's findings, but only in deference to the rulings of the IMT. Hebert accused the majority of having "misread the record in too complete an exoneration and an exculpation even of moral guilt to a degree which I consider unwarranted."[219] He carefully qualified his dissenting opinion:

> I do not agree with the majority's conclusion that the evidence presented in this case falls so short of sufficiency as the Tribunal's opinion would seem to indicate. The issues of fact are truly so close as to cause genuine concern as to whether or not justice has actually been done because of the enormous and indispensable role these defendants were shown to have played in the building of the war machine which made Hitler's aggressions possible.[220]

Judge Hebert believed that the defendants took "a consenting part in the commission of war crimes and crimes against humanity," reasoning that I.G. Farben Industries "has been shown to have been an ugly record which went, in its sympathy and identity with the Nazi regime, far beyond the activities of . . . normal business." He believed all the defendants to be guilty under Count 3: "In my view, the Auschwitz project would not have been carried out had it not been authorized and approved by the other defendants, who participated in the corporate approval of the project knowing that concentration-camp inmates and other slave labor would be employed in the construction and other work."[221] Judge Hebert pointed to the defendants' clear violation of even the customary laws of war: "Under the evidence it is clear that the defendants in utilizing slave labor which is conceded to be a war crime (in the case of non-German nationals) and a crime against humanity, did not, as they assert, in fact, act exclusively because of the compulsion or coercion of the existing Governmental regulations and policies."[222] The sentences in the Farben cases were, as prosecutor Josiah DuBois said, "light enough to please a chicken thief." Not only did the tribunal acquit ten of the twenty-three defendants, none of the convicted were sentenced to more than eight years.[223]

Industrialist Alfried Krupp and executives from his company faced similar charges. On November 12, 1943, the forty-year-old Krupp was named sole owner of the Krupp Armament Works of Essen by a Reich decree called the "Lex Krupp." He and eleven other company executives, including Ewald Loeser, Eduard Houdremont, and Erich Mueller, were also indicted for leading the "secret and illegal rearmament of Germany for foreign conquests."[224] As in the Farben case, this indictment included crimes against peace and conspiracy counts in addition to the spoliation and forced labor charges.[225] The prosecution contended that the Krupp works had played an important role in Hitler's secret rearmament plan. Once the prosecution rested, the defense introduced a motion to drop Counts 1 and 4—crimes against peace and conspiracy to commit crimes against peace.[226] A few weeks later, the tribunal acquitted all the defendants of these counts, following the IMT's acquittal of Schact and Speer on the same charges. This was yet another blow to the aggression precedent. Judge Wilkins wrote: "Giving the defendants the benefit of what might be called a slight doubt, and although the evidence with respect to some of them was extraordinarily strong, I concurred that, in view of Gustav Krupp's overriding authority in the Krupp enterprises, the extent of the actual influence of the present defendants was not as substantial as to warrant finding them guilty of Crimes Against Peace."[227] Judge Anderson of Tennessee agreed, contending that the crimes against peace charge was only for "leaders and policy makers," not "private citizens . . . who participate in the war effort." The defendants argued that they had mistreated slave labor only out of military necessity. The court rejected the doctrine of necessity on the ground that the defendants were not "acting under compulsion or coercion exercised by the Reich authorities within the meaning of the law of necessity," although it acknowledged that the defendants were "guilty of constant, widespread and flagrant violations of the laws of war relating to the employment of POWs."[228]

The tribunal sentenced Alfried Krupp to twelve years in prison and forced him to forfeit all his personal property, while sentencing the other nine defendants to less than ten years each and acquitting one. Judge Anderson filed a dissenting opinion and claimed that the sentences were too severe.[229] After February 1948, the sentences handed down at Nuremberg grew increasingly lenient. This was due to a combination of Cold War pressure and legitimate discomfort with the radical implications of Control Council Law No. 10.

Robert Maguire had assumed that his Nuremberg stay would be no longer than six months. By the summer of 1948, he had been in Germany for nine months, the end was nowhere in sight, and the novelty of Nuremberg had worn off. "Our case moves on but so slowly. We are doing everything we can to hurry it but even so we are not moving or making as much progress as I could wish. However, we go ahead and perhaps we will be able to get it completed someday,"[230] he wrote. When the trial finally ended, the transcript ran to more than twenty-eight thousand pages, with more than nine thousand documentary exhibits.[231] The Ministries case finished with the majority of the courtroom portion of the case on October 7, 1948.

On November 12, while the Ministries case was in recess, the International Military Tribunal for the Far East handed down the verdicts in the Tokyo trial. After an acrimonious two-and-a-half-year proceeding, the eleven-man court handed down yet another split decision. The Cold War had also made an impact on the IMTFE. As early as February 1948, the State Department's George Kennan had warned American leaders that the United States needed to protect Japan from the "penetration and domination" of communism. Kennan was as strongly against the Tokyo trial as he had been against the Nuremberg trials. After a March 1948 visit to Japan, he considered the trials "profoundly misconceived from the start." In a secret report to the Policy Planning Staff, he described the trials as "*procedurally* correct, according to our concepts of justice, and at no time in history have conquerors conferred upon the vanquished such elaborate opportunities for the public defense and for vindication of their military acts." However, to Kennan, like the Nuremberg trials, these were "political trials . . . not law."[232] Soviet and American relations were much worse during the Tokyo trial than they had been during the IMT. The official Soviet news organ, *Pravda*, opined that "Wall Street and its agents, who direct U.S. policy, are resurrecting militarism in Japan and converting the country into a base for the promotion of their insenate plans of world domination."[233]

Again the IMTFE was forced to confront the unresolved issues that lay at the heart of the London Agreement Charter. By 1948, this was an old debate with new players. The points of contention (with some slight deviations) were basically the same as those debated inconclusively in Washington and London in 1944 and 1945 and in Nuremberg from 1945 to 1949 (conspiracy to commit aggression, individual responsibility for acts of state, the criminality of aggressive war, the *ex post facto* character of the law, and the existence of negative criminality). By a majority of eight to three, the IMTFE sentenced seven to death and sixteen to life in prison, two to lesser prison terms, and acquitted none.[234]

All three dissenters agreed that the trial's integrity was compromised by the failure to indict Emperor Hirohito. As John Dower points out in *Embracing Defeat*, the defendants went to great pains to protect the emperor. France's Justice Bernard was very critical of Hirohito's nonindictment and concluded that "a verdict reached by a Tribunal after a defective procedure cannot be a valid one."[235] Although Webb concurred with the majority opinion, he wrote, "the leader of the crime, though available for trial, had been granted immunity. . . . The Emperor's authority was required for war. If he did not want war he should have withheld his authority." Justice Bernard argued that it was unfair to judge Emperor Hirohito "by a different standard," believing that "the present Defendants could only be considered as accomplices."[236]

Justice Röling questioned the validity of the Kellogg-Briand Pact as a precedent for criminalizing aggression. Although he did not reject the aggressive war charges, the Dutch jurist argued that "no capital punishment should be given to anyone guilty of crimes against peace only."[237] Röling stated, "No soldier should ever be found guilty of the crime of waging an aggressive war simply for the reason that he performed a strictly military function. Aggression is a political concept and the crime of aggression should be limited to those who take part in the relevant political decisions."[238]

The most extreme argument of all the war crimes decisions of the post–World War II period came from Justice Radhabinod Pal of India in the IMTFE. He accepted the contention that Japanese foreign policy of the 1930s and 1940s constituted self-defense. Based on this and a radical interpretation of the laws of war, Pal found all of the accused not guilty on every count of the indictment.[239] The implicit and explicit target of Pal's attack was the victorious Allied powers. He believed the word "aggressors" was a "chameleonic" international legal device used to justify a successful war. The Indian judge had spent most of his adult life opposing British colonial rule at home and believed that the international political status quo was inherently unjust because it was established and maintained by force and the oppression of indigenous people. To Pal, the real crime was not totalitarianism, it was imperialism: "The part of humanity which has been lucky enough to enjoy political freedom can now well afford to have the deterministic ascetic outlook of life, and may think of peace in terms of the political status quo."[240]

Pal took up the cause of the peoples that had been traditionally labeled "barbarian" or "savage" and slaughtered like infected livestock: "every part of humanity has not been equally lucky and a considerable part is still haunted by the wishful thinking about escape from political dominations. To them the present age is faced with not only the menace of totalitarianism but the ACTUAL PLAGUE of imperialism."[241] As for the conspiracy to commit aggressive war, he felt that "the story here has been pushed, perhaps, to give it a place in the Hitler series."[242] He considered the Bataan Death March and Rape of Nanking "isolated incidents." If killing civilians was a war crime, then what was the legal status of Curtis LeMay, who knowingly ordered the deaths of hundreds of thousands of Japanese civilians? According to Pal,

> In the Pacific war under our consideration, if there was anything approaching what is indicated in the above letter of the German emperor, it is the decision coming from the Allied powers to use the atom bomb. Future generations will judge this dire decision. . . . It would be sufficient for my present purpose to say that if any indiscriminate destruction of civilian life and property is still illegitimate in warfare, then, in the Pacific war, this decision to use the atom bomb is the only

near approach to the directives of the German Emperor during the First World War and of the Nazi leaders during the Second World War. Nothing like this could be traced to the credit of the present accused.[243]

Judge Pal's strongly anti-Western dissent argued that "natural law" was a Western notion, totally irrelevant to Asian defendants.[244] He viewed the Allied attempt to criminalize aggression as a means by which they could maintain the status quo, or in his words, "repent of their violence and permanently profit by it."[245] The duality in the American-inspired standards of international law was obvious to Pal: "I would only like to observe once again that the so-called Western interests in the Eastern Hemisphere were mostly founded on the past success of these Western people in 'transmitting military violence into commercial profit.' " The Indian judge pointed to the duality in U.S. policy: "As a program of aggrandizement of a nation we do not like, we may deny to it the terms like 'manifest destiny', 'the protection of vital interests', 'national honour' or a term coined on the footing of 'the white man's burden', and may give it the name 'aggressive aggrandizement' pure and simple."[246]

Hideki Tojo accepted his death sentence with the same stoic indifference that Yamashita had exhibited in Manila. Like the Sioux braves in Minnesota who sang and chanted on their way to the gallows, the Japanese officers faced death as warriors. War to them was not a matter of winning or losing, it was a matter of living or dying. In his final statement, Tojo confirmed, "The sentence so far as I am concerned is as deserved." He apologized if his testimony had implicated anyone else—"I am sorry though, that I brought my colleagues trouble. I sincerely regret it"—and made it clear that he was happy to sacrifice his life for Emperor Hirohito: "At least, through the trial, nothing was carried up to the Emperor and on that point I am being comforted." On the day of sentencing, the American prosecutor Joseph Keenan enjoyed a three-hour lunch with Emperor Hirohito.[247]

After a two-week break, the Ministries case reconvened on November 9, 1948, to hear two weeks of final arguments. The High Command case had finished in late October; the Ministries case was the final trial, the last vestige of a bygone era.[248] Robert Maguire anticipated returning to Portland in January 1949, but once the court adjourned and the judges began to debate the verdicts, it was evident that the division between Powers and the other two judges would manifest itself in the tribunal opinion. To match the extent and vigor of Judge Powers's dissent, the majority opinion had to be fortified. This extra labor added several months to Maguire's stay in Europe. His wife, Ruth, mentioned the setbacks in a letter: "Bob says things are moving along now but there have been many discouraging circumstances that have delayed matters."[249] If the tribunal planned to convict any of the five defendants charged with aggression, their opinion would need to be strongly reasoned because it was sure to come under fire.

Though the Nuremberg trials were no longer front-page news in 1949, curiosity was growing about the last trial. On April 12, the defendants entered the courtroom of the Palace of Justice. The first verdicts read concerned the controversial crimes against peace (aggression) charge. There had been no convictions for crimes against peace since the IMT; moreover, the charge had been rejected in the Farben, Krupp, and High Command cases. This was the prosecution's last hope to gain a conviction to bolster the IMT's weak precedent.[250] When Judge Christianson began to read the majority opinion, *Stars and Stripes* reported, "there was a sensation in the courtroom."[251] Even before he got to the charges against the individual defendants, it was obvious that the court had taken the broadest reading of their mandate. Because this was the final trial, there was evidence available to the court (the minutes of the Wansee Conference, the records of the Einsatzgruppen, the Four-Year Plan, and the German Foreign Office) that painted a more graphic picture. The majority opinion began on this point:

> Hundreds of captured official documents were offered, received and considered, which were unavailable at the trial before the International Military Tribunal, which were not offered in any of the previous cases before United States Military Tribunals, and the record here presents, more fully and completely than in any other case, the story of the Nazi regime, its program, its acts.[252]

The majority opinion was that deliberate policies of conquest had long been violations of the customary rules of war. They traced precedents back to Caesar, Frederick the Great of Prussia, Philip II of Spain, Edward I of England, Louis XIV of France, and the colonial powers of the nineteenth and twentieth centuries. According to Maguire and

Christianson, "Every and all of the attackers followed the same time-worn practice. The white, the blue, the yellow, black and red books had only one purpose, namely, to justify that which was otherwise unjustifiable."[253] The judges asked an important question that highlighted the weakness of the defense arguments: "But if aggressive invasions and wars were lawful and did not constitute a breach of international law and duty, why take the trouble to explain and justify? Why inform neutral nations that war was inevitable and excusable and based on high notions of morality, if aggressive war was not essentially wrong and breach of law?"[254]

The majority rejected the pleas of superior orders and sovereign immunity. "To permit such immunity is to shroud international law in a mist of unreality. We reject it and hold that those who plan, prepare, initiate, and wage aggressive wars and invasions . . . may be tried, convicted and punished for their acts."[255] The opinion also went to special pains to reject the many Cold War–inspired *tu quoque* arguments. The tribunal conceded that the Soviets had been fully complicit in the invasion of Poland, but this in no way exonerated Germany:

> But if we assume, *arguendo*, that Russia's action was wholly untenable and its guilt as deep as the Third Reich, nevertheless, this cannot, in law, avail the defendants of the guilt of those of the Third Reich who were themselves responsible. . . . It has never been suggested that a law duly passed becomes ineffective when it transpires that one of the legislators whose vote enacted it was himself guilty of the same practice.[256]

In keeping with this broad reading of Control Council Law No. 10, the court found five men guilty of crimes against peace. These were the first convictions for aggression since the IMT.[257]

Despite the efforts of his five attorneys and high-profile character witnesses, Ernst von Weizsäcker had, in Christianson and Maguire's judgment, crossed an ethical point of no return. They conceded that the diplomat, in his own mind, might have resisted, but that his efforts were too little, too late. The majority asked "how a decent man could continue to hold office under a regime which carried out and planned wholesale barbarities of this kind?"[258] There were a number of factors that undermined the former State Secretary's credibility. Maguire and Christianson were unconvinced by von Weizsäcker's "Jekyll and Hyde" strategy: "The defense that things are not what they seem, and that one gave lip service but was secretly engaged in rendering even this service ineffective . . . is a defense readily available to the most guilty, and is not novel, either here or in other jurisdictions."[259]

The majority opinion found von Weizsäcker's failure to mention his affiliation with the resistance until 1948 "suspicious." The defendant's performance on the witness stand also damaged his case. Although the former diplomat had expertly summarized the details of the Hitler-Stalin Pact from memory during the IMT, when his own trial began, his memory began to falter. This irony was not lost on the tribunal majority: "The exceeding caution observed by the defendant on cross-examination and his claims of lack of recollection of events of importance, which by no stretch of the imagination could be deemed routine, his insistence he be confronted with documents before testifying about such incidents, were not calculated to create an impression of frankness and candor."[260] Maguire and Christianson were unswayed by his repeated claims of resistance, remarking that "he was not a mere bystander, but acted affirmatively, and himself conducted the diplomatic negotiations both with victims and the interested powers, doing this with full knowledge of the facts; silent disapproval is not a defense to action."[261]

Finally, the court ruled that good intentions did not "render innocent that which is otherwise criminal, and which asserts that one may with impunity commit serious crimes, because he hopes thereby to prevent others, or that general benevolence towards individuals is a cloak or justification for participation in crimes against the unknown many."[262] Judges Maguire and Christianson gave an example of the defendant's dishonesty on the stand: his statement that "he thought Auschwitz was merely a camp where laborers were interned, we believe tells only part of what he knew, and what he had good reason to believe."[263] The majority pointed out that the German diplomats were aware of the Einsatzgruppen's activities—"The Foreign Office regularly received reports of the Einsatzgruppen operations in the occupied territories. Many of these were initialled by Weizsaecker and Woermann. They revealed the clearing of entire areas of Jewish population by mass murder, and the bloody butchery of the helpless and the innocent, the shooting of hostages in numbers wholly disproportionate to the alleged offenses against German armed forces; the murder of captured Russian officials and a reign of terrorism carried on with calculated ferocity, all told in the crisp, unimaginative language of military reports."[264]

Ernst von Weizsäcker and Ernst Woermann were found guilty of crimes against peace for their roles in the Nazi takeover of Czechoslovakia. Wilhelm Keppler was convicted for his participation in the invasions of Austria and Czechoslovakia, Woermann for aiding the invasion of Poland, and Koerner for his role in the war against the Soviets. The tribunal majority rejected the defense argument that America's Cold War policy justified Operation Barbarossa. "The plans for the economic exploitation of the Soviet Union, for the removal of the masses of the population, for the murders of the commissars and political leaders, were all part of a carefully prepared scheme launched on June 22 without warning of any kind, and without the shadow of a legal excuse. It was plain aggression."[265] Hans Lammers was the only nondiplomat found guilty of aggression for his role in the invasions of Czechoslovakia, Poland, Norway, Holland, Belgium, Luxembourg, and the Soviet Union. The defendants found guilty of crimes against peace were the type of fifth columnists that the authors of the Nuremberg indictment had had in mind when they broadened the definition of war crimes.[266]

When his turn to read a portion of the majority opinion came, Judge Powers began: "Before resuming the reading, it seems to me appropriate to say that my participation in the reading is merely for the purpose of helping out with the physical task of reading this opinion. It should not be construed as anything so far as my approval is concerned."[267] In his dissent Judge Powers made a conservative interpretation of the court's mandate: "I violently disagree with the opinion that we are engaged in enforcing International law which has not been codified, and that we have an obligation to lay down rules of conduct for nations of the future. . . . It is not for us to say what things should be condemned as crimes and what things should not. That has all been done by the lawmaking authority."[268]

The standard by which Judge Powers measured individual guilt favored the defendants; he wrote, "to establish personal guilt it must appear that the individual defendant must have performed some act which has a causal connection with the crimes charged, and must have performed it with the intention of committing a crime." Powers dissented on all the crimes against peace convictions on the ground that the violations did not occur during wars: "We will have to exclude invasions, because there was no possible basis for claiming that a mere invasion was contrary to international law."[269] Based on this reading, von Weizsäcker was not guilty for two reasons: "One, the invasion of Czechoslovakia was not a crime against peace. Two, he took no part in bringing about or initiating such an invasion." The dissent also cleared Keppler, Lammers, Woermann, and Koerner of any criminal wrongdoing.[270]

For the next two days the verdicts on the various counts of crimes against humanity (3 through 8) were read. The tribunal majority found 14 defendants guilty under at least one count.[271] Ernst von Weizsäcker was found guilty of crimes against humanity for his failure to object to Himmler about the deportation of 6,000 French Jews to Poland. Judge Powers argued that von Weizsäcker and Woermann had not been able to protest because "No grounds, therefore, based on foreign politics existed for objection." He accepted the defense of necessity and mocked the majority's logic: "So the so-called consent of WEIZSAECKER and of Woermann was merely recognition of the fact that conditions were absent which gave them a right to object on the grounds of foreign politics. But the Opinion seems to hold, especially as to WEIZSAECKER, that even in such a situation, he should have taken advantage of the opportunity to deliver a lecture to Ribbentrop on International Law and on morality."[272]

SS General Gottlob Berger was found guilty under Count 3 (war crimes) for the execution of French General Mesny, a reprisal for a German general killed by French underground forces. The tribunal majority accused Berger of lying in his courtroom testimony: "In view of the documents it seems impossible to believe Berger's testimony that he knew nothing of the plans to destroy the Jews or that he never heard of the 'final solution' until after the war." However, the court accepted the defendant's plea that during the final months of the war, "Berger was the means of saving the lives of American, British, and Allied officers and men whose safety was gravely imperiled by orders of Hitler that they be liquidated or held as hostages. Berger disobeyed the orders and intervened on their behalf and in doing so placed himself in a position of hazard."[273] Gottlob Berger was found guilty of transporting Hungarian Jews to concentration camps and recruiting concentration camp guards. Finally, Walter Schellenberg was found guilty of helping create the Einsatzgruppen. In 1941, Schellenberg prevented Jewish immigration to Belgium "in view of the final solution which is sure to come."[274]

Like the defendants in the Justice case, Hans Lammers was convicted for drafting and implementing Nazi legal policies. The majority opinion stated, "Lammers was not a mere postman, but acted solely without objection as a responsible Reichminister carrying out the function of his office. We find that Lammers knew of the policy, approved of it, and took an active, consenting and implementing part in its execution."[275] Edmund Veesenmayer was convicted for war crimes, crimes against humanity, and slave labor for forcing the Hungarian government to deport more than 300,000 Hungarian Jews to concentration camps like Auschwitz.[276] Otto Dietrich was found guilty for providing the anti-Semitic byline that justified the German campaign against the Jews. Steengracht von Moyland was convicted for preventing Jewish immigration and aiding in the extermination of Hungarian Jews. Wilhelm Keppler and Hans Kehrl were found guilty of "resettling" Jews to make room for ethnic Germans, and Richard Darré for removing thousands of Polish and Jewish farmers.[277] Bankers Schwerin von Krosigk and Emil Puhl were convicted of laundering confiscated property and financing the construction of the concentration camps. Regarding Puhl's guilt, the tribunal majority wrote, "The defendant contends that stealing the personal property of Jews and other concentration camp inmates is not a crime against humanity. But under the circumstances which we have here related, this plea is and must be rejected."[278]

Judge Powers dissented on many of the crimes against humanity convictions: "Where a finding of guilt is justified, the opinion so exaggerates the guilt, that I cannot concur in it."[279] He argued that the defendants were guilty of association rather than personal action. The dissent once again cleared diplomats von Weizsäcker and Woermann of criminal wrongdoing because they did not personally commit crimes. Similarly, Powers rejected the convictions of von Moyland, Dietrich, Veesenmayer, von Krosigk, and Puhl. His reasoning for dissenting on von Krosigk's conviction was indicative: "Many of the acts such as Jewish fines took place before the war began and are not within our jurisdiction. It cannot be a crime against humanity because merely depriving people of their property is not such a crime."[280] By the time the tribunal finished handing down their decisions, Judge Powers had dissented on 37 of the 49 convictions. His 124-page opinion opposed all the guilty verdicts other than those for the use of slave labor and membership in the criminal organizations. The Iowan jurist argued that the convictions were a gross misapplication of international law and that it was better to free high-ranking Nazis than to establish misleading precedents.[281]

On April 15, 1949, the sentences were handed down. Once again, they did not match the tone of the opinion. They were not as lenient as those of the Farben and Flick cases, but given the status of the defendants and the body of evidence, the sentences were light. The record was as follows:

Ernst von Weizsäcker: 7 years.
Steengracht von Moyland: 7 years.
Wilhelm Keppler: 10 years.
Ernst Bohle: 5 years.
Ernst Woermann: 7 years.
Karl Ritter: 4 years.
Otto von Erdmannsdorff: Acquitted.
Edmund Veesenmayer: 20 years.
Hans Lammers: 20 years.
Wilhelm Stuckart: Acquitted due to illness.
Richard Darré: 7 years.
Otto Meissner: Acquitted.
Otto Dietrich: 7 years.
Gottlob Berger: 25 years.
Walter Schellenberg: 6 years.
Schwerin von Krosigk: 10 years.
Emil Puhl: 5 years.
Karl Rasche: 7 years.
Paul Koerner: 15 years.
Paul Pleiger: 15 years.
Hans Kehrl: 15 years.[282]

It appeared that the tribunal majority rejected von Weizsäcker's defense of necessity; however, the question was reopened after the judgment was read; the tribunal allowed all of the convicted to file "Motions for the Correction of Alleged Errors of Fact and Law." Among other things, the motion attacked the court's legal legitimacy. "The Tribunal as a whole was never legally established and its said decision and judgment constitutes an arbitrary exercise of military power over each of the said defendants, in violation of the laws of nations and agreements made by the belligerent powers and other countries appertaining thereto."[283]

Because of the court's split decision, the Ministries case was hailed by trial supporters and critics alike. For Brigadier General Telford Taylor, the final year had been a long one; the decisions in the Ministries case provided a limited measure of vindication. Impressed by the strongly reasoned 835-page tribunal opinion, he praised the resolve of the court's concurring members, asserting that "today's judgment, more severe than many of those which have been handed down previously, is perhaps more important than those which went before. It was decided long after the excitement of the war which ended nearly four years ago."[284] The Chief Counsel believed that the trial was both important and redemptive because it "proves that we still mean in 1949 what we meant in 1945."[285] There was also praise for the judge from Iowa. August von Knieriem, general counsel for I. G. Farben and former Nuremberg defendant, described Powers's dissenting opinion as "extensive and carefully motivated." Carl Haensel, a leading Nuremberg defense counsel, viewed the dissent as the high point of the Ministries case: "The leading event of the day of judgment was the news of Judge Powers' Dissenting Opinion. Judge Powers declared that in his Opinion the majority of the defendants should be acquitted."[286]

Ernst von Weizsäcker

All photos courtesy of Constance and Joseph Wilson.

Ernst von Weizsäcker with Adolf Hitler.

Ernst von Weizsäcker (second from right).

Ernst von Weizsäcker discusses the details of the Munich Agreement with British Prime Minister Neville Chamberlain, Berchtesgaden, 1938.

State Secretary Von Weizsäcker greeting Japanese officials in 1941.

Adolf Hitler awards a medal to a German sailor, as defendant Bohle looks on.

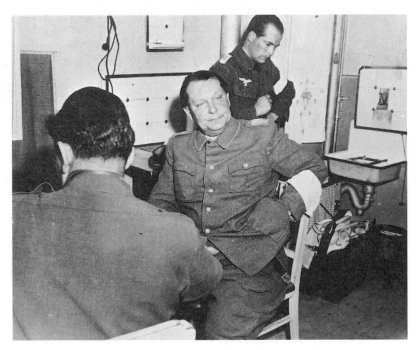

Hermann Goering

Tribunal IV. *Left to right*: Leon Powers, William Christianson, Robert F. Maguire.

Ernst von Weizsäcker confers with his defense team.

Ministries Case defendants: *(left to right, front row)* Ernst von Weizsäcker, Steengracht von Moyland, Wilhelm Keppler, Ernst Wilhelm Bohle, Ernst Woermann, Karl Ritter, Otto von Erdmannsdorf, Edmund Veesenmayer, Hans Lammers, Wilhelm Stuckart, Richard Darré; *(second row)* Otto Dietrich, Gottlob Berger, Walter Schellenberg, Schwerin von Krosigk, Emil Puhl, Karl Rasche, Paul Koerner, Paul Pleiger, Hans Kehrl.

Chapter Five

NUREMBERG: A COLD WAR CONFLICT OF INTEREST

Robert Maguire and William Christianson's extensive majority opinion helped to bolster the reputation of the American Nuremberg trials. Because the two judges convicted defendants under the revolutionary charge of crimes against peace, the American war crimes effort appeared to end with a small victory for the prosecution. The majority opinion in the Ministries case would serve to offset the judgments of the Krupp, Farben, and High Command cases. Although the tone and tactics of the prosecution might have seemed "vindictive" when measured by German or Continental legal standards, the proceedings were fundamentally sound. This unique legal effort ultimately provided a valuable documentary record of the Nazi dictatorship. On the whole the judgments were very conservative; all of the capital sentences in the *Einsatzgruppen* case, the Medical case, and the Pohl case were for violations of the traditional laws of war. The overwhelming majority of the judges rejected or avoided the contentious, or as some might argue *ex post facto*, aggression and conspiracy charges. If anything, given the decisions in the Farben, Krupp, and High Command cases, the original sentences in the American Nuremberg trials appear quite lenient in retrospect.

The guilt or innocence of Ernst von Weizsäcker has continued to be debated until this day. Despite his high-level character witnesses, many questions remained. Had von Weizsäcker, whatever his intentions, crossed an ethical point of no return due to his actions? His son, former West German President Richard von Weizsäcker, recently blamed the failure of his father's complicated defense on the provincial American judges who, he claimed, "were not even familiar with the details of European and German history." However, the loyal son went too far by declaring that his father has been absolved by modern historians: "Since then, the extensive literature on the contemporary history of both Germany and the rest of the world has left little serious doubt about the appropriateness of the charges against my father."[1] But is it that simple? While German diplomatic historian Klemens von Klemperer agrees that Ernst von Weizsäcker may have been part of the resistance, he describes the former State Secretary's behavior as "that of a tired servant of the old school rather than that of an outraged man of principle; it was resistance devoid of firm resolve and conviction"—Klemperer describes it as "social refusal" rather than resistance. German historian Marion Thielenhaus examines the period 1938–41 and portrays Ernst von Weizsäcker as an "ultranationalist" trying to keep the German Foreign Office from being absorbed by the National Socialists and to prevent a larger war from breaking out. Thielenhaus also shows the State Secretary to have been both anti-Czech and anti-Polish. As in Richard von Weizsäcker's recent book, there is no discussion, let alone mention, of the role that Ernst von Weizsäcker played in the deportation of European Jews, or the fact that the State Secretary regularly reviewed the reports of the Einsatzgruppen.[2]

German historian Jörg Friedrich remains totally unconvinced by von Weizsäcker's repeated claims of resistance: "Diplomats had deported foreign Jews because they did not want the Nazis to suspect them of subversion and undermine their position in clandestine peace talks. . . . Aside from the fact that they lied to the courts, those who offered such testimony demonstrated their submission to the victors' value system, exhibiting retroactive opportunism."[3] As for the Roman Jews that Ernst von Weizsäcker helped to deport, on October 18, 1943, approximately 1,200 Italian Jews were packed into railroad cars at Rome's Tiburtina station.

Five days later the train reached its destination—the Auschwitz concentration camp. One hundred forty-nine men and 47 women were retained for slave labor; the remaining 1,060 were killed. Only 14 men and one woman from the deportation survived World War II.[4]

The Ernst von Weizsäcker case took a strange twist in May 1949, when a Senate Armed Services Committee began to "conduct a full and complete study and investigation of the action of the Army with respect to the trial of those persons responsible for the massacre of American soldiers which occurred during the Battle of the Bulge near Malmedy, Belgium." The investigation was a result of Senate Resolution 42 (January 20, 1949).[5] Connecticut Senator Raymond Baldwin headed the hearing. Much to the delight of his German-American constituency, freshman Senator Joe McCarthy of Wisconsin offered his services to the Senate investigation.[6]

When the committee opened their first session on May 4, 1949, Senator McCarthy attacked the conviction of Ernst von Weizsäcker and the opinion of judges Maguire and Christianson: "Before there is any testimony, there is a matter which has come to my attention which I think this committee should go into, and I believe it is of tremendous importance." According to McCarthy, von Weizsäcker's innocence was a well-established fact: "Apparently the evidence is all uncontradicted, there is no question about it. It was to the effect that this was the most valuable undercover man which the Allies had in Germany, starting in 1936." McCarthy argued that the sentences would "do tremendous damage" to the American position in Germany: "If they keep this up, they will make it impossible for us to have any kind of intelligence in the prospective opposition of other nations, potential enemies." Senator McCarthy called for an investigation into the Ministries case and wanted to call Judges Maguire and Christianson before the panel: "I think this committee should see what type of morons—and I use that term advisedly—are running the military court over there. There is something completely beyond conception, and I would like to ask the Chair to go into the matter, and in effect notify the world at this time that the American people are not in approval of this complete imbecility in that area."[7]

In a strategy that later brought McCarthy both fame and censure, the senator claimed to be on the verge of exposing a massive cover-up. He said that the members of *Kampfgruppe* Peiper had been severely beaten by

American captors. McCarthy asked that U.S. Army interrogators Perl, Thon, and Kirchbaum all be subjected to lie-detector tests. He said to Lieutenant Perl, "I think you are lying. I do not think you can fool the lie detector. You may be able to fool us." Perl, a lawyer himself, responded caustically, "If it is so reliable, we should have used it from the beginning. Why a trial at all? Get the guys, and put the lie detector on them. 'Did you kill this man?' The lie detector says, 'Yes.' Go to the scaffold. If it says, 'No,' back to Bavaria."[8]

In the end, the former Wisconsin judge heatedly accused Army prosecutor Burton Ellis of "whitewashing" the "Gestapo and OPGU" interrogation techniques of the U.S. Army:[9] "This committee is not concerned with getting the facts. Further, this committee is afraid of the facts, and is sitting here solely for the purpose of a whitewash of the Army and that phase of the military government in charge of the trials." McCarthy's dramatic attack of the Baldwin committee drew much attention, especially in Germany. Although the subcommittee upheld the convictions resulting from the Malmedy trials, their final report concluded that there had been some minor judicial abuses.[10] The report came down hardest on the trial critics. Historian Frank Buscher describes the report: "More at stake than the Army's conduct in this particular matter, the subcommittee warned . . . that the 'attacks' on the war-crimes trials in general and the Malmedy case in particular were meant to revive German nationalism and to cast doubt upon the U.S. occupation of Germany as a whole."[11] The clamor over the Malmedy trials had a catalyzing effect on many Germans, who saw these exchanges as a green light of sorts. It was now permissible to attack American war crimes policy in a more inflammatory way with the justification that they were merely emulating the tactics of "responsible American statesmen."[12]

Once Germany became the fulcrum of the American plan for the reconstruction of Europe, the question of Landsberg Prison and the fate of the war criminals took on new significance. By 1949, conservative American politicians like Francis Case, Harold Knutsen, John Taber, William Langer, and John Rankin were concluding that alleged improprieties in the Malmedy trial discredited the findings of all the American war crimes tribunals. According to Frank Buscher, by the end of the 1940s, these conservative Republicans had succeeded in establishing "a new Nuremberg philosophy." Many in the United States "had come to accept the conservative argument that the convicted Nazi perpetrators were not criminals, but instead were the victims of the Allied war crimes program."[13]

The dispute in the U.S. Senate over the Malmedy trials gave German nationalists badly needed political ammunition. The tone of their letters to the High Commissioner began to change. Franz Bleucher, the chairman of the right-wing Free Democratic Party, offered a typical expression of "doubt":

> The German public is very much perturbed by the fact that death sentences passed on German Nationals by Allied Special Courts will be executed on German soil six years after the termination of hostilities. The main committee of the Free Democratic Party is definitely of the opinion that crimes committed during the time of the Nazi Terror Regime should be punished, however the committee believes that some of the death sentences were based on trials which were not properly conducted.[14]

On December 12, 1949, judges Maguire, Christianson, and Powers ruled on a series of post-trial defense motions and rejected all but three of them. "The assertion that the Tribunal considered evidence which the defense has never seen, if true, would constitute a grave breach of judicial duty. It is, however, wholly without foundation." Whether this was a result of McCarthy's attack or Maguire's own political candidacy, it is impossible to say. In any case, Judge Maguire reversed his position on the most significant verdict of the Ministries case and joined Judge Powers in opposing the convictions of Ernst von Weizsäcker and Ernst Woermann under the radical charge of crimes against peace. The new tribunal majority of Maguire and Powers announced, "After a careful examination of the entire record concerning his conviction with the aggression against Czechoslovakia, we are convinced that our finding of guilt as to that crime is erroneous. We are glad to correct it. The judgment of guilt against the defendant von Weizsaecker as to Count I is hereby set aside and he is hereby acquitted under Count I."[15] Presiding Judge William Christianson vehemently dissented from the modification of Ernst von Weizsäcker's sentence from seven to five years, not to mention the reversal of a precedent like his aggression conviction: "I cannot agree that the majority of the Tribunal in the original judgment erroneously evaluated the evidence with respect to the said matter as is now indicated to be the view of my colleagues with respect to the defendant von Weizsaecker's conviction under said count one. A re-examination of the evidence with respect to the actions of defendant von Weizsaecker in connection with the aggression against Czechoslovakia deepens my conviction that said defendant is guilty under said count one." Ministries case prosecutor William Caming had a high regard for the judge from Oregon, but to this day remains baffled by his post-trial action. Caming wrote, "Judge Maguire, without plausible explanation reversed his position, joining Judge Powers in setting aside their convictions under Count One. . . . Judge Maguire's Memorandum Opinion is embarrassingly vague and devoid of any rationale for his change of heart. I can only surmise what the impelling personal factors were."[16] Although it is impossible to determine Robert Maguire's motives, his action cast a cloud of doubt over the conviction of Ernst von Weizsäcker.

The pressure to release von Weizsäcker only increased after his aggression conviction was dropped. Former German resistance leader Theo Kordt wrote Lord Halifax on December 13, 1949, calling the von Weizsäcker case "a new Dreyfuss case . . . on an international level." He strongly supported von Weizsäcker's claim that he had accepted the job of State Secretary in 1938 in order to prevent war: "My friends and I felt that he was making a personal sacrifice with a view to preserve the peace and bring about the restitution of legal and decent government in Germany." Kordt ended on an emotional note: "All those who gave their lives, most of them personal friends of mine, considered Weizsacker as their example and their spiritual leader."[17]

By the fall of 1949, Robert Maguire had decided to run as a Republican candidate for the Oregon Supreme Court. This would not be an easy feat, as he had been away nearly two years. Moreover, Nuremberg was still controversial, especially despised by conservative Republicans. Did Maguire employ a bit of strategic legalism to appease the right wing of the Republican Party and to help his candidacy? In November 1949, the *American Bar Association Journal* published a speech delivered by Robert Maguire entitled, "The Unknown Art of Making Peace: Are We Sowing the Seeds of World War III?" at an American Bar Association meeting in St. Louis. In the speech, Judge Maguire traced the ill effects of punitive peace treaties on world history; he examined peace treaties from Wellington to Wilson and concluded that vindictive treaties only lead to more war.

The former Nuremberg judge argued that the time for punishment had ended. "There were crimes of aggression and mass horror beyond description or human realization, and that those who are responsible for, committed or participated in mass war crimes should be punished, I think, is beyond reasonable question. Nevertheless, it is just as unreal to proceed upon the basis that all Germans are monsters. . . . The historical fact is that even the mature German had little or no knowledge of those crimes."[18] He warned against punishing the next generation of Germans: "The terms of peace will not be imposed alone upon the guilty, but they will be imposed upon those who had neither knowledge of nor were responsible for the war, upon the women and children, upon the boys and girls, not only of this generation, but those of future generations."[19] Since his return to the United States, Robert Maguire had grown increasingly critical of postwar American diplomacy: "Yalta, Moscow, and Potsdam have already done untold damage. Much of Europe now writhes under unjust discriminations, seizures of land, and power at the expense of the helpless."[20]

From the vantage point of more than half a century later, the judgments in the American Nuremberg trials appear extremely lenient. Years afterward, Robert Maguire wrote, "One thing I think can be said without question, is that so far as the courts were concerned, the attitude was the opposite of emotional, and that they earnestly endeavored, and I think succeeded, in being entirely objective toward the defendants and evidence."[21] If this was one of the "harshest" jurists at Nuremberg, what of the others? Maguire confirmed the trend toward leniency: "I think that it may be fairly said that not only was every attempt made to give the defendants a fair trial and every opportunity to defend themselves, but that the judges in various cases probably leaned backwards in protecting their rights."[22]

Although the "vindictive" policies of the Nuremberg trials and JCS 1067 summoned memories of Versailles, the analogy between the two settlements was a false one. However, as Jörg Friedrich points out, rationality, law, and facts had little place in this debate—a point that is the key to understanding the second phase of American war crimes policy: "The Nuremberg prosecution, well supplied with documentary evidence, succeeded in refuting these nonsensical excuses and winning convictions. However, the public was not won over." Many Germans simply chose not to believe: "The criminal guilt that was meant to be a wedge between the public and the defendants turned out to form a link between them."[23] Many Germans found not only the actual punishment, but also the manner in which it came, objectionable. Moral guidance from the upstart Americans was too much to bear. By 1949, there was a deep reservoir of German resentment over the subject of war crimes that had yet to be tapped.

During the second phase of American war crimes policy (1949–53), American and West German leaders fashioned two American policies— one public and one private. The public policy was designed to defend the legal validity of the American trials from widespread German attacks, while the private policy sought to release war criminals as quickly and quietly as the political and legal circumstances would allow. The problematic details surrounding the early releases would occupy the State Department's legal advisors until the last German war criminals were released from Landsberg Prison in the late 1950s. The Germans would prove to be worthy foes at the game of strategic legalism. Ironically, they would now launch the same attacks on the legal validity of the Allied war crimes trials that had been rejected by the IMT under Article 3, in 1945.

The first major step toward the restoration of German sovereignty occurred on September 21, 1949, when the Federal Republic of West Germany was officially established. General Lucius Clay had said earlier in the occupation, prior to handing the task of denazification over to the Germans, that the best way to learn democracy was to live it.[24] The Occupation Statute was replaced by West Germany's Basic Law. The former American governing body, the U.S. Military Government, was replaced by the U.S. High Commission for Germany (HICOG), and Clay was replaced by Stimson's former Assistant Secretary of War, John McCloy. Most significantly, American oversight of West Germany shifted from the U.S. Army to the U.S. State Department, and American war crimes policy would soon reflect this change. Throughout 1945, John McCloy had fought passionately for the creation of the IMT and all that it implied. His "certainty and energy" had bowled over even the skeptical British.[25] However, it was now 1949, and the punitive policies of JCS 1067 were not compatible with the new American program for Germany. More than anything else, John McCloy was true to his roots as a third-generation American lawyer-statesman (who had begun his career in Elihu Root and Henry Stimson's Wall Street law firm).

After the establishment of HICOG in 1949, seventy-three-year-old Konrad Adenauer was elected West Germany's first Chancellor. The

State Department was satisfied that he was a sufficiently pro-American representative for the German people. Although Adenauer was committed to German integration into the West, the problem created by the imprisoned war criminals was growing into what Frank Buscher describes as "a major obstacle to the achievement of his foreign policy goals."[26]

Though there were continued cries for a reunified Germany, the possibility looked out of the question in 1949. East Germany had already been militarized by the Soviet Union; its *Volkspolizei* (People's Police) had more than fifty thousand Soviet-trained members.[27] As early as 1949, some of America's most influential foreign policy makers felt that rearming West Germany was inevitable.[28] Because the United States had demobilized so rapidly after the war, the Soviets had what appeared to be a huge superiority in conventional forces in Europe. The United States had barely twelve army divisions, while the Soviets had twenty-four and another seventy in reserve.[29] German rearmament fulfilled the darkest geopolitical prognostications of right-wing German nationalists and unrepentant Nazis—the Soviet Union was the true enemy of Western civilization.

By 1949, a fast-growing segment of the West German population considered *all* the war crimes trials to be a form of political theater with no basis in either fact or law. The Nuremberg trials had become a hugely important symbolic issue, a contemporary version of the Treaty of Versailles' "shame paragraphs."[30] The attacks on Nuremberg were the same as in 1945, but the international political context had changed; now West German goodwill and cooperation were vital to the American plan for Western Europe.

By 1950, all the war criminals convicted by American courts in Germany were incarcerated in Bavaria's Landsberg Prison.[31] Of the 185 men charged in the American Nuremberg Trials, 177 were tried, 35 acquitted, 24 sentenced to death, 20 sentenced to life, 98 given other prison terms, and four committed suicide. In the Dachau and other concentration camp trials conducted by the U.S. Army, 1,672 were charged, 256 acquitted, 426 sentenced to death, 199 sentenced to life, and 791 given other prison terms. In the United Kingdom trials, 1,085 were charged, 348 acquitted, 240 sentenced to death, 24 sentenced to life, and 473 given other prison terms. In the French trials, 2,107 were charged, 404 acquitted, 104 sentenced to death, 44 sentenced to life, and more than 1,000 given other prison terms. There are only the sketchiest details of the Soviet trials. Of 14,240 who were charged, 142 were acquitted, 138 sentenced to death, and more than 13,000 given other prison terms.[32]

The Nuremberg trials had no appellate court to review the sentences. Rather than create a permanent court for the task, John Raymond, Walter Rockwell, and members of the legal staff of the U.S. Military Government did early sentence reviews on an *ad hoc* basis. This board was responsible for the sentences of both the Nuremberg trials and the Army trials. Up until 1949, General Clay had the final word on the fate of the war criminals. Because the trials were being severely criticized in the United States, he took the sentence confirmation process very seriously. Clay knew that whatever they were, his decisions were going to be attacked.

German trial critics did not merely seek clemency; they wanted an apology to assuage their violated sense of honor. Many German veterans considered the war crimes convicts prisoners of war, whose main crime was losing the war.[33] Due to Langer's Senate investigation, Lucius Clay had been unable to carry out all the Nuremberg death sentences, and they were inherited by John McCloy when he took office as High Commissioner in 1949 (those convicted by the army at Dachau were under the jurisdiction of Army Commander-in-Chief Thomas Handy). German criticism of the American war crimes program weighed heavily on McCloy. From his first day as High Commissioner, he was barraged with thousands of letters, telegrams, and postcards begging clemency for those imprisoned at Landsberg, but his largest problem were the handful of men awaiting execution.[34] These convicts had exhausted all channels of appeal and awaited his final decision.

John McCloy refused to admit that politics influenced his treatment of the German war criminals. Until his death in 1989, he doggedly maintained that these were apolitical "legal" decisions.[35] In a climate of changing political priorities, High Commissioner McCloy established the Advisory Board on Clemency for War Criminals (also referred to as the Peck Panel) in 1950. He provided this justification for his decision to review sentences that already had been both reviewed and confirmed by General Clay: "The availability to the individual defendant of an appeal to executive clemency is a salutary part of the administration of justice. It is particularly appropriate that the cases of defendants convicted of war crimes be given an executive review because no appellate court review has been provided."[36]

It was becoming increasingly clear that by 1950, many West Germans still did not accept the legal validity of the American war crimes trials. Among the first to take up the defense of the war criminals were the leaders of Germany's Catholic and Protestant churches. In a letter responding to a plea for a war crimes amnesty from Bishop Fargo A.J. Muench, the Regent of the German Apostolic Nunciature in Germany, High Commissioner McCloy expressed irritation: "I have been somewhat disturbed, however, in examining these petitions, by what appears to be a persistent tendency to question the legal basis for the prosecutions and the judicial soundness of the judgements." McCloy unequivocally rejected the Bishop's call for a war crimes amnesty: "Anything approaching a general amnesty would, I fear, be taken as an abandonment of the principles established in the trials of the perpetrators of those crimes."[37] Jörg Friedrich points to the irony of the German clergy's new position: "The same bishops who had witnessed the murder of more than 4,000 priests and nuns by Nazi courts and kept silent about the deportation and gassing of Jewish converts, now felt the need to confront the occupation authorities with biblical rigor."[38]

On January 19, 1950, President Truman received a letter on behalf of Ernst von Weizsäcker from Lord Halifax. Even though the former State Secretary's aggression conviction had been overturned, his advocates would not rest until he was released from Landsberg Prison. The former British Foreign Minister told Truman that his appeal was based on the trust that he placed in Theo Kordt's word: "But this appeal from Kordt comes to me with the claim based on what I know to have been his own willingness to incur grave danger in the cause that he believed right— namely trying to check the Nazi movement to war—and after anxious thought, and after consulting the Foreign Office here who raised no objection to my so doing, I have decided to submit it to you." Lord Halifax included a copy of the letter from Kordt and stated, "reconsideration of Weizsacker's case, if you felt able to give it, would be both justified on merits and would exercise a powerful affect on those German quarters, where the conviction prevails today that in his case justice has miscarried."[39]

Kordt's letter described Ernst von Weizsäcker as the "spiritual leader" of the German resistance and claimed that he had accepted the job of State Secretary in order "to prevent the greatest crime that had ever been committed in human history." Kordt contended that von Weizsäcker was compelled to collaborate with the Nazis due to an " '*ubergesetzlicher Nostand*' or 'superlegal emergency,' which requires a priority of responsible action with regard to supernational interests, e.g. the prevention of aggressive war."[40]

On January 30, 1950, President Truman wrote Lord Halifax, "I appreciate most highly your letter of January fourth, concerning Herr von Weizsacker. I am looking into the matter to determine what steps should be taken to insure that justice prevails in his case."[41] In early February, Secretary of State Dean Acheson presented Truman with a response to Lord Halifax drafted by the State Department's legal advisors. Although it was little more than a brief outline of the case, the President wrote, "the United States High Commissioner for Germany has the power to mitigate the sentence," and "I am having a copy of your letter and the letter from Doctor Kordt forwarded to the United States High Commissioner for Germany for consideration in connection with the petitions for clemency filed in the case of Herr von Weizsacker." Ernst von Weizsäcker would be released in October 1950.[42]

In late January, High Commissioner McCloy set about establishing the Advisory Board on Clemency for War Criminals to consider the petitions of German war criminals convicted by any American courts. In a confidential memo, State Department Assistant Legal Advisor for German Affairs John Raymond agreed that an "impartial board" review would relieve public pressure. However, Raymond was one of the members of General Clay's review board and believed that the vast majority of the death sentences should stand because these men were truly guilty. The convictions were based not on hearsay but on evidence directly linking the individuals to the crimes. General Clay had taken special care in reviewing the death sentences; he explained:

> When you have the responsibility of whether someone is going to die, before you sign a paper you worry about it an awful lot. And I never signed any of those papers without going through the trial record from A to Z. And if there was any doubt, *any doubt*, I commuted the sentence. In terms of procedure, the Nuremberg trials were much easier to follow; it was much easier to determine whether justice had been done. In Dachau, I had some doubt.[43]

The vast majority of the prisoners facing the death penalty had been Einsatzgruppen leaders.[44]

Former Nuremberg prosecutor Telford Taylor challenged the decision to review the sentences in a February 2, 1950 *New York Post* article entitled, "Stalling Baffles U.S. Prosecutor." In an interview from his law office in New York City, Taylor announced, "The retreat from Nuremberg is on. I fear such a review would work to the benefit of those who have wealthy and powerful influences behind them." Taylor called the "whole concept questionable. Where will the people be found who are qualified to do so delicate a job calling for a high degree of wisdom and detachment?"[45] The next day, Michael Musmanno, the judge responsible for the majority of the death sentences, bolstered Taylor's views in another *New York Post* article. The former judge in the Einsatzgruppen case called the death sentences "eminently just and proper" and was quick to remind the public that Otto Ohlendorf and the other twenty-two defendants in that case were responsible for ordering and overseeing a "total number of killings amounting to 1,000,000."[46]

The same day, State Department legal advisor John Raymond discussed the review board with the State Department's Henry Byroade. He warned Byroade against appointing anyone to the board "who had personal convictions against the Nuremberg trial concept." Raymond also cautioned, "We must also watch the religious aspect."[47] They agreed that "a detailed study of fact, or law is not contemplated," and that the review of the war crimes trials should take "sixty days at a maximum."[48]

In a February 8 cable to the High Commissioner, Secretary of State Dean Acheson expressed his doubts about having one board review the sentences of all the war crimes trials. Acheson recognized that the proposed sentence reviews would reopen the debate over the legal legitimacy of the Nuremberg trials: "Army cable to CINCEUR suggests that same individuals deal with both Nuremberg and Dachau death sentences. This seems undesirable in view of different nature of trials." Acheson warned of the negative impression cast by another review: "Boards of the caliber you suggest would be bound to attract attention and might tend to create impression that legal basis, and procedure of Nuremberg trials under review, or at least be construed as indication of doubt RE Pohl and Ohlendorf cases."[49] McCloy heeded Acheson's advice, and by May 1950, two American war crimes clemency boards had been created. The American Nuremberg trials would be reviewed by a three-man committee that would report to John McCloy. The Dachau and Army cases would be reviewed by Texas Supreme Court

Justice Gordon Simpson, who would report to Army Commander-in-Chief General Thomas Handy.[50]

The legal expert for the High Commission's clemency board was former New York Supreme Court Justice David Peck. Questions about parole and incarceration were handled by the former chairman of the New York Board of Parole, Fredrick Moran. It is interesting to note that Moran was trained in social work and was an outspoken advocate of parole as "an instrument of rehabilitation."[51] The third member of the board was State Department legal advisor Conrad Snow. Their official task was to equalize sentence discrepancies between the various Nuremberg tribunals. The board was authorized only to reduce sentences, not to challenge the legal basis of the decisions. The Peck Panel spent the summer of 1950 in Munich, reading the judgments of the various courts.

Questions over German rearmament overshadowed the question of war crimes and led to a deadlock among the Truman administration's policy makers. The President was not blind to the implications of putting weapons back into the hands of German soldiers. He was quick to remind "the experts" that Germany had taken a 100,000-man paramilitary organization and transformed it into the greatest fighting force in modern history.[52] The stalemate over the West German army continued until, once again, "international communism" lived up to American expectations.

During the early morning of June 25, the State Department in Washington received a cable from the U.S. ambassador in Seoul, Korea: "North Korea forces invaded the Republic of Korea territory at several points this morning. . . . It would appear from the nature of the attack and manner in which it was launched that constitutes an all-out offensive against ROK." Initially, North Korean forces overran the South with ninety thousand troops and Soviet-made T-34 tanks.[53] Some of the darker minds in the U.S. government believed that the action had been ordered by Moscow and that once American forces were mired in Korea, the Red Army would launch a Western offensive. President Truman condemned the invasion in the strongest terms, arguing that "Communism was acting in Korea just as Hitler, Mussolini, and the Japanese had acted 10, 15, 20 years earlier. If this was allowed to go unchallenged it would mean a Third World War."[54] By September 1950 the United States had troops in Korea, and the "conflict" had turned into a full-scale war. Truman's decision to back his rhetoric with U.S. ground forces changed the diplomatic landscape throughout the world, but nowhere more than in Germany. The situation was further complicated by the fact that the West Germans were about to be asked to rearm and possibly fight East Germans.

There was a consensus among the State Department's elite (Acheson, McCloy, Harriman, and Nitze) that Germany needed to be rearmed.[55] High Commissioner McCloy recognized this and, like Clay before him, issued a dramatic warning to Washington. In a "top secret" cable, McCloy warned dramatically, "If no means are held out for Germans to fight in an emergency my view is that we should probably lose Germany politically as well as militarily without hope of regaining. We should also lose, incidentally, a reserve of manpower which may become of great value in event of a real war and could certainly be used by the Soviets against us."[56]

Secretary of State Dean Acheson and High Commissioner John McCloy decided to make Germany part of the Western European Defense Force (EDF), which had been created by representatives of the European powers who had already appointed Dwight Eisenhower Supreme Commander. One of Eisenhower's first assignments was to raise a German army.[57] The man who had once recommended executing the entire German General Staff now actively supported rearmament. Neither England nor France was overly enthusiastic about the idea, but considering the size of the U.S. military commitment in Korea and the amount of American economic aid to Europe, they couldn't afford to voice much opposition. Members of the High Commission met with Chancellor Adenauer to discuss the creation of seven German divisions by the mid-1950s.[58] The Truman administration, the State Department, and Konrad Adenauer were all in favor of rearmament, but both nations had huge domestic obstacles to overcome.[59] They needed the approval of their domestic constituencies and of the governments of Great Britain and France before they could implement any new plan.[60] Once it became official that West Germany would be rearmed, questions pertaining to the war criminals took on new significance as West German leaders from all political parties pointed to America's paradoxical role as occupying ally.

The system of war crimes trial review instituted by the High Commissioner was, like its predecessor, ad hoc. There was little procedure to follow, so the board created their own. Although they were able to review the judgments in each of the twelve American Nuremberg trials, they could not possibly consider the documentary evidence or the actual trial transcripts. It was an impossible task for three men. The transcripts in the Ministries case alone ran to twenty-eight thousand pages, and there were an additional nine thousand documentary exhibits.[61]

By the summer of 1950, the Peck Panel was hard at work. Review board member Conrad Snow reported "substantial progress" and said that the board was "fortunately, in perfect harmony." The board would finish reading the cases by August 4 and would "hear counsel the following week."[62] Despite the official pronouncements of impartiality, there were very basic ways the review process favored the German war criminals. Fifty lawyers representing the majority of the prisoners were brought before the board. Not only were the judges and prosecutors who had tried the cases conspicuously absent, but they did not even know that the sentences were being reviewed for a second time.[63]

The Peck Panel presented its final report to the High Commissioner on August 28, 1950. The report circulated through the High Commission office, and several members of the HICOG staff expressed reservations about their recommendations. State Department legal advisor John Raymond generally approved but considered some of the individual decisions excessively lenient. He felt that some of the sentence reductions called the original verdicts into question. In a confidential memo to State Department legal advisor Robert Bowie on September 11, 1950, Raymond wrote: "The basic difference in the approach adopted by the Board from the one that we took in reviewing cases is that the Board . . . did not feel bound by the findings drawn as conclusions from the facts, whereas we accepted all the findings of the tribunals." Raymond expressed the reservation that the "reduction from death to eight years is perhaps going too far" in reducing the sentences of former Einsatzgruppen Schubert and Seibert.[64]

Robert Bowie, High Commissioner McCloy's trusted legal advisor, also had serious misgivings about the Peck Panel's final report: "I have carefully reviewed the recommendations of the Board and believe that in a number of cases the reductions recommended are excessive. I have serious doubts as to the validity of the 24 recommendations of the Board which seem to me to fail to give sufficient recognition to the seriousness of the crime for which the individuals concerned were sentenced by Tribunals."[65]

Like Acheson, Bowie realized that the issue had moved beyond the legal realm. He concurred with Raymond that the clemency board's decisions called the original Nuremberg sentences into question: "certain statements by the Board suggest that they have striven to be as lenient as possible and I am concerned lest the report as a whole create the impression of a repudiation of the Nuremberg trials."[66]

In November, Secretary of State Acheson informed President Truman that some of the death sentences would probably be upheld by John McCloy: "I informed the President of the action which I proposed to take, saying that I did not wish him to assume responsibility in the matter but that he should know about it and that he could instruct me to the contrary if he thought that desirable. The President thought that the action proposed was correct."[67]

By late 1950, word of the impending sentence reviews reached the United States, and John McCloy was attacked from all sides of the political spectrum. On December 18, 1950, Senator Langer compared the Nuremberg trials to Stalin's purge trials: "These war-trials were decided on in Moscow and they were carried on under Moscow principles. These trials were essentially the same as the mass trials held in the 1930s by Stalin when Vyshinsky used treason trials to liquidate his internal enemies. At Nuremberg the Communists used the war crimes trials to liquidate their external enemies. It is the Communists' avowed purpose to destroy the Western World which is based on property rights." Langer added a new dimension to the critique by claiming that the cases against the industrialists were part of a communist plot "aimed directly at property rights. It was intended to try the accused as aggressors, convict them as having started the war, and then confiscate their property as a penalty."

However, under questioning from Senator McCarran of Nevada, Senator Langer made a rather dramatic and embarrassing factual error that exposed his complete ignorance of the American war crimes program that he was so vigorously attacking. When asked to "differentiate between the first Nuremberg trials and the latter Nuremberg trials," Langer replied, "The first Nuremberg trials were tried by Allied courts. . . . The other trials were conducted by American judges and American prosecutors according to American laws specifically enacted for that purpose." Senator Langer stated that the difference between them was like that "between night and day. For the second Nuremberg trials we sent from all over the United States judges to try between two million and three million Germans who were arrested and tried at what were called the denazification trials."[68]

McCloy spent the remainder of 1950 wrestling with his final decisions as German nationalists continued to lobby for an amnesty on war crimes. Security for McCloy's family was increased, as kidnapping threats were made against his children.[69] In early January the High Commissioner received a secret letter from Henry Byroade objecting to the tone of the clemency board's final report: "While it is an excellent summary of the reasons that led you to order the review . . . the tenor of the statement seems a little more apologetic than it need be or should be." Byroade anticipated a negative reaction to the clemency decision in Germany and believed that "a firm and positive statement will do more to counter the reaction in Germany, which inevitably will be bad."[70]

Of all McCloy's decisions as High Commissioner, these would be the most difficult. On January 9, he met with a West German parlimentary committee for two and a half hours. The delegation included Hermann Ehlers, President of the Bundestag Heinrich Hoefler, Carlos Schmid, Jacob Altmaier, Hans von Merkatz, and Franz Josef Strauss. According to Arthur Krock of *The New York Times*, "Dr. Schmid and his colleagues pointed out the new political developments taking place in Western Germany, said many Germans felt such an amnesty would assuage demands for restoration of the honor of German soldiers."[71] Finally, the West German leaders hit McCloy on a much more vulnerable level by pointing out that West Germany's freshly minted constitution "prohibited the death penalty."[72]

By this time McCloy had lost his patience, and he responded indignantly. The man accused of having a "pathological love for Germany" had been pushed too far.[73] According to *The New York Times*, the High Commissioner stated, "I did not know any good German soldier had lost his honor."[74] McCloy called the West Germans' bluff and reminded them who was holding the cards. "Of this threat Mr. McCloy feels that the Americans would rather not have the Germans if their cooperation depended upon the justification of war crimes or negligence to exact the penalty for them."[75] West German Deputy Minister of Justice Walter Strauss claimed that keeping men on death row for three years was in itself a crime against humanity and presented this paragraph of the Ministries case majority opinion to McCloy: "To permit one sentenced to death to remain for months or even years, without knowledge of his reprieve and untolerable anxiety and mental stress of not knowing whether the next day would be his last day on earth, is a trait typical of the sadism of the Nazi regime, and if anything could be considered a crime against humanity, such a practice is."[76] With rearmament now certain, unrepentant Nazis like Hitler's former bodyguard, Otto "Scarface" Skorzeny, recognized the new bargaining power the German veterans possessed. The Nazi folk hero threatened the Americans from his luxurious sanctuary in Madrid. "In good faith, even with a certain amount of enthusiasm, we have put ourselves at the disposal of the Americans. Yet I repeat in the name of all German officers who are working for the future victory of the West, if Peiper dies we will no longer lift a finger to help but will yield to the opposing point of view."[77]

President Truman reentered the fray on January 18, 1951, after receiving a letter from a personal friend in Kansas City who protested the outstanding death sentences. Truman passed the correspondence to Dean Acheson and asked that he "take a look at it." State Department legal advisor John Raymond drafted a memo on war crimes for President Truman that was a wholesale reaffirmation of the original Nuremberg and Dachau decisions[78] and an unequivocal argument against amnesty: "It is quite incorrect to consider the death sentences in such cases as part of a plan of vengeance or to intimate that it is anti-German. In fact they were imposed by the tribunals in order to bring to justice those who were responsible for such atrocities. Under these circumstances Mr. McCloy, who is well aware of the political considerations involved, could hardly grant a general amnesty."[79]

On January 31, 1951, HICOG released *Landsberg: A Documentary Report*, which included the statements of the Peck Panel, Judge Simpson, High Commissioner McCloy, and General Thomas Handy. John McCloy followed the majority of the board's recommendations and freed one third of the Nuremberg prisoners immediately. He commuted all but five of the outstanding death sentences to prison terms.[80] The primary beneficiaries of the High Commissioner's generosity were the German industrialists. With one stroke of John McCloy's pen, all of the remaining lawyers, executives, and industrialists convicted in the Farben, Flick, and Krupp trials were released.[81] Ministries case defendant Gottlob Berger had his sentence reduced from twenty-five to ten years.

The most controversial of all John McCloy's decisions came in the case of Alfried Krupp.[82] McCloy accepted the defendant's claims even though they were not borne out by the facts of the case. After a nine-month trial, Krupp had been found guilty of playing a leading role in running his family's company, which built factories on the grounds of concentration camps and used slave labor provided by the SS. On July 31, 1948, in an otherwise lenient judgment, Krupp was sentenced to twelve years and stripped of all industrial and financial holdings.[83] High Commissioner McCloy expressed his extreme discomfort with the tribunal's command to confiscate Krupp's property: "One feature of this case is unique, namely, the confiscation decree attached to the term sentence of Alfried Krupp. This is the sole case of confiscation decreed against any defendant by the Nuremberg courts." McCloy believed that singling Krupp out "constitutes discrimination against this defendant unjustified by any considerations attaching peculiarly to him. General confiscation of property is not a usual element in our judicial system and is generally repugnant to American concepts of justice."[84]

The duality in American war crimes policy became clear for all to see on February 3, 1951, when Krupp was set free and his property was restored to him. The irony of this convicted war criminal being greeted like a hero and regaining control of his massive empire was too rich and could not be ignored. His release created "the impression" that the United States was slowly but surely reversing its position on war crimes and told the German people that regardless of American rhetoric, it was back to business as usual.[85] Due in part to his high-level lobbying effort, Ernst von Weizsäcker had been out since December 1950; now his sentence was officially reduced to time served. At the time of his release, Nuremberg prosecutor Robert Kempner stated, "In 1924 I warned the Bavarian Government against the release from Landsberg prison of a certain Adolf Hitler and a certain Rudolf Hess. Today I want to go on record with a warning that the premature opening of the Landsberg gates will loose against society totalitarian subversive forces that endanger the free world."[86]

Suffice it to say, the Landsberg decisions had just the effect that Robert Bowie had anticipated. Nazi apologists who had argued all along that the war criminals were political prisoners felt vindicated by the High Commissioner's action. Several segments of the German population stepped up a well-organized campaign for a war crimes amnesty.[87] However, their most pressing concern was the fate of the men awaiting execution. In the capital cases, not even John McCloy could find grounds for clemency. No amount of strategic legalism could veil the fact that commutations in these capital cases would be viewed with great suspicion. Although High Commissioner McCloy and his army counterpart General Handy spared the lives of twenty-one of the war criminals facing death penalties, seven were still scheduled to hang.[88]

In 1948, General Clay had carefully reviewed the same five death sentences and was absolutely convinced that all the convicts deserved them. The most infamous of those awaiting execution was Otto Ohlendorf, the man who led Einsatzgruppen D into Russia in 1941. In one year, Einsatzgruppen D killed as many as ninety thousand civilians.[89] The tribunal found Paul Blobel responsible for overseeing more than sixty thousand murders.[90] Werner Braune was commander of the unit that committed the Simperpol massacre. Erich Naumann was in charge of a group that operated on the Russian front for sixteen months.[91] The fifth defendant to be executed was Oswald Pohl, the notorious concentration camp administrator. The two convicts under the U.S. Army's jurisdiction (Georg Schallermai and Hans Schmidt) had been particularly sadistic concentration camp guards at Mühldorf and Buchenwald.[92]

The final section of the *Landsberg Report* included the decisions of the U.S. Army in the Malmedy and other trials. General Thomas Handy, Commander-in-Chief of the U.S. Army in Europe, had created a European Command War Crimes Modification Board, headed by Texas Supreme Court Justice Gordon Simpson. Their task, similar to that of the Peck Panel, was to grant clemency where grounds for it existed.[93] The Modification Board reviewed more than four hundred cases. These defendants were soldiers who had violated the laws of war. General Handy stayed the executions of all the perpetrators of the Malmedy Massacre because the acts were committed in the heat of battle: "The commutation has been based upon other facts, which are deemed to mitigate in favor of less severe punishment than death. First, the offenses are associated with the confused fluid and desperate combat action, a attempt to turn the tide of Allied successes. . . . The crimes are definitely distinguishable from the more deliberate killings in concentration camps."[94] However, Handy remained convinced that Kampfegruppe Peiper had committed the atrocities and that Joachim Peiper had ordered them. Handy commuted all of the death sentences to life in prison and reduced 349 of 510 sentences; as a result, 150 men were immediately freed. On the whole, the U.S. Army was reluctant to issue wide-ranging war crimes amnesties and was significantly less lenient than John McCloy and the State Department.[95] The Modification Board was not so quick to brush the Malmedy Massacre under the rug in the name of political exigency.

American statesmen had hoped that these generous acts of clemency would mollify the German people, but ultimately *The Landsberg Report* had the opposite effect. No amount of strategic legalism could hide the fact that the American retreat from Nuremberg had begun. Acts like the High Commissioner's reduction of Einsatzkommando Heinz Hermann Schubert's death sentence to ten years spoke more loudly than legalistic distinctions between clemency and parole. Instead of accepting guilt for the criminal acts of the Third Reich, German nationalists stepped up their attacks on American war crimes policy. After 1951, they focused on the legal validity of the Nuremberg trials.[96]

John McCloy was caught in a public relations crossfire in both Germany and the United States. Like his American lawyer-statesmen predecessors, McCloy instinctively believed that what could be justified legally did not have to be justified morally. The High Commissioner attempted to treat the war crimes problem as a one-dimensional legal question, and it blew up in his face. Like Elihu Root before him, McCloy would interpret law to suit the needs of a rapidly changing American foreign policy. In the cases of Germany's worst convicted war criminals, any potential civil rights or legal improprieties became matters of the greatest concern for the U.S. government. However, contrast that to the civil rights of Japanese-Americans during World War II, U.S. citizens no less. At the time of the Japanese internment, McCloy described America's most sacred document, the Constitution, as "just a scrap of paper."[97]

The Americans had a worthy foe in the West Germans when it came to strategic legalism. By shifting the focus away from the crimes of the accused and forcing the Americans to defend the basic legal validity of their trials, the German nationalists changed the very nature of the debate. After nearly five years of occupation and reeducation, "Germans refused to make any practical distinction between the treatment of those who deserved and those who did not deserve punishment. The distinction that they did make was purely theoretical, allowing them to argue that those who had been punished by no means deserved it. Thus the public called not for clemency and reintegration, but for amnesty and rehabilitation," Friedrich points out.[98] Ironically, the questions that had been prohibited at Nuremberg by Article 3 of the London Agreement Charter were the ones that American officials would now have to debate with West German lawmakers and politicians.

By the early 1950s the Adenauer administration and the German Foreign Office were trying to reject the legal validity of the Allied war crimes trials and to secure the premature releases of the imprisoned war criminals. The prisoners now had a powerful and well-connected group lobbying on their behalf. The *Heidelberg Juristenkreis* was founded by former Nuremberg prosecutor and Bundestag representative (CDU) Eduard Wahl. He considered Control Council Law No. 10, which had created the Nuremberg tribunals, a violation of existing international law. Wahl did not simply seek the release of the war criminals; he also sought legal pardons.[99] Other important members of the *Kreis* included former Nuremberg defense lawyer Otto Kranzbühler, representatives from Germany's Catholic and Evangelical churches, politicians, and leading German jurists.[100] Kranzbühler described his role: "When the trials were finished in 1949, me and a lot of other lawyers who had taken part in those trials felt the obligation to see to it that the defendants sentenced would get out as soon as possible and that the principles of these trials would not be recognized by the coming German government."[101] Kranzbühler would emerge as the group's most formidable legal tactician. Just as he had evaded the Article 3 ruling and entered Admiral Nimitz's testimony at the IMT, he would find a way to reject the legal validity of the Allied war crimes tribunals.

The Juristenkreis had considerable influence and held regular meetings with both Konrad Adenauer and American officials. The group not only served as a clearinghouse for information but also drafted a proposal for the Adenauer administration on the subject of war crimes.[102] In a strategy meeting, Chancellor Adenauer instructed Kranzbühler to "see to it that the leading politicians of the [German] states will follow your views. You have to see them and instruct them."[103]

The Essen Amnesty Committee was a more radical right-wing war criminal advocacy group with a much different approach. It was led by Ernst Achenbach, another former Nuremberg defense attorney who was now a Bundestag representative in the right-wing Free Democratic Party. Freiburg law professor Friedrich Grimm served as one of the group's leaders. Not only did the Essen Amnesty Committee oppose rearmament and Western integration, they also sought a "tabula rasa" on war crimes in the form of an unconditional amnesty. John McCloy would later describe some of the committee's members as representatives of Germany's "right-wing lunatic fringe."[104]

By 1951, not only nationalists and neo-Nazis dismissed the American war crimes proceedings as a "victor's justice."[105] Even after the Landsberg decisions of 1951, letters and petitions continued to flood the offices of General Handy and High Commissioner McCloy, urging the American representatives to stay the executions. The powerful and educated appealed to McCloy on the grounds of Christian charity, arguing that those awaiting execution were guilty but that implementing a now outlawed death penalty would send the wrong message to the German people. Princess Helene von Isemberg pleaded to McCloy in the most melodramatic terms: "Jesus Christ has given the high doctrine to mankind: Forgive us our fault, as we forgive our enemies. Please, be a Christ, Sir."[106]

In one of the thousands of letters, a West German postal inspector urged the United States to free all war criminals and captured the spirit of the new debate on war crimes: "West Germany will then be a *reliable and strong friend* of the western countries. The Russians fear *American equipment* and the *German soldier* most of all."[107] Dean Acheson and Robert Bowie had recognized very early that logic and legal concepts would not placate a large segment of the German population. To nationalists, Nazis, and professional military men, the Third Reich had been vindicated by the postwar action of the United States. The Cold War had forced the United States to follow the anti-Bolshevik path originally cleared by Hitler.[108] Former Nazis spoke of Hitler's historic mission to organize the people of Europe and wage the first crusade of a second just war era. At Nuremberg some had argued that Operation Barbarossa had been a justified defensive action. Alfred Seidl, defense attorney for Reich Chancellor Hans Lammers, stated during the Ministries case in 1948:

> The Chief of the Reich Chancellory could be personally convinced in the year 1941 that the measures being taken by the Russians . . . would make necessary and would justify precautionary measures by the Germans. The development of international relations after the conclusion of World War II . . . has proved, in a way that could hardly have been expected or seemed possible, how justified Dr. Lammers was in his assumption.[109]

In the Bundestag debates of the early 1950s, German lawmakers made an interesting semantic shift. They began to refer to the war criminals (*Kriegsverbrecher*) as "war sentenced" or "sentenced because of war" (*Kriegsverurteiler*).[110]

The Nuremberg trials were also considered an affront to the military honor of the German soldier. There were numerous German veteran organizations whose highest priority in 1951 was to save the men on Landsberg's death row. The veterans considered the Landsberg, Werl, and Wittlich inmates to be prisoners of war. Many former members of the Waffen SS maintained that they had only been soldiers loyally fighting to protect their country. They were especially indignant that membership in the organization had been declared a criminal act at Nuremberg and equated the IMT's action with the Treaty of Versailles' "shame paragraphs." This was part of a larger effort to prove that the German war criminals had been unjustifiably persecuted. Although groups like the *Stahlhelm* were loyal to Bonn, they too were extremely critical of the judicial treatment of Germans in Allied courts.[111] The SS veteran organizations were less numerous and less influential. Membership in the SS had been ruled a criminal offense by the IMT at Nuremberg and the Basic Law ensured that former members were disqualified from obtaining military service pensions.[112]

In 1951, SS General Otto Kumm created an assistance group for former SS members, the Mutual Aid Society (*Hilfsgemeinschaft auf Gegenseitigkeit*).[113] HIAG leaders constantly rallied for the release of German war criminals in Allied custody, proclaiming that as a result of the widespread acts of clemency, the United States had repudiated its war crimes decisions. They stretched this interpretation, arguing that the Nuremberg ruling that the SS was a criminal organization was no longer binding.[114] Both Chancellor Adenauer and High Commissioner McCloy recognized the important swing vote that these seemingly extreme groups would cast.[115] The forty thousand-strong association of ex-soldiers called the *Schutz-Bund Ehemaliger Soldaten* stated in 1951 that the American decision not to grant a general amnesty proved that "the defamation of the German people in the spirit of Morgenthau continues."[116]

Many German veterans felt that American "stupidity" in dealing with the Soviet Union had placed "all of Europe in jeopardy."[117] Former Field Marshall Albert Kesselring became one of the veterans' prominent spokesmen. Originally sentenced to death by a British military court for reprisals that he ordered carried out against Italians, Kesselring would be released from Werl Prison in 1952. In an appeal to U.S. General Matthew Ridgeway, the German general implored his American counterpart to look beyond petty spites of the politicians and to see the larger issue:

> Sir, as officer to officer, I appeal to you, in whose hands the fate of many Germans lies. Help the German people cooperate enthusiastically in the fulfillment of the European cause so that they may eagerly comply with their inevitable historical obligation. Europe—indeed the whole western world— should not break down as a consequence of contrasts and conflicts with [sic] could be eliminated. You will be convinced as I am, of the fact that politics has its limits in military matters and vice versa, and that the war criminal cases should be separated from political matters and placed under the former uniform jurisdiction.[118]

After twenty months in British custody, German General Otto Remer was released; he founded the far right *Socialist Reich Partei*. Remer not only denied that the Holocaust ever happened but even claimed that the ovens had been built after the war and that the concentration camp films were fakes. Remer derided Adenauer and West Germany's American-inspired "shit democracy" with its "chewing gum" soldiers. He violently opposed the American rearmament plan and offered to show the Soviets the way to the Rhine. He adopted Hermann Goering's deathbed slogan, "*Ohne Mich!*" which loosely translates to "Count me out." SRP deputy Fritz Rossler pointed sarcastically to the duality of America's rapidly changing German policy: "First, we were told that guns and ammunition were poison and now this poison has been changed to sweets which we should eat. But we are not Negroes or idiots to whom they can do whatever they want. It is either they or us who should be committed to the insane asylum."[119]

The State Department's public opinion surveys in the weeks following the Landsberg decisions showed that the much-vaunted "lessons" of Nuremberg had been lost on war-weary Bavarians: "According to Bavarian leaders, the reactions of the man-in-the-street do not seem as favorable as those registered by the press and public officials." Some of the motives people offered for America's recent clemency decisions: "1) The

Americans have missed their chance to make good friends of the Germans. 2) Nuernberg has never been accepted by Germans, partic., in this case where the trial procedures were in many cases doubtful." There was special praise for the American decision to free the "*Stahlkoenig*" (steel king) Alfried Krupp. The survey concluded, "A fairly general public view seems to be that all the decisions were a political maneuver rather than an expression of American justice."[120]

On March 6, 1951, the U.S. High Commission released a confidential report entitled "West German Reactions to the Landsberg Decisions." Residents of German cities were asked their opinions of the American clemency decisions. Public opinion in the four Allied zones of Germany was split nearly 50–50. However, those who approved of the action saw it as a goodwill gesture, not a legal act. The report confirmed that "Finally, the legal considerations motivating the American decisions in the Landsberg cases, apparently completely failed to impress the German public. The principle and implications of judicial review and clemency entirely escape urban West Germans." The primary reason those surveyed gave for American leniency was that "They realize the injustice of the trials."[121]

On March 21, the State Department's Office of Public Affairs announced the results of a survey of German *Buergermeisters'* (mayors') views of the Landsberg decisions. Although 56 percent approved, the report concluded that "They apparently do not appreciably depart from the general urban public in their interpretations of American motivations in moderating the sentences." The most conclusive thing that the public opinion surveys showed was that the "lessons" the West Germans had learned from the Nuremberg trials were not the ones that their American reeducators had hoped to teach: "The prevailing interpretations are either that the basic injustice of Nuremberg is now being conceded, or that the revisions were prompted by a desire to win German allegiance."[122] More than 90 percent of the Buergermeisters agreed with the decision to free Alfried Krupp, whom they believed "did no more than war industrialists in other countries." When asked why the United States was reducing the sentences, 37 percent of those polled said it was because the Americans finally "realize the injustice of the trials."[123] Leo Crespi, head American pollster, concluded, "Whatever the stimulus German Buergermeisters might offer for support in the Landsberg decisions, it seems clear that in the *interpretation* of these actions they are, by and large, propagating views varying from an alleged American retreat from Nuremberg to outright political expediency."[124] On March 30, Crespi reached the same conclusion after conducting another survey of eight hundred urban West Germans. He wrote: "The public, for the most part, attributes the postponement of the execution of the death sentences pending the appeal of the U.S. Supreme Court to uncertainty, weakness, or ulterior purpose on the part of the U.S."[125]

As early as 1951, legalistic distinctions like the one between amnesty and parole were lost on the majority of West Germans, who interpreted the American review policy as cynical and politically expedient. Besides, it was not as if the German public had ever accepted the decisions of the Nuremberg trials as legally valid in the first place. The State Department would use strategic legalism to ameliorate the original sentences. In this case, the mechanism, or as the State Department legal advisors described it, "device," was an ever-decreasing set of standards for clemency and parole. American authorities were trying to justify the early releases by citing "modern penalogical principles." These justifications fell on deaf ears because they were only partially true.[126]

A number of pamphlets demanding a reversal of the death sentences appeared in 1951. The most dramatic one was entitled "Germany's Dreyfus Affair." In it, former concentration camp administrator and SS General Oswald Pohl, one of the convicts facing the hangman's noose, published a letter to former SS General Karl Wolff. In a plea bargain of sorts, Wolff had surrendered to the Allies in 1945 and worked with the prosecutors at Nuremberg in exchange for immunity from prosecution. Pohl considered his former comrade a traitor: "Through your treasonous activity in Switzerland in April 1945, you gained for yourself an 'honorary' position at Nuremberg with the innocent American examiners." Pohl believed that Wolff could prove his innocence. He wrote, "In this predicament, I feel exactly as innocent as the famous French patriot, Alfred Dreyfus. But you in my eyes, have behaved yourself like the traitor, Esterhazy, who was likewise responsible for Dreyfus' conviction."[127] This pamphlet, as well as "a number of pieces of mimeographed material in defense of Pohl, Ohlendorf, and other Landsberg defendants,"[128] was published by the Universal Union, a pro-amnesty group led by Frederick Wiehl, Oswald Pohl's attorney. However, these crude tactics were far less successful than the more sophisticated efforts of the Heidelberg Juristenkreis.

By 1951, a majority of West Germans had come to reject the social engineering of the American occupation. Adenauer's willingness to join an American-led military alliance was also a contentious issue.[129] Although McCloy was slow to realize it, he finally conceded that no argument would placate certain segments of the German population.[130] Instead of quelling a mounting wave of criticism concerning the treatment of war criminals, the Peck Panel Report created controversies on both continents.

In a February 1951 *Nation* magazine article entitled "Why Are We Freeing the Nazis?" Eleanor Roosevelt called attention to the premature release of prominent war criminals like Alfried Krupp. After the article appeared, the High Commissioner defended his decisions in a letter to the former first lady published in the June 29, 1951 issue of the U.S. High Commission's *Information Bulletin*: "As for the Krupp case. I find it difficult to understand the reaction on any other basis than the effect of a name. After a detailed study of this case, I could not convince myself that he deserved the sentence imposed on him. There was certainly a reasonable doubt that he was responsible for the policies of the Krupp company, in which he in fact occupied a somewhat junior position."[131] John McCloy could see no justification for taking Krupp's property: "No other person had his property confiscated—not even the worst mass murderers. Why then single this man out for a type of punishment which, as Justice Jackson has pointed out, was entirely foreign to American tradition?"[132] It has been widely noted that John McCloy was especially uncomfortable with the original decisions in the Krupp case. Former Nuremberg prosecutor Benjamin Ferencz attributed this to his background as a Wall Street lawyer.[133] McCloy vehemently denied the fact that politics played a role in his decisions: "What really smarts with me is the suggestion that these decisions were the result of 'expediency', i.e. that they were timed to gain a political objective. . . . If we were moved by expediency would it have been reasonable to release a man with such a world resounding name as Krupp."[134] However, his earnest claims were unconvincing to many.

Once again, Telford Taylor was called upon to defend the American Nuremberg trials. The former Chief Counsel responded to McCloy's letter to Eleanor Roosevelt because it "contains numerous inaccuracies, which are extremely damaging to the Nuremberg proceedings, to the judges who sat at the trials, to General Clay, and, incidentally to me. Several of these misstatements are so serious that they should not be allowed to stand uncorrected." The High Commissioner had not helped his own case by including basic factual errors. Taylor wrote:

> Mr. McCloy states at the outset of his letter to you 'I inherited these cases from General Clay, who, for one reason or another had been unable to dispose of them finally.' This statement is 87–1/2% incorrect. The judgments pronounced at Nuremberg were to be final, but the sentences were subject to reduction at the discretion of the Military Governor. In eleven of the twelve cases, General Clay exercised his responsibilities, and reviewed the sentences prior to his resignation as Military Governor. In one case, in which the judgment was not rendered until a few months before General Clay's departure, he was unable to take action in the time remaining. This case and only this one case was not 'disposed of finally' at the time Mr. McCloy took office. . . .
>
> Nor was General Clay's review of the sentences in the eleven cases in which he acted in any way perfunctory. General Clay was assisted by a very able legal staff, headed by such men as Judge J. Warren Madden, Alvin Rockwell, and Colonel John Raymond, now Deputy Legal Advisor to the Department of State. To my personal knowledge, this legal staff gave extensive and careful consideration to the records and judgments in the Nuremberg trials, and General Clay gave conscientious and perceptive personal attention to their recommendations before he took action.

The former Chief Counsel pointed out how biased the High Commissioner's review had been:

> He made this review on the basis of a totally one-sided presentation of the law and the facts. . . . The Board read the judgments in all twelve cases (but apparently not the records), and heard fifty lawyers representing the criminals confined at Landsberg Prison. No representative of the prosecution was heard, or invited to appear, before either the Clemency Board or Mr. McCloy.[135]

On March 28, in Great Britain, former Nuremberg prosecutor Sir Hartley Shawcross, now British Attorney General, attacked the Landsberg decisions as "mistaken ideas of political expediency or because of the wholly false view that these sentences were no more than vengeance wreaked by the victors upon the vanquished." The American clemency action would undermine "the validity of what has been done." Shawcross rejected the argument that the Cold War somehow justified a shift in war crimes policy: "These Nazis were and are no friends of ours simply because they fought against the Russians during the war. Nothing could do a greater disservice to our cause, at a time when Germany is being led back into the international life of Europe, than at the same time to white-wash the Nazis and what they stood for."[136] The U.S. embassy in London cabled a copy of the speech to Secretary of State Dean Acheson with the following message: "In this connection domestic polit import Shawcross speech shld not (rpt not) be overlooked."[137]

High Commissioner McCloy responded to the Shawcross charges on March 30. "Sir Hartley, of course, has a right to his own opinions and to express them as he sees fit." McCloy took grave exception to the charges that the clemency decisions were politically motivated: "as reported in the press, this speech seems to imply that clemency for the war criminals was based on 'political expediency' and reflects on the Nuremberg trials. . . . I must take issue on both points in view of the seriousness of the charges." The High Commissioner offered his standard defense for the clemency action, but was especially irritated by the charge that he was undermining the legacy of Nuremberg: "Furthermore, as is clear from a reading of the statement which accompanied them, my decisions do not (rpt not) reflect on the Nuremberg proceedings. . . . In view of my substantial part in orig-inating the concept of Nuremberg and in setting up the machinery, any suggestion that my decisions reflect any lack of sympathy for the basis of these trials is as incorrect and unfounded as the implication that my deci-sions were motivated by considerations other than justice and clemen-cy."[138] It was no longer a question of getting the war criminals freed; a steadily growing number of Germans continued to attack the legal valid-ity of the trials themselves. McCloy's decisions were not seen as benevo-lent acts of clemency within a modern legal system but as the cynical abandonment of a failed policy.

On May 25, 1951, the wives of the condemned German war criminals visited their loved ones for the final time. Some wept openly. Elonora Pohl, the wife of Oswald Pohl, maintained her composure inside Lands-berg Prison but collapsed from a nervous breakdown just outside the gates.[139] The State Department ordered the army and the High Commission to stay the executions for five days so that a U.S. District Court in Washington, D.C. could rule on a last-minute injunction. On June 7, High Commissioner McCloy got the word from Washington, and Blobel, Braune, Naumann, Pohl, Ohlendorf, Schallermaier, and Schmidt were quietly hanged at Landsberg Prison.[140] According to Jörg Friedrich, "This was their final *piece de resistance*. The public uproar over the hanging of these blood tainted butchers underlined Nuremberg's failure."[141] The funeral of Otto Ohlendorf took place a few weeks later in Hoheneggelsen, and representatives of all of Germany's right-wing parties attended. When Ohlendorf was lowered into the grave, the mourners gave the Nazi salute.[142] One wreath bore the slogan, "*Uber Galgen Waechst kein Gras*" ("No grass grows over the gallows"); another said, "*Kein Schoenerer Tod auf dieser Welt als ver vorm Feind erschlagen*" ("No more beautiful death in this world than to be struck down before the enemy").[143]

The early public opinion polls conducted by the State Department's Bureau of Public Affairs after the executions drew the same conclusion as the pre-execution polls. In the press accounts from the Wuerttemberg-Baden area, most of the editorial writers "Voiced considerable reserve in regard to the principles and procedures of the Nuremberg, and especially the Dachau, trials. Many papers argue that the commutation of sentences is proof that something was wrong with the sentences." The Deputy Director for the State Department's Bureau of German Affairs, Geoffrey Lewis, predicted that West Germans would continue to use this issue in the coming years: "One must also be prepared for the possibility that right-wing political circles, ranging from the CDU and DVP to the utmost extreme, may warm this issue up if released by international and domestic political situation."[144]

Chapter Six

THE WAR CRIMINALS AND THE RESTORATION
OF WEST GERMAN SOVEREIGNTY

With the last executions of war criminals on German soil accomplished, by the fall of 1951, talks about the complete restoration of West German sovereignty were well under way. Once again, the continued incarceration of war criminals proved to be a very difficult point of contention between Americans and West German leaders. In October, the attorneys of the Heidelberg *Juristenkreis* approached Carlo Schmid, chairman of the *Bundestag*'s subcommittee on POWs, with a proposal for a solution to the war crimes problem.[1] On October 26, former Nuremberg defense attorney Otto Kranzbühler met with the Bundestag's POW committee and outlined a plan to reject the legal validity of all Allied war crimes trials. Under Kränzbuhler's plan, the West German government would simply and steadfastly refuse to recognize the trials' legal validity.[2] In November, Schmid passed Kranzbühler's plan on to Konrad Adenauer with the additional demand that all the prisoners who had served one third of their sentences should be released. On November 19, the committee on POWs offered a resolution calling for an amnesty on war crimes and a transfer of the prisoners to West German custody.[3]

While the Americans were eager to turn the war criminals over to German authorities, it was not that simple. The State Department was fully aware that if the West German government wanted to assume physical custody of the convicts, they would have to recognize the legal validity of the original sentences—which was extremely unlikely. This point was made in a State Department cable to Washington: "This solution wld require recognition by Gers of Nuremberg and similar judgments, which wld be difficult politically as Gers have heretofore consistently contested their validity."[4] It was illogical to assume that the Federal Republic would stand by the American war crimes courts' findings once they obtained custody of the convicts: "they wld probably use their authority to effect release, extended parole or other differential treatment, thus negating effect of sentences."[5] The second approach proposed by the Bundestag committee involved sending the war criminals to "territory of the Allies or another power," but this was rejected due to the potential "violent political repercussions in Germany." Third and fourth options allowed for the war criminals' continued incarceration in Germany: one plan called for Allied control, while the other called for international custody.

The German Foreign Office was alarmed by the implications of the Bundestag committee's resolution because it went way beyond Adenauer's proposal and raised difficult questions. Could the Allies transfer the war criminals into West German custody if the Adenauer administration refused to recognize the validity of the original sentences? In late December 1951, Chancellor Adenauer met with the recently reelected British Prime Minister, Winston Churchill. Although Churchill offered to turn the British prisoners over to the Federal Republic, he made it very clear that if the Germans wanted to assume custody, they would have to acknowledge the legal validity of the sentences handed down by the Allied war crimes court. Another State Department cable reported: "Brit propose Gers should be given custody when contractual arrangements go into effect. Gers will be rquired to recognize validity of sentences. Clemency will be exercised by an advisory clemency tribunal composed of one Ger, one neutral, and one Allied rep." Once again, the Americans tried to rule questions about the Nuremberg trials' legal validity off limits: "Tribunal will have no (rpt no) power to question validity of sentences."[6] British High Commissioner Ivonne Kirkpatrick reduced the British parole requirements and immediately released twenty-five convicted war criminals from British custody in Werl Prison. Kirkpatrick proposed that the Germans should be given custody of the remaining war criminals once the contractual arrangements went into effect in 1952.[7]

On December 21, High Commissioner McCloy met with Chancellor Adenauer to discuss the war crimes question. The High Commissioner asked the West German leader if he had any new proposals: "I recalled his promise to give his personal attention to this subj and to let us have his suggestions at an early date." Adenauer described his meetings with Churchill and Eden in London and endorsed the plan for a mixed clemency board with a neutral chairman. "He indicated he wld be prepared to accept this solution providing Ger was not thereby required to recognize Nuremberg judgments."[8] McCloy asked who would take control of the German prisoners once the contractual agreements went into effect. When Adenauer said that West Germany could, McCloy believed that the Chancellor had "not fully thought this through. When I pointed out to him the difficulty of finding justification under Ger law to hold these individuals in custody, without recognition of validity of these sentences, he offered no (rpt no) solution but thought some way might be found."[9]

By early 1952, the German Foreign Office realized the implications of a custody transfer, as historian Frank Buscher has noted: "this would be tantamount to an official German recognition of the judgments and the verdicts. This, the agency felt, should be avoided at all costs."[10] In conversations with German politicians, Adenauer stated firmly that he would refuse to recognize the Allied verdicts and that he would demand another sentence review board.[11]

The contractual agreements (Bonn Agreements) restored West German sovereignty and did away with the remaining vestiges of the occupation government. Although Konrad Adenauer supported the Heidelberg Juristenkreis plan for an international clemency board composed of Germans and Americans, a number of problems remained, the most prominent of which was the growing duality in American war crimes policy. While John McCloy was able to prevent the uproar over the Landsberg decisions from derailing American foreign policy, the State Department's strategic legalism was beginning to look increasingly pale in the stark light of the Cold War. Many West Germans found it odd that the United States was now excitedly making provisions for a new German army while military leaders like Erich von Manstein, Wilhelm List, Walter Kuntze, Hermann Reincke, Erhard Milch, Herman Hoth, Georg von Kuechler, Hans von Salmuth, and Walter Warlimont remained in prison.[12]

In March 1952, State Department officer Charles Thayer wrote a secret report concerning the ongoing and serious problem posed by the continued imprisonment of German soldiers. "One of the neuralgic points in the relationship between the Germans and the Allied High Commission is the problem of the war criminals in Landsberg and Werl. The case of the top-ranking generals, in particular, seems to enter into almost all discussions of a German defense contribution." He concluded, "It is expected that the case of the German war criminals will assume increased importance in the months to come in connection with more extended public discussion."[13] If anything, the Landsberg decisions demonstrated that the Americans were growing increasingly flexible on the war crimes question. This lack of resolve led many West Germans to demand an amnesty on war crimes as the precondition for rearmament. Thayer wrote, "Release of war criminals is frequently stated to be condition for any German participation in a defense effort, and release of prisoners who are held for alleged war crimes is a condition for defense participation posed by the government coalition in the Bundestag debate on February 8."[14] Thayer anticipated "the case of the German war criminals will assume increased importance in the months to come in connection with more extended public discussion of a German defense contribution."[15]

Soviet leader Josef Stalin made an attempt to prevent German rearmament on March 10, 1952 when he offered to withdraw the Red Army from East Germany, reunify Germany, and hold free elections. Although the Soviet leader did not succeed in his effort to block the passage of the Bonn Agreements, he did strengthen the West German position in its discussions with the United States. As the ratification process neared, the Heidelberg Juristenkreis worked to devise a way for the West German government to reject the legal validity of the Allied war crimes trials.[16] Kranzbühler described their plan: "There was a treaty settling matters of war and occupation. In this, all the acts of the military government were recognized by the German government. In the document that we prepared for the central German government there was a recommendation that the war crimes trials should not be recognized." To Frank Buscher, the debate over sentence validity provides further evidence that the American re-education efforts had failed. "The philosophy of the *Bundestag* was that the inmates of Landsberg, Werl, and Wittlich were almost exclusively honorable soldiers, who had merely followed orders. Such

views, held by the Federal Republic's political elites, were bound to influence the thinking of the general public sooner or later."[17] Kranzbühler
urged Konrad Adenauer and the German Foreign Office to act so "that
the principles of these trials would not be recognized by the coming German government."[18] According to Kranzbühler, in a private meeting with
Adenauer, he and Edward Wahl "convinced Adenauer . . . that it was
about accepting war guilt or not—accepting special law only for Germans and not for anybody else which no government could really do.
Adenauer agreed with that and it was astonishing."[19] The contractual
agreements restoring German sovereignty were signed by the Allies on
May 26 and 27, 1952, in Bonn and thus came to be known as the Bonn
Agreements. West Germany's official position on the legal validity of the
Allied war crimes tribunals can be found in articles 6 and 7 of the treaty's
"Convention on the Settlement of Matters Arising out of the War and
Occupation."

Article 6 established a six-man committee, composed of one representative from each Allied power and three Germans, to make further parole
and clemency recommendations "without calling into question the validity of the convictions." Article 7, section 1 appears to be a straightforward
endorsement of the legal validity of all the Allied war crimes trials: "All
judgments and decisions in criminal matters heretofore or hereafter rendered in Germany by any tribunal or judicial authority of the Three Powers or any of them shall remain final and valid for all purposes under
German law and shall be treated as such by German courts and authorities." However, buried in Article 6, section 11 is an exception: "The provisions of Article 7 of this Chapter shall not apply to matters dealt with in
this Article."[20] In other words, the Article 6 clemency board did not have
to accept the validity of the courts' decisions. According to Kranzbühler,
"It was drafted after we had a conference with Adenauer. A good lawyer
would never do it that way, to put the exception in a different place than
the rule. But it was intended to conceal. Nobody took notice of it, no
press mentioned it." Buscher argues that the confusion created by the
"Convention on the Settlement of Matters Arising out of the War and
Occupation" created a "constitutional gray zone that made it possible for
the lawmakers to couch their obvious biases in legalistic terms. As a
result, they could freely attack the Allies for allegedly violating the provisions of the Federal Republic's constitution when extraditing and executing German citizens."[21]

Walter Donnelly replaced John McCloy as High Commissioner in August 1952. During McCloy's final press conference as High Commissioner, he claimed to be optimistic about West German democracy. However, he warned his audience that the United States would not trade war criminals for German rearmament: "If you are asking if there is to be a jail delivery to get ratification through, the answer is no."[22] Despite his stern words, West German veterans continued to hammer away at the new High Commissioner. On July 14, 1952, more than two million German veterans adopted a resolution calling for a war crimes amnesty.[23] It declared that "no German can be expected to don a military uniform again until the question of 'war criminals' had been satisfactorily settled." On August 10, High Commissioner Donnelly received a copy of a letter written by Gottfried Hansen, the chairman of the Union of German Ex-Soldiers, to U.S. General Matthew Ridgeway, calling for a "speedy and satisfactory solution" to the war crimes problem in the form of a "general amnesty granted to the prisoners."

> But what is oppressing humanity as a whole now is the curse called down at Tehran, Yalta, and Potsdam. It . . . is against this curse that the Western world is struggling. Are Nuremberg and all that followed to become a similar curse? Is this curse to stand in the way of the Western forces being welded into one true force of defense, united by comradeship and respect?[24]

The veterans' resolution was adopted by members of important German groups like the Association of Former Fighter Pilots, the Air Force Circle, German Association of War Wounded, Association of German Soldiers, Association of Former Members of the German Africa Corps, and others. Hansen announced that "The undersigned associations note with satisfaction that Theodor Blank [Adenauer's Security Advisor] . . . has adopted their view that no German can be expected to don a Military uniform again until the question of 'war criminals' has been satisfactorily settled."[25]

In early September, U.S. General Mathew Ridgeway spoke with Konrad Adenauer in Bonn. This account of the meeting in a Bonn daily was telling: "The General's attention was drawn yesterday to the fact that in the eyes of a large part of the German public this problem is the most serious political obstacle to German defense participation."[26] Jörg

Friedrich describes how the rearmament question fundamentally altered America's relationship with the Federal Republic of Germany: "They could not be allies and prison guards at the same time. There was no choice but to pardon and integrate the convicted." Germany's old elites "had to be rehabilitated for reuse."[27]

Eli Debevoise, General Counsel for the U.S. High Commission, issued a secret report on the problems posed by the war criminals on September 6, 1952. "Whether we like it or not, the German politicians and press are making the subject of the war criminals an important factor at this time." The report described the German critics' attacks on the validity of the original sentences: "To the extent that attacks bear analysis, develop along one or more or combinations of the following: (a) There were no crimes and therefore no legal basis for the trials." The German press had erased all distinctions among the various categories of war criminals: "Through the device of lumping all prisoners into the category of soldiers and all common crimes as 'war crimes,' the press has been able to thoroughly mislead and confuse the German public." The report concluded: "It seems clear enough that a German campaign is aimed at unraveling loose threads in the fabric of action taken by the Allies on war criminals, and thus progressively unraveling the fabric."[28] High Commissioner Donnelly shared these sentiments and began to fear for Adenauer's political future. In a cable to Secretary of State Acheson, Donnelly realized that "the problem will not end (rpt not) end with ratification. On the contrary, it will affect both the wholeheartedness of the Ger def effort and the Chancellor's chances of success at the polls in the early summer of 1953 unless problem has been both rapidly and finally solved after EDC comes into effect, and not (rpt not) so soon before the election as to look contrived."[29] Even as early as 1952, Nuremberg critics in Germany were succeeding in shifting the debate away from the crimes of the defendants and back to the legal validity of the Allied trials.

On September 16, High Commissioner Donnelly announced the latest and most depressing German public opinion poll to date. According to the State Department's August survey, only 10 percent of West Germans approved of the handling of the war criminal issue, while 59 percent disapproved. Those screaming the loudest were not the ill-informed and the downtrodden: "Most widely disapproving are opinion leading population elements—men, better educated, and economically better situated." West Germany's social leaders now demanded an amnesty: "Outright release of the Ger generals now held prisoner by Western powers is the remedy most frequently suggested by those disapproving of the present treatment."[30] The biggest short-term problem facing the Americans was putting the Mixed Clemency Board created by Article 6 of the Bonn Agreements into action. The agreements had to be ratified by all three EDC powers, but it did not look like France would, and the West German government was becoming agitated because the clemency board had not yet been established.

On September 17, the Bundestag debated the war crimes question for more than two hours, with West German lawmakers vociferously attacking Allied policy.[31] They maintained that the trials had served political rather than judicial ends. Ironically, the Communists were the only party that did not attack the trials.[32] Despite German dissatisfaction over prisoner releases, the number of war criminals in Allied custody was declining steadily. In one year (December 15, 1951 to September 13, 1952), the population of Landsberg Prison was reduced by 25 percent, from 458 to 338.[33] Because the establishment of the Article 6 Mixed Board was held up by the ratification of the EDC Treaty in the French Assembly, the Heidelberg Juristenkreis proposed the creation of an interim board to review cases until the Article 6 Board could be convened.[34]

In a secret letter to High Commissioner Donnelly, James Riddleberger, director of the State Department's Office of Political Affairs, considered the problem posed by the conflicting goals of American war crimes policy: "Our main objective is to keep the German agitation and resentment on this subject from interfering with ratification. At the same time, we do not wish to take any steps inconsistent with the principle of the war crimes trials, or with the statement made to the President."[35] The State Department officer saw an interim parole board as "a good device" that "made things easier" for Germany and allowed the United States to maintain "all the basic elements of our position." He anticipated trouble from the German board members: "The fact that the Board will not be able to question the validity of the war crimes judgments will be a continuing objection to it in the German view." Riddleberger advised the High Commissioner that the United States had "little to offer" by way of further concessions for convicted war criminals, and to "be careful not to offer it too soon, because we might be pressed for more at a later and more awkward stage."[36]

Rearmament plans gained new momentum when General Dwight

David Eisenhower was elected President of the United States in November 1952. His choice for Secretary of State, John Foster Dulles, would have great implications for Germany. Dulles was another third-generation American lawyer-statesman, the grandson of American diplomat John Foster, the nephew of Secretary of State Robert Lansing, and the brother of American spymaster Allen Dulles. The new Secretary of State was well acquainted with international law; while still a college student, he had served as a recording secretary at the 1907 Hague Convention.[37] Like his hero and uncle, Robert "Bert" Lansing, Dulles was a member of a prestigious Wall Street law firm (Sullivan and Cromwell). In 1911, during World War I, John Foster Dulles joined the State Department as an expert on political and economic affairs. In 1919, at the tender age of thirty-one, he was appointed to the American delegation during the Paris Peace Conference. Dulles served as an assistant in German war reparations, mainly dealing with financial questions.[38] At the Paris Peace Conference, Lansing rejected all efforts to punish suspected war criminals and was especially hostile to the introduction of "the laws of humanity" into the discussion. Thus John Foster Dulles came to his conservatism quite naturally, and his appointment would have a profound impact on the future treatment of German war criminals. McCloy made this observation: "Dulles had very definite views about Germany. He'd spent a good bit of time in Germany, had a number of German clients and he was deeply interested in it."[39] A month later, his brother, Allen Dulles, was appointed director of the CIA.

In his final weeks as U.S. Secretary of State, Dean Acheson observed that the war criminals had become a "highly emotional and political problem of considerable proportions."[40] On December 22, 1952, the High Commissioner (now James Conant) received a report from the State Department's Office of Political Affairs suggesting a "political" solution to the German war crimes question. This sparked a major internal debate within the U.S. State Department. The Political Affairs report outlined the ways in which the war criminals could adversely affect American policy in Germany: "(1) It will affect the political strength of the Chancellor and his party and thus the chances for continuation of present German foreign policy course (2) it will affect the development of the EDC, both in terms of German popular support, and the more specific problem of recruiting experienced officer material for the German contingent of the EDC." The final recommendation was neither new nor groundbreaking:

"We would suggest further that a more lenient system of reduction of sentence and parole be adopted. . . . An alternative which is posed for possible consideration is the use of a large scale clemency device."[41] The report recommended a third review of the Nuremberg and Dachau sentences by a parole board that would have even looser requirements than the previous two. The suggestions were based solely on political expediency: "The memorandum has limited itself to considering the problem as a political one, and not as a juridicial or moral one. . . . The memo is undoubtedly one sided and it is realized that other points of view will have to be considered."[42]

State Department Assistant Legal Advisor John Raymond was among the first to register his dissatisfaction with the proposed use of parole and clemency as a "device" to free war criminals. Raymond been intimately involved with the Nuremberg trials since 1945, he had also served on General Clay's original sentence review board. Raymond was not impressed by the memo and stated plainly, "It seems to me, however, that there are certain basic fallacies in the discussion which I should like to point out." He believed that the proposal "unwittingly accepts the very German psychology which it criticizes. . . . I am satisfied that the thinking behind the dispatch is quite erroneous in the respects above outlined. There are other matters of detail with which I do not agree but these I think are the basic difficulties. They lead to a wholly unsound conclusion as to the course of action to be pursued." He suggested that the authors of the memo had bought into the German logic on war crimes: "The fallacy lies with the basic premise that because they were German soldiers they were tried and convicted. The true premise is that because they committed crimes of murder, atrocities, etc., they were tried and convicted."[43]

Less than a week later, State Department International Relations Officer John Auchincloss also weighed in against a political solution to what he considered to be a judicial question. Auchincloss would emerge as one of the Nuremberg trials' few defenders within the State Department. "The paper advanced a political solution of the war crimes problem, and it might be well to point out certain objections which would apply to any solution of that kind," he argued. Asserting that a political solution would have a corrosive effect on the legacy of Nuremberg, he warned: "Why should others think more highly of them than we? The solution proposed would remove all legal basis for the trials by showing what little respect we have for them; it would discredit everything the Allies have done in this field." Auchincloss was especially irritated by the Political Affairs report's description of clemency as a "device": "The solution recommended in the paper is admittedly a political solution. That is to say, it is designed to meet political requirements and intended to accomplish a political result, rather than to accord with the facts in the individual cases. The solution would not be a true exercise of clemency (the despatch even speaks of clemency as a 'device')."[44]

The State Department officer conceded that "The Germans do not want to be grateful to us, and they do not accept any of the principles behind the war crimes trials." He believed that political clemencies would lower American prestige in Germany and be viewed as an abandonment of America's postwar reform policies outlined in JCS 1067. Auchincloss enumerated the ways in which more releases would discredit and contradict America's radical post–World War II war crimes policy:

> There is so much background to this question—the Moscow Declaration of 1943 issued by President Roosevelt, Mr. Churchill, and Stalin; the trials themselves, with the wide expectation that they would serve the ends of justice and also create new principles of law; the international acceptance of these principles by the adherence of other nations to the Charter of the International Military Tribunal, and by the General Assembly resolution of December 11, 1946 affirming the principles of international law recognized by the Charter of the Nurnberg Tribunal and the judgment of the Tribunal—that an American yielding to a German demand for the release of war criminals would be a concession of uncommon significance.[45]

Most important, Auchincloss warned, "While any political solution will be attended with great difficulty, the particular vice of the one recently suggested is that it is a political solution which pretends to be something else." His warning would prove quite prophetic: "I believe this is one subject on which we have no chance of fooling other people, and we had better not try, or we shall fool only ourselves."[46]

In early February 1953, Secretary of State John Foster Dulles traveled to Bonn to meet with German leaders. The State Department's Division of Political Affairs prepared a series of briefing papers for him. "Political Brief No. 5" described "Political Aspects of the War Crimes Question."

By 1953, the State Department conceded that the Nuremberg trials had failed to "reeducate" West Germans: "From the political point of view, the crux of the war criminals problem in Germany is the refusal of a large number of Germans to accept the principles underlying the trials or the findings of the trials. . . . In spite of all the Western powers have said to the contrary, the trials are generally portrayed as acts of political retribution without firm legal basis."[47] "Political Brief No. 5" warned that the "problem cannot be eradicated, or perhaps even treated effectively, by rational arguments"[48] and predicted that the war criminals would "act as one more constant irritant in the relations of Germany with the United States as well as England. . . . As time goes on, the fundamental, if unavoidable, contradiction between the role of the United States as Germany's ally and friend can be exhibited by unfriendly German politicians and publicists to the detriment of German-American relations."[49]

On May 15, State Department legal advisor John Raymond warned the Department of Defense to limit the jurisdiction of any proposed parole board "to matters of parole (not clemency) and exclude any basis for attempt by German member to reopen cases or question original convictions. Similar precautions should be taken with respect provisions for parole supervision, in which we suppose Germans will also participate, so that we shall have nearest possible equivalent to explicit recognition by Germans of validity war crimes judgments."[50]

German Chancellor Konrad Adenauer traveled to the United States in April 1953 to attend the Washington Foreign Ministers Conference. The State Department knew that he intended to press for the release of more war criminals. A preconference memo described the American policy initiative: "To keep German feeling on the subject of war criminals from adversely affecting U.S.-German relations or a German defense contribution."[51] The memo also acknowledged that "the lessons of Nuremberg" had been lost on the vast majority of postwar Germans: "The German attitude towards the war crimes trials and the confinement of criminals has constituted a problem of continuous difficulty ever since the trials were held. The Germans have not accepted the underlying principles of the trials and do not believe in the guilt of those who have been convicted."[52] According to the memo, rationality and empirical facts meant little in this debate: "Their attitude is strongly emotional and is not influenced by argument or by objective presentation of the facts. They persist in believing . . . that most war criminals are soldiers who have been punished for doing what all soldiers do or may be ordered to do in time of war, and that only a small minority of the prisoners are guilty of atrocities or common crimes." Finally and most important, the memo warned that the war criminals were a problem that "may interfere with good relations between this country and the Federal Republic, which may cause difficulties for the parties of the Chancellor's coalition in the election this year."[53]

In the first meeting of the Foreign Ministers Conference on April 8, Adenauer "pointed out that there were considerable psychological and public opinion problems in Germany connected with the war criminal issue."[54] In the second meeting, the Americans appeared eager to facilitate the Heidelberg Juristenkreis plan: "Ambassador Conant said that the US would hope to have either a mixed board or some new procedure . . . in the near future, and certainly before the September elections in Germany. He suggested that little publicity be given to these plans and that public references be made in only general terms."[55] Secretary of State John Foster Dulles went even further; he "reiterated to the Chancellor that the U.S. would review the policies of its military authorities with a view to a more liberal treatment of war criminals. . . . Returning to the parole board question, he reassured the Chancellor that we anticipated the establishment of the joint parole board or commission prior to general EDC ratification."[56] After the meetings, Chancellor Adenauer announced that he was "extraordinarily satisfied" with the progress made.[57]

During the summer of 1953, the State Department was concerned that the war crimes issue would negatively affect Konrad Adenauer's 1953 reelection campaign. A State Department memo warned that the continued imprisonment of convicted war criminals could hurt Adenauer's CDU (Christlich-Demokratische Union/Christian Democratic Union) Party in the election, not to mention have an "adverse effect upon a German defense contribution."[58] In a secret memo to the U.S. Secretary of State, High Commissioner James Conant wrote: "Chancellor attaches great importance to some accomplishment as regards war criminals for political reasons."[59] Because the EDC Treaty faced an uncertain future in the French Assembly, the Mixed Board still remained unconvened.

A June 4 "Memorandum Regarding Proposed Parole Board for German War Criminals," penned by State Department officers John Raymond and John Auchincloss, warned that the "German war criminal problem has become a serious political issue in the Federal Republic of Germany." While the memo described Chancellor Adenauer as "moderate in his demands," it pointed to the trouble being made by "other political parties, veterans' groups, editors of newspapers." Raymond and Auchincloss warned that "A solution by exercise of clemency is no longer practicable. Reviews of the cases for clemency have been conducted over and over again."[60] They believed that the clemency process was fast becoming farcical under American administration: "Unless a new situation develops in a particular case, such as serious physical condition of the prisoner, it would be a mockery of clemency to strain it further to bring about releases of prisoners or modification of sentences."[61] The memo suggested the creation of an interim parole board composed of Allied and German members. While it was "politically desirable to play up German participation to the maximum extent possible, ultimate control must remain with the United States"[62] to ensure "no compromise whatsoever with the legality of the war crimes program, the validity of the judgments or the propriety of the sentences."[63] Raymond and Auchincloss flatly rejected the political solution that many Germans were screaming for: "it would take the form of a release of prisoners without consideration of individual guilt. . . . It is also the German approach. A solution of a political character would certainly be construed as an admission of original error in the convictions, would greatly impair the value of whatever principles and precedents may have been established in the war crimes trials, and would be a highly undesirable solution."[64]

The U.S. Army also opposed the parole system endorsed by the State Department and the Adenauer administration. In a June 9, 1953 memo, John Auchincloss wrote: "The Army is opposed to this plan, but has not specified the grounds for its objections. It is unlikely that further progress can be made unless the matter is discussed between the Secretaries of State and Defense, or even by the two Secretaries with the President."[65] Auchincloss believed that the disagreement was a basic one: "we want a parole system and the Army does not." Once again, he warned against a political solution to the war crimes problem: "The appearance of a political solution would have, in effect, the same disadvantages as a real political solution, and we should not underestimate what these disadvantages would be."[66] He cut through the legalism that was beginning to cloud the issues: "The United States Government would have put itself in the position of disregarding the principles involved in the original trials, and this would undermine, in retrospect, the entire war crimes program."[67] His memo asked that Secretary of State John Foster Dulles and Secretary of Defense Charles Wilson discuss the war crimes problem, "so that they might jointly put the matter before the President, in order to obtain his authorization for a proposal in which he will be interested, and which has been the subject of doubt and misunderstanding that he can properly be asked to resolve."[68]

Above all, the White House and the German Chancellor wanted a parole board before the September 1953 elections in Germany. In June, the State Department's director of Political Affairs James Riddleberger wrote Secretary of State Dulles a memo from Bonn to alert him about "a difference of view which has arisen between the State Department and the Defense Department regarding the institution of a parole system for the German war criminals held in American custody."[69] Riddleberger asked that "this difficulty be resolved either by yourself and Secretary Wilson, or by a decision of the President." Once again, the memo pointed to the political importance of the war crimes question in German domestic politics: "German resentment over the trial and continued confinement of war criminals has been causing difficulty in Allied-German relations for several years. It would help the Chancellor greatly if some way could be found to improve this situation before the elections in Germany this autumn."[70]

James Riddleberger reported that Adenauer was "strongly in favor" of the proposed parole system for war criminals and was very specific about the validity question: "The parole system would have nothing to do with clemency or with any matters involving the validity of the original proceedings or the guilt of the accused."[71] Although he believed that prisoner releases might "have a useful political effect," he warned that "releasing prisoners selected by the Germans . . . would be a purely political action, which would have no relation to the circumstances of any individual case, which would show that the United States had no interest in the principles involved in the trials, and which would therefore wholly discredit the war crimes program."[72] The memo suggested that the Secretary of State meet with the Secretary of Defense and "convince him" of the merits of the proposed parole plan. However, if Wilson could not be swayed, the two secretaries should "submit the question to the White House. . . . The President is already aware of the general problem and the need of a solution, and it is believed that the advantages of the proposed parole system are of sufficient importance to justify asking him to approve it."[73]

On June 19, 1953, the State Department's director of Political Affairs wrote Secretary of State Dulles a memo prior to his conference with Secretary of Defense Wilson: "Ambassador Conant has stressed to you the political reasons why a solution of this problem is necessary." Riddleberger considered a parole system for German war criminals "fully justified on its own merits." The memo erroneously assumed that the Germans would recognize the difference between amnesty and parole. The Americans would try "a new approach which would apply to the German cases the same modern penalogical concepts and practices which are used with respect to all federal prisoners in the United States."[74] "The proposed action on our part would be of material assistance to Adenauer in the election campaign and would bring about an improvement in public relations from which the entire American element in Germany, civilian and military, would benefit."[75] The director of Political Affairs reported Auchincloss's statement that "The Army appears also to believe that the institution of a parole system would reflect in some way on the conduct of the trials. We do not however think that this point is valid, for parole does not involve a re-examination of the original proceedings."[76] On June 23, 1953, Secretary of State Dulles sent a secret telegram to the High Commission in Bonn. "War criminals problem discussed . . . with President. . . . One more attempt to be made Bermuda persuade French accept creation now repeat now of Mixed Board provided in contractuals. If as expected this move fails, parole system to be established for German war criminals in American custody."[77]

On June 26, as the Americans were beginning to plan their new parole system, Dulles sent a secret cable to the U.S. embassy. The cable, drafted by John Auchincloss, warned, "Board's terms of reference must be carefully defined so as to limit its jurisdiction to matters of parole (not clemency) and exclude any basis for attempt by German member to reopen cases or question original convictions." The West German government was still unwilling to recognize the legal validity of the original convictions. German participation on the parole board would "provide nearest possible equivalent to explicit recognition by Germans of validity war crimes judgments. Such recognition has been and presumably still is politically impossible for Germans to give."[78]

On July 7, 1953, one week before the Allied Foreign Ministers met in

Washington, D.C., the French High Commissioner offered a way around the ratification impasse. André Francois-Poncet suggested that each Allied nation create temporary boards modeled on the Article 6 Mixed Board to review their respective sentences. The three powers agreed to the plan on July 11.[79] On October 14, less than a week before the German elections, the Interim Mixed Parole and Clemency Board (IMPAC) was convened to rule on American war crimes cases until the treaties establishing the Mixed Board were ratified. The IMPAC Board had been created by a joint order of the U.S. High Commission for Germany and the Supreme Commander of the U.S. Army in Europe on August 31, 1953.[80] It consisted of three Americans and two Germans; it did not function like the Peck Panel of 1950 but more like a traditional parole board before which prisoners were allowed to plead their cases twice a year. The chairman was an attorney from Boston (Henry Lee Shattuck), and the other two Americans were an Army Major General (Joseph Muller) and a career State Department officer (Edwin Plitt). Both German representatives (Emil Lersh and Hans Meuschel) were former German high court judges.[81]

New nonjudicial mechanisms helped further loosen parole standards; credit for time served was again increased and the parameters for medical parole were broadened with new provisions for physical health, mental health, old age, and the condition of the prisoner's family.[82] Eligibility for parole on life and death sentences was reduced to fifteen years from the day of arrest.[83] The board's mandate was very explicit: "The Board is authorized, without questioning the validity of the convictions and sentences, to make recommendations to the competent U.S. authorities for the termination or reduction of sentences or for the parole of persons convicted by the War Crimes Tribunals." When the Interim Board was established in the summer of 1953, 312 prisoners remained in Landsberg Prison; 281 were under army jurisdiction, and 71 of those were serving life sentences. Only 31 of the war criminals convicted by the United States at Nuremberg remained in custody.[84]

These bold moves on war crimes were timed to cast a favorable light on Konrad Adenauer during the final days of his election campaign. Adenauer took a firm stand on the subject, demanding the release of all those in Allied custody. Several bills were pushed through the Bundestag granting economic benefits to former SS members and Nazi officials.[85] The Chancellor realized the importance of being on the "right" side of the issue. He even visited Werl Prison (where prisoners tried and convicted by the British were jailed) in the summer of 1953. Adenauer shook hands with the prisoners and assured them that he was doing his best to get them released.[86] Just as the Americans had not been content with only a military victory after World War II, the Germans wanted vindication of their new status as an ally. The Chancellor's active commitment to the German war criminals and application of unrelenting pressure on the U.S. government won him the support of his nation's veterans. Representatives of the military organizations urged all former military men to support the CDU Party. Adenauer received more than 12 million votes in the 1953 election.[87]

After the German leaders produced the political results their American patrons desired, they sought compensation. In a letter to American war crimes officials, Dr. Friedrich Middelhauve, vice president of the Free Democratic Party (FDP), made it clear that now the time had come for the United States to cooperate on the subject of war criminals:

> The Free Democratic Party of West Germany is the motor of German-American teamwork. It constitutes a strong bulwark against Communist infiltration, radicalism from the left and the right. It helped democracy win in West Germany on September 6, 1953 by 3,000,000 votes. Say action should be taken, you can't afford delay: Let your congressman awaken through you—so act to-day! YOUR POSITIVE DECISION—A BLOW TO BOLSHEVISM.[88]

By 1953, the main concern of American officials in charge of implementing war crimes policy in Germany was to keep the parole action as quiet as possible. Chief U.S. Parole Officer Paul Gernert reported to High Commissioner Conant that the German press had helped by not publicizing the release of prominent convicted war criminals: "No problems have been reported, and the German press has been cooperative in avoiding any publicity concerning parolees or their release. . . . There is no evidence of any organized efforts to exploit the war criminal prisoners' problems or to pressure for their release."[89]

In January 1954, the U.S. ambassador to Japan reopened the entire war crimes debate by suggesting a general amnesty for lower-level Japanese war criminals. Although the two war crimes programs had been very different, they were inextricably connected. It was ironic, but Japanese war crimes policy now threatened to determine the course of German war crimes policy. According to historian John Dower, the war crimes trials did not serve to reform and reeducate the Japanese population. Much like the German war criminals during the 1950s, the Japanese war criminals were embraced by their countrymen. "Defendants who had been convicted and sentenced to imprisonment became openly regarded as victims rather than victimizers, their prison stays within Japan made as pleasant and entertaining as possible," wrote Dower. In 1952 alone, there were 114 performances staged for the convicts' entertainment at Sugamo Prison. Ambassador John Allison was suggesting for Japan what State Department legal advisors John Raymond and John Auchincloss had been warning against all along—a political solution to the war crimes problem. If that proved impossible, Allison suggested "an accelerated parole process to ensure the release of those prisoners within two years."[90]

In a secret memo to Geoffrey Lewis at the U.S. embassy in Bonn, Auchincloss stated his now familiar argument. "I am attaching a copy of Tokyo's telegram No. 1821 of January 26, 1954, in case you should want to read it. This is the one which contains Ambassador Allison's recommendations for a general amnesty for class B and C war criminals or, failing that, an accelerated parole process to ensure the release of these prisoners in two years." Auchincloss pointed out, "whatever is done on these lines in Japan will have extensive repercussions in Germany," and predicted three very negative side effects. First, such a major concession would cast a dark shadow over the legacy of Nuremberg: "It would derogate retroactively from the war crimes program as a whole." The State Department felt that in addition to bolstering the far right in Germany, an amnesty would cause "a Congressional problem and also a problem of public opinion."[91] Auchincloss warned his superiors that "The appearance of a political solution would have, in effect, the same disadvantages of a real political solution, and we should not underestimate what these disadvantages would be. The United States would have put itself in the position of disregarding the principles involved in the original trials, and this would undermine, in retrospect, the entire war crimes program."[92]

For John Auchincloss, there was a difference between legal guilt and moral guilt. He dissented from the traditional position of American lawyer-statesmen. He did not believe that what could be justified legally did not have to be justified morally. The State Department advisor raised a question that had traditionally been taboo to American lawyer-

statesmen: "More important than any of these is the question of principle, and I do not think we should hesitate to raise it, even if some people
are likely to find it abstract and uncomfortable." Auchincloss considered
broad-ranging paroles, under any pretext, to be both an abandonment of
and an affront to the original Nuremberg decisions: "The men now serving sentences for war crimes are doing so because we believed at one time
that they deserved to be punished for what they did. Do we still believe
this, or do we not? If we do not, then we should release the men as soon
as possible." Finally, he sought a clarification of American war crimes
policy and added an ominous warning: "We should reexamine our basic
position in order to see whether we believe in what we have done, before
we proceed to undo it. If we believe in it, we should stick to it, for to act
against it would be cynical, if our purpose were to gain a political advantage, or weak, if our purpose were to avoid political pressure."[93] A meeting between the State Department legal advisors and Ambassador John
Allison was scheduled in Washington for the coming weeks.

The State Department officers drafted a preconference memo arguing
strongly against a political solution in Asia because of the dramatic repercussions it would have in Germany. "The Germans have never accepted
the principles of the war crimes trials and do not believe in the guilt of
those still in confinement. Because of the similarity of the two situations,
it is apparent that an amnesty in Japan would inevitably lead to an
amnesty in Germany, and EUR should emphasize strongly that an
amnesty ought not be granted in Japan."[94] The German Office felt that
this action would be seen as pandering to the worst elements of the West
German political spectrum: "We should take into account the possibility
that the Germans, or at least some of them, would interpret an amnesty
as an example of Allied weakness in the face of German pressure."[95] An
amnesty would serve as "an indication that the war crimes trials were
wrong in principle; such an interpretation would provide a vindication of
the convicted men and a justification for evading any sense of responsibility for the war and the atrocities committed in its course."[96]

On February 16, 1954, a war crimes summit was held at the State
Department in Washington, D.C. The attendees included Ambassador
Allison, State Department legal advisors John Raymond and John Auchincloss, former Peck Panel member Conrad Snow, and legal advisors
from both Germany and Japan. Ambassador Allison opened the meeting
with the shocking admission that "the question of war criminals in Japan

was becoming a farce in view of the Japanese Government's laxity of control over the prisoners who were permitted to attend baseball games and other activities in Tokyo." Allison conceded that an amnesty would cause problems in Germany and asked "if it would be possible to take some action less than amnesty with respect to Japanese war criminals." Conrad Snow pointed out that those still in prison had been convicted of "particularly heinous crimes" and would not be eligible for parole until 1960 or 1961. Snow offered a solution to the dilemma, noting "that it would be possible for the Board to change the 'ground rules' so as to make lifers eligible for parole after serving 10 instead of 15 years."[97] However, "Mr. Raymond indicated that Mr. Phleger felt strongly that a grant of amnesty would undermine the entire legal basis of the war crime trials in that an amnesty or pardon had the effect of wiping out the crime. He indicated that the grant of parole or clemency fell into a different category and did not necessarily prejudice the legal basis of the trials."[98] Secretary of State John Foster Dulles officially rejected the proposed amnesty on May 26, 1954: "In view of serious nature crimes committed by remaining war criminals and fact 145 out of 293 have life sentences and 30 have sentences of over 30 years, impossible release any sizeable bloc per your recommendation."[99] However, the Secretary of State did agree to "change the ground rules" by reducing parole eligibility for those war criminals originally sentenced to death from fifteen to ten years.

By May of 1954, the Interim Mixed Parole and Clemency Board was busily reviewing cases and parole plans. Geoffrey Lewis, the director of the State Department's Office of German Affairs in Washington, wrote American IMPAC board member Edwin Plitt to congratulate him on the board's "remarkably fine job," which Lewis attributed to "the hard work and tactful handling by the American employees, particularly, I suspect, yourself." For the moment, the IMPAC board had quieted the controversy: "The fact that we in Washington hear nothing about the War Criminal 'problem' anymore is an indication of your effectiveness."[100] In early June, HICOG Records Officer Richard Hagan sent State Department legal advisor John Raymond an update and informed him of the incoming parole applications. Hagan described "the formula" for keeping the news of war criminal paroles quiet: "no general disclosure of individual parolees' names; no disclosure of the fact of parole release to a person having personal connection with and legitimate interest in any particular person about whom he inquires."[101]

In August, the French National Assembly killed the EDC Treaty and the Allies had to find another way to rearm West Germany. Winston Churchill urged President Eisenhower to absorb the new German army into the NATO forces.[102] Meanwhile, German veterans' groups like the *Stahlhelm* continued to argue that West Germany should refuse to rearm until all the war criminals had been set free. On August 29 in Recklinghausen, former German Field Marshal Albert Kesselring oversaw a Stahlhelm meeting wearing the now outlawed gray uniform and jack boots of the *Wehrmacht*. FDP leader Eric Mende stated that as a former German officer, he personally could not support ratification and rearmament until German military leaders like Field Marshal Eric von Manstein were released from Allied prisons.[103] The Paris Treaties, incorporating Articles 6 and 7 of the Bonn Agreements, would outline the new Allied-German plan. Western leaders signed the conventions in Paris in October 1954. In late December, Chancellor Adenauer wrote U.S. High Commissioner James Conant, requesting a Christmas amnesty for German war criminals. Conant refused on the ground that it "would largely negate what we are trying to accomplish."[104]

On January 18, 1955, *Deutsche Partei* leader Hans Joachim von Merkatz and Admiral Heye, a Bundestag deputy in the CDU Party, met with State Department officials to discuss the continued imprisonment of war criminals on German soil. Admiral Heye argued that the provisions of the Paris Treaties "which reserve Allied sovereignty on the war criminals' issue are a great mistake."[105] Heye believed that the "unresolved issue of war criminals would deter many individuals with a strong sense of honor and duty from volunteering for the new armed forces." Although the admiral was willing to admit that "many of the remaining prisoners had committed criminal acts and deserved punishment," he rejected their sentences' legal validity: "the principle of their guilt could be maintained and, at the same time, the untenable legal position governing their continued imprisonment could be resolved if a general amnesty were extended."[106] Van Merkatz also attacked the war crimes trials "in a very emotional manner." He stated that "many of the trials had not been conducted in accordance with established legal procedure . . . and maintained that the whole sorry episode of war criminals should be concluded by an amnesty for those remaining." The State Department noted that this was the first time in recent months that German politicians had raised the question of an amnesty for war criminals.[107]

The Bundestag debated the subject of the "German Prisoners of War" on February 17, 1955. German State Secretary Hallstein answered questions from Bundestag members. While some, like Countess Fincken- stein of the DP (Deutsche Partei/German Party), still called for "a gener- al amnesty to make a clean sweep for all prisoners of war," the State Sec- retary was more moderate. Hallstein appeared impressed by the American willingness to free convicted war criminals: "These numerous efforts of the Federal Government have met with great understanding. The subsequent releases for which I have quoted figures, have proved that."[108] The State Secretary counseled the German politicians to wait a few months, until the tenth anniversary of the armistice, then "once more to appeal to the custodial powers, but not without expressing appreciation for the understanding and willingness with which they have fulfilled many wishes and proposals of the Federal Government." When asked if the Federal Republic was prepared to assume custody of the war criminals, Hallstein was very coy and did not offer a clear response: "I do not want to make a conclusive statement on this question, but I would like to point out that apart from difficulties resulting from legal provisions in the custo- dial countries, the German legal authorities will be confronted with per- haps nearly insoluble difficulties by the necessity of carrying out such a big number of proceedings under existing circumstances."[109]

U.S. High Commissioner James Conant had already anticipated the problems of transferring the prisoners to German custody. In a January 22, 1955 secret telegram, he wrote to Secretary of State Dulles warning that mass paroles in Japan would "have a most unfortunate and drastic effect here." Conant pointed out that "Federal Government does not wish to rec- ognize sentences of Nuremberg tribunals, on which ultimate analysis parole would be based, as court orders within meaning of basic law and Federal Government would therefore lack legal authority to enforce parole restrictions by re-arrest or otherwise."[110] The German disdain for the Nuremberg trials and the "vindictive" occupation policies of JCS 1067 had hardened by 1955. In a letter to State Department legal advisor John Ray- mond, HICOG's head of Prisons, Richard Hagan, reported his conversa- tion with a former Nuremberg defense lawyer and a representative from a German POW group: "I obtained an admission from the two gentlemen that, were all prisoners to be released, there would be no end to the war criminal problem until in the German mind each act has been justified."[111]

The Federal Republic of Germany regained its sovereignty on May 5,

1955, when the Paris Treaties took effect. What that translated to in clear language was that men sentenced to death in 1948 would soon be eligible for parole. Yet America's lenient war crimes policy won no goodwill from West German politicians. On July 25, Eric Mende, one of the most powerful members of Adenauer's coalition, announced that it would be impossible to recruit decent officers for the new German army "unless a substantial number of war criminals are released." Mende was echoing the views of former Wehrmacht generals like Hans Speidel and Adolf von Heusinger—who had both served as military advisors to the Federal Republic of Germany.[112] According to Frank Buscher, instead of accepting responsibility for Nazi Germany's atrocities, "legislators of almost all parties portrayed the Allies as the villains and the violators of the law."[113]

The parole of German war criminals was further accelerated by yet another revision of parole requirements in July 1955. On July 21, HICOG in Bonn received a cable from the Secretary of State announcing the new requirements: "FYI President has approved recommendation Clemency with sentences over 30 years including life sentences be considered eligible for parole after serving ten repeat ten years."[114] As of March 1, 1955, the United States held 88 war crimes prisoners at Landsberg Prison.[115] By July 11, 1955, only 10 Nuremberg convicts remained in Landsberg.[116] When the Interim Mixed Parole and Clemency Board ceased functioning on August 1, 1955, the United States had released almost 90 percent of the convicted war criminals in its custody and the European Allies were not far behind with clemency programs of their own.[117]

State Department legal advisor John Raymond asked Richard Hagan of HICOG to prepare a statement about the remaining prisoners, or as they had come to be known, the "hardcore" prisoners, that justified their continued incarceration. On April 19, Hagan wrote back that he would prepare reports on the cases of "the really 'hard core' ones." The parole officer offered an anecdote that illustrated how intractable the war crimes problem had become. He described a conversation with two German lawyers lobbying for the continued release of war criminals: "I obtained an admission from the two gentlemen that, were all prisoners to be released, there would be no end to the war criminal problem until in the German mind each act has been justified."[118]

There was an impending crisis over the pending parole of Malmedy Massacre convict Sepp Dietrich. Because he had been tried by the U.S. Army, he was their prisoner and there was little the State Department could do. Ambassador Conant had always followed the IMPAC Board's recommendations, but when it came to the German soldiers involved in the Malmedy Massacre, U.S. Army leaders had consistently refused to consider early releases. It is important to remember that General McAuliffe, the man in charge of the American prisoners, had been surrounded by German soldiers in 1944 at Bastogne and had refused to surrender.[119] State Department legal advisor Knox Lamb cabled Secretary of State Dulles on August 3 to inform him of an impending problem: "The most conspicuous case is that of ex-General Dietrich. The board has twice unanimously recommended that he be paroled and both recommendations were turned down—once by General Hoge and once by General McAuliffe."[120] In a conversation with Ambassador Conant, "General McAuliffe felt that he had a personal responsibility in these cases and that he was not called upon to follow the Board's recommendation if he disagreed with it."[121]

Although General McAuliffe was prepared to reject a third recommendation for Dietrich's parole, it sounded as if the decision to parole Dietrich had already been made: "the U.S. member of the new Board will be as lenient as is appropriate in dealing with the remaining U.S. cases and . . . the British and French members and, of course, the German members will not vote against him on any recommendation for clemency. It is therefore likely that any majority vote will be a unanimous vote."[122] The U.S. Army was the last obstacle to accelerating the war criminal parole program. Knox Lamb stressed the importance of leniency: "if a case should arise where a majority's recommendation is rejected it would undoubtedly have an adverse affect on our relations with the Germans. Therefore we think the recommendations of a majority of the new Board should be accepted."[123]

After the Paris Treaties went into effect in 1955, West Germany regained national sovereignty and the first military legislation was introduced in the Bundestag. According to a State Department memo, "The restoration of German sovereignty through the coming into effect of the Paris Treaties . . . and the introduction of the first military legislation in the Bundestag have strongly revived political and public interest in the question of war criminals imprisoned in the Federal Republic and elsewhere."[124] The memo pointed out the unpleasant fact that most of the West German political and religious elites were now more intent than ever on an unconditional war crimes amnesty even though only a handful of Nazi Germany's most notorious war criminals remained in prison.

Representatives of Germany's political parties (CDU, FDP [Freie Demokratische Partei/Free Democratic Party], BHE, and DP) "made strong appeals during the first reading of the Volunteer's Law to the former occupation powers to release the prisoners they still hold."[125] The leaders of Germany's Catholic and Protestant churches also called for an amnesty. The memo predicted that "the German public will become increasingly sensitive about their status as a sovereign country and the inconsistency between their positions as allies of the United States and the continued existence of the war criminals problem to an extent which will make our efforts to bind Germany to the West more difficult the longer the prisoners are held."[126] By 1955, it was clear that in order to resolve the contradiction of the "occupying ally," the United States would release the remaining "hard core" war criminals.

On August 11, 1955, the long-awaited and much-anticipated Mixed Clemency Board was established. The Mixed Board (also referred to as the Article 6 Board) was responsible for reviewing the parole applications of the remaining forty-four "hard core" war criminals in Landsberg Prison. The six-man board was composed of three Germans and one member from each of the Allied countries. Career State Department officer Edwin Plitt was appointed the American member; he had also served on the Interim Board.[127] The Mixed Board was supposed to be an independent judicial body, and each Allied representative was supposed to rule according to his conscience. The Mixed Board's first major crisis erupted in late 1955, when Malmedy Massacre convict Sepp Dietrich, who had originally been sentenced to death, was granted parole. When word of this symbolically significant release reached the United States, there was a major public outcry.[128]

On November 3, Senator Estes Kefauver called Sepp Dietrich's release a "serious error" and called for a Senate investigation. The State Department in Bonn was startled by the implications of an inquiry into American war crimes policy. Ambassador Conant immediately attempted to contain the public relations damage and wrote Secretary of State John Foster Dulles that "U.S. public reaction Re Dietrich case has reached a point where it may endanger American-German relations to such a degree that I am bringing the matter to your personal attention." The State Department believed that "Any Senate investigation of this case, which would necessarily bring into question Allied policy on war criminals, could do great damage." Conant felt "it essential that a full message be sent to Senator Kefauver. . . . Same statement should be to other Senators who have indicated interest."[129] A November 7 memo from the State Department's European Office recommended that "an officer of the Department, perhaps Mr. Murphy or the Acting Legal Advisor, should get in touch with Senator Kefauver's office and offer to explain the foregoing considerations to the Senator before he takes further action towards an investigation of the Dietrich case."[130] On November 8, Senator Kefauver wrote Secretary of State Dulles, "It is my firm conviction that a serious error has been made in the release of General Sepp Dietrich (Josef). I would urge to propose reconsideration of the matter while there is time yet to rectify the mistake." It appeared that the State Department would be unable to head off this growing controversy: "I am sending an identical letter and reports mentioned to the Secretary of Defense and to the Chairman of the Armed Services asking that they look into the matter."[131]

While the second phase of American war crimes policy failed to appease German veterans, it succeeded in infuriating many former American soldiers. Veterans of Foreign Wars Commander Joseph Lombardo supported Senator Kefauver's call for a Senate investigation. More troubling, Lombardo called for the resignation of American Mixed Board Member Edwin Plitt and an investigation into why he had voted in favor of Dietrich's early release: "It is the thought of this office that the reasons of the American member of the Mixed Board for voting favorably on the release of the Hitlerite Killer should be investigated and his resignation immediately forthcoming to wipe out the dishonor to the memory of our murdered comrades at Malmedy."[132] This request was especially problematic because the decisions of the Mixed Board, when unanimous, were final and not subject to the instructions of the members' respective governments. By November 28, the controversy over Dietrich's release was further fueled by American Legion National Commander J. Addington Wagner's call for Edwin Plitt's resignation.[133]

Above all, the State Department wanted to avoid a public inquiry into the inner workings of the Mixed Board. Legal advisor John Raymond made this point in a November 29, 1955 memo. He offered to help sharpen the official justification for Dietrich's release and urged the State Department to stress the independence of the American member: "I think the end of that paragraph should read substantially as follows: 'The United States member of the Mixed Board is career minister Edwin Plitt, a veteran Foreign Service officer. The members of the Board act independently in formulating their recommendations and are not subject to the instructions of their governments.' "[134] Once again, American war crimes policy was losing a two-front public relations battle and once again, an American diplomat was caught in the crossfire.

Ambassador Conant wrote to Secretary of State John Foster Dulles asking for his "personal attention" on the war crimes problem. According to Conant, the ongoing controversy surrounding the vote of the American member Edwin Plitt "has made effective functioning board difficult and is also damaging German-American relations." The ambassador recommended that Dulles personally put this fire out with "Serious effort through personal conversation or otherwise to convince Wagner, American Legion, Murphy of VFW and Senator Kefauver that their criticism is unjustified." Plitt's role in the parole of Dietrich was "in accord with the policy of the U.S. Government."[135] Conant sensed an impending blowback and believed that the United States had lost a great deal of face due to their mishandling of the war crimes question: "A failure to bring this fact out clearly in previous statements from Washington as well as failure to emphasize nature of parole and unfortunate first statement tending to place the blame on the Army has seriously embarrassed U.S. member of Mixed Board and thus embarrassed U.S. Government in its relation to the French, British as well as the Federal Republic."[136] The duality in American war crimes policy was fast becoming indefensible.

In early December, a State Department brief on Dietrich's parole was prepared for Secretary of State John Foster Dulles. The defense would not be based on the details of the individual case; instead, it would stress that parole, unlike clemency, is a conditional release. As State Department legal advisor John Raymond suggested earlier, Dulles would stress that the Mixed Board was "an independent body" whose rulings, when unanimous, were binding. If asked about the possibility of Plitt resigning, he would offer the following reply: "He was appointed like the other members, to exercise his judgment in formulating the Board's recommendations, without being subject to governmental instructions." Again, the Secretary of State was instructed to keep his responses general and stress the "independence" of the Mixed Board.[137]

On December 10, 1955, Livingston Merchant, the State Department's Assistant Secretary of State for European Affairs, wrote a secret letter to Ambassador Conant about the ongoing controversy over Dietrich's release. "We have been very much concerned about the public reaction in this country to the release of Dietrich. . . . It has, in fact, preoccupied a considerable number of us. We have been troubled, of course, about the effect of this controversy on our relations with the Germans and also about the attacks on Ed Plitt." Merchant argued that the State Department should "rest our defense of what we do about war criminals essentially on the procedures involved"—in other words, shift the debate away from the facts and stress the law and procedure upon which the decisions were based. According to Merchant, "The defense we are making of the Board has come down essentially that it is an independent body of men who make judgments on the basis of such considerations as seem wise to them in the circumstances. We are in no position to defend, or even to state, the criteria on which the board operates or the considerations which have been taken into account in a particular case such as the Dietrich case."[138] However, this defense was problematic in Edwin Plitt's case because he was a career employee of the agency responsible for American war crimes policy. Merchant recognized that "The very fact of his being a Foreign Service Officer to some extent opens up the way to a charge that, whatever the Convention says about his not being subject to instructions from this Government, he will in fact as a Foreign Service Officer carry out our political policy towards Germany and therefore be governed, in the absence of any demonstration that other factors are guiding his judgment, by our political policies towards Germany."[139] Merchant believed that "This fact and the German membership on the Board seems to us to open the way to an attack on the Board and the entire system as being nothing but a mechanism for carrying out a political policy of releasing war criminals, rather than for the administration of justice."[140] The Assistant Secretary of State warned the State Department to prepare for a Senate investigation.

On December 27, 1955, State Department legal advisor John Raymond advised Ambassador Conant not to go before the Senate Foreign Relations Committee to discuss American war crimes policy. The outcry over Dietrich had not died down, and the possible release of his comrade Joachim Peiper would soon compound the State Department's problems.[141] On December 30, Merchant wrote Conant, "We were unaware that the Peiper case was already up for consideration and the leaks of the possibility of Peiper's release have now intensified the controversy greatly." Merchant conceded that the Dietrich release had gone very badly from a public relations point of view—"Looking back, it seems clear that we have not put our best foot forward on the subject"—and warned that the Peiper parole would probably be opposed by the army: "While our relations with the people most directly concerned with the problem at the legal and public information level is good, I should be frank to say that there are people at the higher levels in the Pentagon who are not very sympathetic with the program, which may eventually be a source of difficulty."[142] Merchant informed Ambassador Conant that during an upcoming trip to Washington, they should meet to discuss the ongoing war crimes problem. He also requested that the conversation be held behind closed doors—off the record. "The meeting which is being arranged with members of the interested Committees in substitution for a statement before the Appropriations Committee will provide one occasion to deal with this matter." Conant would also meet with the leaders of America's veteran groups in an effort to quiet them down.[143]

The controversy over Sepp Dietrich's release dragged on into 1956 as the calls for Edwin Plitt's dismissal grew even louder. On January 3, Timothy Murphy, commander of the Veterans of Foreign Wars, called for Plitt's removal. Ironically, now the American Mixed Board member was being defended by prominent German Nuremberg critics like the Papal Nuncio, Bishop Fargo, who lavishly praised him in a letter to Secretary of State John Foster Dulles. "Having discussed this case on a number of occasions with Mr. Plitt, allow me to say that I have learned to admire him for his moral integrity and for his conscientious grasp of the issues involved." Urging the Secretary of State not to cave in to the growing pressure to remove Plitt, the Bishop wrote that he trusted "sincerely that pressure groups will not prevail in their demands. . . . In writing you in this matter I do so with the sole thought that injustice be not done to a red-blooded American such as I know Mr. Plitt to be."[144] Despite Plitt's popularity in Germany, the criticism of his actions in the United States continued to intensify.

On January 6, Minnesota Senator Hubert Humphrey asked Secretary of State Dulles to explain why the U.S. government had failed to prevent the release of Sepp Dietrich. Humphrey also protested the rumor of the impending release of Joachim Peiper. He pointed out that these beneficiaries of American generosity were among the Third Reich's worst war criminals: "When we come to consider murder, torture and general brutality, it is an entirely different matter, and it is the persons guilty of those acts who are now benefitting from what amounts to a general jail delivery approved by the United States Government."[145]

On January 18, the State Department took notice of a small article entitled "The Problem of the Western Prisoners," written by a CDU Deputy Hoefler and published in the CDU's official press service, *Deutschland-Union Dienst.*[146] The article asked for the release of all German war criminals from foreign-controlled prisons. Although moderate in tone, it marked a new direction for Adenauer's normally centrist party: "the CDU has up to now maintained considerable reticence on the general question of war criminals." To Elim O'Shaughnessy in the U.S. embassy in Bonn, "The fact that the CDU has taken the initiative in the matter, in contrast to the usual practice of waiting to be pushed into it, is an index of the political importance which the party attaches to the question."[147]

On January 20, 1956, the British Foreign Office weighed in on the war crimes question. The British hoped to avoid another fiasco like the Sepp Dietrich parole: "Her Majesty's Government wish to do everything possible to assist the Board in meeting public criticism, but they do not believe that the inner workings of the Board, which is an independent body, should be revealed." The British felt that the publication of information justifying the paroles would further undermine the legal validity of the war crimes convictions: "Publication of the considerations underlying a recommendation of the Board could scarcely avoid the casting of doubt on the validity of the original convictions; this is expressly forbidden by the terms of the Bonn Conventions."[148] The State Department continued to refuse to release the details of the Board's decisions arguing that the Mixed Board was not an arm of the State Department, but rather "a quasi-judicial body, and that the purpose of giving its members freedom of action was to enable them to exercise an objective judgment based on the facts of the individual case."[149]

These legalistic justifications did little to dispel the impression that the Mixed Board was another strategic legalist shakeout mechanism. State Department International Relations Officer John Auchincloss's suggested answer to critic Max Meron was very telling: "Here I would say that the Board is an independent body, that the members are not subject to instructions from their governments, and that there is no provision in the applicable procedures for the American authorities to approve or disapprove a unanimous recommendation of the Board."[150] The State Department's legal justifications remained unconvincing to many Americans, and by early 1956, American war crimes policy needed a scapegoat. Mixed Board member Edwin Plitt would serve nicely. On January 24, 1956, the State Department announced that Plitt would be replaced on the Mixed Board by former New Hampshire judge and Senator Robert Upton.

The replacement of Plitt with a prominent jurist helped to restore some of the Mixed Board's credibility in the United States, but it had the opposite effect in West Germany, where Edwin Plitt had been regarded highly by his German colleagues. And why not? Plitt had certainly proved willing to carry out an accelerated parole system designed to release German war criminals. When the three West German members of the Mixed Board got word of his removal, they proposed protesting to Ambassador Conant: "The said members expressed the feeling that the action in transferring Mr. Plitt had been taken because . . . he had voted to transfer Dietrich from prison to parole status and that Plitt's removal was a reflection on the entire membership of the Board." The Germans were calmed by the British Board member, who advised them that any such protest would be "improper" without consulting their respective governments.[151]

In early March, the legal advisors from the State Department began to prepare for another public outcry over the release of Joachim Peiper. In a letter to John Auchincloss about their official position, State Department legal advisor John Raymond wrote, "I have a feeling we do not point up as precisely and emphatically as we should the difficulty in the situation." Raymond considered how to handle the public inquiries: "We cannot possibly tell others it is none of their business to ask such questions nor can we refer them to the Board for an answer. Perhaps we should even stress the fact that if such information is not forthcoming and if further decisions are rendered which cannot be explained and which have a violent reaction in this country, it may jeopardize the whole program."[152]

Senator Robert Upton arrived in Germany in late March 1956 to assume Edwin Plitt's seat on the Mixed Board. Things got off to a bad start for the senator from New Hampshire. Once the Mixed Board reconvened, Upton was shocked to learn that his colleagues had already granted Joachim Peiper parole six months earlier (on October 5, 1955). The only thing standing between Peiper and his freedom was the Mixed Board's approval of his parole plan. Although Senator Upton accepted Peiper's release as a *fait accompli*, he immediately set about distancing himself from the decision. In a letter to State Department legal advisor John Raymond,

Upton commented, "on examining the records . . . the Board had unanimously voted that Peiper be declared eligible for parole now and that he be released upon the submission to the Board of an acceptable parole plan." He made it very clear to the State Department that he would not assume responsibility for Peiper's release: "In any press release by the Department concerning this case I expect you to make it clear that the action authorizing the parole of Peiper was taken before I became a member of the Board." More ominously, Senator Upton expressed strong misgivings about the Mixed Board's view of the parole process: "The other members of the Board have had no experience with parole as it is not recognized in their countries." He believed that his European colleagues saw parole for what it was, a "device" created to release war criminals.[153]

Senator Upton requested some instructions from the State Department on these questions. Legal advisor John Raymond appears to have been startled by the news that Peiper would soon be released. In a letter to John Auchincloss, Raymond wrote, "The attached letter from Senator Upton gives me much concern. Apparently Peiper may be released any day." He "had hoped that the action had not gone so far but Senator Upton could stop it, but apparently he feels precluded from raising any objection." Raymond also expressed his irritation with Edwin Plitt's recent statements to the press that he thought Peiper was the one responsible for the Malmedy Massacre: "I am not clear how he reconciles that with his action in voting for his parole. I wonder if he forgot that the nature of the offense is one of the elements to be considered in connection with granting parole."[154]

Conrad Snow, the former member of McCloy's Peck Panel, was now serving as State Department legal advisor for the Far East, and he was responsible for the Japanese war criminals that remained in U.S. custody. On April 10, Snow responded to Senator Upton's query about parole procedure; he agreed that "the nature of the crime was the most important single element in passing on the question of parole" and believed that "some of the offenses before us have been so heinous that we have not as yet brought ourselves up to granting any parole at all. Maybe we shall change our minds, as time passes on, for we make no unalterable negative decisions, but for the present at least, they are in the 'hard core.' "[155] Although the State Department had sought an independent jurist to boost the Mixed Board's reputation, the new American member was turning out to be more than it had bargained for.

To further complicate matters, on April 12, 1956, the U.S. Army expressed deep misgivings about Joachim Peiper's parole. Army Assistant Judge Advocate General, Major General Claude Mickelwait, took grave exception not only to Peiper's release but also to Edwin Plitt's statements about the U.S. Army's conduct in the Dachau trials: "We are somewhat concerned over certain comments made by Mr. Plitt therein since we believe it reflects unjustly on the Dachau War Crimes Program."[156] Mickelwait charged that both Plitt and the Mixed Board had exceeded the scope of their legal mandate in the Malmedy cases: "While carefully avoiding any direct admission, Mr. Plitt leaves no doubt that the Interim Mixed Board weighed the evidence adduced at the trial, in direct violation of its charter." Finally, the Assistant Judge Advocate General leveled his most serious charge—that the Mixed Board had acted like an appellate or review court. "Mr. Plitt is not only admitting that the Interim Mixed Board illegally constituted itself as an appellate court, but also arrogating to the board an unwarranted conscience, while clearly implying lack of competence and justice on the part of the trial courts." He pointed out that this was "a favorite tactic of those who have found it expedient to attack the German war crimes program."[157] Although the State Department vigorously denied the army's charges, they were preparing for the fallout over Peiper's imminent release.

Because Joachim Peiper had now served ten years, he could be released on parole due to the recent ruling that granted parole on a death sentence after ten years' imprisonment. In mid-April 1956, the Mixed Board received Peiper's parole application—he had been offered a job by Porsche, the German automotive company. His parole plan was approved by the Mixed Board by a vote of five to one, the lone dissenting vote coming from the American member, Robert Upton. He stated his reasons in a letter to State Department legal advisor John Raymond: "I objected to the granting of parole on the ground that such action would be premature. The Board approved the parole plan and recommended that parole be granted by a vote of 5:1. I have completed the minority report and will forward you a copy as soon as the reports in this case are forwarded to the Competent Authority."[158] In his minority report, Senator Upton wrote: "I began an intensive study of the case from which I concluded that Col. Peiper ought not presently to be granted parole. The records before me clearly established that the shooting down of prisoners of war and civilians during the Ardennes offensive was confined to the combat group commanded by Colonel Peiper."[159] Upton cited the opinion of Army General Thomas Handy: "My review of the case leads to the same general conclusions. In my opinion Col. Peiper must be held primarily responsible for the violations of the laws and customs of warfare committed by his combat group. Consequently I am convinced that his release on parole at this time would be premature."[160] The new American Mixed Board member also objected to the specifics of Peiper's parole plan: "The plan calls for his employment in the sales department of the Porsche Company. . . . Because of the widespread and intense feeling for and against Col. Peiper, it is inadvisable that he be employed in a position where he may be in contact with the general public including foreign customers of the Porsche Co."[161] Joachim Peiper's case history provides a telling barometer of the changes in American war crimes policy:

> July 16, 1946—sentenced to death. May 18, 1948—Supreme Court denied petition for a Writ of Habeas Corpus. Apr. 8, 1949—death sentence confirmed. Aug. 29, 1950—commutation of death sentence denied. Jan. 30, 1951—death sentence reduced to life imprisonment. May 12, 1954—life sentence reduced to 35 years. Dec. 9, 1954—clemency denied. Oct. 5, 1955—clemency denied, but Mixed Board voted unanimously that Peiper be declared eligible for parole, his release pending the Board's approval of his parole plan.[162]

On May 8, 1956, Senator Upton wrote State Department legal advisor John Raymond to discuss the progress of the Mixed Board. Upton continued to express dismay over the Mixed Board's parole procedure—"I have abandoned any hope of formulating rules of procedure acceptable to the Board." Senator Upton objected to his colleagues' use of the parole procedure as a mechanism to release war criminals irrespective of their deeds. "A majority of the Board apparently are disposed to hold that on applications for parole by a war criminal eligible for parole the nature of the offense is not considered in determining whether, if parole is granted, the applicant would have been sufficiently punished. In other words, these members hold that if eligible for parole a war criminal has expiated his crime." Robert Upton rejected this as absolutely improper: "This is contrary to the procedure of Parole Boards generally, but probably conforms to the procedure which was here in the Interim Mixed Board." Senator Upton was not optimistic: "We are making rather slow progress

and, as you will see, there have been few unanimous recommendations."[163] On May 10, John Raymond wrote Senator Upton for another
progress report, which he passed on to International Relations Officer
John Auchincloss: "He was able to make use of this information—of
course without attributing it to you or the Board—in a way that I hope
will dispose of the inquiry."[164]

Earlier in May, Senator Upton had informed the State Department
that Edwin Plitt's removal had increased "the pressure on Adenauer for
action looking to the release of all war criminals." According to Upton,
there were now only 33 inmates left in Landsberg Prison, and "These
constitute a 'hard core,' the release of whom, either through clemency or
parole, is likely to extend over years. We also have now 190 parolees, the
majority of whom will not be entitled to a conditional release before
1960."[165] Although the Allies had granted broad concessions to Konrad
Adenauer on the war crimes question, he was still not content. Between
January 31, 1953 and January 31, 1955, the United States had released 82
percent of the convicts in Landsberg Prison, and the European Allies
were pursuing clemency programs of their own.

TABLE 1   German War Criminals in Captivity[166]

In Confinement	8/31/53	1/31/55	% Released
U.S. Army	281	34	87.9
U.S. Embassy (Nuremberg)	31	7	77.4
British (Werl)	82	27	67.0
French	72	18	75.0

Prior to West German Chancellor Konrad Adenauer's visit to Washington in June 1956, the State Department reported a conversation with the
West German Foreign Minister, who informed them that Adenauer wanted
the United States to "speed up releases from Landsberg and (2) Relaxation
conditions those now on parole." The German diplomat "mentioned the
shock felt German Circles when Plitt removed; thought Plitt's government
should have supported him; said removal under pressure home politics had
seriously undermined confidence in independence of Board." It was now
clear that the West German government would not rest until all war criminals in Western captivity were released. Even though the United States had
released all but a handful of war criminals, the foreign minister claimed to

be "gravely concerned" over the "slow progress Mixed Board; at present rate problem will last many years."[167]

Anticipating Chancellor Adenauer's request for more war criminal releases, State Department officers John Raymond and John Auchincloss prepared a position paper entitled "German War Criminals Held By the United States." The State Department suggested that the United States take the position that the Mixed Board should review each war crimes case on an individual basis. Of the thirty-two war criminals left in American custody, twenty-six were under the control of the U.S. Army, and only six were under State Department control. While the State Department was prepared to release more war criminals, they ruled out an unconditional amnesty because it would "require a revision of the Settlement Convention [Articles 6 and 7 of the Bonn Agreements, relating to war criminal sentence validity]. Considering the feeling in Congress last winter about the parole of Dietrich and the possible parole of Peiper, it is hardly likely that there would be any support in the Senate or the House for such a revision."[168] However, it was the resignation of Senator Robert Upton that opened the way for a new approach to the war crimes question.

On June 11, 1956, Robert Upton announced his resignation after less than three months on the Mixed Board. "While the number of war criminals convicted by American tribunals now held at Landsberg is relatively small, it is unlikely that they will be released by 1960, especially as some are serving life sentences." In Upton's opinion, the United States would be overseeing German war criminals for years to come: "many parolees will not be entitled to conditional release until 1962 or later."[169] Once again, he expressed dissatisfaction with the German Mixed Board members' view of the parole process as a shake-out mechanism: "A majority of the Board apparently are disposed to hold that on applications for parole by a war criminal eligible for . . . parole the nature of the offense is not to be considered in determining whether . . . the applicant would have been sufficiently punished."[170] Robert Upton made it clear that the State Department's description of the Mixed Board as a traditional parole board was very inaccurate: "These members hold that if eligible for parole a war criminal has expiated his crime. This is contrary to the procedure of Parole Boards generally. . . . In Germany the Board has come to be regarded as an instrumentality for the release of war criminals rather than an agency for the exercise of clemency or parole in deserving

cases. This view has to some extent been reflected in the attitude of the German members of the Board."[171] According to Senator Upton, this "resulted in frequent disagreements among the members of the Board."[172]

When news of Senator Upton's resignation reached the United States, the American Legion loudly protested. J. Addington Wagner, the Legion's National Commander, wrote Secretary of State John Foster Dulles: "To the very great credit of Senator Upton, he is reported to have cast the single negative vote which blocked the release of Peiper. Now Senator Upton, unfortunately from the American standpoint, has terminated his service on the Board." Wagner warned that the Secretary of State should exercise "great care" in selecting the new Mixed Board member. In closing, the American Legion Commander reminded Dulles of some basic facts that were being obscured by legalistic debates over parole procedure: "Those who may be inclined to sympathize with Peiper would do well to recall that the American soldiers at Malmedy were afforded no trial and no opportunity to defend themselves. They cannot appeal the sentence given them by Peiper's command."[173]

In late July 1956, Senator Upton met with State Department legal advisor John Raymond to discuss the future of American war crimes policy. Upton offered a plan that would rid the United States of the war crimes problem once and for all by marrying a clemency program to the existing parole program. Once paroled prisoners demonstrated "that they are once again law-abiding citizens able to behave themselves," their sentences would be reduced to time served. The former Mixed Board member saw the program as "one of gradual parole for prisoners, and gradual clemency for those on parole." He "thought it was important for his successor to understand a situation that has developed and which will certainly be a problem with which he will be confronted." Raymond admitted that both the IMPAC Board and the Mixed Board were following a flawed parole procedure: "Apparently the Interim Board and the present Board prior to the arrival of Senator Upton proceeded on the theory either that the nature of the offense had no bearing on parole or that it had a bearing merely as reflecting the character of the prisoner and his ability to readjust in society." Although Senator Upton had aggressively argued against this view, he regretfully informed the State Department that he could not convince the other Mixed Board members to revise their procedure: "he has been unable to convert any of the members of

the Board to this point of view, but he believes it is absolutely sound and should be held by the U.S. member."[174]

On July 31, Robert Upton met with State Department officers John Raymond and John Auchincloss and the new American Mixed Board member, Spencer Phenix, in Washington. This time the Americans were taking no chances. Phenix was a veteran State Department officer who would prove to be a master of strategic legalism. From the very beginning, Phenix stated that American war crimes policy needed a scapegoat and he was happy to serve. "Mr. Phenix emphasized that, since the members of the Mixed Board were independent of government instructions, there was an arm's length relationship between the Department and the American member of the Board." Phenix suggested that the State Department should "refer inquiries to him," and "should say little, if anything, in answer to inquiries which it might receive." Phenix understood that the objective of the final phase of American war crimes policy was to release the remaining war criminals. He was prepared to go to far greater lengths to free war criminals than his predecessor Robert Upton and even Edwin Plitt.[175] On September 7, 1956, Senator Upton spoke to his replacement about "the problems which troubled me." Upton wrote: "I left with feelings of regret, but I would not choose to continue as a member of the Mixed Board reviewing the same cases again and again, especially as the work would lose interest for me." He hoped that eventually "the German government will decide to assume responsibility for these prisoners upon terms acceptable to us."[176] However, this would be nearly impossible without reopening the question of the war crimes trials' legal validity.

The Japanese section of the State Department continued to press Washington to release the remaining Japanese war criminals in American custody. However, Ambassador Allison's 1954 proposal for a political solution to the war crimes question in Japan had been rejected by Secretary of State John Foster Dulles, with help from State Department legal advisors John Raymond and John Auchincloss. A November 9 memo defined the problem: "How can what the Japanese desk considers the serious damage done to Japanese-United States relations by the continued U.S. retention of Japanese war criminals be eliminated in such a way that United States relations with West Germany . . . will not be adversely affected?"[177] Once again, the State Department's Japanese bureau proposed that President Eisenhower parole the remaining ninety Japanese war criminals in Amer-

ican custody after each had completed ten years of his sentence. Although Ambassador Conant recommended that "the United States divest itself of the custody of the German war criminals as soon as possible," he warned that "the German war criminal issue is still a highly explosive political question"; any preferential treatment accorded to Japanese war criminals would create a "problem of the first magnitude in U.S.-German relations." Conant pointed out that accelerated releases would require a Presidential recommendation.[178]

The State Department's Office of Political Affairs in Bonn issued a confidential memo on the objectives of the final phase of American war crimes policy on December 12, 1956. The memo assumed that "steps should be taken to eliminate the difficulties which the war criminal situation is causing in our relations with the Federal Republic of Germany and with Japan" and offered two types of solutions, those "to which no legal barriers exist" and those that "could not be put into effect without formal amendment of existing agreements and treaties." While the American President could unilaterally release war criminals in Japan, the State Department noted that legally, things were not quite so simple in Germany: "The Settlement Convention provides rather elaborate machinery . . . for dealing with war criminals while the Japanese Peace Treaty merely reserves to the United States, as sentencing authority, the right to decide upon recommendation of the Japanese Government." Any changes in the Settlement Convention would require the consent of both the Allies and the U.S. Senate, and "To obtain approval of the Senate would present difficulties of such consequence that it seems desirable to adopt a course of action not predicated on such requirement."[179] The State Department memo concluded that if the United States wanted to be protected from domestic criticism "and preserve our position that the trial and sentencing of these criminals was eminently justified then the emphasis may shift from end result to method with a consequent necessity for as similar procedures as possible in order to avoid any dispute" that either Japan or Germany received "a procedure more favorable to one of the two countries concerned."[180] The United States would continue to review the sentences on a case-by-case basis, and those pressing hardest for a war crimes amnesty would be reminded that the remaining prisoners were "the hard core . . . found guilty of heinous crimes."[181] The memo made the point that under the Mixed Board, the terms of parole for war criminals were extremely favorable; "They would not in general be considered eligible for parole or release if normal standards were applied."[182]

On February 8, 1957, newly appointed American Mixed Board member Spencer Phenix offered his appraisal of American war crimes policy in two memos. Memo A, "a statement of the present position as I see it," pointed out that while the United States had reduced the number of war criminals to 23, they were still responsible for overseeing the ongoing paroles of 198 others. Although many had been freed, these had been conditional, probationary releases. The French and British war criminal releases were far less conditional and did not require either nation to provide ongoing parole supervision. But in keeping with America's "modern penalogical principles," "the Board would continue in operation until the deaths of the six individuals serving life terms, or, barring prior death, until 1985." Phenix saw nothing to be gained by such a "dull and profitless operation" as the continued incarceration of *Einsatzkommandos* and other major war criminals originally sentenced to death: "It is not easy to see what political, practical or sociological advantage would be realized by continuing so empty an operation until say 1985." Although Phenix considered turning the prisoners over to the Federal Republic, he pointed back to the sentence validity question, "the German Government has not yet recognized the validity of the convictions of those persons and that non-recognition has constituted a bar to the transfer of any penal responsibility to the German authorities." Memo A recommended that "the time has come to re-examine the present parole procedure with a view to its termination within a reasonable period."[183]

Spencer Phenix's Memo B was an example of strategic legalism *par excellence*, or as he put it, "a statement of what I am prepared to do as the American member of the Mixed Board to facilitate a relatively prompt settlement of the problem." With that Phenix called for the "rapid liquidation of the war crimes problem" and suggested the continued reliance on the strategic legalists' favorite post-trial, nonjudicial "device"—yet another reduction in the parole requirements. If that failed to win approval, he suggested transferring authority over the prisoners to the Federal Republic of Germany.[184] If the Germans' only objection to accepting custody of the prisoners was the sentence validity question, Phenix devised a way around this longstanding impasse that allowed both nations to save face: "it should not be difficult to incorporate in any exchange of notes recording agreement between the two governments some saving paragraph which would cover that point."

Phenix, an old hand at the strategic legalist game, offered an illustra-

tion of what he meant by a "saving paragraph": "Many years ago I negotiated the settlement agreement between British and American Governments covering the 'Disposal of Certain Pecuniary Claims Arising out of
the Recent War', signed 19 May 1927. The discussions centered around
cargo and ship seizure, detentions and confiscation. . . . In those negotiations the British Government found the subject matter at least as sensitive
as the German Government finds the war criminal problem." To get
around this impasse, Phenix "drafted notes exchanged recording the
agreement. . . . These provided that 'the right of each government to
maintain in the future such a position as it may deem appropriate with
respect to the legality or illegality under international law of measures
such as those giving rise to claims covered by the immediately preceding
paragraph is fully reserved, it being specifically understood that the juridical position of neither government is prejudiced by the present agreement.' " At the time, the British believed that this solution provided them
with "sufficient political insurance, and I do not see why the German
Government could not accept a similar paragraph for the same purpose."[185] In other words, both West Germany and the United States could
justify the final war criminal releases however they saw fit.

If the Germans proved unwilling to take custody of the war criminals,
Memo B suggested hiring German prison authorities to oversee the
remainder of the sentences. Phenix believed this "would enable the Germans to accept physical custody during '*Untersuchungshaft*' without admitting the validity of the convictions of the American military courts but it is
a cumbersome procedure and the least attractive of the alternatives I have
been able to think of."[186] In Memo B, the new American Mixed Board
member stated very plainly, "I am prepared to suggest to the Mixed Board
the adoption of the following procedure for the rapid liquidation of the
war crimes problem as it affects the 296 persons for whom the United
States is still responsible." Under the Phenix plan, once the Mixed Board
received "an appropriate 'petition by or on behalf of a person' now on
good conduct time release," the Mixed Board could recommend "the
reduction of the sentence of such person to actual time served in prison,
on parole, and on good conduct time." The Mixed Board would then terminate the sentence "as of the date when the Competent Authority acts
pursuant to the Board's recommendations." Phenix believed that the German Government "will be so pleased with the almost immediate termination of the sentences of 204 of the persons now on parole and good con-

duct time release that they will be willing to accept without further argument or discussion responsibility for the 'custody and carrying out of the sentences' of the remaining 92."[187]

In a cover letter attached to the two memos, the American Mixed Board member stated very plainly that he was prepared to shoulder any and all blame and responsibility for his action: "I feel that the Department, in its own interest, should keep its hands officially out of the war criminal problem and treat it as within the exclusive jurisdiction of the Mixed Board" and "disclaim all responsibility for the decisions of the American member, scrupulously refraining from attempting to explain or justify his action." Phenix noted that although the Mixed Board members were supposed to serve as independent jurists "expressly not subject to the instructions of their governments," he believed that "there is nothing in the Convention or in good sense which prohibits agreement between the government and its appointee." He would be returning to Washington soon, and he requested a meeting with State Department legal advisor John Raymond so that, "Without in any way passing the buck of responsibility back to the Department . . . I could be given an informal indication that the procedure I have suggested in Memorandum 'B' is not unacceptable per se or inconsistent with the Department's basic policies. . . . I hope I can answer all your questions and that between us we can reach substantial agreement on what can and should be done to get this bothersome problem quietly out of the way where it will no longer complicate international relations."[188] Raymond attached a handwritten note to the memo: "Very interesting food for thought. My preliminary reaction is to agree with the first three pages of Memo B."[189]

On March 11 and 12, Spencer Phenix met with John Raymond and State Department officers Raymond Lisle, Robert Creel, Richard Kearney, and Knox Lamb in Washington to discuss speeding the release of the war criminals according to the plan outlined in Memo B. In the memorandum of their meeting, Phenix pointed to the difference in Allied and American parole standards. Under the British and French systems, the prisoners were more or less unconditionally released after ten years in prison. Under the American system, parolees followed designated plans and maintained contact with their parole officers. If the parolee failed to meet the terms of his release, he was supposed to be subject to rearrest. The American Mixed Board member believed that the United States should modify its parole standards to match those of the British and

French. The United States would quickly and quietly end their war crimes program on an especially inauspicious note, "by reducing the sentences of the parolees after they had spent sufficient time on parole to establish the fact of their rehabilitation." Phenix informed the State Department officials that it was "his intention to propose to the Board" yet another plan to offer parolees new opportunities to have their sentences reduced to time served.[190]

The latest strategic legalist mechanism came in the form of "an appropriate petition" stating that the "ultra hardcore" convicts had been "rehabilitated." Although the standards were supposed to vary according to each prisoner's legal status, under Spencer Phenix's direction, the Mixed Board would reserve the right to "recommend reduction of the sentence of such person to actual time served in prison and on parole." Phenix closed the discussions by stating "that in view of his independent status as a member of the Mixed Board he was not seeking the Department's agreement or consent to these plans." However, Phenix did ask for a wink and a nod, "so as to avoid causing any conflict with policy which the Department might have under consideration." After some discussion of the "mechanics by which the plans of Mr. Phenix would be put into operation," the State Department representatives would neither "approve nor disapprove the proposed plans." However, they added "that the plans did not appear to give rise to any conflict with Departmental policies."[191]

The German Foreign Office had already informally raised the question of the war criminals with an American State Department officer in Bonn in February 1957. Richard Balkan of the German Foreign Office asked Robert Creel of the State Department if the United States was "considering any steps to resolve this problem from our own standpoint" and told him that they had received reports that the British and French would release their last war criminals in a matter of weeks. When Creel asked the German diplomat "whether he was bringing this matter up on his own initiative or under instructions from a higher authority," Balkan replied that "the Embassy had received a communication from the Foreign Office suggesting that the matter be discussed informally with the Department on the basis of certain specific points." He handed Creel a typed memorandum from the German Foreign Office entitled, "War Criminals still in custody of the American authorities in Landsberg." The memo stated that the British and French would soon release their last prisoners and presumed that "the US government has also a certain interest in bringing the whole problem of the prisoners to a satisfactory solution, which would relieve the relations between the American and the German peoples from a certain burden still existing." The Germans proposed that the United States "shorten or dissolve the whole parole system at a proper time by bi-lateral negotiations, in order to abolish an institution which is not in accordance with German law" and requested a "general pardone [sic.] for all German prisoners in American custody or a transfer of all prisoners to the German legal authorities could now be taken into serious consideration."[192]

From Germany, Spencer Phenix wrote to State Department legal advisor John Raymond in Washington on April 17, 1957 to inform him of "developments since I was in Washington last month . . . everything seems to be proceeding smoothly in the directions I indicated." During the Mixed Board's April 10 meeting, Phenix had presented his plan to the German members: "On the 11th, after very minor modifications in the suggested procedures, the Board unanimously adopted the resolutions necessary for the implementation of the plan." He was "entirely satisfied by the action taken by the Board which, I feel, has now done its part in pointing the way to a practicable solution of the problem."[193]

Spencer Phenix was a one-man war crimes fixer. Anticipating criticism from the U.S. Army, Phenix spoke to Army Judge Advocate General Rieger about the Mixed Board's unanimous decision to release Joachim Peiper. "In this controversial area I dislike to quote anyone, but I can safely say that I found no opposition to the action taken by the Board." Phenix believed that the army, like the State Department, would be happy to have a scapegoat: "I think the Board's action was something of a relief since being unanimous it has the result of confronting them with recommendations which, under the terms of the Bonn Convention, are binding on the Commander-in-Chief, thereby relieving him of all responsibility." Again, Phenix offered to take the fall if necessary. "They agreed that the Board, as a Board, and particularly I myself as the U.S. member, had shouldered a considerable responsibility however, but we are all hopeful that no controversial publicity will develop."[194]

The American Mixed Board member also met with representatives of the Heidelberg Juristenkreis, the war crimes lobbying group led by Eduard Wahl and Otto Kranzbühler. "What really concerns the Heidelberg authorities seems to be their continued responsibility for the Landsberg prisoners," he wrote. "The Heidelberg Group expressed the opinion that if the Germans refused to accept unqualified custody the next best solution would be to negotiate an agreement whereunder Germany assumed all operational responsibility for the non-paroled prisoners." Phenix told John Raymond that the Mixed Board would make no public announcement of Joachim Peiper's release and "expressed the hope that the Foreign Office will also refrain from publicity at this time. The disadvantages of publicity were pointed out to me by the Heidelberg authorities who quickly agreed and, I am sure, the Department is of the same opinion."[195]

In late April, Richard Hagan, the U.S. parole official in Germany, wrote to the State Department legal advisor to report that there were only 18 prisoners remaining in Landsberg Prison and 193 on parole. Hagan believed that "This problem is well within manageable proportions although much work remains e.g. Drafting orders to carry out the recently adopted policies of the Mixed Board with reference to parole terminations and ending of good conduct status."[196] On May 13, 1957, Spencer Phenix reported to John Raymond that the sentences of 74 individuals paroled on good conduct release had been "reduced to time already served." On July 2, Phenix updated the legal advisor on the Mixed Board's progress. Under his Memo B plan, the United States had reduced their case load from 300 to 148; "Of the 148 remaining American cases 15 are confined in Landsberg, four are on medical parole, one is on good conduct release and 128 are on parole." Phenix estimated that "the number of 'hard core' cases is nine."[197]

In December 1957, President Eisenhower abolished the Japanese war crimes parole and clemency board and transferred authority to the U.S. ambassador in Tokyo and a "responsible non-political Japanese Board to review application for parole of prisoners now in confinement." According to a secret State Department cable, a similar offer had been made to the West German government: "Chapter 1, Article 6, paras 4 and 5 Settlement Convention contemplate transfer of custody of war criminals to German authorities and US is prepared to make immediate transfer if Germans will accept custody. . . . If Germans wish, we would be prepared to raise with other signatories Bonn Conventions possibility amending Settlement Convention by abolishing Mixed Board and replacing it with a German Board along the lines proposed for Japanese." However, once again, the validity question posed a stumbling block: "US cannot agree to any course of action which would bring into question validity of trials of war criminals or sentences imposed on them."[198] The State Department in Bonn responded with a secret cable to the Secretary of State. The ambassador did not believe that the action in Japan would have much of an impact on the situation in Germany. By the end of 1957, only 4 convicts remained in Landsberg and 36 remained on parole. "The four remaining prisoners constitute the ultimate hard core and Phenix believes it highly improbable Board will ever unanimously recommend parole for them."[199] However, Phenix would find a way to release the "ultimate hardcore" by the spring of 1958.

The last four German war criminals remaining in U.S. custody were not ordinary war criminals; in fact, they made the men of *Kampfegruppe* Peiper look like choirboys. During their trial, the prosecution took only two days to present its case, which consisted entirely of the execution squads' reports from the Soviet Union. A former Lutheran clergyman, Ernst Biberstein headed Sonderkommando 6 (part of Einsatzgruppen C). While serving in the Soviet Union, Biberstein admitted, "I personally superintended an execution in Rostov which was performed by means of a gas truck. . . . The truck was then driven to a place outside the town where members of my kommando had already dug mass graves." Adolf Ott was equally candid: "I have already said . . . every Jew who was apprehended had to be shot. Never whether he was a perpetrator or not."[200] On April 14, 1948, Ernst Biberstein, Klingelhoefer, and Adolf Ott were sentenced to death. The Peck Panel spared their lives and reduced their sentences to life in prison during their 1951 review of the *Einsatzgruppen* case.[201]

On April 30, 1958, Spencer Phenix wrote to State Department legal advisor John Raymond to inform him of the Mixed Board's recent action in the four "ultimate hardcore" American war crimes cases. Due to the extreme nature of the defendants' crimes, the Mixed Board could not easily grant them parole. However, because the prisoners had served more than ten years, they were officially eligible for parole under the newly reduced criteria. During the April 29, 1958 meeting of the Mixed Board, the German Foreign Office presented parole requests for the final four prisoners at Landsberg. While the Mixed Board "unanimously decided to deny the parole requests," they did move "to approve the individual clemency requests with the result that it was recommended unanimously that the sentences of the four be reduced to time served." The Mixed Board submitted their formal recommendations to the U.S.

ambassador and the U.S. Army. Phenix informed Raymond that the United States had only 31 parolees left under American jurisdiction. The Mixed Board had already received the "appropriate petitions" from 269 convicts and reduced their sentences to time served.[202]

On May 6, Secretary of State John Foster Dulles received a cable from the U.S. Embassy in Bonn announcing that "As a result of unanimous recommendations by Mixed Board, sentences of four remaining prisoners confined Landsberg (three Embassy Biberstein, Ott, Sandberger, one Army Brinkmann) have been commuted to time served. Planned release prisoners May 9. Following statement will be issued to press 1600 May 9. Begin Text: 'The last four prisoners confined at the war crimes prison at Landsberg were released today following clemency action.' " On May 7, John Raymond wrote to offer Phenix "congratulations on the conclusion of a fine job."[203] The State Department legal advisor added that the United States had also reduced the number of war criminals imprisoned in Japan from 50 in 1957 to 18 in 1958.

On May 9, 1958, the gates of Landsberg prison swung open for the final time as the last four German war criminals in American custody were released.[204] On May 13, Spencer Phenix reported to John Raymond: "It is only fair to say that circumstances played a more significant part than I did. In any case it is pleasant to feel that this diplomatic pebble has been removed from the State Department's shoes."[205] A few weeks later, Raymond offered Phenix "his sincere congratulations on the very capable manner in which you have discharged an exceedingly difficult and delicate assignment."[206] Spencer Phenix had found the final solution to the American war crimes problem.

CONCLUSION

Finally, we are left with two myths: the American myth of the redemptive trial and the German myth of harsh victor's justice. The outcome of the Nuremberg trials does not affirm the contention that political justice is, by its very nature, illegitimate—if anything, America's post–World War II war crimes policies show the many types and gradations of political justice. What is most often overlooked, especially about the American Nuremberg trials, is the leniency of most of the original sentences. Originally convicted and sentenced to twenty and twenty-five years respectively in the Ministries case, high-ranking Nazis like Hans Lammers and Gottlob Berger were both released from Landsberg Prison in December 1951.[1] As for the "ex post facto" laws like those concerning "aggression," all of the Nuremberg courts proved reluctant to apply, much less convict, under these controversial new laws. In the industrialist cases, several of the courts were almost unwilling to punish CEOs whose companies had demanded, utilized, and egregiously mistreated slave labor. The more systematic killing of millions of civilians was a massive violation of both customary military practice and the codified laws of war, not to mention the fact that it was done with a cold-blooded precision that was unique in human history. The Nuremberg trials left a complex and mostly sensible set of military and political standards that were not upheld in the post–World War II era.

It was not enough for American leaders to simply defeat and destroy the Third Reich; they also insisted on reforming their vanquished foes. The assumption that the Germans would denounce their former leaders and embrace their conquerors' value system was erroneous. During the 1950s, die-hard Nazis were allowed to exploit the Cold War and in the end considered themselves unjustifiably persecuted. The most important agents of "persecution" were America's punitive occupation policies, and above all, the Nuremberg trials.

The war crimes trials' initial credibility problems were exacerbated by American leniency—a second policy that contradicted the original, punitive occupation policy (JCS 1067). As a result of this dramatic shift, a very basic debate was reopened. Instead of discussing the shocking atrocities committed by many of the high-ranking convicts, American officials were forced to defend the basic legal legitimacy of the trials. Frank Buscher attributes the shift in German attitude to the hard line taken by West German lawmakers on the sentence validity question in the early 1950s: "Most importantly, during the period between the creation of the Federal Republic and the attainment of sovereignty, the parliament stubbornly refused to accept any responsibility for Nazi Germany's atrocities and war crimes. Instead, legislators of almost all parties portrayed the Allies as villains and violators of the law."[2] It was ironic, as Jörg Friedrich points out, that the convicted war criminals did not want to be "judged by their standards or treated according to their own methods."[3] Strategic legalism in the form of nonjudicial, post-trial sentence reductions allowed the State Department to shift the direction of American war crimes policy without officially contradicting JCS 1067. However, American actions spoke far louder and more eloquently than the State Department's dissembled words. American public opinion polls showed the German public split nearly 50/50 in their opinions of Nuremberg's IMT in 1946, but by the early 1950s West German public opinion had turned sharply against the trials.[4]

However, just as the Allies were releasing their last convicted war criminals in the late 1950s, something amazing did occur. In 1958, the West German government opened the Central Office of the State Ministries for the Investigation of National Socialist Crimes of Violence in Ludwigsburg. The West German government began to try concentration camp staff and *Einsatzkommandos* for violations of German law during World War II. Although men like Treblinka commandant Franz Stangl were sentenced to long prison terms, many West Germans found it odd that their government had chosen to move so far down the chain of command in their own trials. Between 1958 and the end of 1985, West German courts convicted 992 Germans for wartime atrocities. However, many of the sentences were extremely lenient. Historian Jeffrey Herf explains how the American and Allied war crimes clemencies of the 1950s undermined the subsequent German trials: "these decisions had a profoundly negative impact on subsequent trials in German courts because higher-ranking officials who had been amnestied in 1951 offered testimony in trials in the 1960s against lower-ranking officials who bore less guilt. As a result, it became more difficult to gain convictions in these later cases."[5] "They had too many friends," the late Nuremberg prosecutor Robert Kempner explained to the author in a 1988 interview. "The man who wanted parole told their people, 'If you don't sign good things about the parole business, I will tell about you'—very simple—'I will tell about you.' " Kempner offered this telling anecdote about the German trials:

> I was sitting with the Chief German Justice during the Auschwitz case as a spectator. You saw Veesenmayer as a witness for the defense and he was a free man. . . . He told the court stories and this judge next to me asked me, "Who is this man?" and I said, "This is a very nice acquaintance of mine, he was only responsible for 400,000 Jews." "Why is he running around?" I said, "Because he is a defense witness for the Auschwitz case." Veesenmayer came back when he was through and he stopped at me and said, "How are you?" and I said, "We have both grown older." Later I talked with a reserve judge and he said, "It is very bad for us, Veesenmayer is running free and we should judge about the little SS men who killed only two."[6]

Although Edmund Veesenmayer was sentenced to twenty-five years in the Ministries case, he too was released in December 1951.

The idea that the U.S. government took a firm position on the subject of war crimes and in the process, "reeducated" postwar Germans and Japanese was and remains a comforting myth. The U.S. proved unwilling to uphold sentences that were justified and in many cases lenient. Soldiers who individually killed civilians by the thousands, judges who twisted the law to suit the whims of despots, diplomats who were caught double dealing, bankers who laundered the booty of the dead, industrialists who used and abused slave labor, and doctors who mutilated living humans in the name of science—to name only a few—deserved to pay a heavy price for such acts.

During the Cold War, the superpowers defied international authority and took cynical, strategic legalism to new heights. Although there were prominent exceptions, like the Eichman trial (1960) and the Calley and Medina trials (1971). However, on the global level—international law, the Nuremberg Principles, the Hague Conventions, even the customary laws of war—provided little protection for civilians caught on the wrong side of the political dividing line in places like Vietnam, Cambodia, East Timor, Afghanistan, and El Salvador, to name only a few.

Actually, the tragic fate of Cambodia clearly demonstrates the weakness of international law during the Cold War. After the Vietnamese toppled the Khmer Rouge in 1979, it soon became clear that Pol Pot's regime had systematically carried out some of the worst atrocities since World War II. Did the United States call for the prosecution of Pol Pot, Ieng Sary, Khieu Samphan, and other Khmer Rouge leaders? No, quite the opposite: in 1979, Cyrus Vance, the Carter administration's UN representative, voted to allow the deposed, genocidal regime to retain its seat in the UN General Assembly. After the decision, a senior U.S. official justified the decision to journalist Nayan Chanda: "The choice for us was between moral principles and international law. The scale weighed in favor of law because it served our security interests."[7] Deposed Khmer Rouge leader Ieng Sary put it most succinctly in a 1981 interview: "First are the aggressors and expansionists headed by the Soviet Union. . . . It is good that the USA and China are agreed here. We too are on this team!"[8]

The cynicism of American strategic legalism reached new heights in 1985, when the International Court in the Hague agreed to hear the Nicaraguan Sandinista government's case against the United States for mining its harbors and illegally supporting the Contra guerrillas. Rather than contest the charges, the Reagan administration simply withdrew from the International Court's jurisdiction for a two-year period. Although the court ultimately ruled against the United States, this had little effect on Reagan's secret war in Central America and provided a graphic illustration of Thucydides' famous maxim from the Melian dialogue, "the standard of justice depends on the equality of power to compel and that in fact the strong do what they have the power to do and the weak accept what they have to accept."[9]

Former U.S. Senator Daniel Patrick Moynihan argues that by 1990, there was "a certain disorientation in American foreign policy," which grew out of "our having abandoned, for practical purposes, the concept that international relations can and should be governed by a regime of public international law." Though alarmed by America's decision to shed all international legal pretense, Moynihan was more bothered by the fact that "this idea had not been succeeded by some other reasonably comprehensive and coherent notion as to the kind of world order we do seek, or which at all events we do accept and try to cope with."[10] This lack of vision became most apparent after the collapse of the Soviet Union and the end of the Cold War.

The post–Cold War world confronted American leaders with any number of daunting challenges and in the process exposed the limits of American power and vision on the most pressing questions of our time. Although Nuremberg's International Military Tribunal continues to provide an important symbolic model for human rights advocates, the end of the Cold War saw genocidal civil wars in Rwanda and Bosnia vie for the West's increasingly fragmented and unfocused attention. Most shocking about the "postmodern" wars of the 1990s was that the line between soldier and civilian had all but vanished. Michael Ignatieff goes so far as to argue that in "postmodern" conflict, "war crimes and atrocities" became "integral to the very persecution of war."[11]

The strategic legalism of the Reagan and Bush administrations during the final years of the Cold War have been transformed into a more timid, therapeutic form of legalism under the Clinton administration. With genocides in Rwanda and former Yugoslavia, the mantra "Never Again," became, in the words of President William Jefferson Clinton, "I am sorry." At the time of Rwanda's hundred-day massacre (claiming between 700,000 and 900,000 lives and sparking an ongoing civil war in the Congo), his administration did not push for UN intervention, downplayed clear warnings, and even quibbled over using the word "genocide" to describe the clearest example since World War II.[12] However, this did not deter President Clinton from making a postgenocide airport stop in Kigali to apologize to Rwandans for his error in judgment. More distress-

ing than Clinton's day-late, dollar-short "concern" is the growing accep-
tance of the idea that it is permissible to stand aside and watch knowingly as genocide is carried out on live television as long as it is likely that a
dozen or so ringleaders will be solemnly indicted and tried by an international tribunal in the not-too-distant future. As Michael Ignatieff
observes: "The two tribunals were created in 1993 and 1994 by Western
governments who had done little or nothing to stop the crimes the tribunals were set up to punish. Instead of armed intervention, the international community promised the victims justice, in the form of a prosecutor, a panel of judges, and a secretariat of investigators and lawyers."

The duality—the yawning chasm between American rhetoric and foreign policy, the very thing that so infuriated postwar Germans—continues to widen. George Kennan observes, "And thus, extravagantly do we,
like a stern school master clothed in the mantle of perfect virtue, sit in
judgment over all other governments, looking sharply down the nose of
each of them to see whether its handling of its domestic affairs meets our
approval."[13]

Today the American duality is alive and well in the persons of Secre-
tary of State Madeline Albright and U.S. Ambassador for War Crimes
David Scheffer. Their public relationship is not unlike that of President
Woodrow Wilson and his Secretary of State Robert Lansing. While
Albright has strongly advocated the enforcement of international crimi-
nal law and urged the prosecution of everyone from Pol Pot to Slobodan
Milosevic, her top war crimes official has proven considerably more con-
servative.

In 1998 the American duality was forced into the stark light of the
Roman summer. Many of the world's international legal luminaries had
gathered to hammer out the details of the UN's long-awaited international criminal court at the Rome Conference. Finally, much to the dismay of human rights groups and international law advocates, the United
States sided with China, Iraq, Algeria, India, and Israel and refused to
join the one hundred other nations signing the treaty to create a permanent international criminal court. Once again, the American delegates
wanted one set of international laws for the rest of the world and another, more flexible set for the United States. In January 2000, Jesse Helms,
chairman of the Senate Foreign Relations Committee, met with the UN
Security Council and issued an ominous warning: "a UN that seeks to
impose its presumed authority on the American people, without their

consent, begs for confrontation and—I want to be candid with you—
eventual U.S. withdrawal."[14]

Fifty years after the United Nations adopted the "Nuremberg Principles," there remains a great deal of confusion surrounding the issues
raised by these revolutionary trials. Though they certainly served as a
warning to rogue political leaders that under the right set of political circumstances they might find themselves held accountable, other aspects of
the Nuremberg legacy remain far less certain. The UN has not captured,
much less tried, major war criminals in former Yugoslavia and Cambodia. One has to ask whether it is possible to enforce a Nuremberg-based
set of international laws under tense, armed, diplomatic compromises
like the Dayton Accords and the Paris Agreements.

Given the fate of international law since Nuremberg, the time has
come to reconsider the legacy of the Nuremberg trials as more of an
anomaly than a paradigm. In the year 2000, human rights and war
crimes only become considerations for U.S. foreign policy when they cor-
respond with larger policy objectives, or more commonly, when they turn
into public relations problems. Lurching from global crisis to global crisis,
we live in an age when strategic, much less moral, doctrines have been
replaced by pyschobabble, public opinion polls, and that great arbiter of
justice, CNN. Today, Telford Taylor's description of America "as a sort of
Steinbeckian 'Lennie,' gigantic and powerful, but prone to shatter what
we try to save" has never seemed more fitting.[15]

The early to mid-1990s were heady times for those who believed that a
Nuremberg-derived system of international criminal law would soon take
root. However, at the end of the decade and the bloodiest century in
recorded history, the so-called "international community" has grown
increasingly indifferent to and accepting of the horrors suffered by its
most powerless, politically insignificant members. Laws of war professor
Jonathan Bush described the phenomenon: "What was most troubling
about this early 1990s feeling was that it overvalued what trials can do and
completely missed the point of what Nuremberg did and didn't do."

Today, despite the most comprehensive set of laws governing war
and international relations in human history, the oldest and most basic
distinction, the one between soldier and civilian, is fast disappearing. A
nineteenth-century German historian calculated that from 1496
B.C.–A.D. 1861, a span of 3,357 years, only 227 had been years of peace
while 3,130 had been years of war. For every year of peace there had

been thirteen years of war.[16] As Sven Lindqvist suggests in his book *Exterminate All the Brutes*, "You already know enough. So do I. It is not knowledge that we lack. What is missing is the courage to understand what we know and draw conclusions."[17] Having just concluded the bloodiest century in the history of man, is it enough to seek salvation in new codes of international criminal law? More laws are not necessary; what is necessary if we are to avoid an even bloodier twenty-first century is the will to enforce the laws that exist.

Notes

Introduction

1. U.S. District Court for the District of Oregon, "In the Matter of the Memorial to Messrs. Robert F. Maguire and Charles A. Hart, May 17, 1976" (Portland: Federal Court Reporters), 2.

2. Ibid., 13.

3. Telford Taylor, interview by author, tape recording, New York City, 8 April 1987.

4. The Thirty Years War was to the sixteenth century what World War II was to the twentieth; both wrought destruction on an unprecedented scale. It is estimated that half of Europe's German-speaking population was killed by either war or famine during the Thirty Years War. J.F.C. Fuller wrote: "The age of the absolute kings arose from the ashes of the Wars of Religion, which culminated in the Thirty Years War (1648–1648), the latter half of which was a hideous conflict of hastily enrolled mercenaries, as often as not accompanied by hordes of starving people. When, in 1648, the Peace of Westphalia put an end to the anarchy, Central Europe lay in ruins; 8,000,000 people are said to have perished, not counting some 350,000 killed in battle" (*The Conduct of War 1781–1961* [New York: Da Capo, 1961], 15). David Kaiser offers this analysis: "The Thirty Years War, however, was not merely another case of a European monarch trying and failing to increase his authority. No conflict shows more clearly

the continuing power of the European aristocracy and, above all, the ways in which early modern armies served themselves, rather than than their legal sovereigns" (*Politics and War: European Conflict from Philip II to Hitler* [Cambridge: Harvard University Press, 1990], 83). See also Theodore Rabb, *The Thirty Years War: Problems of Motive, Extent and Effect* (Washington, D.C.: University Press of America, 1981).

The Thirty Years War was the result of the Renaissance and the Reformation; both challenged the supreme authority claimed by the Pope and the Holy Roman Emperor. With the modern nation-state came the recognition that war was a constant in human affairs. A good concise account of the changes in warfare is Michael Mann's *States, War, and Capitalism* (Oxford: Basil Blackwell, 1991). Mann breaks the changes in warfare into three "phases." During Phase II, pre-1780, "Making war was formally the private perogative of the medieval prince. . . . Moreover, wars were not devastating, did not involve the mass of the population, and were profitable to most surviving states" (157). Phase II (1780–1945) was something completely different: "The cost of war 'success' also rose phenomenally. Perceptive observers could see the escalation of costs and casualties of war, from the Napoleonic Wars, through the American Civil War" (157). Mann credits democracy and the industrial revolution with bringing about these changes. For a more through account see Kaiser, *Politics and War*. See also Hans Delbrück, *The Dawn of Modern Warfare* (Lincoln: University of Nebraska Press, 1990); Fuller, *The Conduct of War 1781–1961*; and Jeremy Black, *The Rise of the European Powers 1679–1793* (London: Edward Arnold, 1990). See Friedrich Meinecke (*Machiavellianism: The Doctrine of Raison d'Etat and Its Place in Modern History* [Boulder: Westview, 1984], 31). The five states of fifteenth-century Italy (Naples, the Papal States, Florence, Milan, and Venice), each with a permanent embassy and diplomats, provided a preview of the state system that emerged in the aftermath of the Thirty Years War. Statesmen followed fixed rules; everything was considered with a view to its usefulness, above religion or morality. Machiavelli wrote in *The Prince*: "It seemed more suitable to search after the effectual truth of the matter rather than its imagined one . . . for there is such a gap between how one lives and how one ought to live that anyone who abandons what is done for what ought to be done learns his ruin rather than his preservation" (Niccolo Machiavelli, *The Prince* [New York: Oxford University Press, 1984], x). What made the Florentinian unique was his candid acknowledgment of state's reason or *raison d'etat*. Acts considered violent or immoral by Christian standards were justifiable if they furthered the stability and self-sufficiency of the state (xiii). Meinecke writes: "In spite of his outward respect for the Church and Christianity . . . Machiavelli was at heart a heathen, who leveled at Christianity the familiar and serious reproach of having made men humble, unmanly and feeble" (31).

For a dissenting view on the rise of the modern nation-state see Kaiser, who argues that the transition to the modern nation-state was slow and uncertain: "Tilly's argument reflects one of the most common tendencies of modern historians, the tendency to exaggerate the pace of political change, particularly with respect to the growth of central authority" (*Politics and War*, 135). See also Michael Howard, "Can War Be Controlled?" in Jean Bethke Elshtain, ed., *Just War Theory* (New York: New York University Press, 1992), 26. Howard describes the departure from the Christian, just war tradition: "The first of these criteria dominated thinking about war during the era of ecclesiastical dominance which lasted in Europe until the sixteenth century, as clerical apologists, attempting to accommodate the necessities of warfare to the ethical imperatives of the Christian religion, refined the concept of the 'just war.' The second became dominant from the seventeenth to the nineteenth centuries, the age of Grotius, when it was assumed, in the words of Montesquieu, that, 'the law of nations is naturally founded on the principle, that different nations ought in time of peace to do one another all the good they can, and in time of war as little injury as possible without prejudicing their real interests" (26).

5. During the fifteenth and sixteenth centuries the Catholic doctrine was called into question by lay scholars and jurists (Vittoria, Gentili, and Suarez) who challenged the hegemony of both the Pope and the Holy Roman Emperor. All three men denied the Emperor's claim to jurisdiction over princes, citing "the existence of an international community governed by international law." Leo Gross, "The Peace of Westphalia, 1648–1948" *American Journal of International Law* 42(1948): 38. These early scholars shifted the focus of international law away from the just/unjust distinction and prepared the ground for the era of the sovereign nation-state. Vittoria, Gentili, and Suarez shared the belief that "the whole world formed one state, and that all men were fellow citizens and fellow townsmen, like a single herd feeding in a single pasture" ("The Peace of Westphalia," 32). For an excellent modern analysis of sovereignty see George F. Kennan, *Around the Cragged Hill* (New York: Norton, 1993). "Sovereignty was originally a quality attached to the person of a great ruler, normally an emperor or someone equivalent. It was his person, not the country or the people over whom he ruled, who was 'sovereign.' He alone was unlimited in his powers, in the sense that no one else's word could rival his authority. All of his subjects owed him submission and obedience. It was this that made him sovereign" (87). Kennan traces the development of the principle of sovereignty: "In ancient times, and in part down into the modern era, this concept of sovereignty, the supremacy of a single ruler, was often conceived to have universal significance—to be applicable, that is, to all of the known civilized world. . . . In the course of time, these pretensions lost their reality, and it came gradually to be accepted that a ruler, while still being 'sovereign,' would be sovereign only in the territory traditionally accepted as being under his rule, even if it did not include the entire world" (87). See also David Luban, *Legal Modernism* (Ann Arbor: University of Michigan Press, 1994), 337–338 for an interesting discussion of sovereignty's relationship to legal positivism.

6. According to Paul Piccone and G. L. Ulmen, under the traditional rules of European statecraft during the era of the nation-state, "Every recognition in international law was fundamentally an expression of the fact that the state in question had a legitimate spatial dimension and belonged to a recognized spatial order" ("American Imperialism and International Law," *Telos* 72 (Summer 1987). Under the act-of-state doctrine during the era of the nation-state, the leader of a sovereign nation was immune from legal prosecution. There were exceptions: for example, rogues like

Napoleon who refused to play by the rules were punished. Carl Schmitt argued that the removal of the messianic impulse of the just war rationalized and even "humanized" war. See also John Appleman, *Military Tribunals and International Crimes*, 54–59.

Reinhard Koselleck makes a similar observation in *Critique and Crisis* (New York: Berg, 1988): "The termination of religious civil war and the confining of war to an affair between States were two corresponding phenomena rooted in the separation of morality and politics, implicit in one case, explicit in the other. What expressed this separation in terms of international law was that states at war—like men in the state of nature—faced each other as equals with the same rights, beyond any question of the moral *justa causa*, and that regardless of the moral grounds of war, solely by virtue of its statehood, each one understood the other as well as itself as *justus hostis*, a rightful enemy" (43). Koselleck describes international relations in the era of the European nation-state: "The conscience of the sovereign became absolutely free, but his jurisdiction was confined to the inner space of the State he represented. . . . This delimitation of an independent inner space, a space whose moral integrity was shown by Hobbes to lie solely in its character as a State—this was what it took to effectuate the outward evolution of an inter-state, supra-individual commitment" (43–44). Koselleck considers the shift significant: "The *jus publicum Europeaum* was based on strict separation of a State's morally inviolate interior from the mutual external and political relations between States. States were absolutely free, and their sovereigns, like Hobbes's men *qua* human beings, were subject to their consciences alone, without submitting like men *qua* citizens to any common, institutionalized higher authority. . . . Each sovereign had the *jus ad bellum*, the same right to make war, and war became a means of princely politics, guided by *raison d'etat* and reduced to the common formula of a 'European balance of power' " (43–44). Major-General J.F.C. Fuller offers this assessment of military conflict during the nation state period: "Monarchs generally fought wars for limited aims. Publicists frequently accused rival monarchs of seeking total victory over their enemies, and one or two of them briefly dreamed of it, but opportunities for complete victory repeatedly proved illusory, and the peace treaties arrived at reflected an explicit conception of a balance of power" (*The Conduct of War 1781–1961*, 141).

1. The End of Limited War

1. Michael Howard, *War in European History* (New York: Oxford University Press, 1976), 5. On the Battle of Agincourt see John Keegan, *The Face of Battle* (New York: Penguin, 1976). A particularly good example of this tendency are recent journalistic accounts of the Battle of Agincourt. One journalist went so far as to describe it as "an atrocity on a scale and of a horror almost unimaginable, even by contemporary standards." Another journalist called Henry V's order to execute the French prisoners "a violation of the laws of war." Historian John Keegan offers a more complete and satisfactory discussion in *The Face of Battle*, 109–110. Howard and Keegan both agree that greed played a more important role than honor in early European warfare. Howard writes, "But the increasing codification of the laws of war was due less to any search-

ing of Christian, legal, or Knightly consciences than to a different development indeed: the growing commercialism of war. Ransom and booty were no longer agreeable bonuses, but, for a growing number of belligerents, the major object of their activity" (7). Michael Ignatieff describes the restraining role of "warrior's honor" in his book of the same title: "Warrior's honor was both a code of belonging and an ethic of responsibility. Wherever the art of war was practiced, warriors distinguished between combatants and noncombatants, legitimate and illegitimate targets, moral and immoral weaponry, civilized and barbarous usage in the treatment of prisoners and of the wounded" (*Warrior's Honor* [New York: Holt, 1997], 117).

Howard Levie leaves few doubts about the brutality of early European warfare in his encyclopedic study, *Terrorism in War: The Law of War Crimes* (Dobbs Ferry, N.Y.: Oceana, 1993): "In a city taken by storm almost any licence was condoned by the law. Only churches and churchmen were technically secure, but even they were not often spared. Women could be raped, and men killed out of hand. All the goods of the inhabitants were regarded as forfeit. If lives were spared, it was only through clemency of the victorious captain; and spoilation was systematic" (9–10). Levie describes the roles played by ransom and booty in early European warfare: "The prospect of this free run of his lust for blood, spoil and women was a major incentive to a soldier to persevere in the rigors which were likely to attend a protracted siege" (10). Levie also points out that many early European wars ended with an amnesty on war crimes: "In the peace treaties ending the wars of the seventeenth century and thereafter, it became the custom to include in each one an amnesty (or 'oblivion') provision which, in effect, forgave, among other things, any war crimes committed during the course of hostilities which the treaty was intended to bring to an end." Levie cites Article II of the Treaty of Westphalia; Article III of the 1713 Treaty of Utrecht; 1763 Treaty of Paris" as examples of "oblivion provisions" (12).

2. Telford Taylor, *Nuremberg and Vietnam* (New York: Bantam, 1971), 59. Taylor comments on the original paradox of Christianity and organized violence: "During the first three centuries after Christ's death there grew up among his followers a strong school of religious pacifism. Moreover, the early Christians were a religious minority in a pagan state. For this reason the early church leaders condemned all military service as incompatible with Christian life."

3. Howard, *War in European History*, 5. Howard describes war against the heathens as "*guerre mortale* in which not only the property but the lives of the vanquished were at the mercy of their conquerer." Moreover, when Christian knights were fighting pagans, "no holds were barred, and knights indeed could gain remission from their sins by waging it." As Michael Ignatieff points out in *Warrior's Honor*, "Warrior codes were sharply particularist: that is, they applied only to certain people, not to others. The protections afforded by the chivalric code applied only to Christians. Toward infidels, a warrior could behave without restraint" (117).

4. Dee Brown, *Bury My Heart at Wounded Knee* (New York: Holt, 1970), 9. Brown wrote: "About five million of the indigenous American poulation lived in what is now the United States. At the beginning of the nineteenth century, half a million

remained. In 1891, at the time of Wounded Knee—the last great massacre of Indians in the United States—the native population reached rock bottom: a quarter of a million, or 5 percent of the original number of Indians" (114). For more on American Indian numbers see Colin Galloway's *New Worlds for All: Indians, Europeans, and the Remaking of Early America* (Baltimore: Johns Hopkins University Press, 1998). Some estimates run much higher than five million.

5. Richard Drinnon, *Facing West: The Metaphysics of Indian-Hating and Empire-Building* (Norman: University of Oklahoma Press, 1980), xiii. "The basic feature of the white policies is the assault of the strong on the weak, the intention to take their land from them. This phenomenon has taken its most grandiose form in North America. Land-hungry whites crowd in between the weak and partly decayed settlements of the Indians" (Sven Lindqvist, *Exterminate All the Brutes*, trans. Joan Tate [New York: New Press, 1996], 144).

6. Walter McDougall, *Promised Land, Crusader State* (Boston: Houghton Mifflin, 1997), 17. McDougall writes that there are so many references to early America's sense of moral superiority that it is "trite."

7. Edmund Morgan, *American Slavery, American Freedom* (New York: Norton, 1975), 4. See Anders Stephanson, *Manifest Destiny: American Expansionism and the Empire of Right* (New York: Hill and Wang, 1995), 24. For a differing point of view see McDougall, *Promised Land, Crusader State*.

8. Drinnon, *Facing West*, 70.

9. Hugh Brogan, *The Pelican History of the United States of America* (London: Penguin, 1986), 64*n*17.

10. John Keegan, *Fields of Battle: The Wars for North America* (New York: Knopf, 1996), 270. According to Keegan, war played an important part in the day-to-day life of many American tribes before contact with early settlers: "North America, moreover, already had its own bitter military history. Intertribal warfare was a fact of American Indian life long before the coming of the Europeans, as in so many 'hard primitive' societies; Indians fought for honour, revenge, excitement, and in order to replace the casualties of war by seizing and 'adopting' captives from the enemy" (103).

11. Stephen Longstreet, *Indian Wars of the Great Plains* (New York: Indian Head Books, 1970), 113.

12. Keegan, *Fields of Battle*, 273, 283. Carol Chomsky makes the point that women and children had always been fair game in American Indian warfare in "The United States–Dakota War Trials: A Study in Military Injustice," *Stanford Law Review* 43(1)(Nov. 1990): 88.

13. Paul Wellman, *The Indian Wars of the West* (New York: Indian Head Books, 1992), 28*n*4.

14. Jill Lepore, *The Name of War: King Philip's War and the Origins of American Identity* (New York: Knopf, 1998), xiv. "English colonists in New England defined themselves against both the Indians' savagery and the Spaniards' cruelty: between these two similar yet distinct 'others,' one considered inhuman and one human, the English in New

England attempted to carve out for themselves a narrow path of virtue, piety, and mercy."

15. Ibid.

16. Drinnon, *Facing West*, 331.

17. Ibid.

18. Anthony Wallace, *Jefferson and the Indians: The Tragic Fate of the First Americans* (Cambridge: Harvard University Press, 1999), 175. See also Drinnon, *Facing West*, 81.

19. Drinnon, 87.

20. Ibid.

21. Ibid., 82 and Peter Parish, *Slavery: History and Historians* (New York: Harper and Row, 1989), 12–13, 26–28. According to Parish, America's slave population grew from 26,000 in 1700 to 2 million by 1830.

22. McDougall, *Promised Land, Crusader State*, 56.

23. Drinnon, *Facing West*, 76.

24. Stephanson, *Manifest Destiny*, 27.

25. Drinnon, *Facing West*, 99.

26. Elihu Root, *The Military and Colonial Policy of the United States* (New York: AMS Press, 1970), 320–321.

27. Vine Deloria Jr. and Clifford Lytle, *American Indians, American Justice* (Austin: University of Texas Press, 1983), 4.

28. Chomsky, "The United States–Dakota War Trials," 16–17.

29. Ibid., 16. The Minnesota Indian War of 1862 and the trial that followed were brought to my attention by historian John Willand of North Hennepin Community College in Minnesota. He was also kind enough to send me Carol Chomsky's authoritative *Stanford Law Journal* article on the Minnesota Indian War and the ensuing trials. I agree with Chomsky's analysis of President Lincoln's action and his final judgment. I supplemented this with local histories written by Minnesota residents who lived through the period. Most notable of these is the late Marion Satterlee, who spent the better part of a lifetime documenting the history of the massacre. Dee Brown really brought Santee leader Little Crow to life in her classic *Bury My Heart at Wounded Knee*. Bob Primeaux, a Sioux chief and a member of the Hunkpapa Treaty Council, also helped me a great deal in the final stages of the book.

30. Brown, *Bury My Heart at Wounded Knee*, 38. See also Chomsky, "The United States–Dakota War Trials," 16.

31. Brown, *Bury My Heart at Wounded Knee*, 39.

32. Ibid.

33. Ibid.

34. Ibid., 40.

35. Ibid.

36. Ibid.

37. Charles Bryant and Abel Murch, *A History of the Great Massacre by the Sioux Indians in Minnesota* (Millwood, N.Y.: Kraus Reprint, 1977), 315.

38. Brown, *Bury My Heart at Wounded Knee*, 43.

39. Ibid., 44.

40. Ibid.

41. Ibid., 43.

42. Ibid., 44.

43. Marion Satterlee, "A Description of the MASSACRE BY SIOUX INDI-ANS. In Renville County, Minnesota, August 18–19" (Minneapolis: Fisher Paper Co., 1916). This quote came from the section entitled "The Massacre at Redwood Agency," 4.

44. Brown, *Bury My Heart at Wounded Knee*, 45.

45. Kenneth Carley, *The Sioux Uprising* (Minneapolis: The Sioux Uprising Committee of the Minnesota State Historical Society, n.d.), 4.

46. Ibid., 5.

47. Ibid., 4.

48. Wellman, *The Indian Wars of the West*, 28n4.

49. Satterlee, "A Description of the MASSACRE BY SIOUX INDIANS," 4.

50. Ibid., 5.

51. Ibid. The brave ferry boat operator Herbert Millier is called Jacob Mauley in other accounts. Satterlee and others credit him with saving at least forty lives before he was butchered alive.

52. Brown, *Bury My Heart at Wounded Knee*, 45.

53. Ibid., 46.

54. *The New York Times*, August 22, 1862, 1. See also Robert Hays, *A Race at Bay* (Carbondale: Southern Illinois University Press, 1997). This entire book is devoted to *New York Times* editorials on America's "Indian Problem."

55. Brown, *Bury My Heart at Wounded Knee*, 50.

56. Carley, *The Sioux Uprising*, 2–3.

57. Ibid., 4.

58. *The New York Times*, August 24, 1862.

59. Richard Ellis, *General Pope and U.S. Indian Policy* (Albuquerque: University of New Mexico Press, 1970), 6.

60. Chomsky, "The United States–Dakota War Trials," 23.

61. Ellis, *General Pope and U.S. Indian Policy*, 8.

62. Brown, *Bury My Heart at Wounded Knee*, 52.

63. Ibid., 56–57. After the final battle, Little Crow announced that he was embarrassed to call himself a Sioux and believed that the Americans fought "like cowardly women" (58).

64. Wellman, *The Indian Wars of the West*, 39n3.

65. Brown, *Bury My Heart at Wounded Knee*, 54.

66. Chomsky, "The United States–Dakota War Trials," 21n44.

67. Brown, *Bury My Heart at Wounded Knee*, 55.

68. Ibid., 55.

69. Chomsky, "The United States–Dakota War Trials," 22.

70. Ibid., 23.

71. Ibid. 24.

72. Ibid., 50–51. Godfrey was married to an Indian woman. He was reported to have killed seven at New Ulm and the Santee dubbed him "he who kills many." According to Carol Chomsky, he traded his testimony for his life. He testified in fifty-five cases; of those, eleven ended with death penalties.

73. Ibid., 27. On the first day, the Commission sentenced ten to death.

74. Ibid., 23.

75. Brown, *Bury My Heart at Wounded Knee*, 54.

76. *The New York Times*, November 9, 1862, 2.

77. Ibid. On November 23, 1862, *The New York Times* reported an account of the trial written by a reporter from the *St. Paul Press*.

78. *The New York Times*, November 6, 1862.

79. Chomsky, "The United States–Dakota War Trials," 29.

80. Ibid.

81. Ibid., 31.

82. Ibid., 30.

83. Ibid., 32n118.

84. Ibid. *The New York Times*, December 12, 1862, reported President Lincoln's reductions: "We have this morning a message from President Lincoln to the Senate in retaliation to the thirty-nine Minnesota Indians whom he has ordered to be executed one week from today. The President was anxious not to act with so much clemency as to encourage another outbreak of the savages, nor with a degree of severity which should be real cruelty, and therefore at first ordered only the execution of such Indians as 'had proved guilty of violating females.' "

85. Ibid., 33.

86. Ibid.

87. Ibid., 34.

88. *The New York Times*, November 24, 1862.

89. Chomsky, "The United States–Dakota War Trials," 36–37.

90. Michel Foucault, *Discipline and Punish* (New York: Vintage, 1977), 7–8. Foucault points to the disappearance of torture as a public spectacle: "By the end of the eighteenth and the beginning of the nineteenth century, the gloomy festival of punishment was dying out, though here and there it flickered momentarily into life. In this transformation, two processes were at work. They did not have the same chronology or the same raison d'etre. The first was the disappearance of punishment as a spectacle. The ceremony of punishment tended to decline; it survived only as a new legal or administrative practice."

91. Chomsky, "The United States–Dakota War Trials," 36–37.

92. Carley, *The Sioux Uprising*, 66.

93. Longstreet, *Indian Wars of the Great Plains*, 125.

94. Brown, *Bury My Heart at Wounded Knee*, 63–64.

95. Otto Kirchheimer, *Political Justice: The Use of Legal Procedure for Political Ends* (Princeton: Princeton University Press, 1961), 260.

96. Francis Lieber, *Lieber's Code and the Law of War*, ed. Richard Hartigan (Chicago: Precedent, 1983), 2. See also Taylor, *Nuremberg and Vietnam*, 21. Lieber had three sons fighting in the Civil War, two Union and one Confederate. Early in the Civil War, Lieber and General Halleck met at Fort Donaldson, where the professor was visiting a son (the Confederate) whose arm had just been amputated.

97. Levie, *Terrorism in War*, 13; Geoffrey Best, *War and Law Since 1945* (Oxford: Clarendon, 1994), 41.

98. Lieber, *Lieber's Code and the Laws of War*, 14.

99. Ibid., 21. See also Taylor, *Nuremberg and Viet-Nam*, 21.

100. Lieber, *Lieber's Code and the Laws of War*, 22. Hartigan describes its lasting impact: "By the time peace returned, appreciation was growing for Lieber's Code." Lieber's own prediction to Halleck that "It will be adopted as a basis for similar works by the English, French, and Germans' soon proved true." The first three chapters provide a concise overview of the early laws of war. The Prussians modeled their own code after it in 1870. For a more comprehensive account see Leon Friedman, ed., *The Laws of War* (New York: Random House, 1972), I:6.

101. Lieber, *Lieber's Code and the Laws of War*, 49.

102. Ibid., 50.

103. James McPherson, *Battle Cry of Freedom* (New York: Ballantine, 1989), 854. According to the author, 360,000 Union and 260,000 Confederate soldiers were killed in America's bloodiest war.

104. From Charles Royster, *The Destructive War* (New York: Knopf, 1991), 254. Originally in John William DeForest, *Miss Ravenel's Conversion from Secession to Loyalty*, first published in 1867. Martin van Crevald in *The Transformation of War* (New York: Free Press, 1991) dates the period in which a new form of war emerged as between 1793 and 1815. He describes the shift as "smashing the ancien regime to smithereens. In the process, the origin of armed conflict, its strategy and command, not to mention but a few features, were all transformed beyond recognition. More important still, the scale on which war was waged also increased dramatically, and, above all, so did the sheer power with which it was waged" (36).

105. J.F.C. Fuller, *The Conduct of War 1789–1961* (New York: Da Capo, 1961), 111. Fuller has extreme views on many things, including President Lincoln, calling him "none other than a dictator" (99).

106. Ibid., 31. Fuller considers the movement toward "people's wars" a return to tribal warfare. David Kaiser believes that the Enlightenment and revolutionary political ideologies were responsible for the change. However, he argues that: "An intellectual consensus prevailed at the upper reaches of European society from London to St. Petersberg, but the practicality of the new ideas remained questionable. . . . The seductive power of the new ideas tempted the rulers of Europe to new heights of ambition, but the resources of European society could not in the long run satisfy them. In the end the revolutionary and Napoleonic era simply continued the consolidation of European states, while bequeathing the new political and intellectual problems to subsequent generations" (*Politics and War* [Cambridge: Harvard

University Press, 1990], 211–212). See also Quincy Wright, *A Study of War* (Chicago: University of Chicago Press, 1969), I:152; Wright also marks the ideological shifts: "The idea of totalitarian war was developed in the writings of Clausewitz, rationalizing Napoleonic methods. . . . The rise of nationalism, democracy and industrialism and the mechanicization of war in the mid-century re-established the trend toward the nation in arms and totalitarian war" (*A Study of War* 297). Bernard and Fawn Brodie, *From the Crossbow to the H-Bomb* (Bloomington: Indiana University Press, 1972), 125. Rifles and breechloading weapons made armed conflict more destructive than ever.

107. Fuller, *The Conduct of War 1789–1961*, 109. The author sees America's tactics as unique to the nineteenth century and a harbinger of things to come: "For the nineteenth century this was a new conception, because it meant that the deciding factor in war—the power to sue for peace—was transferred from the government to the people, and that peace making was the product of revolution. This was to carry the principle of democracy to its ultimate stage and with it introduce the theory of the psychological attack—in essence Marxist warfare. Of Sherman, Major George Nichols, one of his aides-de-camp, says: 'He is a Democrat in the best sense of the word. There is nothing European about him' " (108). See also Henry Hitchcock, *Marching with Sherman: Passages from the Letters and Campaign Diaries of Henry Hitchcock* (New Haven: Yale University Press, 1927). Royster dissents from this view of Sherman and believes that contemporary scholars have attached too much importance to his harsh and frank words (*The Destructive War* 358). Royster also does an excellent job of summarizing much of the contemporary historiography, 352–356.

108. Michael Walzer, *Just and Unjust Wars* (New York: Basic, 1977), 32.

109. Ibid., 126–128. General Sherman's wartime memoirs are extremely candid and provide a window into an extremely complex and often brutally honest man. "Until we can repopulate Georgia, it is useless to occupy it; but the utter destruction of the roads, houses and people will cripple their military resources. . . . I can make the march and make Georgia howl. . . . Should I be forced to assault . . . I shall feel justified in resorting to the harshest measures, and shall make little effort to restrain my army. . . . I knew, of course, that such a measure would be strongly criticized, but made up my mind to do it, with absolute certainty of its justice, and that time would sanction its wisdom" (William T. Sherman, *Personal Memoirs of William Tecumseh Sherman* [New York: Library of America, 1990], 2:111).

110. Fuller, *The Conduct of War 1789–1961*, 99.

111. J.F.C. Fuller, *Decisive Battle of the U.S.A* (New York: Da Capo, 1993), 305–308. The British military historian offers an extreme view of Sherman's tactics. See Best, *War and Law Since 1945*, 51 on Sherman's march as precedent setting.

112. Sherman, *Personal Memoirs*, 2: 127.

113. For more on Reconstruction see Eric Foner, *Reconstruction: America's Unfinished Revolution 1863–1877* (New York: Harper and Row, 1988), 603. Foner actually used the expression "limits of the possible" in a lecture in his Columbia University seminar on Reconstruction in 1991.

114. Friedman, ed., *The Laws of War*, 783.

115. The biographical information comes from a sympathetic Southern account by James Madison Page, *The True Story of Andersonville* (New York: Neale Publications, 1908), 183.

116. Royster, *The Destructive War*, 26, 325–327; Geoffrey Ward, *The Civil War* (New York: Knopf, 1990), 338.

117. Ibid. For the indictment in the Wirz case see Friedman, ed., *The Laws of War*, 788.

118. McPherson, *Battle Cry of Freedom*, 797. In a letter to the head of the St. Louis Sanitary Commission, General Sherman pointed to lack of medical supplies in the war-torn Confederacy: "These Confederates are proud as the Devil, and hate to confess poverty, but I know they are really unable to supply socks, drawers, undershirts, scissors, combo, soap, etc., which our men in prison need more than anything else to preserve cleanliness and health" (135).

119. Friedman, ed., *The Laws of War*, 788. This collection provides trial transcripts from the Wirz case. I was also fortunate to study this case in Telford Taylor's "Laws of War" seminar at Columbia University Law School in 1992. My analysis also draws on Taylor's lectures and my discussions with him about the case.

120. Ibid., 787.

121. Ibid., 788.

122. Ibid., 789.

123. Ibid., 790.

124. Ibid., 793.

125. Ibid., 786.

126. Ibid.

127. Ibid.

128. Ibid.

129. Levie, *Terrorism in War*, 513.

130. Ibid.

131. Friedman, ed., *The Laws of War*, 798. This unconfirmed rumor comes from Page, *The True Story of Andersonville*, 220.

132. Ibid.

133. McPherson, *Battle Cry of Freedom*, 802. McPherson offers this analysis of the Wirz case: "Whether Wirz was guilty of anything worse than bad temper and inefficiency remains controversial today. In any case, he served as a scapegoat for the purported sins of the South" (797).

134. *Lieber's Code and the Laws of War*, 22.

135. Ibid.

136. Brown, *Bury My Heart at Wounded Knee*, 86.

137. Ibid.

138. Ibid.

139. Wellman, *The Indian Wars of the West*, 70; Brown, *Bury My Heart at Wounded Knee*, 86; Brogan, *The Pelican History of the United States of America*, 63.

140. Brown, *Bury My Heart at Wounded Knee*, 86.

141. Ibid., 86.

142. Ibid.

143. Wellman, *The Indian Wars of the West*, 71n1 and Brogan, *The Pelican History of the United States of America*, 63.

144. Brown, *Bury My Heart at Wounded Knee*, 86.

145. Ibid., 89.

146. Ibid.

147. Ibid.

148. Ibid., 88 and Wellman, *The Indian Wars of the West*, 72–73. My accounts of the Sand Creek and Wounded Knee massacres owe a great deal to my conversations with Bob Primeaux.

149. Brown, *Bury My Heart at Wounded Knee*, 90.

150. Ibid.

151. Ibid.

152. Ibid., 91.

153. Brogan, *The Pelican History of the United States*, 62.

154. Ibid., 69.

155. Wellman, *The Indian Wars of the West*, 56–57.

156. Drinnon, *Facing West*, 329.

157. Brown, *Bury My Heart at Wounded Knee*, 297.

158. Ibid., 298.

159. Ibid., 299.

160. Ibid.

161. Ibid., 300.

162. Ibid.

163. Hermann Hagedorn, *Roosevelt in the Badlands* (Boston: Houghton Mifflin, 1921), 352.

164. Ibid., 355.

165. Brown, *Bury My Heart at Wounded Knee*, 299.

166. Ibid., 446.

167. Phone interview with Bob Primeaux, 16 August 1999.

2. The Changing Rules of War and Peace

1. Richard Hartigan makes this point in *Lieber's Code and the Laws of War* (Chicago: Precedent, 1983).

2. Ibid., 21. Cynics saw the Russians as using humanitarianism to cloak their desire to avoid costly artillery and other expensive military upgrades. George Kennan is quite dismissive of the Czar's humanitarian claims: "This movement [the peace movement] was given a significant filip when Tsar Nicholas II of Russia in 1899 issued a call for an international conference on disarmament. The curious initiative largely the product of the immature dilettantism of the Tsar himself and elaborated by the characteristic confusions of the Russian governmental establishment at the time, was

not a serious one" ("The Balkan Crisis, 1913 and 1993," *The New York Review of Books* 60[13][July 15, 1993]: 3). See also Calvin DeHormond Davis, *The United States and the Second Hague Peace Convention* (Durham: Duke University Press, 1975), 4–5. Rudyard Kipling mocked the idea of Russians coming as bearers of peace and humanitarianism. His poem entitled "The Bear That Walks Like a Man" tells of a wounded bear and a hunter who cannot bring himself to take the final shot: "When he stands up as pleading, in wavering, man-brute guise: / When he veils the hate and cunning of his little swinish eyes, / When he shows as seeking quarter with paws like hands in prayer, / That is the time of peril—the time of the Truce of the Bear!" The hunter feels a twinge of pity and lowers his rifle. The bear rewards the hunter's humanitarianism with a "steel shod" backhand to the head (*The United States and the Second Hague Peace Convention* 7). British Admiral Sir John Fisher was equally cynical; he wrote at the time, "The humanising of war! You might as well talk of humanising hell!" (in Michael Howard, *Restraints on War* [New York: Oxford University Press, 1979], 54). For an American participant's account see Joseph Choate, *The Two Hague Conferences* (Princeton: Princeton University Press, 1913), 5–6 in the 1969 Kraus reprint. The only stated objective of the conference was to limit new armaments systems and thus preserve the nation's "physical and intellectual" strength for more positive enterprises.

3. See Adam Roberts and Richard Guelff, eds., *Documents on the Laws of War* (Oxford: Clarendon, 1989), 35–109 for the texts of both the 1899 and 1907 conventions. For a summary see Leon Friedman, ed., *The Laws of War* (New York: Random House, 1972), 152–153. Even George Kennan recognized the significance of the Hague Conventions: "But it was seized upon with enthusiasm by adherents of the peace movements and had consequences the Czar himself had not anticipated. Of those, the most important were the two Hague Peace Conferences of 1899 and 1907, resulting in a modernization and renewed codification of international law and a significant elaboration, in particular, of the laws of war" ("The Balkan Crisis, 1913 and 1933" 3).

4. William Hull, *The Two Hague Conferences and Their Contribution to International Law* (Boston: Gwin, 1928), 503. Hull says the conferences justified "the belief that the world has entered upon a more orderly process through which, step by step, in successive conferences, each taking the work of its predecessor as a point of departure, there may be continual progress toward making the practice of civilized nations conform to their peaceful professions" (503).

5. Davis, *The United States and the Second Hague Peace Convention*, 15–16. See also Stanley Hoffman, "The Delusion of World Order," *New York Review of Books* 39(7)(1992): 37; Friedman, ed., *The Laws of War*, 14. See also Ann and A. J. Thomas, *The Concept of Aggression* (Dallas: Southern Methodist University Press, 1972) and Julius Stone, *Aggression and World Order* (London: Stevens and Sons, 1958).

6. Hoffman best describes the structural weaknesses of international courts in "The Delusion of World Order": "International society has neither the centralized government, judicial system, and police that characterize a well-ordered state nor the consensus on what constitutes a crime that exists in domestic affairs" (38). See also

Friedman, ed., *The Laws of War*, 14; Thomas, *The Concept of Aggression*; Stone, *Aggression and World Order*. Hull describes his ideal international court: "not only will the idea of such a court henceforth stand behind the wrong of warfare, but it will inevitably rule the future" (*The Two Hague Conferences* 493).

7. Davis, *The United States and the Second Hague Peace Convention*, 25.

8. Ibid.

9. John Keegan, *The First World War* (New York: Knopf, 1998), 17. Keegan, *The First World War*, on the international court at the First Hague Convention: "Some effort had been made to supply the deficiency through the establishment of a code of international law. It remained a weak concept, for its most important principle, established during the Treaty of Westphalia in 1648, was that of sovereignty of states, which left each in effect unfettered by anything but . . . self-interest" (17). "The flaw in the provision for an International Court was that its convening was to be voluntary. 'The greatest thing,' wrote the American delegate about the conference, 'is that the Court of Arbitration . . . shall be seen by all nations [to] indicate a sincere desire to promote peace [and to] relieve the various peoples of the fear which so heavily oppresses all, the dread of a sudden outburst of war at any moment" (18).

10. Choate, *The Two Hague Conferences*, 44. For more on Elihu Root see Richard Leopold, *Elihu Root and the Conservative Tradition* (Boston: Little, Brown, 1954).

11. Richard Drinnon, *Facing West: The Metaphysics of Indian-Hating and Empire-Building* (Norman: University of Oklahoma Press, 1980), xiii.

12. Ibid., 240.

13. Ibid., 238.

14. Anders Stephanson, *Manifest Destiny* (New York: Hill and Wang, 1995), 80.

15. Sven Lindqvist (*Exterminate All the Brutes*, trans. Joan Tate [New York: New Press, 1996]) described the changing justifications for colonial wars: "During the nineteenth century, religious explanations were replaced by biological ones. The exterminated peoples were colored, the exterminators were white." Darwin had seen "the struggle for life" in Argentina in 1832: "The Argentine government had just decided to exterminate the Indians who still ruled the Pampas" (115). Darwin interviewed the Spanish commander in charge: "Everyone here is fully convinced that this is the most just war, because it is against barbarians. Who would believe in this age such atrocities could be committed in a Christian civilised country?" Darwin also visited Tasmania in 1836 and watched Australians wipe out native aborigines (115–116). Drinnon, *Facing West*, 236, 157.

16. Drinnon, *Facing West*, 239–240.

17. Ibid., 238.

18. *Selections from the Correspondence of Theodore Roosevelt and Henry Cabot Lodge 1884–1901* (New York: Scribners, 1925), 313. Captain Alfred Thayer Mahan's *The Influence of Sea Power upon History* was published in 1890 and would have a profound impact on American foreign policy in the coming decade. Thomas Paterson, J. Garry Clifford, and Kenneth Hagan wrote in *American Foreign Policy: A History—1900 to Present*, vol. 2

(Lexington: D. C. Heath, 1988), "It became a treasured volume in the libraries of American imperialists like Henry Cabot Lodge and Theodore Roosevelt. Mahan's thesis was direct: a nation's greatness depended upon its sea power. . . . Ships of war, in turn, required fueling stations or 'resting places' and colonies, which would further enhance foreign commerce and national power. The loop was closed: a great nation required colonies" (163).

19. Ibid., 205.

20. Leon Wolff, *Little Brown Brother* (London: Longman, 1961), 29.

21. Stephanson, *Manifest Destiny*, 88.

22. Lindqvist, *Exterminate All the Brutes*, 140. Wolff, *Little Brown Brother*, 346, 46, 140. This commentator was especially unimpressed by the use of Manifest Destiny as a justification for expansion: "It is nearly three years since the Americans have gone to war with Spain . . . for Cuba, decided that it was their Manifest Destiny to deprive the Philippines of their liberty." For more on European colonialism in Africa see Adam Hochschild, *King Leopold's Ghost: A Story of Greed, Terror, and Heroism in Colonial Africa* (New York: Houghton Mifflin, 1999).

23. Judith Shklar, *Legalism: Laws, Morals, and Political Trials* (Cambridge: Harvard University Press, 1964), 1. Leopold, *Elihu Root and the Conservative Tradition*, 18. In a letter dated August 10, 1899, Theodore Roosevelt described Root as "a great corporation lawyer and retained by Whitney and the street railway men"; *Selections from the Correspondence of Theodore Roosevelt and Henry Cabot Lodge*, 415.

24. Ibid., viii.

25. Ibid.

26. Shklar, *Legalism*, viii. While Shklar rejects the completely politicized view of the law advocated by critical legal scholars, she points to the equally wrongheaded tendency of lawyers to view law as somehow above politics: "The tendency to dismiss both the political provenance and the impact of judicial decisions especially, and of legal practices generally, remains very common in legal theory. This is what I meant by saying that legalism tends to treat law as just 'there,' and that legal formalism has always been the most articulate defense of this stance" (x).

27. Wolff, *Little Brown Brother*, 266.

28. *Selections from the Correspondence of Theodore Roosevelt and Henry Cabot Lodge*, 415.

29. Elihu Root, *The Military and Colonial Policy of the United States* (New York: AMS Press, 1970), 9. For more on Root see Philip Jessup's two-volume biography, *Elihu Root* (Hamden, Conn.: Archon, 1964), and Leopold, *Elihu Root and the Conservative Tradition*.

30. Elihu Root, *The Military and Colonial Policy of the United States*, 9.

31. Ibid., 10. Root dismissed Aguinaldo's claim to Philippine independence and compared Filipinos to the American Indians: "Nothing can be more preposterous than the proposition that these men were entitled to receive from us sovereignty over the entire country which we were invading. As well the friendly Indians, who have helped us in our Indian wars, might have claimed the sovereignty of the West. They knew that we were incurring no such obligation, and they expected no such reward" (39).

32. Elihu Root, "The American Soldier," in *Miscellaneous Addresses* (Cambridge: Harvard University Press, 1916), 12.

33. Wolff, *Little Brown Brother*, 290.

34. Ibid.

35. Charles Burke Elliott, *The Philippines To the End of the Military Regime* (Indianapolis: Bobbs and Merrill, 1917), 118.

36. Wolff, *Little Brown Brother*, 207.

37. Ibid.

38. Ibid.

39. Jessup, *Elihu Root*, 338.

40. Wolff, *Little Brown Brother*, 237.

41. Ibid.

42. Ibid., 253.

43. Herbert Welsh, *The Other Man's Country* (Philadelphia: J. P. Lippincott, 1900), 210.

44. Ibid.

45. Ibid. See also Wolff, *Little Brown Brother*, 237.

46. Brian McAllister Linn, *The U.S. Army and Counterinsurgency in the Philippines War, 1899–1902* (Chapel Hill: University of North Carolina Press, 1989), 23.

47. Henry Graff, ed., *American Imperialism: The Philippine Insurrection* (Boston: Little, Brown, 1969), 76.

48. Wolff, *Little Brown Brother*, 262.

49. Jessup, *Elihu Root*, 333.

50. Drinnon, *Facing West*, 299. Roosevelt compared the Philippine situation to the American Indians several times: "The reasoning which justifies our having made war against Sitting Bull also justifies our having checked the outbreaks of Aguinaldo and his followers." For other comparisons to the Indian Wars see Wolff, *Little Brown Brother*, 331 and Root, *Military and Colonial Policy*, 75.

51. Wolff, *Little Brown Brother*, 303.

52. Ibid., 331.

53. Ibid.

54. Drinnon, *Facing West*, 321.

55. Stuart Creighton Miller, *Benevolent Assimilation: The American Conquest of the Philippines* (New Haven: Yale University Press, 1982), 200; Drinnon, *Facing West*, 322.

56. Ibid.

57. Miller, *Benevolent Assimilation*, 94–95; see also Wolff, *Little Brown Brother*, 200.

58. Miller, *Benevolent Assimilation*, 204; Wolff, *Little Brown Brother*, 203–204.

59. Miller, *Benevolent Assimilation*, 94–95. See also Drinnon, *Facing West*, 324. General Chafee commented on General Smith's appointment, "I am told, is an energetic officer, and I hope he will prove so in command of that brigade."

60. Miller, *Benevolent Assimilation*, 220. Wolff, *Little Brown Brother*, 356 and Friedman, ed., *The Laws of War*, 803–804.

61. Friedman, ed., 803–804.

62. Ibid., 804.

63. Miller, *Benevolent Assimilation*, 220.

64. Friedman, ed., *The Laws of War*, 804.

65. Drinnon, *Facing West*, 325. After receiving news of the executions, Adna Chaffee cabled General Smith, "Smith, have you been having any promiscuous killing in Samar for fun" (Miller, *Benevolent Assimilation*, 227).

66. Drinnon, *Facing West*, 315.

67. Ibid., 326–327. Major Littleton "Tony" Waller had served in Egypt during the Arabian pasha's rebellion against Khedive and in China.

68. Miller, *Benevolent Assimilation*, 207. Bell "followed the disclaimer with a long list of Filipino transgressions against the laws of civilized warfare which reads much like a lawyers brief and related each alleged violation to specific sections of 'the well known law and usage of war as announced in General Order No. 100 (signed by Lincoln),' as though the Filipinos could possibly have known of this document" (207).

69. Graff, ed., *American Imperialism*, 97. This was the testimony of Army Private Leroy Hallock from Boston. After a member of Private Hallock's company named O'Hearn was found hacked and burned to death, the American soldiers tortured twelve suspects until one, according to Hallock, confessed to the crime (97–98).

70. Ibid., 95.

71. Ibid.

72. Ibid., 114.

73. Ibid., 115.

74. Drinnon, *Facing West*, 327.

75. Ibid.

76. Jessup, *Elihu Root*, 342.

77. Miller, *Benevolent Assimilation*, 230. Drinnon, *Facing West*, 327. Waller did not deny the killings; instead he argued that they fell within the scope of Jacob Smith's orders.

78. Miller, *Benevolent Assimilation*, 230; Friedman, ed., *The Laws of War*, 803–804.

79. Friedman, ed., 804.

80. Ibid., 801.

81. Ibid., 804.

82. Ibid.

83. Ibid.

84. Ibid.

85. Friedman, ed., 799–800.

86. Ibid.

87. Jessup, *Elihu Root*, 341–342. Morefield Story, Julian Cadman, and Carl Schurz were the most outspoken critics of America's Philippine policy. The most embarrassing of the antiwar pamphlets was "Mr. Root's Record" by Story and Cadman.

88. Ibid., 342. According to Jessup, the Secretary of War did not take a close look at the atrocities in the Philippines until 1902. On February 18, 1902, Root wrote a memo, "How does it happen that we have no orders on the treatment of natives since

1900, a year and a half ago?" (342). Root was also attacked by old friends like General Grenville Dodge for yielding to squeamish elements who did not understand war. On July 21, 1902, Root wrote Dodge, "I think if you could read the testimony in the Waller case you would change your views. I had very much the same view of the case that you express, but a careful examination of the entire record and evidence was extremely distressing to me" (341).

89. Ibid.

90. Drinnon, *Facing West*, 329.

91. Ibid., 522.

92. Ibid.; Telford Taylor lecture at Columbia Law School, February 3, 1993.

93. Godfrey Hodgson, *The Colonel: The Life and Wars of Henry Stimson* (New York: Knopf, 1990), 50.

94. Wolff, *Little Brown Brother*, 360. Wolff estimates the United States killed approximately 20,000 on the battlefield. However, the Philippine civilians were the real victims in this conflict. It is estimated that out of a prewar population of 8,000,000, approximately 200,000 died of diseases like typhus and dysentery. See also Paterson, Clifford, and Hagan, *American Foreign Policy 1900 to Present*, 2:205.

95. Daniel Patrick Moynihan, *On the Law of Nations* (Cambridge: Harvard University Press, 1990), 23. In 1905, President Theodore Roosevelt negotiated an end to the Russo-Japanese War. Not only did a New York lawyer mediate the dispute, but the meetings were held on Fifth Avenue at the Lotos Club. A club history recalled the event: "Then President Theodore Roosevelt assembled Japanese and Russian arbitrators in America for the purpose of ending the bitter Russo-Japanese war, these dignitaries left a deadlocked conference one afternoon to retire to the Lotos bar where they miraculously found themselves talking the same language. Shortly afterwards, points of agreement reached in the clubhouse were incorporated in the Treaty of Portsmouth, which ended the war" (23).

96. Jessup, *Elihu Root*, 470. In 1915, Elihu Root, then President of the American Society of International Law, referred to a forthcoming American effort to criminalize aggression: "To give international law binding force, a radical change in the attitude of nations towards violations of law is necessary. Up to the present time breaches of international law have been treated as we treat wrongs under civil procedure, as if they concerned nobody except the particular nation upon which the injustice was inflicted and the nation inflicting it. . . . There must be a change in theory, and violations of the law of such a character as to threaten the peace and order of the community of nations must be deemed a violation of the right of every civilized nation to have the law maintained and a legal injury to every nation" (George Finch, "The Progressive Development of International Law," *American Journal of International Law* 41[1947]: 613). American Joseph Choate made this observation about the German resistance to new codes of international law in *The Two Hague Conferences*: "he sees as in a dream a celestial apparition which excites his ardent devotion, but when he wakes and finds her by his side he turns to the wall, and will have nothing to do with her" (63). The German representative was not moved by the American's histrionics. He

pointed to the chasm between the two nations' views of international relations: "To-day, as then I am not a partisan of abstract obligatory arbitration, but a partisan of real obligatory arbitration which can be realized only in the individual system and which I regard as impossible in the world system" (63).

97. Davis, *The United States and the Second Hague Peace Convention*, 282–283. See Roberts and Guelff, eds., *Documents on the Laws of War*, 35–109 for the full texts of both the 1899 and 1907 conventions. For a summary see Friedman, ed., *The Laws of War*, 152–153; Davis, *The United States and the Second Hague Peace Convention*, 15–16. See also Hoffman, "The Delusion of World Order," 37 and Choate, *The Two Hague Conferences*, 44.

98. Davis, *The United States and the Second Hague Peace Convention*, 25, 282. According to Fritz Dickman, such schemes robbed Germany of the most important element of national survival: "Her superior military organization, which affords her a headstart in any general mobilization and which may well prove decisive" (Andreas Hillgruber, *Germany and the Two World Wars*, trans. William C. Kirby [Cambridge: Harvard University Press, 1981], 35).

99. Hull, *The Two Hague Conferences*, 92.

100. Davis, *The United States and the Second Hague Peace Convention*, 11.

101. Hull, *The Two Hague Conferences*, 87. He believed the conferences justified "the belief that the world has entered upon a more orderly process through which, step by step, in successive conferences, each taking the work of its predecessor as a point of departure, there may be continual progress toward making the practice of civilized nations conform to their peaceful professions" (503).

102. Jessup, *Elihu Root*, 310.

103. Hull, *The Two Hague Conferences*, 92.

104. Marc Trachtenberg, *History and Strategy* (Princeton: Princeton University Press, 1991), 77–78. See also Howard, *Restraints on War*, 9. For many years, it was argued that mobilization and blind, almost mechanical forces led to the outbreak of World War I. Progressive historians shifted the onus of guilt to "armament manufacturers" and "big business." Trachtenberg made a strong case that the nations of Europe moved from diplomacy to war, both "consciously and willingly" (*History and Strategy* 11). But by stating the obvious, Howard puts the great debate over the war's origins into perspective: "None of them . . . was prepared to say courageously, 'We only acted as statesmen always have in the past. In the circumstances prevailing, war seemed to be the best way of forwarding or protecting the national interests for which we were responsible. . . . Our guilt does not lie in the fact that we started the war. It lies in our mistaken belief that we could win it' " (*Restraints on War* 9). Sigmund Freud was shocked that "the great ruling powers among the white nations" could not "succeed in discovering another way of settling misunderstandings and conflicts of interest" (from Arno Mayer, *Wilson v. Lenin: The Political Origins of the New Diplomacy, 1917–1918* [Cleveland: World Publications, 1964], 27). Fuller describes the new problems brought on by "people's wars" in *The Conduct of War*: "The experience of 1914–18 . . . showed that war posed new, virtually impossible problems for the modern governments, leading in central and eastern Europe to revolution, the collapse of

traditional political and social arrangements, and eventually to the emergence of totalitarian regimes" (280). Keegan, *The First World War*, 8. Keegan takes a different view. He described World War I as "the Last Civilized War," contending that "it was, despite the efforts by state propaganda machines to prove otherwise, and the cruelties of the battlefield apart, a curiously civilized war." See also Best, *Law and War Since 1945*.

105. J.F.C. Fuller describes the impact of "people's wars" on the governments of the nation states in ibid. David Kaiser makes a similar point in *Politics and War*: "By the twentieth century . . . war had become an aberration, and one which imposed new, unique demands upon the whole society" (280).

106. Martin Kitchen, *Europe Between Wars* (London: Longman, 1988), 67. Herr von Jagow, German Secretary of Foreign Affairs, announced on April 29, 1913 that "Belgian neutrality is provided for by International Conventions and Germany is determined to respect those Conventions." At the same meeting of the Reichstag, Herr von Heeringen, Minister of War, announced, "Germany will not lose sight of the fact that the neutrality of Belgium is guaranteed by International Treaty." Henri Davignon, ed., *Belgium and Germany: Texts and Documents* (Brussels: Belgian Govt. Publication, 1921), 7. Walzer, *Just and Unjust Wars*, 240. See also Hillgruber, *Germany and the Two World Wars*, 231. Alwyn Freeman defines *Kriegsraison* as "the German doctrine of military necessity whose logic conduces inevitably to the abrogation of all restraints upon belligerent activity" ("War Crimes by Enemy Nationals Administering Justice in Occupied Territories," *American Journal of International Law* 41[1947]: 584).

107. Hillgruber, *Germany and the Two World Wars*, 8. See also David Calleo, *The German Problem Reconsidered* (New York: Cambridge University Press, 1978), 8. Hillgruber characterizes the German foreign policy style as "crude and overbearing" (8). James Willis comments on the strategic thinking of the German leadership: "The Germans arrogantly placed too much faith in the potency of sheer military force, failing to recognize that such power necessarily had limits" (*Prologue to Nuremburg* [Westport, Conn.: Greenwood, 1982], 9).

108. Martin van Crevald, *The Transformation of War* (New York: Free Press, 1991), 42. The utilization of national resources like the railroad and the telegraph provided a decisive advantage in 1864, 1866, and 1870–71. In 1871, General Helmuth von Moltke devised the first plan for a war with Russia and France. In 1892, Chief of Staff Alfried von Schlieffen calculated that Germany's adversaries had twice the troops and thus began to develop a strategic plan that would help overcome these odds. See also Manuel DeLanda, *War in the Age of Intelligent Machines* (New York: Swerve Editions, 1991), 91 for a comparison to the Battle Cannae.

109. Kitchen, *Europe Between Wars*, 67.

110. Hillgruber, *Germany and the Two World Wars*, 8.

111. Willis, *Prologue to Nuremberg*, 9. This excellent and comprehensive study of the war crimes issue during World War I helped me a great deal, especially in my analysis of the Leipzig trials.

112. For complete documentation of the Belgian charges see Fernand Passelecq, *Truth and Travesty: An Analytical Study of the Belgian Government to the German White Book*

(London: Sir Joseph Causton and Sons, 1916), 9. For the German response see the German Imperial Foreign Office, *The Belgian People's War: A Violation of International Law* (New York: Press of John C. Rankin, 1915). For more on the Bryce Report see Niall Ferguson, *The Pity of War* (New York: Basic, 1998), 232, 494.

113. Committee on Alleged German Outrages, *Report on Alleged German Outrages* (New York: Macmillan, 1964), 21–22. J.F.C. Fuller offers this view of the role of propaganda in World War I: "The stranglehold of the blockade created a fertile soil for sowing the seeds of propaganda, and—not excepting the American Civil War—in no previous war was it so virulent and vile. . . . War by propaganda is pre-eminently a democratic instrument, fashioned to dominate the mass mind—Rousseau's 'general will.' Its purposes are: (1) to stimulate the mass mind on the home front; (2) to win to one's support the mass minds of neutral nations; and (3) to subvert the mass mind on the enemy's inner front. The first is accomplished by awakening the tribal instincts latent in man, and, in order to focus these instincts, to transform the enemy into the devil" (*The Conduct of War* 179). See Willis, *Prologue to Nuremberg*, 10, quoting from the 5 September 1914 *London Times*. Asquith described the destruction of Louvain as "the greatest crime against civilization and culture since the Thirty Years' War—the sack of Louvain . . . a shameless holocaust." David Kaiser describes the role of public opinion in *Politics and War*: "Because of the spread of literacy, political success also depended to a great extent upon the careful management of public opinion and the press" (273). See also Paul Kennedy, *The Rise of German-Anglo Antagonism, 1860–1914* (London: Allen and Unwin, 1980).

114. John Keegan, *The Face of Battle* (New York: Penguin, 1976), 260. Of the 60,000 casualties, 21,000 died.

115. Ibid., 285. In his recent book *The First World War*, Keegan writes that in the first four months of World War I, 300,000 French were killed and another 600,000 were wounded (6–7). In *Law and War Since 1945*, Best writes, "The First World War very much changed the total context in which the law of war operated and in which alone it can be properly understood. 1919 marks as much of a shock in its history as 1945" (53).

116. Willis, *Prologue to Nuremberg*, 13. The French tried and imprisoned three men for pillaging in 1914; the German government countered by imprisoning six French officers. Their release was pending the release of the Germans convicted of war crimes.

117. Hillgruber, *Germany and the Two World Wars*, 12. Assaults by hot air balloons were a violation of the second Hague Convention, but by war's end each side was attacking cities. This highlighted the dilemma of the laws of war during a time of actual conflict: can a nation be expected to place itself at a strategic disadvantage by unilaterally observing international law?

118. Ibid.

119. Hillgruber, *Germany and the Two World Wars*, 12. See also Willis, *Prologue to Nuremberg*, 8. Again the Germans were largely responsible for their own image. David Calleo agrees, arguing that the German problem was essentially one of appearances: "A

good deal of Germany's reputation for aggressiveness must probably be laid to the prevalent German style—a traditional military stiffness caricatured by middle class imitators" (*The German Problem Reconsidered* 28).

120. Freeman, "War Crimes by Enemy Nationals Administering Justice in Occupied Territories," 591. Freeman notes: "more objectionable would seem to have been the execution of Miss Cavell within a few hours after the trial, to forestall an appeal." She first met her lawyer in the courtroom and did not know of the charges against her until the arraignment. Willis, *Prologue to Nuremberg*, 28. Telford Taylor, lecture at Columbia University Law School, February 11, 1993. Howard Levie, *Terrorism in War*, 225.

121. Willis, *Prologue to Nuremberg*, 27.

122. Ibid. See also Walter Gorlitz, ed., *The Kaiser and His Court: The Diaries, Note Books and Letters of Admiral Georg Alexander von Muller, Chief of the Naval Cabinet 1914–1918* (London: MacDonald and Co., 1961), 115 and Hillgruber, *Germany and the Two World Wars*, 12.

123. Paterson, Clifford, and Hagan, *American Foreign Policy: A History—1900 to Present*, 2:268. See also Willis, *Prologue to Nuremberg*, 17 and Levie, *Terrorism in War*, 21–22, 66–67, 105–107 on submarines and the laws of war.

124. Paterson, Clifford, and Hagan, *American Foreign Policy: A History—1900 to Present*, 2:268; Gray, *The U-Boat War*, 81–83.

125. Ibid., 267–268. The British also mined the North Sea and cut off German imports (food and cotton).

126. Willis, *Prologue to Nuremberg*, 29.

127. Ibid., 30. See also Levie, *Terrorism in War*, 145n20.

128. Edwyn Gray, *The U-Boat War* (London: Leo Cooper, 1973), 243.

129. Ibid.

130. Willis, *Prologue to Nuremberg*, 35.

131. Ibid., 37, 39. Many American clergymen saw the war as "Armageddon and Wilhelm II as the biblical beast of the last days" (272).

132. Elihu Root, *Miscellaneous Addresses*, 293.

133. Root, *Miscellaneous Addresses*, 288.

134. Leopold, *Elihu Root and the Conservative Tradition*, 121.

135. Kaiser, *Politics and War*, 351; Christopher Simpson, *The Splendid Blond Beast: Money, Law, and Genocide in the Twentieth Century* (New York: Grove, 1993), 28. See also Jon Kirakosyan, *The Armenian Genocide* (Madison: Sphinx, 1992); Telford Taylor, *The Anatomy of the Nuremberg Trials: A Personal Memoir* (New York: Knopf, 1992), 13, 18; Ulrich Trumpner, *Germany and the Ottoman Empire* (Princeton: Princeton University Press, 1968).

David Kaiser attempts to fit the Armenian genocide within the context of nationalism, more specifically tribal war. According to Kaiser, this provided the precedent for both Stalin and Hitler: "Curiously enough, the nationalist impulse which finally upset the post-1885 territorial status quo came not from any of the Balkan states but from the Turkish officers of the Turkish Army in Macedonia who staged the Young

Turk Revolt in 1908. Hoping to maintain Turkish preeminence within a newly democratic empire, they announced constitutional rule and called elections to a Parliament throughout the Ottoman Empire" (316). However, "By the time of the Balkan Wars . . . they had abandoned this principle and determined instead to rebuild the empire upon a basis of ethnic Turkish nationalism . . . and to solve the problem of the Armenian minority by exterminating the Armenians. . . . Here the nationalist question entered a new phase" (351). While John Keegan in *The First World War* concedes that the Turkish forced marches of Armenians were acts of genocide, he argues that "the forced marches organized to do them to death belong more properly to the history of Ottoman imperial policy than to that of war itself" (8).

136. Karl Schwabe, *World War, Revolution, Germany, and Peacemaking* (Chapel Hill: University of North Carolina Press, 1985), 164.

137. Willis, *Prologue to Nuremberg*, 72, 117. See also Hoffman, "The Delusion of World Order," 37: "Wilsonian liberalism proposed a third principle." According to Hoffman, "World order would emerge if the world of nation-states was also a world of constitutional governments" ("The Delusion of World Order" 37). Wilson felt the United States provided the "unique moral force" that would lead the world into greener pastures where reason would prevail over brute force (Robert Tucker, "Brave New World Order," *The New Republic* [Feb. 24, 1992]:24). On the eve of his departure to the Paris Peace Conference in 1919, Wilson was most optimistic: "It has come about by no plan of our own conceiving, but by the hand of God who led us into this way. We cannot turn back, we can only go forward, with lifted eyes and freshened spirit, to follow the vision. It was of this that we dreamed at birth. America shall in truth show the way" (Lloyd Ambrosius, *Wilsonian Statecraft* [Wilmington, Del.: Scholarly Resources, 1991], 134). The League of Nations was the institution and collective security was the mechanism that would guarantee the sovereignty and territorial integrity of nations (130). Wilson's problems with skeptical European leaders like Georges Clemenceau of France and domestic critics like Henry Cabot Lodge had less to do with specifics and more to do with Wilson's vision of collective security. The Europeans did not believe that a balance of power could be replaced with a balance of opinion. Sally Marks describes the failure of the Treaty of Versailles in *The Illusion of Peace* (New York: St. Martin's, 1976): "On the whole the peacemakers at Paris did not recognize the danger inherent in a situation where Germany was no longer surrounded and checked by great empires. They assumed erroneously that Germany would abide by their decisions and accept her new neighbors" (16). According to international relations theorist Stanley Hoffman, "Harmony thus was ultimately dependent on the triumph of democracy, because it has been assumed, ever since Kant, that democratically elected governments that respect the rights of citizens would not make war against other democracies" ("The Delusion of World Order," *New York Review of Books* xxxix [7]: 37).

138. Willis, *Prologue to Nuremberg*, 80. See also Schwabe, *World War, Revolution, Germany, and Peacemaking*, 164.

139. Willis, *Prologue to Nuremberg*, 70.

140. Simpson, *The Splendid Blond Beast*, 23.

141. Michael Marrus, *The Nuremberg War Crimes Trials 1945–1946* (New York: Bedford, 1997), 8–10. Although this is a slim volume, it contains some of the key war crimes documents of the twentieth century. Marrus wisely begins by including sections from the Treaty of Versailles and the Kellogg-Briand Pact before turning his full attention to Nuremberg's IMT.

142. Ibid. Even as late as 1919, Lloyd George pressed for the trial. The Kaiser scoffed at the idea from the relative safety of Denmark (Willis, *Prologue to Nuremberg*, 174).

143. Ibid., 8. See also Levie, *Terrorism in War*, 24–25.

144. *The Foreign Relations of the United States: Paris Peace Conference 1919* (Washington: U.S. Government Printing Office, 1945), 568–569. See also Paterson, Clifford, and Hagan, *American Foreign Policy: A History—1900 to Present*, 2:285. American lawyer Paul Cravath took up the issue of Germany's "war indemnity." In a memorandum to the President, he argued that Germany should pay for the destruction they had wrought. The European powers later transformed the peace treaty into something more Carthaginian by charging the Germans with the cost of the entire war (Marks, *The Illusion of Peace*, 13).

145. Ibid.

146. Willis, *Prologue to Nuremberg*, 41, 76.

147. Ibid. See also Schwabe, *World War, Revolution, Germany and Peacemaking*, 163–166.

148. Simpson, *The Splendid Blond Beast*, 24. McDougall, *Promised Land, Crusader State*, says Robert Lansing described the Treaty of Versailles as "thoroughly bad" and the League of Nations as "thoroughly useless" (142). Secretary of State Lansing asked critics: "Had you rather have the Kaiser or the Bolsheviks?" Wilson believed that what Germany needed someone to face the growing socialist movement, someone who "could put it down." According to Schwabe, *World War, Revolution, Germany, and Peacemaking*, "In short, the American legal experts were not willing to abandon the framework of existing international law. That does not mean, however, that they were not convinced of Germany's guilt in starting the war. Miller even spoke of Germany's collective guilt, but he did not think the issue fell under the jurisdiction of the tribunals which would try individual Germans" (164).

149. Willis, *Prologue to Nuremberg*, 24.

150. Marrus, *The Nuremberg War Crimes Trials*, 10.

151. Ibid.

152. See Paul Piccone and G. L. Ulmen, "American Imperialism and International Law," *Telos* 72 (Summer 1987): 60.

153. Ibid.

154. Willis, *Prologue to Nuremberg*, 177

155. Ibid., 60. The most famous and pernicious myths were that the General Staff had been stabbed in the back by weak-kneed politicians and that the war crimes accusations were all false. See also 72, 117. Even as late as 1919, Lloyd George pressed for the trial.

156. Ibid., 60.

157. Taylor, *The Anatomy of the Nuremberg Trials*, 16.

158. Willis, *Prologue to Nuremberg*, 100.

159. Levie, *Terrorism in War*, 27.

160. Ibid., 28.

161. Ibid.

162. John Appleman, *Military Tribunals and International Crimes* (Westport, Conn.: Greenwood, 1971), 54–57. Bismarck offered very pragmatic advice on the treatment of the vanquished. In the Chancellor's eyes, strategy and necessity overruled popular passions and/or morality: "People insist that, in conflicts between states, the conqueror should sit in judgment upon the conquered, moral code in hand, and inflict punishment upon him for what he has done. . . . This is an altogether unreasonable demand. Punishment and revenge have nothing to do with policy. Policy must not meddle with the calling of the Nemesis, or aspire to exercise the judge's office. . . . In such a case as the one referred to, the question would be, 'which of the two will be more useful to us—a badly-used Napoleon or a well-used Napoleon?' " Mortiz Busch, *Our Chancellor* (New York: Scribners, 1884), 1:99; from Fuller, *The Conduct of War*, 305.

163. Claud Mullins, *The Leipzig Trials* (London: H.F.G Witherby, 1921), 99.

164. Ibid., 42.

165. Ibid., 12. The tribunal sternly admonished the defendants, "Don't imagine that you are going to get rid of this terrible affair by trying to put the blame upon a dead man: that won't do."

166. Friedman, ed., *The Laws of War*, 876.

167. Ibid., 880. The judgment read sternly: "The rule of International Law, which is here involved, is simple and is universally known. No possible doubt can exist with regard to the question of its applicability. The Court must in this instance affirm Patzig's guilt of killing contrary to International Law."

168. Ibid., 868.

169. Mullins, *The Leipzig Trials*, 66–67; Levie, *Terrorism in War*, 31.

170. Friedman, ed., *The Laws of War*, 882. See also Willis, *Prologue to Nuremberg*, 135.

171. Mullins, *The Leipzig Trials*, 162.

172. Willis, *Prologue to Nuremberg*, 135.

173. Levie, *Terrorism in War*, 32.

174. Mullins, *The Leipzig Trials*, 162. Taylor, *The Anatomy of the Nuremberg Trials*, 12, 17.

175. Levie, *Terrorism in War*, 32.

176. Ibid., 516n246.

177. "However, with official connivance, and wholehearted public approval, Boldt escaped in November 1921 and Dithmar in January 1922" Levie, *Terrorism in War*, 33.

178. Willis, *Prologue to Nuremberg*, 135.

179. Ibid., 23.

180. Piccone and Ulmen, "American Imperialism and International Law," 62.

181. Quincy Wright, *A Study of War* (Chicago: University of Chicago Press, 1969), 342.

182. Ibid.

183. Ibid.

184. Howard, *Restraints on War*, 11. Howard describes their effort to create not simply laws of war, but laws against war. This was one in a series of treaties written in the late 1920s all aimed at outlawing "aggression."

185. Marrus, *The Nuremberg War Crimes Trials*, 14. See also Finch, "The Progressive Development of International Law," 613.

186. For nearly three hundred years of international relations, war was considered a legally admissible instrument of policy independent of its justness or unjustness (Ulmen, "American Imperialism and International Law," 49). Sally Thomas has argued that the lawful/unlawful distinction was a departure from the concept of just and unjust war. The illegality of resort to war was not a judgment based on "the intrinsic injustice of the cause of war, but of a breach of a formal procedural requirement" (17). Quincy Wright, "International Law and Guilt by Association," *The American Journal of International Law* 43(1949): 753.

Fuller described what he believed to be the intellectual underpinnings of the antiwar movement in *The Conduct of War*: "The same determination to establish a new basis for peace lay behind an entirely different war aim. As the war went on, socialists and liberals increasingly voiced the hope that peace would lead to a more just and peaceful international order based on general disarmament, an end to trade barriers, and perhaps a new world organization. Although many Europeans adopted these views, only the American government based its program of war aims upon them, and President Wilson, of course, became the symbol of the proposed new order during 1918. Wilson's ideas, however, did not command universal support, even in the United States where the Republican opposition, like the other Allied governments, stood for total victory and a harsh peace" (332). George Kennan remarks on the American interest in the peace movement: "There was especially in the United States, a marked surge of interest in and enthusiasm for the negotiation and adoption of treaties of arbitration and conciliation. And the government efforts were supported by a number of private institutional initiatives" ("The Balkan Crisis, 1913, 1993" 3).

187. Hodgson, *The Colonel*, 164.

188. Ibid., 20, 49.

189. Ibid., 164.

190. Ibid.

191. Ibid., 164.

192. Ibid., 158. The Manchurian crisis was "an issue between the two great theories of civilization and economic methods." The Pact's august pronouncements proved hollow when Stimson called on Britain and France "to repair to the standard," joining in the nonrecognition of the Japanese conquest. See also *The New York Times*, August 9, 1932.

193. Ibid., 162. Paterson, Clifford, and Hagan, *American Foreign Policy: A History—1900 to Present*, 1:339. Stimson was less concerned about the fate of China than "the specter of great powers seizing new empires to rescue themselves from economic depression" (339).

194. Hodgson, *The Colonel*, 158; Paterson, Clifford, and Hagan, *American Foreign Policy*, 2:280. Accordingly, Wilson's *raison d'etat* was "the expansion of freedom." However, "freedom" was defined by the Americans. Although the Treaty of Versailles abolished colonialism, the Americans refused to abandon the Monroe Doctrine. Originally written to keep the American continent free from European influence, it became a means by which the United States could retain a free hand in the region. Ambrosius, *Wilsonian Statecraft*, 56. Tucker, "Brave New World Order," 26.

195. Piccone and Ulmen, "American Imperialism and International Law," 63. See also Hodgson, *The Colonel*, 158.

196. Piccone and Ulmen, "American Imperialism and International Law," 63.

197. Ibid., 51. To Schmitt, the American redefinition of "recognition" was of vital importance. "In Schmitt's estimation, such a doctrine had a clearly interventionist character. It meant that the United States could effectively control every governmental and constitutional change in every country in the Western Hemisphere" (63). Although the American delegation pressed for arbitration, there was a conflict of interest: they also wanted their Monroe Doctrine. To Carl Schmitt this was telling: " 'This is the core of the great original Monroe Doctrine, a genuine Grossraum principle, namely the union of a politically awakened people, a political idea and on the basis of this idea, a politically—dominant Grossraum excluding foreign intervention' " (Schmitt quoted in ibid., 51).

198. Paterson, Clifford, and Hagan, *American Foreign Policy: A History—1900 to Present*, 2:375. See also International Military Tribunal, *Trial of the Major War Criminals* (Nuremberg: International Military Tribunal, 1947), 5:322; Ann and John Tusa, *The Nuremberg Trial* (New York: Atheneum, 1984), 21. The conferees felt that the Germans had violated the laws of war so egregiously that drumhead justice would not suffice.

199. Whitney Harris, *Tyranny on Trial* (Dallas: Southern Methodist University Press, 1954), 4.

200. Ibid. See also Robert Conot, *Justice at Nuremberg* (New York: Carol and Graf, 1983), 9.

201. John Lewis Gaddis, *The United States, Russia, and the Origins of the Cold War* (New York: Columbia University Press, 1972), 8.

202. The entire text of the Moscow Declaration can be found in the Trials of the German War Criminals (Washington, D.C.: U.S. Government Printing Office, 1949). Bradley F. Smith, *The Road to Nuremberg* (New York: Basic, 1981), 8–9. President Roosevelt's style was to deemphasize political questions to prevent divisions in the wartime alliance (39). According to Smith, the Roosevelt administration effectively sidestepped contentious issues by adopting a policy that sought to bring quick victory for the least amount of American lives. See also Tusa, *The Nuremberg Trial*, 50–51 and

Taylor, *The Anatomy of the Nuremberg Trials*, 34. Bradley F. Smith offers the most comprehensive account of the pretrial debates in *The American Road to Nuremberg: The Documentary Record* (Stanford: Hoover Institution Press, 1982). Smith is without question one of the world's foremost experts on the creation of the IMT and the international trial. His trilogy was extremely helpful.

203. Frank Buscher, *The U.S. War Crimes Program in Germany, 1946–1955* (Westport, Conn.: Greenwood, 1989), 8. Buscher ably summarizes the historiography of the occupation period. See also John Gimbel, *The American Occupation of Germany* (Palo Alto: Stanford University Press, 1968); John Montgomery, *Forced to Be Free: The Artificial Revolution in Germany and Japan* (Chicago: University of Chicago Press, 1967); and Paul Hammond, "Directives for the Occupation of Germany: The Washington Controversy," in Harold Stein, ed., *American Civil-Military Decisions* (Birmingham: University of Alabama Press, 1963). For German views see Walter Dorn, "*Die Debatteuber die amerikanische Besatzungspolitik für Deutschland* (1944–1945)" *Vierteljahrshefte für Zeitgeschichte* 20(1972): 39–62; and Gunter Moltmann, "*Zur Formulierung der amerikanischen Besatzungspolitik in Deutschland am Endedes Zweiten Weltkrieges*," *Vierteljahrschefte für Zeitgeschichte* 15(1967): 299–322.

204. Hans Morgenthau Jr., *Morgenthau Diaries* (New York: Da Capo, 1974), 2:443–444. The American Jewish Conference expressed a similar view in a letter to Secretary of State Cordell Hull: "This campaign of terror and annihilation has been carried out with unexampled bestiality in consort with Axis allies. . . . These crimes cannot go unpunished without destroying the legal and moral foundations upon which our civilization rests." (For the original text see 30–44 and the introduction to the memo from Henry Morgenthau to President Roosevelt, 5 September 1944, in Smith, ed., *The American Road to Nuremberg*, 27–29.)

205. Smith, *The American Road to Nuremberg*, 8. "On August 28, an additional push was applied in the same direction by John Pehle, a Morgenthau associate and director of the war refugee board." Christopher Simpson offers a more conspiratorial account of the State Department's inaction in *The Splendid Blond Beast*. Presidential Memorandum for the Secretary of War, 26 August 1944, in Smith, ed., *The American Road to Nuremberg*, 20–21. It would be generous to say that FDR waffled on war crimes policy; it had been a detail in a two-theater war. The real focus of American wartime enmity was Japan.

206. Ibid.

207. Ibid., 20–21.

208. From Henry Morgenthau Jr. to President Roosevelt (The Morgenthau Plan), 5 September 1944, in Smith, ed., *The American Road to Nuremberg*, 27–29.

209. Ibid., 28.

210. Taylor, *The Anatomy of the Nuremberg Trials*, 107–111.

211. Ibid.

212. Robert Abzug, *Inside the Vicious Heart* (New York: Oxford University Press, 1985), 44. One veteran recalled how the American soldiers reacted to finding the camp: "Control was gone after the sights we saw, and the men were deliberately

wounding guards that were available and and then turned them over to the prisoners and allowing them to take their revenge on them."

213. Smith, ed., *The American Road to Nuremberg*, 6–8. *The Road to Nuremberg* and *The American Road to Nuremberg* are two different books, both by B. F. Smith.

214. Conot, *Justice at Nuremberg*, 11.

215. Ibid., 13.

216. Secretary of War Henry Stimson to President Roosevelt, 9 September 1944, in Smith, ed., *The American Road to Nuremberg*, 30–31.

217. Smith, ed., *The Road to Nuremberg*, 31.

218. Tusa, *The Nuremberg Trial*, 60.

219. Memorandum, "Major War Criminals" by British Lord Chancellor Sir John Simon, 4 September 1944, in Smith, ed., *The American Road to Nuremberg*, 33–37. Churchill advocated a similar plan (46). The British were adamant about not redefining war crimes in order to punish war criminals. But as victory neared, this conservative approach fell by the wayside (18). In the spring of 1944, Stimson described his plans: "the method of dealing with these and other criminals requires careful thought and a well-defined procedure. Such procedure must embody . . . at least the rudimentary aspects of the Bill of Rights, namely notification to the accused of the charge, the right to be heard and, within reasonable limits, to call witnesses in his defense. The Nazi crimes were profound and widespread and they demanded trial and punishment as all *crimes*, no matter how clear, do" (Tusa, *The Nuremberg Trial*, 54).

220. Ibid., 1. The title of the first chapter is "The Great German War on the Potomac." The Tusas describe the idea for a trial as having "originated in an interdepartmental row in Washington over plans for the future of conquered Germany" (50). Smith describes Roosevelt's treatment of the war crimes question: "The reason for this lack of preparation was simple: Nothing definitive had come down from the White House indicating what Franklin Roosevelt thought should be done with the remains of central Europe once Nazism had been destroyed. The President was still stalling on the question, as he had been stalling since the U.S. entered the war in 1941" (*The Road to Nuremberg* 13).

221. Henry Stimson to Henry Morgenthau, 9 September 1944, in Smith, ed., *The American Road to Nuremberg*, 30. Stimson wrote: "My basic objection to the proposed methods of treating Germany which were discussed this morning was that in addition to a system of preventative and educative punishment they would add the dangerous weapon of complete economic oppression."

222. Ibid.

223. Tusa, *The Nuremberg Trial*, 61.

224. Kai Bird, *The Chairman: John McCloy, the Making of the American Establishment* (New York: Simon and Schuster, 1991), 258.

225. Tusa, *The Nuremberg Trial*, 50.

226. William Bosch, *Judgment on Nuremberg* (Chapel Hill: University of North Carolina Press, 1970), 9. Many believed that the vindictive tenor of the Treaty of Ver-

sailles had fostered a political atmosphere that allowed the seed of National Socialism to germinate and flourish. The twin debacles of the Versailles and the Leipzig trials contained practical lessons for the victors of World War II. At the time, German nationalists described the Treaty of Versailles as the Allies' "hour of reckoning." The final outcome was a "Carthaginian peace par excellence" that culminated with the "crucifixion" of Germany. This view would later play into the hands of post–World War II German nationalists who had long argued after World War I: "The old Germany was suffering on the cross while the terrible punishment of Bolshevism hovered over the world as the Divine vengeance for the Victors. Here was an added feature to the myth—the initial suggestion that the Allies never understood that Germany was the vital bulwark against Bolshevik expansion" (Louis Snyder, *The Roots of German Nationalism* [Bloomington: University of Indiana Press, 1978], 175). Karl-Heinz Janssen makes a similar point in "*Versailles und Nürnberg: Zur Psychologie der Kreigsschuldfrage in Deutschland*"; to Janssen, both Nuremberg and Versailles "refers to a continuity, to a link between World War I and World War II—both have negative connotations despite five years of 're-education' and thirty-eight years of political education. . . . Thus the greater part of Germans have not learned to deal with historical guilt or to recognize the 'continuity of error' " (in *Lichtinden Schatten der Vergangenheit*, eds. Jörg Friedrich and Jörg Wollenberg, Frankfurt/Main: Ullstein Zeitgeschichte, 1987), 26.

227. The Secretary of War to the Secretary of State, 27 October 1944, in Smith, ed., *The American Road to Nuremberg*, 40–41.

228. Tusa, *The Nuremberg Trial*, 52. They describe the Secretary of War's thinking: "He was unwilling to criminalize the entire German nation, but saw a therapeutic value in punishing internationally recognized war criminals" (52).

229. Bird, *The Chairman*, 205. David Wyman, *The Abandonment of the Jews* (New York: Pantheon, 1984), 14. Martin Gilbert, *Auschwitz and the Allies* (New York: Holt, 1981), 94. In 1942 former member of the Polish Foreign Ministry and Warsaw underground leader Jan Karski disguised himself as a concentration camp guard and entered the Belzec concentration camp. Karski wrote a report of what he had seen and traveled to London and Washington in an attempt to impress upon world leaders the magnitude of the atrocities (from Bird, *The Chairman*, 205–206).

In the summer of 1943 Karski traveled to Washington and presented his first-hand account to President Roosevelt, Secretary Stimson, and OSS Chief William Donovan. He also met with Felix Frankfurter, whom he hoped would be a natural ally; the Supreme Court Justice was an active Zionist. But after meeting at the Polish embassy and hearing his account of the atrocities, Frankfurter told the Polish ambassador that he could not believe the stories: "Mr. Ambassador, I did not say that this young man is lying. I said that I am unable to believe him." Frankfurter was not alone; Walter Lippman also met with Karski "but, unlike other columnists who heard Karski's story, he—the only Jew among them—decided not to write about it" (206–207). This letter to Congress, objecting to Jewish immigration, captured the mood in some of the American heartland: "I am writing to you to protest against the entry of Jewish refugees into this country. . . . Their lack of common decency, gross ignorance and unbelievable gall stamps them as undesirables even if they could be assimilated into a common society, which they can't. I see from the papers that 200,000 Refugee Jews in Hungary will not live through the next few weeks. That's too dam bad; what in the hell do we care about the Jews in Hungary" (Buscher, *The U.S. War Crimes Program*, 12). See also "Nazi Mass Killing Laid Bare in Camp," *New York Times*, August 30, 1944.

230. Taylor, *The Anatomy of the Nuremberg Trials*, 42.

231. Ibid.

232. *The Foreign Relations of the United States: The Conference at Quebec, 1944* (Washington, D.C.: U.S. Government Printing Office, 1972), 124–125.

233. *The Foreign Relations of the United States 1945* (Washington, D.C.: U.S. Government Printing Office, 1968), 3:1162–1164. Bernays hoped to try "Nazi organizations themselves rather than individuals and to convict them and all their members of engaging in a criminal conspiracy to control the world, to persecute minorities, to break treaties, to invade other countries and to commit war" (1163).

234. Conot, *Justice at Nuremberg*, 12. As Geoffrey Best observes, the worst atrocities of World War II were not war crimes under the traditional laws of war: "International law at that date held it no crime for a government to murder its own subjects. Civilians had, within the past decade, been killed on so many occasions, in such varied circumstances, and under so many pretexts, that there could be real difficulty in distinguishing the more justiciable instances from the less" (*War and Law Since 1945*, 64).

235. "Trial of European War Criminals," Colonel Murray Bernays, 15 September 1944, in Smith, ed., *The American Road to Nuremberg*, 33–34.

236. David Luban, *Legal Modernism* (Ann Arbor: University of Michigan Press, 1994), 335.

237. Smith, ed., *The American Road to Nuremberg*, 34. The notion that Germans could not be punished for crimes against German Jews highlighted the obsolescence of the laws of war. The bombing of cities was not a war crime; neither the United States nor Germany signed 1925 Geneva accords. There was a sense that executions and court-martials would not reach the root of the problem: "the Bernays plan sought to solve the need to purge German society by means other than the Morgenthau Plan" (55). These acts would not go unpunished under the Bernays plan: "Therefore, such technicalities as the question whether the extermination of fellow Germans by Nazi Germans was unlawful, or whether this could be a 'war crime' if it was perpetrated before there was a state of war, would be unimportant, if you recognize as the basic crime the Nazi conspiracy" (33).

238. Ibid., 35. According to international legal theorists Oppenheim and Lauderpacht, traditional war crimes consisted of: violations of the recognized rules of war, hostilities committed by individuals who are not members of armed forces, espionage, treason, and marauding acts. According to critics, the Allies had no precedent or positive statute to justify trying statesmen and industrialists. (Nuremberg defense attorney Otto Kranzbühler in Wilbourn Benton, ed., *Nuremberg: German Views of the War Trials* [Dallas: Southern Methodist University Press, 1955], 111).

239. Ibid., 35. "Trial of the German War Criminals by Col. Murray Bernays," September 15, 1944, in Smith, ed., *The American Road to Nuremberg*, 33.

240. Ibid., 36.

241. Ibid.

242. Hans Ehard, "The Nuremberg Trial Against the Major War Criminals and International Law," *The American Journal of International Law* 43(1949): 225. Ehard commented on the concept of conspiracy in Continental law: "the concept is not one familiar to continental law. It has developed in Anglo-Saxon customary law" (227).

243. Ibid. See also Tusa, *The Nuremberg Trial*, 57; Taylor, *The Anatomy of the Nuremberg Trials*, 36–37. Telford Taylor described the plan's major deviation as "the Bernays additions."

244. Ibid., 55. Historians John and Ann Tusa point out that it was ironic the trial planners chose to build their case around such a novel and contentious charge when a large body of evidence existed. See also "Memo from Colonel Ami Cutter for Mr. McCloy," October 1, 1944, in Smith, ed., *The American Road to Nuremberg*, 38.

245. "Memo for the President from the Secretaries of State, War and Navy," November 11, 1944, in Smith, ed., *The American Road to Nuremberg*, 41–44.

246. Ibid., 43.

247. Smith, ed., *The American Road to Nuremberg*, 33–35.

248. Ibid. Legal theorist Otto Kirchheimer shared William Chanler's view that the criminal state forfeited the right to be protected by rules it had so egregiously violated: "On the basis of its attitude toward and treatment of the human material under its domination, such a state could not ask that credence be given to its acts and not expect the actions of its servants to be clothed with the presumption of legality" (*Political Justice: The Use of Legal Procedure for Political Ends* [Princeton: Princeton University Press, 1961], viii, 19). According to Chanler, the Germans forfeited protection typically reserved for "a lawful belligerent under international law" (51). Kirchheimer attempted to put the crimes of the criminal state into a larger context. According to him, the extreme nature of the crimes allowed the successor regime great liberties. He considered political justice the most tenuous type, because it could so easily turn to farce: "By utilizing the devices of justice, politics contracts some ill-defined and spurious obligations. Circumstantial and contradictory, the linkage of politics and justice is characterized by both promise and blasphemy" (9). Henry Stimson diary entry, January 19, 1945, in Smith, ed., *The American Road to Nuremberg*, 130.

249. Tusa, *The Nuremberg Trial*, 58. Much of the discussion was stimulated by "Memo on Aggressive War by Colonel William Chanler," November 28–30, 1944, in Smith, ed., *The American Road to Nuremberg*, 69–74. "Willi" Chandler was a neighbor and law partner of Henry Stimson. See also "Memo from General Kenneth C. Royall for the Assistant Secretary of War," December 14, 1944, in Smith, ed., *The American Road to Nuremberg*, 78.

250. Smith, ed., 76–77.

251. "Attorney General's Memo on the Punishment of Criminals," January 5,

1945, in Smith, ed., *The American Road to Nuremberg*, 91. See also Weschler's critique of the aggression charge, 84–90.

252. James Weingartner, *Crossroads of Death: The Story of the Malmedy Massacre and Trial* (Berkeley: University of California Press, 1979), 10. Also see Michael Reynolds, *The Devil's Adjutant: Jochen Peiper, Panzer Leader* (New York: Sarpedon, 1995); Lothar Greil, *Oberst der Waffen SS Joachim Peiper und der Malmedy Process* (Munchen: Schild-Verlag, 1977) and Leo Kessler, *SS Peiper* (London: Leo Cooper, 1986). The exploits of Kampfgruppe Peiper (1941–43) won their leader the Knight's Cross of the Iron Cross. Historian James Weingartner offers this observation of the German commander: "Peiper also provided an example of personal daring which goes far to explain his success as a combat leader; he expected much of his men and more of himself and displayed sangfroid which excited the admiration of his youthful troopers. One of many anecdotes that has survived describes Peiper's destruction of an onrushing T-34 tank with a rifle grenade at a few meters' range. Peiper grinned, observing, 'That should suffice for the close-combat badge, boys' " (Weingartner, *Crossroads of Death*, 118). Originally recorded by Ernst Gunther Kratschmer in "*Der Soldat: Jochen Peipers militarischer Werdegang*," *Der Freiwillige* (Sept. 1976):5.

253. Ibid., 10.

254. Ibid., 65.

255. Tusa, *The Nuremberg Trial*, 30. There is a consensus among Nuremberg historians that the Malmedy Massacre marked a turning point in the debate over America's war crimes policy: "America, thanks to geography, had been insulated against the horrors of the War. Only in December 1944 did the American public have its first direct experience of Nazi brutality. . . . The question of war crimes could be seen as remote and rather abstract; now it was painfully real."

256. Weingartner, *Crossroads of Death*, 12.

257. Smith, ed., *The American Road to Nuremberg*, 89. "Memo from Assistant Attorney General Herbert Weschler to Attorney General Francis Biddle," December 29, 1944, in Smith, ed., *The American Road to Nuremberg*, 84–90.

258. "Presidential Memo for the Secretary of State," January 3, 1945, in Smith, ed., *The American Road to Nuremberg*, 92.

259. "Questions posed by Major General John Weir to Edmund Morgan, January 12, 1945," in Smith, ed., *The American Road to Nuremberg*, 107. Morgan was assigned the following questions: "1. May you rationally use a conspiracy theory of prosecution of the principal leaders of Germany to dominate other peoples by acts violative of the laws and customs of war? 2. If that premise is sound, may you prove as part of the chain of the conspiracy the persecutions of dissident groups of their own nationals committed prior to the beginning of the war on racial, political, and religious grounds?" Morgan wholeheartedly disapproved of the Bernays plan; he found the conspiracy charge "so highly questionable and so novel to international law that it should be entertained only in the most necessitous circumstances." He wrote: "The conspiracy theory is too thin a veneer to hide the real purpose, namely, the creation of a hereto unknown international offense by individuals, *ex post facto*."

260. Ibid.

261. "Diary Entry of Henry L. Stimson," January 19, 1945, in Smith, ed., *The American Road to Nuremberg*, 130.

262. Ibid., 52–53.

263. Tusa, *The Nuremberg Trial*, 18, 19, 66–67. Ironically, this was a reverse of the situation after World War I, when the Americans were clinging to the conservative position as part of a larger effort to thwart the war crimes prosecutions sought by the British, the French, and the Belgians.

264. "The argument for summary process against Hitler and co., Prepared by Lord Simon," in Smith, ed., *The American Road to Nuremberg*, 155–157.

265. Tusa, *The Nuremberg Trial*, 66; Smith, ed., *The American Road to Nuremberg*, 139. Cutter and Rosenman hoped to redraft the proposal to make the proceedings appear more like a trial.

266. Tusa, *The Nuremberg Trial*, 66. See also Smith, ed., *The Road to Nuremberg*, 170–173.

267. Ibid., 66. I left names recognizable to English readers—Goering (Göring), Hoess (Höss), Doenitz (Dönitz)—in their anglicized forms. In the cases of Richard and Ernst von Weizsäcker, I used the German spelling. It became difficult to use the German spellings because so many of the names were anglicized in the American trial records (Waldemar Klingelhöfer and Otto Kranzbühler became Waldemar Klingelhoefer and Otto Kranzbuehler). In the cases of Japanese leaders, I did not use the correct Tojo Hideki, Yamashita Tomoyuki, Homma Masahru, but the more recognizable Tojo, Yamashita, and Homma.

268. Ibid., 66.

269. Ibid., 67. See also "Memo on Proposals for the Prosecution and Punishment of Certain War Criminals and other Offenders," April 25–30, 1945, in Smith, ed., *The American Road to Nuremberg*, 162–172.

270. Tusa, *The Nuremberg Trial*, 69. Jackson did not hesitate to trade his moralist hat for a legalist one if American interests were imperiled. In 1940, then Attorney General Jackson reinterpreted the Neutrality Act of 1917, to help President Roosevelt consummate the destroyer-naval base arrangement with the British. According to Daniel Patrick Moynihan, "Attorney General Jackson gave out a legal opinion that found everything in order. He cited the relevant statute, the Neutrality Act of 1917. In his version of the text, however, a comma was inserted that completely changed the effect of the statute" (*On the Law of Nations* 144).

271. Tusa, *The Nuremberg Trial*, 68.

272. Ibid. 68. In 1941, in a speech before the American Bar Association, Jackson claimed: "We may be certain that we do less injustice by the worst process of the law than would be done by the best use of violence. We cannot await the perfect court before stopping men from settling their differences with brass knuckles. . . . I do not deny that in the 19th century certain rules of neutrality were developed, based on the idea of neutrality, and that these rules have been supplanted by various Hague conventions. The application of these rules has become obsolete. Experiences since the

world war have demonstrated their invalidity. The fundamental principles of the 19th century, according to which all warring parties must be handled equally, have been swept away by the League of Nations to the principal sanctions against aggressors, through the Kellogg-Briand Pact and the Argentina Declaration outlawing war. We must return to earlier and healthier conceptions."

273. Ibid., 69.

274. Taylor describes Jackson's view of the court's legal basis: "Jackson not only invoked the Kellogg-Briand Pact but, more compellingly, the history of the English common law, which developed not primarily by act of parliament but by 'decisions reached from time to time in adapting settled principles to new situations' " (*The Anatomy of the Nuremberg Trials* 55).

275. Ibid.

276. Ibid. Telford Taylor was more of a realist than Justice Jackson. In June 1945, when, according to Bradley Smith, "American idealistic fervor was burning at white heat," Taylor candidly admitted that many of these decisions were political and recognized the necessity of acknowledging this basic fact. He maintained that the *ex post facto* argument was "Not, I believe, a bothersome question if we keep in mind that this is a *political* decision to declare and apply a principle of international law." See also "An Approach to the Preparation of the Prosecution of Axis Criminality by Telford Taylor, early June 1945," in Bradley F. Smith, ed., *The American Road to Nuremberg: The Documentary Record 1944–1945* (Stanford: Hoover Institution Press, 1982), 209. During the pretrial period Taylor wrote a memo arguing that a trial for the German leaders would "give meaning to the war. To validate the casualties we have caused. . . . The conviction and punishment of the Axis war criminals are desirable objectives in themselves, but in order to accomplish the larger objectives the conviction and punishment must be obtained by procedures and for reasons which will help to make the war meaningful and valid for the people of the Allied Nations, and it is not beyond hope for at least some people of the Axis nations" (209).

3. The American War Crimes Program

1. Conrad Crane, *Bombs, Cities, and Civilians* (Lawrence: University of Kansas Press, 1993), 1, 143. This is without a doubt one of the best studies on American bombing during World War II.

2. Ibid., 143. Geoffrey Best on the legality of bombing: "Assessment of the legality of bombardment . . . and bombing . . . can be a delicate undertaking. It requires in effect that each particular event be placed on a graduated scale, of which only the opposite extremities from a permanent affliction of fog. The extreme point at the lawful end is, of course, where the object of attack is beyond reach of dispute. . . . But not all objectives in battle, and rather few in economic warfare, are as simple as that" (*War and Law Since 1945* [Oxford: Clarendon, 1994], 51). On total war and the role of civilians: "the civilian's probable participation in the workings of an economy perhaps totally mobilized for national struggle made it difficult to distinguish him as clearly as the principle of non-combatant immunity required" (51).

3. Otto Kirchheimer, *Political Justice: The Use of Legal Procedure for Political Ends* (Princeton: Princeton University Press, 1961), 336–337. This was really an accusation of hypocrisy and it would be heard more in the coming years. The philosophers (Kirchheimer and Arendt) tend to be more dismissive of *tu quoque* charges than the lawyers. Kirchheimer describes the use of the argument at Nuremberg: "Against the inherent assertion of moral superiority, of the radical difference between the contemptible doings of those in the dock and the visions, intentions, and record of the new master, the defendants will resort to *tu quoque* tactics . . . the argument raises the objection that the new regime is guilty of the same practices with which it now tries to besmirch its predecessor's record. Critics employed this tactic when assailing Nuremberg due to Soviet participation" (336). Kirchheimer finds this argument extremely weak: "In a wider sense, the *tu quoque* argument could be leveled against any type of terrestrial justice. Only the archangel descending on judgment day would be exempt from the reproach that blame and praise have not been distributed according to everyone's due desert" (337). Howard Levie, *Terrorism in War: The Law of War Crimes* (Dobbs Ferry, N.Y.: Oceana, 1993), notes an obvious but often overlooked fact that *tu quoque* was not even a legal principle.

4. Ann and John Tusa, *The Nuremberg Trial* (New York: Atheneum, 1984), 72. The British Foreign Office and the U.S. State Department made similar arguments. George Kennan was another important official who criticized Soviet participation in any trial.

5. Allen Paul, *Katyn: The Untold Story of Stalin's Polish Massacre* (New York: Scribners, 1991), 58. See also Ronald Hingley, *The Russian Secret Police* (New York: Simon and Schuster, 1970), 168–171. On the NKVD under Beria and the first mobile killing squads see Lennard Gerson, *The Secret Police in Lenin's Russia* (Philadelphia: Temple University Press, 1976). For literary accounts see Aleksandr Solzhenitsyn, *The Gulag Archipelago* (New York: Harper and Row, 1985). Both Alan Bullock (*Hitler and Stalin* [New York: Knopf, 1992]) and Conquest claim that between thirteen million and fifteen million died during collectivization (*The Great Terror* 277). Walter Lacquer has described Stalin's actions as "without precedence in peacetime in modern history" (*Stalin* [London: Undwin and Hyman, 1990], 125). He draws on recent Soviet research to reach much higher numbers: "According to an author writing in *Neva* (October 1988), the Leninist periodical, at least 16 million were arrested under Stalin of which some 8–10 million died in camps. If one adds the number of peasants who died as a result of collectivization, one reaches a figure of no less than 20 million." Although these estimates are on the high side of the spectrum, they give a sense of the magnitude of the Stalinist purges.

6. Paul, *Katyn*, 72. According to Troutbeck, the hypocrisy of allowing the Soviets to sit in high judgment would invalidate any precedent set by the International Court: "Surely the Russians had 'entered into a common plan or enterprise aimed at domination over other nations' which involved 'atrocities, persecutions and deportations' on a colossal scale. 'Is not the Soviet government not employed today in the very same thing in Poland, the Baltic States, the Balkan States, Turkey and Persia? (Someone added in the margin: 'And what about Finland?') 'All this,' seethed Troutbeck, 'cannot

be excused on the principle of the housemaid's baby. There have been two criminal enterprises this century—by Germans and Russians. To set up one lot of conspirators as judges of the other robs the whole procedure of the basis of morality.' " For more on Stalin's massacre of Soviet nationals see Lacquer, *Stalin* and Robert Conquest, *The Harvest of Sorrow* (New York: Oxford University Press, 1986). For a comparison to Hitler see Bullock, *Hitler and Stalin*. See also Peter Baldwin, *Reworking the Past: Hitler, the Holocaust, and the Historians' Debate* (Boston: Beacon, 1991), 14 and Sven Lindqvist, *Exterminate All the Brutes*, trans. Joan Tate (New York: New Press, 1996). Lindqvist offers a novel argument about the *Historikerstreit*: "All German historians participating in this debate seem to look in the same direction. None looks to the west. But Hitler did. What Hitler wished to create when he sought *Lebensraum* in the east was a continental equivalent of the British Empire. It was in the British and other western European peoples that he found the models, of which the extermination of the Jews is, in Nolte's words, 'a distorted copy' " (10).

7. Bullock, *Hitler and Stalin*, 497.

8. Richard Lukas, *The Forgotten Holocaust* (Lexington: University of Kentucky Press, 1986), 21.

9. Paul, *Katyn*, 111, x, 58. Wishing to avoid the bloody aftermath with half-dead victims writhing on the floor, the Cheka perfected what the Germans later called *Nackenschuss*, or a shot in the nape of the neck. By the 1930s it had become the standard method used by the NKVD to kill Stalin's purge victims and others.

10. Ibid.

11. Lukas, *The Forgotten Holocaust*, 232. It was difficult for the Allies to denounce Stalin; they had gone to great lengths to reinvent him. In 1943, Allied disinformation reached all-time heights when Stalin was named *Time* magazine's man of the year. *Time* wrote: "We respect the mighty Russian people and admire them. . . . They live under a system of tight, state-controlled information. But probably the attitude to take toward this is not to get too excited about it. When we take account of what the [USSR] has accomplished in the 20 years of its existence we can make allowances for certain shortcomings however deplorable" (Paul, *Katyn*, xi). Paterson, Clifford, and Hagan, *American Foreign Policy: A History—1900 to Present*, 2:372–375.

12. Ibid.

13. Ibid., x. The Allies faced a conflict of moral and strategic interests, and strategic interests clearly prevailed.

14. Robert Abzug, *Inside the Vicious Heart* (New York: Oxford University Press, 1985), 30.

15. Ibid., 52.

16. Ibid., 90.

17. Abzug, *Inside the Vicious Heart*, 90.

18. Ibid., 94.

19. Ibid., 93. David Irving published the photograph in *Nuremberg: The Last Battle*. (London: Focal Point, 1999), 36. According to David Irving, of the 560 Germans captured, all but 40 were killed.

20. Paul Fussell, *Doing Battle: The Making of a Skeptic* (Boston: Little, Brown, 1996), 291.

21. Ibid.

22. Ibid.

23. Telford Taylor, *The Anatomy of the Nuremberg Trials: A Personal Memoir* (New York: Knopf, 1992).

24. Ibid., 63.

25. Tusa, *The Nuremberg Trial*, 76–77.

26. Ibid., 75.

27. Ibid., 77.

28. Tusa, *The Nuremberg Trial*, 78. The Tusas described the Soviet judge's action as "so untypical . . . one wonders if he had been ordered by Moscow to trail a coat."

29. Tusa, *The Nuremberg Trial*, 78. "An Approach to the Preparation of the Prosecution of Axis Criminality" in Smith, ed., *The American Road to Nuremberg*, 211.

30. Taylor, *The Anatomy of the Nuremberg Trials*, 62–63.

31. Ibid., 61.

32. Ibid., 63. According to Taylor, "In all probability Jackson was making a 'show of force,' and in fact he had a lot of force to show" (62–63).

33. Ibid., 81 and Taylor, *The Anatomy of the Nuremberg Trials*, 67. Tusa, *The Nuremberg Trial*, 76–77. Gros rejected the notion that "The prosecutor could come out of the blue with evidences which were completely unknown until the moment of the trial, opening a Pandora's box of unhappy surprises" (77).

34. Taylor, *The Anatomy of the Nuremberg Trials*, 67. In *Aggression and World Order: A Critique of United Nations Theories on Aggression* (Berkeley: University of California Press, 1958), Julius Stone wrote: "What is in debate is not the value of definition in general, but the value of definition of this particular notion in the present state of the international community" (19). He considered the comparison between international and domestic societies to be erroneous: "But in international society no means exist even of collective redress of the gravest wrongs, whether judicial or private, legal or moral, much less of collective adjustment of law to minimum standards of justice. In such a society, this single notion of 'aggression' is being asked to perform within the monstrously wide ambit of all inter-State relations, most of the major tasks of criminal and constitutional law, not to speak of much of the law of property, torts and procedure" (130).

35. Ibid., 66.

36. Ibid.

37. Ibid., 67. See also Tusa, *The Nuremberg Trial*, 73. Jackson argued that "the idea of separate trials for each nation . . . might be the easiest and most satisfactory way of reconciling it."

38. Taylor, *The Anatomy of the Nuremberg Trials*, 70. Dean believed the source of friction was William Donovan, who "clearly does not like the Russians much." Dean believed the Americans were trying "to magnify the differences between their views" and those of the Russians.

39. Taylor, *The Anatomy of the Nuremberg Trials*, 70; Tusa, *The Nuremberg Trial*, 103; Robert Conot, *Justice at Nuremberg* (New York: Carroll and Graf, 1983), 482–485. B. F. Smith also agreed that by the end of the London Conference, Justice Jackson hoped to exclude the Soviets from the proceedings.

40. Taylor, *The Anatomy of the Nuremberg Trials*, 68.

41. Ibid., 70–71. Article VII reads: "The Three Governments have taken note of the discussions which have been proceeding in recent weeks in London . . . with a view to reaching agreement on the methods of trial of those major war criminals. . . . They hope that the negotiations in London will result in speedy agreement reached for this purpose, and they regard it as a matter of great importance that the trial of those major criminals should begin at the earliest date." Whitney Harris, *Tyranny on Trial* (Dallas: Southern Methodist University Press, 1954), 21.

42. Tusa, *The Nuremberg Trial*, 79–80.

43. Jay Baird, ed., *From Nuremberg to My Lai* (Lexington, Ky.: D. C. Heath, 1972), 3–8. This very interesting collection includes both the London Agreement and the Charter.

44. David Luban, *Legal Modernism* (Ann Arbor: University of Michigan Press, 1994), 335n.

45. Ibid.

46. Taylor, *The Anatomy of the Nuremberg Trials*, 648.

47. Ibid.

48. Jörg Friedrich, "Nuremberg and the Germans," in Belinda Cooper, ed., *War Crimes: The Legacy of Nuremberg* (New York: TV Books, 1999), 87.

49. Ibid. Historian John Teschke makes a similar point in *Hitler's Legacy: West Germany Confronts the Aftermath of the Third Reich* (New York: Peter Lang, 1999): "After the treatment the Soviet Union had received at the hands of Nazi armies, the Russian soldiers exercised all of the traditional perquisites of conquerors as a way of settling a few scores" (15).

50. Ibid., 87.

51. Irving, *Nuremberg: The Last Battle*, 161. See also Solzhenitsyn, *The Gulag Archipelago* (New York: Harper & Row, 1978) and Robert Conquest, *The Great Terror* (New York: Oxford University Press, 1990).

52. Ibid., 157.

53. Ibid., 161.

54. Ibid., 161–162.

55. Tusa, *The Nuremberg Trial*, 86.

56. Smith, *Reaching Judgment at Nuremberg*, 303.

57. Wilbourn Benton, ed., *Nuremberg: German Views of the War Trials* (Dallas: Southern Methodist University Press, 1953), 228–230.

58. Ibid.

59. Originally published in the December 1945 edition of *Life* magazine, these articles were also reprinted in Baird, ed., *From Nuremberg to My Lai*, 47–52. American novelist John Dos Passos recounted Jackson's opening statement: "Robert Jackson

steps quietly to the microphone to open the case for the prosecution. He has a broad forehead and an expression of good humor about his mouth. He wears round spectacles. . . . He talks slowly in an even, explanatory tone without betraying a trace of self-importance in his voice: 'The privilege of opening the first trial in history for crimes against the peace of the world imposes a grave responsibility.' . . . With the calm, explanatory voice of a man delivering a lecture in a history course, Jackson begins his exposition of the assault on Europe. . . . His voice firmer and louder, Jackson has launched into the theory, which he is laying down in behalf of the U.S., that aggressive war is in itself a crime under the law of nations. . . . Robert Jackson has finished speaking. The court rises. People move slowly and thoughtfully from their seats. I doubt if there is a man or a woman in the courtroom who does not feel that great and courageous words have been spoken. We Americans rise to our feet with a feeling of pride because it was a countryman of ours who spoke them" (47–52).

60. International Military Tribunal, *Trial of the Major War Criminals Before the International Military Tribunal* (Washington, D.C.: U.S. Government Printing Office, 1949), 2:99. John Alan Appleman, *Military Tribunals and International Crimes* (Westport, Conn.: Greenwood, 1971), 15. See also IMT, *Trial of the Major War Criminals*, 14:462–463. The German attorneys were quick to recognize the revolutionary implications of the Nuremberg trials. Defense counsel Carl Haensel wrote: "The Nuremberg Tribunals place us anew before the problems of whether positivism really represents the final conclusion of wisdom and coronation of jurisprudence, or whether we have entered a new cultural period and thus, also a new period to be comprehended in legal history, in which . . . an argument emerges which is not based solely on positive norms and their interpretation according to the opinion of the lawmaker" (Benton, ed., *Nuremberg: German Views of the War Trials*, 123). The revolutionary implications of Nuremberg were conceded by German attorney Otto Kranzbühler: "In a revolution one will always have to accept violence and injustice. . . . Its worth or worthlessness is determined by what it contains for the future" (107). See also Werner Maser, *Nuremberg Trial: A Nation on Trial* (New York: Scribner, 1979), 287.

61. IMT, *Trial of the Major War Criminals*, 2:99.

62. Ibid.

63. Ibid., 2:101.

64. Ibid.

65. Ibid., 2:102.

66. Ibid., 2:104.

67. Otto Kranzbühler in *Nuremberg: A Courtroom Drama*, a film produced by Michael Kloft for Chronos Films. It first aired in Germany and France in November 1995 on Arte Television. It is a remarkable film because Kloft was able to interview numerous German, American, Russian, and French participants who have since died.

68. Levie, *Terrorism in War*, 55n66.

69. Gustav Gilbert, *Nuremberg Diary* (New York: Farrar, Straus, 1947), 45–46.

70. IMT, *Trial of the Major War Criminals*, 3:99.

71. Ibid., 3:97.

72. Ibid., 3:144.

73. Ibid., 9:307.

74. Gilbert, *Nuremberg Diary*, 66.

75. Telford Taylor in Kloft, *Nuremberg: A Courtroom Drama*. Telford Taylor, *The Anatomy of the Nuremberg Trials*, 247–248.

76. Telford Taylor in Kloft, *Nuremberg: A Courtroom Drama*.

77. Ibid.

78. Marrus, ed., *The Nuremberg War Crimes Trial 1945–1946*, 165.

79. IMT, *Trial of the Major War Criminals*, 4:478–479.

80. Ibid., 4:485.

81. Gilbert, *Nuremberg Diary*, 102–103.

82. Marrus, ed., *The Nuremberg War Crimes Trial 1945–1946*, 93.

83. Ibid., 92.

84. IMT, *Trial of the Major War Criminals*, 7:169.

85. Ibid.

86. Ibid., 7:170.

87. Ibid., 7:190.

88. Ibid. 679,000 million was the odd number offered by the Soviets.

89. Ibid., 8:302.

90. Ibid., 8:307.

91. Ibid., 8:308.

92. Gilbert, *Nuremberg Diary*, 161–163.

93. Marrus, ed., *The Nuremberg War Crimes Trial 1945–1946*, 180.

94. Ibid., 181.

95. Ibid., 182. For the statistics on Goering's weight, see Irving, *Nuremberg: The Last Battle*, 208.

96. Marrus, ed., *The Nuremberg War Crimes Trial 1945–1946*, 98. See also Conot, *Justice at Nuremberg*, 337. According to Goering, the practices of contemporary total war had developed along three lines that left the old laws far behind: "the war of weapons on land, at sea, and in the air; and . . . the propaganda war, which is also an essential part of this warfare."

97. Marrus, ed., *The Nuremberg War Crimes Trial 1945–1946*, 98.

98. Ibid.

99. IMT, *Trial of the Major War Criminals*, 9:311, 364.

100. Ibid., 9:272–273.

101. Ibid., 9:274–275. See also Baird, *From Nuremberg to My Lai*, 57.

102. Ibid.

103. IMT, *Trial of the Major War Criminals*, 9:49.

104. Ibid., 9:507.

105. Ibid., 9:508.

106. Ibid., 9:509–510.

107. Conot, *Justice at Nuremberg*, 412.

108. Kranzbühler interview in Kloft, *Nuremberg: A Courtroom Drama.*

109. Conot, *Justice at Nuremberg*, 417.

110. Ibid.

111. IMT, *Trial of the Major War Criminals*, 11:400.

112. Ibid., 11:398.

113. Conot, *Justice at Nuremberg*, 452.

114. Paul, *Katyn*, 229.

115. Friedrich, "Nuremberg and the Germans," 87.

116. IMT, *Trial of the Major War Criminals*, 10:313.

117. Ibid., 14:283.

118. Ibid., 14: 284–285.

119. Irving, *Nuremberg: The Last Battle*, 229–230. See also Conot, *Justice at Nuremberg*, 420; Taylor, *Anatomy of the Nuremberg Trials*, 417.

120. Ibid., 231. For a more complete refutation of Speer's claims see Matthias Schmidt, *Albert Speer: The End of a Myth*, trans. Joachim Neugroschel (London: Harrap Limited, 1985). See also Gitta Sereny, *Albert Speer: His Battle with Truth* (New York: Knopf, 1995) and Dan van der Vat, *The Good Nazi: The Life and Times of Albert Speer* (New York: Houghton Mifflin, 1997).

121. Bradley F. Smith, *Reaching Judgment at Nuremberg* (New York: Basic, 1977), 218–219.

122. Ibid., 171.

123. Gerald Reitlinger, *The SS: Alibi of a Nation* (New York: Viking, 1957), 266.

124. Marrus, ed., *The Nuremberg War Crimes Trial 1945–1946*, 98.

125. Ibid.

126. Gilbert, *Nuremberg Diary*, 103.

127. Taylor, *The Anatomy of the Nuremberg Trials*, 228.

128. Gilbert, *Nuremberg Diary*, 45–46.

129. Smith, *Reaching Judgment at Nuremberg*, 304–305. Smith considers the court's conservative opinion their greatest achievement: "It should ever live to the glory of the Nuremberg judges that they took a major step toward dissipating this danger. By advancing a conservative and cautious interpretation of the law of the London Charter, the Court sharply limited the utility of such concepts as 'aggressive war' and 'crimes against humanity' in any future victors' trials. Of even greater importance was the Tribunal's achievement in virtually eliminating the collective guilt features by emasculating the conspiracy-common plan charge and the system for prosecuting members of organizations."

130. Ibid., 305.

131. Ibid., 304.

132. David Luban, *Legal Modernism* (Ann Arbor: University of Michigan Press, 1994), 350.

133. Levie, *Terrorism in War*, 417n131.

134. Kranzbühler in Kloft, *Nuremberg: A Courtroom Drama.*

135. Levie, *Terrorism in War*, 57.

136. Irving, *Nuremberg: The Last Battle*, 182. See also Ben Swearington, *The Mystery of Hermann Goering's Suicide* (New York: Harcourt Brace Jovanovich, 1985).

137. Friedrich, "Nuremberg and the Germans," 87.

138. Tusa, *The Nuremberg Trial*, 465. According to the Tusas, the Soviet judges were ordered to dissent: "He [Nikitchenko] confessed to Biddle that he had consulted Moscow about his problems and received orders to dissent—to object to the acquittals, state that Hess should have been hanged and insist that declarations of criminality should have been made against the Reich Cabinet, General Staff and High Command" (465–466). Otto Kranzbühler on the Russians: "The presence of the Russians was a shame by itself. The whole case of aggressive war, the real undisputable aggressive war was the Polish war. They had instigated it. If you apply the *tu quoque* principle there should be no sentences whatsoever" (interview with the author).

139. Friedrich, "Nuremberg and the Germans," 88. Quincy Wright made a very important point about the Nuremberg debates that is still relevant today: "the favorable or unfavorable character of comments upon events related to the theory of international law often depend less upon events related to the theory of international law assumed by the commentator" (William Bosch, *Nuremberg: American Attitudes Towards the Major German War Crimes Trials* [Chapel Hill: University of North Carolina Press, 1970], 41). International relations theorist Hans Morgenthau placed little faith in international law: "The rule of law has come to be regarded as a kind of miraculous panacea which, whenever applied, would heal, by virtue of its intrinsic reasonableness and justice, the ills of the body politic, transform insecurity and disorder into the calculability of a well-ordered society, and put in place of violence and bloodshed the peaceful and reasonable settlement of social conflicts" (149). Kirchheimer was more approving: "The Greek ideal grows sharper in profile precisely because justice in political matters is more tenuous than in any other field of jurisprudence, because it can so easily become a mere farce. By utilizing the devices of justice, politics contracts some ill-defined and spurious obligations. Circumstantial and contradictory, the linkage between politics and justice is characterized by both promise and blasphemy" (vii). On the first Nuremberg trial: "the Nuremberg trial, with all its hypocrisy and grotesqueness deriving from its very subject, does not belong very profoundly in the category of a morally and historically necessary operation" (423).

140. Howard Levie raises important questions about using trials for "reeducation" in *Terrorism in War*. "How much the trials themselves had to do with this transformation from deadly enemies to close friends and partners can only be a matter of conjecture" (8). Best, *War and Law Since 1945*, comments that "The second lesson is that not much effect is to be expected from the prospect of trial and punishment, which the aftermath of the Second World War suddenly made loom so large" (63). See also Robert Wolfe, ed., *Americans as Proconsuls: United States Military Government in Germany and Japan, 1944–1952* (Washington, D.C.: U.S. Government Printing Office, 1978), 246. Many Germans were cynical about the war crimes trials. Nuremberg prosecutor Morris Amchan recalled: "Finally, when the IMT Nuremberg verdict was announced, I walked out of my office

shortly after hearing it on the radio, headed for an elevator and met one of the German publishers we had recently licensed . . . he had just heard the announcement, he had not been down in the street yet or talked to anyone, but he already told me what the Volksmund (public opinion) was saying about the Nuremberg verdict: the three people were acquitted for the reason that Papen was going to forge the alliance for the war against the Russians, Fritsche was going to conduct the propaganda, and Schacht was going to organize the financing" (246). This essay by "Genet" was originally published in *The New Yorker* magazine. Janet Flanner picked up on the German resentment of the proceedings: "While the war was going on, the Allies had a threefold declared aim: to defeat the German Army, to bring the Nazi leaders to trial, and to re-educate the German mind. What the opening Nuremberg defense counsel have just offered is more than a mere display of Grade-B legal talent; it is an absolute first-rate demonstration of the still unreconstructed prewar German mind. The mental qualities the German defense has shown so far sound comical but are no laughing matter; egomania, mythomania, paranoia, superiority complex, and a general falling flat in those areas in which, in civilized men's minds, logic and morality have always been supreme" (57).

141. Although he praises the court's final decision, Bradley F. Smith charges the Americans with gross hypocrisy. The author's reaction to the prosecution's tone is not atypical. Smith concludes: "So the Allies lost the moral triumph over Nazism with a double-edged quid pro quo of saturation bombing and a trial. Nevertheless, the decision to have a judicial proceeding was a boon to both" (*Reaching Judgment at Nuremberg* 305). These criticisms aside, Smith concludes that the proceedings were unique and a departure from the tradition of primitive political justice: "As it was, the Allied governments and the prosecutors prevented an anarchic bloodbath, though had they been able to work their will, Nuremberg might well have been a trial pro forma. The top leaders would have been quickly condemned and the declarations of criminality against the six organizations would have been confirmed, establishing a procedure whereby hundreds of thousands of people might have been punished. This precedent of wartime leaders being punished through mass purge trials would surely have become a major obstacle to ending war once it broke out. . . . The Nuremberg court performed its real service by remedying the most dangerous defects of the Allied war crimes policy" (305). The Tusas argue that the cooperation of the IMT was impressive, despite the Soviet dissent. According to Smith, "Repeatedly, the judges emphasized to each other the vital importance of compromise in order to avoid the unpleasant appearance that would result if a judge wrote a public dissenting opinion. . . . Again, this was especially difficult for the Soviet Tribunal members . . . when a Western judge failed to win a point, it was merely a defeat for his personal interpretation, while a Russian failure may have meant that the judge had not achieved the result desired by the Soviet government. By the end of the trial, but even after a string of defeats on the organization question, he still indicated that he would not make a public dissent. The Court's actions on organizations goaded the Moscow government, though, and shamefacedly, Nikitchenko had to inform the other judges that the Soviet members would write dissenting opinions and make them public, after all" (169).

142. Friedrich, "Nuremberg and the Germans," 88. "At the conclusion of the trial of the major defendants in October 1946, OMGUS surveys indicated that 55 percent of the German population found the guilty verdicts to be just, 21 percent thought them too mild, and only nine percent found them to be harsh. Overall, 78 percent regarded the proceedings as fair" (Herf, Jeffrey. *Divided Memory: The Nazi Past in the Two Germanys*. Cambridge: Harvard University Press, 1997], 206).

143. The Tokyo Charter had not prohibited attacks against the court's legal legitimacy. Like the German lawyers at Nuremberg, "prominent Japanese lawyers, Takayanagi Kenzo and Kiyose Ichiro . . . questioned the very legitimacy of the tribunal" (Dower, *Embracing Defeat*, 462). For an overview of American war crimes policy in the Far East see Philip Piccigallo, *The Japanese on Trial* (Austin: University of Texas Press, 1979), 49–68; Appleman, *Military Tribunals and International Crimes*, 237–267. For critical views of Far Eastern policy see Richard Minear, *Victors' Justice: The Tokyo War Crimes Trial* (Princeton: Princeton University Press, 1972); Richard Lael, *The Yamashita Precedent* (Wilmington, Del.: Scholarly Resources, 1982). Lael offers the most comprehensive examination of the Yamashita case and the novel doctrine of command responsibility. Yamashita's lawyer, Frank Reel, wrote a book entitled *The Case of General Yamashita* (Chicago: University of Chicago Press, 1949); John Dower's recent book, *Embracing Defeat: Japan in the Wake of World War II* (New York: Norton, 1999), provides excellent analysis of U.S. policy in postwar Japan.

The postwar treatment of the Japanese was mentioned in the Potsdam Agreement: "We do not intend that the Japanese shall be enslaved as a race or destroyed as a nation, but stern justice shall be meted out to all war criminals, including those who have visited cruelties on our prisoners" (Dower, *Embracing Defeat*, 445). The Tokyo Charter was a series of laws modeled after the London Agreement by an executive decree of General Douglas MacArthur.

144. William Manchester, *American Caesar: Douglas MacArthur* (Boston: Little, Brown, 1978), 484.

145. Judith Shklar, *Legalism: Law, Morals and Political Trials* (Cambridge: Harvard University Press, 1964), 184. The American prosecutor seemed oblivious to the fact that the natural law tradition had no relevance for the Japanese. Keenan claimed the aggressive war charges were valid on the grounds of "the Christian-Judaic absolutes of good and evil" (184). Shklar observes: "Natural law . . . was a Western notion, meaningless to the men being tried and their fellow citizens. In any case, it cannot serve as the enforceable law of the world community because there is no world community. To enforce the 'common good' internationally is impossible, because no one, certainly not one set of nations, can be the custodian of that good" (186).

146. Nisuki Ando, Chihiro Hosoya, Richard Minear, and Yasuaki Onuma, eds., *The Tokyo War Crimes Trial: An International Symposium* (Tokyo: Kodansha, 1986), 17. Röling described Webb as "Quarrelsome at times, he embarrassed some of the judges with his court behavior" (19).

147. Appleman, *Military Tribunals and International Crimes*, 197. "The attitude of the president of the Tribunal throughout toward defense counsel was one not consistent with standards commonly observed in courts of the United States" (197).

148. Levie, *Terrorism in War*, 386.

149. Ibid., 39. See also Piccigallo, *The Japanese on Trial*, 14. The indictment in the IMTFE was hopelessly complicated. There were twenty different conspiracy counts that stretched back nearly eighteen years. For more on the IMTFE indictment, see Levie, *Terrorism in War*, 389–390.

150. Minear, *Victors' Justice*, 67.

151. Levie, *Terrorism in War*, 289.

152. Ibid., 46.

153. Piccigallo, *The Japanese on Trial*, 21–23.

154. Ibid. See also Minear, *Victors' Justice*, 50–53. If one considered the attack on Pearl Harbor a preventative war, this was consistent with Frank Briand's reading of his own treaty. Briand told Congress in 1928, "I knew that this government, at least, would never agree to submit to any tribunal the question of self-defense, and I do not think any of them [the Allied governments] would" (53).

155. Ibid., 23. See also diplomatic historian Waldo Heinrichs on U.S.-Japanese relations and the events leading up to Pearl Harbor in *Threshold of War: Franklin D. Roosevelt and American Entry into World War II* (New York: Oxford University Press, 1988).

156. Kurt Tauber, *Beyond Eagle and Swastika: German Nationalism Since 1945* (Middletown: Wesleyan University Press, 1967), 1:26. Tauber writes: "The difficulty with these agreements was that there was no vivid understanding of the tacit assumptions underlying them. The agreements clearly meant that Germans had to be punished. But was it merely, negatively, to prevent a recurrence of so tragic a chapter in Western history; or was it rather, positively, to effect *inner* changes, to re-educate the Germans to the ways of peaceful neighborliness and democratic tolerance?"

157. Levie, *Terrorism in War*, 133.

158. Ibid., 179–180.

159. Lael, *The Yamashita Precedent*, 79–95. Lael offers the most comprehensive examination of the Yamashita case and the novel doctrine of command responsibility. For a less temperate view see Manchester, *American Caesar*, 486.

160. Ibid.

161. Lawrence Taylor, *A Trial of Generals: Homma, Yamashita, MacArthur* (South Bend, Ind.: Icarus, 1981), 163.

162. Manchester, *American Caesar*, 487. George Marshall warned MacArthur and his staff "that there was no precedent here for charging a Field Commander with the negligence of duty in controlling his troops" (Manchester, *American Caesar*, 487). See also Levie, *Terrorism in War*, 157.

163. Reel, *The Case of General Yamashita*, 27. See also Levie, *Terrorism in War* for a significantly less sympathetic account.

164. Reel, *The Case of General Yamashita*, 157.

165. Taylor, *A Trial of Generals*, 137. General MacArthur considered the rules of evidence "obstructionist." Article 13 of his "Special Proclamation" stated: "The Tribunal shall not be bound by technical rules of evidence. It shall adopt and apply to the greatest possible extent expeditious and non-technical procedure, and shall admit any evidence which it deems to have probative value" (137).

166. Ibid.

167. Manchester, *American Caesar*, 487.

168. Reel, *The Case of General Yamashita*, 142.

169. Piccigallo, *The Japanese on Trial*, 53–54. See also Taylor, *A Trial of Generals*, 168.

170. Piccigallo, *The Japanese on Trial*, 53–54; see also Taylor, *A Trial of Generals*, 168.

171. Ibid., 162–163.

172. Reel, *The Case of General Yamashita*, 173.

173. Howard Levie describes the professional military's continuing reluctance to reject the doctrine of superior orders in *Terrorism in War*. Over the last fifteen years, Levie has taught the laws of war to approximately 750 officers at the U.S. Naval War College in Newport, Rhode Island; according to Levie, "it would be a liberal estimate to say that half a dozen have supported the idea of denying the validity of the defense of superior orders" (521). General Lucius Clay made a similar point in his oral history at Columbia University: "I've spent most of my life as a soldier, and I could not honestly tell you today, in my own mind, when I could make a distinction between refusing to obey an order because I decided it was not a legal order and, or obeying it because I was a soldier" (568).

174. Manchester, *American Caesar*, 488. Manchester traces MacArthur's view of war back to more chivalrous times: "To him warfare would always be tinged with the romantic tones of Arthurian legend with the magic nimbus of the round table, and he believed that Shinto, Bushido, and the samurai code were extensions of it. In his view, therefore, these two Japanese commanders had betrayed, not just Dai Nippon, nor even Manila's violated Filipinos, but MacArthur's own profession" (488). See also Piccigallo, *The Japanese on Trial*, 53–54; Taylor, *Trial of the Generals*, 168.

175. MacArthur was ordered by the Secretary of War to issue a stay of execution while the Supreme Court reviewed the case.

176. Lael, *The Yamashita Precedent*, 105. According to Chief Justice Stone, the Quirin decision "demonstrated that Congress by passing the articles of war, had recognized and sanctioned the use of military tribunals to try war criminals." Stone went on to claim that the military tribunals were "not courts whose rulings and judgments are subject to review by this court." This limited the Supreme Court to two questions: "Did the government have the right to detain Yamashita for trial? Did the military tribunals have lawful authority in this instance to try to condemn him?" Although Stone privately opposed the war crimes proceedings, he was an advocate of judicial restraint and feared that meddling in the Yamashita case might lead to "unnecessary and unwise judicial interference with the other branches of government" (105). He was

bolstered by Justice Frankfurter. For more on Stone's philosophy see Alpheus Mason, *Harlan Fiske Stone: Pillar of the Law* (New York: Viking, 1956) and C. Herman Pritchett, *The Roosevelt Court: A Study in Judicial Politics and Values, 1937–1947* (New York: Macmillan, 1948).

177. Lael, *The Yamashita Precedent*, 105.

178. Ibid. Both dissenters were outraged by the military commission's inability "to demonstrate that Yamashita had committed or ordered the commission of war crimes." Rutledge pointed out: "It is not in our tradition for anyone to be charged with crime which is defined after his conduct . . . has taken place. . . . Mass guilt we do not impute to individuals, perhaps in any case but certainly in none where the person is not charged or shown actively to have participated in or knowingly to have failed in taking action to prevent the wrongs done by others, having both the duty and power to do so" (105).

179. Ibid. Richard Lael claims, "Murphy's jabs at the military may have been influenced to some small degree by his dislike for MacArthur. When Murphy became high commissioner for the Philippines in the 1930s, he and MacArthur frequently clashed" (*The Yamashita Precedent* [Wilmington, Del.: Scholarly Resources, 1982], 130). For more on Murphy see J. Woodford Howard Jr., *Mr. Justice Murphy: A Political Biography* (Princeton: Princeton University Press, 1968).

180. Manchester, *American Caesar*, 487. For a differing view on the Yamashita case see Gary Solis, "Yamashita Had It Coming," *Proceedings of "Accounting for Atrocities: Prosecuting War Crimes Fifty Years After Nuremberg," October 5–6, 1998* (Annandale-on-Hudson, N.Y.: Bard College Publications, 2000), 37–49.

181. Dower, *Embracing Defeat*, 516; Levie, *Terrorism in War*, 164.

182. Robert Edgerton, *Warriors of the Rising Sun* (New York: Norton, 1997), 14. See also John Dower, *War Without Mercy* (New York: Pantheon, 1986); Yuki Tanaka, *Hidden Horrors: Japanese War Crimes in World War II* (Boulder: Westview, 1996); Iris Chang, *The Rape of Nanking* (New York: Basic, 1997); for a prisoner's account see Gavan Daws, *Prisoners of the Japanese* (New York: Morrow, 1994).

183. Chang, *The Rape of Nanking*, 4–5. Chang estimates the numbers killed in Nanking in the late months of 1937 and into early 1938 ranging between 260,000 and 350,000. This was more civilians than Britain (61,000), France (108,000), and the Netherlands (242,000) lost during the entire war. See also Howard French, "Japanese Call '37 Massacre a War Myth, Stirring Storm," *New York Times*, January 23, 2000.

184. Sheldon Harris, *Factories of Death: Japanese Biological Warfare 1932–45 and the American Cover-Up* (London: Routledge, 1994), 149, 205.

185. Piccigallo, *The Japanese on Trial*, 16; Dower, *Embracing Defeat*, 465; Hal Gold, *Unit 731: Testimony* (Tokyo: Yen Books, 1996), 96.

According to Hal Gold, the men of Unit 731 did their best to destroy their facilities and were able to return to Japan before the Russians could capture them (92–93). When the ship carrying the American biological warfare expert landed in Japan, he was greeted by Naito Ryoichi, a high-ranking member of Unit 731. He offered to broker a trade: Unit 731's research data for immunity from war crimes prosecution. Murray Sanders described meeting Dr. Naito: "My mission was biological warfare. I was to find what the Japanese had done, and when the *Sturgess* docked in Yokohama, there was Dr. Naito. He came straight toward me. . . . I didn't even know what 731 was" (95). Sanders described his first impression of research data provided by Dr. Naito: "It was fundamentally dynamite. The manuscript said, in essence, that the Japanese were involved in biological warfare" (96).

Lieutenant Colonel Sanders took the material to General Douglas MacArthur, the Supreme Commander for Allied Powers. General MacArthur granted Sanders permission to offer the men of Unit 731 a deal—if they surrendered all of their research data, they would be immune from war crimes prosecution. According to Sanders, "This made a deep impression, and the data came in waves after that . . . we could hardly keep up with it" (97). According to Hal Gold and new documents published in a spring 1995 Japanese magazine article entitled, "The Report on Japan's War Responsibility," "This shows that the proposal—made with the involvement of the American president—to grant immunity from war crimes was already on the table less than two months after the war's end" (99).

However, Germany was not the only place where the Cold War caused dramatic changes in the American treatment of fallen foes. In 1948, America shifted away from a punitive policy and adopted one that sought to ally Japan with the West. Just as with Germany, George Kennan was pushing for normalization of relations. The new policy, NSC-13/2, was written by Kennan. According to Awaya Kentaro, professor of history at Rikyyo University, morality proved to be no match for strategy. Kentaro writes: "At the time of the Tokyo trial, the Soviet Union vigorously demanded the investigation of Ishii [commander] and his staff. GHQ did not respond to these demands. It is said that Ishii and others escaped prosecution by turning over to the United States the data on their experiments and their use of germ and chemical warfare in the field. . . . Moreover, behind the immunity granted Unit 731, I detect the national self-interest of the United States, which was willing to grant immunity to criminals in order to secure a monopoly on the most up-to-date information concerning techniques of warfare" (Richard H. Minear, *Victor's Justice: The Tokyo War Crimes Trial* [Princeton: Princeton University Press, 1971], 85–86).

Levie, *Terrorism in War*, 155. Howard Levie rejects the contention that the IMTFE purposely excluded the Japanese biological warfare specialists from prosecution. However, a great deal of new material has been recently published proving otherwise. Years after the trial, Judge Röling charged: "The American military authorites wanted to avail themselves of the results of the experiments, criminally obtained in Japan, and at the same time prevent them from falling into the hands of the Soviet Union" (4). See also John Dower, *Embracing Defeat* and Hal Gold, *Unit 731*.

186. Manchester, *American Caesar*, 488.

187. Ibid., 488. MacArthur's commission was closer to military custom than either of the international tribunals, or as the prosecution described it, "retail justice for wholesale slaughter" (101).

188. Weingartner, *Crossroads of Death*, 75. Weingartner describes the stories: "Again results were meager, a suspiciously large number of men claimed the killings had been ordered by SS Sturmbannführer Walter Pringel, commander of the First Battalion, First Panzer Regiment, who had not survived the war" (75).

189. Ibid.

190. Army Command War Crimes Branch, Cases Tried, General Administration Files, RG 338. National Archives Modern Military Branch, Suitland, Maryland).

191. Ibid.

192. Weingartner, *Crossroads of Death*, 118.

193. Ibid., 104. According to one of Peiper's men, the commander said: "We will fight in the same manner as we did in Russia in the action which will follow" (84). The commander's next statement supports the contention that the rules of war only applied in the West: "The certain rules which have applied in the West until now will be omitted" (84). In his company's prebattle pep talk, Pringel gave similar orders, urging his men to "fight in the old SS spirit . . . I am not giving you any orders to shoot prisoners of war, but you are well-trained SS soldiers. You know what you should do with prisoners without my telling you that" (84). Telford Taylor and many others also make the point that the Wehrmacht fought a more restrained war in the West and disregarded the laws of war in the East (interview by author, 1993).

194. Weingartner, *Crossroads of Death*, 81.

195. Ibid., 89. These were Pringel's orders to Peiper.

196. Weingartner, *Crossroads of Death*, 95–96.

197. Ibid., 98. In regard to evidence, the court was very much like MacArthur's military commission: "no evidence no matter how tenuous was to be excluded if in the opinion of the bench, it had a bearing on the case. The bench was also free to exclude any evidence it considered to be irrelevant" (98).

198. Senate Subcommittee of the Committee on Armed Services, *Investigation of Army Action with Respect to Trial of Persons Responsible for the Massacre of American Soldiers, the Battle of the Bulge, near Malmedy, Belgium, December, 1944* (Washington, D.C.: U.S. Government Printing Office), 1012.

199. Ibid.

200. Weingartner, *Crossroads of Death*, 116. Many of these interrogations were conducted by Austrian-born Jewish lawyer Lieutenant William Perl. It should be mentioned that this trial occurred in 1945, when wartime passions had not yet cooled. The prosecution employed various psychological ploys to get confessions. One German soldier committed suicide, and Perl admitted having threatened to turn him over to the Belgians. Once this became known to the German public, many turned against any and all war crimes proceedings, in the name of upholding the violated civil rights of the German war criminals.

201. Ibid.

202. Ibid.

203. Ibid.

204. Ibid., 130.

205. Ibid., 137.

206. Ibid., 133. A number of the American military men respected and sympathized with Peiper. McCowan claimed, "I have met few men who impressed me in as short a space of time as the German officer" (127).

207. Ibid., 185–187.

208. Ibid., 187.

4. A Shift in Priorities

1. John McCloy, "From Military Government to Self-Government," in Robert Wolfe, ed., *Americans as Proconsuls: United States Military Government in Germany and Japan, 1944–1952* (Carbondale: Southern Illinois University Press, 1984). Assistant Secretary of War McCloy described JCS 1067 as "rather Draconian . . . not as bad as the Morgenthau Plan—but it was pretty negative" (119). The always extreme J.F.C. Fuller on JCS 1067 in *The Conduct of War*: "No steps were taken toward the economic rehabilitation of Germany. And no action that would tend to support the basic living standard in Germany on a higher level than that existing in any one of the neighboring countries was to be taken. In short, Germany was to be converted into a super concentration camp" (306). John Montgomery called the reeducation program an "artificial revolution" because it was not a German initiative. Buscher convincingly argues that the German objection to the program had roots stretching back to the war guilt clause in the Treaty of Versailles: "The historian Hajo Holborn was sent to Germany in 1947, and reported that some Germans he encountered—according to Holborn, predominantly simple and non-intellectual people—were ashamed of their country's wartime deeds. Almost everyone rejected the concept of collective guilt" (109).

2. John Mendelson, "War Crimes Trials and Clemency in Japan and Germany," in Wolfe, ed., *Americans as Proconsuls*, 261. The most comprehensive monograph on America's war crimes policy is Frank Buscher's *The U.S. War Crimes Trial Program in Germany* (Westport, Conn.: Greenwood, 1989) (see 31). Carl Anthony, "Reeducation for Democracy," in Wolfe, ed., *Americans as Proconsuls*, 262. Even Friedrich Meinecke wrote of the need for German reeducation: "So far as the victors try to eradicate National Socialist influences and thereby provide the atmosphere for Christian Occidental sound morals, we must not only recognize that they are fundamentally right but must ourselves help them and try to prevent them only from schematic exaggerations and mistakes" (*The German Catastrophe* [Boston: Beacon, 1950], 104).

3. Buscher, *The U.S. War Crimes Trial Program*, 8–9. For a more comprehensive account of the trial's objectives, see Bradley F. Smith, *The Road to Nuremberg* (New York: Basic, 1981).

4. Howard Levie, *Terrorism in War: The Law of War Crimes* (Dobbs Ferry, N.Y.: Oceana, 1993), 126.

5. Elmer Plischke, "Denazification in Germany," in Wolfe, ed., *Americans as Proconsuls*, 199.

According to Kurt Tauber, "Most serious of all, the very excesses of de-nazification procedure not only unjustly discredited the entire idea in the eyes of a large segment of the population but also created a climate of opinion which the Nazis could use for their own purposes" (*Beyond Eagle and Swastika: German Nationalism Since 1945* [Middletown, Conn.: Wesleyan University Press, 1967], 245).

6. Friedrich, "Nuremberg and the Germans," in Belinda Cooper, ed., *War Crimes: The Legacy of Nuremberg* (New York: TV Books, 1999), 90.

7. Plischke, "Denazification in Germany," 216–217.

8. Hans Schmitt, ed., *U.S. Occupation of Europe After World War II* (Lawrence: Regents Press of Kansas, 1978), 93. Thomas H. Etzold and John Lewis Gaddis, eds., *Containment: Documents on American Policy and Strategy, 1945–1950* (New York: Columbia University Press, 1979).

9. This was a residual effect of the Morgenthau Plan, but the perception was based more on fantasy than fact. However, there were enough Jewish war crimes officials (prosecutors, interrogators, translators, etc.) to provide a germ of truth. There is no evidence to support the contention that these individuals were vindictive in accordance with American policy. If anything, as Peter Grose points out, U.S. policy was moving in a different direction:

"As Major General Stephen J. Chamberlin, director of army intelligence in Washington, informed Eisenhower, 'valuable intelligence on Russia and Russian dominated countries can be developed more rapidly by this method than other.' In the less formal language of an American staff officer in Frankfurt, speaking to journalist John Gunther, 'Are we dealing with our former enemies, or our future allies? We have not yet decided whether we want to win the last war or the next one" (Peter Grose, *Operation Rollback* [New York: Houghton Mifflin, 2000], 25).

10. Schmitt, *U.S. Occupation of Europe*, 35.

11. Columbia University Oral History Project, Benjamin Buttenweiser, 1:28, 2:201. The former Assistant High Commissioner stressed, "our primary goal was to get Germany 'on its feet' as soon as possible" (31). Tauber, *Beyond Eagle and Swastika*, 36. Due to the American mishandling of denazification, "Many . . . seemingly unjustly treated by a badly floundering administration of the law, withdrew in sullen resentment, a ready audience for the irresponsible demagogy of unreconstructed Nazi leaders" (36). Etzold and Gaddis, eds., *Containment*, 118–119. The Policy Planning Staff made the observation in the February 24, 1948 "Review of Current Trends."

12. Louis Snyder, *The Roots of German Nationalism* (Bloomington: Indiana University Press, 1978), 175. Although Snyder is referring to the German reaction to the Treaty of Versailles, this background knowledge is key to understanding the post–World War II nationalists' attitudes toward war crimes. "The old Germany was suffering on the cross while the terrible punishment of Bolshevism hovered over the world as the Divine vengeance for the Victors. Here was the added feature of the myth—the initial suggestion that the Allies never understood that Germany was the vital bulwark against Bolshevik expansionism" (175). This would be the theme of an increasing number of German critiques in the years after World War II. Many Nazis felt vindicated by the turn of events.

13. Robert Jackson, letter to President Harry Truman, 4 December 1945. From

Telford Taylor, *Final Report to the Secretary of the Army on the Nuernberg War Crimes Trials Under Control Council Law No. 10* (Washington, D.C.: United States Government Printing Office, 1949), 262–263.

14. Lucius Clay, *Decision in Germany* (New York: Doubleday, 1950), 251.

15. All of the military directives are contained in the introductory sections of all of the volumes of the Green Series.

16. Jean Smith, ed., *The Papers of General Lucius Clay* (Bloomington: Indiana University Press, 1974), 658. For more on Clay and clemency see Columbia University Oral History Project, Lucius Clay.

17. Jean Smith, *Lucius D. Clay: An American Life* (New York: Holt, 1990), 308. Clay stood firmly behind the trials at several key points. Taylor was impressed: "He would listen and decide quickly and firmly. I liked him. I thought he was a fine commanding officer and I had very high regard for him" (251). Taylor said that General Clay was "Just about the best boss I ever had." Clay recalled, "It was resolved that we would proceed in the United States Zone under Military Government, and Justice Jackson's able young assistant, General Telford Taylor, was persuaded to head the prosecution staff" (251).

18. Telford Taylor, "An Approach to the preparation of the prosecution of Axis Criminality," early June 1945, in Smith, ed., *The American Road to Nuremberg*, 209. Smith praises Taylor's contribution: "Jackson and his staff had also raised the level of legal draughtsmanship, and the new executive agreement was more tightly and precisely composed than any of its predecessors. In addition, among the new faces brought in by the justice were such men as Colonel Telford Taylor, who, although they did not play a part in this drafting, would soon leave their mark by asking tough, direct questions" (142).

19. Many military men were offended by the preponderance of high-ranking, Harvard-educated lawyers at Nuremberg. Tom Bower observes: "But control of the operation was firmly—too firmly some said afterwards—in the hands of a Harvard law school mafia. . . . They diligently tried to covert a group of undistinguished and conservative American judges to a radical theory: that educated, respected and otherwise normal businessmen could be guilty of murder" (*Blind Eye to Murder: Britain, America and the Purging of Nazi Germany—A Pledge Betrayed* [London: Andre Deutsch, 1981], 256).

20. Robert Kempner, interview by author, tape recording, Locarno, Switzerland, 23 February 1988.

21. Ibid. Otto Kranzbühler described Robert Kempner to this author: "He was a divided personality, he really felt as a German, he loved Germany. He was full of hate for Hitler and those who did not allow him to love his country. I had a very good relationship with the opposite points of view. He asked me to defend Hitler's adjunct . . . in a denazification trial. [He] was one of Kempner's proteges and he wanted him to come free—typical Kempner, some people he really helped" (interview with author). Bower, *Blind Eye to Murder*, 278–279.

22. Bower, *Blind Eye to Murder*, 278–279. Some in the prosecution staff (Taylor and Sprecher) worked for New Deal agencies. Former congressman from Indiana Charles LaFollette served as a prosecutor in the Justice case. One can safely assume that the vast majority of the prosecutors were sympathetic to the prosecution's broadened conception of international law.

23. Taylor, *Final Report to the Secretary of the Army on the Nuernberg War Crimes Trials*, 164.

24. Clay, *Decision in Germany*, 251.

25. Ann and John Tusa, *The Nuremberg Trial* (New York: Atheneum, 1984), 69. Julius Stone did not consider international society to be anything like domestic society.

26. Joseph Borkin, *The Crime and Punishment of I. G. Farben* (New York: Free Press, 1978), 139.

27. Robert Conot, *Justice at Nuremberg* (New York: Carroll and Graf, 1983), 517. Other second-generation critics included William Langer, Francis Case, Harold Knutsen, and John Taber. See George F. Kennan, *Memoirs 1925–1950* (Boston: Atlantic Monthly, 1967), 260. The movement away from a vindictive policy also occurred in Japan and also was led by Kennan. Philip Piccigallo observes in *The Japanese on Trial: Allied War Crimes Operations in the East, 1945–1951* (Austin: University of Texas Press, 1979): "United States authorities, in accordance with Kennan's advice, recognized the need to stabilize Japan, politically and economically, and to 'win' that nation to its side in the Cold War" (46). Unlike the Nuremberg trials, which he and other realists like Hans Morgenthau criticized, Kennan made a point of praising the "fairness" of the military commissions in the Far East (46).

28. Kennan, *Memoirs 1925–1950*, 260. Gaddis describes the impact of the Long Telegram: "This 8,000-word telegram from George Kennan probably did more than any other single document to influence the evolution of early postwar United States' foreign policy. The 'long telegram' was both an analysis of Soviet behavior and a prescription for American action. In it, Kennan advanced the now famous argument that Soviet hostility sprang from nothing the West had done, but from the need Russian leaders felt for a hostile outside world as a means of justifying their own autocratic rule" (50).

29. Ibid.

30. Ibid.

31. Ibid.

32. Ibid.

33. Ibid.

34. Christopher Simpson, *The Splendid Blond Beast: Money, Law, and Genocide in the Twentieth Century* (New York: Grove, 1993), 98.

35. Kennan, *Memoirs 1925–1950*, 260.

36. Christopher Simpson, *Blowback: America's Recruitment of Nazis and Its Effects on the Cold War* (New York: Weidenfield and Nicolson, 1988), 41. For a self-serving but highly entertaining first-hand account see Reinhard Gehlen, *The Service* (New York: World

Publishing, 1972). The best study in English is Mary Ellen Reese's *General Reinhard Gehlen* (Fairfax, Va.: George Mason University Press, 1990), 8–9. Gehlen and the captured Germans were interrogated by Captain John Bokor: "During the weeks following Bokor's new assignment Gehlen gradually laid his cards on the table. Not only did he know where the precious archives were buried, but he had also maintained the embryo of an underground espionage operation that could put the records to use against the Soviet Union" (*General Reinhard Gehlen* 41). Bokor kept the details of Gehlen's offer and managed to get his top generals off the Allied war criminal lists. The captain was operating on his own in violation of the Yalta accords, which required the United States to hand over Germans involved in the eastern front.

37. Simpson, *Blowback*, 42. See also Reese, *General Reinhard Gehlen*, 32. The OSS was tipped off about the existence of the microfilm and was soon jockeying for control of the spymaster and his records. According to Simpson, "Gehlen and seven of his senior officers were transferred to the camp [Camp King], where they were constituted as a 'historical study group,' supposedly working on a report on the German general staff. Gehlen's precious cache of records was located and shipped to the interrogation center under such secrecy that not even the CIC's chain of command was informed" (*Blowback* 53). According to Lieutenant Colonel John Bokor, son of the captain: "Nobody had legalized, really, the functions of intelligence in those days. Today maybe things have changed, but back then the intelligence agent was on his own. . . . There wasn't any sheet music for us to sing from in those days. That's how a lot of those guys [former Nazis] got hired" (53).

38. Ibid. The American espionage chief commented on the lack of information: "Even the most elementary facts were unavailable—on roads and bridges, on the location and production of factories, on city plans and airfields." Rositzke credits Gehlen with playing a "primary role" in providing the Americans with this basic information. See also Reese, *General Reinhard Gehlen*, 142.

39. According to Simpson, *Blowback*, Gehlen convinced American officials that war with the Soviet Union was not just possible but imminent. Eventually Bokor won the support of Walter Bedell Smith and Edwin Siebert. Gehlen would soon play a disproportionately large role in shaping American perceptions of the Soviet Union.

40. Martin Lee, *The Beast Reawakens* (New York: Little, Brown, 1997), 30.

41. Reese, *General Reinhard Gehlen*, 69. Reese places the absorption of the Nazi intelligence operation (*Fremde Heere Ost*) into context: "As the Soviets provoked more hostile incidents (what Anthony Cave Brown calls 'flourishes'), and as the Americans began to appreciate how little they understood Soviet intentions and capabilities, Gehlen's confidence began to revive. And with good reason, information about the new adversary was at a premium, and compared with many former Nazis being used by Army Intelligence, Gehlen looked benign as well as smart."

42. The trials were not held one at a time; several were conducted simultaneously. Drexel Sprecher, interview by author, tape recording, Chevy Chase, Maryland, 29 May 1987.

43. Smith, ed., *The Papers of General Lucius Clay*, 252. At the time the Military Gov-

ernor supported the war crimes trials: "In 1947, I urged the Department of the Army to permit the Foreign Ministry, Military Command and Krupp cases to be brought to trial before the program was discontinued, and to find additional judges for the requisite courts. This was approved with the understanding that no further cases would be considered. I was unable to meet my commitment of July 1948 for completion because defense counsel had to be given as much time as it desired to prepare its evidence."

44. Taylor, *Final Report to the Secretary of the Army on the Nuernberg War Crimes Trials*, 118.

45. Ibid., 164.

46. Articles 4 through 20 of the 1907 Hague Conventions specifically prohibit far less extreme types of POW mistreatment. Medical experiments on humans had been outlawed as early as 1907.

47. Taylor, *Final Report to the Secretary of the Army on the Nuernberg War Crimes Trials*, 164. Adam Roberts and Richard Guelff, eds., *Documents on the Laws of War* (New York: Oxford University Press, 1989), 48–49. Article 4 of the 1907 Hague Agreement's Annex to the Convention states: "Prisoners of war are in the power of the hostile Government, but not of the individuals or corps who capture them. They must be humanely treated." Article 6 is more specific: "The State may utilize the labor of prisoners of war according to their rank and aptitude, officers excepted. The tasks shall not be excessive and shall have no connection with the operations of the war."

48. Walter Beals, *The First German War Crimes Trial* (Chapel Hill: Documentary Publications, 1985), 141–185. This book provides a one-page biography of each defendant.

49. Appleman, *Military Tribunals and International Crimes*, 146.

50. Taylor, *Final Report to the Secretary of the Army on the Nuernberg War Crimes Trials*, 177. For the scientific standards see Appleman, *Military Tribunals and International Crimes*, 147–148. See also Robert J. Lifton, *The Nazi Doctors* (New York: Basic, 1983) and Michael Kater, *Doctors Under Hitler* (Chapel Hill: University of North Carolina Press, 1989).

51. Taylor, *Final Report to the Secretary of the Army on the Nuernberg War Crimes Trials*, 118.

52. John Alan Appleman, *Military Tribunals and International Crimes* (Westport, Conn.: Greenwood, 1971), 158 and Taylor, *Final Report to the Secretary of the Army on the Nuernberg War Crimes Trials*, 155. See also *U.S. Military Tribunal Nuremberg, Transcript, Case II, Milch*, 2258.

53. Appleman, *Military Tribunals and International Crimes* provides an extensive discussion of "the Nuremberg defense": "Defense counsel frequently brought out this testimony, in their arguments, that the individual defendants had no choice but to perform the acts charged against them. Particularly in a dictatorship . . . there was but one leader, the rest were followers. They raised the question, with reference to subordinates, of the legal defense of respondeat superior—or, let the master answer, rather

than the servant; and, in the case of those in command, of the doctrine of Act of State—or, in other words, the act of the leader is the act of the sovereign, and the State should answer instead of the individual" (54).

54. Ibid., 147–148.

55. Taylor, *Final Report to the Secretary of the Army on the Nuernberg War Crimes Trials*, 118.

56. Ibid., 175.

57. Ibid., 176–177.

58. Levie, *Terrorism in War*, 301.

59. Appleman, *Military Tribunals and International Crimes*, 167. The quote is from Taylor's *Final Report to the Secretary of the Army on the Nuernberg War Crimes Trials*, 177.

60. None of the defendants was found guilty of aggression or conspiracy. The vast majority of the convictions were for "war crimes" or traditional violations of the codes of war and the broadened conception of "crimes against humanity." Roberts and Guelff, eds., *Documents on the Laws of War*, 48–49.

61. Ingo Müller, *Hitler's Justice*, trans. Deborah Lucas Schneider (Cambridge: Harvard University Press, 1991), 270–271. Müller describes the unintended results of the deaths: "Precisely because the men on trial were not fanatical National Socialists, the ordinary workings of the judicial system during the Third Reich were exposed to view, and it became clear to what extent the largely conservative legal profession and its symbolic figurehead, Schlegelberger, had been profoundly involved in the reign of terror" (271). U.S. Government, *Trials of the German War Criminals Before the Nuernberg Military Tribunals Under Control Council No. 10*, Vols 1–15 (Washington, D.C.: U.S. Government Printing Office, 1949), 966.

62. Taylor, *Final Report to the Secretary of the Army on the Nuernberg War Crimes Trials*, 169.

63. Appleman, *Military Tribunals and International Crimes*, 158.

64. American Nuremberg Trials, *Case 3—United States v. Josef Altstoetter et al.*, 1167.

65. Taylor, *Final Report to the Secretary of the Army on the Nuernberg War Crimes Trials*, 173.

66. Ibid.

67. *U.S. Military Tribunal Nuremberg, Transcript, Case III, Altstoetter* (Nuremberg: Secretariat for Military Tribunals, 1949), 10793–94.

68. Ibid., 966.

69. Taylor, *Final Report to the Secretary of the Army on the Nuernberg War Crimes Trials*, 173–174.

70. Robert Maguire, letter to family, 21 October 1947, Constance Maguire Wilson Papers, Eureka, California (in possession of the author). When the War Department contacted him, there was little doubt as to his decision. He wrote: "Well my dear I have some rather interesting and tremendous news. Last night when I got up to my room there was notice that a long distance call from Washington had come. . . . They finally located the officer who wanted me at his home. He said that General Clay in Germany had cabled asking for my appointment as one of the Judges of the Nurem-

berg Court. . . . My present feeling is to accept if they feel that I can be spared for that period of time. It is an opportunity that comes once in a lifetime. . . . If we go we would have to be in Nuremberg by Oct. 30 or Nov. 30, if we couldn't make the first court" (1). Maguire provided his family with a running commentary on his experiences at Nuremberg. His letters begin in the fall of 1947 and end in December 1948. While he was writing the tribunal opinion, his wife, Ruth, continued the correspondence until their departure in the spring of 1949.

71. Ibid.

72. Ibid., 1. Robert Maguire made numerous reference to the destruction that surrounded him.

73. Ibid., 2.

74. Ibid.

75. Robert Maguire, letter to family, 24 February 1948, Constance Maguire Wilson Papers, 1. The judge described the case and the early courtroom activities: "We have been engaged in analyzing and condensing the indictment which is 75 pages in length relating to 21 defendants, and in making up a classified chart, following each defendant through the mazes of the indictment, and referring to each page on which any of his activities are mentioned, some job." *U.S. Military Tribunal Nuremberg, Transcript, Case XI, Weizsaecker* (Nuremberg: Secretariat for Military Tribunals, 1949), 1:1.

76. Robert Jackson, quoted in Michael Luders, "The Strange Case of Ernst von Weizsaecker," M.A. thesis, Columbia University, 1988, 7. Luders's study was extremely helpful in outlining the defense arguments in the von Weizsäcker case.

77. Ibid.

78. U.S. Government, *Trials of the German War Criminals Before the Nuernberg Military Tribunals Under Control Council No. 10*, Vols 1–15 (Washington, D.C.: U.S. Government Printing Office, 1949), 12:139. Taylor claimed: "The German diplomats of aggression, however, wore the mantle of diplomacy to cloak their nefarious policies which were solely directed toward the realization of the criminal aims of the Third Reich" (148). See also *The New York Times*, January 7, 1948, 10, col. 5. In late February 1948, Robert Maguire met with Professor Weber to discuss the German view of the trial and the role of the government bureaucracy under a dictatorship. Maguire wrote: "Sunday afternoon I went over to call on a Prof. von Eckardt, who holds the chair of sociology and journalism. . . . I wanted to learn from him what the liberals thought of the present situation, what they thought of what we were doing, and what they thought could be done. After expressing his views, he suggested we go see Prof Weber, who, he said was Germany's leading Economist. We did and found a charming, humorous old man past 75, seated in a study whose walls were lined with books and papers, and we talked for over an hour" (Robert Maguire, letter to family, 21 December 1947, Constance Maguire Wilson Papers, 2).

79. Levie, *Terrorism in War*, 386. My student at Columbia University, Greg Lembrich, also pointed this fact out in his paper on the Ernst von Weizsäcker case.

80. Richard von Weizsäcker, *From Weimar to the Wall*, trans. Ruth Hein (New York: Broadway Books, 1999), 92.

81. American Nuremberg Trials, *Case 11—United States v. Ernst von Weizsaecker*, 12:150.

82. William Seabury, *Wilhelmstrasse: A Study of German Diplomats Under the Nazi Regime* (Berkeley: University of California Press, 1954), 14. From Luders, "The Strange Case of Ernst von Weizsaecker," 32. Fritz Stern, *The Politics of Cultural Despair: A Study in the Rise of Germanic Ideology* (Berkeley: University of California Press, 1974). "Even before 1933, the National Socialists had made deep inroads into the ranks of the German elites. Hitler knew how to cultivate their vulnerabilities, how to reassure the elites that he was a German nationalist, the true redeemer" (165).

83. See Buruma, *The Wages of Guilt*, 175.

84. American Nuremberg Trials, *Case 11—United States v. Ernst von Weizsaecker*, 12:151.

85. Ibid., 156–157.

86. Ibid. 157, 160.

87. Ibid., 221.

88. Ibid., 150, 154, 158–160.

89. Ibid., 140–141. The prosecution argued that "Members of the Reich Chancellory were responsible for informing the Fuehrer and Reich Chancellor about current questions of policy and prepare directives" (141). The Tusas have described Hans Lammers's performance in the IMT: "His very appearance might have weighed against his evidence, but then under cross-examination the authoritative, contemptuous bureaucrat gave way. He was so desperate to save himself that he shoveled blame onto Hitler and Bormann—all the time failing to notice or even not caring that every word backed up prosecution charges of criminal policies" (*The Nuremberg Trial* 312).

90. Ibid., 199. Other headlines included FIRING ON ETHNIC GERMANS BY RURAL POLICE.

91. Ibid., 200, 202. *U.S. Military Tribunal Nuremberg, Transcript, Case XI, Weizsaecker*, 28244.

92. Ibid., 193–194. Richard Walter Darré's National Socialist zealotry attracted Hitler in 1930. Darré described the German peasantry as "the Life Spring of the Nordic Race" (194). In 1939 Darré described his prewar objective: "the whole work of agrarian policy since the seizure of power was . . . dominated by the preparation for a possible war" (194).

93. Ibid., 194.

94. Ibid., 205. Stuckart was responsible for the civil administration of Germany's conquered territories. The prosecution contended that "Stuckart looms into prominence in the incorporation of conquered territories into the Third Reich. He headed the central offices for the civil administration of Austria, Sudetenland, Bohemia and Moravia, Alsace-Lorraine, Luxembourg, Norway and the occupied southern territories" (205).

95. *U.S. Military Tribunal Nuremberg, Transcript, Case XI, Weizsaecker*, 28222. Funk made this statement on October 14, 1939. David Kaiser describes the Four-Year Plan in *Politics and War* (Cambridge: Harvard University Press, 1990). In 1936, "Hitler . . .

absolutely refused to slow down rearmament and entrusted Goering with the task of of preparing the German economy and German Army for war in four years. He rejected both a return to the world economy and the satisfaction of Germany's colonial demands by peaceful means. He was proud of having freed Germany, as he saw it, from dependence upon export markets. . . . The Four-Year Plan concentrated upon expanding heavy industrial capacity and developing synthetic substitutes for two critical imported raw materials, oil and rubber. To achieve these goals, Goering rapidly increased state ownership of the economy and reserved the Maximum possible foreign exchange for imports of raw materials" (373).

96. Ibid., 142, 172, 179. Paul Koerner met Hermann Goering in 1926; four years later he went to work in the Offices of the Four-Year Plan, where he also met and aided Heinrich Himmler. In 1936, when the Office of the Four-Year Plan took control of the German economy, Koerner was named State Secretary for the Four-Year Plan.

97. Ibid., 169. See also Tusa, *The Nuremberg Trial*, 272. "Koerner, once State Secretary in the Prussian Ministry, also pressed the line that everyone had seen, heard and spoken no evil, even arguing that since Germany had built up agricultural production in countries she occupied, she had a right to take a little of the 'surplus.' As Dean said in a cable to the Foreign Office that evening, both Koerner and Brauchitsch had 'made a very bad impression' and were too obviously lying."

98. Ibid., 187. The bankers were involved in the intimate details of concentration camp construction and liquidation of confiscated property like gold and glasses. Defendant Rasche played such a prominent role in the rearmament that he earned himself a jingle: "Who marches behind the leading tank? It is Dr. Rasche of the Dresdner Bank."

99. Ibid., 176, 208–210. Schwerin von Krosigk was designated a political heir in Hitler's will. He was Minister of Finance until the fall of the Reich; he was in charge of collecting a one-billion-RM loan and storing concentration camp loot.

100. Ibid., 192.

101. *U.S. Military Tribunal Nuremberg, Transcript, Case XI, Weizsaecker*, 28291–92., 12: 176–177, 193. Puhl attempted to shift the onus of guilt to Funk when he testified before the IMT: " 'Funk told me that he had arranged with Reichsführer Himmler to have the Reichsbank receive in safe custody gold and jewels for the SS. Funk directed that I should work out the arrangements with Pohl, who, as head of the economics sections of the SS, administered the economic side of the concentration camps.' Funk vehemently denied the charges and tried to shift the blame back to Puhl. Funk reeled under the relentless cross-examination of Thomas Dodd: 'I cannot here tell more to the tribunal than I have already said, that is the truth. Let Herr Puhl be responsible before God for what he put in the affidavit. It is absolutely clear that Herr Puhl is now trying to put the blame on me and to exculpate himself. If he has done these things for years with the SS, it is his guilt and his responsibility.' Dodd replied, "You are trying to put the blame on Puhl, are you not?' Funk: 'No. He is blaming me and I repudiate that.' Dodd: 'The trouble is, there was blood on this gold, was there not, and you knew this since 1942?' " (Conot, *Justice at Nuremberg*,

406). This and other shoddy performances on the stand in the IMT case led Conot to conclude: "It was evident that Funk, Puhl, and Thoms were all lying about the extent of their knowledge—though at the beginning they had not been fully aware of the manner in which the SS had acquired their booty" (404–408). For more on Puhl laundering gold and other valuables for the Nazis, see Tom Bower, *Nazi Gold* (New York: HarperCollins, 1997).

102. *U.S. Military Tribunal Nuremberg, Transcript, Case XI, Weizsaecker*, 28378. Chief of Prisoner of War Affairs Gottlob Berger faced a mountain of damning evidence, like the fact that he proposed the "Heu Aktion" project to Alfried Rosenberg. This was the code name for a project to enslave fifty thousand ten- to fourteen-year-olds. Berger was also involved in the formation and activities of the Dirlewanger Brigade.

103. Gerald Reitlinger, *The SS: Alibi of a Nation 1922–1945*, (New York: Viking, 1957), 171. In 1935, Dirlewanger was sentenced to two years' imprisonment for "offenses on a minor." According to Reitlinger, "When he was released, Berger used his influence to get poor old Oskar into the Condor Legion, who were serving in Spain under General Franco. In 1939, when Dirlewanger had to return to Germany, Berger, as head of the SS Staff Office, got him reinstated as a colonel of the general SS Reserve" (172). For more on Dirlewanger see French MacLean, *The Cruel Hunters* (Atglen, Pa: Schiffer Military History, 1998).

104. *U.S. Military Tribunal Nuremberg, Transcript, Case XI, Weizsaecker*, 28393.

105. Reitlinger, *The SS: Alibi of a Nation 1922–1945*, 174n4. At Nuremberg, Berger and others tried to maintain that killing units like the Dirlewanger regiment were not part of the SS. Reitlinger rejects this contention: "The text of Himmler's second Posen speech was only discovered in 1953, and it casts a dubious light on the testimony, given years previously at Nuremberg, by Gottlob Berger. . . . Both fought hard to maintain that the Dirlewanger regiment was not part of the SS at all" (172).

106. *U.S. Military Tribunal Nuremberg, Transcript, Case XI, Weizsaecker*, 218–220. Walter Schellenberg was an SS general and also a close friend and confidant of Heinrich Himmler. For more on Schellenberg, see Richard Breitman, *Official Secrets* (New York: Hill and Wang, 1998), 227, 255.

107. Reitlinger, *The SS: Alibi of a Nation 1922–1945*, 180. Schellenberg's claim that his office was only an information service was greatly undercut by the discovery that many of the executions of Jews and Commissars had been carried out in his offices.

108. Ibid., 351.

109. Ibid., 353.

110. Robert Kempner, interview by author, tape recording, Locarno, Switzerland, 23 February 1988.

111. Robert Maguire, letter to family, 21 December 1947, Constance Maguire Wilson Papers, 2.

112. Robert Maguire, letter to family, 19 January 1948, Constance Maguire Wilson Papers, 1.

113. Ibid. The judge's description of German soldiers is ironic when compared to his description of American soldiers. In a letter of 10 January 1948 (in possession of

the author), he described two German soldiers he met on the train: "The train was crowded to the last inch of space. There were so many Americans going that the only place we could find was a compartment mean [*sic*] to hold six people, but in which eight were crowded, two of them blind Germans, who evidently had lost their eyesight in the war. One was a young man with a handsome refined face, and the other an older man still wearing his army clothes, and accompanied by a seeing eye dog, a beautiful intelligent animal. We gave them . . . cigarettes, for which they seemed quite grateful, the old man saying, time and again, Dankeshon, Camrad, danke schon."

114. Ibid., 2.

115. Ibid.

116. *The New York Times*, 13 January 1948, 9, col. 1. Kathleen McLaughlin described the significance of this testimony: "Her testimony implicated especially the No. 1 defendant, Baron Ernst von Weizsaecker, and Otto Meissner on the trial of Nazi diplomats and officials" (9).

117. Robert Maguire, letter to family, 10 January 1948, Betty Maguire Frankus Papers, 1.

118. Robert Maguire, letter to family, 25 January 1948, Constance Maguire Wilson Papers, 1.

119. This became the crux of von Weizsäcker's defense against the charges of crimes against peace.

120. Robert Maguire, letter to family, 25 January 1948, Connie Maguire Wilson Papers, 1.

121. Walter LaFeber, *America, Russia, and the Cold War* (New York: Knopf, 1985), 71–72.

122. Ibid., 72.

123. Jean Smith, "The View from USFET: General Clay's Interpretation of Soviet Intentions in Germany, 1945–1948" in Schmitt, ed., *The U.S. Occupation of Europe*, 73.

124. Ibid.

125. Clay, letter to General Eisenhower, 28 July 1947, in Jean Smith, ed., *The Papers of General Lucius Clay* (Bloomington: Indiana University Press, 1974), 1:389–390.

126. Ibid., 390.

127. Simpson, *Blowback*, 54. Heinz Hohne of *Der Spiegel* claimed that during the first few years of the Cold War "seventy percent of all the U.S. government's information on Soviet forces came from the Gehlen organization" (54).

128. Ibid., 65. This comment echoes John Kenneth Galbraith, who once observed that the Cold War produced an American James Bondism "based on the thesis that Communist disrespect for international law and accepted standards of behavior could only be countered by an even more sanguinary immorality on the part of the United States" (Galbraith, "The Sub-Imperial Style of American Foreign Policy," *Esquire* 77[1972]: 79–84). J.F.C. Fuller considered the Soviet Union inferior militarily: "Not of two ill-prepared Powers faced with a better prepared one, as at Munich, but of the two greatest industrial powers in the world, at the time rapidly approaching full rear-

mament, faced with an unreliable power crippled by over two years of ferocious war-fare, and almost entirely dependent on their assistance to maintain his armies in the field. Actually, in August 1943, the position of Russia was diametrically opposite of the one posited in the Hopkins document" (288–289).

129. Smith, *Lucius D. Clay*, 75. "In February, while Congress debated the Marshall Plan for European recovery, Czechoslovakia receded further behind the Iron Curtain as the non-Communist members of government were ousted. Doomsayers in Wash-ington believed their prediction fulfilled, although as George Kennan has noted, such a move changed very little and should have been anticipated. On the heels of events in Prague, Lt. Gen. S.J. Chamberlin, Director of Army Intelligence, visited Clay in Berlin. He impressed upon Clay the pitiful unreadiness of U.S. armed forces, the fact that military appropriations were pending before Congress, and the need to galvanize public support for substantial rearmament" (75).

130. Ibid., 75–76. "In fairness to Clay, it must be recognized that he did not envi-sion how the cable would be used or what its effects would be. His intent was to assist the Army before Congress; it was not to create war hysteria in the country. In fact, Clay was appalled when its contents were leaked to the *Saturday Evening Post*. 'The rev-elation of such a cablegram,' he advised Bradley, 'is not helpful and in fact discloses the viewpoint of a responsible commander out of context with many parallel reports' " (Smith, ed., *The Papers of General Lucius Clay*, 2:961–962).

131. Jean Smith, *Lucius D. Clay: An American Life* (New York: Holt, 1990), 76.

132. Michael Howard, "Governor General of Germany," *Times Literary Supplement*, 29 August 1975.

133. Etzold and Gaddis, eds., *Containment*. The Policy Planning Staff saw their objective as returning Germany to self-government: "Thirdly, we must have the courage to dispense with military government as soon as possible and to force the Germans to accept responsibility once more for their own affairs. They will never begin to do this as long as we will accept that responsibility for them" (120). Peter Grose, *Operation Rollback* (New York: Houghton Mifflin, 2000), 96.

134. Taylor, *Final Report to the Secretary of the Army on the Nuernberg War Crimes Trials*, 202–203.

135. Ibid., 203.

136. *Trials of War Criminals before Nuernberg Military Tribunals Under Control Council No. 10* (Washington, D.C.: U.S. Government Printing Office, 1949).

137. Ibid., 789.

138. Taylor, *Final Report to the Secretary of the Army on the Nuernberg War Crimes Trials*, 203. Transcripts, case 7, 10, 446.

139. Ibid., 204. General Taylor's description of the judgment leaves open the possi-bility of legitimate legal differences: "One can easily understand these protests, but, in the writer's view, they have tended to obscure the admirable workmanship of the judg-ment. Furthermore, these were much mooted questions, with highly political over-tones, and it is hard to criticize the court's conservative determination to apply inter-national law, 'as we find it,' not 'as we would have it.' In the long run, this may well

promote the revision of international law along more enlightened lines, which is far more important than the decision with respect to these particular defendants" (207).

140. *U.S. Military Tribunal Nuremberg, Transcript, Case VII, List* (Nuremberg: Secretariat for Military Tribunals, 1949), 10441. The first paragraph read: "In no other way can an army guard and protect itself from the gadfly tactics of such armed resistance. And, on the other hand, members of such resistance forces must accept the increased risks involved in this mode of fighting. Such forces are technically lawful belligerents and are not entitled to protection as prisoners when captured."

141. Ibid.

142. Appleman, *Military Tribunals and International Crimes*, 192; Transcripts, case 7, 10441–2.

143. *U.S. Military Tribunal Nuremberg, Transcript, Case VII, List*, 10446.

144. Ibid. See also Roberts and Guelff, eds., *Documents on the Laws of War*, 48–49.

145. Appleman, *Military Tribunals and International Crimes*, 186.

146. Columbia University Oral History Project, Lucius Clay, 561.

147. *U.S. Military Tribunal Nuremberg, Transcript, Case VII, List*, 10542. Charles Wennerstrum's comments appeared in the conservative *Chicago Tribune* on February 23, 1948. Telford Taylor's rebuttal was printed the same day in a *New York Times* article entitled, "Prosecutor Scores War-Crimes Judge." Tom Schwartz describes the role assumed by the *Chicago Tribune* in the Nuremberg debates: "The conservative Chicago Tribune, with the remarks of Judge Charles Wennerstrum . . . made itself the mouthpiece of the critics of the Nuremberg trials" ("*Die Begnadigung Deutscher Kriegsverbrecher. John J. McCloy und die Haftlinge von Landsberg*" in *Vierteljahrshefte für Zeitgeschichte* 38 [July 1990]: 382).

148. Frank Buscher, *The U.S. War Crimes Trial Program in Germany, 1946–1955* (Westport, Conn.: Greenwood, 1989), 188.

149. "Nazi Trial Judge Rips 'Injustice,' " *Chicago Tribune*, February 23, 1948.

150. Buscher charges in *The U.S. War Crimes Trial Program* that Hal Foust's transmissions were intercepted by the army in violation of U.S. wiretapping laws (35). Taylor described how he received Wennerstrum's comments before they were printed in the United States: "There was a place in Frankfurt where most of the American newspapers had their headquarters where the members of the press hung up what was going out." Telford Taylor, interview by author, tape recording, New York City, 24 February 1993.

151. Telford Taylor, letter to Charles Wennerstrum, 21 February 1948, reprinted in Appleman, *Military Tribunals and International Crimes*, 190–191. "It has come to my attention that yesterday, a few hours before your departure from Nürnberg, you gave an interview to a representative of the *Chicago Tribune*, in the course of which you made a deliberate, malicious, and totally unfounded attack on the integrity of the very trials in which you yourself were a presiding judge. It is clear from the nature of your remarks that you were not speaking on behalf of your Tribunal or in your official capacity, but were volunteering purely personal views. Since your remarks are subversive of the interests and policies of the United States, they must not go unan-

swered" (190). When Wennerstrum arrived back in the United States on February 24, 1948, he was met by the press with a copy of Taylor's comments. The judge stood behind his prior statements. *The New York Times* reported: "Questioned as to his original criticism of persons 'with personal ambitions,' he said they applied 'to the prosecutors and their superior' " (February 25, 1948, 10, col. 3). The other two judges from the Hostage case were with Wennerstrum on the flight back to the United States but were unwilling to side with their colleague, according to the same article: "Accompanying Wennerstrum on the homeward flight . . . were Judge Edward F. Carter . . . and Judge George J. Burke . . . his associates at the trial. They refused to enter the controversy. Both associate judges, however, asserted that they were satisfied with the outcome. . . . Judge Carter's only comment was, 'We heard the case, we wrote an opinion and we think the facts were as we found them.' To this, Judge Burke added, 'The opinion was rather long and well thought out. Beyond that, I have no opinion.'" Telford Taylor, interview with author.

152. Appleman, *Military Tribunals and International Crimes*, 191.

153. *Congressional Record*, December 16, 1948, 11468.

154. As Buscher notes in *The U.S. War Crimes Trial Program*, American criticism provided a pretext for German critics.

155. Schwartz, *"Die Begnadigung Deutscher Kriegsverbrecher,"* 380. Translation by the author and Martin Splichal.

156. Buscher, *The U.S. War Crimes Trial Program*, 35–36.

157. Robert Maguire, letter to Constance Maguire Wilson, 24 February 1948 (in possession of the author).

158. Ibid. Maguire was somewhat pessimistic about the revolutionary impact of the Nuremberg trials: "Personally I have never much been inclined to name calling, and there is a serious question as to whether in being so vigorous we aren't making it more difficult to come to an understanding with Brother Stalin. I think it has become perfectly clear that the late F.D.R. who should have known better, and Harry S., who had no opportunity to know anything about the questions, made terrific and tragic mistakes at Moscow and Potsdam. They were full of benevolence and enthusiasm, and were dealing with exceedingly cool-headed men who knew exactly what they wanted, and proceeded to trade us out of our eye teeth. . . . The more one looks into the history of peoples, particularly those of Russia and the East, the less enthusiastic he is likely to be; they have in the past and they are now, bogged down in the age old jealousies, ideology, racial, religious, and political that have been the eternal causes of war, and the people of each country refuse to examine their own mirrors to see where they have been wrong, but insist on the errors and shortcomings of their neighbors. . . . There is a very natural tendency to say, 'if you didn't then, why should we trust you a second time?' I find no one, and I have heard of no one who has anything good to say of them. Many say that individually they like Russian people, but politically they are utterly ruthless, and without faith. The stories that I hear of what they have done and are doing in the regions here and in other countries are almost unbelievable for horror, cruelty and oppression" (Ibid., 2).

159. Ibid.

160. American Nuremberg Trials, *Case 11—United States v. Ernst von Weizsaecker*, 13:97.

161. James Brand, letter to Robert Maguire, 12 May 1948, Betty Maguire Frankus Papers, 1.

162. Ibid.

163. Walter Rockler, interview by author, tape recording, Washington, D.C., 18 April 1987. Robert Maguire, letter to family, 14 April 1948, Constance Maguire Wilson Papers, 2.

164. American Nuremberg Trials, *Case 9—United States v. Otto Ohlendorf*, 531. The evidence in the Einsatzgruppen case was specific and highly incriminating. The majority of it consisted of the group's reports from the Soviet Union.

165. Appleman, *Military Tribunals and International Crimes*, 202.

166. Ibid. See Christopher Browning, *Ordinary Men* (New York: HarperCollins, 1998).

167. Ibid. On the stand Ohlendorf testified, "I was the leader in Einsatzgruppen D in the southern sector, and in the course of the year . . . it liquidated approximately 90,000 men, women and children. The majority of those liquidated were Jews, but there were among them some communist functionaries" (International Military Tribunal, *Trial of the Major War Criminals* [Nuremberg: IMT, 1947], 4:206).

168. American Nuremberg Trials, *Case 9—United States v. Otto Ohlendorf*, 569, 530–531; Appleman, *Military Tribunals and International Crimes*, 202.

169. See ibid., 202–203, for a summary of Taylor's closing statement.

170. Taylor, *Final Report to the Secretary of the Army on the Nuernberg War Crimes Trials*, 183.

171. Ibid., 181.

172. Ibid., 184.

173. Levie, *Terrorism in War*, 376.

174. Ibid.

175. *Interrogation Report of Carl Schmitt, Nuremberg Office of U.S. Chief Counsel for War Crimes, Evidence Division*, transcript No. 1842. Reprinted in *Telos* 72 (Summer 1987). Although Schmitt offered no substantive comments on Ernst von Weizsäcker, his initial reaction is telling when compared to his responses to other important Nazis like Hans Lammers. Schmitt seemed genuinely surprised by von Weizsäcker's inclusion and the activities in which the diplomat was involved.

176. *Case Eleven—Ernst von Weizsaecker*, XII: 237–238.

177. Robert Louis Stevenson, *The Strange Case of Dr. Jekyll and Mr. Hyde*, from Luders, "The Strange Case of Ernst von Weizsaecker," iii.

178. Von Weizsäcker, *From Weimar to the Wall*, 48.

179. Ibid.

180. Luders, "The Strange Case of Ernst von Weizsaecker," 63–64. In the cases that preceded it, "Unlike in the case of Weizsaecker, in which political resistance played a decisive part in his defense, it had merely been stated as a mitigating circum-

stance that both defendants had occasionally advocated the tempering of certain measures. The key distinction was that in the IMT cases none of the defendants nor their witnesses considered their actions to constitute political resistance" (68n29).

181. Von Weizsäcker, *From Weimar to the Wall*, 95.

182. Klemens von Klemperer, *German Resistance Against Hitler* (Oxford: Clarendon, 1992), 102.

183. Von Weizsäcker, *From Weimar to the Wall*, 90.

184. *Trials of War Criminals before Nuernberg Military Tribunals Under Control Council No. 10*, XII:152–153.

185. Ibid., 154–156.

186. *U.S. Military Tribunal Nuremberg, Transcript, Case XI*, Weizsaecker, 28328; Kaiser, *Politics and War*, 432–433. David Kaiser makes the point that "deportation" became a synonym for execution: "It seems, then, that by the late summer of 1941 deportation meant not deportation and resettlement, but rather deportation and murder" (403–404).

187. John Cornwell, *Hitler's Pope: The Secret History of Pius XII* (New York: Viking, 1999), 300. See also Guenter Lewy, *The Catholic Church and Nazi Germany* (New York: Da Capo, 1964), 300–302.

188. Ibid., 311. According to Cornwell, "The letter indicates the subtle double game that Weizsäcker had played throughout the deportation episode. It was Weizsäcker who helped stop the further arrests of Jews by raising the threat of papal protests that Pacelli had no intention of making. Now that no further arrests were to come, he could speak complacently of the Pope's willingness to remain silent. But what of the thousands who had died?" (312). Ian Buruma on von Weizsäcker's role in the Vatican: "Since 1943, he had served as ambassador to the Vatican—a rather crucial posting, since the Germans wanted to make sure the Pope kept silent about the Final Solution. Whether or not it was due to Weizsaecker's diplomatic skills, the Pope did not disappoint them" (Buruma, *The Wages of Guilt*, 142). See also Michael Phayer, *The Catholic Church and the Holocaust* (Bloomington: Indiana University Press, 2000).

189. *Trials of War Criminals before Nuernberg Military Tribunals Under Control Council No. 10*, XII:148.

190. Ibid., 152.

191. Ibid., 148–153.

192. *U.S. Military Tribunal Nuremberg, Transcript, Case XI*, Weizsaecker, 28331. Parts of Hassell's diary were introduced as rebuttal evidence by the Prosecution (NG 5759, Exhibit C-288, Doc. Bk. 204A); from Luders, "The Strange Case of Ernst von Weizsaecker." For more on the resistance see Hans Gisevius, *To the Bitter End* (Boston: Houghton Mifflin, 1947); Peter Hoffman, *The History of the German Resistance, 1933–1945* (Cambridge: MIT Press, 1979); Allen Dulles, *Germany's Underground* (New York: Macmillan, 1947); Hans Royce, ed., *20 Juli 1944* (Bonn: Heraus-gegeben von der Bundeszentrale für Heimztdienst, 1953).

193. *U.S. Military Tribunal Nuremberg, Transcript, Case XI*, Weizsaecker, 8538.

194. LaFeber, *America, Russia and the Cold War*, 71–72.

195. William Caming, conversation with author, 7 July 1987. William Caming, interviews by author, tape recording, Summit, New Jersey, 9 October 1987, fall 1989. Similar sentiments were expressed to the author by Telford Taylor, Drexel Sprecher, Robert Kempner, Walter Rockler in interviews and conversations. The Italians were in the midst of an election campaign and the Communist Party was running strong. George Kennan and other high-level policy makers were greatly alarmed by the prospect of the Italian Communist Party gaining control of the government through a popular election. The list of men involved in the anti-Communist effort in Italy reads like a Cold War all-star team roster. It included George Kennan, Allen Dulles, James Angleton, Frank Wisner, and William Colby. The Americans worked with the Vatican on behalf of Christian Democrat candidates. Their aid included various types of agitprop, specifically designed to highlight "American munificence and communist atrocities, both real and manufactured." Maguire was unaware of the motor behind the campaigning, but sensed a strange fervor. He wrote, "you never saw such campaigning, and such apparent eager interest . . . they are so close to the fear or love of Russia and Communism that it is all they think of." The Italian election forced him to consider his own views. Maguire wrote, "Communism is an utterly evil thing not because it opposes and would destroy capitalism, but because its primary tenet is the destruction of the right of men to think for themselves, to speak their thoughts, to believe as they will and to criticize the mistakes, real or fancied of those in power."

See Simpson, *Blowback*, 90–91. For more on the CIA's role in the Italian election see William Corson, *The Armies of Ignorance* (New York: Dial/James Wade, 1977); see also Wilson Miscamble, *George F. Kennan and the Making of American Foreign Policy* (New Jersey: Princeton University Press, 1992).

196. Friedrich, "Nuremberg and the Germans," 92.

197. *Defense Brief—Lammers-Meissner-Cross Closing*, X1B11:4, 42.

198. Ibid., 67.

199. American Nuremberg Trials, *Case 11—United States* v. *Ernst von Weizsaecker*, 12:257.

200. Ibid., 358. Edmund Veesenmayer's attorney made a similar argument: "His work there was guided only by the thought of helping his comrades who were fighting desperately against the overwhelming power of the Red Army . . . this man moved along a lonely ridge between life and death in his work, day by day, year by year, motivated by his love for Germany, and moved by the thought of achieving a better European order" (300). *Green Series* vol. XII, 358–359.

201. Ibid.

202. *U.S. Military Tribunal Nuremberg, Transcript, Case XI, Weizsaecker*, 28432. In a speech at a 1935 Nazi Party rally, Dietrich described his view of the press under a modern dictatorship: "The liberalistic age boasted of the Press as a Seventh Power. . . . In National Socialist Germany that kind of press was eliminated with lightning speed by the arm of the law! A fate which it deserved a thousand fold, overtook it on the first day of the revolution. . . . And dear Party Members, we did our full duty by our pro-

gram in this respect also. In National Socialist Germany, enemies of the state and the people are not tolerated in the press; they are exterminated" (28432).

203. The IMT set the precedent followed by the tribunals in the Flick, Farben, and Krupp cases. The majority of the American courts bowed to the IMT's conservative precedents.

204. Schacht was found innocent under Counts 1 and 2 and acquitted. Appleman, *Military Tribunals and International Crimes*, 171–172.

205. *U.S. Military Tribunal Nuremberg, Transcript, Case X, Krupp* (Nuremberg: Secretariat for Military Tribunals, 1949), 13435–37.

206. Taylor, *Final Report to the Secretary of the Army on the Nuernberg War Crimes Trials*, 319.

207. Ibid., 197.

208. Ibid., 319.

209. Borkin, *The Crime and Punishment of I. G. Farben*, 142.

210. Ibid., 144.

211. Ibid., 134.

212. Ibid., 148.

213. Ibid., 149.

214. Ibid.

215. Ibid.

216. Taylor, *Final Report to the Secretary of the Army on the Nuernberg War Crimes Trials*, 198.

217. Borkin, *The Crime and Punishment of I. G. Farben*, 150.

218. Ibid., 151.

219. Ibid. Appleman, *Military Tribunals and International Crimes*, 181. Judge Hebert agreed: "bowing to such weighty precedents as the acquittal by the International Military Tribunal of Schacht and Speer on the charges of Crimes Against Peace; of the acquittal by Military Tribunal III of the leading officials of the Krupp firm on similar charges. . . . I do not agree with the majority's conclusion that the evidence presented in this case falls so far short of sufficiency as the Tribunal's opinion would seem to indicate. The issues of fact are truly so close as to cause genuine concern as to whether or not justice has actually been done because of the enormous and indispensable role these defendants were shown to have played in the building of the war machine which made Hitler's aggressions possible" (181).

220. Ibid.

221. Borkin, *The Crime and Punishment of I. G. Farben*, 155.

222. Levie, *Terrorism in War*, 480.

223. Borkin, *The Crime and Punishment of I. G. Farben*, 154. See Josiah DuBois, *The Devil's Chemists: 24 Conspirators of the International Farben Cartel Who Manufacture Wars* (Boston: Beacon, 1952) for his account of the trial.

224. Appleman, *Military Tribunals and International Crimes*, 211.

225. Taylor, *Final Report to the Secretary of the Army on the Nuernberg War Crimes Trials*, 193. The Krupp Works' use of slave labor violated a number of the convention's articles.

226. *U.S. Military Tribunal Nuremberg, Transcript, Case X, Krupp,* 12380–81.

227. Ibid., 13451–52.

228. Appleman, *Military Tribunals and International Crimes,* 180–181.

229. Taylor, *Final Report to the Secretary of the Army on the Nuernberg War Crimes Trials,* 193. Appleman, *Military Tribunals and International Crimes,* 177–178. The most severe sentences were two eight-year terms. Eleven of the twenty-three defendants were acquitted or released for time served. The weekly *Christ und Welt* of Stuttgart featured a picture of Curtis Shake, presiding judge at the Farben trial, with the following caption: "The president of the U.S. Military Tribunal in the Nuremberg I. G. Farben trial, who excelled by his just conduct of the proceedings, by his absolute objectivity and disregard for all vindictive sentiments, as well as by his endeavor to understand the nature of German conditions between 1933 and 1945." Appleman, *Military Tribunals and International Crimes,* 181n1b.

230. Robert Maguire, letter to Katie Maguire, 27 July 1948 (in possession of the author).

231. *U.S. Military Tribunal Nuremberg, Transcript, Case XI, Weizsaecker,* 28087. The Ministries case transcript was 28,085 pages long, and this does not include the 9,067 pages of documentary exhibits.

232. Dower, *Embracing Defeat,* 453; Piccigallo, *The Japanese on Trial,* 46. This was a political event, even though the United States had been careful to use the "hocuspocus of a judicial procedure which belies its real nature."

233. Levie, *Terrorism in War,* 386.

234. Minear, *Victor's Justice,* 72. The trial lasted thirty-one months, from May 3, 1946 through November 1948. Seven were sentenced to death, sixteen to life, one to twenty years, and one to seven years. There were no acquittals. Five died in prison, while the remaining twelve prisoners were paroled between 1954 and 1956. "In 1958, the last ten were granted clemency following discussions with the former victorious powers" (Dower, *Embracing Defeat,* 450). In Khabarovsk, twelve former members of Japan's infamous Unit 731 were put on trial; all pled guilty and confessed (Dower, *Embracing Defeat,* 449). Levie on the Chabarovsk trial: "Four had been in the Kwantung Army and eight in Units 731 and 100" (Howard Levie, *Terrorism in War: The Law of War Crimes* [Dobbs Ferry, N.Y.: Oceana, 1993], 164). Tanaka, *Hidden Horrors,* 2 and Dower, *Embracing Defeat,* 450. From 1945 to 1951, Allied military commissions in the Far East sentenced 920 to death and 3,000 to various prison terms (vi). U.S. trials in the Pacific were held in the Philippines (215); China (75); Pacific Islands (123); and Yokohama (996) (Piccigallo, *The Japanese on Trial,* 74).

235. Judith Shklar, *Legalism: Laws, Morals, and Political Trials* (Cambridge: Harvard University Press, 1964), 185–186. Shklar points out the weakness of natural law as a basis for the charge of aggressive war: "Many observers have noted that natural law is capable of too many interpretations in any concrete situation to provide an objective and impersonal basis for international criminal trials. At Tokyo there was a telling illustration of this point. Justice Bernard based his dissent on natural law too, but in his view it rendered the charge of waging aggressive war illegitimate. In short, the

very charge which Mr. Keenan's natural law supported, Justice Bernard's natural law rejected" (185). In his dissenting opinion, the French justice wrote that the defendants were only "accomplices," and the "principal author . . . escaped all prosecution." Dower, *Embracing Defeat*, 460.

236. Ibid., 460. See also Piccigallo, *The Japanese on Trial*, 29. For more on Hirohito's wartime role and nonindictment, see Herbert Bix, *Hirohito and the Making of Modern Japan* (New York: HarperCollins, 2000).

237. Piccigallo, *The Japanese on Trial*, 30.

238. Levie, *Terrorism in War*, 390.

239. R. John Pritchard and Sonia Magbanua Zaide, eds., *The Tokyo War Crimes Trials* (New York: Garland, 1981), 21:1226. Pal wrote: "For reasons given in the foregoing pages, I would hold that each and every one of the accused must be found not guilty of each and every one of the charges in the indictment and should be acquitted of all those charges. . . . I believe that this is really an appeal to the political power of the victor nations with a pretense of legal justice. It only amounts to piecing up want of legality with matter of convenience" (1226).

240. David Luban, *Legal Modernism* (Ann Arbor: University of Michigan Press, 1994), 340–341. Levie wrote that Judge Pal "went to Tokyo prepared to strike a blow for Asia's freedom from European colonization" (*Terrorism in War* 152).

241. Ibid., 341.

242. Piccigallo, *The Japanese on Trial*, 31.

243. Pritchard and Zaide, eds., *The Tokyo War Crimes Trials*, 1091. Dower, *Embracing Defeat*, 473.

244. Shklar, *Legalism*, 186–187.

245. Ibid., 187.

246. Pritchard and Zaide, eds., *The Tokyo War Crimes Trials*, 279; Dower, *Embracing Defeat*, 473.

247. Pritchard and Zaide, eds., *The Tokyo War Crimes Trials*, 279; Dower, *Embracing Defeat*, 460.

248. Robert Maguire, letter to Katie Maguire, 27 July 1948, 1. Maguire knew his trial would be the last to finish in the summer of 1948 when he wrote his mother: "Our case moves along but not very rapidly to my disgust and disappointment but there is little we can do about it. Two of the Tribunals close this week, Krupp and Farben, and the High Command Case will probably finish sometime about the middle of August but we can look forward to no such luck. However, one of these days, it is likely we will be hopping on the steamer for the U.S.A. and particularly, Portland and Birdshill" (2).

249. Ruth Maguire, letter to Katie Maguire, 9 November 1948, Betty Maguire Frankus Papers, 1.

250. Ruth Maguire, letter to Katie Maguire, 13 January 1949. Now it was clear Powers would not concur with the majority opinion, and this added several months to the Maguires' stay. Ruth informed her mother-in-law of the delay: "you are probably wondering when we are leaving Nurenberg. We do not know the actual date,

but Bob is working hard and hopes to leave by the end of the month. It is a long, drawn-out affair, this 'Ministries Case' and sometimes I guess he wishes he had taken the 'High Command Case' for he would have been thru . . . 2 or 3 months ago. If he had known that he would have to stay as long as this he said he would not have come. However, when it's all over, I think he will be glad to have had the experience over here—in spite of the grueling last months" (1). Ruth makes no specific mention of the divided court.

251. *Stars and Stripes*, April 12, 1949.

252. American Nuremberg Trials, *Case 11—United States v. Ernst von Weizsaecker*, 14:316.

253. *U.S. Military Tribunal Nuremberg, Transcript, Case XI, Weizsaecker*, 28092–93.

254. Ibid., 28093.

255. Ibid.

256. Ibid., 28096–97. Jack Raymond of *The New York Times* observed this in an article entitled "Five High Nazis Guilty of Helping Hitler to Violate Peace": "The court rejected the defense claim that the Soviet-German treaty disclosed that the Soviet Union was just as guilty as Germany of waging aggressive war" (*New York Times*, April 12, 1949, 1, col. 1).

257. *U.S. Military Tribunal Nuremberg, Transcript, Case XI, Weizsaecker*, 28097. *The New York Times* reported the convictions for crimes against peace: "The conviction on the aggressive war count was the first in the twelve trials conducted by the United States since the International Military Court at Nuremberg convicted Hermann Goering and other makers of Nazi high policy" (Raymond, "Five High Nazis Guilty," 1).

258. *U.S. Military Tribunal Nuremberg, Transcript, Case XI, Weizsaecker*, 28121. Jack Raymond described the court's reasoning: "Although the court conceded Weizsaecker 'continuously discouraged Ribbentrop's penchant for aggressive war,' a 'radically different' attitude was attributed to him after the Munich pact. 'The reason for this we think is obvious,' the court declared. 'Before Munich he feared that France and England would take up arms in defense of Czechoslovakia and that if it did so, Germany would suffer defeat. After Munich he felt danger to Germany had vanished and he looked with complaisance if not approval on the future fate of Czechoslovakia' " (Raymond, "Five High Nazis Guilty," 1).

259. *U.S. Military Tribunal Nuremberg, Transcript, Case XI, Weizsaecker*, 28121.

260. Ibid.

261. Ibid., 28140.

262. Ibid., 28122.

263. Ibid., 28293.

264. Ibid., 28292.

265. Ibid., 28096–97.

266. Powers rejected the charges on the grounds that these acts were not traditional war crimes because they were not committed by combatants or (in the cases of Austria and Czechoslovakia) during wartime.

267. *U.S. Military Tribunal Nuremberg, Transcript, Case XI, Weizsaecker*, 28116.

268. American Nuremberg Trials, *Case 11—United States v. Ernst von Weizsaecker*, 14:877.

269. Ibid., 14:872. See Levie, *Terrorism in War*, 95 for the Powers quote.

270. American Nuremberg Trials, *Case 11—United States v. Ernst von Weizsaecker*, 14:890.

271. Appleman, *Military Tribunals and International Crimes*, 222–223.

272. U.S. *Military Tribunal Nuremberg, Transcript, Case XI, Weizsaecker*, 28285.

273. Ibid.

274. American Nuremberg Trials, *Case 11—United States v. Ernst von Weizsaecker*, 12:219–220.

275. "Report of the Advisory Board on Clemency for War Criminals to the U.S. High Commission for Germany Advisory Clemency Report," RG 59, Box 5 (Clemency Board on German War Criminals), 13, NA.

276. Ibid.

277. Appleman, *Military Tribunals and International Crimes*, 223.

278. Levie, *Terrorism in War*, 478n136.

279. American Nuremberg Trials, *Case 11—United States v. Ernst von Weizsaecker*, 14:931. According to Judge Powers's conservative reading of the laws of war: "To be guilty—I repeat—the defendant must have participated in the initiation of a war of aggression. In order to do that, he must have committed some act intended to have some effect in bringing about a war, knowing it would become a war of aggression. That evidence is conspicuous by its absence here" (894). Jack Raymond analyzed the Powers dissent in an article entitled "Nuremberg Judge Dissents on Guilt" (*The New York Times*, April 14, 1949, 8, col. 1): "Most of the court's verdicts were immediately condemned by one of its members, Judge Leon W. Powers. He said in a dissenting opinion that his two colleagues were endorsing a 'strange doctrine' of attributing guilt to those who merely had knowledge of a crime. . . . Judge Powers' contention that 'guilt is personal and individual and must be based on personal acts of an individual charged,' was in direct contradiction to the majority view that those who did the planning and administrative work of the crimes were 'equally guilty' with concentration camp commanders and other implementers of the crimes."

280. American Nuremberg Trials, *Case 11—United States v. Ernst von Weizsaecker*, 14:930.

281. Ibid. 14:931.

282. Ibid. 14:866–871.

283. William Caming, paper delivered at University of South Carolina College, September 11, 1998, 13; American Nuremberg Trials, *Case 11—United States v. Ernst von Weizsaecker*, 14:947. "Ernst Von Weizsaecker, Gustav Adolf Steenracht von Moyland, Wilhelm Keppler, Wilhelm Stuckart, Richard Walter Darré, Otto Dietrich, Gottlob Berger, Walter Schellenberg, Lutz Scherin von Krosigk, Emil Puhl, Paul Koerner, Paul Pleiger, and Hans Kehrl presented to and filed with the Tribunal a motion to set aside the decision and the judgment of conviction 'on the grounds that said decision and judgment is contrary to the facts, contrary to law, and against the weight of the

evidence; on the ground that this Court has no jurisdiction to hear and determine the alleged charges, and on the further ground that the facts alleged and the facts found do not constitute an offense against the law of nations or against the laws of the sovereign power of the United States,' and on the ground 'that the rulings made are not in conformity with the principles of the due process of law, and the Constitution and laws of the United States, the international law, and the rules of law generally applicable to the trial of criminal cases" 14:946–947.

284. *Stars and Stripes*, April 15, 1949, 1.

285. Ibid.

286. Wilbourn Benton, ed., *Nuremberg: German Views of the War Trials* (Dallas: Southern Methodist University Press, 1953), 197.

5. Nuremberg: A Cold War Conflict of Interest

1. Richard von Weizsäcker, *From Weimar to the Wall*, trans. Ruth Hein (New York: Broadway Books, 1999), 90, 95.

2. Klemens von Klemperer, *German Resistance Against Hitler* (Oxford: Clarendon, 1992), 26. A review of Marion Thielenhaus' study of a group of German diplomats, *Zwischen Anpassung und Widerstand: Deutsche Diplomaten, 1938–1941* (Paderborn: Ferdinand Schoningh, 1985) by Gerhard Weinberg (*Journal of Modern History* 9 [Sept. 1987]: 638) raises many of the same questions as the tribunal majority in the Ministries case: "The state secretary is in many ways the central figure in the book. If Thielenhaus is rather sympathetic to him in her presentation, she certainly shows him to have been vehemently and continually anti-Czech and positively hysterical in his hatred of Poland. He is portrayed as what might be called a conventional ultranationalist, and—in view of his inability to comprehend from his excellent vantage point that it was Hitler who was driving German foreign policy in 1938 and 1939—quite extraordinarily stupid. . . . The sketch in the first chapter of German diplomats in the early years of Nazi rule includes no discussion of the Jewish question, and no conclusions are drawn by the author from her observation that (p. 88) only one document in the whole Foreign Ministry archives revealed an effort to assist the persecuted. If she had extended her scope to include at least minimal reference to von Weizsäcker's regular review of the reports of the murder squads (Einsatzgruppen), his role in the extraction of Jews from all over Europe for dispatch to the killing centers, his rejection out of hand of the Swedish government's offer to accept the Norwegian Jews to prevent their being murdered, and his postwar admiring comment on one of the leaders of the murder squads, she might have seen more clearly a side of the central figure in the book that is entirely blocked out by the tunnel vision of this monograph."

Michael Luders, "The Strange Case of Ernst von Weizsaecker," refuses to offer an opinion on the diplomat's innocence or guilt, but gives this Robert Louis Stevenson quote as a preface. Dr. Jekyll's description of himself applies fittingly to the former State Secretary: "Though so profound a double-dealer, I was in no sense a hypocrite; both sides of me were in dead earnest; I was no more myself when I laid aside restraint and plunged in shame, than when I laboured, in the eye of day, at the furtherance of knowledge or the relief of sorrow and suffering" (iii).

3. Jörg Friedrich, "Nuremberg and the Germans," in Belinda Cooper, ed., *War Crimes: The Legacy of Nuremberg* (New York: TV Books, 1999), 92. *U.S. Military Tribunal Nuremberg, Transcript, Case XI, Weizsaecker* (Nuremberg: Secretariat for Military Tribunals, 1949), 28122; see also 28328.

4. John Cornwell, *Hitler's Pope: The Secret History of Pius XII* (New York: Viking, 1999), 310.

5. Hearings before a Subcommittee on Armed Services, U.S. Senate, 81st Congress, 1st Session, pursuant to Senate Resolution 42, *Investigation of Army Action with Respect to Trial of Persons Responsible for the Massacre of American Soldiers, Battle of the Bulge, near Malmédy, Belgium, December, 1944*, 102. See also Frank M. Buscher, *The U.S. War Crimes Trial Program in Germany, 1946–1955* (Westport, Conn.: Greenwood, 1989), 41; Glenn Smith, *Langer of North Dakota: A Study in Isolationism* (New York: Garland, 1978), 148–150.

6. David Oshinsky, *A Conspiracy So Immense: The World of Joe McCarthy* (New York: Free Press, 1983), 74.

7. *Investigation of Army Action with Respect to Trial of Persons Responsible for the Massacre of American Soldiers, Battle of the Bulge, near Malmedy, Belgium, December, 1944*, 352.

8. Ibid.

9. Ibid., 102. The German magazine *Die Strasse* filed this brief for the men of Kampfegruppe Peiper: "Americans and Germans demand Review. . . . The gallows wait for the accused of the Malmedy Trial for four years. Twenty-eight prisoners of the Landsberg Prison had been sentenced to death; six of these prisoners were sentenced to death in the Dachau Malmedy Trial. These six men had nothing to do with concentration camps, neither had they been assigned to liquidation squads, but they were soldiers of the 6th Armored Army, who participated in the final German Eifel Offensive. American politicians and lawyers had tried for years to obtain a Review of the Malmedy Trial. Petitions for Clemency were submitted, although innocent men need no pardon, only justice" (January 21, 1947). McCarthy bore into one witness with his most famous statement during the hearings: "I assume that you and I would agree that an innocent man will scream about as loudly as a guilty man if you are kicking him in the testicles, and an innocent man will perhaps sign the same confession that a guilty man will if you kick him long and hard enough" (Oshinsky, *A Conspiracy So Immense*, 50).

An American newspaper article reported McCarthy's outrageous behavior: "At one point, Senator McCarthy alleged that Senator Baldwin had been 'criminally wrong' in continuing as chairman of the investigation of the group while his law partner, former Major Dwight Fanton, who had headed a military government team that extracted the confessions from accused Nazis, was under charge. A protest, based on Senate rules, was laid by Senator Charles W. Tobey, Republican of New Hampshire. Mr. McCarthy conceded that he might have gone too far in his language" ("Malmedy Inquiry Held 'Whitewash,' " *The New York Times*, July 27, 1949, 1, col. 1).

10. Oshinsky, *A Conspiracy So Immense*, 80.

11. Buscher describes how the Malmedy investigations played into the hands of the German propagandists: "The Board of Review report would undoubtedly have been of great value to the German anti-war crimes propaganda. But the bishops did not really need such confidential information to criticize the operation. Fortunately for them, there were the Malmedy hearings in the spring and fall of 1949, which lent themselves to this purpose. The German Protestant bishops became downright theatrical during this phase of the Malmedy controversy" (*The U.S. War Crimes Trial Program* 100).

12. Alfred Seidl offered this characterization during the Ministries case. Martin Hillenbrand, "The United States and Germany," in Wolfram Handrider, ed., *West German Foreign Policy 1949–1979* (Boulder: Westview, 1990), 74–75. See also Buscher, *The U.S. War Crimes Trial Program*, 37, 93–95. Buscher writes, "The clemency program of the American war crimes operation can be divided into two parts. During the first phase from 1946 to January 1951 . . . American officials thought that the early clemency programs should serve another purpose. Since U.S. authorities in Germany viewed the war crimes program as an important part in their effort to reform and reeducate the German people, the post-trial treatment of war criminals, in addition to the trials themselves, became a vital part of this educational device. The United States intended to use the proceedings against war criminals to demonstrate to the Germans the horrendous crimes Nazism had inflicted on its victims. . . . In contrast, sentence review and clemency were meant to promote the superior values of democratic society, which entitled even the perpetrators of mass murder to fair treatment" (69).

13. Buscher, *The U.S. War Crimes Trial Program*, 37.

14. Franz Bluecher, letter to Thomas Handy, 21 May 1951, RG 466, U.S. High Commission for Germany, Security Segregated Records 1949–1952, Box 28, 321.6, NA.

15. American Nuremberg Trials, *Case 11—United States v. Ernst von Weizsaecker*, 14:952; "The defendants von Weizsaecker and Woermann insist that our judgment against them on count five is based upon the false hypothesis that at the time they had knowledge of the extermination program established at Auschwitz. Such is not the fact. We were and are convinced beyond reasonable doubt that both were aware that the deportation of Jews from occupied countries to Germany and the East meant their ultimate death. No one can read the record concerning the Dutch Jews and have any question as to the facts." The tribunal majority reaffirmed their rejection of the defense argument that the German diplomats thought that Auschwitz was merely a labor camp: "In an attempt to persuade us that these concentration camps, including Auschwitz, were merely labor camps and not murder factories until after 1942, the defense has offered much testimony. An analysis reveals that great care was exercised not to state that prior to that time Jews were merely labored and were not murdered, but to emphasize that the mass murder program had not been instituted until after 1942, when convoys of Jews were driven into the gas chambers immediately on arrival

at the camps" (American Nuremberg Trials, *Case 11—United States v. Ernst von Weizsaecker*, 14:952, 957–958).

16. Ibid., 14:960; William Caming, "The Nuremberg Prosecutors Reflect on the Triumph of Justice and Morality," September 26, 1997; paper delivered at the University of South Carolina, 1998, 14.

17. Theo Kordt, letter to Lord Halifax, 13 December 1949, RG 59, Box 16 (War Crimes 1949, 1950, October 16, 1952–December 31, 1952), NA.

18. Robert Maguire, "The Unknown Art of Making Peace: Are We Sowing the Seeds of World War III?" *American Bar Association Journal* 35 (Nov. 1949): 907.

19. Ibid.

20. Ibid., 973.

21. Robert Maguire, letter to Kathy Bomke, 29 April 1959, 2 (in possession of the author).

22. Ibid. While praising the fairness of the Nuremberg trials, von Knieriem made a very important observation concerning the obsolescence of the laws of war: "No one who occupies himself with the legal problems of the Nuremberg trials can avoid a consideration of the laws of warfare. But what has happened to these rules of law during the last decades? Have they not perhaps disappeared? Each modern war has been more radical and more horrible than the preceding one; each war has swept away a part of the international law of warfare" (Wilbourn Benton, ed., *Nuremberg: German Views of the War Trials* [Dallas: Southern Methodist University Press, 1953], xxi).

23. Friedrich, "Nuremberg and the Germans," 92. See Tauber, *Beyond Eagle and Swastika*, 40: "Apart from the program of de-nazification, the Allied policy which aroused the most intense public controversy . . . and which most affected the development of radical nationalism was undoubtedly the trial and conviction of the top Nazi leaders before the International Military Tribunal at Nuremberg. . . . Without a doubt, the vast majority of Germans were disabused of certain illusions, some of them deeply rooted, about the Nazi regime." Tauber makes an important point about the irrationality of this debate: "from a nonlegal point of view, the Allies made a mistake when they decided in Moscow and London to bring war criminals before their own courts. Horrendous and overwhelming as the evidence against the Nazi leaders was, or perhaps *because* it was so horrendous and overwhelming, there was a widespread inclination to discount it as propaganda. It must be appreciated that the Germans had been surfeited with the Big Lie for twelve long years. They had, on the whole, developed a certain skeptical immunity to it. When the Allies, in apparent ignorance of that fact, began their publicity campaign for the trials, nationalists and bitter opponents of the occupation regimes quickly exploited this widespread suspicion to cast doubt on the entire procedure" (40).

24. Clay, *Decision in Germany*, 258–259. Clay proved to be a more stalwart supporter of the trials than John McCloy. In 1949, when several of Germany's leading bishops sent the Military Governor a letter criticizing the Nuremberg trials and comparing them to Hitler's trials of the German officers involved in his assassination attempt, Clay "rebutted the bishops' statement point by point. The military governor was

deeply disappointed that even Germany's bishops, as the highest moral authorities, had learned little or nothing from the tragic evidence presented at the trials. . . . Clay argued he could not understand how the review of the evidence could lead the Evangelical church to sympathize with the perpetrators of mass murder" (Buscher, *The U.S. War Crimes Trial Program*, 107).

25. Ann and John Tusa, *The Nuremberg Trial* (New York: Atheneum, 1984), 66–67; Thomas Alan Schwartz, *America's Germany: John J. McCloy and the Federal Republic of Germany* (Cambridge: Harvard University Press, 1991), 42–43. See also McCloy obituary, *The New York Times*, March 12, 1989.

26. Buscher, *The U.S. War Crimes Trial Program*, 56. See also Walter LaFeber, *America, Russia, and the Cold War* (New York: Knopf, 1985),71–72.

27. Thomas Schwartz, "From *Occupation to Alliance*," 137; LaFeber, *America, Russia, and the Cold War*, 73. East Germany held war crimes trials of its own. "In 1964 the East Germans noted that of a total of 12,807 convictions related to the Nazi era, 11,274 took place between 1948 and 1950. In 1950 alone the Waldheim trials led to 4,092 convictions, including 49 executions, 160 life sentences, and 2,914 sentences longer than ten years. The Waldheim trials took place from April to June 1950. Trumpeted as an example of East German determination to confront the Nazi past, the trials instead did more to undermine East German claims to upholding the rule of law. Many cases were decided on the basis of past membership in organizations such as the Nazi Party, the SS, or the Wehrmacht, rather than demonstration of individual responsibility for crimes" (Jeffrey Herf, *Divided Memory: The Nazi Past in the Two Germanys* [Cambridge: Harvard University Press, 1997], 73).

28. Ibid., 306. Paul Nitze, George Kennan, H. Freeman Matthews, and Averell Harriman all urged Secretary of State Dean Acheson to rearm Germany. Tom Bower, *Blind Eye to Murder: Britain, America and the Purging of Nazi Germany—A Pledge Betrayed* (London: Andre Deutsch, 1981) states that the German influence increased "in direct proportion to the rising tension in Europe." German scorn for the trials initially stemmed from the Allies' "association with Stalin's Russia." Their hurt feelings of national honor could not be ignored "after the murder of Masaryk and the communist coup in February 1948" (253). David Kaiser describes the unprecedented political aims of both Cold War protagonists in *Politics and War* (Cambridge: Harvard University Press, 1990): "Both the Soviet and American governments, to begin with, have proclaimed foreign policy goals of extraordinary scope. The official premises of the Cold War make even the dreams of Napoleon look relatively restrained. Since the proclamation of the Truman Doctrine in 1947, the government of the United States has theoretically committed itself to the maintenance of non-Communist regimes throughout the world, without reference to their particular strategic importance. At times American policies have gone further, suggesting that the security of the United States required the disappearance of communism. The Soviet government has claimed to be assisting the gradual transition of the entire world from capitalism to socialism and communism. Both powers, in short, have put themselves forward as a model which the rest of the world must inevitably follow" (423).

29. Ibid., 305. There is considerable fluctuation in the estimates of Soviet military strength. Schwartz's numbers make the differentiation between battle-ready divisions (27) and reserve divisions (75). Stephen E. Ambrose claims in *The Rise to Globalism* (New York: Penguin, 1980) that the ratio of Soviet superiority in ground forces was ten to one. Schwartz, "*Occupation to Alliance*," 265. Adenauer stated in an interview with an American newspaper that the United States would have to assume the burden of defending West Germany.

30. See Schwartz, "*Occupation to Alliance*," 266–267 for more on Adenauer and rearmament. For more on the rise of Konrad Adenauer see Richard Hiscocks, *The Adenauer Era* (New York: Lippincott, 1966). In the first elections of the West German Bundestag in 1949, the Christian Democratic Union took a majority of seats and Adenauer was elected Chancellor by one vote. See "Judge Advocate General to the Assistant Secretary of War, November 22, 1944," in Bradley F. Smith, *The American Road to Nuremberg: The Documentary Record 1944–1945* (Stanford: Hoover Institution Press, 1982). Cramer's suggestions are interesting given the final fate of the German war criminals and the more recent efforts to revise the history of the Third Reich: "I feel quite strongly that the world cannot afford to dispose of the war guilt question by compelling the vanquished nations to make an admission under duress, as it did in article 231 of the Versailles Treaty in 1919. There must be convincing proof of guilt, which should be preserved in such form that the record of trial can be widely distributed" (58).

31. On April 1, 1950, Landsberg Prison held 663 war criminals convicted by American courts (ibid., appendix B).

32. For a detailed, case-by-case analysis of the verdicts and sentences see Telford Taylor, *Final Report to the Secretary of the Army on the Nuernberg War Crimes Trials* (Washington, D.C.: U.S. Government Printing Office, 1949) and John Alan Appleman, *Military Tribunals and International Crimes* (Westport, Conn.: Greenwood, 1971). See also Jean Smith, ed., *The Papers of General Lucius Clay* (Bloomington: Indiana University Press, 1974), 962. Contrary to the claims of the High Commissioner, General Clay had ordered his legal staff (Alvin Rockwell, Judge Madden, and Colonel Raymond) to review all of the death sentences in an effort to see if any grounds existed for commutation. After his legal staff issued their report, General Clay reviewed each case and upheld all but one death sentence. McCloy's premise for creating a clemency board was that no review had been provided. That was a false statement. There were a number of death sentences in the Medical case (7), the Pohl case (3), and the Einsatzgruppen case (13). Levie, *Terrorism in War*, 135–136.

33. Buscher, *The U.S. War Crimes Trial Program*, 107. According to Buscher, "The veterans and refugee groups clearly equated the . . . war criminals with regular POWs," 106–7.

34. Because the IMT was in the hands of the four powers and the Germans were incarcerated in Spandau Prison, their sentences were not easily manipulable because their modification required a consensus. The Russians were not as forgiving in the cases of major war criminals.

35. The High Commissioner made this point most strenuously in his letter to Eleanor Roosevelt and maintained it until his death.

36. Office of the U.S. High Commissioner for Germany, *Landsberg: A Documentary Report* (Frankfurt: U.S. Army, 1951), 18. This report was the first official pronouncement of the High Commissioner's decisions regarding clemency for the German war criminals. It was included in the February 1951 issue of the High Commissioner's "Information Bulletin." McCloy decided to review the sentences of the now "controversial" American war crimes program and offered this justification for his action: "Since my arrival in Germany I have received many letters and petitions asking clemency for war crimes prisoners convicted at Nuremberg and confined in Landsberg Prison. It is a fundamental principle of American justice that accused persons shall be given every opportunity to maintain their innocence." General Clay intended to execute those on Landsberg's death row. He did not want to pass the burden to his successor, John McCloy. Langer's Senate resolution forced the Military Governor to await the findings of the Baldwin committee (a Senate investigation) before proceeding (Smith, ed., *The Papers of General Lucius Clay*, 1012).

37. High Commissioner's press release, 11 January 1950. RG 59, Box 16 (War Crimes 1949, 1950, October 16, 1952–December 31, 1952), NA.

38. Friedrich, "Nuremberg and the Germans," 93. According to Buscher, the German clergy's disapproving statements about American war crimes policy "clearly showed that U.S. efforts to use the trials to reeducate the Germans were in serious trouble. American officials, convinced that National Socialism had resulted from Germany's authoritarian and militaristic past, hoped that the war crimes program would underscore the need to democratize German society. In contrast, the Germans interpreted war crimes trials as attempts to prove their collective guilt. Wurm and Dibelius's attitudes confirmed that the Germans viewed themselves as victims of arbitrary and cruel occupation policies, and not as a people ready and willing to assume responsibility for the Holocaust and other Nazi atrocities" (Buscher, *The U.S. War Crimes Trial Program*, 101–102).

39. Theo Kordt, letter to Lord Halifax, 13 December 1949. This letter was included with Lord Halifax's 19 January 1950 letter to President Truman. RG 59, Box 16 (War Crimes 1949, 1950, October 16, 1952–December 31, 1952), NA.

40. Ibid.

41. President Truman, letter to Lord Halifax, 10 February 1950, RG 59, Box 16 (War Crimes 1949, 1950, October 16, 1952–December 31, 1952), NA.

42. Ernst von Weizsäcker was released from Landsberg Prison on October 16, 1950, several months before the McCloy sentence revisions were announced. Army Commands War Crimes Branch, Cases Tried—Miscellaneous Administration Files, RG 338, NA.

43. Smith, ed., *The Papers of General Lucius Clay*, 305.

44. John Raymond warned, "Any presentation of new evidence by the defendants without the prosecution being represented would be *ex parte* and open to criticism." John Raymond, letter to Colonel Byroade, 2 February 1950, RG 59, Box 16 (War Crimes 1949, 1950, 1952), NA.

45. John Hohenberg, *New York Post*, February 2, 1950.

46. John Hohenberg, *New York Post*, February 3, 1950.

47. John Raymond, memo of conversation, 2 February 1950, RG 59, Box 16 (War Crimes 1949, 1590, 1952), NA.

48. Ibid.

49. Dean Acheson, confidential cable to HICOG, RG 59, Box 16 (War Crimes 1949, 1950, October 16, 1952–December 31, 1952). Dean Acheson, letter to John McCloy, 5 February 1950, RG 466, U.S. High Commission for Germany, Security-Segregated General Records 1949–1952, Box 28, 321.6, War Criminals File, NA.

50. Office of the U.S. High Commissioner for Germany, *Landsberg: A Documentary Report*, 3.

51. Ibid.

52. Schwartz, "Occupation to Alliance," 286.

53. Political theorist Robert Jervis has written that in international politics the pre-conceptions and expectations of the observer are often as important as the empirical facts. "The perceiver's expectations and needs strongly influence what he will see. Subtle messages are easily missed; when they are not, they are usually assimilated to the perceiver's pre-existing beliefs." Robert Jervis, *The Logic of Images in International Relations* (New York: Columbia University Press, 1989), xix. Robert Leckie, *The War in Korea* (New York: Random House, 1963), 20–21. Walter LaFeber, "NATO and the Korean War: A Context," *Diplomatic History* 3 (Spring 1986): 461. LaFeber considers this an example of American preconceptions being confirmed: "The conflict in Korea was a watershed in the history of American foreign policy, but like all watersheds, it had indispensable tributaries. The war did not mark an abrupt break or turn in President Harry S. Truman's foreign policy plans, but formed part of a continuum that had its more important origins ten months earlier when the Soviets exploded their first atomic device and it became clear, with the writing of the State Department White Paper, that the United States had to accept the conquest of China by the Communists. So too, important changes in the NATO alliance did not suddenly become real after June 1950, but had begun in the fall and winter of 1949 when (despite the absence of Soviet military threats to Western interests—an absence acknowledged by top State Department experts) the United States began the institutional restructuring of its foreign policy" (*America, Russia, and the Cold War* [New York: Knopf, 1985], 461–462).

Jervis attaches more importance to the Korean War in "The Impact of the Korean War on the Cold War," *The Journal of Conflict Resolution* 24(4)(Dec. 1980): "the Korean War shaped the course of the Cold War by both resolving the incoherence which characterized U.S. foreign and defense efforts in the period 1946–1950 and establishing important new lines of policy. Second, if the war had not taken place, no other events were likely to have occurred that would have produced the effects that Korea did. . . . Thus without Korea, international history would have been very different" (563). Theodore White most famously described what the Korean War brought for Germany: "quick, complete and unconditional profit" (*Fire in the Ashes* [New York: William Sloan

Associates, 1953], 157). This is probably the single most widely quoted statement concerning the impact of the Korean War on German reconstruction. William Manchester, *The Arms of Krupp* (New York: Bantam, 1968), 751. Manchester's best-seller was extremely helpful because it clearly laid out the events of the Peck Panel and the first clemency procedure for German war criminals. But in trying to write a gripping narrative, Manchester offers a conspiracy theory that blames the Korean War, Washington, and John McCloy for the release of Alfried Krupp and other German war criminals. Though there is some truth to his argument, it is overstated (208–209). For a differing point of view on the impact of the Cold War and the war criminals, see Geoffrey Herf.

54. Robert Divine, *Since 1945: Politics and Diplomacy in Recent American History* (New York: Knopf, 1985), 35.

55. Schwartz, *Occupation to Alliance*, 306. Thomas H. Etzold and John Lewis Gaddis, eds., *Containment: Documents on American Policy and Strategy, 1945–1950* (New York: Columbia University Press, 1978), 383–384. Gaddis argues that the new American strategic doctrine, outlined in "NSC-68 constitutes the most elaborate effort made by United States officials during the early Cold War years to integrate political, economic and military considerations into a comprehensive statement of national security policy. In response to a presidential directive to analyze the combined implications of the Communist victory in China, the Soviet atomic bomb, and the American decision to construct a thermonuclear weapon, a special State and Defense department group headed by Paul Nitze (who in January 1950 had replaced Kennan as head of the Policy Planning Staff) drafted NSC-68 in February and March 1950. The completed study, compromising some seventy single-spaced, legal-sized typed pages, was forwarded to President Truman on April 7, 1950. . . . NSC-68 can be viewed as a 'call to arms' to stave off that prospect by significantly upgrading Western defense capabilities. It can also be seen as an argument in favor of what later came to be known as 'flexible response' " (383–384; for text of NSC-68 see 385–442). For more on NSC-68 see Paul Hammond, "NSC-68: Prologue to Rearmament," in Warner Schilling, Paul Hammond, and Glenn Snyder, eds., *Strategy, Politics and Defense Budgets* (New York: Columbia University Press, 1962), 267–378.

56. Isaacson and Thomas, *The Wise Men*, 513. This is one of McCloy's most famous statements as High Commissioner. Many have accused him of engaging in convenient hyperbole. Like Clay's cable before, he used the cable to influence policy. McCloy made a rather abrupt shift in 1950. As early as February he told a West German audience, "there will be no German army or air force." Drew Middleton, "McCloy Warns the Germans Against a Revival of Nazism," *The New York Times*, February 7, 1950.

57. Manchester, *The Arms of Krupp*, 753. The official decision to rearm Germany came on September 11, 1950, in NSC-82. It initially called for a European defense force with Soviet participation.

58. Hiscocks, *The Adenauer Era*, 220.

59. Ibid., 220.

60. Buscher, *The U.S. War Crimes Trial Program*, 44.

61. *U.S. Military Tribunal Nuremberg, Transcript, Case XI, Weizsaecker*, 28087.

62. Conrad Snow, letter to State Department legal advisor Jack Tate, 26 July 1950, RG 59, Box 18 (War Crimes Clemency 1950–1955), NA.

63. Manchester, *The Arms of Krupp*, 756.

64. John Raymond, confidential memo to Robert Bowie, 11 September 1950, RG 59, Box 18 (War Crimes Clemency 1950–1955). Fredrick Moran reflected on his experience in Germany in a letter to Conrad Snow in October 1950: "I reduced the material to a minimum, but the human beings in Landsberg are still in my mind. I can't forget the 'Generals' who are sick old men, existing in a world which has discarded the values by which they formerly lived. These men are the only people at Landsberg towards whom I wish we had been more generous in our recommendations."

65. Robert Bowie, letter to John Raymond, 11 September 1950, RG 59, Box 18 (War Crimes Clemency 1950–1955), NA.

66. Ibid.

67. Confidential memo of conversation with the President, 16 November 1950, RG 59, Box 29, NA.

68. William Langer with Senator McCurran, *Congressional Record*, December 18, 1950 (Washington, D.C.: U.S. Government Printing Office), 16707–9.

69. Columbia University Oral History Project, Benjamin Buttenwieser, 112.

70. Secret letter from Henry Broade to John McCloy, 6 January 1951, RG 59, Box 18 (War Crimes Clemency, 1950–1955), NA.

71. Jack Raymond, "Bonn Legislators Press McCloy for Amnesty for War Criminals," *The New York Times*, January 10, 1951. This January 12, 1951, cable from a liaison officer to High Commissioner McCloy described the mood of the Bundestag leaders: "During informal conversation January 11, Bundestag President Ehlers stated McCloy's interview regarding Landsberg executions made a strong and favorable impression on Parliamentary delegation. Germans were especially impressed with High Commissioner's sincere and honest desire to explore even the slightest bit of evidence in favor of condemned war criminals. . . . Only disappointment voiced by delegation after interview, according to Ehlers, centered around refusal of High Commissioner to accept German argument based Article 102 Basic Law (abolition of death penalty)" (Samuel Reber to McCloy, 12 January 1951, Misc. Administration File, RG 338, NA).

72. Ibid.

73. *Der Spiegel* magazine (1/31/51) accused John McCloy of having "an almost pathological love for Germany."

74. *The New York Times*, January 10, 1951.

75. Ibid. See also Samuel Reber to John McCloy, 12 January 1951, Misc. Administration Files, RG 338, NA, Misc. Admin. Files, Misc. Files, Modern Military Branch, Suitland.

76. Bower, *Blind Eye to Murder*, 368.

77. Martin Lee, *The Beast Reawakens* (New York: Little, Brown), 69. See also *The New York Times*, "Defends War Criminals: Skorzeny Hitler Aide, Warns in Spain Against Executions," January 13, 1951. See also Rand C. Lewis, *A Nazi Legacy: Right-*

Wing Extremism in Postwar Germany (New York: Praeger, 1991). Buscher describes the early resurgence of post–World War II German nationalism: "Nonetheless, German nationalism between 1946 and 1955 . . . differed from its aggressive predecessor during the Third Reich, although it bore some features which were reminiscent of the widespread post-World War I reaction to the Treaty of Versailles" (91).

78. Adrian Fisher to Dean Acheson, and a draft of a letter to President Truman on the subject of the German war criminals, 25 and 31 January, 1951, RG 59, Box 18 (War Crimes Clemency 1950–1955), NA.

79. Ibid.

80. Office of the U.S. High Commissioner for Germany, *Landsberg: A Documentary Report*, 55.

81. Buscher, *The U.S. War Crimes Trial Program*, 63.

82. Manchester, *The Arms of Krupp*, 756. Once again, McCloy's interpretation was not borne out by the facts. Krupp and his father wholeheartedly aided the Nazi rise. Manchester shows how McCloy repeats the arguments made by Krupp's defense team. Moreover, these arguments were largely rejected by an extremely conservative American war crimes tribunal in 1948. Manchester's accusation that the clemency was "illegal" is incorrect, but he does point to the weakness of the High Commissioner's legal arguments. On McCloy's letter to Eleanor Roosevelt, Manchester writes: "At times the explanations which went out over his signature bordered on sophistry; the confiscation decree had 'already been partially rescinded by General Clay' (Clay had merely pointed out that he couldn't enforce it outside the American zone), and in his reference to foreign workers he merely mentioned Krupp's 'use' of them, never Krupp's *treatment* of them, the hard rock upon which Telford Taylor had built his case" (766). Thomas Schwartz's most thorough analysis of the war crimes question is "*Die Begnadigung Deutscher Kriegsverbrecher. John J. McCloy und die Haftlinge von Landsberg*" in *Vierteljahrshefe für Zeitgeschichte* 38 (July 1990).

83. Appleman, *Military Tribunals and International Crimes*, 219.

84. Office of the U.S. High Commissioner for Germany, *Landsberg: A Documentary Report*, 55.

85. Manchester described the Krupp Works as "a hallowed institution of war" (*The Arms of Krupp*, 766).

86. *The New York Times*, February 2, 1951.

87. Buscher considered the reason to be that "The Germans did not think that their actions in the East were considerably different from what other powers had done in the countries they had occupied. This was coupled with a tendency to blame Germany's post-war problems, such as the loss of the Eastern territories and the economic hardships of the immediate post-war years, on an Allied conspiracy, instead of viewing them as one of the consequences of military defeat. In short, the Germans viewed themselves as a victimized nation. Such an interpretation of the recent past was bound to affect the war crimes program. As early as 1946 there were indications that even the average German was at least indifferent, if not opposed, to American education attempts in that area" (91–92).

88. Office of the U.S. High Commissioner for Germany, *Landsberg: A Documentary Report*, 64.

89. Ibid.

90. Ibid., 63–64.

91. Ibid., 64.

92. Ibid.

93. Ibid., 3. Judge Gordon Simpson reaffirmed the findings of the Army court: "I am likewise convinced that Peiper was the motivating spirit of the terror spreading, killing-prisoner-of-war procedure of this spearhead. The record of the trial is detailed and voluminous. The evidence is compelling and has convinced everyone who has read it objectively that these criminals committed the acts as found by the court which tried them."

94. Ibid., 65.

95. Ibid., 67.

96. Kurt Tauber, *Beyond Eagle and Swastika: German Nationalism Since 1945* (Middletown, Conn.: Wesleyan University Press, 1967), 1:39. This book describes the important role of the German veteran groups in the early 1950s.

97. McCloy defended his role in the Japanese concentration camps similarly. In 1981, he testified before a congressional committee on Japanese internment. McCloy biographer Kai Bird describes the debacle: "He mistakenly thought he would be accorded the usual deference and courtesy of an elder statesman. Things did not work out that way. When he tried to describe conditions in the internment camps as 'very pleasant,' the audience burst into spontaneous laughter. . . . McCloy felt misunderstood. . . . He didn't understand why anyone would think he ever had the power to decide these issues. 'I was just a leg man,' he protested. He was further annoyed when *Harper's* magazine profiled him in a long cover story as 'the most influential private citizen in America.' He tried to stop the publication of the article and, failing that, vigorously protested its treatment of his role in the internment, Auschwitz, and Krupp decisions" (*The Chairman: John J. McCloy, the Making of the American Establishment* [New York: Simon and Schuster, 1992], 659–660).

Jacob Heilbrunn makes a simple, yet often overlooked point: "Certainly McCloy's lack of compassion for the Jews trapped in Auschwitz contrasts curiously with his solicitude for their prosecutors" ("The Real McCloy," *The New Republic* [October 16, 1992], 44). Heibrunn's statement about McCloy's role in the deportation of Japanese Americans is telling. "The cunning with which McCloy carried out the internment of the issei and the nisei, first- and second-generation Japanese respectively, proved that he was a good student of Root's on flouting the Constitution and abdicating moral responsibility." Heilbrunn was not impressed by McCloy's strategic legalism: "Once again McCloy was more papist than the pope. He came down on the Army's side. 'If it is a question of the safety of the country, [or] the Constitution of the United States,' he exclaimed, 'why the Constitution is just a scrap of paper to me' " (42). Many years after leaving Germany, McCloy best described the mindset of the American lawyer-statesmen: "I saw my public service in terms of getting things done. . . . I never considered myself a politician, but rather a lawyer, so the question I asked myself in the various jobs I had was 'What should we do to solve the problem at hand?' then I tried to solve the problem" (*New York Times* obituary, March 12, 1989). In 1951 his objectives were to rearm and realign Germany with the United States. One fast-growing "problem at hand" was the continued imprisonment of German war criminals.

98. Friedrich, "Nuremberg and the Germans," 98.

99. Buscher, *The U.S. War Crimes Trial Program*, 118. Buscher describes the shortcomings of the American system: "However, this system was without a foundation due to the absence of a more general long-range punishment policy encompassing all aspects of the occupation. . . . A second important shortcoming was the lack of any planning for an appellate court" (22). Tom Schwartz places the lack of careful planning into the larger context of American foreign policy: "The historical memory of the Americans, as is well known, is very short, and just as the prohibition of fraternization with the German people was abandoned, the passionate anti-German posture did not last as long as the trials dragged on" ("*Die Begnadigung Deutscher Kriegsverbrecher*" [translation by the author and Martin Splichal] 378). Buscher describes the role that sentence review played in the post-trial period: "Most importantly, these operations put in place a mechanism which made the political abuse of sentence reviews and clemency possible in the coming years. It is not surprising that the Allies and the Germans decided to rely on this method of sentence reduction after January 1951" (*The U.S. War Crimes Trial Program* 59). Bower, *Blind Eye to Murder*, 368. The most prominent German private interest group was the *Heidelberger Juristenkreis*, or Heidelberg circle of jurists. According to Frank Buscher, "The group maintained close ties with Adenauer and his government, and it carried enough political weight to arrange conferences with American occupation authorities. This allowed the Juristenkreis to work as a clearing house for information and to draw up policy proposals for the German government regarding possible solutions to the war criminals problem. As a result, this secretive organization credited itself with two major developments in the early 1950s: the Article 6 Allied-German mixed clemency commission in 1952 and the concept of the interim mixed boards in 1953" (*The U.S. War Crimes Trial Program* 101). The less respectable advocacy group was Ernst Achenbach's *Vorbereitender Ausschuss für die Herbeifuhrungeiner Generalamnestie* (Preparatory Committee for a General Amnesty, also known as the Essen Amnesty Committee). Their argument was "*Nach totale kreig, totale Amnestie.*" The Essen Amnesty Committee wanted all war criminals freed, regardless of their crimes (101).

100. Ibid., 101.

101. Otto Kranzbühler, interview by author, tape recording, Tegensee, Germany, 16 August 1996.

102. Ibid.

103. Ibid.

104. Buscher, *The U.S. War Crimes Trial Program*, 105. American Consul General LaVerne Baldwin to State Department, Washington, 28 February 1952, RG 59, Box 29, NA.

105. An interesting report was issued by the Political and Public Affairs Section of the American Consulate General, August 20, 1951, and classified all the clemency appeals according to the interests of the petitioning parties. RG 466, Box 28, 321.6. See also Buscher, *The U.S. War Crimes Trial Program*, 91–92. A 1952 HICOG survey, "Current West German View on the War Crimes Issue," indicated that the powerful and educated were most aggressive in their rejection of the trials and imprisonment of the war criminals (HICOG Office of Public Affairs, Research Analysis Staff, 8 September 1952, RG 338, Box 469).

106. Princess Isemberg was given the sobriquet "the mother of the red jackets" and waged a one-woman battle to win freedom of the convicted German war criminals. She sent telegrams to President Truman, Secretary of State Acheson, and Mrs. McCloy (who was a distant cousin of Konrad Adenauer). According to *Der Spiegel*, the Princess even dined with the McCloys and pleaded the case of the condemned for two and a half hours. She argued that "the red jackets had suffered horrible torment in fear of death and are almost insane." According to one account, Mrs. McCloy sent the princess a check to aid the prisoners and wrote: "I too feel that we have to bridge our mutual problems, and I assure you, it was for Mr. McCloy and myself not only an honor but also a great joy to have you as our guest" (*Der Spiegel*, 31 January 1951; quoted in Haren Tetens, *The New Germany and the Old Nazis* [New York: Random House, 1961], 209). See also Princess Helene von Isemberg, telegram to General Handy, 11 September 1951, RG 338, NA.

Much of the German historiography concurs: "Recent studies indicate that the West German elites provided the most resistance to Allied occupation policies and reform efforts. Wolfgang Benz described this phenomenon in his survey on Allied initiatives to reform the civil service" (92; see also Wolfgang Benz, "*Versuche zur Reform des öffentlichen Dienstes in Deutschland 1945–52: Deutsche Opposition gegen alliierte Initiativen*," *Vierteljahrshafte für Zeitgeschichte* 29 [1981]: 216–245; Verena Botzenhart-Viehe, *The German Reaction to the American Occupation 1944–1947*, Ph.D. diss., University of California-Santa Barbara, 1980). Botzenhart-Viehe also documents the role of German elites in "instigating the opposition to American reeducation efforts" (from Buscher, *The U.S. War Crimes Trial Program*, 115). Thomas Schwartz makes a similar point: "One of the main problems remained the extent to which a significant portion of the political, economic, ecclesiastical and economic elites of the new Federal Republic sympathized with the condemned war criminals. This solidarity undermined the attempt of the Americans" ("*Die Begnadigung Deutscher Kriegsverbrecher*" 379).

107. Herman Guthard, letter to General Handy, 25 January 1951, Army Command War Crimes Branch, Misc. Admin. Files, RG 338, NA.

108. Tauber, *Beyond Eagle and Swastika*, 356.

109. *Defense Briefs, Lammers and Meissner, Cross/Closing, XIB*, (Nurenberg: Secretariat for Military Tribunals, 1949), 67.

110. Buscher, *The U.S. War Crimes Trial Program*, 118.

111. Tauber, *Beyond Eagle and Swastika*, 259.

112. Article 131 of the Federal Republic of Germany's Basic Law denied members

of the Waffen SS their military pensions. Waffen SS veterans would later argue that they had been collectively branded with guilt by association.

113. Tauber, *Beyond Eagle and Swastika*, 346.

114. Ibid., 349. Former SS officer and veteran group organizer Harald Milde embodied this tendency to an extreme degree: "One should not debate about Adolf Hitler. That man was too great to be judged by any old hack writer. . . . Men like Adenauer and Heuss shall not be mentioned in the same breath with a man like Adolf Hitler. . . . There is perhaps only one chance and that is that we soldiers, we front-line soldiers of all nations join together before it is too late." Milde was a former SS major and right-wing activist. He argued that all former soldiers should remain aloof from party politics and join together in one all-embracing Wehrmacht. Buscher describes the military's attitudes toward the issue of war crimes: "The former military men considered the release of the war criminals a prerequisite to a German contribution to the EDC. The veterans condemned the Allied war crimes trials, and particularly those involving Wehrmacht officers, as a direct attack on the honor of the German soldier. One critic, Infantry General Schack called this alleged defamation of Germany's military the '*kulturschande*' (cultural disgrace) of the twentieth century. . . . The German response to the punishment of the war criminals strongly points to a continuity in German nationalism. The 1945 surrender evidently did not lead to a clean break and a completely new national identity, even though post-war German nationalism did not contain the militaristic and authoritarian features of its predecessor" (*The U.S. War Crimes Trial Program* 91–92).

115. Ibid. "In addition, U.S. officials wanted Adenauer to win the September 1953 federal elections. But the war criminals problem had put the chancellor in the very awkward position of appearing to be more pro-Allied than pro-German" (148).

116. "Bavarian Reactions to Decisions Concerning Landsberg War Criminals," 2 February 1951, RG 59, Box 18 (War Crimes Clemency 1950–1955), NA.

117. Tauber, *Beyond Eagle and Swastika*, 259.

118. Field Marshal Kesselring's letter was restrained in comparison to the more zealous nationalists, but he struck the same anti-Soviet chords: "However, I am sure, Sir, that you are as interested in the formation of first-class troops as I, the former German leader, am interested in seeing the German troop contingent formed. Our neighbor in the East whose disadvantages and advantages I know quite well, will easily find out whether or not the new German soldier will equal the one of 1940 to 1945. The Kremlin will draw its conclusions accordingly. . . . It seems to me, Sir, the time to change courses. It is not only the former German soldiers who would be happy to see the problem of war criminals solved; we will all be grateful to you if you order further releases and thereby make the public understand that the course has been changed. Time is against us." "It is our duty as soldiers to abandon our usual reserve in order to tell the politicians very clearly that the direction taken in 1945 will result in severe damage and disadvantages to the soldiers of today and tomorrow—damage which will make the difference between victory and defeat in war" (Kesselring to Eddy, 31 December 1952, Army Command War Crimes Branch, Misc. Admin. Files, RG 338, NA).

119. Lee, *The Beast Reawakens*, 65.

120. "Bavarian Reaction to Decision Concerning Landsberg War Criminals," 9 February 1951, RG 59, Box 18 (War Crimes Clemency 1950–1955), NA.

121. "West German Reactions to the Landsberg Decisions," U.S. High Commission confidential report, 6 March 1951, RG 59, Box 5 (Clemency Board on German War Criminals), NA.

122. "German Buergermeisters and the Landsberg Decisions," State Department Office of Public Affairs, 21 March 1951, RG 59, Box 18 (War Crimes Clemency 1950–1955), NA.

123. Ibid.

124. Ibid.

125. "Further Findings on West German Reactions to the Landsberg Decisions," State Department Office of Public Affairs, 30 March 1951, RG 59, Box 18 (War Crimes Clemency 1950–1955), NA.

126. *The New York Times* quoted Governor Dewey's description of Peck Panel member Fredrick Moran in his obituary, "a pioneer leader in parole."

127. "Germany's 'Dreyfus Affair': I Accuse! An open letter from General Oswald Pohl (in Landsberg Prison) to General Karl Wolff," RG 59, Box 29, NA.

128. HICOG Bonn to State Department Washington, 24 May 1951, RG 59, Box 29, NA.

129. Buscher, *The U.S. War Crimes Trial Program*, 91–92.

130. Ibid., 125–127.

131. John McCloy, letter to Eleanor Roosevelt, 12 March 1951, 2, Roosevelt Library, Hyde Park, New York.

132. Ibid., 2–3.

133. Ibid. As the years went by McCloy grew prickly about his more controversial legacies (the Landsberg decisions, the concentration camps in California, and the decision not to bomb the railways leading to Auschwitz). The Landsberg decisions were the worst of his career, and McCloy knew it. In the late 1970s he still clung to the position that there was "not a goddamn bit of truth" to the contention that international politics had motivated his decisions. When William Manchester presented the former High Commissioner with the case against him, he merely looked at the paper and replied, "That's ancient history" (Manchester, *The Arms of Krupp*, 770).

What further complicates the McCloy case is the number and prominence of his supporters. Benjamin Ferencz, the former Chief Counsel in the Einsatzgruppen case, defends the High Commissioner. In a letter to the author, Ferencz wrote: "Sure, some U.S. leaders were primarily interested in getting Germany re-armed but that does not mean that releasing war criminals was the negotiated price deliberately paid for German cooperation. As misguided as the commutations may have been, and as detrimental to the Nuremberg proceedings as they were, it is my own considered judgment that as far as McCloy is concerned, there were other motives that were decisive, and the re-armament consideration—if it existed at all—was rather a sub-conscious desire to get the past behind us and move on to a new Germany as part of a unified western alliance" (Benjamin Ferencz, letter to author, 23 February 1990). McCloy wrote Ferencz a most revealing letter in the spring of 1980: "At long last I acknowledge receipt of your book which I have read with great interest. It opened up a number of facts which were new to me. I am much impressed by the research that must have gone into it. If I had all the facts I now have, I might have reached a more just result. It was an ordeal that I would not care to repeat" (John McCloy, letter to Ben Ferencz, 10 April 1980 [courtesy of Benjamin Ferencz]). Although there was a hint of regret in this personal letter, publicly McCloy stubbornly refused to concede his past errors, which seemed to provoke as much irritation as his actual decisions. His lack of contrition irritated author Peter Irons. In a letter to the *New York Times Book Review*: "Forty years apart, John J. McCloy made telling comments about the internment. Responding to an Army general who questioned its legality, he said, 'The Constitution is just a scrap of paper.' Before the Presidential commission in 1981, he defended the internment as 'retribution' for the Pearl Harbor attack. His lack of repentance gives McCloy a unique and unenviable place in American history" (Peter Irons, *New York Times Book Review*, July 5, 1992, 4). *The New York Times*, John McCloy obituary, March 12, 1989. Jacob Heilbrunn, "The Real McCloy," *The New Republic*, May 11, 1992, 40.

134. John McCloy, letter to Eleanor Roosevelt, 12 March 1951, Roosevelt Library, Hyde Park, NY, 2.

135. *New York Herald Tribune*, March 29, 1951. The *Information Bulletin* refused to print Telford Taylor's response to McCloy's Eleanor Roosevelt letter.

136. "Shawcross Condemns Leniency Granted to War Criminals," *New York Herald Tribune*, March 29, 1951.

137. State Department London to Secretary of State, 29 March 1951, RG 59, Box 18 (War Crimes Clemency 1950–1955), NA.

138. John McCloy, telegram to Dean Acheson, 30 March 1951, RG 59, Box 18 (War Crimes Clemency 1950–1955), NA.

139. *The New York Times*, May 25, 1951.

140. *The New York Times*, June 8, 1951.

141. Friedrich, "Nuremberg and the Germans," 98.

142. American Vice Consul Ernest Ramsaur, confidential cable to State Department, 29 June 1951, RG 59, Box 29, NA.

143. Ibid.

144. Ibid.

6. The War Criminals and the Restoration of West German Sovereignty

1. Frank Buscher, *The U.S. War Crimes Trial Program in Germany, 1946-1955* (New York: Greenwood, 1989), 132–133.

2. Ibid.

3. Ibid., 135.

4. State Department Bonn, secret cable to Secretary of State, 30 October 1951, RG 59, Box 29, NA.

5. Ibid. See also Jörg Friedrich, "Nuremberg and the Germans," in Belinda Cooper, ed., *War Crimes: The Legacy of Nuremberg* (New York: TV Books, 1999), 99.

6. U.S. Embassy London (Gifford), secret cable to Secretary of State, 21 December 1951, RG 59, Box 24 (War Crimes Clemency July 1952–December 1953), NA.

7. Ibid.

8. High Commissioner McCloy, secret cable to Secretary of State, 21 December 1951, RG 59, Box 29, NA.

9. Ibid.

10. Buscher, *The U.S. War Crimes Trial Program in Germany*, 75.

11. Ibid., 135.

12. Kurt Tauber, *Beyond Eagle and Swastika: German Nationalism Since 1945* (Middletown: Wesleyan University Press, 1967), 259.

13. Charles Thayer, secretary report to the State Department, 12 March 1952, RG 59, Box 29, NA.

14. Ibid.

15. Ibid.

16. Otto Kranzbühler, interview by author, tape recording, Tegernsee, Germany, August 1996. See also Friedrich, "Nuremberg and the Germans," 99.

17. Otto Kranzbühler, interview by author, tape recording, Tegernsee, Germany, August 1996.

18. Ibid.

19. Ibid.

20. Friedrich, "Nuremberg and the Germans," 102–105. The treaty articles related to war crimes are reprinted in Cooper, ed., *War Crimes*.

21. Otto Kranzbühler, interview by author, Tegernsee, Germany, August 1996; Buscher, *The U.S. War Crimes Trial Program in Germany*, 127. From Richard Hiscocks, *The Adenauer Era* (New York: Lippincott, 1966): "The Brussels Treaty of 1948 was to be extended to include the German Federal Republic and Italy and was to become known as the Western Eruopean Union; the Federal Republic was to become a member of NATO; and the Bonn agreements of May 1952, subject to certain minor alterations, were to come into force. These arrangements, known as the Paris treaties, were ratified in February 1955 by the Federal Republic and in March by France. They went into effect on May 5. The Western occupation of Germany came to an end; the Allied high commissioners became ambassadors; subejct only to the reservations agreed upon in May 1952, the Federal Republic attained full sovereignty; and it became a member of the Western alliance" (39).

22. "McCloy Confident on West Germany," *The New York Times*, July 17, 1952; see also Buscher, *The U.S. War Crimes Trial Program in Germany*, 141.

23. Admiral Gottfried Hansen to Matthew Ridgeway, 10 August 1952, RG 59, Box 29, NA. See also a *Frankfurt Allgemeine* article of 18 August 1952, "A Mortage of a Special Kind," by Adelbert Weinstein.

24. Ibid.

25. Ibid.

26. *Anzeiger*, September 3, 1952, RG 59, Box 29, NA.

27. Friedrich, "Nuremberg and the Germans," 97.

28. HICOG, Secret Report on War Criminals to State Department, 6 September 1952, RG 59, Box 29, NA.

29. Ibid.

30. State Department Office of Public Affairs August Flash Survey, 16 September 1952, RG 59, Box 29, NA. See also Buscher, *The U.S. War Crimes Trial Program*, 109.

31. Buscher, *The U.S. War Crimes Trial Program in Germany*, 144. See also State Department Bonn to Secretary of State, 17 September 1952, RG 59, Box 29, NA.

32. Buscher, *The U.S. War Crimes Trial Program in Germany*, 144.

33. Ibid., 143. See also appendix B.

34. Ibid., 80.

35. James Riddleberger, secret letter to Walter Donnelly, 13 October 1952, RG 59, Box 16 (War Crimes 1949, 1950, October 16, 1952–December 31, 1952), NA.

36. Ibid.

37. Christopher Simpson, *The Splendid Blond Beast: Money, Law, and Genocide in the Twentieth Century* (New York: Grove, 1993), 20–22.

38. Ibid.

39. Ibid., 25; Columbia Oral History Project: John McCloy, 21.

40. Buscher, *The U.S. War Crimes Trial Program in Germany*, 149.

41. "War Criminal Question" Report from HICOG written by various staff members of the State Department's Office of Political Affairs, 22 December 1952, RG 466, Box 28, 321.6, NA.

42. Ibid., 3.

43. State Department deputy legal advisor John Raymond to Brewster Morris, 5 January 1953, RG 59, Box 18 (War Crimes Clemency 1950–1955), NA.

44. John Auchincloss to John Raymond, 9 January 1953, RG 59, Box 16 (War Crimes 1949, 1950, October 16, 1952–December 31, 1952), NA.

45. Ibid.

46. Ibid.

47. "Political Brief No. 5: Political Aspects of the War Criminal Question," 1 February 1953, RG 59, Box 17 (War Crimes 1953–1959), NA.

48. Ibid.

49. Ibid.

50. John Raymond to the Department of Defense, 15 May 1953, RG 59, Box 18 (War Crimes Clemency 1950–1955), NA.

51. Preconference memo on the war criminals prepared by State Department legal advisor John Auchincloss, 31 March 1953, RG 59, Box 17 (War Crimes 1953–1959), NA.

52. Ibid.

53. Ibid.

54. "U.S.-German Political Talks, April 8, 1953: Minutes—Second General Meeting," RG 59, Box 18 (War Crimes Clemency 1950–1955), NA.

55. The minutes of the talks are also in *The Foreign Relations of the United States: Germany and Austria 1952–1954* (Washington, D.C.: U.S. Government Printing Office, 1983), 434. Townsend Hoopes, *The Devil and John Foster Dulles* (Boston: Little, Brown, 1973), 67. Dulles was a consummate strategic legalist whose Wall Street firm had strong ties with German industrialists. Historian Michael Coles describes Dulles in an unpublished review of Hoopes's book: "The book deals with Dulles, the righteous Christian crusader against the devil in the guise of communism. It also deals with Dulles the lawyer who was at his best in dealing with the immediate tactical needs of his client and possibly at his worst in assessing the long term impact of those tactics" (Coles, unpublished book review, 1990, 1). Christopher Simpson offers a more conspiratorial treatment of the Dulles brothers and their relations with German big business and its impact on the prosecution of the German war criminals in the *The Splendid Blond Beast*. However, Simpson's contentions are not without some footing in historical fact.

56. Ibid., 434, 442–443.

57. *The New York Times*, July 14, 1953.

58. "U.S.-German Political Talks, April 8, 1953: Minutes—First General Meeting," RG 59, Box 18 (War Crimes Clemency 1950–1955), NA.

59. James Conant to Secretary of State, 1 April 1953, RG 59, Box 18 (War Crimes Clemency 1950–1955), NA.

60. "Memo Regarding Proposed Parole of German War Criminals," 4 June 1953, RG 59, Box 18 (War Crimes Clemency 1950–1955), NA.

61. Ibid.

62. Ibid.

63. Ibid.

64. Ibid.

65. Confidential Memo on the Parole System for German War Criminals in U.S. Custody, 9 June 1953, RG 59, Box 18 (War Crimes Clemency 1950–1955), NA.

66. Ibid.

67. Ibid.

68. Ibid.

69. James Riddleberger to Secretary of State John Foster Dulles, 15 June 1953, RG 59, Box 18 (War Crimes Clemency 1950–1955), NA.

70. Ibid.

71. Ibid.

72. Ibid.

73. Ibid. "The military objections are firmly held, and there is no prospect of overcoming them by further argument at the same level."

74. James Riddleberger to John Foster Dulles, 19 June 1953, RG 59, Box 18 (War Crimes Clemency 1950–1955), NA.

75. Ibid.

76. John Auchincloss to John Raymond, 29 June 1953, RG 59, Box 17 (War Crimes 1953–1959), NA.

77. John Foster Dulles to U.S. High Commission in Bonn, 25 June 1953, RG 59, Box 17 (War Crimes 1953–1959), NA.

78. Memo on war criminal paroles written by John Auchincloss and John Raymond for Secretary of State John Foster Dulles, 26 June 1953, RG 59, Box 17 (War Crimes 1953–1959), NA.

79. Buscher, *The U.S. War Crimes Trial Program in Germany*, 81–82.

80. Colonel Howard Levie (JAG Chief of Internal Affairs) to Brigadier General George Gardes, 5 March 1956, Army Command War Crimes Branch, Misc. Admin. Files, RG 338, NA. See also Buscher, *The U.S. War Crimes Trial Program in Germany*, 81–84.

81. Levie to Gardes, 5 March 1956. See also RG 59, Box 17, War Crimes: 1953–1959, "Briefing for Secretary's Press Conference December 6, 1955."

82. Levie to Gardes, 5 March 1956.

83. Ibid.

84. Ibid.

85. Michael Balfour, *West Germany: A Contemporary History* (Connecticut: Croom & Helm, 1982), 190. By 1952, Chancellor Adenauer publicly vowed to wage an all-out effort to free the German war criminals. Alan Cowell, "Germany Defends Pensions for SS Veterans," *The New York Times*, May 9, 1999: "More than half a century after World War II, the German authorities have acknowledged that war disability pensions are still being paid to members of Waffen-SS units and even to war criminals."

86. From T. H. Tetens, *The New Germany and the Old Nazis* (New York: Random House, 1961), 65–66.

87. Ibid., 67.

88. Dr. Friedrich Middelhauve to Thomas Handy, RG 466, 321.6, NA.

89. Paul Gernert, U.S. Parole Officer to the High Commissioner, 23 April 1954, Army Command War Crimes Branch, Misc. Admin. Files, RG 338, NA. Frank Buscher considers the action of the IMPAC board a sell-out of American war crimes policy. But the Americans were not alone; the British and French instituted similar programs: "Although IMPAC did not release all war criminals from American custody, it sufficiently reduced the problem so that German rearmament and sovereignty were no longer in jeopardy. The United States had sold out its war crimes program— so had the British and French. Thus, the trial operation, which was to punish the perpetrators and, at the same time, teach the Germans the virtues of democracy by demonstrating the evils of Nazism, simply fell by the wayside" (*The U.S. War Crimes Trial Program in Germany* 85).

90. Dower, *Embracing Defeat*, 514, 453; State Department legal advisor John Auchincloss to Geoffrey Lewis at the U.S. embassy in Bonn, 28 January 1954, RG 59, Box 16 (War Crimes 1949, 1950, October 16, 1952–December 31, 1952), NA.

91. Ibid.

92. Ibid.

93. Ibid.

94. Drafted by John Auchincloss for Cecil Lyon to James Bonbright, State Department, 16 February 1954, RG 59, Box 17 (War Crimes 1953–1959), NA.

95. Ibid.

96. Ibid.

97. "Memorandum of Conversation: General Amnesty for Japanese War Criminals, February 16, 1954," RG 59, Box 18 (War Crimes Clemency 1950–1955), NA. The participants in this meeting included State Department Far East heads Ambassador John Allison and Walter Robertson. State Department legal advisor John Raymond, former Peck Panel member Conrad Snow, and Cecil Lyon represented the State Department's German interests.

98. Ibid.

99. Secretary of State John Foster Dulles to Ambassador Allison, 26 May 1954, RG 59, Box 18 (War Crimes Clemency 1950–1955), NA.

100. Geoffrey Lewis to Edwin Plitt, 25 May 1954, RG 59, Box 18 (War Crimes Clemency 1950–1955), NA.

101. Richard Hagan to John Raymond, June 1954, RG 59, Box 18, NA.

102. Buscher, *The U.S. War Crimes Trial Program in Germany*, 149–151. See for a good summary of the death of the EDC Treaty.

103. *The New York Times*, August 30, 1954.

104. Ambassador Conant to Secretary of State, 20 December 1954, RG 59, Box 18, NA.

105. State Department Bonn Memorandum: "Conversation with Von Meratz and Heye," 18 January 1955, RG 59, Box 18, NA.

106. Ibid.

107. Ibid.

108. Elim O'Shaughnessy, director of HICOG political affairs office, to State Department Washington, 2 March 1955, RG 59, Box 16 (War Crimes 1949, 1950, October 16, 1952–December 31, 1952), NA.

109. Ibid.

110. James Conant to Secretary of State Dulles, 22 January 1955, RG 59, Box 18, (War Crimes Clemency 1950–1955), NA.

111. Richard Hagan, secret letter to John Raymond, 4 March 1955, RG 59, Box 18, NA.

112. *The New York Times*, July 26, 1953.

113. Buscher, *The U.S. War Crimes Trial Program in Germany*, 153.

114. Secretary of State, cable to State Department Bonn, 25 July 1955, RG 59, Box 19 (War Crimes Clemency January 1956–1959), NA.

115. Colonel Howard Levie to Brigadier General George Gardes, 5 March 1956, 2, Army Command War Crimes Branch, Misc. Admin. Files, RG 338, NA.

116. Ibid.

117. Ibid.

118. Richard Hagan to John Raymond, 19 April 1955, RG 59, Box 18 (War Crimes Clemency 1950–1955), NA.

119. See Stephen Ambrose, *Citizen Soldiers* (New York: Touchstone, 1997), 224–225, for more on Bastogne.

120. Knox Lamb, U.S. Embassy Bonn to State Department, 3 August 1955, RG 59, Box 16 (War Crimes 1949, 1950, October 16, 1952–December 31, 1952), NA.

121. Ibid.

122. Ibid.

123. Ibid.

124. American Embassy Bonn to State Department Washington, 3 August 1955, RG 59, Box 17, NA.

125. Ibid.

126. Ibid.

127. State Department Bonn to State Department Washington, 16 September 1955, Box 18 (War Crimes Clemency 1950–1955), RG 59, NA.

128. For more on Dietrich, see Reitlinger, *The SS: Alibi of a Nation*, 56–57.

129. Ambassador Conant to Secretary of State, 4 November 1955, RG 59, Box 18 (War Crimes Clemency 1950–1955), NA.

130. State Department Bonn to Washington, 7 November 1955, RG 59, Box 18 (War Crimes Clemency 1950–1955), NA.

131. Estes Kefauver to John Foster Dulles, 8 November 1955, RG 59, Box 18 (War Crimes Clemency 1950–1955), NA.

132. Veterans of Foreign Wars Commander Joseph Lombardo to Secretary of Defense Charles Wilson, 8 November 1955, RG 59, Box 18, (War Crimes Clemency 1950–1955), NA.

133. Ibid.

134. State Department legal advisor John Raymond, press release to Mr. Wilkinson, 29 November 1955, RG 59, Box 17 (War Crimes 1953–1959), NA.

135. Ambassador Conant to Secretary of State, 30 November 1955, RG 59, Box 18 (War Crimes Clemency 1950–1955), NA

136. Ibid.

137. "Briefing for Secretary's Press Conference," 6 December 1955, RG 59, Box 17 (War Crimes 1953–1959), NA.

138. Livingston Merchant to James Conant, 10 December 1955, RG 59, Box 18 (War Crimes Clemency 1950–1955), NA.

139. Ibid.

140. Ibid.

141. John Raymond, secret memo to Ambassador Conant, 27 December 1955, RG 59, Box 17 (War Crimes 1953–1959), NA.

142. Livingston Merchant to Ambassador Conant, 30 December 1955, RG 59, Box 17 (War Crimes 1953–1959), NA.

143. Ibid.

144. Papal Nuncio Archbishop Fargo to Secretary of State Dulles, 6 January 1956, RG 59, Box 19 (War Crimes Clemency January 1956–1959), NA.

145. *Stars and Stripes*, January 6, 1956.

146. Report by Elim O'Shaughnessy, U.S. Embassy Bonn, 18 January 1956, RG 59, Box 19 (War Crimes Clemency January 1956–1959), NA.

147. Ibid.

148. British Embassy Washington to State Department, 1 January 1956, Box 19 (War Crimes Clemency January 1956–1959), RG 59, NA. "It would be contrary to long-established precedent in the United Kingdom to publish the reasons on which the recommending majority bases advice to the executive authority on the exercise of clemency."

149. John Auchincloss to Max Meron, 3 February 1956, RG 59, Box 19 (War Crimes Clemency Jan. 1956–1959), NA.

150. Ibid.

151. State Department general counsel Knox Lamb to State Department, 13 February 1956, RG 59, Box 19 (War Crimes Clemency January 1956–1959), NA.

152. State Department legal advisor John Raymond to assistant legal advisor John Auchincloss, 8 March 1956, RG 59, Box 19 (War Crimes Clemency January 1956–1959), NA. See also "258 Germans under American Law in the Sovereign Federal Republic" in *Der Stern*, March 17, 1956.

153. Robert Upton to John Raymond, 29 March 1956, RG 59, Box 19 (War Crimes Clemency January 1956–1959), NA: "for the average case rather than the exceptional case in which the granting of parole would defeat the ends of justice."

154. State Department legal advisor John Raymond to assistant legal advisor John Auchincloss, 11 April 1956, RG 59, Box 16 (War Crimes 1949, 1950, October 16, 1952–December 31, 1952), NA.

155. Conrad Snow, chairman of the Clemency and Parole Board for War Criminals, to Senator Robert Upton, 10 April 1956, RG 59, Box 19 (War Crimes Clemency January 1956–1959), NA.

156. Major General Claude Mickelwait to State Department legal advisor John Raymond, 12 April 1956, RG 59, Box 19 (War Crimes Clemency January 1956–1959), NA.

157. Ibid.

158. Senator Robert Upton to State Department legal advisor John Raymond, 29 March 1956, RG 59, Box 19 (War Crimes Clemency January 1956–1959), NA.

159. Ibid.

160. Ibid.

161. Ibid.

162. Ibid.

163. Robert Upton to John Raymond, 8 May 1956, RG 59, Box 19 (War Crimes Clemency January 1956–1959), NA.

164. John Raymond to Robert Upton, 10 May 1956, RG 59, Box 19 (War Crimes Clemency January 1956–1959), NA.

165. Robert Upton to John Raymond, 17 May 1956, RG 59, Box 19 (War Crimes Clemency January 1956–1959), NA. Robert Upton to John Raymond, 8 May 1956, RG 59, Box 19 (War Crimes Clemency January 1956–1959), NA.

166. Numbers from Colonel Howard Levie to General George Gardes, 25 January 1956, Parole Report, Army Command War Crimes Branch, Misc. Admin. Files, RG 338, NA.

167. Elim O'Shaughnessy, State Department Bonn, to Secretary of State, 9 June 1956, RG 59, Box 19 (War Crimes Clemency January 1956–1959), NA.

168. "Chancellor Adenauer Visit, Washington: German War Criminals Held by the United States," 8 June 1956, RG 59, Box 19 (War Crimes Clemency January 1956–1959), NA.

169. Robert Upton to John Raymond, 11 June 1956, RG 59, Box 19 (War Crimes Clemency January 1956–1959), NA.

170. Ibid.

171. Ibid.

172. Ibid.

173. American Legion National Commander Addington Wagner to Secretary of State John Foster Dulles, 15 June 1956, RG 59, Box 19 (War Crimes Clemency January 1956–1959), NA.

174. "Memorandum of Conversation: The Mixed Board," 26 June 1956, RG 59, Box 19 (War Crimes Clemency January 1956–1959), NA. The participants in this meeting were Robert Upton, John Raymond, and Robert Creel from the State Department's German section.

175. "Memorandum of Conversation: Public Information in German War Crimes Cases," 31 July 1956, RG 59, Box 19 (War Crimes Clemency January 1956–1959), NA. The participants in this meeting were John Raymond, John Auchincloss, Spencer Phenix, Mr. Kearney, and Mr. Lampson.

176. Robert Upton to John Raymond, 7 September 1956, RG 59, Box 19 (War Crimes Clemency January 1956–1959), NA.

177. Edward Lampson, State Department Germany, to Mr. Lisle, 9 November 1956, RG 59, Box 17 (War Crimes 1953–1959), NA.

178. Ibid.

179. State Department Memo, "War Criminals," drafted by Richard Kearney, 12 December 1956, RG 59, Box 19 (War Crimes Clemency January 1956–1959), NA.

180. Ibid.

180. Ibid.

181. Ibid.

182. Ibid.

183. Spencer Phenix to John Raymond, 8 February 1957, RG 59 Box 19 (War Crimes Clemency January 1956–1959), NA. There was a cover letter and memos A and B.

184. Ibid.

185. Ibid.

186. Ibid.

187. Ibid.

188. Ibid.

189. John Raymond's handwritten comment was clipped to the Phenix cover letter, 14 March 1957, RG 59, Box 19 (War Crimes Clemency January 1956–1959), NA.

190. Spencer Phenix, secret letter to John Raymond, 17 April 1956, RG 59, Box 19 (War Crimes Clemency January 1956–1959), NA.

191. Spencer Phenix, secret letter to John Raymond, 21 July 1957, RG 59, Box 19 (War Crimes Clemency January 1956–1959), NA.

192. "Memorandum of Conversation: Informal Approach by German Embassy on German War Criminals," 18 March 1957, RG 59, Box 19 (War Crimes Clemency January 1956–1959), NA.

193. Spencer Phenix to John Raymond, 17 April 1957, RG 59, Box 19 (War Crimes Clemency January 1956–1959), NA.

194. Ibid.

195. Ibid.

196. Richard Hagan to John Raymond, 30 April 1957, RG 59, Box 19 (War Crimes Clemency January 1956–1959), NA.

197. Spencer Phenix to John Raymond, 2 July 1957, RG 59, Box 19 (War Crimes Clemency January 1956–1959), NA.

198. Ambassador Bruce, secret cable to Secretary of State, 14 December 1957, RG 59, Box 19 (War Crimes Clemency January 1956–1959), NA.

199. Ibid.

200. American Nuremberg Trials, *Case 9—United States v. Otto Ohlendorf*, vol. 4, 542, 562, 569.

201. See Office of the U.S. High Commissioner for Germany, *Landsberg: A Documentary Report* (Frankfurt: U.S. Army, 1951) for a breakdown of the individual cases. RG 59, Box 19 (War Crimes Clemency January 1956–1959), NA.

202. Spencer Phenix to John Raymond, 30 April 1956, RG 59, Box 19 (War Crimes Clemency January 1956–1959), NA.

203. Ambassador Bruce to Secretary of State, 6 May 1958, RG 59, Box 19 (War Crimes Clemency January 1956–1959) and John Raymond to Spencer Phenix, 7 May 1958, RG 59, Box 19 (War Crimes Clemency January 1956–1959), NA.

204. Robert Wolfe, ed., *Americans as Proconsuls: United States Military Government in Germany and Japan, 1944–1952* (Washington, D.C.: U.S. Government Printing Office, 1978), 238. See also Dower, *Embracing Defeat*, 514.

205. Spencer Phenix to John Raymond, 13 May 1958, RG 59, Box 19 (War Crimes Clemency January 1956–1959), NA.

206. John Raymond to Spencer Phenix, 23 June 1958, RG 59, Box 19 (War Crimes Clemency January 1956–1959), NA.

Conclusion

1. "Inactive Inmates—201 Files to Be Retired," Cases Tried—Misc. Administration Files: Correspondence and Reports—U.S. Parole Supervisor (Misc. Files), RG 338, NA.

2. Frank Buscher, *The U.S. War Crimes Program in Germany, 1946–1955* (Westport, Conn.: Greenwood, 1989), 153.

3. Jörg Friedrich, "Nuremberg and the Germans," in Belinda Cooper, ed., *War Crimes: The Legacy of Nuremberg* (New York: TV Books, 1999), 93.

4. Jeffrey Herf, *Divided Memory: The Nazi Past in the Two Germanys* (Cambridge: Harvard University Press, 1997), 206.

5. Ibid., 296. According to Raul Hilberg, between 1958 and 1977, the West German government formally charged 816 and sentenced 118 to life; 398 were sentenced to prison terms, but there were no convictions in 300 cases. For more on the West German post–1958 trials, see Raul Hilberg, *The Destruction of the European Jews* (New York: Holmes and Meier, 1985), 1086–1088; see also Adalbert Rückerl, *The Investigation of Nazi Crimes: 1945–1978* (Hamden, Conn.: Archon, 1980).

6. Interview with author, Locarno, Switzerland, 17 January 1990.

7. Nayan Chanda, *Brother Enemy: The War After the War* (New York: Harcourt, Brace, Jovanovich, 1986), 377.

8. *Die Angkar* produced and directed by Heynowsky and Scheumann Studios, 1981. Sary was interviewed by an East German camera crew in 1981.

9. There are many interpretations of the Melian dialogue found in Thucydides' *The History of the Peloponnesian War*. Michael Walzer considered the "dialogue between the Athenian generals Cleomedes and Tisias and magistrates of the island state of Melos . . . one of the high points of Thucydides' *History* and the climax of his realism. . . . His spokesmen are two Athenian generals, who demand a parlay and then speak as generals have rarely done in military history. Let us have no fine words about justice, they say. . . . We will instead talk about what is feasible and what is necessary" (Michael Walzer, *Just and Unjust Wars* [New York: Basic, 1977], 5).

The powerful Athenians attempt to coerce the isolated Melians into accepting a deal: "Instead we recommend that you should try to get what it is possible for you to get, taking into consideration what we both really do think; since you know as well as we do that, when these matters are discussed by practical people, the standard of justice depends on the equality of power to compel and that in fact the strong do what they have the power to do and the weak accept what they have to accept" (Thucydides, *History of the Peloponnesian War* [New York: Penguin, 1972], 401–402). When the Melians resist these efforts, the Athenians speak more frankly: "Do not be led astray by a false sense of honour—a thing which often brings men to ruin when they are faced with an obvious danger that somehow affects their pride. . . . And, when you are allowed to choose between war and safety, you will not be so insensitively arrogant as to make the wrong choice. This is the safe rule—to stand up to one's equals, to behave with deference towards one's superiors, and to treat one's inferiors with moderation. Think it over again . . . you are discussing the fate of your country, that you have only one country, and that its future for good or ill depends on this one single decision which you are going to make" (406–407). The Melians refuse to submit, so the Athenians build a wall around the city of Melos. After a few skirmishes, more Athenian forces arrive and "siege operations were carried on vigorously" (408). The story grows tragic: "the Melians surrendered unconditionally to the Athenians, who put to death all the men of military age whom they took, and sold the women and children as slaves. Melos itself they took over for themselves, sending out later a colony of 500 men" (408).

10. Daniel Patrick Moynihan, *On the Law of Nations* (Cambridge: Harvard University Press, 1990), 1.

11. Michael Ignatieff, *Warrior's Honor* (New York: Holt, 1997), 6.

12. For more on the UN and U.S. responses to Rwanda, see *Report of the Independent Inquiry into the Actions of the United Nations During the 1994 Genocide in Rwanda*, UN document, December 15, 1999.

13. Michael Ignatieff, *Virtual War* (New York: Holt, 2000), 118. George Kennan, *Around the Cragged Hill* (New York: Norton, 1993), 206.

14. Barbara Crossette, "Helms, in Visit to U.N., Offers Harsh Message," *The New York Times*, January 21, 2000, 1.

15. Telford Taylor, *Nuremberg and Vietnam: An American Tragedy* (New York: Bantam, 1971), p. 207. See also Peter Maguire, "War Criminals Have Little to Fear," *New York Newsday*, January 22, 1999.

16. Eugene Davidson, *The Nuremberg Fallacy* (New York: Macmillan, 1973), 9.

To Kurt Vonnegut, World War II veteran and survivor of the Dresden firebombing, neither war nor law was the problem—rather, it was man. In his novel *Jailbird*, Walter, an American army official at Nuremberg, describes the "new era" being born: "The world has learned its lesson at last, at last. The closing chapter to ten thousand years of madness and greed is being written right here and now—in Nuremberg. Books will be written about it. Movies will be made about it. It's the most important turning point in history." Ruth, a concentration camp survivor, is more circumspect: " 'Walter,' she said, 'sometimes I think you are only eight years old.' 'It's the only age to be when a new era is being born.' . . . 'Well,' said Ruth. . . 'when you eight-year-olds kill Evil here in Nuremberg, be sure to bury it at a crossroads and drive a stake through its heart—or you just might see it again at the next full mooooooooooooooooooooooon.' "

17. Sven Lindqvist, *Exterminate All the Brutes*, trans. Joan Tate (New York: New Press, 1996), 2.

Glossary

Auchincloss, John Office of German Political Affairs, 1951–June 1953; thereafter International Relations Officer, Office of German Affairs, 1952–54

Bonbright, James Counselor of the U.S. Embassy in Paris; Deputy Assistant Secretary of State for European Affairs, 1951

Bowie, Robert Chief of the Office of the General Counsel, HICOG, 1951–May 1953; thereafter Director of the Policy Planning Staff

CC10 Control Council Law Ten

CDU Christlich-Demokratische Union (Christian Democratic Union)

Clay, General Lucius U.S. Military Governor, 1947–49

Conant, James B. U.S. High Commissioner, January 1953–May 1955

Byroade, Colonel Henry Director of the Bureau of German Affairs, 1949–April 1952

DDR Deutsche Demokratische Union (German Democratic Republic)

Dean, Patrick Head of the German Political Department, British Foreign Office

Donnelly, Walter U.S. High Commissioner, July 1952–January 1953

DP Deutsche Partei (German Party)

Ebert, Friedrich Member of the Politburo of the German Socialist Unity Party

EDC European Defense Community

EDF European Defense Force

Ehard, Hans Minister President of Bavaria

Elbrick, Burke Deputy Assistant U.S. Secretary of State, 1955–58

EUCOM European Command, United States Army

FDP Freie Demokratische Partei (Free Democratic Party)

François-Poncet, André French High Commissioner

GDR German Democratic Republic

Handy, General Thomas Commander in Chief, EUCOM after 1949

HICOG U.S. High Commission for Germany

HICOM U.S. High Commissioner for Germany

IMPAC Interim Parole and Clemency Board, 1953–55 (U.S. zone)

IMT International Military Tribunal

IMTFE International Military Tribunal Far East

JAG Judge Advocate General

JCS Joint Chiefs of Staff

Kennan, George Director, Policy Planning Staff; Chairman of the Steering of the NSC Subcommittee on the German Question, 1949

Kirkpatrick, Ivonne British High Commissioner

Landsberg Prison U.S. prison for convicted war criminals

Lewis, Geoffrey Assistant to Assistant U.S. Secretary of State for Occupied Areas, 1948; Deputy Director, Bureau of German Affairs 1951–53; Acting Director, Office of German Affairs, 1952–54

Lyon, Cecil Special Assistant to the U.S. Commander in Berlin; Director, Berlin HICOG 1951; Director, Office of German Affairs from 1954

Mathews, H. Freeman Director, Office of European Affairs, Department of State December 1944–July 1947; Deputy Under-Secretary of State

McCloy, John J. U.S. High Commissioner June 1949–July 1952

McNarney, General Joseph U.S. Military Governor 1945–47

Mickelwait, Colonel C. B. EUCOM Theatre Judge Advocate

Merchant, Livingston Deputy Assistant Secretary of State for Far Eastern Affairs until November 1951; Special Assistant for Mutual Security Affairs; Assistant Secretary of State for European Affairs, 1953–56

Morris, Brewster Secretary, Office of the U.S. Political Advisor for German Affairs from 1952; Officer in Charge of German Political Affairs, Office of German Affairs, November 1953–June 1954

NATO North Atlantic Treaty Organization

NSC National Security Council

OMGUS Office of United States Military Government

Raymond, John Assistant Legal Advisor for German Affairs, 1952–54

Reber, Sam Director of Political Affairs, HICOG Office of Political Affairs until July 1953

Reinstein, Jacques Special Assistant to Assistant U.S. Secretary of State, Economic Affairs, 1948; Special Assistant to Assistant U.S. Secretary of State for European Affairs until August 1955; thereafter Director, Office of German Affairs

Riddleberger, James Chief, Division of Central European Affairs, State Department January 1944–July 1947; Counselor of Mission, Office of the U.S. Political Advisor for German Affairs from October 1947; Counselor of the Mission of the U.S. Political Advisor for Germany at Berlin, 1948; Director of the Office of Political Affairs, Office of Military Government for Germany, OMGUS; Political Advisor to USHC, 1949; Director of Political Affairs, Office of Political Affairs; Director of Bureau of European Affairs May 1952–July 1953

Royall, Kenneth Under-Secretary of War 1945–47; Secretary of War July–September 1947; Secretary of Army from September 1947

Snow, Conrad Acting Assistant Legal Advisor for Far Eastern Affairs

SCAP Supreme Commander Asia-Pacific U.S.

SHAEF Supreme Headquarters, Allied Expeditionary Force (1944–45)

SPD Sozialdemokratische Partei Deutschlands (Social Democratic Party of Germany)

USAREUR U.S. Army, Europe

Voorhees, Tracy Special assistant to U.S. Secretary of War

VOPOS Volkspolizei

Wahl, Eduard CDU member of the Bundestag and member of the Heidelberg Juristenkreis

Werl British prison for war criminals

Wittlich French prison for war criminals

Bibliography

Primary Sources

National Archives Modern Military Branch, Suitland, Maryland
Record Group (RG) 338 General Administration Files
RG 446

National Archives, College Park, Maryland
RG 59
  Box 5: Clemency Board on German War Criminals
  Box 16: War Crimes 1949, 1950, October 16, 1952–December 31, 1952
  Box 17: War Crimes 1953–1959
  Box 18: War Crimes Clemency 1950–1955
  Box 19: War Crimes Clemency January 1956–1959
  Box 24: War Crimes Clemency July 1952–December 1953
  Box 29

Columbia University Oral History Project, New York
Benjamin Buttenweiser
Lucius Clay
John Foster Dulles
John McCloy

Franklin D. Roosevelt Library, Hyde Park, New York
Papers of Eleanor Roosevelt

Unpublished Nuremberg Trial Records

Case No. 111, Document Books. Nos. 58A, 58B, 59, 60A, 90A, 90B, 91, 120, 203, 204, 204A. Nürnberg: Secretariat for Military Tribunals, 1949.

Defense Briefs: Lammers and Meissner, Cross/Closing, XIB. Nürnberg: Secretariat for Military Tribunals, 1949.

Prosecution Briefs: Individual 1–2, Lammers and Stuckart. Nürnberg: Secretariat for Military Tribunals, 1949.

U.S. Military Tribunal Nuremberg, Transcript, Case XI, Weizsaecker, 1–28085. Nürnberg: Secretariat for Military Tribunals, 1949.

Official Documents

Belgium and Germany: Texts and Documents. Ed. Henri Davignon. Brussels: Belgian Government Publication, 1921.

Committee on Alleged German Outrages. *Report on Alleged German Outrages.* Reprint, New York: Macmillan, 1964.

The Foreign Relations of the United States: Paris Peace Conference 1919. Washington, D.C.: U.S. Government Printing Office, 1945, vols. I–IV.

The Foreign Relations of the United States: The Conference at Quebec, 1944. Washington, D.C.: U.S. Government Printing Office, 1972, 124–125.

The Foreign Relations of the United States: 1945. Vol. 3. Washington, D.C.: U.S. Government Printing Office, 1968.

The Foreign Relations of the United States: European Security and the German Question 1951. Vol. 3. Washington, D.C.: U.S. Government Printing Office.

The Foreign Relations of the United States: Germany and Austria 1952–1954. Vol. 7. Washington, D.C.: U.S. Government Printing Office, 1983.

German Imperial Foreign Office. *The Belgian People's War: A Violation of International Law.* New York: Press of John C. Rankin, 1915.

U.S. Chief of Counsel. *Nazi Conspiracy and Aggression: Opinion and Judgment.* Washington, D.C.: U.S. Government Printing Office, 1947.

High Commission Reports

Documents on Germany Under Occupation 1945–1954. London: Oxford University Press, 1955.

Office of the U.S. High Commissioner for Germany. *Landsberg: A Documentary Report.* Frankfurt: U.S. Army, 1951.

———. *Report on Germany, September 21, 1949–July 31, 1952.* Cologne: Greven and Bechtold, 1952.

Published Trial Records

U.S. Government. *Trials of the German War Criminals Before the Nuernberg Military Tribunals Under Control Council No. 10.* Vols 1–15. Washington, D.C.: U.S. Government Printing Office, 1949.

Case 1. *The United States v. Karl Brandt et al.* (the Medical case)

Case 2. *The United States v. Erhard Milch* (the Milch case)

Case 3. *The United States v. Josef Alstoetter et al.* (the Justice case)

Case 4. *The United States v. Oswald Pohl et al.* (the Pohl case)

Case 5. *The United States v. Fredrich Flick et al.* (the Flick case)

Case 6. *The United States v. Carl Krauch et al.* (the Farben case)

Case 7. *The United States v. Wilhelm List et al.* (the Hostage case)

Case 8. *The United States v. Ulrich Greifelt et al.* (the RuSHA case)

Case 9. *The United States v. Otto Ohlendorf et al.* (the Einsatzgruppen case)

Case 10. *The United States v. Alfried Krupp von Bohlen und Halbach et al.* (the Krupp case)

Case 11. *The United States v. Ernst von Weizsaecker et al.* (the Ministries case)

Case 12. *The United States v. Wilhelm von Leeb et al.* (the High Command case)

Jackson, Robert. *The Nürnberg Case as Presented by Robert H. Jackson, Chief of Counsel for the United States, Together with Other Documents.* New York: Knopf, 1946.

Malmedy Massacre Investigation: Hearings Before a Subcommittee of the Committee on Armed Services, United States Senate, Eighty-First Congress, First Session Pursuant to Senate Resolution 42. Washington, D.C.: U.S. Government Printing Office, 1949.

Taylor, Telford. *Final Report to the Secretary of the Army on the Nuernberg War Crimes Trials.* Washington, D.C.: U.S. Government Printing Office, 1949.

Trials of the Major War Criminals Before the International Military Tribunal, Nuernberg, Germany: 14 November 1945–1 October 1946. 42 vols. Nürnberg: International Military Tribunal, 1947–1949.

Trials of War Criminals Before the Nuremberg Military Tribunals Under Control Council Law No. 10. 15 vols. Nürnberg: International Military Tribunal, 1953.

Dissertations and Unpublished Materials

Botzenhart-Viehe, Verena. "The German Reaction to the American Occupation, 1944–1947." Ph.D. diss., University of California-Santa Barbara, 1980.

Clark, Harry H. "The Laws of War, Prisoner of War Policy, and United States Practices." Ph.D. diss., The Catholic University of America, 1987.

Luders, Michael. "The Strange Case of Ernst von Weizsaecker." Masters thesis, Columbia University, 1988.

Schwartz, Thomas. "From Occupation to Alliance: John J. McCloy and the Allied High Commission in the Federal Republic of Germany, 1949–1952." Ph.D. diss., Harvard University, 1985.

Newspapers and Periodicals

Stars and Stripes 1946–1949

The New York Times
Chicago Tribune
New York Herald Tribune 1946–1949
Paris Herald Tribune 1946–1949
Newsweek 1946–1949
Time 1945–1949
Der Spiegel 1981
Abenend Post 1952

Letters

Brand, James. Letter to Robert Maguire, 17 February 1948. Betty Frankus Maguire Papers, Portland, Oregon.

Caming, William. Letters to author, 24 June 1987, 14 October 1987, 5 February 1990, 14 September 1998.

Ferencz, Ben. Letter to author, 23 February 1990

Kempner, Dr. Robert. Letters to author, 5 November 1987, 12 October 1988, 17 January 1990.

Koblitz, Robert. Letter to author, 20 May 1996.

Kranzbühler, Otto. Letter to author, 11 July 1996.

Maguire, Robert. Letters to friends and family from Europe, September 1947–May 1949. In possession of the author.

Olsen, Ron. Letter to author, 5 June 1990.

Preston, William. Letter to author, 1 September 1990.

Schwartz, Thomas. Letter to author, 8 July 1990.

Shonfeld, Peter (for Richard von Weizsäcker). Letter to author, 12 April 1989.

Sprecher, Drexel. Letters to author, 27 December 1987, 20 February 1992, 9 June 1994.

Taylor, Telford. Letter to author, 13 May 1988.

Willand, John. Letter to author, 20 January 1995.

Interviews

Brand, Thomas. Interview by author. Tape recording. Portland, Oregon, 2 December 1993.

Caming, William. Interviews by author. Tape recording. Summit, New Jersey, 9 October 1987 and 20 September 1990.

Frankus, Betty. Interviews by author. Tape recording. Portland, Oregon, 20 March 1987 and 16 August 1987.

Friedrich, Jörg. Interview by author. Tape recording. Berlin, Germany, 21 September 1995 and 16 August 1996.

Hampsten, Alfred. Interview by author. Tape recording. Portland, Oregon, 19 March 1987.

Kempner, Dr. Robert. Interview by author. Tape recording. Locarno, Switzerland, 23 February 1988.

Kester, Randolph. Interview by author. Tape recording. Portland, Oregon, 19 March 1987.

Koenig, Werner. Conversations with author. Trancas, California, 10 July 1987 and 20 August 1993.

Kranzbühler, Otto. Interview by author. Tape recording. Tegernsee, Germany, 15 August 1996.

Kremen, Hattie. Interview by author. Tape recording. Salem, Oregon, 15 August 1987.

Maguire, Robert Jr. Interviews by author. Tape recording. Carpenteria, California, 27 March 1987 and 13 September 1987.

Olson, Ron. Conversations with author. Los Angeles, California, 1988–1991.

Primo, Bob (Standing Rock Sioux Tribe official elder). Conversations with author. Summer 1999.

Rockler, Walter. Interview by author. Tape recording. Washington, D.C., 18 April 1987.

Rockwell, Alwyn. Interview by author. Tape recording. San Francisco, California, 21 July 1988.

Sprecher, Drexel. Interviews by author. Tape recording. Chevy Chase, Maryland, 29 May 1987 and 11 October 1990.

Taylor, Telford. Interviews by author. Tape recording. New York City, 8 April 1987, 21 October 1988, 8 March 1989, and spring 1993.

Wilson, Constance Maguire. Interviews by author. Denver, Colorado, 30 March 1987 and 12 September 1987.

Wilson, Joseph. Conversations with author. Jalama, California, 12 September 1987.

Secondary Sources

Books

Abzug, Robert. *Inside the Vicious Heart*. New York: Oxford University Press, 1985.

Adenauer, Konrad. *Memoirs*. Chicago: H. Regenry, 1966.

Ambrose, Stephen E. *Citizen Soldiers*. New York: Touchstone, 1977.

———. *Eisenhower and Berlin, 1945: The Decision to Halt at the Elbe*. New York: Norton, 1967.

———. *Eisenhower: The President*. New York: Simon and Schuster, 1983.

———. *Rise to Globalism*. New York: Penguin, 1980.

Ambrosius, Lloyd. *Wilsonian Statecraft*. Wilmington, Del.: Scholarly Resources, 1991.

Anderson, Gary and Alan Woolworth, eds. *Through Dakota Eyes: Narrative Accounts of the Indian War of 1862*. St. Paul: Minnesota Historical Society Press, 1988.

Ando, Nisuki; Chihiro, Hosoya; Richard H. Minear; and Yasuaki, Onuma, eds. *The Tokyo War Crimes Trial: An International Symposium*. Tokyo: Kodansha, 1986.

Appleman, John Alan. *Military Tribunals and International Crimes*. Indianapolis: Bobbs-Merrill, 1954.

Arendt, Hannah. *Eichmann in Jerusalem: A Report on the Banality of Evil*. New York: Penguin, 1977.

Bailey, Thomas Andrew. *The Man in the Street: The Impact of American Public Opinion on Foreign Policy*. New York: Macmillan, 1948.

Baird, Jay, ed. *From Nuremberg to My Lai*. Lexington: D.C. Heath, 1974.

Baldwin, Peter, ed. *Reworking the Past: Hitler, the Holocaust and the Historians' Debate*. Boston: Beacon, 1990.

Balfour, Michael. *West Germany: A Contemporary History*. London: Croom Helm, 1982.

Beals, Walter. *The First German War Crimes Trial*. Chapel Hill: Documentary Publications, 1985.

Benton, Wilbourn, ed. *Nuremberg: German Views of the War Trials*. Dallas: Southern Methodist University Press, 1953.

Bernstein, Victor. *Final Judgment: The Story of Nuremberg*. New York: Boni and Gaer, 1947.

Best, Geoffrey. *War and Law Since 1945*. Oxford: Clarendon, 1994.

Bird, Kai. *The Chairman: John J. McCloy, the Making of the American Establishment*. New York: Simon and Schuster, 1992.

Black, Jeremy. *The Rise of the European Powers 1679–1793*. London: Edward Arnold, 1990.

Blum, John Morton. *From the Morgenthau Diaries*. 3 vols. Boston: Houghton Mifflin, 1967.

Borkin, Joseph. *The Crime and Punishment of I. G. Farben*. New York: Free Press, 1979.

Bosch, William. *Judgment on Nuremberg*. Chapel Hill: University of North Carolina Press, 1970.

Botting, Douglas. *From the Ruins of the Reich: Germany 1945–1949*. New York: Crown, 1985.

Bower, Tom. *Blind Eye to Murder: Britain, America and the Purging of Nazi Germany—A Pledge Betrayed*. London: Andre Deutsch, 1981.

Boyd, Robert. *How the Indians Fought by a Survivor of the Battle of Birch Cooley*. Minneapolis: Pamphlets in American History, c. 1930.

Brackman, Arnold. *The Other Nuremberg: The Untold Story of the Tokyo War Crimes Trials*. New York: Morrow, 1987.

Brodie, Bernard and Fawn Brodie. *From Crossbow to H-Bomb*. Bloomington: Indiana University Press, 1973.

Brogan, Hugh. *The Pelican History of the United States of America*. London: Pelican, 1987.

Brown, Dee. *Bury My Heart at Wounded Knee*. New York: Holt, 1970.

Browning, Christopher. *Ordinary Men*. New York: HarperCollins, 1998.

Bryant, Charles and Abel Murch. *A History of the Great Massacre by the Sioux Indians in Minnesota*. Millwood, N.Y.: Kraus Reprint, 1973.

Bullock, Alan. *Hitler, a Study in Tyranny*. New York: Macmillan, 1967.

———. *Hitler and Stalin*. New York: Knopf, 1992.

Buruma, Ian. *The Wages of Guilt: Memories of War in Germany and Japan*. New York: Penguin, 1994.

Buscher, Frank M. *The U.S. War Crimes Trial Program in Germany, 1946–1955*. Westport, Conn.: Greenwood, 1989.

Calleo, D. *The German Problem Record*. New York: Cambridge University Press, 1978.

Caridi, Ronald. *The Korean War and American Politics: The Republican Party as a Case Study*. Philadelphia: University of Pennsylvania Press, 1968.

Carley, Kenneth. *The Sioux Uprising of 1862*. Minneapolis: Minnesota State Historical Society, 1961.

Cesarani, David. *Justice Delayed*. London: William Heineman, 1992.

Chambers, John Whiteclay, ed. *The Eagle and the Dove: The American Peace Movement and United States Foreign Policy 1900–1922*. Syracuse: Syracuse University Press, 1991.

Chanda, Nayan. *Brother Enemy: The War After the War*. New York: Harcourt Brace Jovanovich, 1986.

Chang, Iris. *The Rape of Nanking*. New York: Basic, 1997.

Choate, Joseph. *The Two Hague Conferences*. 1913; reprint, New York: Kraus Reprint, 1969.

Clausewitz, Karl von. *War, Politics, and Power: Selections from* On War, *and* I Believe and Profess. Trans. Edward M. Collins. Washington, D.C.: Regnery Gateway, 1962.

Clay, Lucius. *Decision in Germany*. New York: Doubleday, 1950.

———. *The Papers of General L. D. Clay 1945–1949*. Bloomington: Indiana University Press, 1978.

Cole, Hugh. *The Ardennes: Battle of the Bulge*. Washington, D.C.: U.S. Government Printing Office, 1965.

Cookridge, E. H. *Gehlen: Spy of the Century*. New York: Random House, 1971.

Conant, James Bryant. *Germany and Freedom, A Personal Appraisal*. Cambridge: Harvard University Press, 1958.

Conot, Robert. *Justice at Nuremberg*. New York: Carroll and Graf, 1983.

Conquest, Robert. *The Great Terror: A Reassessment*. New York: Oxford University Press, 1990.

Cooper, Belinda, ed. *War Crimes: The Legacy of Nuremberg*. New York: TV Books, 1999.

Corbett, Percy Elwood. *The Individual and World Society*. Princeton: Princeton University Press, 1953.

Cornwell, John. *Hitler's Pope: The Secret History of Pius XII*. New York: Viking, 1999.

———. *The Study of International Law*. Garden City, N.Y.: Doubleday, 1955.

Corson, William. *The Armies of Ignorance*. New York: Dial/James Wade, 1977.

Cox, General Jacob. *Sherman's Battle for Atlanta*. New York: Da Capo Reprint, 1994.

Craig, Gordon. *Germany 1866–1945*. Oxford: Oxford University Press, 1980.

Crane, Conrad. *Bombs, Cities, and Civilians*. Lawrence: University of Kansas Press, 1993.

Dastrup, Boyd. *Crusade in Nürnberg: Military Occupation*. Westport, Conn.: Greenwood, 1986.

Davidson, Eugene. *The Trial of the Germans*. New York: Macmillan, 1966.

———. *The Death and Life of Germany: An Account of U.S. Occupation*. New York: Knopf, 1959.

Davignon, Henri. *Belgium and Germany: Text and Documents*. London: T. Nelson and Sons, 1915.

Davis, Calvin DeHormond. *The United States and the Second Hague Convention.* Durham: Duke University Press, 1975.

Daws, Gavan. *Prisoners of the Japanese.* New York: Morrow, 1994.

De Landa, Manuel. *War in the Age of Intelligent Machines.* New York: Swerve Editions, 1991.

Delbrück, Hans. *The Dawn of Modern Warfare.* Lincoln: University of Nebraska Press, 1961.

Deloria, Vine Jr. and Clifford Lytle. *American Indians, American Justice.* Austin: University of Texas Press, 1983.

Dettremond, Calvin. *The United States and the Second Hague Peace Conference.* Durham: Duke University Press, 1975.

De Zayas, Alfred M. *The Wehrmacht War Crimes Bureau, 1939–1945.* Lincoln: University of Nebraska Press, 1979.

Dickinson, Edwin. *Law and Peace.* Philadelphia: University of Pennsylvania Press, 1951.

Divine, Robert. *Since 1945: Politics and Diplomacy in Recent American History.* New York: Knopf, 1985.

Dower, John. *War Without Mercy.* New York: Pantheon, 1986.

———. *Embracing Defeat: Japan in the Wake of World War II.* New York: Norton, 1999.

Drinnon, Richard. *Facing West: The Metaphysics of Indian-Hating and Empire-Building.* Norman: University of Oklahoma Press, 1980.

Dulles, Allen. *Germany's Underground.* New York: Macmillan, 1947.

Edgerton, Robert. *Warriors of the Rising Sun.* New York: Norton, 1997.

Eisenhower, Dwight D. *Crusade in Europe.* New York: Doubleday, 1948.

Elliott, Charles Burke. *The Philippines: To the End of the Military Regime.* Indianapolis: Bobbs and Merrill, 1917.

Ellis, Richard. *General Pope and U.S. Indian Policy.* Albuquerque: University of New Mexico Press, 1970.

Elshtain, Jean Bethke, ed. *Just War Theory.* New York: New York University Press, 1992.

Etzold, Thomas H. and John Lewis Gaddis, eds. *Containment: Documents on American Policy and Strategy, 1945–1950.* New York: Columbia University Press, 1978.

Ferencz, Benjamin. *Less Than Slaves.* Cambridge: Harvard University Press, 1979.

———. *Enforcing International Law: A Way to World Peace.* New York: Oceana, 1983.

Ferguson, Niall. *The Pity of War.* New York: Basic, 1998.

Ferrell, Robert. *Peace in Their Time: The Origins of the Kellogg-Briand Pact.* New York: Yale University Press, 1952.

Fleming, Gerald. *Hitler and the Final Solution.* Berkeley: University of California Press, 1982.

Foucault, Michel. *Discipline and Punish.* New York: Vintage, 1979.

Foner, Eric. *Reconstruction: America's Unfinished Revolution 1863–1877.* New York: Harper and Row, 1988.

Friedman, Leon, ed. *The Laws of War,* vol. 1. New York: Random House, 1972.

Friedmann, Wolfgang. *The Changing Structure of International Law*. New York: Columbia University Press, 1964.

Friedrich, Carl Joachim. *The Philosophy of Law in Historical Perspective*. Chicago: University of Chicago Press, 1958.

Friedrich, Jörg. *Die kalte Amnestie*. Frankfurt: Fischer, 1984.

Friedrich, Jörg and Jörg Wallenberg. *Licht in den Schatten der Vergangenheit*. Frankfurt/Main: Ullstein, 1987.

Fritzsche, Hans. *The Sword in the Scales*. Trans. Diana Pyke and Heinrich Freenkel. London: Wingate, 1953.

Fuller, J.F.C. *The Conduct of War 1789–1961*. New York: Da Capo, 1961.

———. *Decisive Battles of the U.S.A.* New York: Da Capo Reprint, 1993.

Fussell, Paul. *Doing Battle: The Making of a Skeptic*. Boston: Little, Brown, 1996.

———. *The Great War and Modern Memory*. New York: Oxford University Press, 1975.

Fyfe, Sir David Maxwell, ed. *UN War Crimes Commission, The Belsen Trial*. New York: Howard Fertig, 1983.

Gaddis, John. *The United States and the Origins of the Cold War, 1941–1947*. New York: Columbia University Press, 1972.

Gatske, Hans. *Germany and the United States: A Special Relationship?* Cambridge: Harvard University Press, 1980.

Gehlen, Reinhard. *The Service: The Memoirs of General Reinhard Gehlen*. Trans. David Irving. New York: World, 1972.

Genovese, Eugene. *Roll, Jordan, Roll: The World the Slaves Made*. New York: Vintage, 1976.

German Imperial Foreign Office. *The Belgian People's War: A Violation of International Law*. New York: Press of John C. Rankin, 1915.

Germany Reichsgericht. *German War Trials: Report of Proceedings Before the Supreme Court*. London: H.M. Stationary Office, 1921.

Gerson, Leonard. *The Secret Police in Lenin's Russia*. Philadelphia: Temple University Press, 1976.

Gilbert, Gustav. *Nuremberg Diary*, New York: Farrar, Straus, 1947.

Gilbert, Martin. *Auschwitz and the Allies*. New York: Holt, 1981.

Gimbel, John. *The American Occupation of Germany: Politics and the Military, 1945–1949*. Palo Alto: Stanford University Press, 1968.

Gisevius, Hans. *To the Bitter End*. Boston: Houghton Mifflin, 1947.

Glueck, Sheldon. *The Nuernberg Trial and Aggressive War*. New York: Knopf, 1946.

Goebbels, Josef. *The Goebbels Diaries*. New York: Eagle, 1948.

Gold, Hal. *Unit 731: Testimony*. Tokyo: Yen Books, 1996.

Gorlitz, Walter, ed. *The Kaiser and His Court: Note Books and Letters of Admiral Georg Alexander von Muller, Chief of Naval Cabinet 1914–1918*. London: MacDonald, 1961.

Graebner, Norman A., ed. *The National Security: Its Theory and Practice, 1945–1960*. New York: Oxford University Press, 1986.

Graff, Henry, ed. *American Imperialism: The Philippine Insurrection*. Boston: Little, Brown, 1969.

Gray, Edwyn. *The U-Boat War*. London: Leo Cooper, 1973.

Greenspan, Morris. *The Modern Law of Land Warfare*. Berkeley: University of California Press, 1959.

Greenfell, Russell. *Unconditional Hatred: German War Guilt and The Future of Europe*. New York: Devin Adair, 1953.

Greil, Lothar. *Oberst der Waffen SS Joachim Peiper und der Malmedy Process*. München: Schild-Verlag, 1977.

Grotius, Hugh. *De Jure Belli Ac Pacis Libri Tres, The Classics of International Law*. Trans. Francis W. Kelsey. Ed. James Brown Scott. Oxford: Clarendon, 1925.

Griffith, Robert, ed. *Ike's Letters to a Friend 1941–1958*. Lawrence: University of Kansas Press, 1984.

Hagedorn, Hermann. *Roosevelt in the Badlands*. Boston: Houghton Mifflin, 1921.

Halle, Louis. *Dream and Reality: Aspects of American Foreign Policy*. New York: Harper, 1958.

Handrider, Wolfram, ed. *West German Foreign Policy 1949–1979*. Boulder: Westview, 1990.

Harbutt, Fraser. *The Iron Curtain*. New York: Oxford University Press, 1986.

Harris, Sheldon. *Factories of Death: Japanese Biological Warfare 1932–45 and the American Cover-Up*. London: Routledge, 1994.

Harris, Whitney. *Tyranny on Trial: The Evidence of Nuernberg*. Dallas: Southern Methodist University Press, 1954.

Hart, B. H. Liddell. *Strategy*. New York: Penguin, 1991.

Hartigan, Richard, ed. *Lieber's Code and the Laws of War*. Chicago: Precedent, 1983.

Hartle, Anthony. *Moral Issues in Military Decision Making*. Lawrence: University of Kansas Press, 1989.

Hastings, Max. *Bomber Command: The Myths and Reality of the Strategic Bombing Offensive 1939–45*. New York: The Dial Press/James Wade, 1979.

Hays, Robert. *A Race at Bay*. Carbondale: Southern Illinois University Press, 1997.

Heinrichs, Waldo. *Threshold of War: Franklin D. Roosevelt and American Entry into World War II*. New York: Oxford University Press, 1988.

Heckscher, August. *Woodrow Wilson*. New York: Scribners, 1992.

Henkin, Louis. *How Nations Behave: Law and Foreign Policy*. New York: Columbia University Press, 1968.

Herf, Jeffrey. *Divided Memory: The Nazi Past in the Two Germanys*. Cambridge: Harvard University Press, 1997.

Heydecker, Joe J. and Johannes Leeb. *The Nuernberg Trial: A History of Nazi Germany as Revealed Through the Testimony at Nuernberg*. Ed. R. A. Downey. Cleveland: World, 1952.

Hill, Alfred. *The History of Company E of the Sixth Minnesota Regiment of Volunteer Infantry*. St. Paul: Pioneer, 1899.

Hillgruber, Andreas. *Germany and the Two World Wars*. Trans. William C. Kirby. Cambridge: Harvard University Press, 1981.

Hingley, Ronald. *The Russian Secret Police*. New York: Simon and Schuster, 1970.

Hiscocks, Richard. *The Adenauer Era*. New York: Lippincott, 1966.

Hitchcock, Henry. *Marching with Sherman*. New Haven: Yale University Press, 1927.

Hitler, Adolf. *Mein Kampf*. Trans. Ralph Manheim. Boston: Houghton Mifflin, 1971.

Hobsbawm, E. J. *Nations and Nationalism Since 1780: Programme, Myth, Reality*. Cambridge: Cambridge University Press, 1990.

Hodgson, Godfrey. *The Life and Wars of Henry Stimson*. New York: Knopf, 1990.

Hodos, George H. *Show Trials: Stalinist Purges in Eastern Europe 1948–1954*. New York: Praeger, 1987.

Hoedeman, Paul. *Hitler or Hippocrates: Medical Experiments and Euthanasia in the Third Reich*. Sussex: Book Guild, 1991.

Hoffmann, Peter. *The History of the German Resistance, 1933–1945*. Cambridge: MIT Press, 1979.

Holmes, Richard. *Acts of War: The Behavior of Men in Battle*. New York: Free Press, 1985.

Hoopes, Townsend. *The Devil and John Foster Dulles*. Boston: Little, Brown, 1973.

Hovannisan, Richard, ed. *The Armenian Genocide In Perspective*. New Brunswick, NJ: Rutgers University Press, 1986.

Howard, Michael. *Restraints on War*. New York: Oxford University Press, 1979.

————. *War in European History*. New York: Oxford University Press, 1976.

Howard, Michael, George Andreopoulos, and Mark Shulman. *The Laws of War*. New Haven: Yale University Press, 1994.

Hoyt, Edwin. *Three Military Leaders: Togo, Yamamoto, Yamashita*. Tokyo: Kodansha, 1993.

Hull, William. *The Two Hague Conferences and Their Contribution to International Law*. Boston: Ginn, 1908.

Hyde, Harlow A. *Scraps of Paper: The Disarmament Treaties Between the World Wars*. Lincoln: Media Publishing, 1988.

Iggers, Georg. *The German Theory of History*. Middletown: Wesleyan University Press, 1968.

————. *Leopold von Ranke and the Shaping of the Historical Discipline*. Syracuse: Syracuse University Press, 1990.

Ignatieff, Michael. *Warrior's Honor*. New York: Holt, 1997.

Irving, David. *The Last Battle*. London: Focal Point, 1999.

Isaacson, Walter and Evan Thomas. *The Wise Men*. New York: Simon and Schuster, 1986.

Jervis, Robert. *The Logic of Images in International Relations*. New York: Columbia University Press, 1989.

Jessup, Phillip. *Elihu Root*. Hamden, Conn.: Archon, 1964.

Jung, Susanne. *Die Rechtsprobleme der Nuremberg Prozesse: Dargestellt am Verfahren gegen Friedrich Flick*. Tubingen: J.C.B. Mohr, 1992.

Kaiser, David. *Politics and War*. Cambridge: Harvard University Press, 1990.

Kaplan, Fred. *The Wizards of Armageddon*. New York: Touchstone, 1983.

Kaplan, Morton and Nicholas de B. Katzenbach. *The Political Foundations of International Law*. New York: Wiley, 1961.

Kater, Micahel. *Doctors Under Hitler*. Chapel Hill: University of North Carolina Press, 1989.

Keegan, John. *The Face of Battle*. New York: Penguin, 1976.

———. *Fields of Battle: The Wars for North America*. New York: Knopf, 1996.

———. *The First World War*. New York: Knopf, 1998.

Keen, Maurice. *Nobles, Knights, and Men-at-Arms in the Middle Ages*. Ohio: Hambaldon, 1996.

Kelsen, Hans. *General Theory of Law and State*. Cambridge: Harvard University Press, 1949.

———. *Law and Peace in International Relations*. Cambridge: Harvard University Press, 1942.

———. *Peace Through Law*. Chapel Hill: University of North Carolina Press, 1944.

———. *Principles of International Law*. New York: Rhinehart, 1959.

Kempner, Robert M. W. *Ein Advokat für die Humanität*. Osnabrück: Universität Osnabrück, 1986.

Kennan, George F. *Around the Cragged Hill: A Personal and Political Philosophy*. New York: Norton, 1993.

———. *American Diplomacy, 1900–50*. Chicago: University of Chicago Press, 1953.

———. *Memoirs 1925–1950*. Boston: Atlantic Monthly, 1967.

———. *Realities of American Foreign Policy*. Princeton: Princeton University Press, 1954.

Kennedy, John Fitzgerald. *Profiles in Courage*. New York: Harper, 1961.

Kennedy, Paul. *The Rise of German-Anglo Antagonism, 1860–1914*. Boston: Allen and Unwin, 1980.

Kessler, Leo. *SS Peiper*. London: Leo Cooper, 1986.

Kochavi, Arieh. *Prelude to Nuremberg: Allied War Crimes Policy and the Question of Punishment*. Chapel Hill: University of North Carolina Press, 1998.

Keohane, Robert O., ed. *Neorealism and Its Critics*. New York: Columbia University Press, 1986.

Kerruish, Valerie. *Jurisprudence as Ideology*. New York: Routledge, 1991.

Kessler, Leo. *SS Peiper: The Life and Death of SS Colonel Jochen Peiper*. London: Leo Cooper, 1986.

Kirchheimer, Otto. *Political Justice: The Use of Legal Procedure for Political Ends*. Princeton: Princeton University Press, 1961.

Kirakosyan, Jon. *The Armenian Genocide*. Madison: Sphinx, 1992.

Kitchen, Martin. *Europe Between Wars*. London: Longman, 1988.

Klee, Ernst, ed. *The Good Old Days: The Holocaust as Seen by Its Perpetrators and Bystanders*. Trans. Deborah Burnstone. New York: Free Press, 1988.

Klemperer, Klemens von. *German Resistance Against Hitler*. Oxford: Clarendon, 1992.

Kneeshaw, Stephen J. *In Pursuit of Peace: The American Reaction to the Kellogg-Briand Pact, 1928–1929.* New York: Garland, 1991.

Knieriem, August von. *The Nuernberg Trials.* Trans. Elizabeth Schmitt. Chicago: Regnery, 1959.

Koch, H. W. *In the Name of the Volk: Political Justice in Hitler's Germany.* New York: St. Martin's, 1989.

Koselleck, Reinhard. *Critique in Crisis.* New York: Berg, 1988.

Kreiger, Wolfgang. *General Lucius D. Clay.* Stuttgart: Klett-Cotta, 1987.

Lacquer, Walter. *Stalin.* London: Undwin and Hyman, 1990.

Lael, Richard. *The Yamashita Precedent.* Wilmington, Del.: Scholarly Resources, 1982.

LaFeber, Walter. *America, Russia, and the Cold War.* New York: Knopf, 1985.

Lansing, Robert. *The Peace Negotiations: A Personal Narrative.* Port Washington, N.Y.: Kennikat, 1969.

———. *War Memoirs of Robert Lansing, Secretary of State.* Indianapolis: Bobbs-Merrill, 1935.

Leckie, Robert. *The War in Korea.* New York: Random House, 1963.

Lee, Martin. *The Beast Reawakens.* New York: Little, Brown, 1997.

Leopold, Richard. *Elihu Root and the Conservative Tradition.* Boston: Little, Brown, 1954.

Lepore, Jill. *The Name of War: King Philip's War and the Origins of American Identity.* New York: Knopf, 1998.

Levie, Howard. *Terrorism in War: The Law of War Crimes.* Dobbs Ferry, N.Y.: Oceana, 1993.

Lewis, John. *Uncertain Judgment: A Bibliography of War Crimes Trials.* Santa Barbara: ABC-Clio, 1979.

Lewis, Rand C. *A Nazi Legacy: Right-Wing Extremism in Postwar Germany.* New York: Praeger, 1991.

Lifton, Robert J. *The Nazi Doctors.* New York: Basic, 1983.

Lindqvist, Sven. *Exterminate All the Brutes.* Trans. Joan Tate. New York: New Press, 1996.

Linn, Brian McAllister. *The U.S. Army and Counterinsurgency in the Philippines War, 1899–1902.* Chapel Hill: University of North Carolina Press, 1989.

Longstreet, Stephen. *Indian Wars of the Great Plains.* New York: Indian Head, 1970.

Lorenz, Konrad. *On Aggression.* Trans. Marjorie Kerr Wilson. New York: Bantam, 1966.

Luban, David. *Legal Modernism.* Ann Arbor: University of Michigan Press, 1994.

Lukas, Richard. *The Forgotten Holocaust.* Lexington: University of Kentucky Press, 1986.

Mahan, Alfred Thayer. *Armaments and Arbitration: The Place of Force in the International Relations of States.* New York: Harper and Bros., 1912.

Maier, Charles S. *The Unmasterable Past: History, Holocaust, and German National Identity.* Cambridge: Harvard University Press, 1988.

MacLean, F. L. *The Cruel Hunters.* Atglen, Pa.: Schiffer Military History, 1998.

Manchester, William. *American Caesar: Douglas MacArthur 1880–1964.* Boston: Little, Brown, 1978.

————. *The Arms of Krupp 1587–1968*. New York: Bantam, 1968.

Mann, Abby. *Judgment at Nuernberg*. New York: New American Library, 1961.

Mann, Michael. *States, War and Capitalism*. Oxford: Basil Blackwell, 1991.

Manstein, Erich von. *Lost Victories*. Novato, Calif.: Presidio, 1994.

Marks, Sally. *The Illusion of Peace*. New York: St. Martin's, 1976.

Marrus, Michael. *The Holocaust in History*. New York: Penguin, 1987.

————, ed. *The Nuremberg War Crimes Trial 1945–1946*. New York: Bedford, 1997.

Maser, Werner. *Nuremberg Trial: A Nation on Trial*. New York: Scribners, 1979.

Mason, Alpheus. *Harlan Fiske Stone: Pillar of the Law*. New York: Viking, 1956.

Mayer, Arno. *Wilson v. Lenin: The Political Origins of the New Diplomacy*. Cleveland: World, 1964.

McDougall, Walter. *Promised Land, Crusader State*. Boston: Houghton Mifflin, 1997.

McGeehan, Robert. *The German Rearmament Question: American Diplomacy after World War II*. Urbana: University of Illinois Press, 1971.

McNeill, William H. *The Pursuit of Power: Technology, Armed Force, and Society Since A.D. 1000*. Chicago: University of Chicago Press, 1982.

McPherson, James. *Battle Cry of Freedom*. New York: Ballantine, 1989.

Meinecke, Friedrich. *The German Catastrophe: Reflections and Recollections*. Boston: Beacon, 1950.

————. *Machiavellism: The Doctrine of Raison d'Etat and Its Place in Modern History*. Boulder: Westview, 1984.

Mendelson, John. *The Use of Seized Records in the United States Proceedings at Nürnberg*. New York: Garland, 1988.

Merrit, Richard. *Democracy Imposed: U.S. Occupation Policy and the German Public, 1945–1949*. New Haven: Yale University Press, 1995.

————. *Public Opinion in Occupied Germany: The OMGUS Surveys 1945–1949*. Urbana: University of Illinois Press, 1970.

Middleton, Drew. *The Struggle for Germany*. Indianapolis: Bobbs Merrill, 1949.

Miller, Stuart Creighton. *Benevolent Assimilation: The American Conquest of the Philippines, 1899–1903*. New Haven: Yale University Press, 1982.

Minear, Richard H. *Victor's Justice: The Tokyo War Crimes Trial*. Princeton: Princeton University Press, 1971.

Miscamble, Wilson. *George F. Kennan and the Making of American Foreign Policy, 1947–1950*. Princeton: Princeton University Press, 1992.

Montgomery, John. *Forced to be Free: The Artificial Revolution in Germany and Japan*. Chicago: University of Chicago Press, 1957.

Morgan, Edmund. *American Slavery, American Freedom*. New York: Norton, 1975.

Morgenthau, Hans. *In Defense of National Interest: A Critical Examination*. New York: Knopf, 1951.

————. *Politics Among the Nations: The Struggle for Power and Peace*. New York: Knopf, 1961.

————. *Scientific Man vs. Power Politics*. Chicago: University of Chicago Press, 1946.

Morgenthau, Hans Jr. *Morgenthau Diaries Vols. I–II*. New York: Da Capo, 1974.

Morse, Arthur D. *While Six Million Died: A Chronicle of American Apathy.* Woodstock, N.Y.: Overlook, 1983.

Moynihan, Daniel Patrick. *On the Law of Nations.* Cambridge: Harvard University Press, 1990.

Müller, Ingo. *Hitler's Justice: The Courts of the Third Reich.* Trans. Deborah Lucas Schneider. Cambridge: Harvard University Press, 1991.

Mullins, Claud. *The Leipzig Trials.* London: H.F.G. Witherby, 1921.

Murphey, Robert. *A Diplomat Among Warriors.* New York: Doubleday, 1964.

Murray, Williamson. *Luftwaffe.* Baltimore: The Nautical and Aviation Publishing Company of America, 1985.

Musicant, Ivan. *Empire by Default: The Spanish-American War and the Dawn of the American Century.* New York: Holt, 1998.

Myers, Frank. *Soldiering in the Dakota Among the Indians 1863–1865.* Huron, Dakota: Huronite Press, 1888.

National Council of the National Front of Democratic Germany. *White Book on the American and British Policy Intervention in West Germany and the Revival of German Imperialism.* 1951.

Neave, Airey. *On Trial at Nuremberg.* Boston: Little, Brown, 1978.

Nelson, Walter. *Germany Rearmed.* New York: Simon and Schuster, 1972.

Neumann, Inge. *European War Crimes Trials: A Bibliography.* New York: Carnegie Endowment for International Peace, 1951.

Neumann, Sigmund. *Germany: Promise and Perils.* New York: Foreign Policy Association, 1950.

New York Constitutional Convention 1938. *Proceedings of the Constitutional Convention of the State of New York Commemorative of the Life and Public Service of Elihu Root.* Albany: J. B. Lyon, 1938.

Nobleman, Eli. *American Military Courts in Germany: With Special Reference to Historic Practice and Their Role in the Democratization of the German People.* Fort Gordon, Ga.: U.S. Army, Civil Affairs School, 1961.

Noltke, Ernst. *The Three Faces of Fascism.* New York: Holt, Rinehart, and Winston, 1966.

Nyiri, Nicolas. *The United Nations' Search for a Definition of Aggression.* New York: Peter Lang, 1989.

Olsen, Marvin E. and Martin Marger, eds. *Power in Modern Societies.* San Francisco: Westview, 1993.

Orwell, George. *A Collection of Essays.* New York: Harcourt Brace Jovanovich, 1946.

Oshinsky, David. *A Conspiracy So Immense.* New York: Free Press, 1983.

O'Toole, G.J.A. *The Spanish War.* New York: Norton, 1984.

Pagden, Anthony and Jeremy Lawrance, eds. *Francisco DeVitoria: Political Writings.* Cambridge: Cambridge University Press, 1991.

Page, James Madison. *The True Story of Andersonville.* New York: Neale Publications, 1908.

Parish, Peter. *Slavery: History and Historians.* New York: Harper and Row, 1989.

Passelecq, Fernand. *Truth and Travesty: An Analytical Study of the Belgian Government to the German White Book.* London: Sir Joseph Causton and Sons, 1916.

Paterson, Thomas, J. Garry Clifford, and Kenneth Hagan, eds. *American Foreign Policy: A History—1900 to Present.* Vol. 2. Lexington: D. C. Heath, 1988.

Paul, Allen. *Katyn: The Untold Story of Stalin's Polish Massacre.* New York: Scribners, 1991.

Piccigallo, Philip. *The Japanese on Trial: Allied War Crimes Operations in the East, 1945–1951.* Austin: University of Texas Press, 1979.

Plischke, Elemer. *The Allied High Commission for Germany.* Bad Godesberg: HICOG, 1953.

Pound, Roscoe. *Interpretations of Legal History.* New York: Macmillan, 1923.

Pridley, Russell. *Charles E. Flandrau and the Defense of New Ulm.* New Ulm, Minn.: Brown County Historical Society, 1962.

Pritchard, R. John and Sonia Magbanua Zaide, eds. *The Tokyo War Crimes Trial.* New York: Garland, 1981.

Pritchett, C. Herman. *The Roosevelt Court: A Study in Judicial Politics and Values, 1937–1947.* New York: Macmillan, 1948.

Rabb, Theodore. *The Thirty Years War: Problems of Motive, Extent and Effect.* Washington, D.C.: University Press of America, 1981.

Ramsey, Paul. *The Just War: Force and Political Responsibility.* Savage, Md.: Littlefield Adams, 1983.

Rappaport, Armin. *Henry Stimson and Japan.* Chicago: University of Chicago Press, 1963.

Reel, Frank. *The Case of General Yamashita.* Chicago: University of Chicago Press, 1949.

Reese, Mary Ellen. *General Reinhard Gehlen: The CIA Connection.* Fairfax, Va: George Mason University Press, 1990.

Reitlinger, Gerald. *The SS: Alibi of a Nation 1922–1945.* New York: Viking, 1957.

Reynolds, Michael. *The Devil's Adjutant: Jochen Peiper, Panzer Leader.* New York: Sarpedon, 1995.

Riley-Smith, Jonathan. *The Crusades: A Short History.* New Haven: Yale University Press, 1987.

Roberts, Adam and Richard Guelff, eds. *Documents on the Laws of War.* New York: Oxford University Press, 1989.

Robertson, Richard. *The Development of RAF Strategic Bombing Doctrine, 1919–1939.* Westport, Conn.: Praeger, 1995.

Rodnick, David. *Post-War Germans.* New Haven: Yale University Press, 1948.

Röling, B.V. A. and Antonio Cassese. *The Tokyo Trial and Beyond.* Cambridge: Polity, 1993.

Root, Elihu. *Addresses on International Subjects.* Cambridge: Harvard University Press, 1916.

———. *Elihu Root, President of the Century Club Association, 1918–1927.* New York: The Century Club, 1937.

———. *Men and Policies.* Cambridge: Harvard University Press, 1925.

———. *The Military and Colonial Policy of the United States.* New York: AMS Press, 1970.

———. *Miscellaneous Addresses.* Cambridge: Harvard University Press, 1917.

Ropp, Theodore. *War in the Modern World.* New York: Collier, 1962.

Royster, Charles. *The Destructive War: William Tecumseh Sherman, Stonewall Jackson, and the Americans.* New York: Knopf, 1991.

Rückerl, Adalbert. *The Investigation of Nazi Crimes, 1945–1978.* Hamden, Conn.: Archon, 1980.

Satterlee, Marion. "A Description of the MASSACRE BY SIOUX INDIANS. In Renville County, Minnesota, August 18–19." Minneapolis: Fisher Paper Co., 1916.

Scheingold, Stuart A. *The Politics of Law and Order: Street Crime and Public Policy.* New York: Longman, 1984.

Schellenberg, Walter. *The Labyrinth.* New York: Harper, 1956.

Schilling, Werner, Paul Hammond, and Glenn Snyder, eds. *Strategy, Politics and Defense Budgets.* New York: Columbia University Press, 1962.

Schlesinger, Arthur, Jr. *The Cycles of American History.* Boston: Houghton Mifflin, 1986.

Schmidt, Matthias. *Albert Speer: The End of a Myth.* Trans. Joachim Neugroschel. London: Harrap, 1985.

Schmitt, Carl. *The Concept of the Political.* New Brunswick: Rutgers University Press, 1976.

Schmitt, Hans, ed. *U.S. Occupation of Europe after World War II.* Lawrence: Regents Press of Kansas, 1978.

Scott, James Brown. *The Hague Peace Conferences of 1899 and 1907.* New York: Garland Library of War and Peace, 1972.

Schwabe, Karl. *World War, Revolution, Germany and Peacemaking.* Chapel Hill: University of North Carolina Press, 1985.

Schwartz, Karl. *World War, Revolution, Germany and Peacemaking 1918–19.* Chapel Hill: University of North Carolina Press, 1985.

Schwartz, Thomas Alan. *America's Germany: John J. McCloy and the Federal Republic of Germany.* Cambridge: Harvard University Press, 1991.

Schwarz, Hans Peter. *Die Ara Adenauer: Gründerjahre der Republik.* Stuttgart: Deutsche Verlags-Anstalt; Wiesbaden: Brockhaus, 1983.

Seabury, William. *Wilhelmstrasse: A Study of German Diplomats under the Nazi Regime.* Berkeley: University of California Press, 1954.

Sereny, Gitta. *Albert Speer: His Battle with Truth.* New York: Knopf, 1995.

———. *Into That Darkness: An Examination of Conscience.* New York: Vintage, 1983.

Settel, Arthur. *This is Germany.* New York: Sloane, 1950.

Sherman, William T. *Personal Memoirs of William Tecumseh Sherman.* Vol. 2 New York: Library of America, 1990.

Shirer, William L. *The Rise and Fall of the Third Reich: A History of Nazi Germany.* New York: Fawcett Crest, 1950.

Shklar, Judith N. *Legalism: Laws, Morals, and Political Trials.* Cambridge: Harvard University Press, 1964.

Simpson, Christopher. *Blowback: America's Recruitment of Nazis and Its Effects on the Cold War.* New York: Weidenfield and Nicolson, 1988.

———. *The Splendid Blond Beast: Money, Law, and Genocide in the Twentieth Century*. New York: Grove, 1993.

Smith, Bradley F. *The American Road to Nuremberg: The Documentary Record 1944–1945*. Stanford: Hoover Institution Press, 1982.

———. *Reaching Judgment at Nuremberg*. New York: Basic, 1977.

———. *The Road to Nuremberg*. New York: Basic, 1981.

Smith, Glenn. *Langer of North Dakota: A Study in Isolationism*. New York: Garland, 1978.

Smith, Jean Edward. *Lucius D. Clay: An American Life*. New York: Holt, 1990.

Smith, Jean, ed. *The Papers of General Lucius Clay*. Bloomington: Indiana University Press, 1974.

Snyder, Glenn. *Strategy, Politics and Defense Budgets*. New York: Columbia University Press, 1962.

Snyder, Louis. *The Roots of German Nationalism*. Bloomington: Indiana University Press, 1978.

Solzhenitsyn, Aleksandr. *The Gulag Archipelago*. New York: Harper and Row, 1985.

Spector, Ronald. *Eagle Against the Sun: The American War with Japan*. New York: Vintage, 1985.

Speer, Albert. *Inside the Third Reich: Memoirs*. Trans. Richard and Clara Winston. New York: Collier, 1970.

———. *Spandau: The Secret Diaries*. Trans. Richard and Clara Winston. New York: Macmillan, 1976.

Sprecher, Drexel. *Inside the Nuremberg Trial*. New York: University Press of America, 1999.

Stein, Harold, ed. *American Civil-Military Decisions*. Birmingham: University of Alabama Press, 1963.

Stephanson, Anders. *Kennan and the Art of Foreign Policy*. Cambridge: Harvard University Press, 1989.

———. *Manifest Destiny: American Expansionism and the Empire of Right*. New York: Hill and Wang, 1995.

Stern, Fritz. *Dreams and Delusions: The Drama of German History*. New York: Vintage, 1989.

———. *The Politics of Cultural Despair: A Study in the Rise of Germanic Ideology*. Berkeley: University of California Press, 1974.

Stimson, Henry and McGeorge Bundy. *On Active Service in Peace and War*. New York: Harper, 1947.

Stone, Julius. *Aggression and World Order: A Critique of United Nations Theories on Aggression*. Berkeley: University of California Press, 1958.

———. *Legal Controls of International Conflict*. New York: Rhinehart, 1959.

Swearingen, Ben. *The Mystery of Hermann Goering's Suicide*. New York: Harcourt Brace Jovanovich, 1985.

Taft, Robert. *A Foreign Policy for Americans*. Garden City, N.Y.: Doubleday, 1951.

Tanaka, Yuki. *Hidden Horrors: Japanese War Crimes in World War II*. Boulder: Westview, 1996,

Tauber, Kurt. *Beyond Eagle and Swastika: German Nationalism Since 1945*. 2 vols. Middletown: Wesleyan University Press, 1967.

Taylor, A.J.P. *The Origins of the Second World War*. New York: Atheneum, 1961.

Taylor, Lawrence. *A Trial of Generals: Homma, Yamashita, MacArthur*. South Bend, Ind.: Icarus, 1981.

Taylor, Telford. *The Anatomy of the Nuremberg Trials: A Personal Memoir*. New York: Knopf, 1992.

———. *Nuremberg and Vietnam*. New York: Bantam, 1971.

Teschke, John. *Hitler's Legacy: West Germany Confronts the Aftermath of the Third Reich*. New York: Peter Lang, 1999.

Tetens, T. H. *The New Germany and the Old Nazis*. New York: Random House, 1961.

Thielenhaus, Marion. *Zwischen Anpassung und Widerstand: Deutsche Diplomaten, 1938–1941: die politischen Aktütaten der Beamteng um Ernst von Weizsäcker im Auswartigen Amt*. Paderborn: Ferdinand Schöningh, 1984.

Thomas, Ann and A. J. Thomas. *The Concept of Aggression*. Dallas: Southern Methodist University Press, 1972.

Thucydides. *History of the Peloponnesian War*. New York: Penguin, 1972.

Trachtenberg, Marc. *History and Strategy*. Princeton: Princeton University Press, 1991.

Trumpner, Ulrich. *Germany and the Ottoman Empire*. Princeton: Princeton University Press, 1968.

Turner, Henry Ashby, Jr. *The Two Germanies Since 1945*. New Haven: Yale University Press, 1987.

———. *German Big Business and the Rise of Hitler*. New York: Oxford University Press, 1985.

Tusa, Ann and John Tusa. *The Nuremberg Trial*. New York: Atheneum, 1984.

Thomas, Evan and Walter Isaacson. *The Wise Men*. New York: Simon and Schuster, 1986.

Thomas, A. J. *The Concept of Aggression*. Dallas: Southern Methodist University Press, 1972.

Utley, Freda. *The High Cost of Vengeance*. Chicago: Regnery, 1949.

Vidal-Naquet, Pierre. *Assassins of Memory: Essays on the Denial of the Holocaust*. Trans. Jeffrey Mehlman. New York: Columbia University Press, 1992.

Van Creveld, Martin. *The Transformation of War*. New York: Free Press, 1991.

Veale, F.J.P. *Advance to Barbarism: How the Reversion to Barbarism in Warfare and War-Trials Menaces Our Future*. Appleton, Wisc.: C. C. Nolan, 1953.

Vetter, Charles. *Sherman: Merchant of Terror*. Gretna, La.: Pelican, 1992.

Vitoria, Francisco de. *Political Writings*. Cambridge: Cambridge University Press, 1991.

Wallace, Anthony. *Jefferson and the Indians: The Tragic Fate of the First Americans*. Cambridge: Bell Knapp, 1999.

Walzer, Michael. *Just and Unjust Wars*. New York: Basic, 1977.

Waltz, Kenneth N. *Man, the State and War: A Theoretical Analysis.* New York: Columbia University Press, 1954.

Ward, Geoffrey. *The Civil War.* New York: Knopf, 1990.

Weingartner, James. *Crossroads of Death: The Story of the Malmedy Massacre and Trial.* Los Angeles: University of California Press, 1979.

Weitz, John. *Hitler's Diplomat: The Life and Times of Joachim von Ribbentrop.* New York: Ticknor and Fields, 1992.

Weizsäcker, Richard von. *From Weimar to the Wall.* Trans. Ruth Hein. New York: Broadway, 1999.

Wellman, Paul. *The Indian Wars of the West.* New York: Indian Head, 1992.

Welsh, Herbert. *The Other Man's Country.* Philadelphia: Lippincott, 1900.

West, Rebecca. *A Train of Powder.* New York: Viking, 1955.

White, Theodore H. *Fire in the Ashes: Europe in Mid-Century.* New York: William Sloane Associates, 1953.

————. *In Search of History: A Personal Adventure.* New York: Harper and Row, 1978.

Whiting, Charles. *Massacre at Malmedy.* New York: Stein and Day, 1971.

Williams, Emilio. *A Way of Life and Death: Three Centuries of Prussian-German Militarism.* Nashville: Vanderbilt University Press, 1986.

Willis, James. *A Prologue to Nuremberg.* Westport, Conn.: Greenwood, 1982.

Wilson, Robert Renbert. *The International Law Standard in Treaties of the United States.* Cambridge: Harvard University Press, 1953.

Wittner, Lawrence. *Cold War America.* New York: Praeger, 1974.

Woetzel, Robert. *The Nuernberg Trials in International Law.* London: Stevens, 1960.

Wolfe, Robert, ed. *Americans as Proconsuls: United States Military Government in Germany and Japan, 1944–1952.* Carbondale: Southern Illinois University Press, 1984.

Wolff, Leon. *Little Brown Brother.* London: Longmans, 1961.

Wright, Quincy. *Problems of Stability and Progress in International Relations.* Berkeley: University of California Press, 1954.

————. *The Role of International Law in the Elimination of War.* Manchester: Manchester University Press, 1961.

————. *The Study of International Relations.* New York: Appleton-Century-Crofts, 1955.

————. *A Study of War.* Chicago: University of Chicago Press, 1969.

Wyman, David S. *The Abandonment of the Jews: America and the Holocaust, 1941–1945.* New York: Pantheon, 1984.

Zink, Harold. *The U.S. Military Government in Germany.* New York: Macmillan, 1947.

————. *The United States in Germany, 1944–55.* Princeton, N.J.: Van Nostrand, 1957.

Articles

Alderman, Sidney. "Background and High Lights of the Nuremberg Trial." *I.C.C. Practitioners' Journal* 14 (Nov. 1946): 99–113.

Benz, Wolfgang. "*Versuche zur Reform des öffentlichen Dienstes in Deutschland 1945–1952: Deutsche Opposition gegen alliierte Initiation.*" *Vierteljahrshafte für Zeitgeschichte* 29 (1981): 216–245.

Bernays, Murray. "Legal Basis of the Nuremberg Trials." *Survey Graphics* 35 (Jan. 1946): 390–391.

———. "Letters of Fortune: The Nuremberg Novelty." *Fortune* 33 (Feb. 1946): 10–11.

Biddle, Francis. "Nuremberg: The Fall of the Supermen." *American Heritage* 13 (Aug. 1962): 65–76.

———. "The Nuremberg Trial." *Virginia Law Review* 33 (Nov. 1947): 679–696.

———. "Report from Francis Biddle to President Truman." *Department of State Bulletin* 15 (Nov. 24, 1946): 956–957.

Borchard, Edwin. "International Law and International Organization." *American Federation of International Law* 41 (Jan. 1947): 106–108.

Brand, James. "Crimes Against Humanity and the Nürnberg Trials." *Oregon Law Review* 28 (Feb. 1949).

Briggs, Herbert. "New Dimensions in International Law." *American Political Science Review* 46 (Sept. 1952): 677–698.

Caravajal, Doreen. "History's Shadow Foils Nanking Chronicle." *Los Angeles Times*, May 20, 1999, .

Chomsky, Carol. "The United States-Dakota War Trials: A Study in Military Injustice." *Stanford Law Review* 43 (1) (Nov. 1990).

Doman, Nicholas. "The Nuremberg Trials Revisited." *American Bar Association Journal* 47 (Mar. 1961): 260–264.

———. "The Political Consequences of the Nuremberg Trial." *Annals of the American Academy* 246 (July 1946): 81–90.

Dorn, Walter. "*Die Debatte über die amerikanischen Besatzungspolitik für Deutschland 1944–5.*" *Vierteljahrschefte für Zeitgeschichte* 20 (1972): 39–62.

Dulles, John Foster. "International Law and Individuals, A Comment on Enforcing Peace." *American Bar Association Journal* 35 (Dec. 8, 1945): 1–3, 7.

Ehard, Hans. "The Nuremberg Trial Against the Major War Criminals and International Law." *The American Journal of International Law* 43 (1949).

Elbe, Joachim Von. "The Evolution of the Concept of the Just War in International Law." *American Journal of International Law* 33 (Oct. 1934): 665–688.

Emmet, Christopher. "Verdict on Nuremberg." *Commonweal* 45 (Nov. 22, 1946): 138–141.

Eulau, Heinz. "The Nuremberg War-Crime Trials, Revolution in International Law." *New Republic* 113 (Nov. 12, 1945): 625–628.

Falk, Richard. "The Realities of International Law." *World Politics* (Jan. 1962): 353–363.

———. "The Fallen Eagles." *Time* 46 (Dec. 3, 1945): 28–30.

Ferencz, Benjamin. "The Nuremberg Procedure and the Rights of the Accused." *Journal of Criminal Law and Criminology* 39 (July-Aug. 1948): 144–151.

Finch, George. "The Nuremberg Trial and International Law." *American Journal of International Law* 41 (Jan. 1947): 20–37.

———. "The Progressive Development of International Law." *American Journal of International Law* 41 (July 1947): 611–616.

Freeman, Alwyn. "War Crimes by Enemy Nationals Administering Justice in Occupied Territories." *American Journal of International Law* 41 (July 1947).

Gault, P. F. "Prosecution of War Criminals." *Journal of Criminal Law and Criminology* 36 (Sept.-Oct. 1946): 180–183.

Genet (Janet Flanner). "Letter from Nuremberg." *The New Yorker* 21 (Mar. 23, 1946): 78–84.

———. "Letter from Nuremberg." *The New Yorker* (Mar. 30, 1946): 78–84.

Gimbel, John. "The American Reparations Stop in Germany. An Essay on the Political Uses of History." *Historian* 37 (1974/75): 276–296.

Glueck, Sheldon. "The Nuremberg Trial and Aggressive War." *Harvard Law Review* 59 (Feb. 1946): 396–456.

Gross, Leo. "The Peace of Westphalia, 1648–1948." *The American Journal of International Law* 42 (1948).

Harris, Whitney. Review of *Nuremberg Trials*, by August von Knieriem. *American Journal of International Law* 54 (April 1960): 443–444.

Hauser, Ernst. "The Backstage Battle at Nuremberg." *Saturday Evening Post* 218 (Jan. 19, 1946): 18, 19, 137.

Heilbrunn, Jacob. "The Real McCloy." *The New Republic* (Oct. 16, 1992).

Hirsh, Felix. "Lessons of Nuremberg." *Current History* 11 (Oct. 1946): 312–318.

Hobbs, Malcolm. "Nuernberg's Indecent Burial." *Nation* 169 (Dec. 3, 1949): 634–635.

Hoffman, Stanley. "International Systems and International Law." *World Politics* 14 (Oct. 1961): 205–237.

———. "The Delusion of World Order." *The New York Review of Books* 7 (1992).

Hoover, Glenn. "The Outlook for 'War Guilt' Trials." *Political Science Quarterly* 59 (Mar. 1944): 40–48.

Howard, Michael. "Governor General of Germany." *Times Literary Supplement*, 29 August 1975.

Hubert, Cecil. "Nuremberg—Justice or Vengeance?" *Military Government Journal* 1 (Mar. 1944): 11–14.

Hula, Erich. "Punishment for War Criminals." *Social Research* 13 (Mar. 1945): 1–23.

———. "The Revival of the Idea of Punitive War." *Thought* 82 (Sept. 1946): 405–434.

Hull, Cordell. "Indefensibles' Defense." *Time* 47 (Mar. 18, 1946): 29.

———. "Indictment of War Criminals." *American Bar Association Journal* 31 (Dec. 1945): 645–646, 673.

———. International Military Tribunal. "Judgment and Sentences." *American Journal of International Law* 41 (Jan. 1947): 172–333.

Jackson, Robert. "Final Report to the President from Supreme Court Justice Jackson." *Department of State Bulletin* 13 (Oct. 27, 1946): 771–776.

———. "Nuremberg in Retrospect, Legal Answer to International Lawlessness." *American Bar Association Journal* 25 (Oct. 1949): 814–815, 881–881.

———. "The Nuremberg Trial, Civilization's Chief Salvage from World War II." *Vital Speeches* 13 (Dec. 1, 1946): 114–117.

Jackson, William. "Germany's Dance of Death." *Saturday Review of Literature* 30 (May 10, 1947): 15, 34.

Jaffe, Sidney. "Natural Law and the Nuremberg Trial." *Nebraska Law Review* 26 (Nov. 1946): 90–95.

Jervis, Robert. "The Impact of the Korean War on the Cold War." *Journal of Conflict Resolution* 24 (Dec. 1980): 563–592.

Jessup, Phillip. "The Crime of Aggression and the Future of International Law." *Political Science Quarterly* 62 (Mar. 1947): 1–10.

Karsten, Thomas and James Mathias. "The Judgment at Nuremberg." *New Republic* 115 (Oct. 21, 1946): 512.

Kennan, George F. "The Balkan Crisis, 1913 and 1993." *The New York Review of Books* 60 (13) (July 15, 1993).

Kunz, Josef. "Bellum Justim et Bellum Legale." *American Journal of International Law* 45 (July 1951): 528–534.

———. "The Swing of the Pendulum: From Overestimation to Underestimation of International Law." *American Journal of International Law* 44 (Jan. 1950): 135–140.

LaFeber, Walter. "NATO and the Korean War: A Context." *Diplomatic History* 3 (Spring 1986): 461–477.

Leonhardt, Hans. "The Nuremberg Trial, A Legal Analysis." *Review of Politics* 11 (Oct. 1949): 449–460.

Leventhal, Harold, Sam Harris, John M. Woolsey Jr., and Warren Farr. "The Nuremberg Verdict." *Harvard Law Review* 60 (July 1947): 857–907.

Levin, Bernhard. "Bertrand Russell: Prosecutor, Judge and Jury." *New York Times Magazine* (Feb. 19, 1967): 24, 55, 57, 60, 62, 67, 68.

Lippmann, Walter. "The Meaning of the Nuremberg Trial." *Ladies Home Journal* 63 (June 1946): 32, 188–190.

McDougal, Myres. "The Role of Law in World Politics." *Mississippi Law Journal* 20 (May 1949): 253–283.

Maguire, Robert. "The Unknown Art of Making Peace: Are We Sowing the Seeds of World War III?" *American Bar Association Journal* 35 (Nov. 1949): 905–909, 972–973.

Moltmann, Gunter. "*Zur Formulierung der amerikanischen Besatzungspolitik in Deutschland am Ende des Zweiten Weltkrieges.*" *Vierteljahrschefte für Zeitgeschichte* 15 (1967): 299–322.

Morgenthau, Hans, Eric Hula, and Moorhouse F. X. Millar. "Views on Nuremberg: A Symposium." *America* 76 (Dec. 7, 1946): 266–268.

Neumann, Franz. "The War Crimes Trials." *World Politics* 2 (Oct. 1949): 137–147.

Piccone, Paul and G.L. Ulman. "American Imperialism and International Law." *Telos* 72 (Summer 1987).

Schick, Franz. "The Nuernberg Trial and the International Law of the Future." *American Journal of International Law* 41 (Oct. 1947): 770–894.

Schuster, George. "Hanging at Nuernberg: The Truth Was Not Allowed to Emerge." *Commonweal* 45 (Nov. 15, 1946): 110–113.

Schwartz, Thomas. "*Die Begnadigung deutscher Kriegsverbrecher. John J. McCloy und die Haftlinge von Landsberg.*" *Vierteljahrshefte für Zeitgeschichte* 38 (July 1990): 382.

Schwarzenberger, Georg. "Settling the Issue of War Guilt, Conclusive Verdict Against Nazis." *United States News* 21 (Oct. 11, 1946): 24–25.

Solis, Gary. "Yamashita Had It Coming." *Proceedings of "Accounting for Atrocities: Prosecuting War Crimes Fifty Years After Nuremberg," October 5–6, 1998.* Annandale-on-Hudson, N.Y.: Bard College Publications, 2000, 37–49.

Stimson, Henry. "The Nuernberg Trial, Landmark in Law." *Foreign Affairs* 15 (Jan. 1947): 179–189.

Storey, Robert. "Nuernberg Trials." *Tennessee Law Review* 19 (Dec. 1946): 517–525.

Taft, Robert. "Equal Justice Under Law." *Vital Speeches* 13 (Nov. 1, 1946): 44–48.

———. "The Republican Party." *Fortune* 39 (April 1949): 108–118.

Taylor, Telford. "Nuremberg War Crimes Trials: An Appraisal." *Academy of Political Science* 23 (May 1949): 239–254.

Thompson, Dorothy. "Germany Must Be Salvaged." *American Mercury* 56 (June 1943): 647–662.

———. "The Trial Begins." *Newsweek* 69 (May 2, 1967): 64.

———. "Trial by Victory." *Time* 48 (Aug. 5, 1948): 31.

Tucker, Robert. "Brave New World Order." *The New Republic* (Feb. 24, 1992): 26.

Vambery, Rustem. "Criminals and War Crimes." *Nation* 160 (May 19, 1945): 567–568.

———. "Law and Legalism." *Nation* 61 (Dec. 1, 1945): 573–575.

———. "The Law of the Tribunal." *Nation* 163 (Oct. 12, 1946): 400–401.

Walkinshaw, Robert. "The Nuremberg and Tokyo Trials, Another Step Towards International Justice." *American Bar Association Journal* 35 (April 1949): 299–302, 362–363.

Walsh, Moira. "Crime and Punishment." *America* 106 (Jan. 20, 1962): 542–544.

Weinberg, Gerhard. Book review. *Journal of Modern History* 9 (Sept. 1987): 638.

West, Rebecca. "Reporter at Large." *The New Yorker* 22 (Sept. 7, 1946): 34–47.

———. "The Birch Leaves Fall." *The New Yorker* 22 (Oct. 26, 1946): 93–105.

———. "Will Nuernberg Stop New Aggressors?" *Saturday Evening Post* 219 (Nov. 2, 1946): 164.

Williams, Walter. "United States Indian Policy and the Debate over Philippine Annexation: Implications for the Origins of American Imperialism." *The Journal of American History* 66 (Mar. 1980): 810–831.

Winner, Percy. "The Atom at Nuernberg." *Commonweal* 43 (Mar. 22, 1946): 566–569.

Wright, Quincy. "The Crime of 'War Mongering.' " *American Journal of International Law* 40 (April 1946): 398–406.

———. "Due Process and International Law." *American Journal of International Law* 40 (April 1946): 128–136.

————. "International Law and Guilt by Association." *American Journal of International Law* 42 (Jan. 1947): 38–72.

————. "The Law of the Nuernberg Trial." *American Journal of International Law* 42 (Jan. 1947): 38–72.

————. "The Nuernberg Trial." *The Annals of the American Academy* 246 (July 1946): 72–80.

————. "Outlawry of War and the Law of War." *American Journal of International Law* 39 (April 1945): 257–285.

————. "War Criminals." *American Journal of International Law* 39 (April 1945): 257–285.

Index

American Nuremberg trials *(cont.)*
assessment of fairness and leniency, 203, 209; Brandt (Medical)
case, 153–54; civilians as defendants, 149–50, 156, 158–59,
160–63; Cold War causing change
in prosecutory climate, 184–85;
concentration camp administrators' trials, 155–56; conservative
reading of law and narrowing of
legal mandate, 170–71, 172; Continental versus American legal systems, 107, 343*n*9; Control Council
Law No. 10 mandating, 148, 172,
176, 190, 195, 225; crimes against
humanity charge against German
nationals, dismissed, 176; criticisms from U.S. judges 172–75;
criticisms from Kennan, 151–52;
defenses offered, 156, 157, 178–79,
180, 184–85; distracted by Soviet
takeover of Czechoslovakia and
Berlin blockade, 167, 184; evidentiary base unprecedented, 164;
Farben case, 159, 186, 222; Flick
case, 2, 186, 222; guerrillas/parti-
sans *(franctireurs)* as war criminals,
171; High Command case, 159;
Hostage case, 170; Justice case,
155–57; justifications and supporters, 147–48; Krupp case, 159, 186,
189–90, 222, 229; legacy of scientific standards for medical
research on human subjects, 154;
Milch case, 154–55; military defendants, 170; Ministries *(Wilhelmstrasse)* case, 15, 158–67, 179–201;
overview, 14–15; Pohl case, 155;
pressure to finish, 184; prosecution's need for legal innovation,
159; prosecution staffing, 148–49,
153, 157–58, 170, 172; reprisals
defined broadly, 171; "retroactive

law" defense, 96, 156, 176–77;
"subversive diplomats" defense,
166; "superior orders" defense, 41,
154, 155, 195, 338*n*173; Taylor's
statement of goal, 175–76; tension
between prosecution and bench,
172–75; verdicts, dissenting opinions, and sentences, 157, 178,
188–90, 194–200, 211; Weizsäcker
case, 15, 147, 160, 179–84, 195–99;
see also Anti-Nuremberg efforts of
West Germans; Charges; Defenses; Nuremberg trials; Sentence
reductions
American political ideology: abrupt,
contradictory shifts of 1950s, 18;
conquest, credit, and debt, 23–24;
egalitarianism versus imperialism,
6–9; failure to join in creation of
international criminal court, 290;
fear of Bolshevism after World
War I, 10, 12, 78, 315*n*148, 343*n*12;
impact of Kennan's "Long
Telegram," 343*n*8; justifying
Philippine colonialism, 8, 51–52;
Manifest Destiny, 8, 49–51, 57;
Monroe Doctrine, 10, 78,
318*n*194&197; post–World War I
interests, 10; Stimson Doctrine
(nonrecognition of "illegitimate"
governments), 11, 84–85; timidity
in face of 1990s genocides,
287–89; war crimes as public
relations problems, 289; *see also*
American Indians; International
law
American war crimes program: awkward questions raised by, 101;
defendants, 113; problem of Continental versus American legal systems, 107; problem of definition of
war crimes, 108–9; *see also* American Nuremberg trials; Nuremberg